WELLINGTON'S GUNS

OSPREY
PUBLISHING

Dedication

To my Mother who gifted me the pen and to my Father who guided
me to the sword.

In Memoriam:

Professor/Brigadier Edward Richard Holmes CBE, TD, JP.
29 March 1946 – 30 April 2011.
A friend and unique inspiration.

WELLINGTON'S
GUNS

*The Untold Story of Wellington and his Artillery in the
Peninsula and at Waterloo*

NICK LIPSCOMBE

First published in Great Britain in 2013 by Osprey Publishing,
Midland House, West Way, Botley, Oxford, OX2 0PH, UK
43-01 21st Street, Long Island City, NY 11101, USA
E-mail: info@ospreypublishing.com

Osprey Publishing is part of the Osprey Group

A CIP catalogue record for this book is available from the British Library

ISBN: 978 1 78096 114 9
E-pub ISBN: 978 1 4728 0469 3
PDF ISBN: 978 1 4728 0468 6

Typeset in Adobe Garamond Pro and Copperplate
Cartography by Nick Lipscombe
Index by Zoe Ross
Originated by PDQ Digital Media Solutions, UK
Printed in China through Worldprint

13 14 15 16 17 18 10 9 8 7 6 5 4 3 2 1

Osprey Publishing is supporting the Woodland Trust, the UK's leading woodland conservation charity, by
funding the dedication of trees.

www.ospreypublishing.com

Cover: The Duke of Wellington on the road to Quatre. (Corbis)

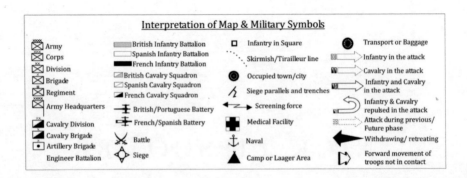

Contents

Appendices

List of Images

Between pages 296 and 297
1. Colonel Sir Augustus Frazer. (RAI)
2. Major General Sir Hoylett Framingham. (RAI)
3. Major General Sir George Bulteel Fisher. (RAI)
4. Major General Sir John May. (RAI)
5. General Alexander Cavalie Mercer. (RAI)
6. Second Captain Richard Bogue. (RAI)
7. Captain Charles Sillery. (RAI)
8. Lieutenant General Sir Thomas Downman. (RAI)
9. Captain William Webber. (RAI)
10. General Sir Edward Whinyates. (RAI)
11. Second Captain William Swabey. (RAI)
12. Colonel Charles Dansey. (RAI)
13. Major Henry Baynes. (RAI)
14. Major Robert Ord. (RAI)
15. Major General John Boteler Parker. (RAI)
16. Lieutenant Henry Mussenden Leathes. (RAI)
17. Lieutenant William Lempriere. (RAI)
18. Lieutenant General Sir Burke Cuppage. (RAI)
19. Second Captain George Silvester Maule. (RAI)
20. Second Captain John Edmund Maunsell. (RAI)
21. Colonel William Robe. (Author's Collection)
22. Lieutenant William Robe. (Author's Collection)
23. The tombstone of Major (William) Norman Ramsay at Musselburgh, Edinburgh. (Author's Collection)
24. A drawing of the headstone of Lieutenant General Sir Edward Howorth at Banstead Church, Surrey. (RAI)
25. Three pictures of the Dickson Memorial. (RAI/Author's Collection)
26. Dickson, aged 21. (RAI)
27. Dickson in the uniform of a Portuguese Artillery Officer. (RAI)
28. RHA headdress worn in the Peninsula and at Waterloo. (RAI)
29. A Royal Artillery Sabretache. (RAI)
30. Coat of arms of the Board of Ordnance. (RAI)

List of Maps

Acknowledgements

I am indebted to so many who enabled me to bring this three-year study to conclusion. On the military side, I am extremely grateful to General Sir David Richards, GCB, CBE, DSO, ADC Gen, for writing the foreword. From the Royal Regiment of Artillery I have received tremendous support; the generosity of the Royal Artillery Institute in making so many paintings, pictures and engravings available for reproduction has been the icing on the cake. I am indebted to the Regimental Secretary, Colonel Nick Quarrelle, and his Assistant, Major Bob Begbie RA, who have been hugely supportive throughout. To the serving Regiment: Major Iain Harrop RHA and Captain Neil Radford RHA from 1st Regiment Royal Horse Artillery; Major Chris Gent RHA from 3rd Regiment Royal Horse Artillery; Major Rob Alston RA and Captain Chris Bulmer RA from 4th Regiment Royal Artillery; Major David Walker RHA, Major Al Searle RHA and Warrant Officer (BSM) D. J. Homer from 7th Parachute Regiment Royal Horse Artillery; Major Neil Henderson RA from 12th Regiment Royal Artillery; Captain Alice Wheeler RA and Captain Ben Rees RA from 14th Regiment Royal Artillery; Major Garrett O'Leary RA from 16th Regiment Royal Artillery; Lieutenant Colonel Andrew Dawes RA and Captain Pete Alexander RA from 19th Regiment Royal Artillery; Captain Paul Hazell RA from 26th Regiment Royal Artillery; Captain Aodhan O Tuairisg RA from 32nd Regiment Royal Artillery; and Captain James Burnett RA from 47th Regiment Royal Artillery. Thank you so much, all of you.

Thanks also to the many who have provided information, guidance or both. To Brigadier Ken Timbers, Chairman of the RA Historical Society, and Mark Smith, Curator of the Firepower Museum and the author of Appendix 3 to this work. I am also indebted to the staff at the James Clavell Library at Woolwich for all their help and I would like to mention Teresa Brookes in particular. Huge thanks to Professor Charles Esdaile, Richard Tennant, Ian Fletcher and Nick Haynes for your snippets, ideas and for playing devil's advocate – when required! I am grateful to Wilgha Edwards at the Australian Defence Forces Academy Library (Canberra) for tracking down Bowyer Lane's memoir, to Mr. John Calverley for a copy of Tom Scott's diary, to Hans Ebke and Gabriele Eilert-Ebke for their work on Andrew Cleeves's life as an officer in the King's German Legion (Artillery) and to Dr. Stephen Summerfield for his notes on Dickson's interview in 1823. Furthermore I am indebted to Colonel João Vieira Borges for lending me copies of Teixeira Botelho's *História da Artilharia Portuguesa;* these rare books provided essential information on the Portuguese guns and gunners.

I am very grateful to David Rowlands, Chris Collingwood and Dawn Waring for providing some brilliant examples of their work for the plates section. I am hugely appreciative of Richard Sullivan, Kate Moore, Marcus Cowper and Emily Holmes at Osprey Publishing.

I am beholden to four people who have been an immense help. To Colonel Desmond Vigors whose unpublished work on the History of the Royal Artillery 1716–1853 has sadly gone unrecognised. It is an extraordinarily detailed account covering 140 years of the Regiment's history which deserves to see the light of day. Desmond's help throughout has been colossal and I am immeasurably grateful. To Paul Evans, the Head Librarian at the James Clavell Library, who has provided similar assistance over the last three to four years despite numerous other pressures on his time and expertise; again I am immensely appreciative. Finally, I want to give very special thanks to Sarah and Robin King who have read and re-read my work, made suggestions and corrections, and provided encouragement, support and material above and beyond the call of duty. I could not have crossed the Rubicon without them.

Nick Lipscombe
Lisbon, December 2012

Foreword by General Sir David Richards

GCB, CBE, DOS, ADC Gen, Chief of the Defence Staff

The fighting component of a Napoleonic army consisted of the triad of infantry, cavalry and artillery. The mark of a good general was the skill and decisiveness with which he brought these three components together on the field of battle. The cohesion of that force was all important: cohesion was, and remains, one of the most enduring principles of war. Yet 200 years ago one key element of the triad, the artillery, had a separate chain of command. It is not difficult to imagine how challenging this would have been to the Gunners and to the commander of a British force, many miles from home, during a long and unrelenting campaign.

Wellington's difficult relationship with his Gunners is well known. Less familiar are the real reasons for this impenetrability: the relationship of the Gunners to their commander-in-chief and their frustration with their own chain of command through the Board of Ordnance. It is not surprising, therefore, that a book has been written on the matter. What is quite astonishing is that, after 200 years, this is the first book which really addresses the issue. It is a fascinating story; one of epic courage and devotion above and beyond the call of duty; of new artillery tactics, from creeping barrages to 'danger close' fire missions; of the development of new branches of the British artillery (above all, the Royal Horse Artillery); of the introduction of new equipment ranging from heavier and more lethal guns mounted on more manoeuvrable carriages to the more dramatic but less successful Congreve rockets; and of the force-multiplication effect of Shrapnel's new shell. Interwoven in this story is the complex relationship with a commander-in-chief who possessed an uncompromising and often abrupt style of leadership. And of how one young Gunner officer, in time, broke through this barrier to become both Wellington's artillery commander and one of his trusted advisors.

Histories of both the Peninsula and Waterloo campaigns abound. None have done justice to the Royal Regiment of Artillery and the indubitable contribution it made to Wellington's army. Sir Charles Oman's seminal work on the Peninsular War remains, to this day, the definitive history of that conflict. Yet his coverage of the British artillery is at best sporadic and at worst non-existent. This compelling story of the relationship between one of the country's greatest military commanders and the Royal Regiment of Artillery is therefore long overdue.

David Richards
London, December 2012

Preface

Why, after 200 years, is a history devoted to the Duke of Wellington and his artillery necessary? The answer is twofold. General Sir David Richards, in the foreword to this work, emphasises that the fighting components available to a general of the era consisted of three distinct but ultimately interwoven parts: the infantry, the cavalry and the artillery. The skill on the field of battle was in the weaving. Period and modern-day studies of Napoleonic armies, and the battles they fought, demonstrate a clear understanding of this principle, with one notable exception: the British coverage of Wellington's army and tactics in the Peninsular War.

Andrew Roberts in his excellent work on *Napoleon and Wellington* wrote that 'History might not repeat itself, but historians repeat one another…'. And so it has been when recording the role and accomplishments of Wellington's artillery. Leaving aside Robert Southey's work (*History of the Peninsular War*, London 1823–1832) which rather withered on a fragile vine, it is with a degree of regret that I find myself directing criticism towards a great Peninsular soldier, but less able historian, William Napier. His work, while colourful and stirring, was infantry centric and xenophobic. Of course there was mitigation; Wellington and his army did not enjoy the large cavalry formations or numbers of artillery guns that Napoleon and his generals had at their disposal, or that indeed were at the disposal of most other central European armies of the era. Furthermore, in Britain the chain of command of the infantry and cavalry differed from that of the artillery. Nevertheless, this in no way alters the fact that the fighting component consisted of three parts and any record of events, to be balanced and accurate, must consider all those parts to judge the performance of the whole. With far more trepidation I pass judgement on Sir Charles Oman's seminal study of the Peninsular War which, despite largely redressing the role of the cavalry, still fails to take adequate account of the third element of the fighting component – namely the artillery. Oman's book *Wellington's Army* is 400 pages in length but just a single page is devoted to the artillery with the opening, 'only a short note is required as to Wellington's use of artillery'. Historians ever since have compounded this neglect.

Professor Jeremy Black, when reviewing Andrew Uffindell's *National Army Museum Book of Wellington's Armies* in the *RUSI Journal* (April 2004), summed up the situation succinctly. 'Whereas, only 17 per cent of Wellington's British troops in the Peninsula campaign were cavalry, in the Museum's sources for the campaign the infantry and cavalry are equally well represented, and the artillery (15 per cent of the troops) not at all.' So has the problem been due to a lack of material sources? A brief glimpse at the first section of the Bibliography to this work dismisses that hypothesis. Another recent work on Wellington's army devotes chapters to the infantry and the cavalry and one to the ordnance, in which he includes the artillery and engineers lumped together, signifying a fundamental misunderstanding of the fighting components. Yet firepower, then and now, is a vital component; it was not sidelined or forgotten by soldiers on the field of battle and it follows, therefore, that it should not be overlooked in the subsequent histories. Those who struggle to comprehend the importance of (direct fire) artillery in conflict would benefit from a brief study of the Special Air Service action at Mirbat on the 19th July 1972, where the range and lethality of a single 25-pounder gun dominated the judgements and conduct of both attacker and defender.

It is curious that this same mistake has not been made in primary or secondary accounts of Napoleon's army and the battles in which his *Grande Armée* fought, whether written by French or (mainly in the case of secondary accounts) by British historians. Was this because Napoleon was an artilleryman by education, who therefore attached greater importance to firepower? 'It is with artillery alone' and 'Great battles are won by artillery' are quotations attributed to the great general. Wellington, by contrast, started military life as an infantryman so perhaps it is no surprise that histories and historians have concentrated on his use of this aspect of the triad at the expense of the others. There is no doubt that the British infantryman was formidable; however, myopic adoption of this theme does the Duke of Wellington a huge injustice. He too was a great general. He would not have been so had he not understood his fighting components and employed them decisively on the fields of battle. He did not merely accept his army as a fighting instrument, but gauged its strengths and limitations and devised his tactics accordingly. One way or another, he overcame the paucity of his cavalry and guns and his frustrations with different chains of command and made what he had work as a team to win. Details of that synergy have been largely ignored in the histories of the Peninsula (not the case for Waterloo) and that is why a book on Wellington and his Gunners and Guns is long overdue.

Why does this work not open with Wellesley in India?[1] Simply, it is a study of Wellington's relationship with the Board of Ordnance and the Royal Regiment of Artillery as much as an examination of Wellington's skill at handling his guns in battle and during sieges. In India, at this time, artillery was provided by the Honourable East India Company (not subordinate to the Board of Ordnance) and it was not until 1861 that these batteries, or at least those that remained, were absorbed into the Royal Artillery. Of course, India is where Arthur Wellesley 'cut his teeth', providing some interesting observations on his use of artillery. But in fact, artillery in

---

1   Sir Arthur Wellesley was elevated to (Lieutenant General) Viscount Wellington following his
     victory at Talavera in July 1809.

India were still being deployed as 'battalion guns' (see Introduction), a concept which reduced the flexibility and personal intercession by battlefield commanders. A more difficult argument to deflect is why the study does not start in 1807 with the bombardment of Copenhagen and the battle of Køge. The reason is not only to keep the book to a manageable length; it also seems logical to open events at the commencement of the war in Iberia where Wellington really honed his trade and made his name as arguably Britain's greatest general.

Finally, it is not the aim of this work to describe the British ordnance and artillery uniforms in any detail. There are many other works that have successfully achieved this, namely: Carl Franklin's *British Napoleonic Field Artillery and British Rockets of the Napoleonic and Colonial Wars*; General Hughes's *British Smooth-Bore Artillery*; Robert Wilkinson-Latham's *British Artillery on Land and Sea 1790–1820*; Kevin Kiley's *Artillery of the Napoleonic Wars 1792–1815*; Anthony Dawson's, Paul Dawson's and Stephen Summerfield's *Napoleonic Artillery* and Chris Henry's two books on *British Napoleonic Artillery 1793–1815*. I commend all of these to anyone interested in the subject.

Introduction

One lesson stands out to me at this juncture when, once again, big cuts are being proposed to our defence budgets – when it comes to planning military force now and in the future, there can be no substitute for firepower, because this is what matters most in any conflict. Concepts of flexibility and manoeuvrability are sensible notions, but won't help our forces win unless they have the necessary kinetic resources at their disposal.

John Hutton (Defence Secretary) *Daily Telegraph* 7th August 2011

In 1783 amidst political and social chaos George III asked the young William Pitt to form a government. The successful revolt of the American colonies had shattered the complacency of 18th-century England. Pitt, deeply influenced by Adam Smith's *The Wealth of Nations*, was the first English statesman to extol the principles of Free Trade; he saw this as a means of rebuilding the British Empire through new markets in Canada, India and the Antipodes. The national debt stood at £250 million and another £40 million voted by Parliament for war purposes could not be accounted for. Pitt was determined to stand clear of the impending European conflict, placing himself on a collision course with those eager for a national military response to enlightened despotism. The navy was reduced within limits, for commercial wealth depended on the fleet, but the army was pared to the bone.

The Royal Artillery, which had reached full strength of 5,337, was decreased by 2,000 men; the existing four battalions of ten companies were retained but manning reduced to a mere 67 men per company.[1] The 'Invalid' battalion was also retained at an unchanged establishment; these companies were already much smaller than their 'marching' counterparts and were principally intended for home defence, garrison duties at Woolwich, Fort George and the Channel Islands.[2] So it remained, virtually unchanged, until the commencement of the Revolutionary Wars. However, Pitt's determination to remain neutral was shattered in January 1793 by the execution of Louis XVI and the subsequent French declaration of war on Britain and Holland. Within weeks the British Prime Minister had outlined his first proposals to tackle the crisis and conceded war finance and resources; it was a problematic responsibility for a man who knew nothing of war or military strategy and, in the penning of those plans, neither he nor the Tory party could have had any idea that the nation would be at war for over 20 years. 'The English never prepared for war. Yet they never doubted they would be victorious.'[3] The British Army which emerged following the ultimate defeat of Napoleon's *Grande Armée* on the field at Waterloo had changed radically from that which now struggled to cobble together a few thousand men to move in support of their Dutch allies. Nowhere were those changes more apparent than in the Royal Regiment of Artillery, which had transformed itself with improved procedures and far greater mobility, permitting them, after 400 years of gunpowder artillery, to stamp their undeniable influence on the land battle.[4]

From 1716, when the first two companies of artillery were formed by Royal Warrant, to 1757 the only permanent unit of the Royal Artillery was the company, known by the name of its commander. In 1757, the companies were grouped in numbered battalions, but being the first company in the first battalion did not, in any way, signify any order of precedence. Of course, as the company commander changed, so did the name of the company – an additional source of confusion and occasional misrepresentation, which was not resolved until after 1815 when artillery sub units were numbered for the first time. A company of guns was purely an administrative grouping of officers and men and their personal weapons (small arms); the company had no guns integral to its establishment. When the foot artillery were provided between six and 12 guns and or howitzers, and the means to transport them, they were known as 'brigaded'. Artillery companies without guns, allocated to the park or stores or to fixed point defence, were, by the same token, not 'brigaded' and executed their role as companies of artillery. Brigades of guns, formed by one or more companies, could be further broken down into pairs of guns known as divisions; this naturally causes confusion with infantry terminology and is further complicated by the fact that within the Anglo-Portuguese army in the Peninsula a division of artillery represented a grouping of artillery brigades. The establishment of horse artillery in the Royal Artillery in 1793 provided the basis for major organisational change across the board; the Royal Horse Artillery (RHA) sub unit was termed a 'troop' and to distinguish it from its foot-borne counterpart was *de facto* permanently 'brigaded'. That is, its guns, horses and drivers were integral to the troop; these fully integrated troops provided the basis for the foot brigades of artillery that had evolved by the start of the Peninsular War and laid the foundations for the modern 'battery'.[5]

The Royal Artillery companies which served on the continent in the early campaigns of 1793–95 were not employed as complete companies but were split up and allocated to the infantry or retained to support the Park of Artillery.[6] Each infantry battalion was provided two guns in direct support, commanded by a subaltern with a non-commissioned officer (NCO) and a few gunners, hence the term 'battalion guns'. The company commander, normally a captain but possibly a major, commanded the groups of battalion guns within the infantry brigade. These guns were by requirement lightweight, 3-pounder or the light 6-pounder, as they had to be manhandled by the small group of attendant gunners, assisted in their task by infantrymen. Guns packeted in this fashion were not maximising the effects of mass and lacked any form of centralised control and, as such, could not be moved around the battlefield and brought to bear at critical geographical points and moments in time. Furthermore, they were under command of the infantry battalion to which they were attached and, therefore, entirely reliant on that infantry commander for their efficient utilisation. This arrangement may have had evident advantages to King Gustavus Adolphus in his reorganisation of the Swedish Army in the early 17th century and subsequently to Frederick the Great in the mid-18th century, but by the commencement of the Revolutionary Wars it was defunct.

The four artillery battalions of ten companies grew at an alarming rate; two had been added by 1799 and then, owing to the Act of Union of Great Britain with Ireland in 1801, ten companies of the Royal Irish Artillery were incorporated as the 7th Battalion.[7] By the start of the Peninsular War, there existed ten battalions of ten companies; they were spread across the globe, from Ceylon to the Cape of Good Hope and from Barbados to Quebec but the majority were either already deployed or preparing to embark for service on the continent. The concept of ten companies to each battalion was an extension of the Roman system of tens and hundreds, which had been adopted by the infantry, and many variations of guns and gunners were tried and tested in the latter years of the 18th century, but by 1804 brigades of foot artillery were designed around the single company and the number of guns settled at six. Conceptually, a brigade supported an infantry division and was generally task organised as such. This was certainly a huge advance on battalion guns and provided far greater concentration of fire but the paucity of guns in the Peninsula often resulted in there being insufficient brigades of guns to support each division and the system relied upon a centralised artillery command and control which was far from mature at the commencement of the war. It was often impossible to cover the entire divisional frontage with a single brigade of guns, leading to a tendency to break up the fire unit to two or three 'gun divisions', reducing concentration of fire and, to all intents and purposes, returning to a re-branded form of battalion guns.[8]

The problem of positioning gun brigades in support of the infantry on a Napoleonic battlefield was further complicated by the space requirements, both across the frontage and in depth. An interval of 20 metres (21 yards) between guns was adopted to enable the guns to traverse, left and right, facilitating coverage of wide arcs of fire without being impeded or impeding the neighbouring gun.[9] Thus a brigade of guns required a frontage of 100 metres (110 yards) and, as the practice of firing over the heads of infantry deployed in line was not commonplace, the artillery had to fit between the infantry battalions, which often resulted in the brigade being split, to either flank, to reduce the footprint on the ground. This, however, complicated re-supply for the limbers and ammunition wagons were to the rear of the guns; shot and shell were heavy and charges volatile, the movement from wagon to gun was time consuming and labour intensive, and the positioning of the ammunition wagons a sensitive all-arms real estate issue. Consequently, the relationship between, and interaction with, the artillery and infantry and cavalry was a far more complex issue than it may appear at face value. Brent Nosworthy's excellent work on Napoleonic battle tactics concluded that 'at close range, artillery was generally unable to inflict a greater number of casualties than competent well-led infantry occupying the same frontage'. The complications of providing that intimate level of artillery support to infantry or cavalry in the advance or retreat, or during manoeuvre operations, were instrumental in driving change. Nosworthy summed up the problem, 'artillery although able to break enemy infantry when sufficiently massed or carefully orchestrated to achieve converging fire, was unable to exploit its own success'.[10] That inability to *exploit* was directly related to mobility, or a lack of it, and was addressed in Britain, gradually but methodically, by improvements to artillery guns and equipment, by the militarisation of the artillery drivers and, most significantly, by the introduction of mobile or horse artillery.

In 1788 Charles, Duke of Richmond, the then Master General of the Ordnance, established a committee (largely composed of serving artillery officers) to consider how best to meet the opportunities afforded by mobile artillery. In fact Britain was behind the European power curve in terms of adopting mobile guns; on the 1st August 1759, at the battle of Minden, Frederick the Great had used his reserve artillery in a mobile role to support a flanking movement but despite his undoubted military genius he cannot claim to be the inventor of mobile artillery. There is some evidence to suggest that he copied the idea from the Austrians, Russians or even the Swedes.[11] Nevertheless, from the end of the Seven Years' War (1756–63) development across Europe appears sporadic; the Russians, Prussians, Austrians and certain German states experimented with three types of system: the horse mounted, the vehicle mounted and the semi vehicle mounted.[12] The British had also tested various ideas in India with the so called 'galloper guns' but national interest was accelerated with news that the French had formed two companies in 1791 and the following year the Duke of Richmond took matters into his own hands. He adopted one of the three establishments being considered, with the following provisoes: both gunners and drivers would have to be unified under a single command; guns, carriages, limbers and wagons would have to be of a light, robust and manoeuvrable design; all this equipment, the men to crew and service it and all the horses required to move it must be owned by the government (i.e. Board of Ordnance); and, above all, a common drill must be fashioned to train, hone and deliver the capability.

The new *arme d'élite* was titled the Royal Horse Artillery (RHA); the first two troops were raised in January 1793 and two more by November of the same year. Captain Robert Lawson was given command of 'A' Troop, 'the formation of the three others was superintended by him, and he arranged the drill, so as to enable them to conform to the movements of the cavalry'.[13] Undoubtedly, supporting the cavalry was the *raison d'être* of the RHA but it was by no means the *sine qua non*; a mobile self-contained artillery unit has considerable utility both on and off the Napoleonic battlefield. Howie Muir in his introduction to Captain Hew Ross's *Memoirs* provides an excellent appraisal of the efficacy and flexibility of horse artillery of the day:[14]

> During its service from 1809–1815, Ross and 'A' exemplified the varied roles for which horse artillery was genuinely suited. In order to join the Peninsular field army in August 1809, in the immediate aftermath of the battle of Talavera, 'A' Troop accomplished a march, the rapidity of which is often obscured by attention

given to that made by Brigadier-General Robert Craufurd's Light Brigade just ahead of it, but one difficult to match by an RA [Royal Artillery] brigade.

'A' Troop was thereafter attached to Fane's cavalry brigade for several months. In December, the troop was placed under Craufurd, then commanding the 3rd Division. Subsequently it followed Craufurd when his brigade of light infantry united with two battalions of Portuguese *Caçadores* to form the Light Division, in February 1810. Ross's troop remained attached to the celebrated command until sometime in August 1813, sharing fully in the Light Division's hazards and successes. In early December 1813, the troop was attached to Lieutenant-General Rowland Hill's command; by late February 1814 it was with the 6th Division; in March it was supporting Lieutenant-General Dalhousie's command (7th Division and Vivian's brigade of hussars) at Bordeaux. Intermittently, it was detached on other duties: in July 1812, to support the cavalry during the Salamanca campaign; again in late June and early July 1813, for the pursuit after the battle of Vitoria; portions of the Pyrenean campaign found the troop quartered well behind the main line; late autumn 1813 found 'A' Troop collected in [artillery] division to support the 4th and 7th divisions at the Nivelle. Throughout, the troop demonstrated horse artillery's ability to support not only cavalry, but infantry commands, participating both in detached duties of light corps and punishing battle-work of a general engagement.[15]

All too often the role of (British) horse artillery has been simply dismissed as supporting the cavalry and, while General Sir John Moore and Wellington had a paucity of both cavalry and horse artillery in the Peninsula, even the briefest of studies reveals how well these two great commanders exploited the versatility of this new and exciting capability which extended well beyond galloping off in support of the cavalry. However, it was the decision to organise this new artillery into tactical self-contained units that was more of a revolution than the introduction of the horse artillery itself.[16] The militarisation of the civilian drivers and horses was the key. The horse artillery troops had arguably the most demanding task in the army: for them to be able to drag tons of gun and carriage over difficult terrain in support of a mobile operation, most likely under fire, then bring that equipment into action still under fire, engage the enemy, bring the guns out of action and retire (if necessary) required teamwork and courage of the highest order. Any suggestion that such discipline and *esprit de corps* could be fostered by a union of gunners and civilian drivers was immediately dismissed by Richmond's committee. There were far too many instances in the recent past where the gunners had been left in the lurch, in the heat of battle, by their civilian drivers who had quit the field when the action became a touch too personal for their liking. Despite best intentions, even in the RHA, animosities remained between gunners and drivers, who were, after all, still just civilian employees of the Board of Ordnance, although dressed in uniform and subject to military jurisdiction.

Nevertheless the concept was sound and in 1794 the Board of Ordnance ceased the practice of hiring civilian drivers and horses for the foot artillery and a special corps was raised to provide a pool of drivers and horses for the artillery companies. Fortescue commented that 'it was a peculiar distinction of the Horse Artillery that its drivers formed part and parcel of each troop; and it is difficult to say why the like organisation was not adopted for the Field Artillery'.[17] The answer, in fact, was simple; the cost would have been prohibitive. Nevertheless the Royal Warrants established this new corps as a separate organisation and not integral to the Royal Artillery; this, as it turned out, was to be a mistake. It was raised as the Corps of Captains, Commissaries and Drivers but became the Corps of Gunner Drivers in 1801 and then settled as the Corps of Drivers, Royal Artillery in 1806 and remained that way until its disbandment in 1822. In 1806 there were 11 troops of five divisions; establishments fluctuated throughout the period but, at the commencement of the Peninsular War, troop strength was about 550 with 198 officers' horses and 859 riding horses.[18] In theory each division was designed to provide the necessary driver and support personnel and horses to an artillery company but this rarely happened in practice and often divisions were cobbled together from all available manpower and resources; for example Maxwell's Company had elements from 'C', 'E', 'F' and 'L' troops when in support of Hill's Division during the campaign in the Pyrenees in 1813. This was not uncommon and made any form of identity, both to their own corps and to the artillery they were supporting, very difficult to achieve. Discipline suffered accordingly. Second Captain Robert Cairnes recounted the problems in a letter to his stepfather (General William Cuppage) from Salamanca in 1813:

They leave England paid in advance, sell half their necessaries when lying at Portsmouth and the other half either at Lisbon, or on the road. Thus they join the Brigade perfectly naked, and being paid up three or four months in advance of the army they must be in a wretched state for a considerable time afterwards. I have got the Paymaster to advance money on account to get them shirts, flannels and overalls, and I have at this moment about six Drivers without stockings, shoes or boots; positively without them, that is barefoot in the literal sense! In my establishment of 100 Drivers I have men of three different Troops, whose accounts I may hope to get hold of at the end of six months: however, I am resolved to do no more than superintend their money matters and see that my Officer of Drivers (Lt. Dalton) does his duty in supplying them with necessaries, soap and salt. This is all that I allow him to interfere with. My own officers look to the stable duties and inspect the Drivers' Kits of their Divisions every Saturday, with those of the gunners, their Mess Accounts etc. The poor Drivers are sadly to be pitied. Considering the labour of taking care of two horses and their harnesses (and often sometimes three) they are worse paid than any other troops, and when left entirely to the management of their own Officers, they are less-luck indeed. By being with a Brigade, there is some hope of instilling into them the idea that they are soldiers and, when they find themselves looked after and treated precisely as the Gunners of the Brigade, they certainly evince a difference.[19]

By the end of the war in the Peninsula the level of professionalism of the Corps of Drivers was still far from resolved and the Commander Royal Artillery (CRA) wrote to Regimental headquarters in the frankest terms on the issue:

I am sorry to have to add generally that the discipline and arrangements of this corps is so bad that I despair of ever seeing matters properly put to rights … many of the Officers are negligent, and indifferent to their duty. I may say worse indeed, for they are constantly giving their names in sick and in several instances absenting themselves without leave. Under these circumstances nothing but vigorous measures will do and these of necessity I must use.[20]

By 1808, the establishment of the artillery company had settled and consisted of five officers (a captain company commander, a second captain and three subalterns), four sergeants, four corporals, nine bombardiers (lance corporals), three drummers and 124 other ranks. That of an RHA troop comprised five officers, two staff sergeants, three sergeants, three corporals, six bombardiers, 75 gunners, 60 drivers, seven artificers and a trumpeter. The enlisted personnel remained with either the horse artillery or marching companies to which they were apportioned following their basic training. Until 1772 this training had taken place at the 'Warren' at Woolwich Dockyard, on the shores of the River Thames; that year the Board of Ordnance purchased Mr Bowater's estate on Woolwich Common and a new, considerably larger barracks was constructed there between 1774 and 1803. Soldiers recruited for the infantry, cavalry or artillery were all drawn from the same pool, the defining rationale being which of the three arms happened to have a recruiting team in the area when a young man decided to take the King's Shilling.[21]

For officers, however, the selection criterion was markedly different; the infantry and cavalry obtained rank through the purchase of a Commission, for the artillery and engineers it was through selection and ability. The system of purchase was 'thoroughly rotten' at the commencement of the Revolutionary Wars; prior to the turn of the century, some 20 per cent of all commissions were purchased for men under 15 years of age, others might command a battalion as a lieutenant colonel within days of entering the army.[22] Contrast this with the system in the 'scientific' corps where selection for a place at the Royal Military Academy was keenly contested and where a commission was earned by attaining the required level of expertise. The main reason for the significant variation was the difference in respective chains of command. The artillery came under the second largest state department, the Board of Ordnance. This Board, created by Henry VIII and initially concerned with the manufacture and supply of guns to the British Army and Navy, controlled the Ordnance Corps which embraced the Royal Artillery and Royal Engineers. It was independent from Horse Guards, which exercised control over the rest of the army. The Board was, to all intents and purposes, a government department: the appointment of the Master General of the Ordnance (MGO) politically motivated and worthy of a Cabinet seat; command and control of its assets never absolute to any other than the Board. It was a situation that, understandably, infuriated commanders-in-chief on operations. Wellington, in particular, was especially incensed by this check on his military charge; he begrudged the 'back-door' political interference and, accordingly, resented the officers and men who operated under its cloak.

Such prejudice inevitably, and sadly, coloured Wellington's perception of Gunners but in fact his bias ran deeper. Professor Hew Strachan asserts that purchase of

Commissions provided more than just a symbol of aristocratic dominance, it was also a guarantee of political neutrality, for promotion which depended on purchase negated reliance on preferment by political patronage and therefore those officers who had secured their rank by such means did not seek such elevation.[23] Wellington's personal staff were handpicked from the 'right' sections of society and all were well aware of Wellington's views on the 'lower-bred' officers of the technical arms. Revolutionary France had just spawned such a group of military revolutionaries from bourgeois families who had 'no connection with property'. Wellington distrusted them, he questioned their motives and the fact that Bonaparte himself had emerged from an artillery academy was evidence enough to convince him that he was right.[24]

Few today would question selection on ability in preference to birth but, at the turn of the 19th century, the Age of Liberalism remained a distant vision. The criterion of aptitude was, however, driven by a clear (technical) need rather than a chosen desire; moreover as many technical officers were to lament, there was a significant drawback. Once commissioned, promotion was through seniority; the average service to attain the rank of lieutenant colonel in the artillery was 24 years, captain 17 years and second captain 11 years. This was to become much worse following Waterloo and, while commissioning through ability had clear merit, promotion through seniority alone certainly did not.

> As a result both corps [Artillery and Engineers] had at their head a collection of senior officers too old to go on active service. Their juniors could only wait patiently until they died in their beds. In 1809 no regimental lieutenant-colonel in the Royal Artillery had less than 26 years' service after leaving Woolwich. None of them was less than a year older than Lieutenant General Sir Arthur Wellesley.[25]

The system of promotion by seniority from the rank of lieutenant colonel onwards applied to those who had attained the rank by purchase or seniority; but the date a man attained his lieutenant colonelcy was critical for it was this date which dictated his seniority for the rest of his life. If it were not for brevet promotions it would have been virtually impossible for officers who worked for the Board of Ordnance to rise above the rank of colonel.[26]

What then of the artilleryman's tools of trade? During the period 1790–1820 there was a bewildering array of British ordnance in land service.[27] For a cursory appraisal these are best broken down into light equipment, used in the field, and heavy equipment, used for sieges. The former category included the field 3-, 6- and 9-pounder guns as well as the 5½-inch howitzers, while the latter encompassed the 12-, 18- and 24-pounder guns, the heavy 8-inch and 10-inch howitzers (including the iron 24-pounder howitzers) and the 8- and 10-inch mortars.[28] Poundage referred to the weight of the projectile while the measurement in inches referred to the diameter of the smooth bore. In simple terms a gun was designed to impart the highest practicable muzzle velocity to its projectiles to maximise range and lethality; howitzers were required to throw as heavy a projectile as possible on a curved trajectory and were therefore larger in calibre than a gun, but since velocity was less important they could be shorter in the barrel and could fire in the low and high angle; finally, mortars exaggerated the characteristics of the howitzer, being purely designed for high angle fire.

The lightweight 3-pounder guns came into their own during the war in the Peninsula with demi-brigades of mountain guns, as they were termed, being used on the east coast in 1813 and, more extensively, during the Pyrenean campaign and in southern France in 1813–14. There was, at the time, much debate regarding the suitability of the lighter ordnance and a clear preference for heavier pieces. This debate was, to an extent, fuelled by the fact that the standard French field gun, from the Grimbeauval system, was an 8-pounder. Major General Alexander Dickson, the ultimate CRA in the Peninsula, summed up the situation ten years after the war:

> Light guns in my opinion are merely to suit certain difficulties of country, when they are not likely to be opposed by ordnance of a better class; for otherwise the precision and effect of light guns is so unsatisfactory, that I think it infinitely better to bring fewer pieces into the field, provided they are guns of decided effect … The light 5½in. howitzer is good for nothing; indeed it should be abolished in our service … [The heavy 5½-inch] is a good howitzer and it was not found too heavy for quick movements … the 9-pounder is the most efficient gun, and I have no doubt will always be the piece most used by us on continental service. In the latter campaigns in Spain, with the exception of the horse Artillery and one battery of long 6-pounders, all the rest were 9-pounders; and at Waterloo, both foot and horse Artillery, almost all had 9-pounders.[29]

Mortars were mounted on beds designed to take the shock of firing; however, guns were mounted on carriages and it is here that overseas and domestic designs varied widely. The bracket carriage was the most common; it consisted of a heavy wooden axle tree and two substantial timber planks set on edge, parallel to one another. For howitzers such a design was essential to allow the barrel to tilt back and through the gap in order to fire in the high angle. However, for guns such tilt was not essential and so General Thomas Desaguliers was tasked to consider another form of carriage consisting of a single block trail. In fact Desaguliers's design was based upon a French 3-pounder captured in Martinique in 1761 and early trials at Woolwich were very promising. The block trail certainly provided greater manoeuvrability to the gun, limber and horse team and it was not long before Colonel William Congreve, the Inspector of Military Machines and Carriages, and Colonel Griffiths Williams, Commanding the Park of the RA, realised the potential of this new trail for the horse artillery. Not only was the turning circle greatly reduced but as soon as the gun was unhooked from the limber it could be fired. It is again worth noting Dickson's views on this equipment:

> The equipment of field Artillery during the whole of the Peninsular war, was with block trail carriages, and four wheeled ammunition limber wagons, according to the convenient system adopted in British service, by which the wagon limbers being packed and fitted exactly the same as those for the guns, the former can be substituted for the latter in time of action, without the waggon's being brought

much in fire, and most disastrous consequences from explosions are thereby avoided. The block trail carriages were found much superior to the cheek trailed or bracket carriages, in strength and durability, in facility of limbering and unlimbering, and in pointing whilst in action; they also admitted of more close turning in manoeuvres and on the march.[30]

Another area where the British artillery enjoyed superiority over their French counterparts was in their span of projectiles. Round shot, common shell and grape shot were universal but there were two types of canister or case shot.[31] Short range canister was first developed for naval use and consisted of a tin with carbine (later musket) balls, which ruptured soon after leaving the muzzle to produce a shot-gun effect in the immediate frontage of the weapon. Range was increased by altering the size of the shot within the tin but developers soon hit problems with tins rupturing prematurely or the balls fusing together from the initiation. A longer range canister round was developed, with a stronger tin casing containing balls wrapped in sawdust, designed to rupture on impact at range. The effects of long range canister were dubious at best as most of the balls ploughed into the ground while those that continued to the target had questionable velocity and lethality. Most European armies had both rounds and could therefore cover point blank to about 330 yards with short range and up to 820 yards with long range canister. The British, however, only used short range canister and experimented instead to improve on the poor performance of the common shell and to develop a universal projectile with a widespread effect at the target at longer range.

In 1784 Lieutenant Henry Shrapnel RA produced his first prototype spherical case shot which later became known as the shrapnel shell.[32] The essential difference was that Shrapnel's shell was an air-burst munition incorporating a bursting charge initiated by a fuse that shattered the casing which, along with the tightly packed lead balls, carried on its trajectory to engulf the target. The shell entered service in 1803 and coincided with the development of French infantry tactics of deploying larger numbers of skirmishers in front of densely packed columns (or *ordre mixte*, i.e. a mixture of line and column) which would then deploy into line, to maximise musketry firepower, outside of the range of short range canister or grape. A projectile which could be fired from a gun, which had far greater effect than long range canister, was relatively simple to use and provided greater reach to disrupt the infantry formations just prior to attack, would inevitably make its mark. And so it was. First used in anger at the battle of Vimeiro on the 21st August 1808, this new weapon greatly assisted the disruption of the first two French infantry brigade attacks upon the hill and then wreaked havoc on General François Kellermann's subsequent attack.[33] Throughout the Peninsular War and up to, and including, the battle of Waterloo the shrapnel shell was to provide the British Gunners with a force multiplier which went some way to compensate for the correspondingly fewer guns they were able to field. The French detested this 'black rain', as they had no means of reply and attempts to develop their own ended in failure as they could not perfect the fuses.

The range of projectiles is, however, an area fraught with controversy. Range depended on the size (and quality) of the powder charge and the elevation of the gun but contemporary firing tables varied widely in their assessments. Effective range was a relative concept but it was more applicable than maximum range for at the latter the effectiveness of the projectile would be negligible. There was a range beyond which it was no longer cost-effective to engage and the following table has been compiled based on effective range, that is, the maximum range beyond which the effectiveness of the projectile is less than 30 per cent.

British Field Guns/Howitzers – Effective Ranges

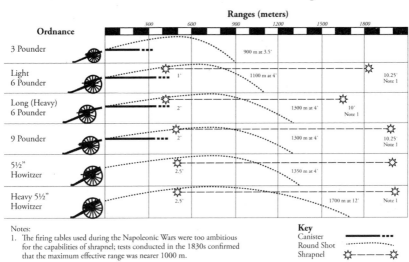

Ranges (meters)

Ordnance	300	600	900	1200	1500	1800	
3 Pounder			900 m at 3.5˚				
Light 6 Pounder	1˚		1100 m at 4˚				10.25˚ Note 1
Long (Heavy) 6 Pounder	2˚			1300 m at 4˚	10˚ Note 1		
9 Pounder	2˚			1300 m at 4˚			10.25˚ Note 1
5½" Howitzer	2.5˚			1350 m at 4˚			
Heavy 5½" Howitzer	2.5˚			1700 m at 12˚			Note 1

Notes:
1. The firing tables used during the Napoleonic Wars were too ambitious for the capabilities of shrapnel; tests conducted in the 1830s confirmed that the maximum effective range was nearer 1000 m.

Key

Canister	▬▬▬ ▪▪▪
Round Shot	··················
Shrapnel	✬─ ─ ─✬

Sources: Compilation from Adye, Jones, Hughes, Dickson, Wilkinson-Latham and Colquhoun.

British inventiveness introduced another weapon system to the Napoleonic stage – the Congreve Rocket. William Congreve was the eldest son of Colonel (later General) William Congreve and he certainly benefited from that connection and his friendship with the Prince Regent in the development of his rockets. Rockets were not a new weapon system, having been used for many centuries by the Chinese and Indians. During the latter wars against the Indian princes, the British witnessed the effect of rockets during the siege of Seringapatam in 1799. Captured rockets were transported back to Woolwich but early trials were less than successful and in 1804, following his failure to establish a small but outspoken newspaper, Congreve (junior) threw himself into rocket development. 'In the year 1804, it first occurred to me that … the projectile force of a rocket … might be necessarily applied, both afloat and ashore, as a military engine, in many cases where the recoil of exploding gunpowder made the use of artillery impossible.'[34] Early trials were mixed and the first use in combat in 1805 at Boulogne was a failure, prompting relentless criticism, but with Congreve's high-level political support, and internal patronage, the project was afforded another chance. The second attempt on Boulogne in April 1806 was a success and it was followed by accomplishment at the siege of Copenhagen in 1807 where the fires, caused by the combustible material in the rockets, proved to be a decisive factor in forcing the Danes to capitulate. The greatest triumph of Congreve's rockets was undoubtedly at the 'Battle of Nations' at Leipzig in October 1813 when the Rocket Troop under Captain Richard Bogue terrified 2,500 into surrender at the moment Bogue was killed. Their success in the Peninsula and at Waterloo was less convincing, not helped by the fact that Wellington had little time for the weapons, despite having witnessed them in India.

For a general who did not merely accept his army as a fighting instrument, Wellington's attitude towards the artillery, the third element of his fighting component, is curious. Not a technical man by nature, he nevertheless grasped the limitations of the main infantry weapon of the day; he acknowledged the limitations of his cavalry, the paucity of his artillery and the dominant characteristics of the soldiers in each component and devised his tactics accordingly. His linear tactics demanded artillery dispersion, which was just as well for, other than perhaps at Waterloo, he never fielded sufficient artillery to establish mass batteries in the Napoleonic style. Following the comprehensive defeat of the French forces at Vitoria in 1813, where ironically some form of artillery massed duel did in fact evolve, comparisons between Wellington and Napoleon are more frequent and thorough. Much emphasis, then and now, has been placed upon Napoleon's artillery roots, his understanding of the arm, his ability to combine its strengths and limitations to best effect on the field of battle. Artillery was integral to the whole and not merely a supporting arm for the infantry and on occasion the cavalry. He embraced and involved himself in the technological advances of all aspects of artillery from the calibre of guns to the axle-width of the limbers and caissons. Many of his lieutenants were Gunner officers commanding all-arms formations; his system of *corps d'armée* fostered an *esprit de corps*.

Wellington, with his army, by contrast appears less convincing; indeed suggestions proliferate that Wellington deliberately undermined the achievements of the Royal Regiment of Artillery in the Peninsula and at Waterloo. Yet, the Regiment's undoubted and undeniable accomplishments in the two campaigns initiated five battery honour titles, firmly established the Royal Horse Artillery in the army's organisation, provided the perfect proving ground for Shrapnel's shell culminating in the 'danger-close' missions to clear the woods in front of the farm at Hougoumont, shaped tactics for the use of mountain guns during the Pyrenean campaign, witnessed the first example of creeping barrage at the siege of San Sebastian, capitalised on the manoeuvrability offered by Congreve senior's block trail and provided a less successful stage for Congreve junior's new rockets. Still, a cloud hangs over its memory. Wellington is accused of over-exerting his influence on artillery matters in the field, of failing to appreciate the need to mass his guns and of lacking sufficient technical knowledge to conduct siege warfare. His personal relations with his artillery commanders were overshadowed by his autocratic and dictatorial manner and his inability to suffer fools gladly, while his treatment of certain individuals, namely Norman Ramsay (see Chapter 17), exemplifies that he was a thankless master to serve. However, it was his treatment and lack of recognition of the Regiment in his Waterloo dispatch which really rankled. In 1872, some 50 years after the battle, upon the publication of the Duke's *Supplementary Letters and Dispatches,* the old wounds reopened and debate raged once again for in the publication appeared a letter from Wellington to the Master General of the Ordnance, Lord Mulgrave, dated 21st December, 1815, in which he wrote 'that to tell you the truth, I was not very pleased with the Artillery at the battle of Waterloo'. He went on to justify his statement by recounting that the artillery, instead of taking shelter in the squares during the French cavalry charges, ran off the field, taking with them their limbers and ammunition carts, thereby denying his artillery support to engage the cavalry when they retreated. They also fired upon the French artillery which he had expressly forbidden.

A few years after the release of the supplementary letters John Fortescue, the Historian of the British Army, summed up the situation:

> The quarrel between the Artillery and Wellington, begun by his unceremonious treatment of his senior officers in the Peninsula, continued by his taking away horses from batteries and giving them to the pontoon-train, embittered by his harshness to Norman Ramsay, and made irreconcilable by his dispatch after Waterloo, renders it difficult to speak of the relations between the two. There can be no doubt that no love was lost between the General and his gunners, but I find it difficult to believe that all the faults were on one side.[35]

Why was this relationship between a commander-in-chief and his artillery component so tempestuous? Were the faults one-sided? The answer lies in a thorough, and long overdue, assessment of Wellington and his Gunners, and the review begins, in August 1808, off the west coast of Portugal ...

Notes

1. The fourth battalion had been established by Royal Warrant in 1771, by raising eight entirely new companies (contrary to Duncan, vol. I, p.251).
2. The Invalid battalion had been established by Royal Warrant in 1779.
3. Bryant, p.80.
4. The term 'Royal Regiment of Artillery' dates back to 1722 and encompassed both the Royal Artillery (RA) and the Royal Horse Artillery (RHA). It is, however, confused by the fact that the term 'Royal Artillery' and abbreviation 'RA' are often used when describing or encompassing the Regiment as a whole.
5. The term battery also existed at the time. The original military term of a battery was derived from the 'battering' guns used to pound enemy strongholds, a task that was undertaken from protected positions known as 'batteries'. In the mid-19th century, following the Indian 'Mutiny', the Indian Presidential armies were reorganised and brought under the Crown resulting in the disbandment of the native artillery and the balance being absorbed into the RA. This provided the catalyst for considerable change and two years later, in 1859, the terms 'brigade' and 'battery' replaced the RA 'battalion' and 'company' and RHA 'troop' – the latter already having the nomenclature 'brigade' for a number of troops of horse artillery. See Hughes, HHT, p.5.

6. The 'Park' was an old term which essentially referred to the artillery attached to the army. In the Napoleonic era it was a depot which contained the heavier and/or spare guns and moved with the army, from where ammunition was re-supplied and repairs were made to guns, carriages, limbers and ammunition wagons.

7. Graham, p.25.

8. Hughes, HOF, pp.54–55.

9. Ibid., p.25.

10. Nosworthy, p.378.

11. See Kiley, p.112; Dawson, Dawson & Summerfield, p.278; and Hughes, HOF, pp.40–45, the last of these for an excellent account of the battle of Minden.

12. The vehicle mounted system consisted of a *'wurst'* which enabled the gun crew to ride on top of the ammunition chest mounted on the trail. See Dawson, Dawson & Summerfield, pp.278–86.

13. Asquith, biographical notes, p.231. There were three Robert Lawsons at that time: the one referred to was No. 369, who attained the rank of lieutenant general; the second, his son, No. 943, saw service throughout the entire Peninsular campaigns and features richly in this history; finally the third, No. 731, died as a young captain at Woolwich in 1802. 'B' Troop was commanded by John MacLeod who became Deputy Adjutant-General Royal Artillery (DAG RA) and who played a pivotal role in all artillery matters during the Revolutionary and Napoleonic Wars.

14. Capt. Hew Dalrymple Ross had assumed command of 'A' Troop in 1806. Despite Duncan's (and others') repeated reference to The Chestnut Troop RHA during this period the Troop's correct title is 'A' Troop until the mid-19th century.

15. Ross, *Memoirs* – introduction by H. Muir, pp.xxv–xxvi.

16. Rogers, p.75.

17. Fortescue, vol. IV, part 2, p.914.

18. Vigors, vol. II, app.J, table 2.

19. Dickson, vol. V, p.895.

20. Dickson, vol. VI, p.1099.

21. Coss, E., app.A. pp.244–63. Coss uses the *British Soldier Compendium* to examine the sample of recruits from 14 infantry regiments, four cavalry regiments and three sources representing a pool for 'unspecified artillery battalions'. The average Gunner recruit is almost identical to his infantry and cavalry counterparts in terms of height (66.52in.), slightly younger in age. (18.89 years compared to 20.48 for the cavalry and 23.40 for the infantry); the Gunners had (as a percentage of enlistees) more English than the other two arms at 69.2%, fewer Irish at 12.2% and more Scottish at 18.4%.

22. See Haythornthwaite, pp.22–42 for a good assessment of the failings of this system.

23. Strachan, p.20.

24. Urban, p.48 and p.230.

25. Glover, p.26.

26. There were four types of rank in the British Army at the time. Substantive rank was the rank that governed pay and allowances (including pension); acting rank provided the rank and pay into which one was 'acting'; temporary rank was just that; and finally brevet rank, which was not a commissioned rank (i.e. could not be sold), could be awarded by a field commander (although only through the MGO in the case of

Gunner or Sapper officers) – it was a permanent rank in that an officer could not be 'demoted' from a brevet rank and as such provided officers the advancement that seniority alone so often denied them.

27. Ordnance is the term used to describe all types of artillery including guns (or cannons), howitzers, mortars and carronades.

28. There were many other types of ordnance used during this period but these were the main pieces used in the Peninsula and at Waterloo.

29. Parlby, pp.136–47. Interview notes of General Dickson by an officer of the Bengal Artillery, dated 17th January 1823.

30. Ibid.

31. A recent publication on Napoleonic Artillery has led to some confusion on the issue of the two types of canister; this has been compounded by an even more recent account of Waterloo. The former leads the reader to understand that canister rounds were only the long range type which burst on impact – unfortunately, the Russian data supplied has no source. Furthermore, it is clear from Smirinov that short range canister was also in use by the Russian artillery.

32. Other nations and inventors have also claimed to have invented the spherical case shot but these assertions have been largely dismissed by later studies and investigations. See Dering Majendie.

33. In fact, these shells had been first used four days earlier at the combat of Roliça on 17th August 1808.

34. Winter, p.35.

35. Fortescue, vol. X, p.216.

CHAPTER 1

Robe's Frustrations

From the deck of the transport *Kingston* Lieutenant Colonel William Robe surveyed the Portuguese coastline; it was a beautifully clear day and the green foliage contrasted starkly with the white quintas[1] and golden sand. On board the atmosphere was good-humoured; the men of Henry Geary's Company were, after five weeks at sea, eager to get back to dry land and equally eager to get to grips with the French. Only six weeks earlier Captain Geary and his men had been enjoying home service at Portsmouth when they received orders to join the transports moving forces from Harwich and Ramsgate to Cork. The force on the east coast had been assembled as the nucleus of a raiding force destined for Boulogne and were redirected to join another force assembling at Cork, which had been likewise redirected from operations in South America. The French invasion of Portugal at the back end of the preceding year and the manifestation of French intentions in Spain in early 1808 provided the British government, eager for a foreign policy success, the perfect opportunity. Lieutenant General Sir Arthur Wellesley was earmarked as the commander of this force:

> The occupation of Spain and Portugal by the troops of France, and the entire usurpation of their respective governments by that power, has determined His Majesty to direct a corps of his troops … to be prepared for service, to be employed, under your orders, in counteracting the designs of the enemy, and in affording to the Spanish and Portuguese nations every possible aid in throwing off the yoke of France.[2]

The transport *Kingston* left Portsmouth harbour on the 20th June and mustered at Cork on the 1st July where she was joined by the transport *Caldicott Castle*, which had left Plymouth in mid-June carrying the second artillery company destined for the force, that of Captain Richard Raynsford. On the 12th July the entire force lifted anchor and sailed south, arriving off the Portuguese coast on the 23rd opposite the landing site at Mondego Bay. Distributed between the two transports were five 9-pounders, ten light 6-pounders, three 5½-inch howitzers (two light, one heavy) and slightly more than 2,500 rounds of various calibres, which the gunners and officers and soldiers of the Field Train aboard the *Kingston* were now busy preparing for disembarkation.[3] Wellesley's orders, written the day prior aboard HMS *Crocodile*, had been received by the artillery commander that morning; there were 15 arrangements. Two were of particular significance to Robe:

> 7th. The commanding officer of artillery is to land the three brigades of artillery, each with half the usual proportion of ammunition, the forge cart, &c. He will also land 500,000 rounds of musket ammunition for the use of the troops, for which carriage will be provided.
>
> 12th. The horses of the Irish commissariat to be handed over, when landed, to the commanding officer of the artillery, who will allot the drivers to take charge of them; and then the officers and drivers belonging to the Irish commissariat to place themselves under the orders of Mr. Pipon.

William Robe's selection to command the artillery was a clear endorsement of his standing in the Regiment; he had every reason to be optimistic and yet he knew full well that his force was inadequately equipped and in danger of being shamed. He had expressed concerns on the dockside at Portsmouth in mid-June; the lack of ordnance stores and equipment, and the requisite means to carry them, preyed heavily on his mind. He examined Wellesley's orders and, having considered them, retired to his cabin and penned a letter to Brigadier General John MacLeod, the Deputy Adjutant General (DAG), RA.

> I shall therefore take the liberty of mentioning to you some points which it may be essential should on future occasions be put right on the embarkation of Artillery … It appears to me necessary that the officer appointed to command Artillery on any expedition should know something more of the nature of the service intended than I did, and that he should not be made to take upon trust that everything necessary for his service will be found on board his ships. Our equipment is not yet arrived at the state of perfection to render such a mode efficient; and if it is practised, the commanding officer of Artillery will find, as I have, that his brigades will be wanting in articles extremely necessary, and be very short indeed in stores intended for repair or for keeping them in good order. He will perhaps find also, as I have, that entrenching tools, and even platforms, are sent with the Engineer's department for a species of service for which he has not a gun, nor a mortar, nor a round of ammunition. I do not make this a matter of complaint to you. I complain not of anything, because I can go no further than use to the best of my ability the means put into my power; but I confess it would have been much more satisfactory to me had I been permitted an opportunity of stating before I

embarked what might have been sent with me for the real benefit of the service, and I don't think it would have occasioned an hour's delay to the embarkation, or have added a shilling of expense to the country, because the essential articles, if not supplied, must be purchased. I have so often mentioned horses that I ought perhaps to apologise for again recurring to that subject; and perhaps it may be said that I have no reason to mention them, having the horses of the Irish Commissariat ordered to be turned over to me on landing. Fortunate, indeed, I think myself to have even them. I know not what figure we should have cut without them; but when you learn that they are acknowledged to be cast horses from the cavalry turned over to the Commissariat, you will readily think that we are not likely to make a very capital figure with them. I have been also fortunate enough to obtain with them a promise of shoes from that branch, sufficient, with the one hundred sets supplied to me, to shoe them on first going off. Future service must be supplied as it can, and I shall not let it go unsupplied.[4]

Robe's concerns were transmitted to the Board of Ordnance but, as we shall see, they received rather a customary bureaucratic rebuff. A month earlier Wellesley, who had also harboured considerable misgivings about the Board and their separate chain of command for some considerable time, had penned similar qualms to Lord Castlereagh, the Secretary of State for War:

> I declare that I do not understand the principles on which our military establishments are formed, if, when a large corps are sent out to perform important and difficult services, they are not to have with them those means of equipment which they require, such as horses to draw artillery, and drivers attached to the commissariat.[5]

Robe had witnessed the same lack of stores and equipment during the siege of Copenhagen in 1806 and, like his commander-in-chief, was acutely aware that the policy of procurement in theatre was a political expedient with significant military shortcomings. Such *contretemps* were quite commonplace in the British Army of the day. With the letter written and his conscience clearer Robe now set about the task at hand. News of a significant Spanish victory over the French at Bailén in mid-July reached Wellesley on the 31st July and, from his temporary quarters aboard HMS *Donegal*, he quickly redirected this welcome report to his force.

The disembarkation commenced on the 1st August; the shores of Mondego Bay are broad and gradual and at right angles to the Atlantic swell. The area had been chosen by Wellesley following his meetings with the Bishop of Oporto, the *de facto* military commander in the city, and Admiral Sir Charles Cotton, the commander of the Portuguese station,[6] who had concurred that to attempt the establishment of a beachhead further south, nearer General Jean-Andoche Junot's cantonments and on less favourable terrain, would be inadvisable. The harbour at Mondego was far from ideal but it was guarded by the fort

1. The Iberian Peninsula and Theatre of Operations

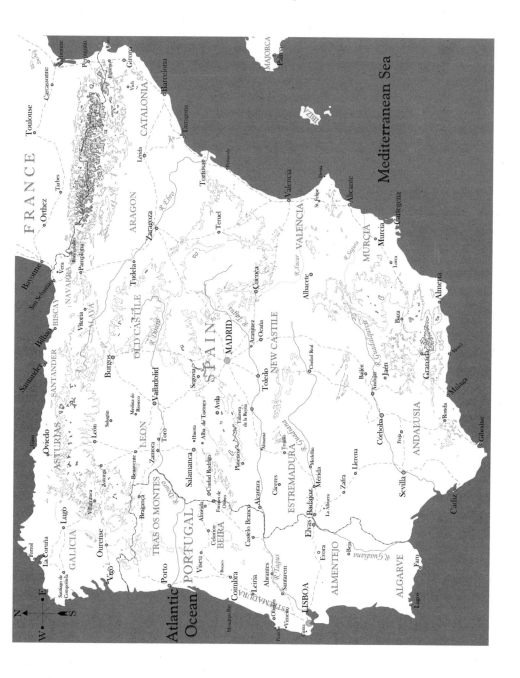

of Figueira, which had been gallantly captured by Portuguese irregulars in the run-up, and was now garrisoned by 300 British marines. It was a beautiful day but the onshore breeze was enough to create reasonable surf across the bar, providing an exhilarating experience for the troops as they rode high on the waves in their flat bottomed boats. Some of the initial boats were upset and a few infantry perished; soldiers and sailors, stripped to the skin, helped with the landing by throwing ropes to the boats and assisting them over the bar and onto the beach.

Once ashore the infantry formed up on the sand and, when companies were complete, they marched inland a few miles, each man carrying three days' pre-cooked rations, and established a makeshift camp just north of Lavos. The artillery, ammunition and heavier stores were landed further up the Mondego estuary and were assisted in their task by the Portuguese bullock-drivers who cut striking figures with their tanned appearance, long black hair and over-large three-cornered hats. Robe mustered the artillery contingent and received, as ordered, the cast horses from the cavalry upon which his worst fears were realised. On the 7th August, from the camp located just north of Lavos, he penned another letter to MacLeod.

… I now deem it my duty (which were I to neglect I should be highly culpable) to point out to you in the strongest manner the impolicy [sic] of sending Artillery to a foreign country without horses. Even the horses we have now, old, blind, and casts from the Cavalry as they are, we find superior to what we can obtain from the country. The latter are good of their kind, but small, and not of sufficient weight for our carriages. Three hundred good horses would have cost the country no more for transport than as many bad ones, and what we shall do for the brigade now to be landed remains to be decided … I must also mention the proportion of general stores which you, sir, know Artillery cannot do without, and which ought to be sent out with every embarkation. Had I been made acquainted with what was to have been embarked, I should not have gone on board ship till the proper proportion had been furnished. I did everything in my power to obtain the information from the Board, and was referred to Mr. Wild, who himself at the time was not furnished with any information. I did at hazard request Mr. Spencer to put on board one hundred sets of horse-shoes and some nails, thinking them an addition to what would be provided for us. These are all I have had for the horses of three brigades; and had I not obtained some more from the Commissary-General, belonging to the horses delivered to us, the horses must have taken the field barefoot. I have made demands for some, and for such things as are most immediately required, and what may be wanted in the meantime must be purchased here.

I write this to you officially, and must not be considered as individually complaining or making difficulties. My people of all classes exert themselves, and I am determined to get on; but I know that, engaged in a department where much is expected, I am doing my country greater service by pointing out what may render that department as complete as it is supposed to be, than if I were to remain for ever silent on the subject.[7]

It had long been the plan at the War Office to supplement Wellesley's force of 9,000 men from Cork with an additional 4,500 from Cadiz and Gibraltar and to this it was hoped to add a further 5,300 regular Portuguese troops under General Bernardino Freire. Wellesley estimated Junot's army at 18,000 men (in fact it was nearer 26,000) and was confident to commence operations at numerical parity, secure in the knowledge that the French commander would have to leave substantial numbers in Lisbon to hold the capital. As it transpired, Wellesley was unable to agree terms for the use of Freire's force; furthermore, the War Office, suspecting the estimates of French strengths in Portugal to have been underplayed, dispatched another 16,000 men to the Peninsula. Two brigades, under Brigadier General Robert Anstruther and Brigadier General Wroth Acland, had sailed on the 19th July while the balance of the reinforcement, consisting of Lieutenant General Sir John Moore's force, which had returned from a failed expedition to the Baltic, would commence south as soon as practically possible. Such enhancement to the size of the British Expeditionary Army would inevitably rob Wellesley, the army's most junior lieutenant general, of overall command.

Observing the initial stages of the disembarkation from the decks of HMS *Donegal*, Wellesley received notification of London's intentions; the Governor of Gibraltar, Lieutenant General Sir Hew Dalrymple, was to be the overall commander and his second in command was to be Lieutenant General Sir Harry Burrard. It was a bitter blow to Wellesley who knew only too well that Sir John Moore's arrival would demote him even further but, for now, he was in command and the shortcomings of the commissariat were becoming all the more apparent.

On the 5th August, the troops had arrived from Andalusia under Major General Sir Brent Spencer and included a half company of artillery with six light 6-pounders which joined Robe at Lavos on the 7th August.[8] Rather confusingly this was Captain Robert Lawson's half company from Gibraltar under the command of Captain William Morrison. Captain Thomas Hughes, the previous commander, had died at Gibraltar on the 18th May 1808; a few days before his death, half the company, under Second Captain Henry Fauquier, had moved to Sicily (never rejoining) while the other half was dispatched from Gibraltar to Cadiz under Spencer and temporary command ceded to Morrison. Lawson was not promoted until the 29th June 1808 and did not catch up with his command until later in the year. Morrison was delighted at the opportunity to escape the Rock where he had served for nearly five years but his enthusiasm was to be cut short when he realised the chronic shortage of horses on his arrival at the camp at Lavos. Every effort was being made by both Wellesley's staff and the commissariat to procure more local livestock. In the interim, Robe submitted his plans for the allocation of half brigades to support the six Brigades of Line, and outlined his intentions to keep the 9-pounder half brigades in reserve. His plans, which were approved by Wellesley on the 8th August, were as follows:[9]

CRA: Lt. Col. W. Robe RA
Staff: Maj. J. Viney RA
Brigade Major: Vacant

Infantry Brigade	Guns Commanded by	Equipment
Maj. Gen. Hill	Capt. Raynsford	2 x 6-pounders 1 x heavy 5½-inch howitzer
Maj. Gen. Ferguson	Lt. Locke	2 x 6-pounders 1 x 5½-inch howitzer
Brig. Gen. Fane	Capt. Geary	2 x 6-pounders 1 x 5½-inch howitzer
Brig. Gen. Bowes	Lt. Festing	3 x 6-pounders
Brig. Gen. C. (Catlin) Craufurd	Capt. Morrison	2 x 6-pounders 1 x 5½-inch howitzer
Brig. Gen. Nightingall	Lt. Graham	3 x 6-pounders
Reserve half brigades of guns – Maj. Viney to superintend		
Capt. Gardiner and Lt. Johnson		3 x 9-pounders
Second Capt. Eliot and Lt. Hawker		2 x 9-pounders 1 x heavy 5½-inch howitzer

Source: Robe

The same day Robe wrote two letters to Wellesley requesting permission to increase his civil establishment and to appoint Geary as his Brigade Major, RA. Wellesley's prompt reply serves to reinforce the inadequacies of the extant chain of command of the period and the common frustrations experienced by those who endured such arrangements in the field:

I have the honor [*sic*] to acknowledge the receipt of your letter of this date, representing the inadequacy of the assistance in the Civil department of the Ordnance with which you have been provided for this service; the same being only one clerk of stores, who is also Paymaster, and five conductors of stores, two of whom have never yet joined. I have to acquaint you, in reply thereto, that although I fully concur with you in considering the establishment insufficient for the performance of all the duties required of it, yet I do not consider myself warranted in giving my authority for the increase of the same, or of granting any allowance to persons holding the temporary appointments in the Ordnance department, until the sanction of the Board be obtained. It is, therefore, not in my power to make the appointment pro tempore, specified in the scale annexed to your letter. I have likewise to acquaint you, in reply to your letter of this date, respecting the appointment of a Brigade Major, in consequence of the junction of the two detachments, by the arrival of Major General Spencer's corps, that however the extension of your duties may render the assistance of such a Staff Officer necessary, I have it not in my power to make the appointment, nor to issue allowance to any Officer acting in that capacity, without the concurrence of the Board of Ordnance.[10]

Wellesley's reply came as no surprise to Robe who now had a more pressing problem on his hands. Lawson's half company had arrived with no horses, one corporal, one artificer and only 12 drivers. With no horses, and none to be had from local sources, the consequences were plain and unavoidable: Wellesley summed up the situation in his report to Viscount Castlereagh, later the same day.

> I shall be obliged to leave Spencer's guns behind for want of means of moving them; and I should have been obliged to leave my own, if it were not for the horses of the Irish Commissariat. Let nobody ever prevail upon you to send a corps to any part of Europe without horses to draw their guns. It is not true that horses lose their condition at sea.[11]

Wellesley had also requested 150 draught mules from Oporto but alas they were not to arrive in time and early on the 9th August the six small brigades under generals Rowland Hill, Ronald Ferguson, Miles Nightingall, Barnard Bowes, Catlin Craufurd and Henry Fane moved south on the coast road to Vieira. The light 6-pounder brigade from Gibraltar was left at Lavos but Morrison's gunners manned the 9-pounder guns brought from England and formed the reserve under Craufurd. Raynsford and Geary were both equipped with light 6-pounder brigades (consisting of five light 6-pounders and one light 5½-inch howitzer) and moved as brigades with the army (for the better preservation of the guns and stores[12]) but stood ready to deploy in half brigades to their respective army brigades as required. Wellesley met the Portuguese regional commander, General Freire, at Leiria but the two were unable to agree terms for the amalgamation of the two forces and Wellesley parted, somewhat disgruntled, with an *ad hoc* group of 2,300 Portuguese under the command of Colonel Nicholas Trant, a British officer in Portuguese service. Wellesley's decision to keep his force near to the coast was predicated on his desire to keep in touch with the fleet for reasons of supplies and to simplify the link-up with the two brigades that were *en route* from England.

Junot was well aware of the arrival of a British force to the north and as early as the 1st August had already recalled Loison and his division from their position on the Spanish border, facing Badajoz, with instructions to march with all haste to join the main French force. General Henri Delaborde was equally smartly dispatched from Lisbon with orders to observe and (if necessary) contain Wellesley until the French had concentrated. Delaborde had pushed as far north as Alcobaça and as the British approached on the 14th August he had considered making a stand to get better intelligence as to the strength of the force. However, the position offered little by way of defensive qualities and he elected to pull back to Roliça, leaving an advance post at Obidos. A brief infantry skirmish took place just outside the northern walls of the medieval town on the 15th August, but it was to be another two days before Wellesley's forces were up, in position and ready to advance against Delaborde's divisional sized force at Roliça. Reconnaissance revealed that the French position could be easily turned on either flank and Wellesley drew up orders to try and envelop the defenders.

The plan of attack was formed accordingly, and the army, having broken up from Caldas this morning, was formed into three columns. The right, consisting of 1200 Portuguese infantry, 50 Portuguese cavalry, destined to turn the enemy's left, and penetrate into the mountains in his rear. The left, consisting of Major General Ferguson's and Brig. General Bowes's brigade of infantry, three companies of riflemen, a brigade of light artillery, and twenty British and twenty Portuguese cavalry, was destined, under the command of Major General Ferguson, to ascend the hills at Obidos, to turn all the enemy's posts on the left of the valley, as well as the right of his post at Roliça. This corps was also destined to watch the motions of General Loison on the enemy's right, who, I had heard, had moved from Rio Mayor towards Alcoentre last night. The centre column, consisting of Major General Hill's, Brig. General Nightingall's, Brig. General C. Craufurd's, and Brig. General Fane's brigades (with the exception of the riflemen detached with Major General Ferguson), and 400 Portuguese light infantry, the British and Portuguese cavalry, a brigade of 9 pounders, and a brigade of 6 pounders, was destined to attack General Laborde's [Delaborde's] position in the front.[13]

Robe allocated the left flank to Raynsford, while Geary remained in the centre with Morrison and the heavier guns were kept to the rear in reserve. The French held their ground until the flanking manoeuvres were well developed and then fell back to a more defendable position atop the Columbeira heights. Despite Wellesley's intention to hold the centre until his flanking forces had advanced sufficiently to commence their turning movement, the British infantry had the bit between their teeth and the 29th, spurred on by their somewhat rash commanding officer, quickly found themselves rather isolated in one of the many gullies that ascended to the top of the feature. They were speedily supported by the 9th and the 5th but any chance of enveloping Delaborde's force evaporated as the fighting concentrated on extracting the 29th before pushing on. Delaborde hung on for two hours before the British flanking forces began to threaten; he then ordered his force to retire, which they did, hard pressed all the way through the pass at Azambujeira, and in the ensuing confusion he was forced to abandon three of his guns. Heavily outnumbered it was not a great victory; Delaborde had only intended to delay the British, and this he achieved, but the action nevertheless provided all the British commanders, not least Robe, a chance to measure their men. Raynsford had not been employed but Geary and Morrison, despite the problems of elevation up to the heights from the village of Columbeira, had been in the thick of it. During the second phase of the attack Robe had ordered Geary's guns to fire two shrapnel shells, the first ever fired in action. Their target was Delaborde's battery and the effect was immediate: the French guns ceased firing canister, which was having a devastating effect on the red-coated infantry, and loaded round shot, concentrating their fire against the British guns.

A brigade of artillery being required in front of the attacking columns a rush was at once made by two of the batteries disengaged to be first at the point of honour.

40

Captain Geary's battery was, however, the first to cross the small stone bridge over the Columbeira, and the other at once retired. In a short time the top of the heights was reached by this battery, and the guns were prepared for action. The French skirmishers advanced to within sixty yards of the guns, and Geary having fired one gun charged with canister, as he pointed the second said, "I'll be properly into them this …" time he would have added, but he raised his hand half way to his head and fell to the ground perfectly lifeless. A shot had passed through his head, having entered half an inch above his left eyebrow.[14]

Lieutenant William B. Patten, Robe's adjutant, led the funeral service that evening at 2000 hours at which Geary's body was rolled in a sheet and buried by the officers of the artillery and engineers. Robe's report to MacLeod the following day paid tribute to his brother officer:

> Our own loss, though small in number, is irreparable, our friend Geary being the only sufferer. He was by his own desire, and as senior Captain, in charge of the guns with the light brigade, and was killed while pointing his gun, within one or two hundred yards of the Enemy. I regret him as an Officer, for he was invaluable, and as a friend, and old fellow campaigner, by no means less. His loss to his family cannot be appreciated, but it will always be a comfort, that he died as he lived, in the very act of doing his duty to his Country, and a true Christian.
>
> I do not know how this will go, and we are again on the march after the Enemy. I shall therefore, defer saying what I have to say about our equipment and only desire that the Spherical Case, some time ago demanded, may be sent forthwith. I never will leave England again provided in the manner I have been, nor with less than half my whole stock in that Ammunition.
>
> All our Officers and men are well and hearty, not a man sick.[15]

Wellesley's dispatch to Viscount Castlereagh was more thorough, the closing paragraphs characteristically highlighting the strengths of his officers and men:

> I cannot sufficiently applaud the conduct of the troops throughout this action. The enemy's positions were formidable, and he took them up with his usual ability and celerity, and defended them most gallantly. But I must observe, that although we had such a superiority of numbers employed in the operations of this day, the troops actually engaged in the heat of the action were, from unavoidable circumstances, only the 5th, 9th, 29th, the riflemen of the 95th and 60th, and the flank companies of Major General Hill's brigade; being a number by no means equal to that of the enemy. Their conduct therefore deserves the highest commendation.
>
> I cannot avoid taking this opportunity of expressing my acknowledgments for the aid and support I received from all the General and other Officers of this army: I am particularly indebted to Major General Spencer for the advice and assistance I received from him; to Major General Ferguson, for the manner in

which he led the left column; and to Major General Hill, and Brig. Generals Nightingall and Fane, for the manner in which they conducted the different attacks which they led.

I derived most material assistance also from Lieut. Colonel Tucker and Lieut. Colonel Bathurst, in the offices of Deputy Adjutant and Deputy Quarter Master General, and from the Officers of the Staff employed under them. I must also mention that I had every reason to be satisfied with the artillery under Lieut. Colonel Robe. I have the honor to enclose herewith a return of killed, wounded, and missing.[16]

Wellesley's perfunctory inclusion of the performance of the Royal Artillery was to become an all too familiar theme in his dispatches throughout the war and up to and including Waterloo. By and large it derived, not as a personal slight against the officers and men of the artillery, but as a result of the Gunners' separate chain of command which he found undeniably hard to accept and understandably difficult to manage. Robe had every reason to be content and proud of his men; for had Wellesley found reason to be dissatisfied with the performance of the Royal Artillery that fact would have been made unashamedly clear. For now, with Junot closing from the south, General Louis Henri Loison from the east and the lack of ammunition, equipment and horses, the Commander Royal Artillery (CRA) had other things on his mind.

Following their opening engagement, the British Army had moved south, and established a defensive position in and around the village of Vimeiro facing south. Anstruther's Brigade had arrived from Ramsgate and had disembarked, slightly further north, at Paimogo, while that of Acland, from Harwich, had landed at Porto Novo, just to the west of Vimeiro. Both were ashore by last light on the 20th August and were incorporated into the overall scheme of defence. Neither brigade had brought artillery, which was probably just as well for, had they have done so, there would have been no means of moving the guns. Robe's three brigades constituted the army's artillery; Captain William Granville Elliot had stepped up to command Geary's Company and morale, while high, was tinged with apprehension for all the men were well aware that events at Roliça were a mere soupçon.

The new commander of the British Army had arrived at the tail end of Acland's convoy but was in no great hurry to come ashore and give up the comforts afforded on board the sloop *Brazen*. Well aware that Sir John Moore and his force were *en route* from the Baltic, Sir Harry Burrard[17] was content to wait for their arrival before getting embroiled. Wellesley, beating back across the surf from his meeting with the commander elect, was elated; Junot was closing and the likelihood of a major engagement was high. At around midnight the sounds of an approaching force became all the more apparent and, soon after first light, the first elements of the French columns became visible. It soon became evident that their axis of advance was not towards the village of Vimeiro but well to the east forcing a rapid redeployment of the British lines; the speed and composure of this reorganisation was an early glimmer of Wellesley's self-possession and tactical genius. Junot conversely demonstrated considerably less aptitude: following a token reconnaissance he split his force, and then executed a rather matter-of-fact attack in the centre combined with a decidedly optimistic right flanking manoeuvre. He paid the price.

The British artillery had played a crucial role in disrupting and dispersing both French attacks in the centre prompting William Napier to record the 'solid firmness and resolute thrust of the Infantry, and the wonderful skill and precision of the Artillery'.[18] During the attack on the village of Vimeiro, General Fane had concentrated one half brigade of 9-pounder guns (from the reserve) and another of 6-pounders, which played on the advancing French columns with 'such a shower of shell and grape as might have been sufficient to stop any troops'.[19] Despite making it to the summit of the hill south of Vimeiro, they were so 'shattered by the terrible fire of Robe's Artillery' that the soldiers of the 50th Foot were able to drive them back down the hill with relative ease. Both Thomières's and Charlot's brigades broke and fled, hotly pursued by the jubilant British infantry who chased them for many hundreds of yards, capturing seven French guns from Prost's battery in the process. While waiting for Brigadier General Antoine Brennier's and Brigadier General Jean-Baptiste Solignac's right flanking manoeuvre to unfold, Junot dispatched General François Kellermann with a column of the grenadier reserve to maintain the momentum in the centre. Kellermann would have clearly seen the guns in support of Acland's Brigade on the hillside to the right of his advance but, at a range of 750 yards, would have accepted the anticipated damage from standard projectiles. He had not expected the 'black rain' that followed. The shrapnel shells, air bursting over the French ranks as they filed forward in the narrow entrance to the village, were causing an alarming number of casualties. General Maximilien-Sébastien Foy recalled that 'the Shrapnel-shells at the first discharge struck down the files of a platoon, and then exploded in the platoon that followed'.[20] The fight for the village was a brutal affair but there can be little doubt that the demoralising and disruptive effect of Shrapnel's shells on Kellermann's grenadiers played a crucial part in convincing the aged but capable commander to call off the attack. During the subsequent French extraction, the British cavalry were provided their first opportunity for action but, unfortunately, the 20th Light Dragoons grossly overextended their pursuit and many, including their commanding officer, were cut off and killed.

The flanking movement to the north was as tardily executed as it was conceived with the two French brigades of Brennier and Solignac becoming separated. Expecting only a token force they were outwitted by Wellesley who had moved, in dead ground, three brigades and two half brigades of (light 6-pounder) guns. Initially Solignac was picked off and subsequently Brennier, when Bowes's Brigade joined those of Ferguson and Nightingall, and the artillery was particularly effective in neutralising the three French guns. With both attacks soundly beaten and his force separated by a distance of one and a half miles, Junot was in the most precarious position; with the French at his mercy Wellesley, despite a paucity of cavalry, was poised to strike but Burrard, no doubt stirred by sounds of battle, had ventured ashore and reined in the ambitions of the younger general. With the French in full retreat and the way to Lisbon open, Burrard's decision was not well received by the officers and men, although Robe must have received this news with an element of sanguinity, as the artillery mounts would have been hard pressed to keep up with the chase. The euphoria of victory was quickly replaced by a more sombre disposition involving the completing of post-conflict organisation and administration. That evening, from the camp at Vimeiro, Robe wrote a lengthy letter to MacLeod:

I wrote to you an account of the attack made by our army at Roliça, and of its success, and of the unpleasant news of my worthy friend Geary – I have now to inform you that the enemy having retired, our army came to this place to protect the landing of two brigades under Major General Anstruther, and Brigadier General Ackland, which joined yesterday and today: the enemy reconnoitred our posts last night, and kept us on the alert, and this morning attacked us in form, having a numerous cavalry; of the results of the attack you will be informed by the following accounts. I shall only tell you, that their advance was so apparently determined, that I was obliged to return my guns to a neighbouring height, then being well supported by the 50th Regiment the matter was soon settled – similar occurrences took place on the left – 500 prisoners, 1000 killed and wounded, 12 pieces of cannon, now already sent to the ships … never was man better supported by his officers and soldiers than I have been – I would not change one of them from the major to the youngest subaltern for any thing [sic] in the world …

I have now from experience a right to speak, of what the whole army have witnessed the good effect in every instance … Shrapnel's Spherical Case Shot – the man must be blind who does not allow its authority, and I mean to demand if left with me on any future occasion, half of my whole stock in this sort of ammunition for any guns – this with some other points will be the subject of a future letter. Mean time [sic] I am happy to say my loss today has been *only* [italics added] two drivers, and two horses killed and one gunner and two horses wounded.[21]

Robe had every reason to be pleased; his men had performed well, his losses were light, Shrapnel's new shells had exceeded expectations, the French were on the ropes and, later in the day, the artillery reinforcements (379 officers and men) landed with the two brigades from England. Sadly no horses or artillery stores were included in the manifests and while Burrard handed over command to Sir Hew Dalrymple, and the army adjusted to its third commander in less than a day, Robe was more concerned with the immediate welfare of his men and preparing to hand over command of the Royal Artillery to a more senior Gunner officer who was just days away. In the interim he also found time to write to Colonel Henry Shrapnel.

I have waited a few days to collect what information I could as to the effects of your Spherical Case in two actions which have taken place with the enemy on the 17th and 21st instant, and can now tell you it is admirable to the whole army … I should not do my duty to the service were I not to attribute our good fortune to a good use of that weapon with which you have furnished us. I told Sir A Wellesley I meant to write to you and asked if it might be with his concurrence, his answer was 'you may say anything you please, you cannot say too much, for never was artillery fired with better effect'. I have no objection to your making what use of this letter you think proper. I have already stated my opinion of it to the Deputy Adjutant General and shall do so to the Board from where I should have demanded a very large proportion had I have remained [*sic*] in command.[22]

Junot, relieved by the failure of the British Army to capitalise on the fruits of victory, dispatched his most able negotiator to seek terms. Kellermann, who had served as an attaché in the French Embassy in the United States in 1791, spoke excellent English and was well suited to his task. He was relieved to discover that Wellesley no longer held the immediate reins of command and surprised to detect that Moore's force had not yet landed. Furthermore, he quickly grasped that Dalrymple was decidedly uneasy about how to proceed. Kellermann, who had been happy to save the French Army at all costs, sensed the opportunity and now began to haggle about much of the finer detail. The resulting Convention of Cintra so ludicrously favoured the French that it infuriated the Portuguese, puzzled the Spanish, angered the Admiralty, baffled the Army and, slightly later, provoked a 'frantic rage' with the British public and establishment. Dalrymple, Burrard and Wellesley were summoned home to explain themselves while, to make matters worse, Junot's army was repatriated to France in Royal Naval vessels. Despite this, Portugal had been liberated and Napoleon's plan to enforce the Continental System on Britain's oldest ally was in ruins.

Notes

1. Portuguese farm or manor house.
2. WD, vol. IV, pp.16–19. Castlereagh to Wellesley, dated 30th June 1808.
3. The Field Train was a corps attached to the RA, whose officers wore RA uniforms and held comparative rank in the army, according to their respective grades. The Field Train was responsible for preparing and delivering the battering trains and field brigades of artillery: it was part of the Commissariat and came under the Ordnance Commissary and, as such, received instructions from the Board of Ordnance. See Henegan, vol. 1, p.17.
4. Robe Papers.
5. SD, vol. IV, p.87. Wellesley to Castlereagh, 29th June 1808.
6. The Admiralty had established three naval commands. The north coast of Spain and the Bay of Biscay were the responsibility of the Channel Fleet; the Portuguese station was initially exclusive to Gibraltar and Cadiz; and the Mediterranean Fleet stretched from Cape St. Vincent eastwards.
7. Robe Papers.
8. This was Lawson's half company from Gibraltar. Bredin's and Skyring's companies had also departed Gibraltar in August but they did not disembark at Mondego, perhaps due to the chronic shortages of horses and equipment, and instead mustered at Cascais on the 1st September. There is some confusion as to whether these two companies

accompanied Wellesley in August or whether they were at the battles of Roliça and Vimeiro but Leslie (LRA), ch.1, pp.7–16, provides good evidence that they were not.

9. Robe Papers.

10. WD, vol. IV, p.71. Wellesley to Robe, dated 8th August 1808.

11. WD, vol. IV, pp.72–73. Wellesley to Castlereagh, dated 8th August 1808.

12. Robe Papers.

13. WD, vol. IV, pp.96–97. Wellesley to Castlereagh, dated 17th August 1808.

14. Browne, pp.131–32.

15. PRO WO 55/1193 p.490, battle of Roliça.

16. WD, vol. IV, pp.96–99. Wellesley to Castlereagh, dated 17th August 1808.

17. In fact Harry Burrard had begun his military career in the RA, having entered the Military Academy in April 1768. He was commissioned in June 1772 but resigned that commission four years later and bought into the 60th Regiment.

18. Napier, vol. I, p.213.

19. Ibid., p.218.

20. Foy, vol. II, p.521.

21. Robe Papers.

22. Ibid. Letter from camp near Torres Vedras, dated 25th August 1808.

CHAPTER 2

Harding's Preparations

Sir John Moore and his force, of 10,000 men, had been redirected to the Peninsula after he had failed to reconcile his military instructions with the military aspirations of the unbalanced King of Sweden, Gustavus IV.[1] They arrived off the Portuguese coast on the 24th August, running close to the shore from the mouth of the Douro to the Mondego; the next day they anchored in Maceira Bay and commenced disembarkation. Despite the good weather it was to take a full five days to get all the men and equipment ashore; the Royal Navy had been supplied with flat-bottomed landing boats which struggled in the Atlantic surf. Lieutenant Richard Henegan, attached to Moore's force as the Military Commissary in the Field Train, takes up the story.

A rapid succession of these boats, closely packed with human beings, went tumbling through the surf, discharging on the beach their living cargoes, with little damage beyond a complete drenching. But as the day advanced, the surf increased, and each succeeding boat encountered increasing difficulties in reaching land. At one moment upwards of twenty boats were struggling with the waves, and an awful anxiety for their fate was experienced on board the ships they had left, and by those who awaited on shore. The sea had grown higher and higher, and the foaming billows broke furiously over the beach, raising a cloud of spray along its margin. Some of the boats were raised high upon the mountain waves, and dashed by them in safety on the shore; but others, less fortunate, came broadside and the next moment were floating bottom upwards.

The soldiers, encumbered with their heavy packs, could make but feeble and ineffectual efforts to save themselves, and drowning men, in all the horrors of unavailing struggles, were seen in all directions convulsively buffeting with the waves. Some were picked up by the lighter and better managed craft of the men-of-war; others were saved by the intrepid endeavours of their comrades on shore, who disencumbering themselves of their kits, plunged through the boiling surf to the rescue.

The foremost in this enterprise of danger was a young Scotch [*sic*] gunner, in Captain Drummond's company of artillery, of the name of McNeil. Three times he had returned to land in safety, bearing at each return an exhausted comrade in his arms. Another boat upset in bounding through the dangerous whirlpool; McNeil heard the cry of despair from the crew and although his strength was subdued by great exertion, threw himself into the raging element, to return, alas! No more. The noble fellow had grasped the arm of one of the imploring suppliants, when the prow of the ship's launch, impelled by a heavy sea, struck him a fatal blow upon the head. He sank, and towards the evening the tide left his inanimate body on the shore. It was interred the same night, the funeral service being read over it by one of his own officers.[2]

Moore's force included over 700 men of the Royal Artillery and the King's German Artillery (KGA) under the command of Colonel John Harding, who was destined to assume command of artillery from Robe. With Harding were two brigades of artillery under captains Edward Wilmot and Percy Drummond and three companies of artillery from the King's German Legion (KGL) under Major George Julius Hartmann, KGA;[3] despite being better equipped with horses than Robe's original group, the unfortunate creatures had been confined to ship for many weeks and took a considerable time to regain suitable condition and their land legs.[4] Robe wasted little time in writing to Harding and informing him of the inadequacies of the artillery; on the 1st September, from a camp near Sobral, Robe informed his commander 'that no less than 250 horses would be required to render the artillery of Sir A. Wellesley's Division efficient'.[5] In fact Wellesley was, understandably, having difficulty coming to terms with his new subordinate position and had written, only the day prior, to Lord Castlereagh, the Secretary of War, outlining his feelings. 'I assure you, my dear Lord, matters are not prospering here; and I feel an earnest desire to quit the army. I have been too successful with this army ever to serve with it in a subordinate situation, with satisfaction to the person who shall command it, and of course not to myself. However, I shall do whatever the Government may wish.'[6] With the negotiations for the Convention of Cintra concluded by the 30th August, Wellesley, despite his unease and frustration, entered into considerable correspondence updating the new commander-in-chief on the key issues. One of the first to receive consideration was the lack of suitable mounts for the artillery, and on the 1st September, he wrote to Dalrymple.

As it is probable that you will take an early opportunity of communicating with England, I think it proper at this time to submit to you the enclosed state of the horses attached to the artillery, with the corps which has hitherto been under my command. As it was not deemed expedient that I should take with me horses belonging to the artillery, horses belonging to the Irish Commissariat were embarked for the purpose of drawing the artillery, which horses were of a very inferior description, being either cast horses from the dragoons, or horses purchased in Ireland at a very low price, viz., 12/. or 13/. each ... They have however performed the service hitherto, but with the aids and losses stated in the enclosed papers; and you will observe that there are at this moment seventy six of them with incurable diseases. As these horses were never intended to perform the service of the artillery, and as I have every reason to believe that mules will not answer to draw our ordnance carriages, and that the country does not afford horses of a proper description, I cannot avoid recommending to you to call the attention of His Majesty's Government to this subject at an early period; and to require an immediate supply of 300 artillery horses to draw the brigades of ordnance which have been hitherto attached to this corps, if you should have reason to expect that you shall require any further active service from those guns. I had already apprised the Secretary of State of the inadequacy of these horses to the service required of them. While writing upon this subject, it is proper to remind you, that there is another brigade of 6 pounders belonging to the corps hitherto called mine, three pieces of which are in the ships, and three were left at Leyria [Leiria], as the horses were unable to draw them on.[7]

By mid-September 1808, the British Army had concentrated in and around Lisbon and, with the evacuation of the French and the repatriation of the Russian sailors and confiscation of their squadron ongoing,[8] Dalrymple busied himself with the establishment of an emergency government and the reorganisation of the army from brigades to divisions. Wellesley's advice concerning these matters was constantly ignored and his optimism and loyalty waned accordingly. Dalrymple, sensing Wellesley's unease, suggested that he go to Madrid to discuss options with the Spanish, an offer that Wellesley bluntly turned down on the basis that 'he did not possess the confidence of those who employed him'.[9] On the 20th September he set sail for England and landed at Plymouth on 4th October to be greeted with the welcome news that both Dalrymple and Burrard had been summoned home to explain the circumstances of the Cintra Convention but to his horror discovered that he too was considered no less culpable. General Sir David Dundas headed the Board of Inquiry, which commenced on the 14th November and concluded just over a month later. Burrard and Dalrymple were deemed unfit to ever again appear in the field, while Wellesley was marked as a man with ability and resourcefulness, eminently fit to be employed again; it was to be a visionary judgement.

In early October, as the last of the French troops embarked, Sir John Moore had assumed command of the British Army and immediately set about preparing to move the force east in support of the Spanish. Additional forces had continued to arrive throughout September and the artillery organisation was as follows:

CRA: Col. J. Harding
Staff: Lt. Col. W. Robe
Lt. Col. G. A. Wood

Maj. J. Viney
Brigade Major: Capt. R. W. Gardiner

Companies	Notes	Equipment
Lawson's Company	Half company, commanded by Capt. Morrison.	3-pounders
Raynsford's Company		9-pounders
Geary's Company	Geary was KIA at Roliça – Capt. R. Carthew now in command.	Light 6-pounders
Drummond's Company	Landed end August as part of Moore's force.	Light 6-pounders
Wilmot's Company	Landed end August as part of Moore's force.	Light 6-pounders
Crawford's Company	Landed August and September.	Light 6-pounders
Thornhill's Company	Arrived September to act as Park and Stores Company.	No guns
Bredin's Company	Arrived September.	Light 6-pounders
Skyring's Company	Arrived September to act as Advanced Depot.	No guns
1st Gesenius's Company KGA	Landed end August as part of Moore's force.	Medium 12-pounders
2nd Teiling's Company KGA	Landed end August as part of Moore's force.	Light 6-pounders
4th Heise's Company KGA	Landed end August as part of Moore's force.	Light 6-pounders
Detachment RA Drivers	From 'A', 'C', 'E', 'H' and 'I' troops.	

Sources: Compilation from Laws, Dickson, Duncan, Vigors and Leslie.

Harding and his staff were busy establishing batteries in the forts at Cascais, São Julião and Belem and arranging equipment and stores for the artillery group that was to accompany Moore's army. Lieutenant Henegan recalls the arduous nature of this duty:

> The first orders I received in Portugal were to proceed with a party of gunners to the fortress of Belem, which had been evacuated the previous evening by the French, who had embarked on board our transports for their own country, in accordance with the Convention of Cintra. This service occupied three days, during which we waged a most unsuccessful warfare against a countless host of enemies, in the shape of fleas … We finished this inglorious campaign by returning to Prazzo d'Arcos, where the artillery was encamped, and there making a report to the commanding officer, Colonel Wood, of one hundred and twenty brass guns, mounted upon garrison carriages, a very considerable quantity of ammunition, and an innumerable number of French fleas, prisoners of war, being in a serviceable state in the Fortress of Belem.[10]

At Yeovil, on the 9th December 1795, Sergeant Somerville of the Royal Artillery West Country recruiting team had recognised the ability of a young 20-year old lad who presented himself to the squad. Benjamin Miller could read and write; a very rare talent among village boys of the day. He was immediately enlisted and, following his basic training at Woolwich, had volunteered for service in Gibraltar where he joined Captain John Bradbridge's Company of the 4th Battalion. In 1808, Miller was a bombardier and part of Captain George Skyring's Company, which landed in the Tagus estuary on the 1st and 2nd of September and quartered at the Fort São Julião, along the coast about 10 miles west of Lisbon. Skyring had no guns and was essentially brought to the Peninsula to act as an artillery reserve unit. Miller did not have to wait long for orders to deploy.

> I was now ordered to Lisbon and from thence, with an officer of Artillery, 1 Sergeant, 1 Corporal, 2 Bombardiers, and 30 Gunners, to join the 6th Regiment of Foot, to proceed to Almeida and take possession of it, as the French refused to give it up to the Portuguese ... As we were the first British troops that had marched through any of the towns, we were much caressed, and saluted with cries of 'Viva Engles', 'Bueno Englies', 'Rumpu Francies', and in some of the large towns, of which we went through a great number, we were saluted with rockets, fires, and firing of fowling pieces, and the women covered us with flowers and laurel leaves; the ladies even threw laurels and flowers from the windows on us ... At a town called Larica [Lerida] I went and saw the church where the French soldiers shot five friars at the altar. The blood was still to be seen, likewise the shot holes in the altar ... We arrived in sight of Almeida on 1 October, 1808, after a long and tiresome march of 300 miles and took up our abode in the Friar's Convent. Next morning we formed up at the gates of the fortress. The French marched out prisoners of war and we took possession of it.[11]

Colonel Harding and his staff worked tirelessly during the month of September; there was much to do and, as if preparing his artillery to join Moore's force and taking stock of the defences of the forts in and around Lisbon was not enough, he was also called upon to re-equip the artillery of the Spanish division under General Juan Carrafa which was to be transported by the Royal Navy to Catalonia.[12] The whole army sought suitable draught and pack animals; not only were those in short supply, but the owners of those few that existed had no intention of contracting their services or their animals to the frontier let alone into Spain. Inevitably, Harding was forced to leave a number of batteries in Lisbon including the three from the KGA as well as Andrew Bredin's and Robert Lawson's companies. The Germans were instructed to hand over all their serviceable horses to the British to bring the five gun batteries up to strength.[13] Robe, who was left in charge of the artillery at Lisbon, had only 64 horses and seven mules and most of those were sick or lame. He wrote to MacLeod on the 6th November, by which time numbers had fallen to 40, and stated that 'to meet the demands from the front a reserve of 600 horses would be required'.[14] This chronic lack of mounts would inevitably have shaped Harding's decision to leave the KGA as the 12-pounder guns required ten draughts and the long 6-pounder guns eight draughts, compared to six for the light 6-pounder. Ironically, in the French Army there was no question of providing horses for the artillery from cast cavalry mounts, as was often the British solution and yet the magnificent opportunity, following the Convention of Cintra, of obtaining numerous fit French artillery horses was let slip.

Harding's Brigade Major RA, Captain Robert Gardiner, had already seen considerable service and had been at Roliça and Vimeiro, but his excitement at the possibility of more action was hard to contain. In a letter to his good friend Captain Frank Bedingfield he wrote:

> Sir John Moore proceeds to Spain with 20,000 men to act with the troops embarked under Sir D Baird. The first columns move forward in the course of two or three days. Our route lies towards Burgos by Almeida on the borders of Portugal. The march and season, at present so unfavourable, will I fear greatly reduce our numbers, but I earnestly hope and trust we shall arrive in time to render the Spaniards a benefit. The distance, nearly 700 miles, is alarming but the passes of St. Jean de Port and others of the Pyrenees offer as many obstacles to the route of Napoleon's troops as we are threatened with.[15]

In fact Moore had more than 20,000 men but in addition to his problems of how to move and sustain them, he was unsure of how best to advance the force geographically. Despite Dalrymple's being empowered (by Lord Castlereagh) to commence planning as early as the 2nd September, no plan had been drawn up and no reconnaissance of routes ordered. Of particular concern to the British commander was the suitability of routes for the artillery; as Gardiner pointed out, the season was against them. Moore consulted a number of officers from the old Portuguese Army who, to a man, informed him that the roads via Almeida were unfit for artillery.

> It is, therefore, only necessary to observe, that the Portuguese authorities at Lisbon showed a contemptible ignorance of the topography of their own country, and the state of its roads; and as Sir John Moore was under the necessity of forming his plans for the march of his troops, in a great measure, on this erroneous information, serious evils necessarily resulted.[16]

Henegan's singular criticism of his Portuguese hosts was not entirely fair for Moore also consulted British officers, whom Dalrymple had dispatched towards Almeida to assist the Portuguese in requisitioning the fort from the French garrison, and they corroborated the Portuguese reports. As a result, six of the seven batteries were sent on a southerly route via Elvas, along with the (only) two cavalry regiments and four infantry battalions acting as escort; all under the command of General Sir John Hope. Only Wilmot's light 6-pounder battery remained with the main body of the army, which travelled on three more north-easterly routes. It was to be a costly error, for the main body arrived at Salamanca on the 13th November, while the balance of the guns and all the cavalry did not appear for another three weeks and Moore, devoid of artillery and cavalry, had been unable to commence operations. By the time the army was complete, Madrid had fallen, and the situation had altered considerably.

While Moore had been grappling with the finer detail of his advance in support of Spain and her cause, a reserve force of divisional strength was being assembled in England and Ireland. It was to be commanded by Major General Sir David Baird, an officer who had earned a reputation in India as a hard taskmaster but unswerving operator. His division was to be 12,000 strong and included two troops of horse artillery and four field artillery companies as well as three cavalry regiments. On the 6th September, Lieutenant Colonel George Cookson was exercising the horse artillery on Woolwich Common when the adjutant rode up to him with the order to report to Major General MacLeod without delay.

> It was to acquaint me that Lieutenant General Sir David Baird had named me to be the Commanding Officer of Artillery to go on Service with him to Spain and that Lord Chatham [Master General of the Ordnance] had approved of it and wished to see me as soon as possible at the Ordnance Office. I attended accordingly and after thanking his lordship for appointing me to Commanding Officer upon the intended Service I was informed I was to have two troops of Horse Artillery in the first instance, one Lieutenant Colonel, one major and four companies and a large proportion of the Corps of Artillery Drivers under my command and that our destination was Corunna.[17]

On 22nd September, Cookson was poised to embark from Ramsgate with Captain George Bean's and Captain Robert Truscott's companies of artillery when he received a letter from Lord Chatham telling him to wait for the embarkation of the two horse artillery troops and accompany them to Iberia. Three day prior, two additional companies of artillery, Captain Harcourt Holcombe's and Captain Adam Wall's, had set sail from Cork via Falmouth and arrived at Coruña on the 13th October. However, the Galician Junta refused the British force permission to land and it was a full three weeks before permission had been sought and provided from Madrid so that the first elements of this force were allowed to disembark. In the meantime, they remained frustratingly anchored in the harbour of the Galician port and at the mercy of the autumn storms. Perhaps fortuitously, Cookson's fleet was held up by bad weather and did not sail until the 31st October; on board the transports *Country Squire*, *Niaid*, *Mary Malvira and Spencer* were Cookson and his staff, 'B' Troop commanded by Captain Thomas Downman, 'C' Troop commanded by Captain Henry Evelegh, the Quarter Master and stores, artillery wagons and the Corps of RA Drivers.

Second Captain Richard Bogue was serving in 'B' Troop, and recorded his impressions as the fleet approached Coruña.

> The approach to Coruña is more beautiful than can be described. High and picturesque hills on each side of a deep bay. These are barren and mountainous, but beautiful. The light house (or iron tower) [this is the Tower of Hercules, originally built by the Romans] is a very fine object in entering the site. The town [is] very old but beautifully situated. We anchor'd [sic] at about 12 o'clock having joined the 7th, 10th and 15th Regiments [of Light Dragoons] who sailed from Spithead on

Monday, 31st October. The confusion of nearly 200 sail ships entering a small bay is not to be described – ships running foul, Spanish boats with the most miserable looking men in them rowing in all directions.[18]

By the 10th November the horse artillery troops were ashore and Cookson issued the following Brigade Order:

Lieutenant Colonel Cookson feels considerable pleasure in communicating to the Royal Horse Artillery his entire satisfaction at their uncommonly good appearance, as also every horse, notwithstanding their having been upwards of five weeks on board ship; and the Lieutenant Colonel takes this opportunity of expressing his delight at the prospect of going into active service with them against the enemy that boasts of carrying everything before them. The whole British Army is anxious to know how this corps will answer the wishes of its country, and Lieutenant Colonel Cookson feels confident that their utmost expectations will be fully gratified; doubtless the Service we are about to employed in will require the utmost vigilance of all parties; and very particularly from the Royal Artillery services, as much of the success of every action will greatly depend upon the attention and steadiness of this most essential part of the Corps of Royal Horse Artillery.[19]

The four field artillery companies had landed days earlier and Bean's and Wall's companies had already moved up country towards Lugo. Cookson's command was as follows:

Lt. Col. G. Cookson

Staff: Lt. Col. J. Sheldrake (in Coruña)

Maj. R. Beevor

Brigade Major: Capt. T. Greatley

Troops/Companies	Notes	Equipment
'B' Troop	Commanded by Capt. T. Downman RHA.	Light 6-pounders
'C' Troop	Commanded by Capt. H. Evelegh RHA.	Light 6-pounders
Bean's Company		Light 6-pounders
Truscott's Company		Light 6-pounders
Wall's Company		Light 6-pounders
Holcombe's Company	Remained in Coruña.	Without guns
Detachment RA Drivers	From 'A', 'E', 'F', 'H', 'G' and 'K' troops.	

Sources: Compilation from Laws, Duncan, Vigors and Leslie.

Wall, a practical, no-nonsense officer, had landed his company on the 5th November and almost immediately received orders to march for Lugo.

We arrived in the evening at Betanzos, an ill-built town, and few good houses. I parked the guns, and billeted the men and horses; the forage disagreed with the horses, and one died in consequence. Major General Manningham arrived on the 7th, and directed me to march on the 8th with the 81st Regiment; to encamp two nights, and arrive at Lugo on the 10th … On the 10th, struck our tents and marched to Lugo.[20]

'B' Troop followed five days later, having been quartered in Coruña for nearly a week, and arrived at Lugo on the 18th November where Bogue was to receive a better reception than that afforded to Wall.

Marched at ten o'clock leaving a forge cart & several horses at Baamonde to join us as soon as they were shod. Reached Lugo (4 leagues) at 4, where all of us, Officers, men and horses quartered ourselves in a convent. After the first business of coming into it against the inclination of the Friars was got over, they were very kind and attentive to us. Slept in the chapel.[21]

At the head of the advance, Wall and Bean were at Astorga where Wall was given orders for the next phase of the operation:

On the 24th inst., at 5 o'clock in the morning, the Adjutant-General came to my quarters and gave me written orders, which described that the Army should march at different hours during the day, being divided into three Brigades, and a Brigade of Artillery in front and rear. Sir David Baird directed that Captain Bean and myself should arrange which Brigade should march in front; therefore according to arrangements made on the evening of the 22nd, I marched with the First brigade under Colonel Hay, composed of the 1st or Royals, 26th and 81st Regiments, at 10 o'clock in the morning. This Brigade was ordered to move by the same route we had advanced. Here a transaction occurred which was ill-judged indeed (whether orders had been issued or not I cannot say); but prior to the moving of the troops from the town of Astorga, the stores were destroyed. This occasioned such a scene of confusion as I believe was never witnessed before; – the streets flooded with rum, casks of beef and pork, and bags of biscuits strewed in every street, the troops conveying the rum in camp kettles, and drinking it to horrid excess. Fortunately I arrived on the ground where the guns were parked, just as great quantities of rum were brought in by the drivers; I ordered the whole to be destroyed, but notwithstanding, drunkenness was very prevalent … On the morning of the 25th, before we marched, a drum-head Court-martial was assembled by order of General Manningham; the irregularities committed at Astorga here became punishable, and the Staff-Sergeant of the drivers attached to my Brigade was broke and received corporal punishment.[22]

Notwithstanding the Gunners' jaundiced view of their artillery drivers, such behaviour was a suggestion of even greater excesses and ill-discipline that were soon to consume large elements of Moore's army. Meanwhile, back in Portugal, young Henegan was cajoling the locals, their boats and beasts, and battling with the elements to bring forward the ammunition.

When these movements were decided upon, I was appointed, at Lisbon, to organise the reserve ammunition for this army under orders for Spain. It consisted of two millions, five hundred thousand rounds of ball cartridges, and a large supply for the artillery. The stores were to be conveyed, in the first instance, by water from Lisbon to Abrantes, in fifteen boats, provided by the Regency, of about forty tons each, and such was the clumsy negligence, or want of proper information, on the part of the authorities, that instead of reaching Abrantes, it was found impracticable to ascend the Tagus in large boats beyond Santarem, not half the distance. The river, even long before that point, loses its majestic breadth, and narrowing into an insignificant stream, becomes only navigable for small craft, propelled by poles … From Abrantes the convoy of ammunition was conveyed on bullock wains [wagons], over rugged mountains and wretched roads to Castelo Branco, by the route of Nizza, and the almost impassable defile of Villa Velha, where a flying bridge was thrown over the Tagus. The wet season had commenced, and should any of the gallant fellows of the thirty-second [allocated to provide escort] be still alive, they will not have forgotten this breaking into the hardship of a soldier's life, of eleven days exposure, without intermission, to a drenching rain.[23]

Henegan's experiences, and those of the 32nd Foot, were a mere soupçon of what was yet to come. In mid-November, Cookson had called forward Truscott's Company and by the end of the month the situation was as follows. Lieutenant Colonel John Sheldrake remained in Coruña with Holcombe. Cookson was with Baird at Astorga along with Lord Henry William Paget and the majority of the cavalry, 'B' Troop, Wall's and Bean's companies; 'C' Troop was 40 miles shy of Astorga at Bembibre and Truscott was at Lugo. Plans were already being discussed for the link-up with Moore's force when, on the 1st December, that all changed and Baird's force were given the most unbelievable and morale-sapping of orders to return to the Galician port and prepare for immediate embarkation.

Moore had reached Salamanca on the 13th November with his six infantry brigades and Wilmot's Company of guns, but Hope's column with the balance of artillery and all the cavalry was still three weeks away and Baird, held up by the Galician authorities in October, had only just arrived at Astorga.[24] The situation was not satisfactory but it was far from critical; however, within two weeks the circumstances had altered entirely. By mid-October Napoleon had resolved his differences with Tsar Alexander, freeing the Emperor and tens of thousands of troops who were now on the move for Spain. By the 23rd November the Spanish armies of the Left and Centre had been comprehensively beaten at Espinosa, Gamonal and subsequently Tudela, the road was open to Madrid and there were no allied troops between Napoleon and Moore at Salamanca or Baird at Astorga. Furthermore, if Baird were to continue to move south-east to link up with his commander-in-chief he would expose his left flank, inviting attack from the 2nd Corps under Marshal Nicolas-Jean de Dieu Soult, Duke of Dalmatia, or the 4th Corps under Marshal François Joseph Lefebvre, Duke of Danzig, both of whom lay two days' march to the east of Baird's line of advance. Conscious that he was commanding Britain's only field army and one considerably smaller than the forces at Napoleon's disposal,

Moore felt compelled to order a general retreat: Baird back to Coruña and his force into northern Portugal. It was a bitter blow; the officers and men of Moore's army were flabbergasted and furious. Many of the senior officers tried to get him to change his mind and these appeals, having been curtly dismissed, were followed by similar petitions by the Spanish commanders, the Spanish emergency government and military authorities and by Mr. John Hookham Frere, the British ambassador. Moore, for now, was not to be swayed; he needed more time to determine Napoleon's future intentions.

Notes

1. A direct descendant of Gustavus Adolphus (Gustav II) who was considered, by many, to be the 'Father of Artillery'.
2. Henegan, vol. 1, pp.15–16.
3. These were the 1st, 2nd and 4th foot batteries of the King's German Artillery; the 1st and 4th had been part of Moore's expeditionary army sent to Sweden. The term King's German Artillery is used to denote the artillery of the King's German Legion; it is not an official title.
4. Ludlow Beamish, vol. 1, pp.148–49.
5. Robe Papers.
6. WD, vol. IV, pp.96–99. Wellesley to Castlereagh, 30th August 1808.
7. Ibid. Wellesley to Dalrymple, 1st September 1808.
8. At the end of 1807 Russia and France were allies and, *ipso facto*, enemies of Britain. The capture of this Russian squadron, anchored in Lisbon Bay, was an added bonus to the British who (under the terms of the Treaty of Cintra) repatriated the Russian sailors but impounded their ships.
9. WD, vol. IV, pp.152–3. Wellesley to Dalrymple, dated 10th Sepeptember 1808.
10. Henegan, vol. 1, p.19.
11. Miller, entry for 1808.
12. Carrafa's division had been one of three Spanish divisions which had supported Junot's invasion of Portugal in November 1807. It had been disarmed and imprisoned by the French in Lisbon following Spain's declaration of war on its former ally. The other two divisions, located in the north and east of the country, were able to escape back to Spain.
13. Ludlow Beamish, vol. 1, p.151.
14. Robe Papers.
15. Gardiner, letter dated 9th October 1808.
16. Henegan, vol. 1, p.20.
17. Cookson Journal, 6th September 1808.
18. Bogue Diary, 8th November 1808.
19. Cookson Journal, 10th November 1808.
20. Wall Diary, pp.1–2.
21. Bogue Diary, 18th November 1808.

22. Wall Diary, p.5.
23. Henegan, vol. 1, pp.20–21.
24. Oman, OHP, vol. 1. p.511. This outlines an interesting but unproven story, from the memoir of 'T. S.' of the 71st, that Hope had ordered six guns to be buried at Peñaranda de Bracomonte as the 'horses were so done up'. It is most unfortunate that none of the Gunner officers or NCOs in Moore's group maintained diaries (in complete contrast to the many Gunner works from Baird's Division) as this story cannot be substantiated. However, as Col. Harding (who was with this group) made no mention of this in his letters, as all the guns were all present a few days later, and given that Peñaranda is only 12 miles from Alba de Tormes, I consider it unlikely to be true.

CHAPTER 3

Cookson's Powder Keg

Turning Baird's large British division around was a relatively straightforward affair for the infantry but was to present a real challenge for the Gunners; the huge stores of ammunition and powder at Lugo and Villafranca had already been removed and were well advanced on the road to La Coruña. Sheldrake and Major Robert Beevor had come forward from the Galician port to Lugo in order to orchestrate the reversal and were now working flat out to realise the turnaround in concert with Master Commissary General Coope, both organisations competing for the ever-scarce wagons and prime movers. Since the 1st December, when Moore had issued his order to retreat, his main force had remained static in and around Salamanca waiting for Hope to link up before withdrawing back into Portugal. In the interim some of the outlying garrisons had been ordered to concentrate. Bombardier Miller had been two months at Almeida, when in early December he:

> … was ordered to join a brigade of guns which were going with the army to Spain … Went in pursuit of the French army in Spain. First day's march, ran my sword through a mule that I could not get along. Very wet day. Second day halted at [Ciudad] Rodrigo; remained there two days; from thence to Salamanca … The house where our ammunition was took fire; the drum beat to arms and all the artillery and the 52nd Regiment went to secure it … At the Gate of Salamanca, there hung the head of a man, and his quarters hung at four cross roads. He had been a traitor.[1]

Traitors too were the British, who, following Moore's order to retreat, had received a torrent of accusation and taunts from their Spanish hosts; some in isolated locations felt the full brunt of this feeling. Henegan had arrived with the ammunition at Ciudad Rodrigo the day after Christmas Day, where he found the place deep in preparation to receive the invaders of their nation.

Amid these warlike preparations, it may naturally be supposed that our small band were looked upon by the Spaniards as staunch and certain allies, in this hour of their need; and their unsuspecting reliance on our valorous intentions in their favour, had caused them to raise the draw-bridges that connected the town with the country; never contemplating the possibility of our requiring to make a sortie. The astonishment they felt, when orders were given for the opening of our march, was expressed in the most unequivocal language, and they boldly refused to allow us egress from their walls, for what they denominated as a base desertion. And here it may not be out of place to add, that there were many among us, who warmly shared the feelings of the Spaniards, and would gladly have avoided a movement which looked very much like running away.[2]

Napoleon's initial objective, in his simple but characteristically able plan, was always the capture of Madrid. Moore and the British force were a mere distraction; indeed, as he crossed the Guadarrama he had no idea that the British were only 60 miles to his west. On the 4th December the French entered Madrid; the day prior Hope had joined Moore, bringing with him the cavalry and artillery as well as information of Napoleon's apparent intentions, none of which indicated a westerly purpose. Moore consequently rescinded the order to pull back and issued a new plan of action to attack the French lines of communication at Valladolid. Both his and Baird's forces now began to move in that direction. By the 11th December he received news that Madrid had fallen and any hopes of a prolonged siege or organised resistance, like Saragossa, were dashed, and yet Moore was acutely aware of the need to do something for Spain and therefore elected to continue with the scheme. His divisions moved north and by the 13th December were split between Zamora and Toro where he received news of the content of another captured communiqué, from the Emperor to Soult, in which the former tasked the latter to move with his 2nd Corps into León and drive the remnants of the Army of Galicia back into its native mountains.[3] Moore elected to link up with the General Pedro Caro y Suredo, 3rd Marquis of La Romana's Spanish Army, and attack Soult's Corps in the area of Sahagún and Mayorga; orders were sent to Baird whose force was, by now, spread widely from Galicia and into León. On the 19th December, Moore and Baird finally met up and discussed plans for operations and the organisation of the army. The 1st Division was allocated to Baird, the 2nd to Hope, the 3rd to Major General Alexander Fraser and the 4th Reserve Division to Major General Edward Paget, and two light brigades were placed under brigadier generals Charles Alten and Robert (Black Bob) Craufurd, while the cavalry was organised into two brigades under Lord (Henry) Paget.[4]

Harding now assumed command of all the artillery and at Mayorga on the 25th December he wrote to MacLeod.

We fully expected to have engaged the enemy on the 23rd, about five leagues from Sahagún; the army was in full march at 8 o'clock on the night of the 23rd, and hoped to have fallen in with them early in the morning of the 24th. An intense hard frost, and the whole of the roads one sheet of ice from the snow thawing during the day, was much against the march of Artillery, as we had not time to rough all the horses. The march of the troops was stopped an hour after they marched off; some of the troops, particularly Downman's troops, were out till 2 in the morning. The General received some information immediately after the troops marched off, which caused their sudden return. We now seem to be pointing towards Corunna, and forming depots that way. Our movements have lately been so intricate and unexpected, that if I had had time to write to you, I could give you little information ... Lieutenant-Colonel Cookson has the command of the three brigades on the right of the line, Evelegh's, Bean's, and Wilmot's. Lieutenant-Colonel Wood has charge of those on the left of the line, Downman's, Drummond's and Carthew's. Four reserve brigades with the park are Raynsford's (9-pounders), Crawford's, Brandreth's, and Wall's (light 6-pounders) brigades. The park, stores, and ammunition are under Major Thornhill. The depots advanced are under Captain Skyring. There is a brigade of mountain guns somewhere, which I hope will not join us, but return to Corunna. We have lately received 59 prize horses, which, although not good, are a great help to us, from our great loss.[5]

Cookson stepped down from his post as commander of Baird's artillery but assumed command of the horse artillery; he was clearly disappointed but he had also begun to publicly doubt the plans of his commander-in-chief. It was an error which was to cost him dearly.

Left Astorga and ... Fell in with the Messenger [correspondent] Mr Mates who was on his way to England with important dispatches. He told me that the two Armies, General Sir J Moore's and Sir D Baird's were about to be united and were to march and attack Marshal Soult's Army near Carrion ... I requested he would take charge of a few pencil lines to Mr Remmington my father in Law, by all Means Sir, he replied, he is my banker and I will give them to him as soon as possible after I have delivered the dispatches. I got off my horse and wrote as follows: 'You will be informed in England that the Spaniards are in great force and that we are marching to attack Marshal Soult's Army at Carrion but mark before you receive this scrawl that we shall be in full retreat for Corunna etc.' These hasty lines unfortunately for me and very imprudent in Mr R were published in the News paper and my name attached to them in full length. The following letter from Sir Wm [William] Congreve will prove why it was unfortunate in as much that if I had sent those lines to him instead of Mr R it as things turned out might have been a feather in my cap. The fact is I was so engaged in my duties for the good of the Service that I never once thought of Sir Wm's letter, if I had it is not very unlikely I might have shared some of the honors [sic] that were distributed among my brother officers.[6]

Congreve's letter, dated 4th October 1808, had requested that Cookson keep in touch as the Prince of Wales was keen to receive information from 'Officers of Rank'. It would certainly have done Cookson no harm to have his exploits aired to His Royal Highness, but instead he was branded a 'croaker', or moaner; his subsequent entries seem to confirm that suspicion and appear to have resulted in him being overlooked when it came to recognition following future military action. However, if this were not enough, the next few days were also to take a toll on his physical well being:

A heavy fall of snow sent the Horse Artillery to Valderes and with my Brigade Major Captain Greatley galloped on through the snow to Mayorga and arrived at 4 PM having passed the Foot Guards and Captain Bean's Brigade of Artillery near Valderes; at 9 PM Generals Manningham and Leith's division and Captain Brandreth's Brigade of Artillery arrived and great was the bustle for billets, forage and shoeing our horses. At 11 PM being completely exhausted I lay down in my wet clothes upon an old bedstead up a loft to which I ascended by a steep ladder. I was awoke[n] by Major [Captain] Greatley begging I would partake of Salt and Pork and some warm rum and water. I got up and not being thoroughly awake, I descended head foremost upon the floor which was paved with pebbles and having my bear skin helmet on saved my life. I lay stunned for some time. The brass edge of the helmet was forced with such violence in my forehead as to leave a severe wound. The agony for a considerable time was dreadful – and my fears of not being able to go with the Army augmented my uneasiness, however after the wound was dressed I was able to wear a great silk handkerchief round my head and I marched the next morning with the Horse Artillery through the snow cutting a curious figure without a hat or helmet.

Harding had arranged the artillery in three groups in an attempt to provide some structure for the Gunner support to the reorganised army.

CRA: Col. J. Harding
Brigade Major: Capt. R. W. Gardiner

Troops/Companies	Equipment
Right of the Line – Lt. Col. G. Cookson (Commander of the RHA)	
'C' Troop RHA (Evelegh)	Light 6-pounders
Bean's Company	Light 6-pounders
Wilmot's Company	Light 6-pounders
Left of the Line – Lt. Col. G. A. Wood	
'B' Troop (Downman)	Light 6-pounders
Drummond's Company	Light 6-pounders
Carthew's Company	Light 6-pounders
Reserve Brigades – Maj. J. Viney	
Raynsford's Company	9-pounders
Crawford's Company	Light 6-pounders
Wall's Company	Light 6-pounders
Truscott's Company Commanded by Brandreth[7]	Light 6-pounders
Park, Stores and Depot	
Maj. Thornhill	Park, stores and ammunition
Capt. Skyring	Advanced depots

Sources: Compilation from Laws, Duncan, Vigors and Leslie.

However the CRA's plans did not survive first contact. As Moore's army manoeuvred north to engage Soult, surprise was lost following the gallant cavalry engagement at Sahagún on the 21st December. It was a bitterly cold morning and a deep snow lay on the ground as Lord Paget moved north with the 10th and 15th Light Dragoons (Hussars) supported by Downman's Troop of guns. Bogue recorded that four guns were with the 10th Hussars and the other two with Lord Paget and the 15th Hussars.

> Reached Sahagún, where we knew the French had a position, by ½ past 6, when we found they had received news of our approach, & were drawn up (700 cavalry) ready to receive us. The 15th Dragoons met them first & 400 of them charged them. We came up at the time they were dispersing and assisted in taking them.[8]

This small but clinically executed action at Sahagún was the first cavalry triumph of the war and it is frustrating that the horse artillery's contribution is somewhat vague. Moore halted at Sahagún for two days to allow the rear divisions to close up on the vanguard before advancing to Carrion in order to deliver their sychronized blow on the 13rd December. Meanwhile Soult had wasted little time in concentrating his corps and calling up General Jean-Thomas Lorges's Division of Dragoons and General Henri-François Delaborde's Infantry Division from the 8th Corps. Moore advanced on the 23rd December, later in the day than anticipated and was thereby forced to delay any engagement until the 24th. However, late on the 23rd, he received news that all available French forces were reported marching from the capital, over the Guadarrama, and were headed in the direction of the Anglo-Spanish force. The game was up, and Moore immediately ordered the forces to retrace their steps and await further orders. Cookson, Evelegh and Bogue take up the story:

> The column had been marching slowly on till about 12 at night when a dispatch arrived from General Sir J Moore. I was with Sir J Hope at the head of the column at the time. He asked me for a light which I instantly brought him one from the guns. The General read the dispatch and said 'we are to retreat, halt your guns and desire the word to be quietly passed to the rear of the column'. He then gave orders that three guns of the Horse artillery, a squadron of cavalry and a light brigade of infantry should remain upon the ground all night and to push some patrols near to Carrion.[9]

> At 8 p.m. march'd with Gen Hope's Brigade [Division] to make a joint attack with the army from Sahagun on Marshal Soult at Carrion (about 10,000 men). Drummond's Brigade and my troop taken about a mile beyond the town before dark. Raynsford's 9 pdr. Brigade arrived before we march'd and came on in the rear. On the march, however, an order arrived to advance the rifle corps and half my troop to Pozurama [Pozo de Urama], a village about a league from Villada, and for the remainder to go back. I therefore went on with Walcott, Barlow, the Doctor and three guns. Chester and Webber, who had a bad fall, with his mare in

consequence of the frost, and was a good deal bruised in the face etc., returned to Villada.[10]

We however proceeded forward until overtaken by a dispatch from Sir J Moore ordering us to return to our old quarters at Sahagún. When we had retraced about one third of our route a counter came from Ld Paget & we were wasted a full hour in one of the coldest nights I have ever experienced, till it was determin'd that we should go back to Sahagún, which we reached between one & two, but were obliged to take our guns on by hand the last ½ mile as the horses could not stand the draught.[11]

Moore ordered the divisions of Baird, Hope and Fraser to pull back to Astorga, where he intended to make a stand, and left Paget with the Reserve Division and the two light brigades to act as a rearguard, while the cavalry formed a screen to their front. On the 26th and 27th December Soult ordered the cavalry brigades of Lorges and General Jean-Baptiste Franceschi to close with the British rearguard; within hours Napoleon's vanguard had began to arrive and General Auguste-François-Marie de Colbert's Cavalry Brigade and the cavalry of the Emperor's Guard entered the fray. Every one of Lord Paget's five cavalry regiments was involved in delaying the advance of the 2,500 French cavalry who probed and harassed the British positions. On the 28th December Black Bob Craufurd's Light Brigade blew the bridge over the River Esla at Castrogonzalo and pulled back to Benevente where preparations were ongoing to make a stand. Cookson and the two RHA troops were integrally involved but the commander of the horse artillery was not enjoying the best of relationships with the commander of the British cavalry.

December 26th: … nearly the whole day the rain was very heavy and we entered Valderas cold and wet through. I waited upon Lord Paget and reported my arrival. He rose up from a kind of couch and said 'You have lost a wagon of shrapnel shells', I answered yes my Lord, but not till every possible exertion had been made to save [it] and finding it impossible the shells were thrown into the river. 'It is my orders, Sir, that you go yourself with a party and endeavour to bring back the wagon.' I replied I was sorry I could not obey His Lordship's orders, that I would send a captain or a non-commissioned officer with a party to make this trial but as the Commanding Officer I must decline going myself. His Lordship said 'Do you know who you are speaking to?' I said Yes My Lord, it is Colonel Cookson Commanding the Horse Artillery speaking to Lord Paget Commanding the Cavalry, 'Very well Sir, you will hear from me in the morning, I have not forgotten your conduct at Astorga respecting the horse artillery.'

I took my leave and after a miserable nap in an old chair shivering with cold, I paraded the Horse artillery a little before day light in front of the cavalry upwards of 2000, Lord Paget came to me and said 'Colonel place Captain Downman's Troop of Horse Artillery between the 10th and the 7th Hussars and Captain Evelegh's Troop of Horse Artillery between the 10th and 15th'. The morning was very foggy; upon its clearing away I discovered with my glass a line of troops drawn up on our left front. I was desired to bring all the guns to the front. Upon a nearer view it proved to be Sir John Hope's Division of the Army that had unfortunately been made obliged to make a retrograde movement, the river being so swollen where they were to have forded across; upon approaching the bridge at Castro Gonsalo [Castrogonzalo], Lord Paget rode up to me and gave me orders to march to Benevente with the two Troops of Horse Artillery and remain there until further orders – not a word transpired upon what passed in His Lordship's room early this morning.

December 29th: In telescoping the advanced pickets at dawn near the bridge at Benevente, I discovered the French cavalry fording the river, I instantly ordered the two troops of Horse Artillery to fall in and no orders having been arrived for me I took upon myself the responsibility of moving them out of the town and perceiving the French crossing in force I marched them off towards the river placing Captain Evelegh's Troop upon a favourable spot to cover a retreat in case of necessity and galloped along the main road with the other Troop to the attack which had commenced when Captain Downman called out to me 'Sir if we do not proceed in a direct line we shall not get into action'. I was rather indignant at the remark, but aware of the motive I ordered him to take a 6 Pounder in the direction he pointed out (over plowed [sic] ground) observing it would stick by the way. The rapidity of our movement through some pieces of water splashed out the *slow match* under the first gun. Lord Paget came to me with one of his pistols to procure a light – at this instant a lighted port fire was brought from one of the other guns, and I began throwing shrapnel shells into the enemy column. I pointed the first 3 rounds myself. Almost immediately Downman joined me but without the gun as predicted.[12]

Interestingly, neither Bogue with 'B' Troop nor Evelegh with 'C' Troop saw the action in quite the same way:

The bridge last night was blown up, & no ford known within three of four miles of it each way. At nine our outposts were driven in close up to the town, by a body of upwards of 600 French Dragoons of Bonaparte's Imperial Guard headed by General Lefebvre ... On their again forming on the other side of the river I had the pleasure of firing several rounds at them (the first guns fired in Spain) as well as Downman and [Lieutenant] Lempriere, when they made off leaving their killed and wounded. We remained in their front all night, when all but the picket retreated. We destroyed a bridge on the road, & reached La Bañeza soon after daylight.[13]

At Benevente – an alarm at 9 a.m. The French cavalry forced the River and attacked our piquet there which consisted of about 94 men on the 7th and 10th and Germans under Colonel Quinton of the 10th who charged the French very nobly three times tho', so superior to him in numbers, and kept fighting 'till a reinforcement arrived. The enemy re-crossed the river with the loss of General Lefebure [Lefebvre], Colonel of the Imperial Guard, who commanded, and about

60 killed and wounded. B Troop and mine went down from Benevente, but mine was ordered back to take a position on a hill. D[ownman] fired 2 or 3 shot and they went off. About two p.m. we marched for Puente de Vizana – 3 leagues off, to protect the bridge. B Troop remained, and came to us at night. I made preparations for destroying the Bridge and we marched off at two a.m.[14]

It is curious that neither Evelegh nor Bogue mention Cookson during this or subsequent events; Cookson's recollection of events places him firmly at the centre of the action and even suggests that during the withdrawal to La Bañeza his diligence may have saved the rearguard from possible destruction. Little wonder that he (but he alone) questions his subsequent lack of recognition:

Who would suppose it possible that Lord Paget should have forgotten that I commanded the Artillery in this affair? That His Lordship did forget is unfortunately too true, as the Gazette of the tenth of January 1809 clearly proves which: 'I have forwarded the prisoners to Baneza [La Bañeza], on the other side of the river the enemy formed again. At this instance their guns there were 5 of Captain Downman's Troop of Horse Artillery arrived which did considerable execution.' The French had no field pieces in the above affair – what might not have been the consequence had I not brought forward the 12 guns belonging to the Horse Artillery.[15]

What indeed! The blown bridge at Castrogonzalo held the French follow-up until repairs were completed after noon on the 30th December, by which time Paget's Division had linked up with the balance of the British Army at Astorga where Moore had indicated earlier intention to make a stand. They were joined the same day by the remnants of La Romana's Spanish Army that had withdrawn in haste following Soult's mauling of the Spanish 2nd Division at Mansilla. The passes beyond Astorga offered unquestionable opportunities to thwart the French pursuit but Moore had made up his mind; he had lured Napoleon from moving on the emergency executives at Lisbon and Seville and had no intention of losing *the* British Expeditionary Army in the bargain. Late on the 30th orders were issued for Baird's, Hope's and Fraser's divisions to make best speed for Villafranca; Paget and the two light brigades were to follow the next day. This seemingly inexplicable decision provoked unrestrained criticism from the officers and men, both British and Spanish, and when British soldiers began to take out their frustrations on the local inhabitants, their officers did little to restrain them. The abundant military stores were pillaged and while the rum was enjoyed to excess, the shoes and blankets were largely ignored. Both decisions were to have grave consequences over the next few days. Some of the redcoats were so drunk that they were still incapable of being 'beaten out of the place' by the cavalry when they left the town later the next day. All the field artillery departed the town on the 30th December and Wall, attached to Fraser's Division, takes up the story:

December 31st marched to Bembibre and villages adjoining. This day's march was very harassing, a distance of thirty-four miles without halting a minute; a deep snow over the whole of the mountain of Manzanal; our sickness increased, and I was obliged to carry nine men in a spring wagon in a delirious fever. We continued a precipitate retreat until the 4th January, through a country completely destitute of supplies, from the number of troops that had passed and re-passed since the landing of the British Army. The mountains covered with snow, and the weather extremely cold, our troops began to drop as we marched along, and thousands were left to die in the snow, or fall into the hands of the enemy. The roadside was strewed with the carcasses of horses, mules, and oxen; the troops without shoes, marching barefoot, and horses without forage, exposed at night in this severe season of the year.[16]

Bombardier Miller, with Skyring's Company, was a few miles ahead of Wall and was having to cope with the weather, the terrain, an old war wound, the French and open hostility from the local people.

I was several times in danger of being taken prisoner, for being very wet weather and the roads very bad with so many horses and carriages passing, it was dreadful travelling, and one half of the army without shoes … Frosty weather now came in, which did not make it much better for us, for we were now getting on the mountains where the snow frequently lay all summer, which froze some of the men to death.

When we came to Villafranca, the Spaniards shut their houses on us, and we were ordered to break them open (after all the Convents and Churches were full) and make our lodgings good for the night. Me and four more broke into a house where they had plenty of wood but they would not give us any. I went down stairs to take some, but they had some Spanish soldiers to guard it. They said one to the other kill him, and began to push me about. I asked them in Spanish, if that was the treatment they meant to give us after fighting for them. One of them very luckily pushed me against the stairs. I immediately ran up and told the four men to be on their guard or we should all be killed. One placed himself behind the door, and I and the other three stood with our swords drawn. In a few minutes after up came 3 Spanish soldiers with large staves and knives. The man behind the door ran one of them through, and I cut down another, and the third had 3 swords on him. We left them all for dead … We made the door secure inside and kept all in, the man of the house and his family. We then pulled down a partition that went across the room and broke up chairs and stools, to warm our selves. We saw some hams hung up, and a basket of eggs. We asked them to sell us some, and offered double the value, for we had nothing to eat all day, but they refused. But we took one ham, and as many eggs as we could eat, and fried it [sic]. We also saw a pig's skin full of wine in the room. We offered money for some, and the Spaniard finding that he might as well take the money as not, sold us as much as we chose to drink. We took care not to drink too much, for fear of the Spaniards taking advantage of us.[17]

Such hostility from the Spanish was not universal, as Wall was to discover:

On the 7th at daybreak, we marched and reached Betanzos at 1 o'clock p.m., and during the time my horses were feeding, I paid a visit to my host, whom I was billeted on my first advancing up the country; I met with the kindest reception. A young woman, his wife, was under the greatest alarm, having heard that the French committed horrible excesses during the pursuit of our Army, and with much trouble I persuaded them to the contrary. They fancied their children would be put to death. They prepared something as refreshment, after which I left this unfortunate family. I could not help being under apprehensions for this man, as he held the situation as Corregidor [some form of town official] and was extremely active in forwarding supplies etc., to the British Army.[18]

While the main body of Moore's army were struggling over the mountains Paget's gallant reserve division and the two light brigades were keeping the French at arm's length; just short of Villafranca they fought an action at Cacabelos on the 3rd January and again at Constantín on the 5th January; on both occasions they were closely supported by Evelegh's Horse Artillery.

Monday 2nd at 7 a.m. marched for Villafranca two guns covering the rear of the Army with the 20th under Col Ross. The French pressed us very close during the march. Guns came into action several times. On arrival at Cacabelos found orders to halt with the reserve under M G Paget. Pickets engaged continually during the night. The French cut to pieces 60 stragglers and drunken men.

Tuesday 3rd, under arms at 4 a.m., moved to the top of the hill and took a position. Found the horses just done up and sent Walcott forward to Villafranca for assistance, he found Webber there exceedingly ill. Walcott soon returned with an answer from Capt Downman, who commanded the artillery there, saying he could not assist me with one horse, I must do the best I could. About 2 p.m. received accounts that the French were advancing with large columns of cavalry. Sir J. Moore came back to us from Villafranca in consequence, and the reserve took a strong position on the hill throwing out many detached bodies of riflemen. About 3 [1500 hours] the French mounted rifle men and cavalry drove in our Picket of cavalry; followed them briskly through the town and killed a great many men who had not time to get out of it … We also retired – the riflemen still engaging. The rest of the reserve and 5 of my guns continued their retreat unmolested by the enemy, the other gun with Chester, Walcott and [my]self and the 95th Regiment playing on them during the time about a mile from Villafranca.

Thursday 5th, pickets drove in about 7 in the morning. We retired over the bridge which Pasley [Captain Charles William Pasley RE] attempted to blow up, but did not succeed. Chester and Barlow remained with two guns to defend the blowing up of the bridge. Proceeded on our march to Lugo closely pressed the whole way, guns prepared for action several times. Rifle men constantly engaged. About 4 p.m. reached Constantino [Constantín] and took a position between that and Bazille [Baralla]. One gun came into action in the road half way up the hill – large bodies of French cavalry appeared and made disposition for charging us, the gun then opened and dispersed them after the 3rd round. Ranie and

Craig [Rannie and Craigie] wounded at the gun on this occasion, the French rifle men got quite around our right flank. Remained in that position till dark when we retired to the top of the hill (about two miles) and lay upon our arms about 3 hours in the village.[19]

Napoleon had arrived at Astorga on the 1st January 1809, and was greatly disappointed to discover that Moore had elected not to make a stand; furthermore, the main body of Moore's force was a day and a half's march ahead of the French vanguard. He decided to relinquish command to Soult, convinced that the British would reach their naval transports and complete embarkation without serious molestation. The task of pursuit no longer befitted the Emperor, it was now a task for his subordinates; nevertheless his expectations of Soult, and Marshal Michel Ney, Duke of Elchingen, who was following up with his 6th Corps, were far from yielding. The British were to be pressed actively and enthusiastically and as many as possible were to be prevented from ever seeing England again. Colbert, Ney's cavalry commander, took his Emperor's words to heart and pressed slightly too enthusiastically at Cacabelos, where he was shot in the head by Rifleman Thomas Plunkett.

At Villafranca, Moore had sent the two light brigades on a more southerly route to Vigo, while the main body continued to Lugo where the commander-in-chief had elected to rest the force in an attempt to allow the stragglers to close and discipline to be restored. The CRA had ordered Bean and Captain George Crawford to remain with their light 6-pounder brigades; they would be joined by the two horse artillery troops when the rearguard arrived, while the remainder of the artillery brigades and park began their movement towards La Coruña. Wall's Company was one of the last to march.

Colonel Harding, Commanding the Artillery, arrived with Sir John Moore at Lugo, when a number of troops were employed with the Artillery in destroying ammunition, provisions and stores, which had been brought from Coruna, and for want of a mode of conveyance could not be removed; the quantity of musquet [musket] ammunition was immense, together with a number of Artillery carriages; the conflagration through the whole day appeared as if the whole of the city was on fire; during the day I was busily employed in getting my horses shod, and harness repaired. The fever still continued with great violence amongst the men, but there was no alternative, I was obliged to drag them along in a horrid state, sooner than leave them to the mercy of the enemy. At 12 o'clock at night, finding the Farrier had made great progress, I reported to Colonel Harding, and proposed marching immediately, which he consented to; I got the horses to the guns, again set out for Coruna, and just as I was leaving Lugo the advanced guard of General Fraser's Division was marching in, having been re-called from its route to Vigo.[20]

This unfortunate division had marched an extra 30 miles due to a mix-up in orders and were none too pleased. They arrived in time to receive Moore's 'General Order' which lambasted the lack of command and appealed for officers to do their duty as 'it was chiefly from their negligence, and from the want of proper regulations in the regiments, that crimes and irregularities were committed'. The fact that the same could not be said of the artillery was undeniable; subsequent reports confirmed that of the 2,627 men who had strayed from their colours, none were Gunners, prompting Moore to write that 'The Artillery consists of particularly well-behaved men'. At this juncture Moore had not met Bombardier Miller, that was to happen on the day of the impending battle, and while Miller's loyalty to his colours were unquestioned, calling him, albeit collectively, 'well-behaved' might be stretching things a touch. The vigorous NCO made no secret of the fact that 'on our road to Coruña we burnt down a village because the people would not sell us anything'.

Anger and frustration quickly gave way to eager anticipation as word spread that Moore was to make a stand against Soult; marauders returned and sick men seemed revived at the prospect of some action. However Soult had other ideas; he came up against the British force at Lugo early on the 7th January and spent most of that day and the next in half-hearted probing and ineffectual skirmishing. The road to La Coruña had taken equal toll on both retreating and advancing forces and Soult needed time to allow his stragglers to catch up and felt inclined to wait for Ney before committing to any serious engagement. In the interim, a French battery, which unlimbered opposite the British centre, was immediately silenced by the fire of three batteries, reinforcing Soult's situational appreciation. A feint against the British right was equally quickly dispatched by the Guards supported by 'C' Troop RHA. By last light on the 8th January Moore realised that Soult was waiting for Ney, a situation he could ill afford. Taking the offensive was equally unattractive and so during the evening orders were promulgated for a resumption of the retreat. Captain Thomas Downman's Troop remained with the rearguard while Bean, Crawford and Evelegh set off with Cookson to La Coruña.

> It was so intensely dark and the ground so heavy that I was apprehensive at one time that I should never have gotten in the Main Road with my Brigades. The guns frequently stuck fast in going over the plow'd [*sic*] ground which from the heavy rain was completely saturated – however by great exertions tho' very late we reached [the] Corunna gate out of Lugo; here the confusion of men, horses, carriages etc. forcing their way out of the town was far beyond description. Not far from the gate a number of Spanish field pieces were collected together and their carriages etc. on fire to prevent their being useful to the enemy.[21]

Cookson and his group arrived on the outskirts of the Galician port late on the 10th January and he was 'not a little surprised to find the Fleet to receive us on board was not arrived from Vigo'. Nevertheless, Cookson was afforded a billet in the castle; Bombardier Miller, who arrived the next day, was equally surprised at the lack of Royal Naval presence but he was obliged to encamp on the heights, without any tents, about 3 miles from town. Evelegh was not overly concerned with Miller's predicament announcing that on the 11th January he 'Had a holyday [holiday] at

Corunna and received letters by Humphrey's [Captain Commissary Humphrey's Royal Artillery Drivers]. Tea etc. My guns were embarked.' While the latter may be slightly premature, Evelegh's holiday was certainly short lived, for the very next day his troop were dispatched to assume command of Downman's guns at the bridge at El Burgo. Or more precisely, the blown bridge at El Burgo, which Paget's Division was holding in order to buy time for the fleet to arrive and to enable all manner of other preparations to be undertaken such as the destruction of the great stores of powder which were housed in two magazines on the outskirts of the port. Harding tasked Cookson to deal with the magazines; it is an interesting story.

I was put in orders to move 300 barrels of powder in Corunna. I placed the officers and men at a distance of 10 yards asunder to hand the barrels on to about 200 yards off to the wagons as it was very dangerous to have them nearer owing to the quantity of powder scattered about the magazines. I had removed about 200 barrels when I heard a murmuring among the men saying after such a distressing half starved long march to be made porters of was too bad. This was followed up by swearing they were completely knocked up and throwing the barrels down, some of them burst and made the situation still more dangerous. I thought it better not to notice this almost mutinous conduct, and gave the word at the instant for the officers to pass the order for no more powder to be removed, fall in. After this unpleasant duty was settled an order was brought to me to prepare for blowing up the magazine. I remained on the ground till 12 at night; cleared away the powder near the two magazines, fixed soaking wet blankets round the doors inside and outside – sliced two *portfires* together for each magazine and with my own hands fixed them under the doors, and then I retired to where the Horse Artillery were and lay down till an hour before daylight then visited the magazines and finding all was as safe as I had left them although it rained all night. I went in search of General Sir J. Moore and I found him in the company with Sir J. Hope on the road to Batanza. I reported that the magazines were quite ready to be blown up – well then Colonel, let them be blown up immediately, only take care that the neighbourhood and the troops are made acquainted with it so that there may be no lives lost … after taking every precaution to prevent accidents I placed two steady Non-Commissioned Officers of Artillery between the two magazines with *portfires* in their hands and just before I ordered them to be lighted, I thought it better to make sure of the smaller magazine blowing up first, the larger one having twice the quantity of powder. I therefore cut half an inch off the sliced *portfire* fixed to the smaller magazine. Had the larger one blown up first, I feared the confusion would shake off the *portfire* of the other. I now went up to the Non-Commissioned Officers and desired the *portfires* to be lighted and to proceed to the magazines and that when I held up my handkerchief to immediately set fire to the priming and then walk away quietly and join me, assuring them that the explosion would not take place under 20 minutes or more. When we were about a quarter of a mile off I mounted my horse and rode to a position to have a full view of the explosion and looking at my watch I found the *portfires* had been lighted 23 minutes. The surrounding officers said that something must have happened to the train of powder. They had scarcely finished the sentence when the smaller magazine blew up followed by the larger immediately.

The sight of 12,000 barrels of powder, the quantity stated by the Spaniards, was terrifickly [sic] grand. The explosion from the well which was filled with barrels of powder had a very curious effect; some barrels absolutely blew up in the air. The running fire upon the ground was curious. The inhabitants of Corunna ran out of their houses exceedingly alarmed fancying the French were bombarding the town. The town and suburbs were covered in dust in consequence of the explosion.[22]

While there is no evidence to support Napier's claim that the explosion 'killed many persons who had remained too near the spot',[23] there is perhaps much to substantiate Oman's assertion that 'the explosion was so powerful that well-nigh every window in Corunna was shattered'. Nevertheless, Cookson had every reason to be smug, although it remains subject to debate as to whether he had sufficiently informed the troops and neighbourhood as ordered in person by the commander-in-chief. The reaction of the town's inhabitants would indicate otherwise. Indeed, an account of the incident by August Schaumann, the Deputy Assistant Commissary-General, seems to justify their fears that their world was coming to a premature end in a manner that was anything but 'terrifickly grand'.

On the 13th January I was sitting in my office attending to some orders, and three hussar quartermasters were standing in front of my table, when suddenly two such fierce flashes of lightening [sic] and claps of thunder burst over the town that my windows flew into our faces in a thousand pieces, the doors sprang open, the slates rolled from the roof, while I, who had just been rocking myself in my chair and talking, was flung backwards by the gust of hot air that poured in at the window. Even the quartermasters, who believed a bomb had fallen in the room and burst, ducked under the table. We were almost deaf and the house had been, so to speak, shaken in its foundations. Pulling ourselves together, we stared at each other in dumb amazement, when the streets were suddenly filled with piteous cries. The whole population, particularly the women, who perhaps believed that an earthquake was going to swallow them up, dashed out of their houses with despair written on their faces, and shouting like maniacs tore the hair from their heads.[24]

The next day a far more agreeable sight greeted the collective eyes of Moore's force, when Rear Admiral Sir Samuel Hood sailed around the headland past the ancient Tower of Hercules, at the head of the fleet of transports. Moore wasted little time in ordering the sick and wounded to embark along with the artillery, less for two brigades of light 6-pounders, and the cavalry. Those Gunners not required loading the guns, and what was left of the artillery horses and draught cattle, were put to work distributing new muskets and musket ammunition and destroying the guns and mortars on the Coruña battlements and the island within the bay. On Moore's instructions, Harding had replaced four of the light 6-pounders with four of the heavier Spanish 8-pounders on the 15th January. A roster was in place to man these two brigades and early on the 16th January, Downman's Troop was manning the picket guns.

> At seven o'clock our troop went on the advance picquet; at ten, we saw at least ten thousand fresh troops join the enemy lines, and as they appeared much disposed to strengthen their left, we fired several shots at them from Lieut. Lempriere's guns, which were posted on the right of our lines, when the French, who had endeavoured to bring up more guns, desisted & fell back into their own lines with precipitation and disorder. Between eleven and twelve Truscott, with two companies of foot artillery came up to relieve me by order of Col Harding, as we were then to march on foot to Coruña & embark our horses & men by one o'clock.[25]

Major James Viney was the field officer in charge of the two brigades of guns supporting Moore's army, which were now manned by Truscott's and Wilmot's companies. Both companies had a number of sick so personnel from other companies were warned for duty. One of these was Bombardier Miller.

> On 16 January, 1809, I was ordered out with the guns attached to the 'Forlorn hope' Picquets to keep the enemy's advance picquet at bay. Our shipping had now come round from Vigo, where they had sailed to from Coruña, having received intelligence that our army was retreating to Vigo instead of Coruña, which proved very unfortunate, for had the shipping been at Coruña on our arrival we should all have been safe on board before the enemy would have been able to attack us, and we were in a very poor state to wish for a battle, but, however bad our condition, fight we must, or be driven into the sea, for the enemy, perceiving our shipping [had] come and [was] ready for us to embark, and that we were sending off some of our guns and making preparations to embark, they sent out strong parties to oppose our 'Forlorn hope' picquet. We began to fire on them thinking they were only going to relieve their night picquet, but finding they advanced past their piquet and [were] beginning to fire, we began to think it a signal for general action (or a 'killing day' as we soldiers term it). Some sharp skirmishing took place between the picquets and several men killed and wounded; we drove them back to their lines and continued firing, until Generals Moore and Baird, who were standing by the gun which I commanded, came over and looked over the wheel of the gun with a spy-glass, and said to me 'don't fire any more, Artillerymen, for I don't think it will come to a general engagement to-day'. But he found to the contrary, for he was killed by a French cannon ball that evening and General Baird's arm was shot off.
>
> The action began about 2 o'clock in the afternoon. The enemy came down in a great fury, but our troops charged them so gallantly several times, even charged through their ranks, that they knew not what to make of us, and in place of driving us into the sea, as they expected, we fairly beat them back to their lines, and gained a complete victory, after a retreat of so many miles from Toro to Coruña, over an army five times our number, but with the loss of a great many brave men, who unfortunately lost their lives in such an unequal contest, after

withstanding so many battles and hardships in the country, and were just on the point of leaving it.[26]

By last light the British were in possession of the little hamlet of Elviña, which had changed hands several times; it had provided a pivotal point to the bloody engagement that had raged for nearly four hours. About an hour after dark the French retired and the army began to withdraw under cover of darkness, trudging wearily down the road to the port and the waiting transports.

Captain Truscott's Company came in at night with the army, and occupied the Citadel with the Spanish Brigade. Capt Willmott's [Wilmot's] retired at the same

2. The Battle of La Coruña ~ 16th January 1809

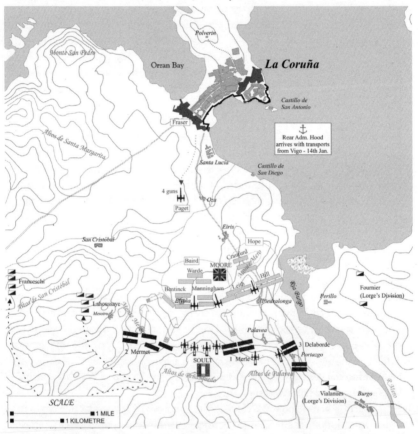

Major Viney RA was left in charge of the artillery group with Moore's army consisting of eight light 6-pounder guns and four Spanish 8-pounder guns. The exact distribution of these guns is unrecorded. It is assumed that the four guns with Paget were 6-pounders which would leave the balance of four 6-pounders and the Spanish guns in the three forward positions. At the time of the French attack all these guns were manned by gunners from Truscott's and Wilmot's companies.

time, but could not embark the guns, owing to the Boats being occupied in embarking the remainder of the troops, during the night. Major General Beresford, with 3 Regiments of the Line, and 3 Companies of artillery under Major Beevor, formed the rear guard, to embark on the night of the 17th instant. At the time I embarked on the 17th, boats were sent to embark Willmott's [Wilmot's] guns at a cove in the rear of the town; but the wind blew so strong, and the swell was so high that I fear they could not embark before the evening; when it became more moderate.[27]

Once on board the transports the ordeal was far from over:

17 Tuesday – At day light this morning our picquets were withdrawn, and at nine o'clock the French entered the suburbs of Coruña and Santa Lucia. By ten they had got some heavy field guns on an eminence, & begun to make a dreadful havoc amongst our shipping, at least 300 sail of which were still in the harbour, & some thousand troops still to be embarked. After pausing in this situation some time, the ships began to cut their cables, & then the confusion that ensued became dreadful beyond description, anxiety for those embarked as well as for the poor fellows still on shore, being wound up to the highest pitch, as there were some dangerous rocks to pass, & several of our finest ships had got so far into the harbour that it was impossible to move them as the wind then blew … The noise & disorder that now ensued was truly distressing, embarking troops under heavy & incessant fire – ships cutting their cables others striking on the rocks, some sinking.

Towards night, Lieut. Debenham of the Navy, one of the agents for the transports, came on board us, but could not tell us if Vigo or England was our destination, but Portugal was the general belief, & the more so as the Commodore made the signal to steer S. by W.

18 Wednesday – This morning a signal was made for *all masters*, and on the return of ours we found to our great happiness, that the destination was Spithead, so that we have again a chance of seeing our dear, dear friends in England, which for some time past we did not think likely.[28]

Notes

1. Miller, entry for 1808.
2. Henegan, vol. 1, p.22.
3. This was Blake's army which had been categorically defeated at Espinosa de los Monteros on the 10–11th November 1808 and had withdrawn into the mountains to the north.
4. Lord Paget and Edward Paget were brothers. Henry, 2nd Earl of Uxbridge (later Marquis of Anglesey) was Wellington's cavalry commander for part of the Peninsular War and Waterloo, where he lost a leg. Edward commanded the reserve division during this part of the war, lost an arm four months later at Wellington's crossing of

the Douro and returned to command the 1st Division in 1812 but was captured within days of arriving back in the Peninsula.

5. WO55/1194 Letters of Col. J. Harding, dated 25th December 1808. The mountain guns mentioned at the end of the correspondence are a mystery: Vigors considers them to be a detachment of Capt. Holcombe's Company. The Muster Roll for January 1809 shows 2nd Capt. F. Knox (1027), two corporals, three bombardiers and 35 Gunners marked 'M Brigade'. Browne, p.135, states that the 'Six 3-pounders were abandoned during the retreat. These guns were landed at Corunna without the general's knowledge; they never went beyond Villa Franca, and not being horsed, they were thrown down the rocks when the troops quitted that town'; see Cookson, 3rd January 1809.

6. Cookson, 18th December 1808.

7. T. A. Brandreth was Bean's second captain but appears to have assumed command from Captain Truscott; there is nothing, in any correspondence or official records, which states why this was the case.

8. Bogue, 21st December 1808. It is unclear as to whether 'B' Troop unlimbered and fired their guns. Given Bogue's description it seems unlikely: this is reinforced by the fact that and no other eyewitness source (Tale, *Jottings from my Sabretache* (London, 1847) or Gordon, *A Cavalry Officer in the Corunna Campaign* (London, 1913)) mentions the horse artillery during or after this action. Contrary to some records, 'C' Troop was not present at this action. This is supported by the fact that Downman and the 'B' Troop officers received the dual clasp *Sahagún and Benevente*, while Evelegh and his officers received only *Benevente*.

9. Cookson, 23rd December 1808.

10. Evelegh, 23rd December 1808.

11. Bogue, 24th December 1808.

12. Cookson – entries dated 26th and 29th December 1808.

13. Bogue, 29th December 1808.

14. Evelegh, 29th December 1808.

15. Cookson, 29th December 1808.

16. Wall, p.12.

17. Miller, January 1809.

18. Wall, pp.13–14.

19. Evelegh, entries dated 2nd, 3rd and 5th January 1809. Gunner Joseph Craigie and Gunner James Rannie; the latter had curiously been reduced to the ranks from sergeant at his own request on the 7th December 1808. Both men survived the campaign.

20. Wall, p.13.

21. Cookson, 8th January 1809.

22. Ibid., 12th January 1809. The actual date this incident took place is a subject of conjecture; most historians state the 13th January and, indeed, Cookson himself indicates this date and is supported by Bogue. However, Harding's letter of the 29th January (see Appendix I) states the 14th January and it is this source that Leslie uses in his history, while Wall states that the explosion took place on the 15th January. Evelegh makes no mention of the incident (as he is sick confined to bed that day)

while Miller's brief notes are unclear. However, an earlier letter written by Col. Harding on the 13th January at Coruña confirms that the magazines were blown this day (i.e. the 13th) which seals the matter. See PRO WO55/1194 pp.146–47.

23. Napier, vol. I, p.500.

24. Schaumann, p.134.

25. Bogue, 16th January 1809.

26. Miller, January 1809.

27. Col. Harding's letter, addressed to the Deputy Adjutant General (DAG), RA, from Spithead on 24th January 1809 (PRO WO55/1194 pp.153–59). Duncan, vol. II, p.219 states that Col. Harding wrote, 'The weather would not permit it; the guns were spiked; the carriages destroyed; and the whole thrown over a precipice into deep water'. However, I can find no evidence to support this in Harding's letters.

28. Bogue, entries 17th and 18th January 1809.

CHAPTER 4

Howorth's Arrival

His duty done, Moore lay dying in a modest lodging in the Canton Grande, within the town of Coruña; his fading thoughts were for his men and his nation, 'I hope that my country will do me justice', but whether his country honoured his dying application is unhappily debateable. Irrespective, his loss was felt deeply and across the force; Gardiner noted:

> General Hope's dispatches will acquaint you with our afflicting loss; you will imagine how severely it was felt: I saw him after he received his wound, but he was talking with such firmness, that I did not apprehend the danger he was in.[1]

The Gunners had certainly played their part and to suggest, as Oman does, that 'they had come off easily' is incongruous. True, infantry losses were at about 15 per cent while those of the artillery were nearer 9 per cent but mere statistics seldom tell the whole story. Captain Robert Carthew, Second Captain William Romer, Lieutenant John Wilson and Lieutenant George Lear all died during the voyage back to England, and Harding, racked with illness, only survived until the following June. Captains John Chester and Henry Evelegh were badly affected with illness for many months and Cookson's dysentery and rheumatism laid him low on several occasions following his return. Nevertheless, despite his afflictions, this officer wasted little time in seeking an audience with the MGO Lord Chatham, to sing his own praises and lament his failure to gazette.[2] When this failed Cookson beat a path to MacLeod's door where he was shown correspondence, forwarded by Sir David Baird, from both houses of Parliament to the Royal Artillery, expressing their thanks and a letter from Lord Chatham in which 'he avails himself of this occasion to express the sense he entertains of the zealous and highly meritorious conduct of the Corps of Royal Artillery during the late service and arduous campaign in Portugal and Spain'.

Cookson, far from impressed, was incensed that his earlier audience had solicited no advancement toward profitable reward and recognition. He penned an immediate and lengthy letter to Lord Chatham in which he emphasised the critical part he had played; concluding that 'one might without much vanity have flattered oneself that something was due for my arrangements as well as Lieutenant Colonel Harding's in the two advances and retreats with the Horse Artillery …'. Two subsequent attempts to pay a call on the MGO were unsuccessful and no reply was forthcoming: then, on 1st April, Cookson was summoned to MacLeod and informed that 'His Lordship had spoken of Cookson in the highest possible terms' and that 'as proof of his feelings towards him had appointed him to the Command of Sussex District'. Furious at this cold shoulder and his continued lack of recognition he took up his post within days; on 6 May he began his visiting inspection 'as far as Selsea Bill near Chichester westward and as far as Newington in Kent eastward'. On the 29th May he sent in his *lengthy* report to the Master General and the Board of Ordnance – at which juncture, Lord Chatham probably regretted his decision, although his mind was equally likely on other matters: he had just been warned off to command the army for the pending campaign at the Scheldt.

The remnants of Moore's army arrived at a number of south coast ports in a dreadful state; starved, half clothed and gripped by fever, their tales of victory at Coruña against the might of the *Grande Armée* were difficult to believe. Wall and Miller recall the experience of their home coming:

In a few days the Company arrived at Chatham, and disembarked in a horrible situation, most of the men attacked by fever, and obliged to be carried to the hospital in carriages, where many survived but a short time. During the campaign, and of the fever after our arrival, my losses amounted to thirty-two, but as five of that number are not accounted for, except as missing in Spain, they may be forthcoming; but many of those who survived was [*sic*] so completely worn out by fatigue, that they will never be effective for service.[3]

Numbers of our men began to die on board the ships with the Spanish fever breaking out among us. But to our great joy on the 27 January, 1809, we came in sight of England, the first sight of British land I had seen for 14 years … Went into Portsmouth harbour, where a great many troops landed, but we were so ragged and lousy, that we were not permitted to land, but [had] to sail to the ports nearest to our different quarters. Neither were our troubles to end here. We buried several men here, who died in the fever. Our Pay-Serjeant went on shore and brought us some slop shirts, shoes, stockings etc. etc., which were soon as lousy as the old ones. We would frequently pull off our clothes and stamp on them with the heels of our shoes to kill the lice. We now began to muster the men from different ships, but our Company, that embarked at Gibraltar 110 strong, we could only muster 40 men, so that we lost 70 men out of one Company in 6 months … On our arrival at Woolwich we were all taken to the hospital and inspected by the surgeon [who] ordered a warm bath and a basin of *Caudle*. Served with clothes and all our old clothes burnt before we went to the Barracks.[4]

Portland's Tory administration had been dealt another foreign policy blow; the debacle in Buenos Aires in 1807 followed by the national outrage at the Convention of Cintra in 1808 and now the expulsion of the army from Spain in early 1809 played directly into the hands of the Whig opponents to continued prosecution of the war in Iberia. To make matters worse, the Tories were split on how best to proceed and the ailing Portland struggled to contain a fractious group of ministers from within. The situation became so serious that it ended, later in the year, with his Foreign Secretary, Lord Canning, fighting a duel against his Secretary for War, Lord Castlereagh. This quarrel had centred on whether to support the campaign at the Scheldt, thereby opening another front in support of Austria's struggle against France during the War of the Fifth Coalition, or to re-engage in Iberia in support of the Spanish in Andalusia or the Portuguese via the British garrison that still remained at Lisbon.[5]

By mid-December 1808 General Sir John Cradock had arrived in Lisbon to assume command of the garrison and within days he had received news of Moore's decision to countermand the retreat and prosecute renewed operations in northern Spain. Cradock immediately mobilised and deployed forward all the troops that he could spare, retaining a mere 4,000 in Portugal under his command. However, by the beginning of January it was clear that Moore's intentions were undone and that the reinforcements from Portugal would not reach the retreating army in time. Cradock thus issued an order for the forces to withdraw, concentrate north of Lisbon and await further instructions. The disarray and disagreement within the British government delayed and complicated the situation further; such instructions appeared to indicate the redeployment of this force elsewhere in the Peninsula. This was a decision which met with Cradock's approval as he considered Portugal a lost cause: the Regency had, at that time, not been suitably empowered by the Portuguese Court in Brazil; there was no funding which could be used to provide defence; the remnants of the Portuguese Army were useless and he, like Moore, considered the Portuguese border too long and porous to defend. Cadiz was deemed the most suitable future base from which to prosecute operations and in January, in accordance with the mood music emanating from London, Cradock dispatched Major General John Mackenzie with 4,200 troops, by land and sea, in that direction.[6] However, the Spanish had not been consulted and had no intention of opening up the possibility of a second Gibraltar. Despite Canning's instructions, Frere, the British ambassador, had not opened discussions on the issue with the Junta and, to exacerbate the situation, Canning, without waiting for the outcome of Frere's consequent negotiations, dispatched another 4,000 men under General Sir John Coape Sherbrooke to the region.[7]

This political and diplomatic ineptitude confined Mackenzie's force to their transports, within the limits of the harbour at Cadiz, until early March by which time the shambles had played out and they received orders to return to Lisbon. They arrived at much the same time as Sherbrooke's force from Ramsgate, which had lost a month in transit due to heavy storms, and Cradock now found himself at the head of 16,000 men. The farce did, however, serve a purpose for the cabinet 'elected not to commit forces to the heart of Spain without a fortress to fall back on'; quite why

Gibraltar would not suffice was not explained. It was of little immediate consequence to Anglo-Spanish relations but the *quid pro quo* was a declaration to reinforce the British Army in Portugal. This followed hot on the heels of an Anglo-Portuguese agreement to appoint a British officer as commander-in-chief of the regular Portuguese Army and a British commitment to train, equip and pay the force. The results of these decisions were twofold: as early as the middle of the year an Anglo-Portuguese army emerged which fought, as such, until the end of the campaign in southern France in 1814 and secondly, it reopened the debate on the ability of such a force to defend Portugal and *ipso facto* provide the British government the foothold in Iberia they desired.

The leading proponent of this policy was none other than Sir Arthur Wellesley; he had survived the Cintra Court of Inquiry and his views on the question were now sought by Lord Castlereagh. In London, on the 7th March, he laid out his memorandum for the defence of Portugal. It opened:

> I have always been of opinion that Portugal might be defended, whatever might be the result of the contest in Spain; and that in the mean time the measures adopted for the defence of Portugal would be highly useful to the Spaniards in their contest with the French. My notion was, that the Portuguese military establishments, upon the footing of 40,000 militia and 30,000 regular troops, ought to be revived; and that, in addition to these troops, His Majesty ought to employ an army in Portugal amounting to about 20,000 British troops, including about 4000 cavalry. My opinion was, that even if Spain should have been conquered, the French would not have been able to overrun Portugal with a smaller force than 100,000 men; and that as long as the contest should continue in Spain this force, if it could be put in a state of activity, would be highly useful to the Spaniards, and might eventually have decided the contest.

Lieutenant Colonel Robe, who was commanding the artillery in Portugal throughout the winter of 1808–09, was still struggling with officialdom. The Board of Ordnance had, by October 1808, replied to the justifiable concerns he had raised following the mounting of the artillery for the earlier campaign. It would have done little to raise his hopes, but would certainly have raised his blood pressure:

> In reply to the parts of your public correspondence in which you have so very warmly complained of some omissions and deficiencies, particularly in the Light Brigade of Artillery shipped at Plymouth, I am to say that his Lordship has, upon inquiry, ascertained that there were some irregularities in the embarkation, and that he has, in consequence, expressed his displeasure through the Board to the parties concerned, in a manner to make a lasting impression. His Lordship has, besides, issued such order, and made such regulations, as must effectually preclude every plea or excuse for irregularity or omission in future. The Master General, in desiring me to give you the above information, has directed me to add that, although he is willing to ascribe much of the style and many of the expressions in the letters to your known zeal for the service, and the anxiety attending an officer

during the moments of preparation for the field, yet his Lordship cannot but regret that, instead of forwarding a complaint, which it would be the wish and the interest of the Ordnance to attend to, you should have allowed yourself to arraign, with such improper and unmerited asperity, the conduct of the Ordnance Department in general.[8]

To a man like Robe, such bureaucratic nonsense, edged with thinly veiled threats of displeasure, was like a red rag to the Spanish bull. His professionalism continues to emanate from his correspondence with MacLeod as he struggled to cope with order and counter-order to defend Lisbon, support Moore's main force, assist the Portuguese in their national defence, gather intelligence on the feasibility of routes within Portugal (presumably prompted by the debacle which predicated Moore's earlier order in October 1808), latterly to assist in the withdrawal of ammunition and stores sent back by Harding and, ultimately, to prepare the artillery for embarkation should the situation require. In addition, he was ordered to test some of William Congreve's new rockets, the first trial causing no little alarm to the inhabitants of Benfica (a suburb of Lisbon) when some fell perilously close to their dwellings. Although Robe had 52 pieces of field ordnance at his disposal, he struggled to equip the five brigades as directed by Moore prior to his departure from Lisbon.[9]

> The Lieut. General has directed me, in the interim, until he can more fully decide upon what will be required, to demand an immediate supply of drivers, horses, harness and stores to complete the five Brigades, *viz.* Two light six pounder Brigades, British, two light 6 pounder, and one medium 12 pounder, German Artillery, to a similar establishment with those gone forward into Spain …[10]

Throughout the winter months some of these stores and a few mounts arrived at Lisbon and Robe had made efforts to bring Lawson's half company up to full strength.[11] However, the British government's decision to prosecute the war in defence of Portugal resulted in three additional companies of artillery being dispatched in January and February. They arrived together in early March and by the end of the month the situation was as follows:

> The following is the disposition I have proposed to make of the several Companies of Artillery on this service, and perhaps with some small alterations they will be attached accordingly, as horses or other means of moving the Brigades can be obtained.
>
> Captain Sillery's Company takes up the Light 6 Pr. Brigade, now at Lumiar, and for the right wing of the Army, as the 3 Prs. are completed with horses or mules to attend the Cavalry.
>
> Captain Bredin's Company has the duties of Lisbon & Fort Belem, and will take charge of the reserve Brigade of 6 Prs. in Lisbon, for which at present there are no horses. [Bredin had accompanied Mackenzie's force to Cadiz and returned on the 12th March.]
>
> Captain May's Company will have a Brigade of 6 Prs. with the Guards, as soon as they can be supplied with horses.

Captain Glubb's Company will occupy Cascaes [Cascais]. Such men of it are disposable will be employed in transport duties of ammunition & stores.

Captain Lawson's Company will have the Light 3 Pr. Brigade with the Cavalry, as soon as it can be put into movement. I have allotted them to this Brigade, as being formed of the men who have been longest in the country, many of whom also in action.

Of the German Artillery, Captain Gesenius's Company has St. Julian's and the forts depending, and would, if horses could be obtained, man another Brigade attached to the German part of the Army [i.e. the King's German Legion infantry and cavalry].

Captain Teiling's Company has a Brigade now at the advanced posts, but which on the 3 Pounder Brigade going there, will form with the left wing of the Army.

Captain Heise's Company will take up a Brigade of heavy guns of position, should such be required.[12]

Robe's letter highlights the chronic shortage of artillery mounts; in reality only Captain Charles Sillery's and Teiling's (commanded by Captain Charles von Rettberg) companies were equipped as brigades ready for field duty. It was a damning indictment of the failings of the Board of Ordnance and the Commissariat as well as an indication of the lack of suitable livestock from within Portugal. Indeed Cradock, almost in desperation, had ordered officers (including Captain Andrew Cleeves KGA) to travel to North Africa in order to attempt to procure animals there. To add to his concerns, Robe was now asked to give up some of his more capable officers for secondment to the Portuguese artillery; captains John May and Victor von Arentschildt KGA and Second Captain William Eliot were the first to be selected.[13] William Carr Beresford had been appointed by the Portuguese government council (acting in the name of the Prince Regent) to modernise, reorganise and train the Portuguese Army. He had arrived in early March, assumed the Portuguese rank of (field) marshal, and set about his task immediately and enthusiastically. Another Gunner officer was also keen to gain employment in the Portuguese service. Captain Alexander Dickson had set sail from Portsmouth on the 15th March aboard HMS *Champion* and arrived at Lisbon on the 2nd April. Dickson had recently returned from the ill-fated expedition to the Rio de la Plata, where General John Whitelocke's questionable leadership had resulted in the British Army's humiliating surrender to an army of part time local soldiers in the burning wreckage of Buenos Aires. The young Gunner officer was desperate to put this military fiasco behind him and had volunteered for operational duty at the first opportunity.[14] Dickson had met Beresford at Monte Video following the latter's release from capture, and capitalising on that association wrote to him, and Sir John Cradock, asking for employment with the Portuguese artillery. He was to be disappointed; 'I found that neither had received notification respecting me', Dickson was to write in his first letter to MacLeod, 'nor did the latter [i.e. Beresford] express any wish on the subject'.[15]

Lord Chatham and the Board of Ordnance had no intentions of leaving Robe in charge of the eight companies of artillery; they had selected and dispatched Brigadier General Edward Howorth as the replacement CRA. Howorth arrived at much the same time as Dickson and, as luck or circumstance would have it, 300 excellent horses and a draft of 170 artillery drivers from Ireland. Robe could have no complaints about being superseded but the coincidental arrival of the artillery horses must have irked. Nevertheless, the brigades could now be equipped for field service and Howorth wasted little time seeking Robe's advice and instigating his recommendations. Howorth also offered the post of Brigade Major to Dickson, which he gratefully accepted, and by early April the artillery organisation was as follows:

CRA: Brig. Gen. E. Howorth

Staff: Lt. Col. W. Robe RA

Lt. Col. H. Framingham RA

Brigade Major: Capt. A. Dickson RA

Companies	Notes	Equipment
Lawson's Company		6 x light 3-pounders
Sillery's Company	Commanded by 2nd Capt. Lane (Sillery was commanding Park and Reserve).[16]	4 x light 6-pounders 2 x 5½-inch howitzers
May's Company	Commanded by 2nd Capt. Baynes (May seconded to Portuguese artillery).	5 x light 6-pounders 1 x 5½-inch howitzer
2nd Rettberg's Company KGA	Formerly Teiling's Company.	5 x light 6-pounders 1 x 5½-inch howitzer
4th Heise's Company KGA		5 x heavy 6-pounders 1 x 5½-inch howitzer
Manning the Forts at Lisbon Command: Lt. Col. G. B. Fisher		
Bredin's Company	Cascais Fort.	Exact ordnance unknown
Glubb's Company	Fort São Julião.	Exact ordnance unknown
1st Gesenius's Company KGA	Garrison at Lisbon.	Exact ordnance unknown

Sources: Compilation from Dickson, Vigors, Laws and Leslie.

Before he departed Iberia in mid-January, Napoleon had issued his strategic vision and operational plan which was to be conducted on three fronts. The first concentrated on the north-east and east of Spain, culminating in the capture of the vital sea port of Valencia; the other two fronts were interlinked and designed to subdue, firstly, the whole of Portugal and then, secondly, Andalusia and southern Spain. Conceptually, the plans were sound but practically, when undertaken over the Iberian terrain in winter, against nations in arms and with limited or nonexistent lines of communication between individual forces, and *ipso facto* contact between commanders, they were flawed. Soult, having driven Moore's army from the Peninsula, was given a leading role in the execution of the Emperor's plan; he was to commence his capture of Portugal from the north, taking Oporto and then linking up with Marshal Claude Victor, Duke of Bellune's 1st Corps, which would cross the Portuguese border from (Spanish) Estremadura, and the two would then move on Lisbon. All of this was, according to Napoleon's timelines, to have been completed by mid-February! Soult had commenced his advance from Galicia on the 30th January and immediately ran into problems with the Galician insurgents and the Portuguese *ordenança*, or home guard. Crossing the River Miño and the mountains of northern Portugal added to his woes but by the end of March he had succeeded in capturing the city of Oporto, although he was now down to less than 16,000 men. With the first part of his plan completed he was well behind schedule but nevertheless decided to wait for word from General Pierre Lapisse at Salamanca or, more crucially, Victor in Estremadura. He was to hear nothing; the month of April passed but unbeknown to Soult, the situation in southern Portugal had now changed dramatically.

On the night of the 14th April HMS *Surveillante* narrowly escaped shipwreck off the coast of the Isle of Wight; on board the frigate was Sir Arthur Wellesley, returning to Portugal with the support of the Secretary for War and great expectations on his shoulders. He arrived on the 22nd April to discover that Cradock had moved the army north to block Soult but he had few troops facing east to cover any attempt by Victor. Wellesley wasted little time instructing Cradock to go firm at Leiria, calling for his key staff, including the commander of the artillery, and then issued subsequent orders for an immediate advance north and for a containing force under Mackenzie to move astride Abrantes.

It is my intention to advance forthwith upon Soult; accordingly, I request you, as soon as you shall receive this letter, to send an Officer of the Quarter Master General's department to Coimbra, to arrange the quarters there for the whole of the British army with you, including the 16th light dragoons, which are ordered forward, excepting Major General Mackenzie's brigade, which you will find otherwise disposed of in this letter. The Officer will arrange at Coimbra for the reception not only of the British troops, but of about 6,000 Portuguese troops, including 350 Portuguese cavalry.

You will then commence your march on the 29th as follows: General Hill's corps, with the cavalry under General Cotton, to Condeixa; Guards, and Stewart's brigade, German light dragoons, and one brigade of artillery, from Leyria to Pombal; the troops at Alcobaça to Leyria; and the troops at Caldas to Alcobaça. On the 30th, General Hill's corps, and General Cotton's cavalry to Coimbra; Guards, Stewart's brigade, cavalry, and artillery, to Condeixa; Tilson's and Campbell's brigades of infantry and one brigade of artillery to Pombal; General Murray's and General Sontag's brigades to halt at Leyria; General Cameron's brigade from Alcobaça to Leyria. On the 1st of May, Guards, &c., cavalry and artillery to Coimbra; Tilson's and Campbell's brigades and artillery from Pombal to Condeixa; General Murray's and General Sontag's brigades and artillery from Leyria to Pombal; General Cameron's halt at Leyria. On the 2nd of May, Tilson's and Campbell's brigade and artillery to Coimbra; General Murray's and Sontag's brigades and artillery from Pombal to Condeixa; General Cameron's brigade from Leyria to Pombal. On the 3rd of May, General Murray's and Sontag's brigades and artillery to Coimbra; General Cameron's from Pombal to Condeixa. On the 4th of May, General Cameron's brigade to Coimbra.

General Mackenzie's brigade, and a brigade of 6 pounders [May's Company under Baynes], to march on the 29th to Ourem, where he will halt till he shall find that the Portuguese troops have passed on their march from Thomar to Coimbra. He will then march to Thomar. He shall receive further instructions from me for his guidance.[17]

In addition to Mackenzie's screen, Wellesley had dispatched Beresford with a force of nearly 6,000 men to undertake a wide flanking manoeuvre in order to get in around the back of Soult and cut off his retreat. Soult established a screen force south of the Douro, comprising General Julien-Augustin Mermet's Infantry Division and Franceschi's Cavalry Brigade; they had clear instructions to delay and not to hold the advancing army. Soult was confident that the wide and fast flowing River Douro, coupled with extensive plans to remove or destroy all the available boats and the solitary pontoon bridge, would bring Wellesley's designs to recapture the city to an abrupt halt. The first major engagement between the French covering force and Wellesley's troops took place near the village of Grijó; Dickson recalls the incident:

11. Thursday … Discovered a corps of the enemies [sic] Cavalry posted at the edge of a wood on the right of the road going to Oporto, a little short of Grijo: on advancing found they were the advance of a body of French which were posted on a strong hill to the left of [the] road with a wood in front. Sir Arthur formed Brig. Gen. R. Stewart's [Brigade] supported by squadrons of cavalry, and the light troops commenced the action with those of the enemy in the wood; this lasted some time and those of the enemy made a vigorous stand; in the mean time Sir A. conducted the German legion into the wood on the right of the road and they, by making a detour, turned the flank of the enemy at the same time as Stewart's attacked them in front; the Battalion 16th Portuguese Regiment charged up the hill where a Corps of Infantry was posted, when they fled and the pursuit continued beyond Grijo; they then entered a wood when the infantry were halted but the cavalry pursued, came up with them and, with the loss of three or four men killed and a few wounded, killed and took prisoners a good number. At the commencement of the thing the 3 Prs. were brought up and the first shot compelled the Corps of French Cavalry to retire which we first observed.[18]

Wellesley's army was thus an Anglo-Portuguese force and was to remain so until the final French defeat at Toulouse in April 1814. In terms of Beresford's training and reorganisation of the Portuguese, it was still early days; nevertheless the commander-in-chief was both delighted and relieved at the performance of the 16th Portuguese Regiment. In response to Mackenzie's concerns at having so many Portuguese in his covering force, Wellesley was to reply: 'You are in an error in supposing that the Portuguese troops will not fight. One battalion has behaved remarkably well with me; and I know of no troops that could have behaved better …'[19]

The guns had been brigaded with pairs of infantry brigades during the advance but on the eve of battle Wellesley made some adjustments. Sherbrooke commanding Henry Campbell's, Alexander Campbell's and John Sontag's brigades was allocated

Captain Henry Lane; Hill commanding his own and Alan Cameron's brigades received
Rettberg; while (Edward) Paget commanding Richard Stewart's and John Murray's
brigades had the companies of Lawson and Lieutenant Henry Heise. Early in the
morning of the 12th May, Wellesley ordered Murray with a composite force, including
two of Lawson's 3-pounders, to move to Avintes to try and find alternative means of
crossing the river.[20] The allied commander then moved to the convent on the Serra
heights to conduct a full reconnaissance; he was joined by several of his staff and many
locals including several of the monks from the Convento. Dickson joined the throng
and described the scene and the events that followed:

> The Douro at Oporto runs something in a serpentine form, the channel of the
> river being sunk and the banks on both sides steep and high. The bridge was
> completely burnt and dispersed, and on the Quays of the river on the opposite side
> I could observe several French guards and sentries at different points, which
> appeared quite at ease, and not as if they were on the point of marching away …
>
> In the meantime several boats were sent down from General Murray to a place
> a short way above Villa Nova, where the bend of the river prevented those in the
> town from seeing what was going on … Sir Arthur then ordered some guns to be
> brought up to the convent where we were which would command the landing of
> our troops on the opposite side and would protect their formation; these guns
> were ordered to remain concealed until wanted.[21]

Soult's confidence that the Douro represented an intractable obstacle to Wellesley's
progress was sorely misplaced. Ever mindful of the ubiquitous nature of the Royal Navy
he had deployed numerous cavalry patrols between the city and the Atlantic, along the
north bank of the Douro, but the balance of French guards and patrols, within the city
and east, seemed to share in their commander's confidence that an attempt to force the
crossing in broad daylight was not viable. These same soldiers had equally tardily
executed Soult's order to destroy, secure or remove to the north bank, all the boats,
ferries and pontoons that could be exploited. Wellesley had, early in the day, dispatched
his intelligence officers to scour the southern banks of the river in search of such craft;
they soon uncovered a repairable ferry pontoon, but more significantly they brought
reports of four unguarded wine barges on the north bank and, by returning in the very
skiff belonging to the Portuguese barber who had rowed across bringing the incredible
news in the first instance, the means to collect them.

> General Hill's Brigade then moved towards the point where the boats were, and a
> cargo went over which I don't suppose exceeded 300 men. If the enemy had had
> any conception of the thing, passing in that way would have been totally
> impracticable; they continued the passage until the Brigade was nearly over, when
> a strong column was discovered advancing from Oporto against them. The first
> two guns that were brought up the hill to our convent were Portuguese 6 Pounders,
> having been the nearest in the streets leading to the convent; these were brought
> forward and opened by Col Framingham who directed them himself with such
> effect, that it checked and drove back the column for a time and assisted the troops

in their formation; Captain Lane's Brigade immediately afterwards got up to the same place. A brisk attack was now made by the enemy in great force on General Hill's Brigade which defended itself nobly; I have heard the Buffs particularly mentioned. Our troops assisted by a large unfinished building [Seminary], completely protected the passage across by which more troops were joining them, and general Paget was somewhere about this time wounded in advancing to drive back the enemy. More troops soon got over to enable us to be the assailants in our turn; the enemy then abandoned the town and the English began crossing over from Villa Nova [the suburb on the south bank]. I was then sent to the rear for ammunition and saw no more, but the enemy were soon afterwards driven out of the field and retired by the road to Amarante; a detachment of our cavalry that got over charged a considerable body of French infantry in line and completely forced them, to the wonder and admiration of the French, which Capt Goldfinch Royal Engineers then a prisoner (but afterwards escaped) heard them express.[22]

Whether the French had time to admire this virtually suicidal charge by the 14th Light Dragoons is debatable but *wonder* they certainly would have entertained; wondering how on earth they had allowed themselves to be driven out of a position as defensively strong as Oporto, from a southerly attack, across the fast flowing and steep-sided River Douro in broad daylight. The Gunners had played their part and Lane recalled that 'the French brought a gun down to the river side evidently to flank our troops in crossing, a shrapnel shell from a 5½-inch howitzer directed by Lieut. W. C. Johnson [Johnston] burst whilst the party were in the act of unlimbering, [it] dismounted the gun and killed or wounded every man or horse attached to it'.[23] Wellesley wrote in his subsequent dispatch to London that he 'had every reason to be satisfied with the artillery and the Officers of the engineers'.[24] The recognition was a bit lukewarm but to be fair the recapture of Oporto was, in the main, an infantry affair. The cavalry charge and follow-up later in the battle would undoubtedly have benefited from horse artillery support; it was an area of deficiency the commander-in-chief had already noted two weeks previously when the second shipment of horses arrived at Lisbon.

> I have received a very bad report indeed of the state of the artillery horses lately arrived from England with the heavy dragoons, being very old, diseased, and out of condition. I shall receive it officially probably in a day or two, when I shall transmit it to England. In the mean time, I think it proper to acquaint you with the state of these horses, and to recommend that for that reason, as well as because it would be very desirable to attach a troop of horse artillery to so very large a body of cavalry as we shall have, that a troop of horse artillery should be sent out.[25]

Within weeks captains Hew Ross and Robert Bull, commanding 'A' and 'I' troops of the horse artillery respectively, had been warned for service in the Peninsula but for now, Lawson's 3-pounders were the most manoeuvrable ordnance available to the force. Wellesley's initial pursuit of Soult's demoralised army was leisurely; his flanking manoeuvre by Beresford had long since failed but latest intelligence had the French marshal's escape route, over the bridge at Amarante, in French hands making Soult's task effectively routine. However, when Wellesley discovered that Loison, holding the crossing, had been dislodged following an indecisive encounter with Beresford and Major General Francisco da Silveira on the 11th May, he headed north to Braga with all speed in an attempt to cut off his adversary.[26] Soult cut the corner and headed off into the mountains with Wellesley in hot pursuit, but at Montalegre the allied commander called off the chase amidst rumours of Victor stirring in Estremadura. Lawson's Company had managed to keep up with the pursuing infantry all the way to Montalegre over some very demanding terrain; the other three companies of artillery had not advanced further than Braga. The CRA, in his letter to MacLeod, recalled the adventure:

> The extraordinary rapidity of events in this country, which have been accompanied by a succession of the most triumphant operations against the enemy, left me no leisure to communicate them as they occurred. However, I am at last returned here, after passing eight days in continued marches over the worst roads I ever saw, through incessant rain, a depopulated country, quartered in uninhabited houses, and with no supplies whatsoever, but what was scantily provided by the Commissariat Department. During the greater part of the march the luxury of a bed, or a change in clothes, which were always wet, was unknown to me ... We pursued to Mantalagree [Montalegre], where the enemy turned short to the left, over the mountains, and took the shortest way to Galicia.[27]

The Commissariat, the whipping dog of the British Army, certainly had their shortcomings but failing to provide succour under these circumstances was explicable and excusable. Schaumann, Assistant Commissary General to the 14th Light Dragoons, highlighted both his plight and that of the retreating French.

> Towards evening I reached the bridge of Saltador [Salvador], and shortly afterwards I passed two farm houses and Campa Ruivas [ruined cottages], where I intended to spend the night. But all the houses were chock full of men of the Coldstream Guards and the light cavalry, together with General Wellesley's staff. Here at last I reached the 14th Regiment, and reported myself to its commander, Colonel Hawker. It was quite impossible to obtain either provisions or forage for the troops. All around there was nothing but hills and rocks, and every house for miles had been plundered by the French ... The cruelties perpetrated at this period by the Portuguese hill-folk against the French soldiers who fell into their hands are indescribable. In addition to nailing them up alive on barn doors, they had also stripped many of them, emasculated them, and then placed their amputated members in the victims' mouths – a ghastly sight![28]

Such atrocities were becoming all the more commonplace as the anti-French feeling and consequent French reprisals began to spin out of control. All the same, the Portuguese had every reason to be satisfied: their country had, for a second time, been liberated from the burden of French occupation. Leaving the Portuguese forces under General Silveira to cover the northern border and those of the Loyal Lusitanian

Legion under Colonel Sir Robert Wilson to cover the north-east, Wellesley headed back to Oporto to consider how best to tackle Victor's 1st Corps that was just beginning to stir after a winter of relative inactivity in Spanish Estremadura.

Notes

1. PRO WO55/1194 pp.149–52.
2. In other words, to be published in the *London Gazette*. Being 'gazetted' means that your award is included in the official record of honours and awards for public service and military accomplishment. Lord Chatham was John Pitt, the 2nd Earl of Chatham, elder brother of William Pitt (the Younger), the Prime Minister until his untimely death in 1806.
3. Wall, p.17.
4. Miller, entries for January and February 1809.
5. The campaign at the Scheldt or Walcheren expedition as it is better known was nothing short of a disaster. Over 4,000 troops (10 per cent of the force) died, only 106 in combat: the balance succumbed to the 'Walcheren Fever'. See *The Expedition to Walcheren 1809* by 2nd Capt. Henry Light RHA.
6. This force consisted of the 2/9th, 3/27th, 1/29th, 2/31st and Capt. Bredin's Company RA by sea and the 1/40th overland from Elvas. Fortescue, vol. VII, p.118 indicates that a second company of artillery was embarked a few days later but I can find no evidence to support this.
7. 1st Coldstream Guards, 1/3rd Guards, 2/87th, 1/88th and three companies of artillery, Glubb's, May's and Sillery's who all sailed from Plymouth in January or February.
8. Duncan, vol. II, pp.200–01
9. PRO WO55/1194 p.52. Letter from Robe to MacLeod, 1st November 1808. There were 9 x medium 12-pounders, 5 x long 6-pounders, 21 x light 6-pounders, 4 x light 3-pounders, 4 x heavy 5½-inch howitzers and 9 x light 5½-inch howitzers.
10. PRO WO55/1194 p.48. Letter from Robe to MacLeod, 5th November 1808.
11. Half this company, under Capt. Fauquier, had proceeded to Sicily (from Gibraltar) in 1808; in March 1809, these men were transferred to other companies enabling Lawson's half company in Portugal to be brought up to strength.
12. PRO WO55/1194 p.265. Letter from Robe to MacLeod, 23rd March 1809.
13. May was selected by the Hon. Mr. Villiers, the British Agent in Lisbon and 2nd Capt. Eliot was part of Carthew's Company and had been left behind to undertake 'intelligence tasks' when Moore's army marched to Spain. In addition, Lt. Charles was attached to the Loyal Lusitanian Legion (a force raised by Sir Robert Wilson) and Capt. Campbell and Lt. Wills were attached to the Spanish Army at Seville and Cadiz respectively.
14. Beresford had captured Buenos Aires in June 1806 which prompted the British government to exploit the success and additional forces were duly sent to join Beresford and the British garrison at the Cape of Good Hope. Dickson's Company

was part of this force, which set sail in October, unaware that Santiago Liniers had already defeated Beresford's force and that the Spanish had reassumed control of the city. Dickson's ship, the transport *Harriet*, arrived off the Argentine coast on the 5th January 1807, and the young captain assumed overall command of the artillery when Capt. Watson returned to the Cape. Gen. Auchmuty's force took Monte Video as a preliminary operation to the re-taking of Buenos Aires and Dickson was to be mentioned in the commander's General Order following the successful capture of the town. However, at this juncture overall command of the force passed to Gen. Whitelocke. The subsequent operation was a complete disaster, Whitelocke being an officer entirely incapable of accomplishing the mission.

15. Dickson, vol. I, 1809, p.3. Letter from Dickson to MacLeod, Lisbon, 12th April 1809.
16. In fact Sillery was ill; he died at Badajoz on the 30th September 1809 and Capt. Thomson assumed command of the company. In the interim it was commanded by 2nd Capt. Henry Bowyer Lane.
17. WD, vol. IV, pp.277–78. Wellesley to Sherbrooke, 27th April 1809.
18. Dickson, vol. I, 1809, pp.19–20.
19. WD, vol. IV, p.350. Wellesley to Mackenzie, 21st May 1809.
20. Interestingly, Wellesley in his subsequent dispatch records this as two 6-pounders, but Dickson states they were 3-pounders and Browne (p.139) records that the (three guns) were commanded by Capt. Taylor, Lawson's second captain.
21. Dickson, vol. I, 1809, p.20.
22. Ibid., pp.20–21.
23. Lane letters, p.10. This is mentioned in Oman, vol. II, p.338, where he refers to 18 guns at the Serra furnished by Lane, Lawson and one KGL battery; but he provides no source for this. We know that two of Lawson's guns were with Murray's flanking assault; therefore it is more likely that the guns were provided by Lane (known to be the case), Rettberg and Heise with the balance of Lawson's guns in reserve ready to cross the river at a moment's notice. The fact that Dickson reports two Portuguese guns being directed by Lt. Col. Framingham is an additional puzzle.
24. WD, vol. IV, pp.322–26. Wellesley to Castlereagh, Oporto, dated 12th May 1809.
25. WD, vol. IV, p.281. Wellesley to Castlereagh, 27th April 1809.
26. This was also news to Soult who had not been informed of this decision by his subordinate; he first heard early on the morning of the 13th May.
27. Letter from Howorth to MacLeod, dated 24th May 1809. PRO WO 55/1194 pp.341–47.
28. Schaumann, p.156.

CHAPTER 5

Wellington's Cold Shoulder

Wellesley returned his army to Oporto and began planning to move south, to Abrantes, for the possible union of his army with that of the Spanish commander of the Army of Estremadura, General Gregorio García de la Cuesta y Fernandez de Celis. Some of the more scattered brigades moved directly to the latter town, while the balance made use of the stores and resources in Oporto. Howorth used the time to write to MacLeod suggesting a series of improvements to the organisation, structure and equipment of the artillery for the Peninsular Army; he also requested additional 3-pounder brigades, on the basis that they had been the only ordnance capable of keeping pace with the infantry over the rugged terrain in northern Portugal. Proposed improvements included: double instead of single draught for both guns and wagons; that brigades should have four instead of six guns; that howitzers should be dispensed with completely and a liberal amount of spherical case be issued for the guns in their stead; that an integral forge, mounted on a small limber, should be provided with each brigade; that the span of wheels should be narrowed to 4½ feet and, to prevent instability from this modification, that a 'bare iron axletree' should be adopted; and finally that spare shafts, wheels, axles, spokes, felloes and pintails should be provided as standard. Most of these ideas belonged to Robe; some made perfect sense and some did not, but their inclusion in the post-operational report in the wake of the second liberation of Portugal and being based on experiences of soldiering in Iberia thus far was, at least, understandable. Within weeks, on the battlefield at Talavera, the army was lamenting the lack of heavier guns with which to answer, in kind, the considerable French firepower.

Lawson's 3-pounder guns had taken such a hammering that they had to remain at Braga to be refitted. Once routes had been cleared and confirmed as suitable for the artillery, the Gunners were dispatched and as early as the 22nd May Heise's heavy 6-pounder brigade was already on the move to Coimbra via Ovar.

The greatest part of the army have marched again from this place for Coimbra, and we follow in a day or two. Nothing further has been heard of Victor. I therefore conclude he has gone back again finding it was all over with Soult. We begin now to imagine that this army may find its way into Spain, and the orders of Sir Arthur do not hold out any speedy probability of being in quarters. It certainly is a fine body of men, and with very little rest and a good supply of shoes will be equal to anything. I wish I could say the same for the artillery horses: these bad roads and rapid marches have cut them up very much.[1]

In fact Victor's Corps were having the most dreadful time trying to sustain themselves in the largely barren region of Estremadura and it was this insufficiency, and not the southerly movement of Wellesley's forces, which preyed uppermost on the marshal's mind. Uppermost on Dickson's mind, however, was how to extract himself from Howorth's staff; the relationship between the CRA and his Brigade Major was far from harmonious.

On my arrival here I found Captain May and other officers serving in the capacity for which I came out, and no opening having been given for being employed in a similar way, I was glad to accept General Howorth's offer of being Major of Brigade, and during the few days we remained at Lisbon making the preparations for the campaign, everything went on so well that I felt quite satisfied with my situation. But immediately after taking the field a total altercation took place in the temper and manners of the General; he became excessively irritable and dissatisfied, and in his line of deportment immediately towards me unhandsome, and I may say frequently ungentlemanlike, finding fault with almost everything I did or said, shewing [sic] an impatience and contempt if ever I ventured an opinion, and if I asked a question even on the most trivial of subjects scarcely condescending a reply, and then perhaps made with a sneer, at the same time shewing an evident want of confidence in me, and suspicion that I could be capable of deceiving him … Under these circumstances I have struggled on through all with the full determination of relinquishing the Office as soon as I could properly do so.[2]

Dickson's opportunity was to manifest itself within days. Major John May had accepted Portuguese service on his arrival in theatre, ceding command of the company to Second Captain Henry Baynes, which had then been task organised as the direct support brigade for Mackenzie's covering force. In the meantime, May had discovered that life with the Portuguese artillery was not quite what he imagined and when he received confirmation that his application for brevet rank had been turned down (from England) his mind was set. However, the problem for both May and Dickson was that the key decision makers, the MGO and DAG RA, were both embroiled in personal preparations for the Walcheren expedition prior to their own individual deployments across the North Sea. On 15th June, Dickson arrived at Abrantes and found May, with his two Portuguese brigades of guns, in the town; the two compared notes and following an office call with Beresford, who was also (fortuitously for the pair) in town, an exchange of posts was agreed. Handover was swift and by the 15th June Dickson was already back on the road, with his new charge, *en route* to Castelo Branco. He quickly realised that his lack of rank was going to hamper his aspirations to influence and improve the Portuguese artillery amidst jealousy and antipathy from the Portuguese officers and NCOs and a general lack of support from the Portuguese Artillery Department. His determination was ignited when, at Castelo Branco, he encountered (acting) Major Arentschildt, who had joined the Portuguese service at the same time as May and now, despite being considerably junior to Dickson, outranked and commanded the latter and indeed received all the orders for the artillery through the Portuguese chain of command. Dickson made application to Beresford, but the commander of the Portuguese Army was having none of it; he had made application to England, outlining his decision to release May and requesting acting rank for Dickson and, until such time as the instructions were forthcoming, Dickson was to get on with things.[3]

While Wellesley waited for a response from Cuesta as to future combined operations, he issued orders for the Portuguese forces to concentrate; thus the two brigades which had marched with Beresford, the four battalions which had been at the crossing of the Douro and the brigade which had been with Mackenzie's covering force, along with the all the Portuguese gunners and cavalry, were to form a corps of observation along the border between the rivers Douro and Tagus.[4] Victor had remained conspicuously inactive for many months but in early May moved against a battalion of the Loyal Lusitanian Legion which had ventured across the border to Alcántara only to discover Cuesta's forces capitalising on his absence by making a move on Mérida. Victor was well aware that just lingering indefinitely in Estremadura would not meet with Napoleonic approval and, with a lack of provisions and his force demonstrating levels of sickness at unprecedented rates, he decided to submit a cogent case to Madrid requesting reinforcement or repositioning. He was granted the latter, and between the 14th and the 19th June he withdrew to the north bank of the Tagus and established his corps between Almaraz and Talavera, confident that the river and his defensive position would be sufficient to hold any attack by Cuesta's Army of Estremadura.

In the meantime, Wellesley was finding Cuesta a difficult partner but it was far from his only distraction: funds had dried up from London delaying the release of replacement shoes and rations for his men and fodder for the horses; those replacements that were available were held up for want of transport; and the long awaited reinforcements were taking for ever to arrive.[5] Furthermore, pay for the army was many months in arrears and some of his men were misbehaving, plundering the Portuguese, seizing their livestock and forcing them to repurchase the beasts as well as stealing the army's horses (mainly from the cavalry) and then selling them on to the Commissariat.[6] To make matters worse, none of Cuesta's proposals for future operations particularly appealed to Wellesley; furthermore Victor's northerly movement had complicated plans. Nevertheless, early in July the British Army moved north across the border into Spain with a small column of Portuguese, under Wilson, providing flank protection. The army had been organised into four infantry divisions, a cavalry division and a five brigades of guns.

Wellesley continued to be concerned about the lack of mounts for the RA and as early as the 5th June he had written to Lieutenant Colonel Hoylett Framingham:

> I hope that your horses on their arrival on the Tagus will not be in the unserviceable state in which you expect they will be. If they should be so, I must relinquish that important branch of our equipment, the British artillery; and I have requested General Beresford to have some brigades of Portuguese artillery in readiness to join and do duty with the British army on its entry into Spain.

Wellesley's words were not an idle threat and, had the long-awaited mounts been insufficient in number and quality to move the RA brigades, then the inconceivable could have become reality and the British Army could have marched to its first major campaign of the war without its own national artillery in direct support. This state of affairs highlighted the failings of the Board of Ordnance's policy to equip and supply the artillery force in theatre; however, as it transpired, the policy of just enough, just in time, sufficed to stave off a crisis for the Board and spare the blushes of many a Gunner. The following artillery took to the field and proceeded with Wellesley's army into Spain:

CRA: Brig. Gen. E. Howorth
Staff: Lt. Col. W. Robe RA
Lt. Col. H. Framingham RA
Lt., the Hon. W. Arbuthnott RA (Adjutant to Framingham)
Brigade Major: Capt. J. May RA – not present at Talavera

Companies	Notes	Equipment[7]
Lawson's Company		6 x light 3-pounders
Sillery's Company		4 x light 6-pounders 2 x 5½-inch howitzers
May's Company	Commanded by 2nd Capt. Baynes.	5 x light 6-pounders 1 x 5½-inch howitzer
2nd Rettberg's Company KGA		5 x light 6-pounders 1 x 5½-inch howitzer
4th Heise's Company KGA		5 x heavy 6-pounders 1 x 5½-inch howitzer

Sources: Dickson, Laws and Leslie.

On the 10th July, Wellesley met Cuesta at Almaraz; it was not the most amicable of congregations and was conducted through interpreters as Wellesley spoke no Spanish and Cuesta apparently refused to converse in French. Cuesta's intransigence is often misinterpreted and misunderstood by British historians; General Charles William Vane, the Marquis of Londonderry, recalled that 'Cuesta was a person of no talent whatsoever; but he was a brave, upright and honourable man, full of predjudices, and obstinate to a great degree, and abhorring the French with the hatred of personal rancour'.[8] He was also well aware that the British ambassador was openly trying to elevate Wellesley to the position of *Generalissimo* of the Spanish forces and that many in the Spanish junta at Seville supported the idea. Not the happiest of circumstances to open central dialogue on future allied cooperation. Nevertheless, the two commanders concluded a plan which placed their left flank in a dangerously exposed position and their right flank in the hands of another Spanish general, the commander of the Army of La Mancha, General Francisco Javier Venegas. The commencement of operations was delayed to enable sufficient time for orders to be disseminated to Venegas, for his troops to get into position and for them to engage and hold the attentions of General Horace-François Sebastiani and his 4th Corps while Wellesley and Cuesta joined forces and moved east to engage King Joseph and Victor's 1st Corps.[9]

The combined Anglo-Spanish armies totalled 56,000, Joseph's and Victor's force no more than 35,000; it seemed like a sound plan but it was to backfire. Firstly, Venegas's encounter was mishandled and mistimed, allowing Sebastiani to break clean and join the main French force. Secondly, plans to execute a combined attack on the French position on the plains north of Talavera on the 23rd and again on the 24th July failed when Cuesta refused to get embroiled. Not the best of starts to Anglo-Spanish operations in the campaign to rid the Peninsula of the *Grande Armée*. What followed was equally theatrical: the French withdrew, now equipped with the knowledge that they were facing a numerically superior force which included the British and, following another verbal bust-up between the two commanders, Cuesta followed the French but Wellesley did not. Early on the 26th July, Cuesta discovered the size of the French force he had just chased up the high road to Madrid and, conversely, the French discovered that only Spanish troops lay to their front. The hunter became the hunted and the Spanish were shortly in full retreat, pursued, rather tardily, by the French cavalry and the whole returned to the environs of Talavera where Wellesley was still ensconced. Wellesley sent forward two divisions under Sherbrooke and Mackenzie to assist the Spanish back across the River Alberche and into their positions on the allied right. During this manoeuvre, Mackenzie's Division was given a rude introduction to events by Lapisse's Infantry Division, which had crossed the river further north and then swung south unobserved and into the flank of the 31st, 87th and 88th. Wellesley, who had ridden up to the area just prior to the encounter, was able to rally the broken battalions and extract them but not without loss.

The depleted and dispirited British battalions assumed their respective places in the allied defensive line and, along with the rest of the forces, began their battle preparation for the impending confrontation. Wellesley had taken a direct hand in the deployment of his guns: Lawson's Company was to the south, adjacent to the Spanish 3rd Division, and located on a small rise in the ground called the Pajar de Vergara, which had been hastily fortified; to their left, behind Cameron's Brigade, was Sillery's Company, whose guns were not in reserve but in position; to their left, in between Alan Cameron's and Ernest Langwerth's brigades, was May's Company under Bayne's command; on the Medellin heights was Rettberg's Company; and the second KGA brigade, under Heise, was in reserve in the centre rear of the British position near the cavalry. The allies held a 3-mile long line from the River Tagus, north through the town of Talavera de la Reina and up to the Medellin heights; the

British held the northern mile from the Pajar de Vergara to the Medellin and the Spanish the south to the river including the town and the Basilica del Prado. The Spanish had the same number of batteries as the British providing for a total of 60 allied guns. They faced 66 French guns in 13 batteries, a situation which, on paper, balanced the odds but many of the French guns were the heavier and longer ranged 12-pounders and Victor wasted little time in grouping nearly half of all the French artillery on the Cerro de Cascajal, an elevation at the north end of the French deployment approximately 600 yards from the Medellin.

During the evening of the 27th July, even before the guns were in place, the French executed an opportunist assault in an attempt to capture the Medellin prior to Hill's Division being properly established thereon. Had General François Ruffin's Division succeeded in their task, the loss of the Medellin would have rendered the allied defensive position untenable, bringing the curtain down upon any ambition for a full scale engagement the following day. Despite valiant efforts on the part of the 9e Léger, the British and German troops managed to counter the French advance and hold the feature. At first light the contest resumed, preceded by a thunderous and effective artillery bombardment and counter-battery engagement which afforded the added advantage of screening the French troops as they advanced, once again, to tackle the Medellin. Wellesley ordered the infantry to move back behind the crest but no such luxury was afforded the Gunners; as a result, their losses were proportionately the highest for all the Peninsular battles and only surpassed by Waterloo.

> The dawn of July 28th saw more than 100,000 men standing ready to slay one another. None but those who have been in similar circumstances can even guess what is felt. Just as the sun shot his first beams over the mountains on our left, *bang* went the first gun from the enemy, and *bang* was the answer from our battery on the hill. Battery after battery now opened, that on our right joining in the fray, and firing over our heads. Who the gunners were in our battery I don't know, but an unlucky shot from it killed a Brunswick rifleman by tearing out his bowels.[10]

Fusilier John Spencer Cooper's view of the Gunners was typical of the day, highlighting the divide, not just between infantry and artillery but between soldiers (and officers) under the wing of Horse Guards and those from the Board of Ordnance. Not quite Kipling's 'East is East, and West is West, and never the twain shall meet' but, nevertheless, in complete contrast to the French *corps d'armée* system whereby the artillery was integral to the division, and sometimes brigades of the corps, and well known to them. Cooper's account also confirms that Lawson's guns were firing against the French columns in enfilade and along the frontage of the British and German infantry, in the very area where the strong line of allied skirmishers would have been operating, just like the unfortunate Brunswicker.

Baynes, commanding May's Company, was on the periphery of the infantry assault on the hill but was subject to vicious counter-battery fire. The Gunners soon began to take heavy casualties and when Baynes was immobilised the CRA appointed Second Captain William Granville Eliot to command the guns, much to the relief of

Lieutenant William Elgee who was the company's next senior officer. Eliot had been serving with the company as a volunteer since becoming detached from Carthew's Company in 1808 when, during Moore's advance to Spain, he had been sent, along with captains John Taylor and George Brander Willis, to act as intelligence officers gathering information on suitable routes for the movement of the artillery. Eliot recalled that 'in this first day's action I endeavoured to make myself useful by assisting the different Brigades, and carrying orders for General Howorth, and in the second, when Captain Baynes was wounded, had the command of his Brigade given to me, with which I continued in action the whole of that day'.[11] Shortly later Lane was also injured, when:

> A French shell burst directly under the gun I was pointing [and] killed Nos. 7 & 8, took a leg off No. 9 and knocked me backwards with a contusion of the head, a graze of the sinews of the left thigh and another of the left foot. Before this, having been obliged to serve the sponge for some time, I was nearly exhausted as were the

3. The Battle of Talavera ~ Positions at Midday, 28th July 1809

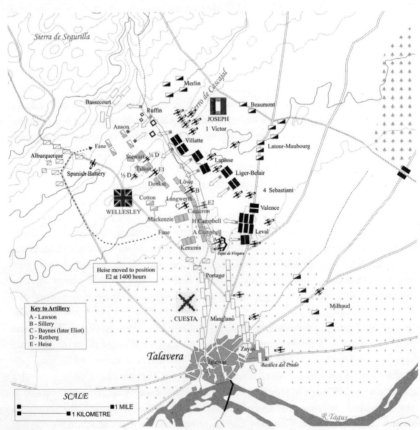

men from the fight ... I lay for some time insensible between the guns and limbers, when Sir I. Sherbrooke perceiving my situation dismounted from his horse and poured the contents of a small phial of brandy and bark down my throat, which brought me to my recollection and I was enabled, by the cessation of all firing about this time, to stand-to the guns again in the afternoon.[12]

Howorth realised that additional firepower was required in this area of the field and ordered Heise to move the reserve artillery to the left of the KGL; the guns were soon in action and the heavier 6-pounder brigade quickly made its presence felt.[13]

Ruffin's second attempt on the Medellin also failed and the French commanders paused to consider their options. Ruffin's regiments had been badly mauled and the French high command was split on how best to proceed with the attack – if at all. An informal truce of sorts evolved with men from both sides filtering down to the Portiña stream to drink and fill canteens and for breakfast to be consumed. For more than two hours stretcher-bearers recovered their wounded. Victor was determined to resume hostilities and was furious at the earlier failures and equally furious, perhaps, at his rather bull in a china shop approach to events thus far. It was clear that any subsequent attacks would have to be made across the frontage and accompanied by some form of manoeuvre. As the French repositioned their forces for just such an attack, Wellesley was able to witness their progress and counter-move. George Anson's and Henry Fane's cavalry brigades were moved into the valley behind and below the Medellin; General Luis Alejandro Bassecourt's Spanish Infantry Division were sent well to the north, on to the forward slopes of the Sierra de Segurilla; General José Miguel Cueva Velasco y La Cerda, Duke of Alburquerque's Spanish Cavalry Division moved (slightly later) to a position behind the British cavalry, supported by its horse artillery battery; Rettberg's Brigade was split into two troops, with the second troop falling back to a position on the far left of the British line; and finally another Spanish 12-pounder battery was split, with four guns to the Pajar de Vergara in support of Lawson's lighter 3-pounder battery and the other two guns to the left of Rettberg's left hand troop. The scene was set.

At 1400 hours Joseph gave orders for the gunners to commence proceedings and about 60 guns, in forward positions, opened up. Only 36 allied guns could respond and the closeness of the French batteries to the lines of allied infantry had an instant effect. Fifteen minutes later the advance commenced: firstly on the French left, then in the centre about 45 minutes later and finally on the right at about 1530 hours. The allies were engaged across the frontage but the French flanking manoeuvre, into the valley to the north of Medellin, provided the greatest cause for concern and Anson's cavalry were dispatched in order to disrupt the French infantry advance. They were supported by the artillery on the Medellin:

Captain von Rettburg's battery being stationed on the hill came more immediately under the observation of the commander-in-chief, who condescended particularly to notice the precision with which a bombardier named Dierking directed the fire of one of the guns of the battery. [He] was so pleased at the precision with which the German bombardier executed his task, that his lordship clapped him on the back and said, 'Very well, my boy'.[14]

Major Hartmann, who was commanding the KGA, witnessed the effectiveness of his own men but had to lend a helping hand to the Spanish gunners who were manning the two heavier Spanish 12-pounder guns to the left of the feature. These guns were bright new brass cannon from the arsenal at Seville but their sighting system was 'a century out of date'. Hartmann dismounted and assisted the young Spanish lieutenant, destroying a French gun in the valley with his first shot; after which the contribution of the heavier artillery was brought to bear with good effect.[15] Although many of the 23rd Light Dragoons came to grief on an unseen ditch, running the width of the valley floor, the French attack in this sector was thwarted.

In the centre, both General Louis Liger Belair and Lapisse had drawn up their divisions in two lines, the front in column of division and the second in column of battalion. They crossed the Portiña and advanced towards Sherbrooke's four brigades on the forward right face of the Medellin. They were met with a barrage of fire from both Eliot's and Sillery's guns and engaged in the flank by Lawson to the south. At some stage they were joined by Heise's long 6-pounder brigade, which Lieutenant William Unger (of the KGL engineers) recalls was moved soon after 1400 hours. 'At 2 o'clock a very heavy cannonade began, the Guards were attacked by a Division, the heavy brigade 6 pr was then ordered to the right of the KGL to past the Guards and in half an hour's time the French retired in disorder after the Guards had charged them with the bayonett [sic].'[16] During this fierce encounter Sillery, who was suffering badly from diarrhoea, was violently attacked by the complaint. Turning to an officer near him, he said, 'I shall not go to the rear, it may be said I was afraid.' He then deliberately walked 100 yards in front of the brigade, and dropping his overalls, yielded to the irresistible necessity of the case; after readjusting his dress, and calmly putting on his sword and sash, he returned leisurely to his post. The transaction excited a good deal of mirth, and a Gunner exclaimed, 'By my soul, our Captain is a sound and a staunch one!'[17]

General Jean-François Leval's attack on the far left of the French line was intended to occupy the forces to their front, but he soon lost control of his German and Dutch troops as they advanced through the olive groves and thickets. The French manoeuvre was not so much in column but more of a huge and confused mass of skirmishers which quickly pushed back the pickets of the 7th and 53rd which withdrew behind the front lines of Alexander Campbell's forward brigade. The ten guns in the redoubt fired canister into the Germans and Dutch as they broke cover and closed on the British and Spanish lines to their front. The casualties in the Baden battalions were extensive and the first attack stalled, then fell back and six French guns, brought forward to counter the ten in the redoubt, were captured and spiked. A second attack made slightly better progress and, at one stage, it penetrated the redoubt but was quickly driven back by James Kemmis's Brigade which had been brought forward to assist the front brigade which was begging to wane. Fusilier Spencer Cooper was in the thick of this action and recalled the moment:

> One of these [columns], after threading its way among the trees and grape vines, came up directly in our front, and while deploying called out *Espanholas*, wishing us to believe they were Spaniards … the Fusiliers and 53rd regiment delivered such a fire, that in a few minutes the enemy melted away, leaving 6 pieces of cannon behind, which they had not had time to discharge. The 6 pieces were immediately rendered unfit for use, as our balls were too large for their bore.

The muster roll of Lawson's Company, following the battle, depicts three men being taken as prisoners of war, most likely during this action, along with a number of the Fusiliers. During the second attack the Spanish cavalry Regiment del Rey engaged the retreating Germans in the flank and in the process came upon a half battery; they cut down the gunners and pulled the four guns back to the redoubt. Leval brought up two more batteries to support a third attack but the supporting infantry was driven back and these guns were also lost in similar fashion. In all Leval had now lost 17 guns indicating a questionable understanding of how to use and support this arm in battle; Napoleon's fury at this shameful incompetence led to a cover-up from which Leval and his corps commander, Sebastiani, were lucky to avoid retribution.[18] There is little doubt that the British and King's German artillery had been handled with far greater adroitness, despite being outnumbered by two to one in that sector of the field. As the light faded the battle died down but the cannonade was maintained and it was at this time that the long grass at the foot of the Medellin caught fire and, being fanned by the gusting wind, the flames began to spread with alacrity. Many of the wounded who were lying in the grass were caught in the inferno, which also began to threaten the ammunition wagons. Sergeant Bostelmann, with four gunners and four workmen, was in charge of the ammunition re-supply and was forced to act quickly and with great courage to avoid disaster.

> Bostelmann … considering that the loss of the ammunition might have a material effect on the result of the battle, as the battery to which it belonged was posted on the key of the allied position, against which the enemy's main efforts were directed, determined to attempt the preservation of the waggons, regardless of the personal danger with which the effort would evidently be attended. Of his assistants, the four gunners only were available, the workmen, expecting every moment an explosion, having run away; and with the aid of these four men, Luttermann, Zingreve, Warnecke, and Lind, the gallant sergeant succeeded in removing the heavily loaded ammunition waggons through the burning heath, and placing them on a spot in the rear, which a little trench had yet preserved from the flames.[19]

Bostelmann deservedly earned the Royal Guelphic Order for his actions but for now he would have been lamenting the loss of so many of his countrymen who had fought so valiantly on the Cerro de Medellin. The KGA suffered one sergeant and two men killed and three sergeants and 27 men wounded; while the RA lost one officer and seven men killed and four officers and 21 men wounded. Within the overall British totals of 801 killed, 3,915 wounded and 649 missing, the artillery losses were small but no less significant. May's Company had remained at the front of the British centre throughout the 27th and 28th and faced almost constant counter-battery fire from the concentration of French guns on the Cerro de Cascajal. It is not surprising therefore that many of the casualties were in this brigade: Lieutenant Henry Wyatt had been killed while commanding his section of guns and the commander, Second Captain Baynes, was also injured early on the second day at much the same time as Second Captain Lane. Second Captain John Taylor was injured while assisting Lawson in the redoubt; he was left behind in the hospital in Talavera following the battle and was subsequently captured by the French and taken prisoner until the end of the war.[20] Eliot, who had taken command of May's Company, recalled in a letter to his wife that 'after the most long running battle ever fought, I have again escaped without a wound, altho' twice hit in my clothes, and my horse, also twice wounded, the artillery has suffered considerably'.[21] Framingham was also injured during the battle; although his injury was quite severe he was able to remain with the army when it withdrew from Talavera a few days later. Howorth was very appreciative of Framingham's actions that day and wrote to MacLeod accordingly in the hope of securing an increment to the officer's pension.

Wellesley's appreciation of the services of the artillery was apparent, if a touch brief, in his dispatch to Castlereagh following the battle. 'The artillery, under Brig. General Howorth, was also throughout these days of the greatest service ...' The truth was that Wellesley had little time for the CRA, he considered him a ditherer and it is clear (but not well documented) that the moves of artillery on the battlefield that day were orchestrated and ordered by Wellesley himself. Some time later Howorth was to write and complain to Wellesley that he had received insufficient recognition for his services at Talavera, a most unwise decision on his part for it was well known that Wellesley was loath to heap praise on subordinates he considered not fully deserving. Howorth's letter clearly rankled and impelled Wellesley to mention the affair in a letter to his brother. 'As for Lord Howorth, I might as well claim the credit for the loss of the horses myself. Howorth was standing on the hill, which I had occupied for most of the battle, when a shell burst killing two of his, and a great number of other people's horses which were standing behind it. I said as much about Howorth as he deserves, for I believe myself lucky if he does not get me into a scrape yet.'[22]

Dawn on the 29th July revealed the vacated French positions but the fields to their front were deep with the dead and severely wounded. The allied armies were exhausted but the need to bury the corpses and care for the injured denied the men the badly needed rest they had earned. The force received the first of the reinforcements from Lisbon that same morning; Black Bob Craufurd had arrived with the three battalions of his newly formed Light Division. Craufurd was desperate to reach Talavera in time to take part in proceedings and had completed the last 43 miles of his journey (from Lisbon) in an almost unbelievable 22 hours. Unbelievable maybe, but the fact that Captain Hew Dalrymple Ross's Troop of Royal Horse Artillery was only a few days behind the infantry is even more remarkable.

I marched from Lisbon on the 9th of last month with my troop alone, with orders to join the army as soon as I could. I consequently used all diligence, and though opposed by many difficulties from want of forage and provisions, as well as being deficient in horses, and having the heat of the climate to endure, which at this season is intense, I reached the army at Talavera on the 2nd August, without having suffered one hour of ill health, and left by the road only two men from sickness. You will easily imagine my vexation on finding I was too late to share in the actions of the 27th and 28th ...[23]

Wellesley and Cuesta were aware, some days earlier, of a French force massing to the north but they were undecided on how to deal with this threat while continuing to contain Victor's force to the east. In the end Wellesley agreed to move north in an attempt to link up with the Spanish force under Bassecourt and block Marshal (Adolphe) Édouard Mortier's Corps at the pass of Puerto de Baños. However, by the 5th August it was clear that the force bearing down from the north consisted of not just Mortier's Corps but also the corps of Soult and Ney: 50,000 men in total, intelligence which changed the situation entirely. Craufurd's light troops were dispatched post-haste to secure the bridge and crossing at Almaraz and the balance of the army followed, while Cuesta evacuated Talavera leaving 1,500 British wounded who received nothing but the kindest handling from the French when they recaptured the city; which is more than can be said of the treatment meted out to some of the Spanish.

Victor has treated all the prisoners he has taken with the greatest attention and kindness, and has, I am told, assured Sir Arthur by an officer left for the purpose of requesting, that every act of humanity and attention shall be shewn to the sick and wounded. Since we left Talavera, we have performed a wonderful march, and crossed mountains which it is hardly possible to suppose artillery could have been got over. We are now four leagues from Truxillo, to which place I believe we shall march tomorrow, unless it is found necessary to wait for stragglers and the stores to come up. Our arrival here today has given us new life, in the hope of having better food. For four days we have had only one biscuit and half a pound of flour between every six men; now we look for something that may make up for the past, by getting into a more plentiful country. I really believe we should have starved had we continued a week longer in the mountains. How thankful I ought to be for possessing such a constitution. Every one of my officers has at times been ill, from fatigue of [the] climate, but I have not had even a moment's uneasiness. By the march we have made, and the start we have got of the French army, it is not thought that we shall be close followed, particularly as they may be anxious to annihilate the remains of the infamous Spanish army. The world, it is hoped, will now give credit to Sir John Moore's opinion of the state of this country, and I have no doubt will see the rashness of venturing so far as we have done with so small a British force.[24]

Despite the, by now, rather questionable success of the Talavera campaign and, for the second time, the less than flourishing relationship between the allies, Wellesley remained determined to create the conditions for continued cooperation. However, during the days that followed the allied victory at Talavera, both General Cuesta and the Spanish authorities did little to reciprocate that benevolent aspiration; the entire British force was suffering through want of provisions and the artillery and cavalry were particularly vulnerable.

We have got thirteen pieces of French artillery, which I wish to give over to the Spanish army; the other seven you have already got. I shall be obliged to you if you will urge General Cuesta to desire the Commanding Officer of the Spanish artillery to receive charge of them from the Commanding Officer of the English artillery. We want ninety artillery horses to complete the number required to draw the guns we have in the field. Could you give us any assistance in this way, either in draught horses or mules?

During the action of the 28th many of the horses of our dragoons and of the artillery strayed, and were taken possession of by the stragglers from the Spanish army who were in the rear of the town. I see English horses, with short tails, in possession of many of the Spanish troops; and I shall be very much obliged to you if you will urge General Cuesta to give an order that all persons having in their possession English horses, or horse appointments, such as saddles, bridles, &c., should take them to the English cavalry lines forthwith.[25]

Not surprisingly, perhaps, no horses or accoutrements were returned and by the 8th August Cuesta had lost all the newly acquired French guns, in addition to 16 of their own pieces, when he was caught ill prepared by Soult at the crossing of Arzobispo. Wellesley's resolve to continue allied operations was fast waning; his army was starving and his claim to his brother Henry, who had recently assumed the post of Ambassador to Spain, that he might have to abandon some of his artillery, was far from idle.

Having asked General Cuesta after the battle of Talavera, to assist me with 90 mules, to draw the British artillery, in lieu of those lost in the action, he refused to give me any, notwithstanding that there were hundreds in his army employed in drawing carts containing nothing. The consequence is, that I shall now be obliged to send back to Portugal, one, if not two brigades of artillery drawn by bullocks, if I should be able to procure these animals; if I should not, I must destroy them.[26]

Within days, Cuesta resigned having suffered a trapped nerve and mild paralysis, but requests to the new commander General Francisco Ramón Eguia, while more amicable in nature, still failed to produce tangible results. Indeed Wellesley's assertions that without rations and fodder he would be forced to withdraw to Portugal were met with a tacit concurrence. Following the French defeat of General Francisco Javier Venegas's Spanish Army in New Castile, Joseph rejected proposals to follow up the British or Spanish Army of Estremadura; instead he elected to consolidate French defences around Madrid and to send Ney back north to assist Kellermann, who had long since reported increasing activity by the Spanish Army of Galicia. The immediate threat to Wellesley's army had faded but nevertheless the problems facing the force were far from over and all soldiers, despite being weakened by starvation, were required to assist in repairing the roads and helping the exhausted horses of the artillery to drag the guns. All the guns, bar one, were saved.

> The whole of his brigades of Artillery returned from Talavera complete, with the exception of one 6-pounder gun which had been damaged in the battle on the 28th, and which the General [Howorth] wrote, had been *privately buried*, perhaps out of consideration for Spanish deportment also. But all the spare ammunition and stores had to be abandoned, as the carts were required to carry the sick. No less than 150 carts were so employed; for the sickness during the retreat, and even after the troops went into cantonments at Merida, was very great.[27]

Losses in 'A' Troop were particularly high. Ross recorded on the 2nd September that 'during the first two days my troop were on this ground, I lost eight horses – that is to say, four dropped down on the march from Medellin, and four died in the lines the following day. Both men and horses continue very unhealthy.' By mid-October Ross had been ordered by the CRA to leave two of his 6-pounder guns with the reserve as 'he can give me neither men nor horses'. Second Captain George Jenkinson, Ross's second in command, summarised the dire situation:

> Our situation is lamentable, we have lost 12 of our best men, and have at present 30 sick, the majority of which will I fear never recover, and that diminution of men, with the loss of 40 of our very finest horses, will give you an idea of the condition we are in ...[28]

By this time 'I' Troop under the command of Captain Robert Bull had arrived prompting Howorth to recall in his letters to MacLeod that he had 'one troop of Horse Artillery, Bull's, and one-half a one, Ross's'.[29] Curiously, the other brigades of guns do not seem to have suffered quite so dramatically. With the failed Spanish autumn offensive, Wellesley was forced to withdraw deeper into Portugal and, by the end of the year, Lawson's Company was at Badajoz, May's at Coimbra and Sillery's at Viseu; while Charles Sillery had succumbed to his lengthy illness and died at Badajoz on the 30th September and Lane had taken temporary command of the company. Andrew Bredin's and Frederic Glubb's companies were still near Lisbon at Cascais and Fort São Julião respectively. Ross moved in mid-December to Arronches, where he linked up with Craufurd's Light Division, and Bull remained at Elvas. Of the KGA, George Gesenius's Company continued to act as the depot and stores for the other two 'active' companies of the KGA and was based in Lisbon and Oporto, while Rettberg wintered with the 2nd Division at Elvas and Campo Mayor and Heise with the 4th Division at Guarda.

Wellesley had learned many lessons from the Talavera campaign; he realised that future allied operations would have to be orchestrated with care but, for the time being, he intended to concentrate on the defence of Portugal and to achieve this he needed to make better use of his Portuguese Army. However, reports from Beresford were far from encouraging, posing a dilemma for the British commander. He summarised the situation in correspondence with the Secretary of War:

> Things are much altered lately, and notwithstanding that the pay has been increased, I fear that the animal is not of the description to bear up against what is required of him; and he deserts most terribly … supposing the Portuguese army to be rendered efficient, what can be done with it and Portugal, if the French should obtain possession of the remainder of the Peninsula? My opinion is, that we ought to be able to hold Portugal, if the Portuguese army and militia are complete. The difficulty upon this whole question lies in the embarkation of the British army. There are so many entrances into Portugal, the whole country being frontier, that it would be very difficult to prevent the enemy from penetrating; and it is probable that we should be obliged to confine ourselves to the preservation.[30]

With this at the forefront of his mind, Wellesley, now elevated to (Lieutenant General) Viscount Wellington following his victory at Talavera, returned to Lisbon in mid-October and on the 20th of the month penned his lengthy memorandum to his chief engineer, Lieutenant Colonel Richard Fletcher Royal Engineers (RE).[31] This followed an extensive reconnaissance of the hills north of the city with Fletcher and his two Quarter-Master generals (QMGs), and provided the impetus for what were to be known as the Lines of Torres Vedras. The reconnaissance and subsequent communiqués with Fletcher demonstrated a very different relationship between the commander-in-chief and his chief of engineers than that with his chief of artillery. Jenkinson summed up the situation succinctly and in remarkably frank terms for the period.

> Nothing can be possibly conceived worse than the terms the Commander of the forces and our chief are on, indeed I should state it in better language did I say that they are on no terms at all, all their communications are of the most formal nature, and the noble Viscount repeatedly gives out regimental orders, two instances have recently occurr'd; one was an order given by the Commander of the forces, stating that that Captains of Brigades would be held responsible by him (which certainly supposes no commanding officer of that corps) for the good appearance of their brigade, and condition of horses attached to them, and called on them to see that the officers of the artillery drivers do their duty. A few days afterwards another made an appearance, directing that the artillery horses should go together in watering order, and be accompanied by their artillery driver officer, both of which orders our chief took very cooly [sic], comforting himself with the reflection that it took all responsibility out of his hands. Whatever fault may attach to him, and certainly great blame does, yet nothing can excuse the conduct of the noble Viscount, who it is pretty easy to see has no affection for the Corps; and I think I can safely state that there is no love lost. Not one single thing will our Brigr. give us that he can possibly help, he repeatedly says, 'why did you not come out here better supplied?' As if Ross had been entrusted with the arrangement of everything when he was ordered for the service, and when any wants are represented to him,

which there may be some difficulty in supplying, he threatens to send the troop to Lisbon, or to make a foot brigade of it, thereby hoping to quash any future representation, tho' there is not a man who would complain more bitterly than he would if any deficiency appeared which he had not been acquainted with – in short he is an old woman.[32]

Notes

1. Dickson, vol. I, 1809, p.28. Letter from Dickson to MacLeod, Oporto 25th May 1809.
2. Ibid., p.31. Letter written 28th May 1809 at Oporto but it is not signed and it is unclear if it was ever sent.
3. Within weeks this subject was to occupy much of the commander-in-chief's time as it began to cause animosity across the force; officers who received advancement by one rank for taking up Portuguese service were now gaining a second elevation through receiving Portuguese commissions elevated by yet another rank. Hence captains suddenly found themselves as Portuguese lieutenant colonels and, when working alongside their British counterparts, outranked them despite being very much their junior.
4. This provided a force of about 14,000 men: 18 battalions, four cavalry regiments and five or six gun batteries. Col. Sir Robert Wilson's Loyal Lusitanian Legion was excluded from this grouping and it continued to operate independently along the border and inside Spain. It consisted of three battalions, a cavalry regiment and a gun battery and numbered about 8,500.
5. Including the new Light Division under Gen. Robert Craufurd, consisting of the 43rd, 52nd and 95th, as well as Ross's and Bull's troops of the RHA and the 48th and 61st of Foot and 23rd Light Dragoons.
6. This was mainly the Irish regiments, the 87th and 88th Foot.
7. There is considerable confusion as to the exact ordnance taken into Spain. Fortescue (vol. VII, p.205) misinterprets Duncan (vol. II, pp.248–49) when he outlined the *desire* to dispense with howitzers. However, Fortescue, Oman, Napier and Duncan are all clear that there were 30 guns and, as there were five brigades, it seems reasonable that they still had their guns and howitzers. To have refitted each brigade with a gun would have been possible but I can find no evidence of this; if they had taken guns (i.e. light 6-pounders) from the Portuguese artillery, Dickson would have certainly mentioned this. Nowhere in Wellesley's dispatches does he refer to the howitzers being left behind, and he most certainly would have considered this an issue worthy of mention. Indeed, Wellesley instructs that howitzer ammunition is to be brought forward in his dispatch of the 5th June. Hughes, HOF, pp.65–72 talks about 25 guns – this must be an error, based on the confusion over the brigades not taking their howitzers, as mentioned (incorrectly) in Fortescue. Even if this were true, we know that Lawson had six guns (3-pounder) and no howitzers so the total would have been 26 in this case and not 25 guns. Indeed, in Hughes, HFI, p.129, 30 guns are

mentioned and Unger's map, to which Hughes refers, certainly shows six guns at each battery position.

8. Vane, vol. I, p.385.

9. Joseph was Napoleon's elder brother who had been crowned King of Naples in March 1806 but then moved, on Bonaparte's instruction, to assume the throne of Spain in April 1808.

10. Spencer Cooper, p.21.

11. Extract of a letter from Eliot to MacLeod, dated 9th October 1813 from Eastbourne. Leslie, p.99. This was supported in a letter sent by Eliot to his wife from Talavera de la Reyna, dated 29th July 1809 – NAM 1959-03-127-1 p.18.

12. Lane letters, pp.11–12.

13. This movement is recorded in the only detailed eyewitness account of the battle: that of Lt. Unger on his map – see James Clavell Library MD 228. Unger recalls, 'In the morning at day light the enemy attacked our left again in order to gain the hill but was repulsed / the heavy artillery was sent from the right of the 4th Divn to the left of KGL'. The move of these guns is supported by other accounts both primary and secondary.

14. Ludlow Beamish, vol. I, p.216.

15. Oman, OHP, vol. II, pp.545–46.

16. From Unger's map – see also Hughes, HFI, pp.134–35.

17. Lane letters, pp.13–14. Sillery had not been well for months and was struggling to cope with the demands of campaigning; he succumbed to his illness two months later on the 30th September 1809 while camped at Badajoz.

18. See Oman, OHP, vol. II, pp.536–38.

19. Ludlow Beamish, vol. I, pp.217–18.

20. See Boothby, *A Prisoner of France*, London Adam and Charles Black, 1898. Boothby was a sapper captain who was also captured by the French at the same time and he often refers to Taylor.

21. Letter from Eliot to his wife, dated 29th July 1809 – NAM 1959-03-127-1 p.18.

22. Raglan Papers, Wellington A/20, Wellington to Wellesley-Pole, dated 13th September 1809.

23. Ross, pp.5–6. Letter to his sister from Gasiesigo [Jaraicego], dated 9th August 1809.

24. Ibid., p.6.

25. WD, vol. IV, p.552. Wellesley to Gen. O'Donoju, 1st August 1809.

26. WD, vol. V, p.22. Wellesley to Marquis Wellesley (who had recently assumed the post of British Ambassador to Spain), 10th August 1809.

27. Duncan, vol. II, p.259.

28. Jenkinson, letter to Sandham from Elvas, dated 20th October 1809.

29. Duncan, vol. II, p.259.

30. WD, vol. V, pp.88–89. Wellesley to Castlereagh, 25th August 1809.

31. Following his victory at Talavera, the British government elevated Wellesley to a peerage with the title of Viscount Wellington of Talavera. He signed his first dispatch 'Wellington' on the 16th September 1809.

32. Jenkinson, letter to Sandham from Elvas, dated 8th December 1809.

CHAPTER 6

MacLeod's Labours

The Spanish central government was quick to accuse the British of desertion but did little to provide the badly needed supplies requested by Wellington. The autumn offensive, when it commenced, caught the French slightly off-guard as their military command had equally concluded that the Spanish position, particularly without the support of the ally, was not one from which to launch a large scale attack against five French corps. Initial success for the Spanish at Tamames (18th October) was quickly reversed by catastrophic defeats at Ocaña and Alba de Tormes on the 19th and 28th November respectively. The Spanish armies of the Centre (La Mancha), Galicia and Estremadura were largely rendered ineffective, the credibility of the Central Junta was in ruins and the way was now open for French advances into Andalusia and to the border forts.

By the time the French subjugation of southern Spain commenced in January 1810, Wellington's army was established within and on the border of Portugal. Wellington's aims were threefold: to defend Portugal, to establish the Anglo-Portuguese army on a firmer footing and finally, to provide better provisions and sufficient equipment to enable the force to function efficiently. During the winter months considerable correspondence passed between Wellington's headquarters and London concerning the cost of the war; not just the business of clearing the arrears but also the projected increase in costs for the continued prosecution of operations. Whig opposition to Wellington's plans to remain in theatre and defend Portugal grew daily; the British Cabinet had been taken by surprise at the overall costs of the war in the Peninsula resulting from the training and equipping of the newly raised Portuguese forces and the abnormally high cost of transport and supply generally. Nevertheless, Wellington was granted more funds, a third of the arrears to the Portuguese government were cleared and the annual subsidy raised to just shy of a million pounds per annum. Spencer Perceval, who had taken over as Prime Minister in October 1809 from Portland, admitted to Wellington that 'if he had foreseen in the winter of 1809 the demands that would be made upon the Treasury in 1810, he would never have dared sanction the continuance of the war upon the scale which it actually attained, from the sheer inability to supply funds to support it'.[1]

An equally difficult issue, in the wake of the failed expedition to Walcheren, was the subject of reinforcements.[2] Wellington was well aware that he had to balance every additional man against the added logistical and financial burden that accompanied any enhancement. Five thousand men were, however, requested and supplied and within months another 8,000 were also dispatched from England, North America and the Mediterranean. The French subjugation of Andalusia stalled at the very gates of Cadiz and the British government was determined to assist the Spanish in holding this strategic position and the emergency Spanish legislature which had been established therein. Reinforcement to the artillery forces was significant, with an additional six companies of artillery and one troop of horse artillery arriving between January and April 1810. Howorth's force, including drivers, rose from 1,957 at the end of 1809 to 3,068 by the 1st July of the following year.[3] The lion's share of this enhancement had been immediately directed to Cadiz.

CRA: Brig. Gen. E. Howorth
Staff: Lt. Col. H. Framingham RA
Lt. Col. W. Robe RA – Commanding the Corps of Drivers, Royal Artillery
Lt. Col. G. B. Fisher – Commanding Artillery in Lisbon
Brigade Major: Maj. J. May RA
ADC to CRA: Lt. J. Weatherall Smith RA
Lt. L. Woodyear RA (Adjutant to Robe)
Lt., the Hon. W. Arbuthnott RA (Adjutant to Framingham)

RHA Troops	Notes	Equipment
'A' Troop (Ross)	Arrived in theatre July 1809.	5 x light 6-pounders 1 x 5½-inch howitzer
'D' Troop (Lefebure)	Arrived March 1810 but following a disastrous voyage was being refitted in Lisbon. The troop officers were serving with 'A' and 'I' troops.	5 x light 6-pounders 1 x 5½-inch howitzer
'I' Troop (Bull)	Arrived in theatre August 1809.	5 x light 6-pounders 1 x 5½-inch howitzer

RA and KGA Companies	Notes	Equipment
Lawson's Company	Lt. Fosting was standing in for 2nd Capt. Taylor – POW in France.	6 x 9-pounders
Thomson's Company	Formerly Sillery's – Sillery died at Badajoz on 30th September 1809. Thomson joined the company in February 1810 and relieved 2nd Capt. Bowyer Lane who departed on sick leave to the UK from March to September 1810.	4 x light 6-pounders 2 x 5½-inch howitzers
May's Company	Commanded by 2nd Capt. Baynes (Maj. May was Brigade Major).	5 x light 6-pounders 1 x 5½-inch howitzer

2nd Rettberg's Company KGA		Light 6-pounders
4th Heise's Company KGA		Light 6-pounders
Lisbon		
Bredin's Company	Alhandra.	Exact ordnance unknown
Glubb's Company	Torres Vedras.	Exact ordnance unknown
1st Gesenius's Company KGA	Lisbon and Oporto – acting as depot for the other two KGA companies.	Nil
Cadiz		
P. Campbell's Company	Arrived February 1810: Acting Lt. Col. Campbell was serving with the Spanish; 2nd Capt. Hunt commanding the company.	Not brigaded
Owen's Company	Arrived February 1810.	Not brigaded
Hughes's Company	Arrived March 1810.	Not brigaded
Dickson's Company	Arrived April 1810. Capt. Birch in command – Dickson was serving with the Portuguese artillery.	Not brigaded
Shenley's Company	Arrived April 1810.	Not brigaded
Roberts's Company	Arrived April 1810.	Not brigaded

Sources: Compilation from Dickson, Duncan, Laws and Leslie.

MacLeod and his staff at Woolwich worked tirelessly to meet the needs of this considerable reinforcement while maintaining the six companies at Gibraltar, three in Malta and five in Sicily. Operations in the Peninsula and Walcheren had a devastating effect on the horses of both the RA and the Corps of Drivers: 2,786 had either died or been destroyed and with the paucity of suitable mounts in theatre, the burden fell on MacLeod to resolve the situation. A total of 3,367 were purchased and sent to Portugal in 1810 and the consequent increase in numbers of RA drivers resulted in the establishment of a field officer's post to command them. Robe assumed this duty, with cavalry pay.[4] The field companies in Portugal remained largely unchanged, as did the three companies providing garrison artillery at both Lisbon and Oporto. MacLeod, sensitive to the need for greater mobility to support Wellington's force, had earmarked a replacement horse artillery troop to relieve 'A' Troop, which had never recovered from the sickness that had swept through the men and horses while at Merida during the retreat from Talavera. Ross was devastated that his Peninsular foray was to be cut so inconclusively short:

Jan. 12th, 1810 – Receive a letter from Colonel Framingham, informing me that Captain Lefebvre's troop is ordered to relieve mine, and that after completing Bull's deficiencies, the remainder will be embarked for England.

Jan. 13th. – Answer Colonel Framingham's letter, and request that he will use his endeavours to induce the Commander of the Forces to detain my troop while there exists so early a prospect of active operations.

> Jan. 20th. – Receive a very kind letter from Framingham, lamenting that he cannot without propriety counteract the orders of the Master-General [MacLeod], by making an application to Lord Wellington to detain my troop. So all hope is fled.[5]

Hope, as fate played out, was far from fled. For 'D' Troop, after many months of uncertainty, were ordered on the 4th February to march from their barracks at Canterbury to Portsmouth and from there embark to Lisbon. On the 16th the fleet of some 60 ships weighed anchor but was soon hit by a violent storm off the west coast of Portugal. The *Camilla*, one of the transports carrying the troop, lost her mast, caught fire and then drifted for two weeks in the Bay of Biscay. The men of the troop assisted the crew in rigging jury-masts and the disabled vessel limped into Bantry Bay on the 18th March having lost all but four of the 36 horses on board. Under assistance, she made her way to Cork; the detachment were transhipped and on the 1st May set sail again into the face of a persistent south-westerly which delayed arrival in Lisbon until the 20th May. The *Camilla* had long since been given up as lost and with Captain George Lefebure's RHA Troop incomplete, Howorth had little choice but to use what had arrived of 'D' Troop to complete the establishments of 'A' and 'I' troops and he issued orders accordingly in early May. Ross received the news on the 15th May: 'receive[d] a letter from Colonel Framingham, stating that General Howorth had directed my troop to be completed immediately from Lefebvre's, desiring me to send Fisher a return of what I wanted, and him a copy of it'.[6] Sixty-eight men and 56 horses were to join Ross and 39 men and 25 horses to join Bull but as they prepared to leave Lisbon, the balance of 'D' Troop arrived; it made no difference, the revised orders were executed and 'D' Troop, with the remnants of the sub unit (37 men and 49 horses) remained as a depot in Lisbon until their future was decided.[7]

At first the French conquest of Andalusia made rapid, virtually unhindered, progress. It was Joseph's opportunity to convince Napoleon and the uncooperative marshals and generals in Iberia that he possessed a martial side to his nature. Napoleon once wrote of his older brother, 'He is of a gentle and kind disposition, possesses talent and information, and is altogether a very amiable man'. It was an accurate description and, having placed such an 'amiable man' on the throne, it is an indication of just how deeply Napoleon had misread the situation and the tenacity of the Spanish people. What is perhaps more puzzling is that Napoleon did little to help his brother and often undermined his authority, failing to sanction and back him as commander-in-chief of all the French armies in theatre. The invasion of Andalusia was, therefore, of critical importance to Joseph. Having commenced operations on the 7th January 1810, he arrived at the outskirts of Seville on the 29th January and the city, largely undefended at this stage, surrendered on the 31st. It was a good start. Seville was not just the capital of Andalusia: it had, since mid-1808, housed the Spanish executive, which now fled (a week prior to capitulation) and established itself in Cadiz. The Duke of Alburquerque, with the vastly diminished remnants of the Army of Estremadura, pulled back with the government and provided the requisite force to prevent French entry along the narrow isthmus on the Isla de Leon to the city and port of Cadiz; an action which, without doubt, saved southern Spain.[8] Despite repeated attempts by Victor to force entry, it was quickly apparent that any attempt at capture, without naval support, was improbable. Joseph was beside himself, defeat at the final hurdle was unthinkable; he asked his brother to release the French Fleet at Toulon to facilitate an attack on the city. Napoleon simply ignored his brother's request and Joseph, utterly disconsolate, returned to Madrid. Spanish reinforcements arrived by sea, escorted and (in some cases) transported by the Royal Navy and Frere, the British ambassador, moved to the city where he received immediate and enthusiastic requests for British support.

Captain Humphrey Owen's and Captain Patrick Campbell's companies were the first artillery reinforcements to arrive. The former company arrived complete, having sailed from Portsmouth with a brief stop-over at Lisbon *en route*; while the latter arrived, as a half company, from Gibraltar where the company had been stationed since 1802. In fact, Campbell himself had been serving for some months with the Spanish artillery and in his stead the company had been led by Second Captain Arthur Hunt.[9] The British engineers proposed that the small fort of Matagorda, which the Spanish had abandoned and blown up as the French arrived, was an important defensive structure and elected to reoccupy it. This was undertaken by a company of the 94th and a detachment of Gunners from both Owen's and Campbell's companies. On the 26th March Lieutenant General Sir Thomas Graham arrived to assume command of the British defence of Cadiz from Major General William Stewart and, within days, additional reinforcements arrived.[10] Framingham should have been the officer sent to command the five artillery companies but Howorth deemed his services 'impossible to spare' and so Major Alexander Duncan, who had accompanied the three additional companies of Alexander Dickson (commanded by Captain Robert Cairnes), William Shenley and William Roberts, had the great fortune to command this considerable artillery grouping. They arrived in Cadiz on the 31st March and Duncan immediately wrote to MacLeod outlining the requirements to equip the companies.

I have been directed by General Graham on my return from viewing the defences of the island of Leon, to report on the quantity of Artillery required for its defence, at the same time informing me, that he had already made a demand for four Brigades of Light artillery complete and one troop of horse artillery. Such a force of Artillery would certainly be of the utmost service considering the great want of the Field Artillery in the Spanish Army here. I am at the same time perfectly aware of the difficulty of procuring so great a supply from England, and should the Island be lost before its arrival, they would no longer be of any use in the defence of Cadiz. We are at present entirely without the means of acting with a Light 6 pounder Brigade, that was sent here from Lisbon, in consequence of the want of horses. There are also two 3 pounder brigades (English) belonging to the Junta. Captain Owen gave a receipt for one of them, in hopes of being able to act, as mules were promised, but no such promise has been kept, the Brigade remains useless. The great reason for the General being so anxious for a large proportion of Field Artillery is the total want of that arm in the Spanish Army, as I have already mentioned. What can be sent from England, I take the liberty of saying must be complete in horses, drivers and camp equipage, and I fear we must in a great measure, if not entirely, depend on England for forage; there is some idea of constructing redoubts on or near the river St. Pietro [Sancti Petri]. In that case a few Medium 12 pounders would be of great service, at least twelve. I understand from general Graham that a large proportion of heavy guns are on their way. I cannot conclude without informing you that the difficulties we meet with here, in the Ordnance Department *particularly*, are far beyond any conception.[11]

Quite what MacLeod was to make of all this can only be surmised; having himself recently returned from commanding the artillery at Walcheren, he must have been left scratching his head as to exactly what was required. Sir Thomas Graham's wish list would have provided him with as much artillery as Wellington had enjoyed in fighting the battle at Talavera and Duncan's letter provided little by way of clarity as he does not appear to have conducted his appreciation against military criteria. Nevertheless, MacLeod dispatched 18 guns, enough to equip three companies, along with 74 horses; 'a small supply ... to form a nucleus of a larger establishment'.[12] A paucity of Spanish field artillery was certainly the case but at this juncture, defence was a far greater priority than an offensive capability, and heavier guns the Spanish possessed in large numbers within the forts and citadel. However Duncan was left somewhat exasperated by the hosts' lack of activity and, in a subsequent letter on the 25th April he expressed a hope that 'the Spaniards will be more active than hitherto, in erecting batteries. Instead of exertions from them, we obtain *nothing* but conversation ... the town is full of men *doing nothing*'.[13]

Lieutenant William Brereton, who had arrived as part of Owen's Company in February, found himself commanding the artillery in Fort Matagorda when 'one night [21st April] the French opened with death and destruction'. Brereton was often exposed to the French fire from about 20 guns as he was on an elevated platform and spotting fall of shot; the young Gunner subaltern later noted that 'the parapet vanished, leaving only the naked rampart ... the men fell so fast that the staff bearing the Spanish flag was broken six times within the hour ... the bombardment continued for thirty hours unceasingly'. General Graham ordered the structure to be abandoned and, following a fairly eventful extraction of the force, Captain Archibald Maclain (87th Foot) wrote to General Graham and mentioned 'the services of that excellent officer, Lieutenant Brereton of the Royal Artillery for his unremitting attention to his duty, and the masterly style in which he kept up his fire on the enemy'.[14]

By this time an additional two companies of artillery had arrived at Gibraltar to replace the three that were diverted to Cadiz; thus the situation at the British dependency was as follows:

CRA: Maj. Gen. J. Smith
Staff: Lt. Col. G. Ramsey RA
Lt. Col. R. Wright RA

Companies	Notes	Equipment
Godby's Company	Since 1796.	Garrison guns
Dodd's Company	Since 1790.	Garrison guns

Smyth's Company	Since 1803.	Garrison guns
Morrison's Company	Since 1805.	Garrison guns
Birch's Company	Arrived April 1810.	Garrison guns
Fead's Company	Arrived April 1810.	Garrison guns
P. Campbell's Company	Half company.	

Sources: Compilation from Duncan and Laws.

Another *ad hoc* group of Gunners was sent, with a few British infantry companies, to support the Spanish garrison at the fort of Tarifa which housed over 20 guns of various calibres. Lieutenant Edward Michell was seconded from Morrison's Company to command the assembly. He had left as early as the 12th April and the balance, bringing his independent command to 67 men, departed two weeks later. They remained in the scenic, if windswept location until February the following year. In October 1810, a rather motley international group was collected under the command of Major General Lord Blayney to execute a diversionary attack on Fuengirola, aimed at disrupting French operations at Cadiz. The group, consisting of four companies of the 89th, a Spanish regiment from Ceuta and 500 Polish, German and Italian deserters from the *Grande Armée*, were joined by an RA detachment at Gibraltar, commanded by Second Captain James Lloyd (Morrison's Company) and consisting of two officers and 33 NCOs and gunners. The operation did not start well; Blayney discovered that the majority of the Spanish soldiers had no firelocks and not one man possessed any ammunition. Once rectified, the transports continued along the coast but things only got worse for on arrival it was discovered that the small fort was a considerably more formidable structure than hitherto reported and that the small French garrison, which had been recently reinforced, were both aware of the attack and well prepared to receive it. With news of a large French relieving force *en route*, Blayney withdrew but not before the three light guns and one 32-pounder carronade had been captured by the French during a sortie. According to Fortescue the RA was not manning the guns at the time; nevertheless three guns and the carronade were lost bringing this rather questionable episode to a close.[15]

Throughout 1809, Beresford had been rebuilding the Portuguese forces and had quickly concluded that the infantry, cavalry and artillery units and sub units required British field officers and captains (but not subalterns) to ensure cohesion and functionality. However, there was little to tempt British officers to volunteer (although this was less of a problem in the artillery) and so, by way of encouragement, a volunteer received not just a step in British rank but also a further step in rank in the Portuguese service. Hence, in theory at least, a British captain found himself as a British major and a Portuguese lieutenant colonel, a situation that caused considerable offence within Wellington's British Army and was deeply resented by Portuguese officers. Horse Guards changed, or perhaps clarified, the ruling in July 1809, by allowing elevation of one step in rank in the Portuguese service but not applying a step in rank to their British commissions. Irrespective of the strong sentiments attached to the policy in general, it worked, and if Wellington was to be able to defend Portugal and meet a French invasion force on anything approaching equal terms, he needed to hone his Anglo-Portuguese force to the task. A British force alone would simply be inadequate and reliance on Spanish support for the defence of their neighbour both unlikely and unwise.

At the commencement of the war, the Portuguese artillery consisted of four regiments: 1st Regiment, based at São Julião, Lisbon; 2nd Regiment at Faro; 3rd Regiment at Estremoz; and 4th Regiment at Oporto. Portuguese Daily Orders of the 24th October 1809 laid down the new organisation of the Portuguese artillery; the four regiments remained but they were all now structured along similar lines. Each regiment comprised a staff, seven artillery companies, one company of miners, one of firemen and one of pontoon engineers. Each artillery company was made up of 112 personnel: one captain, three subalterns, six sergeants, eight corporals, two drummers and 92 gunners.[16] By February 1810 there were seven (mobile) brigades of Portuguese artillery as follows:

Companies	Equipment
Maj. Dickson's Division	Three brigades each with light 6-pounder
Maj. Arentschildt's Division	Three brigades, one of 3-pounder, one 6-pounder and one 9-pounder.
Cabreira's Company	In reserve consisting of 5 x 9-pounders and 1 x 5½-inch howitzer.

Sources: Compilation from Dickson and Vieira Borges.

Dickson was clearly enjoying the independence of his command; missing out on events at Talavera the year prior rankled and the continual supply and transport problems for his brigades tested his patience but he was content with his lot.

January 6 1810 – This day being *Festa dos Reis* [Festival of Three Kings] the detachment went to church. I took a walk with a physician to who I was this day introduced, and Lieutenants Paulino and Demetrio, to the *Ermida* [chapel] de Bom Fim, about 2 miles from the town, on a height from which the view was magnificent, although the day was unfavourable. From this can be seen a great extent of the Tagus, with many towns on the other side … In the evening went to a dance at Captain Mors. There were 8 or 9 couple[s], and we had a very pleasant dance. Got home about one o'clock.[17]

Equipped with mules and bullocks for transport, Dickson trained and tested his brigades. However, the persistent problem of supplies remained ever present and for Dickson making up the shortfall from 'the bad state of the Commissariat and the want of money' was an ongoing distraction, not helped by the fact that 'the farmers and country people have no confidence in the Government to advance anything on credit'.[18] Wellington had written to the new Secretary for War, Lord Liverpool, in similar vein.

I believe that Portugal has never produced a sufficient quantity of grain for its consumption … the part of the country in which the scarcity is stated to exist is among the most fertile and best cultivated in Portugal. I conceive, therefore, that the difficulty in procuring provisions, if it exists, is to be attributed to the want of money by the Government. In fact the Portuguese Government have, since the restoration, been in the habit of taking provisions from the inhabitants of the country without paying for them, or even settling accounts. The people now conceal their provisions, and refuse to continue to furnish supplies, and the troops are distressed.[19]

In early February Dickson received orders that he was to provide the artillery support to General Hill's 2nd Division; it was a task organisation that was, later in the year, to enable the ambitious young artillery officer to see his first action in the Peninsula with Wellington's forces.[20] In the intervening months Dickson was charged to visit the majority of the key border forts and castles and document their ordnance and defensive attributes; it was a potentially tedious task but Dickson undertook to execute it with his customary zeal. His notes were meticulous and, as luck would have it, this knowledge was to provide the break he needed the following year. At Campo Maior he found the place occupied by a Spanish force under General Gabriel Mendizabal and that 'much work had been done', the 'breach made in 1801 had been repaired' and that 'nothing is now wanted but heavy artillery'.[21]

The heavy guns, vital for Wellington's plans to defend the Portuguese capital, had been removed to Elvas and from there to Lisbon. This plan was predicated on a line of forts and redoubts known as the Lines of Torres Vedras. It was a massive undertaking, involving 45 miles of fortifications, including 150 forts employing 600 pieces of ordnance. Wellington, characteristically, left no stone unturned in ensuring that the enterprise had the greatest chance of success, and that every available avenue to supply the men and equipment was explored and, if necessary, exploited. On the 6th March he wrote to Vice Admiral George Berkeley, Commander of the Royal Navy's Portuguese station.

Having found, upon referring to the returns of the ordnance and ordnance carriages in possession of the Portuguese Government, that there are not a sufficient number of guns, with carriages, to arm the different works in front of Lisbon which are now constructing, and which it is intended to construct, to the northward of Lisbon, even with the addition of the heavy ordnance on travelling carriages embarked in the store ships in the Tagus, I shall be much obliged to you if you will place at my disposition the ordnance, the carriages, and the stores belonging to the Russian ships of war still in the Tagus.

If you should consent to adopt this proposition I shall request you further to make them over to Colonel Fisher, the commanding officer of the British artillery at Lisbon.[22]

The French preparations were equally impressive. With the failed British Walcheren expedition and victory over Austria at Wagram, Napoleon set about releasing large numbers of men to reinvigorate the Peninsular campaign. In excess of 100,000 men were destined for Iberia and Napoleon clearly intended to command them personally until French offers of an Austrian marriage were unexpectedly accepted, compelling him to remain in France to supervise both his divorce and his impending wedding. Notwithstanding, in the spring of 1810, Wellington had every reason to be content; everything in his power was being undertaken to counter the threat and an inevitable third French invasion of Portugal. He was even satisfied with the progress of the Portuguese element, writing to Lord Liverpool that 'the pains taken by Marshal Beresford, and all the British officers serving under his command, to bring the Portuguese army to the state in which it now is, are highly deserving of his Majesty's approbation'.[23] Both Dickson and Arentschildt, commanding their divisions of Portuguese artillery, certainly considered it so. Their test was not long in coming.

Notes

1. Fortescue, vol. VII, p.437.
2. The last of the troops were not withdrawn from Walcheren until December and, early the following year, 11,000 of those who returned were still on the sick list.
3. Duncan, vol. II, pp.268–69.
4. Ibid., p.267.
5. Ross, p.9.
6. Ibid.
7. Whinyates, *WCS*, pp.55–58.
8. Lipscombe, *Wellington's Gunner in the Peninsula*, pp.152–55.
9. Laws, LBR, p.145, note 28 and 72. 2nd Capt. A. Hunt was accompanied by two subalterns, two sergeants, two corporals, four bombardiers and 50 gunners. The remainder of the company – 4 NCOs, 31 gunners and two drummers – sailed from Gibraltar to Cadiz on the 20th October 1810, and the company was again complete.
10. Gen. Sir Thomas Graham, KB, the first and last Lord Lynedoch.
11. PRO WO55/1195 pp.25–27. Letter from Duncan to MacLeod, dated 4th April 1810.
12. Duncan, vol. II, p.280 refers to PRO WO55/1201. Letters from MacLeod to Duncan, dated 23rd April and 8th May 1810.
13. PRO WO55/1195 pp.38–40. Letter from Duncan to MacLeod, dated 25th April 1810.
14. Brereton, p.iv.
15. Fortescue, vol. VII, pp.397–403.
16. Vieira Borges, pp.28–36.
17. Dickson, vol. II, p.142.
18. Ibid., p.193.
19. WD, vol. V, pp.385–86. Wellington to Liverpool, 28th December 1809.
20. Dickson had volunteered for service in the Peninsula following a rather slow start to his military career. His brief command and success at Monte Video was overshadowed by Whitelocke's total failure to re-capture Buenos Aires and Dickson was keen to distance himself from this fiasco. However, he was beginning to regret

his decision to join the Portuguese artillery when he missed out on events at Talavera. See Lipscombe, *Wellington's Gunner in the Peninsula*, pp.8–9.

21. Dickson, vol. II, p.201. The breach made in 1801 was made by the Spanish during their support of the French invasion (many Portuguese call this the first invasion) which took place in that year, as part of the War of the Oranges.

22. WD, vol. V, p.529. Wellington to Berkeley, 6th March 1810. See also note 7, ch. 2.

23. WD, vol. V. p.399. Wellington to Liverpool, Coimbra, dated 4th January 1810.

CHAPTER 7

Shrapnel's Duck Shot

Command of the French Army of Portugal, earmarked for the third invasion, was given to Marshal André Masséna, Duke of Rivoli, Prince of Essling; a wily campaigner who, by his own admission, was now past his prime. His command consisted of the 2nd, the 6th and the newly formed 8th Corps under Junot; the latter had, of course, been defeated by Wellesley at Vimeiro but General Jean-Louis Reynier (commanding the 2nd Corps) had also experienced defeat against the British, at Alexandria in 1801 and at Maida in 1806. Ney, conversely, had an altogether different opinion of the British having chased Moore's army 'into the sea'; he harboured no respect for the redcoats, and the Portuguese, as a fighting force, were scarcely worthy of mention. However, it was Ney's attitude to his new commander which was to overshadow all. Ney rarely obeyed anyone other than Bonaparte and viewed Masséna's appointment as a huge personal disappointment and major inconvenience. Masséna did not help matters, often ignoring Ney's advice in favour of Major Jean Jaques Pelet, his young and capable chief of staff. This all led to an unhappy mix of physical and mental factors which were to play a pivotal role in the French command group's dynamics and decision making during the impending campaign.

Wellington had to deploy his Anglo-Portuguese forces to cover the length of the border from a possible invasion in the north by Masséna's Army of Portugal, or in the south from Soult's Army in Andalusia. Hill's 2nd Corps covered the southern approaches, while the newly formed Light Division under Craufurd covered those in the north between the mighty rivers Douro and Tagus. The Portuguese brigade, under Colonel Carlos Frederico Lecor, was stationed between the two divisions and the balance of Wellington's British and Beresford's Portuguese troops were positioned in the centre of the country, poised to react to events as they unfolded. The artillery was largely deployed forward in support of the screening formations as follows:

RHA Troops	Notes	Equipment
'A' Troop (Ross)	Gallegos de Argañan – attached to Light Division. 2 guns under Lt. Elgee (May's Company) in reserve at St. Jago.	5 x light 6-pounders 5 x light 6-pounders
'I' Troop (Bull)	Pinhanços – attached to the Cavalry.	5 x light 6-pounders 1 x 5½-inch howitzer

RA and KGA Companies	Notes	Equipment
Lawson's Company	St. Jago – in reserve.	5 x 9-pounders 1 x heavy 5½-inch howitzer
Thomson's Company	Baraçal – with the Light Division.	5 x light 6-pounders 1 x 5½-inch howitzer
2nd Rettberg's Company KGA	Portalegre – attached to 2nd Division.	5 x light 6-pounders 1 x 5½-inch howitzer
4th Heise's Company KGA	Guarda – attached to 4th Division. Heise resigned on 10th June and Cleeves assumed command.	5 x light 6-pounders 1 x 5½-inch howitzer

Source: Dickson from Howorth's return dated 4th June 1810.[1]

By this time the numbers of fielded, mobile Portuguese artillery brigades had increased to 11, and were distributed as follows:

Maj. Dickson's Division	Two brigades, each with light 6-pounder, near Portalegre.
Maj. Arentschildt's Division	Four brigades, one of 3-pounder, one 6-pounder, one 9-pounder and one mountain brigade stationed to the north near Celorico and Guarda.
Cabreira's Company	5 x 9-pounders and 1 x 5½-inch howitzer at Santarém.
Brigade	Formerly under Dickson's command consisting of light 6-pounder stationed at Golegã.
Brigade	3-pounder, at Castello Branco.
Three brigades	3-pounder and 6-pounder at Trás-os-Montes.

Sources: Viera Borges and Teixeira Botelho.

As French reinforcements began to assemble near Salamanca Wellington surmised that an attack in the north was the most likely French course of action. As early as March 1810 he had outlined his intentions for Black Bob Craufurd and his elite Light Division.

I am desirous of being able to assemble the army upon the Coa if it should be necessary; at the same time that I am perfectly aware that, if the enemy should collect in any large numbers in Estremadura, we should be too forward for our communication with General Hill even here, much more so upon the Coa. But till they shall collect in Estremadura, and till we shall see more clearly, than I can at present, what reinforcements they have received, and what military object they have in view, and particularly in the existing disposition of their army, I am averse to withdrawing from a position so favourable as the Coa affords, to enable us to collect our army to prevent the execution of any design upon Ciudad Rodrigo. I wish you, then, to consider of the posts to be occupied in front of and upon the Coa, to enable me to affect that object ... I intend that the divisions of General Cole and General Picton should support you on the Coa, without waiting for orders from me, if it should be necessary; and they shall be directed accordingly.

French designs on Ciudad Rodrigo began in earnest at the end of May and Craufurd's forward position, centred on the tiny village of Gallegos, was subject to heavy probing by French reconnaissance forces throughout June. Wellington's initial plans were for Craufurd to fall back on Fort Concepción but when the strength of the French Army of Portugal was apparent he ordered the fort to be demolished and the guns moved there (in May) to be withdrawn back to Almeida. In the meantime, the Light Division remained covering the main road and approaches to Portugal. Ross had four guns up and then, in early June, dispatched his second in command, Captain George Jenkinson, to bring up the balance of the brigade from St. Jago. On the 15th June, Captain Edward Charles Whinyates and Lieutenant William Dunn arrived from Lisbon to assist 'A' Troop.[2] The next day Ross recorded: 'The enemy have made considerable advances in their approaches to Rodrigo. Their lines appear in a state of forwardness, and they are constructing mortar batteries – though we do not learn that their artillery are yet arrived.'[3]

Jenkinson had returned a few days earlier.

I returned last Sunday from St. Jago whither I had been to receive our reinforcement, and I am happy to say brought up all the men and horses quite fit for the most active campaign ... What Lord Wellington's intentions are, we are quite at a loss to guess, but they must surely soon develop themselves; he would in my opinion endeavour to relieve the town if he was certain of being able to provision the army here, but that appears to me not only doubtful, but impossible. However the weather is now settled and things coming to a crisis, so that we must either advance of fall back.[4]

In fact Wellington was quite clear as to his intentions and he delivered them to his divisional and brigade commanders a few days later. 'In case the enemy should attack General Craufurd with a superior force, I wish him to retire upon Almeida, and eventually, should he find it necessary, across the Coa, holding the high grounds on the left of the river, and Valverde, and keeping open the communication with the fort as long as may be practicable.'[5] Notwithstanding, Craufurd was a man desperate for personal recognition; such ambition encouraged the likelihood to risk taking and, on the 4th July, when Masséna decided to push back the forward outposts, it very nearly resulted in the loss of two of 'A' Troop's guns.[6]

The village of Gallegos was defended by this little force for a considerable time; a party of dismounted men, under cornet Cordemann, maintaining a small bridge in front, while two other parties of hussars under George von der Decken and Schaumann observed two fords on the flanks. One of these fords was at length passed by the enemy in considerable force, while the hussars were at the same time hard pressed in the village. Captain Krauchenberg, therefore ordered the guns to the rear with directions to unlimber on the other side of the town at a bridge which led from Gallegos to Alameda, and from whence the retreat of his squadron could be protected. This movement was well executed by lieutenant Macdonald; and Krauchenberg, as soon as he saw the guns were nearly in position, led his squadron off at the gallop to gain the bridge.[7]

Only two days earlier, Jenkinson had expressed a widely held view that the division was too far forward and exposed to flanking manoeuvres; his opinion of the divisional commander was all too apparent.

Ld Wellington who visited this post the other day, was, as most sensible men would be, struck with the danger of the position, and ordered our self opinionated, obstinate, ignorant, spiteful, unmanly Brigr. to retire, and we have in consequence retrograded to this place, with a full view to fall still further back the moment Ciudad falls …[8]

When Ciudad Rodrigo finally fell on the 10th July, another incident near Barquilla led to widespread criticism of 'Black Bob'. Ross was, however, more guarded than his second in command in his criticism of Craufurd and the way he handled his force:

Jul 10th – An unfortunate affair occurred, in which Colonel Talbot, of the 14th Light Dragoons, a Quartermaster and 9 men were killed and 9 wounded, and 40 horses of the 14th, the Hussars, and the 16th, killed or rendered unserviceable in an attempt to surprise a patrol, which from daily observation was known to exceed 30 dragoons and 200 infantry. Add to this, the scene of the action was a plain, where Horse Artillery could have been used to the greatest advantage, and were not called upon; and that officers posted in command at different places were left ignorant of the points from whence they were to look for support.
   Jul 12th – Sent for [by] the General [Craufurd] in the evening, who inquired if I had got my ammunition, and after some time spoke of the affair … and said it was very unfortunate, and appeared desirous of drawing from me my opinion respecting that artillery might have been made use of, and hinted that he thought they would not. In answer, I remarked, in such open country we could move with great facility; upon which he dropt [sic] the conversation …[9]

Masséna's orders for the commencement of the third invasion of Portugal were issued to Ney on the 21st July and from that date onwards it would have been clear to the Light Division commander that the French were in the final stages of preparing for the offensive. Yet he chose to dwell in and around Almeida on the east of the River Coa, with his back to the river and with a single bridge providing his only escape route. On the 24th July Ney decided to make the arrogant British commander pay for his temerity. Ross takes up the story:

> The night extremely wet. March to our alarm posts at daybreak, and all appearing quiet we return to our quarters, when the enemy advance, and we are ordered to meet them. I join the guns on piquet with two more sending Jenkinson to the right, on the road to Junça with the 2nd Division. The enemy advances rapidly, and takes possession of the commanding height with their cavalry and two guns, from whence they return the fire which we had opened upon them, but without doing us any mischief from this ground. I am ordered to retire by General Crawford [Craufurd]. We occupy a rocky height in front of the town for some time, but the French kept beyond our reach, sending riflemen up close to our position, when General Crawford directed me to retire on the town [Almeida]. About this time the guns under Captain Jenkinson were ordered from the right to join me at the town, and immediately afterwards the enemy's columns of cavalry and infantry advanced upon our right, occupying the ground we had just vacated. They charge the 95th, and endeavour to cut off the 52nd Regiment, which the skilful conduct of Colonel Barclay alone brought off, together with the piquets of the 95th, and one of the 3rd Cacadores. Finding that his right was completely turned, and that there was every prospect of their getting betwixt him and the brigade, General Crawford ordered a retreat. Lieut. Bourchier, of the Artillery [from Glubb's Company who were in Lisbon], brought me the order 'to retire as rapidly as in my power across the bridge, and get my guns into position on the opposite heights'. At this time we had five guns in action, firing upon a heavy column of cavalry moving apparently with the intention of charging us down the Junça road. Our fire was excellent, and broke them two or three times. Upon receiving the order to retire, I instantly sent to desire the Quartermaster to move off with the wagons, which were still under the walls at Almeida; for, notwithstanding that I requested General Crawford's leave twice during the morning to send them across the river, he would not permit me to do so.[10]

Craufurd's actions flew in the teeth of Wellington's direct orders; on the 11th July he had added the critical word *threaten* to his earlier dispatch.

> That is to say, it will run 'In case the enemy should *threaten* to attack General Craufurd'. In short, I do not wish to risk any thing beyond the Coa, and indeed, when Carrera is clearly off, I do not see why you should remain any longer at such a distance in front of Almeida.[11]

In the panic that ensued, one of Ross's ammunition carriages upset on the narrow road leading to the bridge and threatened closure to the only escape route available to the divisional all arms group.

We were singularly fortunate in getting all the carriages across. One wagon was overset, but by the exertions of McDonald and Bourchier, it was got safe off. During the time we were passing down the hill and up the heights on the other side, the enemy kept up an incessant but ineffectual fire upon us. The cavalry followed the artillery and the infantry, standing their ground wherever they could, and giving us time to get off. It was about nine o'clock when we crossed the bridge. The enemy pursued the infantry close down to it, possessing themselves of every wall as our people fled from it, and persevered in their efforts to force the bridge until three o'clock. They succeeded in getting about thirty men over, but they could get no further; when, concealing themselves behind rocks, they kept up a destructive fire. They brought four guns to bear upon us, but they could not stand our fire …[12]

The intimate, direct fire support of Ross's guns on the west bank undoubtedly saved the situation and with it Craufurd's reputation. The pouring rain played havoc with the sustained fire of the infantry, turning their powder into a solid mass and rendering it virtually impossible to ignite.[13] The effectiveness of 'A' Troop's fire in supporting their infantry and driving off the French artillery is also recorded by Jenkinson.

As soon as we had crossed the bridge we pushed up the hill, and found the most delightful positions for our guns having greatly the advantage of ground on the left bank, we then opened our fire upon their advancing infantry with spherical case, which cut them up and broke them perpetually, and occasionally gave their artillery such discharges of it as compell'd them to shift their ground seven times and then retire altogether, they having fired several times in vain attempted to annoy us …

Our loss though not above half the enemy's was considerable, nearly thirty officers killed and wounded and between two and three hundred men killed, wounded and missing, we were particularly fortunate, not having an officer or man touched, and having only four horses killed – Bouche [Bourchier] who happened to be with us that morning had his horse killed under him – I had the honor [sic] of a tumble under the wheel of a galloping gun, which passed over my helmet, but found my head hard enough to resist it.[14]

Napier majestically described the scene: 'the artillery on both sides played across the ravine, the sounds were repeated by numberless echoes, and the smoke rising slowly, resolved itself into an immense arch, spanning the whole chasm, and sparkling with the whirling fuzes of the flying shells'.[15] Wellington, who had defended Craufurd's decisions following the Barquilla affair, was now hard pushed to deflect the justifiable criticism of his behaviour in front of the Coa. Craufurd's report made no mention of the role of Ross's Gunners and as Wellington forwarded his field commander's report without any additional comment, the contribution by the Horse Gunners has been largely overlooked. Ross was a very different man to Howorth and it was only to his brother that he confided his disappointment and his related concerns about Craufurd's handling of his division, adding that this 'is not the way in which any, much less the British army, can be commanded'. With the French invasion now in motion, few had time to debate the issue further. Almeida was by now invested by Ney's Corps, Junot remained near Ciudad Rodrigo but it was the location of Reynier's Corps, about 45 miles south which was concentrating the commander-in-chief's mind. A two-pronged advance with Ney and Junot to the north along the Mondego and Reynier to the south along the Tagus meant that the Anglo-Portuguese force would have to remain divided to counter. Wellington spent the last few days of July issuing orders for his formations to move to cover any eventuality. Such instructions included very detailed movement of the ordnance, one suspects not always following consultation with his chief of artillery. Guns were moved from throughout Portugal and from Cadiz and Gibraltar to support the defensive lines along the border and the new defensive lines being constructed in front of Lisbon. The extent to which he gave consideration to his artillery can be seen in a dispatch to Admiral Berkeley, as early as April 1810, in which he has given due consideration to the possibility of being able to take the offensive should the opportunity arise.

I am also anxious to have in the Mondego four of the heavy guns, with their travelling carriages and ammunition, in case circumstances should enable me to make a dash at the magazine at Salamanca, that I may not be disappointed in my object, by the want of ordnance, to breach a convent which the French have fortified there. The commanding officer of the artillery has given his directions to Colonel Fisher. The whole that is required will be in one ship, and I shall be very much obliged to you if you will send her to the Mondego.[16]

Dickson, commanding his three brigades of Portuguese artillery, remained attached to Hill's 2nd Division, and was positioned in and around Portalegre and Castelo Branco. He had spent the early months of the year wisely, training and retraining his brigades and by July both he and Beresford had every reason to be pleased with the remarkable transformation of the Portuguese troops. Dickson was desperate not to miss out on the action as he had done the year prior at Talavera; he was hoping that Reynier's movement to within a few miles of the Portuguese border was a precursor to a major attack into Hill's sector. It was not to be; Reynier's independent manoeuvring, against orders and purely in search of provisions for his starving force, had merely resulted in a series of frustrating moves and counter-moves for Hill's men. The premature capitulation of Almeida, after the ignition of the town's magazine, did little to ease minds and clarify the situation.

Considerable uncertainty followed; Wellington, anticipating an immediate advance by the Army of Portugal, withdrew his headquarters to Celorico and all his (infantry) divisions, less for Hill, into the valley of the Mondego. Masséna, however, was realising just how difficult it was to campaign in Iberia; provisions were desperately low and the massive expenditure of 900,000 cartridges in the taking of Ciudad Rodrigo had left the supplies at critically low levels. Furthermore his losses in men needed to be addressed but his request for a division from the newly forming

9th Corps was ignored, leaving him no option but to withdraw Reynier north and sever his lines of communication with Soult in the south. Jenkinson pieced together the potential strengths of Masséna's force with cunning accuracy.

> … what will it leave Massena after the deduction of the garrisons of Almeida and Rodrigo, and his losses in taking those places? I will even allow him another division or corps, and then I am certain he has not above 60,000 men; and they are said to be disposed of along the frontier of the country; viz: Ney at Sabugal and Penamacor with 30,000 men; Regnier [Reynier] at Zarza with 15,000, and the remainder under Massena upon the Coa.[17]

In fact Masséna had 65,000 men and with the autumn rains approaching he was well aware that he had better get on with things. On the 10th September Reynier entered Portugal and headed north; five days later he was at Guarda. The same day Ney broke camp and headed west followed by the cavalry and guns; Junot was already on the move slightly further north but by the 17th September it was clear that all three corps were converging on Viseu.

> On the 15th September the French advanced with their whole army in two columns, the one on the Francosa, the other upon Celorico, apparently with the intention of penetrating Coimbra by both routes, and compelled our cavalry to retire, which was followed by a movement of our whole army the next day … for the French having been joined by Regniers [Reynier's] Corps from the Tagus, and having instead of proceeding by way of Celorico, suddenly crossed the Mondego at Fornes [Fornos de Algodres], and formed a junction of their two corps at Montualdi [Mangualde], Ld W to counteract it, as suddenly crossed that river, and appeared in the plain in front of the position (where probably a battle will be fought) to the great surprise I suspect of the enemy … and on the 20th we saw an army collected near Mortagoa [Mortágua], sufficient as it will doubtless be proved, to defend the pass on that road against Massena's army. A very considerable force under Genl Spencer collected and posted at Malhada [Mealhada], and most unexpectedly the arrival of Genl Hill with his corps …[18]

By the 25th September, Ross's Troop were at the north end of the Buçaco Ridge near the Carmelite convent; to their left and right were in excess of 50,000 troops of Wellington's Anglo-Portuguese army. There were 11 brigades of artillery posted on the ridge, distributed as follows:

CRA: Brig. Gen. E. Howorth
Staff: Lt. Col. W. Robe RA
Lt. Col. H. Framingham RA
Brigade Major: Maj. J. May RA
ADC to CRA: Lt. J. Weatherall Smith RA
Lt., the Hon. W. Arbuthnott RA (Adjutant to Framingham)
Lt. L. Woodyear RA (Adjutant to Robe)

RHA Troops	Notes	Equipment
'A' Troop (Ross)	Attached to the Light Division.	5 x light 6-pounders 1 x 5½-inch howitzer
'I' Troop (Bull)	Attached to Cole's (4th) Division.	5 x light 6-pounders 1 x 5½-inch howitzer

RA, KGA and Portuguese Companies	Notes	Equipment
Lawson's Company	Located near to Pack's independent Portuguese Brigade and stationed to the right of Ross.	5 x 9-pounders 1 x heavy 5½-inch howitzer
Thomson's Company	Attached to Picton's (3rd) Division in the centre of the feature.	5 x light 6-pounders 1 x 5½-inch howitzer
2nd Rettberg's Company KGA	Attached to Spencer's (1st) Division between the Light and 3rd divisions	5 x light 6-pounders 1 x 5½-inch howitzer
4th Cleeves's Company KGA	Located near to Coleman's independent Portuguese Brigade to the right of Ross.	5 x light 6-pounders 1 x 5½-inch howitzer
Portuguese Artillery[19]		
Dickson's 'Division'	Pinto's Company – attached to Hill's (2nd) Division. Da Costa e Silva's Company – attached to Hill's (2nd) Division.	Light 6-pounders Light 6-pounders
Arentschildt's 'Division'	Porfirio da Silva's Company – attached to Picton's (3rd) Division. Augusto Penedo's Company – attached to Picton's (3rd) Division.	Light 6-pounders 9-pounders
De Sousa Passos's Company	Located near to Coleman's independent Portuguese Brigade to the right of Ross.	Light 6-pounders

Sources: Dickson, Leslie, Chambers, Oman, Chartrand, Teixeira Botelho and Vieira Borges.

Jenkinson noted that the entire army were to their front and that Wellington had gone 'out himself and disputed every inch of the very favourable ground in front of the position'.[20] He described the almost continual skirmishing that remained active throughout the day as the French probed for strengths and dispositions and the allies endeavoured to deny them that knowledge. Reynier pushed the allied rearguard back and came up against the dominating ridge in the early afternoon and then, that evening, moved south as Ney's formations closed in from behind. Casualties began to mount on both sides; on the allied side those injured were already being transported back to Coimbra and on the road they exchanged pleasantries with a young Gunner officer who was making his way to join his new company. Lieutenant William Bates Ingilby had exchanged places with Second Lieutenant Henry Forster in Lawson's Company and had arrived at Lisbon on the 15th September and moved north, post haste, to join up with Wellington's army and Lawson's Company.

Our guns were placed at the most commanding point of the position, near the walls of the Convent of Busaco, and gave us the most extensive view of the country, which appeared as an immense plain below us, for many leagues. Columns of the French were opposite, upon the edge of the plain, but much lower, and the valley which ran between their columns and the foot of the ridge of Busaco, on which Lord Wellington had taken up his position, was deep and rugged, and difficult to pass from the steepness of both sides.

At a considerable distance we could perceive the other Corps of the French [8th] advancing, and, as they successively arrived in the evening, the advance posts engaged. We fired a few rounds with good effect; a sergeant of the Company was wounded in the head by a musket ball, but not dangerously. The routes by which the French marched, as far as the eye could discern, by the villages on fire and still smoking. A finer situation could not be imagined to behold the first armies I have ever seen.[21]

For young Ingilby it must have conjured an extraordinary mix of emotions: excitement at the inevitable clash of arms; fear as to the consequences; apprehension at his own performance and a feeling of isolation. He was, after all, an unknown quantity to his fellow officers and men; and men kept their distance from new soldiers (new officers were no exception) until it could be determined whether they were 'shooters or shakers'.[22] Even the more battle-hardened Gunners could not hide their awe and apprehension at the vista that played out to their front; the soldiers of the *Grande Armée*, conquerors of Italy, victors against the martial forces of Prussia at Jena and the conquerors of the Austrians at Austerlitz wore an unmistakable air of invincibility.

Ranging the guns was essential, particularly when firing from a steep hill as at Buçaco. Each gun number one, a non commissioned officer, would need to be quite clear as to the range a round shot would attain at zero tangent elevation and, for each half degree (up and down) thereafter, for a set charge. To gain some depression (into the valley) the Congreve block trail would have been raised at the tail and would have laboured under such demands, rendering the gun and limber liable to be 'overthrown by their own recoil'.[23] Canister was less precise but spherical case shot, or shrapnel, fired from an elevated platform was the devil to perfect. It relied on a fuse being cut to an exact length to ensure the air burst occurred at the right height a few yards short of an intended target; on flat ground that was difficult enough, on undulating ground it was even more complicated; but on ground where the gun is on a higher elevation, and the target on ground which falls away sharply (as at Buçaco), the efficiency of the bursting shot would be reduced to a point where the energy was spent before reaching that target as it would have had to have been fired at a much higher angle. Standard firing tables were virtually worthless and experience and a 'feeling' for their trade the only successful substitute. French gunners conversely, were facing different challenges; the effect of round shot fired at an exaggerated angle of elevation, with a correspondingly abrupt angle of descent would have been almost negligible. No amount of artillery ranging would reduce this disadvantage and so it was pointless bringing the guns within range of the allied artillery until it was absolutely necessary.

The battle on the 27th September was fought in two parts: Reynier commenced with an attack in the centre of the ridge opposite the pass of Santo António de Cântaro and Ney followed up with an assault on the ridge to the north by the Buçaco convent. At the earlier engagement, Major General Étienne Heudelet's Division advanced against Major General Thomas Picton's 3rd Division at the pass and against Colonel Mackinnon's and Colonel José Champalimaud's brigades supported by Arentschildt's two brigades of guns. In the early morning fog visibility was poor but the massed ranks of the advancing French provided an easy target. The Portuguese gunners opened with ball and grape, carving bloody lines of death and destruction in the four battalion columns of the 31e Léger, switching to canister as the French closed. It was enough to break the French momentum of this attack and Picton now turned his attention to events further north where Reynier's second division, that of Major General Pierre-Huges Merle, making best use of the mist, was moving up the ridge in an attempt to outflank the 'Fighting' 3rd. Picton had pre-empted this exploitable gap the night prior and had redeployed the Connaught Rangers to a position between the pass and the next adjacent brigade, that of Major General Stafford Lightburne. Early the following morning half the battalion of the 45th had also moved to support the Irish. With the situation stabilised at the pass itself, Picton now moved north, taking with him the 8th Portuguese and five more companies from the 45th. At much the same time Wellington, who had been observing events from a high point, ordered Captain George Thomson to detach two 6-pounders and move them in support of Picton's blocking manoeuvre. Lane and Lieutenant Frederick Bayly moved the guns to a knoll on lower ground below and to the south of the high plateau from where they could support the action; their deployment was critical for the tirailleurs had driven back the allied light companies who were outnumbered and retiring in disorder. Picton rallied the troops and Major William Smyth of the 45th led the counter-attack; the fire of the guns forced the right-hand French battalion (36e Léger) to swerve to their left and into the path of the 2e Léger who continued the motion, thus creating confusion and causing the French attack to lose momentum. Lane describes the action:

> My men did their duty. Lieutenant F. Bayly's conduct was admirable. It was the first time he had been in action, and no old soldier could have acted better. The French voltigeurs of the 34th Regt. [in fact the 36th] came close to the guns; and one was killed only eight paces off. An immense French column showed themselves in the ravine, we, with three cheers, gave them a few rounds of case and round shot together, at about seventy paces distance, which drove them back.[24]

Reynier's guns could do little to support the infantry as the elevation reduced the effectiveness and accuracy but this did not deter the French gunners from trying and, at one stage, they succeeded in dismounting two of Arentschildt's guns, but a shell fired in response shortly afterwards set fire to a French ammunition caisson which exploded, forcing the French to abandon the battery.[25] Reynier, witnessing the failure of his second attack, ordered Foy to assume the offensive at the pass but by this time reinforcements were arriving from the southern end of the ridge under Major General James Leith. Two of Dickson's guns were with this group and they began to provide some badly needed support to Arentschildt's guns that were, by now, running short of ammunition. To all intents and purposes this brought an end to Reynier's attack but at the north end of the ridge another contest had commenced.

Ney's three-pronged attack quickly ran into trouble; Loison's two brigades on the French right were separated from those of Major General Jean-Gabriel Marchand on the left by a deep ravine but both divisions had to attack a steep ridge and their approaches were covered by the artillery. The ability of the French guns to fire in support was also severely curtailed by the extent of the slope but more crucially the French lacked the range and lethality provided by Shrapnel's spherical case shot. As the brigades of Édouard François Simon and Claude-François Ferey scrambled up the ridge they were taken in the flank by Bull's Troop to the north and Ross's Troop, who after a while were unable to actually see the foe but who continued to fire spherical case over the brow of the hill. Ross's brother, Captain George Ross, an officer in the Royal Engineers who fell at Ciudad Rodrigo, wrote:

> I will venture to assert, and Lord Wellington I am certain could not deny it, that the greatest loss the enemy sustained was by our artillery; and the guns which had the most duty, and I believe I might say that were best placed for effect – even if nothing is said of the admirable manner in which the guns were fought – were those of Hew's troop … Several officers who remained on the field the day after the retreat, amongst others General Crawford [*sic*] himself, were convinced more than those who only looked on it from the heights, of the immense slaughter the enemy sustained from shrapnel shells thrown from my brother's guns, aided for a short time by those of Captain Bull's troop.[26]

To the south Marchand's division was faring little better; as they left the road and began their ascent they came under sustained and accurate artillery fire from the gun brigades of Andrew Cleeves, Antonio De Sousa Passos and Robert Lawson. To this was added fire from Ross's guns once Loison's attack had been beaten back to their front. Maucune's Brigade, leading the division, sought shelter in a small wood which, to their horror, they discovered was full of skirmishers from Denis Pack's Brigade. The French swung left in an attempt to outflank but headed into the jaws of Lawson's 9-pounder guns; the brigade commander was killed along with the colonel of the 6e Léger and the brigade, severely mauled, was ordered back by Ney – the battle was lost. Ingilby stationed with Lawson witnessed the scene:

> The French advanced in three columns to force our position, but were defeated. We commanded their whole attack with artillery and caused them an immense loss in killed and wounded; 300 prisoners were taken, and amongst them was a General Officer. Firing was kept up until night, and recommenced next day from the artillery and advanced posts of both Armies, but the French did not renew their attack seriously.

In the evening [28th September] their columns seemed to be moving off to their right and at night we quitted our position and begun to descend the hill of Busaco, our left being threatened to be turned. The road was bad, and passing through a wood, the excessive darkness of the night obliged us to use torches, and the heads of the columns of infantry were provided in the same manner. We had not proceeded far, when suddenly the drag chains of a gun gave way, and, the descent being very steep, the two wheel horses were not a match to keep the gun back, and the force of its weight was rapidly hurrying the whole down the hill. They had already rushed upon the gun preceding it, for, as a precaution, a considerable distance was allowed between each, when it swerved out of the track of the road and a limber wheel caught the stem of a small tree.

The sudden jerk threw all the leading horses down the declivity that was to the left, but contrary to apprehensions neither the drivers [n]or horses in this instance

4. The Battle of Buçaco (Ney's Attack) ~ Positions at First Light, 27th September 1810

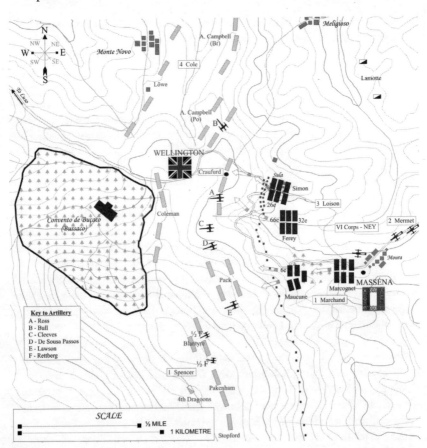

suffered any serious injury whatsoever. We had eight horses in each gun – 9 prs. Two others were a little while afterwards, at a difficult turn on coming out of the convent garden, upset, and, one rolling over, the wheel driver was so much hurt he died in hospital from his bruises.[27]

Jenkinson with 'A' Troop in a letter to his friend Captain Charles Freeman Sandham at Woolwich Barracks outlined his delight at the army's recent victory.

John Bull will not give us credit for a victory, because we are now retrograding, but we are fighting for a kingdom not a town … it is indeed the only fault of the numerous advanced positions in Portugal, that our flanks are unprotected either by impassable rivers or mountains, and consequently an enemy can if he chooses to decline fighting always march round you, such was the case at Busacos [sic], they were beat and nobly beat, and taught to respect and admire the bravery of the Portuguese troops as well as the British … he flattered himself with the hope of getting between us and Lisbon, and when we arrived at Coimbra, he was surprised to see Ld W had arrived there too.[28]

From Coimbra Wellington had penned his report of the battle to the Earl of Liverpool; he had much to praise. The performance of the Portuguese had exceeded expectations and the individual and collective acts of the British infantry and many of Wellington's generals and staff had been exemplary. Surprisingly, and unfairly, the artillery receives scant recognition; Arentschildt is singled out for particular mention and later in the dispatch Wellington adds that he 'is particularly indebted to a host of staff officers' and 'to Major Gen. Howorth and the artillery'. However, a picture now begins to emerge of a commander who, through an aversion to an individual, unfairly disadvantages the group. Fortescue is not the only historian to admit 'that the part played by the allied artillery at Bussaco has been undervalued'.[29] However, he quite rightly condemns Captain Francis Duncan's attack on Wellington, in his *History of the Royal Regiment of Artillery* (London, 1873), as going too far. Duncan wrote:

In the battle that followed, Lord Wellington displayed an ignorance of artillery tactics, from the results of which he was happily saved by the intelligence and gallantry of the representatives of that arm. This want of knowledge, which he never overcame, was the cause of a not unfrequent [sic] irritation against Artillery as an arm, and a tendency to depreciate its value. At Busaco, instead of massing his Artillery in reserve until the attack should develop itself, the guns were placed, as a rule, in the easiest parts of the position, where it was supposed the French *would* attack; and they were massed in these positions so as to form an excellent mark for the enemy's fire'.[30]

This unfortunate ramble is correct in one aspect alone, that Wellington, as we can now unequivocally demonstrate, undervalued his artillery in post-battle dispatches. However, there is no evidence to suggest he depreciated their value on the field of battle, indeed quite the opposite. As to the other claims, massing artillery to cover a ridge 10 miles long would have been very unwise indeed. Wellington had his engineers cut a lateral road along the (rear of the) crest to enable his infantry to move quickly in support of other formations but moving artillery would have been a far more troublesome and time consuming business. Nor does Duncan admit that two of the points where Wellington deployed the artillery were, indeed, the very places where the French chose to attack or that, in both cases, the artillery was well positioned to repel those attacks. Furthermore, Wellington's linear defensive tactics often resulted in brigades of guns having to be split 'either ends of the line' to make best use of their range, leading to greater dispersion and complicating re-supply.

It is true that guns deployed on a forward slope are easy targets for counter-battery fire but there is little evidence that the French guns were able to effectively engage the allied gun positions on the ridge due to the difficulties of elevation.[31] Allied artillery losses of just two killed and 18 wounded would support this argument. What is perhaps most perplexing is Wellington's reluctance to acknowledge the force-multiplication effect of shrapnel; he was to refer to General Simon's injuries from shrapnel as trifling:

> I saw Gen. Simon who was wounded by the balls of Shrapnell's [sic] shells, of which he had several in his face and head; but they were picked out of his face as duck shot would be out of the face of a person who had been hit by accident while out shooting, and he was not much more materially injured.[32]

The size and weight of shot in spherical case (shrapnel) was, of course, far heavier than that used in duck shot and the limitations of firing such munitions from elevated platforms have already been described.[33] However, the nature of Simon's injury is not the issue here; the fact that he was injured at all is, nevertheless, central. For an injured soldier on the battlefield is a far greater burden than a dead one. Granted, Shrapnel's shells were more likely to maim and injure than kill, but that should not have been seen as a point of criticism or disappointment by Wellington, in fact quite the opposite. It was not the nature of Simon's injury but the impact, both short- and mid-term. This was borne out following the battle at Vitoria in 1813 when Wellington was compelled to write:

> The commander of regiments and the officers and non-commissioned officers of companies must take care that no man falls out of the ranks under pretence of taking care of the wounded, who is not ordered to fall out by the officers commanding the company, and those officers must take care that no more men are employed on this duty than are absolutely necessary to perform it.

Questioning Wellington's tactical use of his artillery following the contest at Buçaco is, therefore, unfounded but there certainly appear grounds for questioning his acceptance that tactical procedure was profoundly influenced by human sentiment and the role that Shrapnel's new shell could play to enhance that influence.

Notes

1. Dickson, vol. II, pp.218–19. Return of the RHA, RA and KGA and drivers in the field under the command of Brig. Gen. Howorth, Celorico 4th June, 1810.
2. These officers were part of 'D' Troop, the remnants of which were in Lisbon – still awaiting their fate.
3. Ross, p.10.
4. Jenkinson, letter from Gallegos, dated 18th June 1810.
5. WD, vol. VI, p.239. Memorandum for Maj. Gens. Picton, Cole, and Slade; Brig. Gens. Campbell and Craufurd. Alverca, 2nd July, 1810.
6. Craufurd was one of the few commanders in whose ability Wellington had huge confidence; nevertheless, promotion had been slow in coming, despite considerable operational service, much of which had been coupled with failure and missed opportunities. He had been military attaché during the Austrian Wars in 1794, and participated in the failed Dutch expedition in 1799 and the unhappy Buenos Aires campaign in 1807, where he surrendered his brigade but was cleared of blame at the subsequent court martial. He did not participate at the battle at La Coruña (as Moore had sent his brigade to Vigo) and had missed Talavera by a matter of hours.
7. Ludlow Beamish, vol. I, pp.275–76.
8. Jenkinson, letter from Gallegos, dated 2nd July 1810.
9. Ross, p.10.
10. Ibid.
11. WD, vol. VI, p.259. Wellington to Craufurd, Alverca, half past 7 p.m. 11th July, 1810.
12. Ross, p.11.
13. Coss, p.163.
14. Jenkinson, letter from Celorico, dated 31st July 1810.
15. Napier, vol. III, p.292.
16. WD, vol. VI, p.64. Wellington to Berkeley, Celorico 29th April 1810.
17. Jenkinson, from Vinho, 12th September 1810.
18. Ibid., from Mortagoa, 22nd September 1810.
19. It is fair to state that the participation and particulars of the British and German batteries/brigades need no more explanation as their details have been accurately and consistently reported immediately after and since the battle. However, the participation and denomination of the Portuguese batteries/brigades need examination and explanation. There has been much debate on the number of Portuguese brigades which took part in the battle and this has served to confuse, not just which companies were present, but the total number of allied guns on the ridge that day. It is important to point out that there were other Portuguese brigades in the area (one, or possibly two, 3-pounder brigades with Col. Lecor south of the Mondego) but they did not take an active part in proceedings and are therefore not listed or considered further. Chambers enters this debate with incredible detail but he was lacking some of the pieces of the jigsaw in his work of 1910. Dealing firstly with Dickson's brigades: he certainly started the year with three brigades, but his 3rd Brigade commanded by Capt. da Cunha Preto was detached from his immediate command on 3rd March

1810 (see Dickson, vol. II, p.169). Ignacio José, who was commanding his 2nd Brigade, 'having represented from his age and bad health was not equal to active duties' was relieved and replaced temporarily by Capt. (on promotion) Rozierres, who was Dickson's adjutant (Ibid., p.185). At some stage he was also relieved, although this is not recorded by Dickson. José Justino Teixeira Botelho, himself a general in the Portuguese artillery, has written the only full history of the Portuguese artillery (see bibliography) and he lists the 2nd Brigade as being under the command of da Costa e Silva; this is the only reliable source and so I have listed the 2nd Brigade under his command for the battle. It is regrettable that Dickson, who is generally so meticulous, seems to have lost interest in detailing the Portuguese artillery at an earlier stage in the year. I should add that Teixeira Botelho shows Dickson as having four brigades at Buçaco – this is, without doubt, a mistake.

Victor von Arentschildt's brigades are far more complicated. Teixeira Botelho also lists Arentschildt as having four brigades at Buçaco – this again is a mistake. Only René Chartrand has ever listed what I consider to be the correct brigades under Arentschildt's command that day (see *Bussaco 1810*, Osprey). Many historians (other than Teixeira Botelho above) have listed Arentschildt as having a single brigade of guns which supported Picton at the Pass of San Antonio against Reynier. This is most likely because Arentschildt commanded both brigades personally. The key, however, is in Beresford's dispatch to the Portuguese Secretary of War (30th September 1810) in which he states that 'two brigades of Artillery, 9 and 6 pounders under the personal orders of Major Arentschildt, much distinguished themselves'. We know that Arentschildt had four brigades under his command, all from the 2nd Portuguese Regiment of Artillery; the first was a 3-pounder brigade, the second and third 6- and 9-pounder respectively, and the fourth was a mountain brigade – the latter was added later in 1810 to his command. Teixeira Botelho lists captains João Porfirio da Silva and João Maximiano Augusto Penedo as commanding the second and third brigades respectively and it is therefore reasonable to assume that these two officers were present on the ridge, with their guns, that day. Oman mentions that Leith arrived with one battery of four 6-pounders; as Leith did not have any guns (there were none left that he could have had under command) it is possible that these were the balance of Arentschildt's 6-pounder brigade which he may have left to the south near the Lusitanian Legion but it is more likely that they were the guns which Maj. Dickson brought up from the southern end of the ridge. This is Oman's conclusion – vol. III, p.375. Whether there were two or four guns remains unclear.

20. Jenkinson to Sandham, Convent of Bussaco, dated 25th September 1810.
21. Ingilby, 26th September 1810.
22. See Coss, p.206.
23. See Hughes, HFI, p.145. Two of Arentschildt's were reported as having been 'dismounted by French guns' but it is more likely that they overturned through the force of their own recoil while artificially elevated at the rear in order to engage in depression.
24. Lane letters, p.14.
25. Chambers, *Bussaco*, p.57.
26. Ross, p.12.

27. Ingilby, 27–30th September 1810.
28. Jenkinson, letter while retreating to the Lines, Leyria [Leiria], dated 3rd October 1810.
29. Fortescue, vol. VII, p.531.
30. Duncan, vol. II, pp.276–77.
31. Hughes, HFI, p.145. Hughes is quite clear that the French guns would have been firing at an angle of elevation of 10 degrees and that to increase this to 13 degrees (to reach the summit) would have necessitated digging-in the gun trail.
32. WD, vol. V, p.544. Wellington to Liverpool from Elvas, dated 12th March 1812.
33. These balls were originally carbine ammunition (slightly smaller than a musket ball) and were replaced with musket balls in 1813. The size of shell determined the number of balls; a 6-pounder had around 50 balls, while the 5½-inch howitzer housed 208 balls.

CHAPTER 8

Ross's Agitation

Wellington did not dwell overly long at Coimbra; Brigadier General Charles Sainte-Croix's Dragoons had driven away Trant's small Portuguese force covering the pass at Boialvo and Junot's infantry, forming the vanguard, were a few hours' march behind the cavalry. Early on the 30th September, John Slade's, George De Grey's and George Anson's cavalry brigades pulled back through the town, preceded by Craufurd's Light Division, supported by 'A' Troop, which formed the allied rearguard. The wealthy and picturesque town of Coimbra now lay at the mercy of the French; despite Wellington's timely instructions, the vast majority of the 40,000 townsfolk had not vacated their houses and they now attempted escape by whatever means available. August Schaumann described the sight:

> Old people, lame and sick people, women just risen from childbed, children, and whole families with all their belongings, packed either on bullock carts, mules, horses or donkeys, were to be seen mixed up with all kinds of beasts, among which pigs, owing to their unruliness and horrible cries, were the most conspicuous. And this throng, marching to the wailing and lamentation of the fugitives both from town and country, presented a scene I shall never forget.[1]

This hasty departure inevitably resulted in the abandonment of many valuable possessions but also, more significantly to the half-starved French force, large amounts of provisions. Masséna, realising the need to regulate the distribution of the latter but, with an indubitable personal eye on the former, forbade entry to the town, an order which Junot, in an act of rank insubordination, personally ignored and 'with this example before them, the soldiery could not be kept out'. An orgy of theft, destruction and drunkenness followed and the mob of soldiers had to be restrained from shooting the commissary-generals who were trying to protect and regulate the valuable food stores. These distractions in Coimbra bought precious time for the Anglo-Portuguese army to fall back on their pre-prepared defensive positions in front of Lisbon and it was not until the 4th October that Masséna re-commenced the pursuit. In the interim, the French higher command had argued over the best course of action; Ney and Junot had advised a stay at Coimbra to rest the force, re-supply provisions and ammunition, re-open lines of communication with Almeida and to await the arrival of the reinforcements from the newly raised 9th Corps. Masséna, however, was confused by the behaviour of his adversary. Having fought so ferociously at Buçaco, why had he made no attempt to fight at Fornos or to hold Coimbra? Was Wellington's plan just to pull back to Lisbon and, like Moore at Coruña, extract his army by sea? A week later, when he came up against the Lines of Torres Vedras, his questions were answered.

The Lines of Torres Vedras, Wellington's plan for the defence of Lisbon and *ipso facto* the Portuguese executive, consisted of a series of defensive fortifications, in lines, to protect the capital and, as a last resort, the point of embarkation. The lines were not continuous, rather they were a series of fortified camps and closed earthworks, heavily armed and constructed for mutual support with interlocking and overlapping arcs of fire. Any obstacles which hindered this defensive fire or which provided cover for an attacker were removed and the wood and other materiel used to construct obstacles and *abattis*. The French delay in invading Portugal had provided Wellington and his engineers more time to elaborate on their original aims and by October 1810, four lines had been constructed which incorporated 126 enclosed works equipped with 521 artillery pieces of varying calibres. To man the fortifications Wellington did not use any of his British or Portuguese regulars other than officers and troops from the artillery and engineers. The majority of his defenders thus came from the Portuguese militia and *ordenança*; his main force (34,000 British, 28,000 Portuguese and 8,000 Spanish) was concentrated in areas behind the first two lines; able to reinforce any point at short notice.[2] It was, without doubt, a pioneering venture supported by a sound tactical plan which stunned and enraged Masséna.

> Indeed one of the most amazing features of the project was the secrecy in which it was carried out. The Lines were a year in building; they cut across the four principal highways from Lisbon to the north; and they were built entirely by locally recruited Portuguese labour. Yet, not only was Masséna ignorant of their existence until four days before they were sighted by his advance guard, but the British Ministry in London and all but a few staff officers in the British Army were equally unaware of their construction. Even the British minister in Lisbon, little more than 20 miles away, appears to have had no knowledge of them.[3]

The psychology of the defeat at Buçaco was now about to play a vital role in the French commanders' decision-making process. Masséna now understood why Wellington and, more specifically, the Portuguese element of the allied army had withdrawn with such alacrity. Furthermore, the motivation for the devastation and depopulation of the countryside also became evident: for Wellington had ordered an area, 20–25 miles in front of the forward line of forts, to be stripped of all inhabitants and livestock and for the systematic destruction of all their associated agriculture, mills, stores, fruit trees, vineyards and anything which could be utilised to sustain the French forces. Masséna was quick to realise the significance of such a brutal policy and, while it undeniably caused enormous and understandable resentment with the Portuguese people and their government, it was essential, for without it the Lines of Torres Vedras would likely not have succeeded. The evacuation of the towns and villages and the ruination of livelihoods was, however, a harrowing affair for all concerned: young August Schaumann recorded the gravity and desolation.

> The roads were littered with smashed cases and boxes, broken wagons and carts, dead horses and exhausted men … The nearer the procession came to Lisbon, the greater was the number of animals belonging to the refugees that fell dead, either from fatigue or hunger; and very soon ladies were seen wading in torn silk shoes or barefoot through the mud. Despair was written on all faces. It was a heartrending sight.[4]

Captain Robert Bull, in penning a letter to his wife Harriet, was evidently acutely affected by what he saw and clearly contemplated the consequences of such a humanitarian tragedy closer to home.

> The state this country is in, at the moment, beggars all description – it is a most distressing heartbreaking scene. The people flying in all directions with their little savings on their heads, poor girls brought up in plenty of affluence marching on foot 15 and 20 miles a day to escape ravishment and murder, women leaving their children on the roadside to escape themselves, in short the scenes of the last week will never be effaced from my memory. England little knows the miseries of war and long, very long, may she be a stranger to them.[5]

During the retreat, Bull had been grouped with the cavalry, and had fought a sharp skirmish at Pombal in order to thwart the progress of Sainte-Croix's Dragoons and Colonel Auguste Lamotte's light horse. Lieutenant General Sir Stapleton Cotton wrote to Wellington the next day in praise of the cavalry and acknowledged the support of Bull.[6] Lieutenant Ingilby meanwhile was with Lawson's Company attached to the 1st Division; he recalled the trials of this retreat and his first impressions of the Lines.

> The inhabitants of every town and village quitted their homes and preceded or accompanied the march of troops, and they having left much valuable property in many houses, the soldiers were tempted to quit their ranks in search of plunder … a soldier of the 50th Regiment, which then newly joined the Army from England, who had been detected more than once in plundering … was executed by the Provost Marshal, by order of the Commander-in-Chief, on being taken in the act of robbing … The inhabitants deserted their homes by order of their Government, though terror at the approach of the French Army might probably have been as effectual in causing universal flight …

The Brigade [Lawson's] moved to Zebreira [Zibreira]. Sir B. Spencer had the headquarters of the Division in the village. We bivouacked on our post in the line, and masked the guns with field works. The whole of the French Army arrived and took up position in bivouac occupying Sobral in great strength. A rough deep valley separated the outposts in our front. The extreme right of our line rested upon the Tagus, and the left was at Torres Vedras. Every height was crowned with a permanent redoubt well mounted with guns, and the intermediate spaces between them along the whole front of the line was [sic] strengthened with entrenchments and abattis.[7]

As Wellington's forces arrived behind the Lines they took up their allocated positions and received reinforcement and re-supply from recently arrived troop ships and transports. Two additional companies of British artillery arrived in mid-October and the situation with the RA and KGA was as follows:

CRA: Brig. Gen. E. Howorth
Staff: Lt. Col. H. Framingham RA
Lt. Col. W. Robe RA – Commanding the Corps of Drivers, Royal Artillery
Lt. Col. G. B. Fisher – Commanding Artillery in Lisbon
Brigade Major: Maj. J. May RA

RHA Troops/RA and KGA Companies	Notes	Equipment
In Support of the Army Behind the Lines of Torres Vedras or in/around Lisbon		
'A' Troop (Ross)	In support of the Light Division near Arruda.	5 x light 6-pounders 1 x 5½-inch howitzer
'I' Troop (Bull)	In support of Stapleton Cotton's Cavalry Division south of Alverca.	5 x light 6-pounders 1 x 5½-inch howitzer
Lawson's Company	In support of the 1st Division near Sobral.	6 x 9-pounders
Thomson's Company	In support of the 3rd Division near Torres Vedras.	4 x light 6-pounders 2 x 5½-inch howitzers
May's Company	Commanded by 2nd Capt. Baynes and located near Alverca – not in direct support of a division.	5 x light 6-pounders 1 x 5½-inch howitzer
2nd Rettberg's Company KGA	In support of the 2nd Division near Alhandra.	5 x light 6-pounders 1 x 5½-inch howitzers
4th Cleeves's Company KGA	In support of the 4th Division near Pero Negro.	5 x light 6-pounders 1 x 5½-inch howitzer
Bredin's Company	Alhandra – not in direct support of a division.	Exact ordnance unknown
Glubb's Company	Torres Vedras – not in direct support of a division.	Exact ordnance unknown

Hawker's Company	Arrived Lisbon 19th October 1810 and moved to Cabeça de Montachique – not in direct support of a division.	Exact ordnance unknown
Meadows's Company	Arrived Lisbon 19th October 1810 and remained in Lisbon.	Exact ordnance unknown
'D' Troop (Lefebure)	Received notification in December 1810 that the troop would stay in the Peninsula. Based in Lisbon.	5 x light 6-pounders 1 x 5½-inch howitzer
1st Gesenius's Company KGA	Lisbon and Oporto – acting as depot for the other two KGA companies.	Nil

Sources: Compilation from Dickson, Oman, Laws and Leslie.

The Lines were divided into six districts and Wellington, in his memorandum to his chief engineer Lieutenant Colonel Richard Fletcher, had allocated the regular British and Portuguese artillery, the *ordenança* artillery, the infantry militia and the 'regulating' Royal Engineers to be assembled in each district.[8] British Gunners were allocated as follows: to District 1 at Torres Vedras 70 personnel; to District 2 at Sobral 40 personnel; to District 3 at Alhandra 60 personnel; to District 5 at Cabeça de Montachique 50 personnel; and to District 6 at Mafra 40 personnel. None were allocated to District 4 at Bucellas where instead there were 80 Portuguese regular and 500 *ordenança* artillery. The 260 RA personnel were furnished from Bredin's, Glubb's and (James) Hawker's companies, leaving the troops and brigades from the Buçaco order of battle intact. They, in turn, were allocated to the cavalry division and in direct support to five of the seven infantry divisions. Only May's Brigade of guns remained as a reserve. The Portuguese artillery under Dickson and Arentschildt had concentrated with Hill's 2nd Division at Arruda and Hamilton's Portuguese Division at Alhandra respectively. Early on the 8th October, Wellington gave precise orders as to how Dickson's charge was to be redistributed:

I request you [Hill] also, to-morrow morning, to send a brigade of Portuguese 6 pounders (which you were to have sent to Gen. Leith in exchange for the 9 pounders), and two 6 pounders belonging to the brigade with Maj. Gen. Leith, which you brought from Nuestra Senora del Monte, from Villa Franca, through Alhandra and Arruda to Sobral de Monte Agrao, where the 6 pounder brigade is to join the 6th division of infantry; and the two 6 pounders are to be sent on to Ribaldeira, to join the 3rd division of infantry. I also request you to send from Villa Franca, through Alhandra and S. Antonio do Tojal to Cabeça de Montachique, the Portuguese 9 pounder brigade which has been with your corps; where it is to remain in reserve, and in readiness to move at short notice. The other Portuguese 6 pounder brigade with your corps and the 3 pounder brigade with Col. Le Cor [Lecor], must be brought to Alhandra.[9]

Thus all the infantry and cavalry divisions had been allocated direct support artillery brigades leaving May's Brigade of light 6-pounders and a brigade of Portuguese

9-pounders to form the reserve.[10] The discovery and extent of the Lines was, of course, as much of a surprise to Wellington's men as it was to Masséna's; Jenkinson was greatly impressed by the initiative and confident that it would bring the French to their knees.

> Of the enemy's force … deducting about ten thousand men since their first advance – they are now in front of us and throwing up works, but I am rather apprehensive that they will not attack us, though if any credit can attach to what [French] deserters say, they must starve if they remain where they are; they also say that it is held out to them that they have only one line to force to get to Lisbon, and that when they reach it they shall receive 100 [? per] man; that I think will not happen for some time, for never was there an army so confident in its chief and in such high spirits.
>
> Indeed … I think Ld Wellington's movements have been most able and in whatever light I view Marshal Massenas [*sic*] situation, I am convinced he is in the most serious scrape; if he fights, he must be, unless some unforeseen and very improbable accident occurs, dreadfully beat, and if he retires he will have all Portugal at his heels … and will be utterly unable to procure provisions, or draw off his artillery.[11]

However, not all members of Wellington's force shared the same optimism. Captain John Kincaid, with the 95th Rifles, was convinced that allied armies had 'kicked the French out of more formidable-looking and stronger places; and with all due deference be it spoken, I think that the Prince of Essling [Masséna] ought to have tried his luck against them [the Lines] as he could only have been beaten by fighting as he afterwards was without it!'[12] Nonetheless, other than two probing attacks in front of Sobral on the 13th and 14th October, Masséna did not try his luck; his heavy repulse at Buçaco ridge inevitably preyed heavily on his mind. Instead he instructed Foy to draw up a report, which he was to deliver in person to Napoleon, summing up the situation. 'The Marshal Prince of Essling has come to the conclusion that he would compromise his army of His majesty if he were to attack in force lines so formidable, defended by 30,000 English and 30,000 Portuguese, aided by 50,000 armed peasants.'[13] Such sentiments, only a few weeks previously, would have been unthinkable and Napoleon, on receipt of the report, was enraged; he was unable to comprehend how the *Grande Armée* in Iberia, reinforced with more than 1,000 men, was unable to drive out the small British Expeditionary Army, annihilate the troublesome Spanish and Portuguese armies and subjugate their people. On the face of it such sentiments were understandable but then Napoleon had neither witnessed the Portuguese soldiers at Buçaco nor had he seen, first hand, the most extraordinary feat of military engineering of the era.

> The French General frequently reconnoitred our position, but hesitated, and at length seemed unwilling to hazard an attack upon an Army thus strongly posted. The troops were under arms every morning an hour before dawn, and remained so until it was ascertained that there was no appearance of an intention to attack, or any formation whatever amongst the troops of the enemy.[14]

After a stand-off lasting nearly a month, Masséna's forces pulled back during the night of the 14th November and were able to conceal their movement well into the early hours of the following day, aided by an early morning fog and by the construction of a number of 'dummy sentinels'. Wellington, when aware of the deception, gave chase with the 1st, 2nd and Light divisions and Pack's Portuguese Brigade supported by the cavalry. Bull was again with the cavalry while Ross was with Craufurd's Light Division; his second captain takes up the story:

> We marched on the 16th and overtook their rear guard at Villa Nova, and pressed them somewhat harder than they did us, under similar circumstances; we continued to harass and torment them until they reached Santarem, having taken about five hundred prisoners. At first it was thought they did not intend to make a stand there, but it has since proved to be otherwise, and although it is said Massena is gone to Abrantes with two Corps, yet I suspect the material strength of the Santarem position will enable the other corps to maintain it, and deter Lord W from attacking it, as he would even if successful suffer such a loss as would materially cripple him in future operations … I consider this as a great triumph to Ld. Wellington, inasmuch as he drew the French down to make fools of them, and made Massena by his retreat declare to the world his inability to attack our strong and now celebrated lines, and has absolutely turned the tables upon him … We are very strongly posted, having our right on the Tagus and the left at Rio Maior, in front of the line runs a river, not fordable at this season of the year, and which being covered by a range of high hills, the approaches to which are very narrow, renders it very strong.[15]

Over the coming days, more of Wellington's army followed north, supported by both British and Portuguese artillery but the strong French position at Santarem, the poor state of the roads, the onset of winter, the lack of communication with Major General Francisco da Silveira's Portuguese forces to the north coupled with the uncertainty as to Masséna's future intentions and the possibility of a flanking manoeuvre down the east bank of the Tagus all contributed to Wellington's decision to go firm. He informed the Earl of Liverpool of his intentions in a dispatch on the 21st November; within the same correspondence Wellington heaped praise upon Fletcher and the officers of the Royal Engineers for their 'ability and diligence' in a convivial manner the Royal Artillery were rarely to enjoy from the Commander's pen.

Wellington viewed his decision not to close with Masséna's forces as a continuation of his policy to starve out the French, and here the matter lay quiescent, bar the odd low level skirmish, into the following year. The intervening months were, however, not without incident as both sides probed opposing lines and foraged for provisions. Schaumann was attached to the 1st German Hussars KGL at Rio Maior; the unit had constructed a dummy gun position south of the village made of camp kettles. Originally intended as a bit of a joke, the dummy guns certainly served their purpose for the French attacked the post in some strength and, after some considerable time, 'seeing that the battery did not fire, the French *tirailleurs*, taking courage, stormed the kettles and took them'.

The Duke of Wellington, a copy of the painting by Sir Thomas Lawrence. (RAI)

Major General Sir Alexander Dickson. (RAI)

Lieutenant General John Macleod. (RAI)

Field Marshal Sir Hew Dalrymple Ross. (RAI)

Major Norman Ramsay. (RAI)

Major General Sir George Wood. (RAI)

General Sir Robert Gardiner. (RAI)

Field Marshal, The Viscount Henry Hardinge GCB. (RAI)

Lieutenant General Henry Shrapnel. (RAI)

Major Charles Freeman Sandham. (RAI)

'B' Troop RHA at Sahagún, December 1808. The extent of the Troop's contribution to the action is unclear. ('B' Battery, 1 RHA)

Captain Wilmot's Brigade RA during the retreat to Coruña, January 1809. (Dawn Waring)

Captain Sillery's Company RA at the battle of Talavera, 28th July 1809. (David Rowlands)

OPPOSITE Captain Truscott and his Gunners manning Spanish guns at the battle of La Coruña, 16th January 1809. (Dawn Waring)

Captain Lloyd's Company RA at Waterloo, 18th June 1815. (David Rowlands/RAI)

Captain Sandham's Company RA at Waterloo, 18th June 1815. (Dawn Waring)

OPPOSITE 'G' Mercer's Troop RHA at Waterloo, 18th June 1815. (Chris Collingwood)

Sir Alexander Dickson's medals. (Firepower Museum/Author's Collection)

Sir John May's medals. (Firepower Museum/Author's Collection)

The rotation of artillery units does not appear to have been orchestrated with particular diligence or zeal and by the end of December Ross was becoming increasingly agitated.

> Within these few days we have put on a more active appearance. Drouet's corps, consisting of 3,000 cavalry and 12,000 infantry, is approaching Massena. The head of his column, it is said, would reach Thomar yesterday [28th December 1810]. In consequence of this reinforcement, all the bridges of the Rio Major [Maior] have been mined, and the necessary precautions for their eventual destruction taken. Measures have also been taken within these two days to have the way clear for a speedy retreat to our position [within the Lines of Torres Vedras], should they shew [sic] any intention of disturbing us in our present cantonments ... Whatever change takes place must be in my favour, for my troop has been so hardly [heavily] and unfairly worked since here, that any alteration must be for the better. I have the mortification of seeing my troop alternatively in the highest health and condition, and the very reverse, through the most absurd misapplication of the service. At present we are stuck as artillery of position on heights looking towards Santarem, where we are certainly much more for show than use, and where both men and horses have suffered extremely from the exposure to weather, which for some time was very severe.[16]

In the centre and north of Portugal, the balance of the Portuguese forces was fully committed to disrupting French reinforcements and re-supply from their bases in Leon. The newly established French 9th Corps had a difficult start with many men and much materiel destined for the formation often being redirected. Following Foy's audience with Napoleon in November, orders to General Jean-Baptiste Drouet d'Erlon, the 9th Corps commander, were not long in arriving, instructing him to march to the assistance of the commander of the Army of Portugal without delay. However, by December only one division had made it through to Masséna's area of operations and their arrival added little by way of offensive capability but merely served to add to Masséna's already chronic logistic woes.

Both armies, therefore, remained at high levels of reactionary preparedness but settled down into winter cantonments and tried to establish as comfortable a routine as the circumstances provided. For many, it presented an opportunity for reflection on the year's events and a chance to catch up on correspondence with loved ones. Bull wrote a brief but sentimental letter to his wife and daughters in London:

> My Dearest Harriet, whilst things remain in their present state I will omit no opportunity of writing. Give my love to all my friends. Kiss and bless my darlings for their own fond father and above all keep yourself quiet and composed placing your trust in the Almighty that we shall meet again in peace and happiness.[17]

Following the capture of Minorca in 1798 Dickson had remained on the island until May 1802. He was soon captured by the beauty of the daughter of Don Stefano Briones, a Minorcan businessman, and in 1801 he was to marry Eulalia Rita Barbara at the Catholic Church in the island's capital.[18] Her letters to her husband provided an interesting mix of family and regimental matters, interspersed with some marvellous English idiosyncrasies.

> I shall inclose in this monthly army list, and a few presents from the dear children … By the first you will be able to see how things are going on in the army, and by the second you will judge whither Jane and William are improving. I think William writes better than Jane; he is very much improve, since I have put him to School … I have very little regimental news to give you. Major Godfrey has resigned but his place is not yet filled up, inconsequences of the Kings illness. Major Downman it is said in this place will have the Horse Majority, and Wilmot is to have the troop of Major Evelegh. If this takes place I shall let you know.[19]

The dreaded system of seniority or 'dead man's shoes' within the officers' corps of the artillery and engineers resulted in an unhealthy indulgence in lists, which clearly occupied the wives as much as it did their husbands. However, the situation was far worse in the artillery than the engineers and the following year Ross wrote about the issue in the most forthright terms.

> I fear we are far behind our sister corps in overcoming old prejudices in it. They have lately taken advantage of the opportunities offered, to establish precedents which cannot fail to be of the utmost service to them, whilst our senior officers have grown grey themselves in the subaltern ranks, cannot endure the thoughts of their followers being more fortunate, instead of considering it an advantage to their corps that individuals should have the stimulus of brevet promotion held out to them in common with the rest of the army. They reckon upon what they absurdly call the hardship suffered by others whose service may not put them in the way of obtaining it, and cry out against it as an unjust innovation.[20]

It was a damning but fair and accurate indictment of the senior officers within the Royal Artillery and was a situation that was exploited by both the Board of Ordnance and Wellington. It understandably sapped the morale of Gunner officers at the middle and lower ranks and increasingly featured in their correspondence from, and to, the Peninsula. The policy also served to hands-tie MacLeod in recommending a replacement to Howorth in spite of the strained working relationship between the commander-in-chief and his CRA being public knowledge. In the meantime, there was still much for the CRA and his staff to be getting on with. Notification had arrived in December that 'D' Troop would remain with the Peninsular Army and receive, from home, a complete remount in men and horses.[21] These began to arrive the following spring and the Troop joined the 2nd Division but good horses continued to be a problem.

> Two more brigades of artillery commanded by Hawkes [Hawker] and Meadows are about to be formed, the one a nine, and the other a six pounder, but Alas! It

is at present a vain boast in truth, not a horse, not one horse, not half a horse, not a hair of horse, but, I beg pardon, I forgot, horses are not wanted to draw guns, they will move without any aid, or they would not suit our present artillery system ...[22]

Captain James Hawker's Company were withdrawn from duties on the Lines to Lisbon where they joined Captain Philip Meadows's Company and were re-fitted, as far as possible, as brigades for field service. In October Howorth also received notification from MacLeod's office that 'Lieut. Lindsay, two Non Commissioned Officers and twelve Gunners, are embarked in the *Charlotte* Transport for Lisbon, in charge of an Equipment of Congreve's Rockets. The Master-General having approved of their being employed on this Service, you will be pleased to afford Lieut. Lindsay such further aid as may be requisite, and in your power.'[23] Wellington was, understandably, not best pleased that he had not been consulted by the Board of Ordnance in advance of shipment but he accepted that they were, at least, worthy of a trial and he wrote to Admiral Berkeley to arrange their release and continued transportation.

It is not necessary that I should enter into any discussion on the comparative merits of Congreve's rockets and carcasses; or that I should enter into any defence of the former, of the merits or demerits of which I have no experience, never having seen them used. I should hope, however, that the Master General of the Ordnance would have urged His Majesty's government not to send any to this country, if they are what you describe; but Capt. Beresford having mentioned to me that he had some of them on board the *Poictiers*, I shall be very much obliged to you if you will allow some of them, with some seamen of the *Poictiers* to be sent over to Major Gen. Fane, in order that they may, at least, be tried against the collection of the enemy's materials for their bridge at Santarem and Barquinha ...[24]

Wellington had experienced rockets during his time in India and entertained little by way of expectation. Nevertheless, he identified a potential target for Lieutenant William Lindsay and his rocketeers. He wrote again to Berkeley:

I assure you I am no partisan of Congreve's rockets, of which I entertain but a bad opinion, from what I recollect of the rockets of the East Indies, of which I believe those of Congreve, are an imitation. It is but fair, however, to give every thing a trial, more particularly as I have received the orders of government to try these machines. I don't think it would answer any purpose to try them here; but I understand the enemy have 7 boats on the square at Villa Franca, which might possibly be reached by the rockets fired from Hill's advanced piquet, and they might be tried there.[25]

It would appear that Lindsay's trial was not the greatest success; no doubt soliciting a wry smile from Wellington. Dickson shared the commander's misgivings.

I have at this moment in my quarter Lieut. Lindsay who is on his march to Lisbon with his rocket apparatus which he has been trying against Santarem. From what I can learn he only fired a few of the carcass rockets and without much apparent effect, except putting to the route a large convoy of baggage marching towards Golegam [Golegã], amongst whom a rocket fell. I do not know the motive of the trial at all, as it would by no means be a wise measure to burn such a town the property of our own friends, though occupied even by the enemy.[26]

Dickson had a point.

Notes

1. Schaumann, p.255.
2. Gen. La Romana had moved to behind the Lines from (Spanish) Estremadura in early October with two divisions.
3. Norris and Bremner, p.12.
4. Schaumann, p.261.
5. Letter from Capt. Bull to his wife Harriet Bull written on the 4th October from an unknown location.
6. WD, vol. IV, pp.329–30. Report from Lt. Gen. Sir S. Cotton to Lt. Gen. Viscount Wellington from Miguel, 6th October 1810.
7. Ingilby, entries dated from 3–11th October 1810.
8. Jones, vol. III, lists seven districts but WD, vol. IV, p.317 shows six districts and as it is Wellington's figures that are being used here only six districts are mentioned.
9. WD, vol. IV, p.323. Orders to Lt. Gen. Hill, from Arruda, dated 8th October 1810.
10. Dickson had been allocated this Portuguese 9-pounder brigade at the conclusion of the battle of Buçaco and immediately found it to be 'in a very disorganised and undisciplined state for field service'. Fortunately for Dickson, Lt. Braun of the KGA had, at much the same time, expressed a desire to serve with the Portuguese artillery and so was placed in command. See Dickson, vol. II, p.297.
11. Jenkinson, letter from Euxara de dos Cavalheros (Enxara dos Cavalleiros), dated 18th October 1810.
12. Kincaid, KAR, pp.13–14.
13. Girod de L'Ain, Appx, p.343.
14. Ingilby, 15th October 1810. (The date is slightly odd given that Ingilby refers to an action on the 14th November 1810.)
15. Jenkinson, letter from One League from Santarem, dated 21st November 1810.
16. Ross, p.12. Letter from Ross to Sir Hew Dalrymple, dated 29th December 1810.
17. Letter from Capt. Bull to his wife Harriet Bull written on the 4th October from an unknown location.
18. It is curious that Dickson always spelt her first name Eularia and indeed that is how it is spelt on her tombstone at Plumstead churchyard (now St. Nicholas Church, Plumstead), although the correct spelling is undoubtedly Eulalia.

19. All three letters appear in Dickson, vol. II, pp.310–12.

20. Ross, p.20. Letter from Ross to Maj. Downman, Commanding the RHA, from Las Agallas, dated 31st August 1811.

21. Whinyates, WCS, p.58.

22. Jenkinson, letter from One League from Santarem, dated 16th December 1810.

23. PRO WO 55/1201 p.134. Letter from DAG RA's office to Gen. Howorth, dated 9th October 1810.

24. WD, vol. IV, pp.386–87. Wellington to V. Adm. Berkeley from Pero Negro, dated 3rd November 1810.

25. Ibid., p.399. Wellington to V. Adm. Berkeley, from Pero Negro, dated 6th November 1810.

26. Dickson, vol. II, p.304. Letter from Dickson to MacLeod from below Santarem, dated 29th November 1810.

CHAPTER 9

Duncan's Determination

As early as October 1810 Napoleon had acknowledged that Masséna required more support than the 9th Corps alone. His imperial dispatches began to suggest that Soult might stir from his Andalusian siesta and, with a suitable force, march west. Indeed the Emperor even hinted that he might have followed in La Romana's wake and surprised Wellington by entering Lisbon through the back door. Soult, ever mindful of his vice regal status in the region, coupled with a jealous reluctance to leave either Victor or Sebastiani alone to their own devices, cooked up all manner of excuses. These sufficed to pass Napoleonic muster until the end of the year and Soult's subsequent sop, to capture Estremadura and the southern key of Badajoz, satisfied Paris but created new problems for the Duke of Dalmatia. Estremadura was cavalry country and Badajoz was a formidable objective: the former necessitated the collection of a large cavalry grouping and the latter a substantial siege train. This was to take time.

At the head of 20,000 men, Soult headed north in early January leaving Victor with a force of about the same number to contain Cadiz and continue siege operations. Sebastiani, centred on Granada with a smaller force, had instructions to protect the region's eastern border from incursions from Murcia but curiously received no instructions to watch Victor's back. Intelligence of these readjustments did not take long to reach the allied commanders in Cadiz and plans were soon crafted to exploit these modifications. Initial attempts to land a force in Victor's rear were frustrated by the weather but by the 27th February the Anglo-Spanish force was concentrated north of Tarifa. It numbered about 12,000 with the British element, under Lieutenant General Sir Thomas Graham, providing just over 5,000 men. Graham split the infantry into two brigades and kept the two squadrons of the KGL cavalry and his artillery under his direct command; the make-up of the latter being a rather *ad hoc* affair.

The companies of artillery at both Cadiz and Gibraltar had not changed since April the previous year (see Chapter 6) with the exception of half of Patrick Campbell's Company left at Gibraltar which joined the other half at Cadiz in October 1810.[1] The garrison duties at both strongpoints would need to continue in the absence of this expeditionary force and so Major Duncan, the artillery commander, decided to establish a composite company to man the nine guns and three howitzers of Graham's force. Duncan was also acutely aware that three of his six companies were from the recently established 10th Battalion, with many of the young Gunners experienced at manning the guns in the Cadiz defences but entirely unfamiliar with moving and manning guns in the field. The need for this force to move with speed over difficult terrain and get in behind Victor's lines was going to be backbreaking work and Duncan needed the very strongest men for the task. Aware of the small British detachment at Tarifa, which included a half company of artillery under Lieutenant Edward Thomas Michell, he added these men to his overall force. Three brigades of guns were formed: the first under Captain Philip Hughes with three 6-pounders and one 5½-inch howitzer; the second under Captain William Roberts with the same ordnance; and finally the three heavier 9-pounders with a 5½-inch howitzer under Second Captain Robert Gardiner.[2] The exact manning of these three brigades is unknown but the majority of other ranks came from the older, more established companies.

CRA: Maj. A. Duncan RA
Adjutant: Lt. P. J. Woolcombe RA
Quartermaster: Lt. G. H. Mainwaring RA

RA Companies	Capt.	2nd Capt.	Lt.	ORs[3]	Total	Distribution of Officers
Campbell's Company			2	49	51	S. P. Brett and H. Pester
Owen's Company		1	2	71	74	W. Cator, W. Brereton and G. H. Mainwaring
Hughes's Company	1	1	1	49	52	P. J. Hughes, F. Bedingfeld, C. Manners
Dickson's Company		1	2	5	8	R. M. Cairnes, P. J. Woolcombe and W. A. Raynes
Shenley's Company			1	36	37	B. Maitland
Roberts's Company	1	1		2	4	W. Roberts, R. Gardiner
Total Cadiz	2	4	8	212	226	
Gibraltar Detachment at Tarifa						
Godby's Company				14	14	
Dodd's Company				19	19	
Smyth's Company				14	14	
Morrison's Company		1		19	20	E. T. Michell
Total Gibraltar		1		66	67	

Source: Laws.

Assembling the men was, however, far easier for Duncan than resourcing suitable and sufficient horses. At the start of the year detachments from the 4th and 5th divisions of 'E' Troop Royal Artillery Drivers were stationed at Cadiz; the two divisions were commanded by lieutenants G. Wilkinson and J. Howell and they had 130 drivers and 235 horses between them. As the howitzers and 6-pounder guns would each require six-horse teams and the heavier 9-pounders eight-horse teams, coupled with the need for teams to draw the (artillery and infantry) ammunition carts, it is probable that the entire RA Drivers detachment was embarked.[4] Nevertheless, Duncan was forced to leave two 6-pounders behind at Tarifa for want of sufficient horses.

> From our scarcity of horses and the necessity of attaching six to each six pounder & its carriages, and eight to each nine pounder, we were obliged to thus curtail the Brigades. On the 25th and 26th, the army arrived and landed at Algeciras and proceeded to Tarifa, the road to which being impracticable for artillery, the guns and horses went round by sea, and the detachments marched. As many mules as we could get together here in addition to our horses, were embarked for the conveyance of our reserve gun ammunition and that for the troops, trusting that as we advanced in the country we might purchase and procure others, but in this I was disappointed, so much so as to be obliged to leave at Tarifa a gun from each of the six pounder brigades (the General [Graham] being particularly desirous that the nine pounders should move complete) in order to forward a sufficient quantity of rifle and musket ammunition.[5]

Overall command of the Anglo-Spanish force fell to General Manuel La Peña on the basis that the Spanish contribution was marginally larger than that of Graham. The Spaniard quickly demonstrated questionable leadership and dubious military skill, marching the force at night over waterlogged terrain. One of the lieutenant commissaries attached to the force was Richard Henegan.

> On the 28th of February we commenced our march to Barrosa, having previously been joined by the Spanish force under General La Peña ; and on the second day's march we fell in with an outpost of the enemy, on the heights of Vegar [Vejer]; they had two guns in position, and made an effort at defence, but we soon dislodged them, and bivouacked that night on the plain below …
>
> It was on the 5th March, at about 9 o'clock, on a fine clear morning, that we entered the plain of Barrosa. The troops had been upon the march upwards of seventeen hours; an unnecessary infliction of fatigue, that can only be accounted for by the circumstance of General La Peña having assumed the chief command of the allied army.[6]

The French dragoons dislodged from Vejer returned hot-foot with news that the force was advancing west on the coast road but conflicting reports had the allied column on the interior road and it was not until (Spanish) General José Pascual Zayas threw out a pontoon bridge at the south end of Isla de Leon that Victor was able to predict allied plans. He correctly concluded that the garrison of Cadiz would emerge over the bridge; the two forces would link up and then, outnumbering the besiegers, attack the defensive lines. Victor kept his nerve and ordered an attack on the *tête-du-pont* which forced the Spanish back, although they were able to save the pontoon bridge in the process; he then posted Major General Eugene-Casimir

Villatte's Division to block the coast road and moved inland to Chiclana with the divisions of Ruffin and Leval, which were to emerge and take the allies in the flank when they came up against Villatte.

> Between eleven and twelve o'clock the Spaniards were engaged with a body of French [Villatte's] troops immediately on the sands opposite Santi Petri, and in the woods fronting our position; then they pushed forward nearly their whole force to assist those engaged, and general Graham was ordered to follow with our troops for the purpose of taking up a position between S. Petri and the enemy.
>
> No sooner had the British entered the wood, which was of considerable extent, than the main body of the French troops who must have been well concealed, marched rapidly to possess themselves of the ground we had left. General Graham on being apprised of this (not however until we had considerably advanced into the wood) instantly turned back to meet them. The whole of our brigades amounting to ten pieces were marching together in column near the front of the troops; they immediately counter-marched with the rest and got out of the wood with all speed. As soon as we cleared it the enemy were seen to be within 1100 yards, and deploying into line, and in the midst of high furze [gorse]; such was the General's anxiety for the artillery to get into action that we did so before our troops were up, so that for more than 20 minutes, while our Light Corps engaged the enemys [sic] on their right flank, the ten guns (formed together in line) carried on a most destructive fire against their centre and left flank. The ground admitted of no manoeuvring so that the action very quickly became general and I believe a warmer one never took place. Our guns were much exposed to the enemy's light troops and were, besides, enfiladed from the beginning by their artillery on our right flank.[7]

The difficult terrain undoubtedly hampered the ability of the Gunners to move their guns and howitzers in direct support of both flanks. By the time the British emerged from the woods Ruffin's Division was firmly lodged on the Cerro de Puerco and within minutes Brigadier General William Dilkes's Brigade attempted to dislodge them. The infantry from both sides were soon locked in a close range musketry duel. Much of the feature, upon which the bulk of the French troops were positioned, was also out of effective range of the British guns so, instead, Duncan concentrated his fire against Leval's Division on the French right in support of Colonel William Wheatley's Brigade, and in the process provided one of the best examples of direct artillery fire support of the entire war. So eager were the Gunners to get their pieces into action against the 8e Ligne that 'one team tore up by the roots a pine-tree in which its gun had become entangled'.[8] Henegan, who had been on the Cerro de Puerco with the cavalry before being dislodged by Ruffin's assault, watched the whole unfold.

> The rifles and Portuguese companies running to the right in skirmishing order, commenced the action on our side, while, at the same time the 87th formed into line, having on its left, some companies of the guards. During this formation, the

artillery commanded by Major Duncan had been brought up, and taking a position in the centre, unlimbered within two hundred and fifty yards of the enemy. Never were guns better served, and the gaps in the enemy's ranks showed the precision with which the spherical shells were thrown. It was the moment that General Graham called out 'Give them the steel, my boys'.[9]

The 87th got their just rewards when Sergeant Masterson captured the eagle of the 8e Ligne, the first such trophy of the war, but there were countless other examples of similar tenacity and bravery which turned the tide in favour of Graham's men. In short, two brigades had defeated two divisions, despite the French having both surprise and the better ground to their advantage. Victor, an accomplished field commander, had been beaten and by a man who had taken up the sword late in life but who had shown determination, a cool head and no small amount of leadership. Graham had taken a professional interest in his guns and Gunners from the outset and when he had turned around his force in the woods one of his immediate thoughts was the manoeuvrability of his guns. He earmarked two companies of the 2/47th to assist the Gunners and, on emerging from the wood, took in the confusing scene with remarkable clarity and having issued hasty orders to his brigade commanders encouraged Duncan to unlimber the pieces with great haste to support.[10] Comparable leadership was not, however, demonstrated by the force commander who, positioned less than an hour's march to the north-west, refused to stir, despite the protestations of General Zayas. La Peña's actions were, in short, a disgrace to Spain and her cause and, although many attempts have been made to explain his actions, the shameful stain remains ineffaceable.

In his dispatch to the Earl of Liverpool, Graham outlined the extent of the victory:

> ... An eagle, 6 pieces of cannon, the Gen. of Division Ruffin and the Gen. Of Brigade Rousseau, wounded and taken; the chief of staff, Gen. Bellegarde, an aide de camp of Marshal Victor, and the Colonel of the 8th regt, with many other officers, killed; and several wounded and taken prisoners; the field covered with dead bodies and arms of the enemy attests that my confidence in this division was nobly repaid.
>
> Where all have so distinguished themselves, it is scarcely to discriminate any as the most deserving of praise ... I owe too much to major Duncan, and the officers and corps of the Royal artillery, not to mention them in the highest approbation; never was artillery better served.[11]

Graham concluded by recommending seven officers, including the bearer of the dispatch, for promotion: one of those officers was Major Duncan. Notwithstanding the outstanding achievements of Duncan and his men, this dispatch contrasts plainly with Wellington's post-battle dispatches in recognising the contribution made by the officers and men of the Royal Artillery and this, in itself, speaks volumes.

Eight out of the 15 officers of artillery were injured that day: Captain Philip Hughes, Second Captain William Cator, lieutenants Edward Thomas Michell,

Robert Woollcombe, William Brereton, Charles Manners, Brownlow Maitland and Henry Pester. One gun from Gardiner's Brigade lost most of its detachment to enemy fire and had to be kept in action by a sergeant of the RA Drivers. Five gunners were killed during the battle and a number of the 49 wounded officers and men died within days.

It is extraordinary that under such a fire our loss in killed should be so trifling, altho' that of wounded is most severe, the whole of the enemy's fire being for a considerable time from the commencement of the action directed against the battery formed by our guns; indeed their whole force seemed to be directed towards us, and occasioned general graham [sic] to make his formation in rear of the guns, so that much of the fire intended for us reached them and caused dreadful destruction ...

I am most truly concerned to state that Lieut. [P. J.] Woolcombe, the acting adjutant to the Detachment, died this evening of the wound he received yesterday. A more gallant zealous officer never existed; to his personal exertions I am so indebted that for every reason both public and private I must most deeply regret his loss. Lieut. Maitland received also a severe wound but from the report of the surgeons to night there is much hope that he may yet recover, and, that a most valuable and promising young man as he is, may be saved to the service ... Lieut. Pester's wound was from a musket ball through the calf of the leg, but is doing extremely well; the other officers are in the fairest way of recovery and no unpleasant doubts whatever entertained to the contrary.

I must not omit to commend the exertion of Lieut. Wilkinson of the Drivers Corps and the steadfastness of the men under his charge, exposed and unoccupied as they were remaining stationary during the greater and severest part of the action.[12]

Indeed, another contrast from the battle on the gorse-covered hills outside Cadiz seems to be the accolades heaped upon the RA Drivers. Besides the sergeant who kept Gardiner's guns in action, another sergeant from Captain William Roberts's Company was reported missing having returned into the wood in search of the ammunition wagons. He was most likely caught and killed by a French cavalry patrol. The sergeant from Hughes's Company received three wounds and was specially recommended for his gallantry during the fighting. Although all three of these senior NCOs were ex-artillerymen themselves it was nevertheless significant that all three officers commanding brigades of guns found the time to write to the Commandant of the RA Drivers in Woolwich and emphasise the steadfastness of the corps on the day of battle. Gardiner recommended his sergeant for promotion to staff sergeant but admitted that 'he did not know what sort of pen man he is, but his merit [was] in overcoming difficulties that occur in the course of active service'.[13]

Graham, furious at La Peña's indolence, refused to serve under the Spaniard and withdrew his force back to Cadiz. One in four men had fallen and although French losses were marginally higher, the fact remained that the British losses had been largely in vain; Anglo-Spanish relations were badly damaged and Victor was able to re-occupy his lines and even declare that the battle had been successful in thwarting the allied attempt to lift the siege. Duncan closed his report to MacLeod with two familiar themes: the first was an emphatic endorsement of the effectiveness of spherical case; the second a plea for fresh horses, 'hopefully slightly younger than their predecessors'. In closing this chapter on Barrosa, and the contribution made by Duncan and his 300 men, it is a great pity that the two companies of artillery, which might reasonably expect to bear the honour title, were disbanded shortly after Waterloo. Like so many of the actions in the Peninsula, which did not directly involve Wellington's forces, they have been dismissed as a side-show, and their achievement and memory have faded with time.

Another 'side-show' had been ongoing on the east coast of Spain, albeit sporadically, since Marshal Bon-Adrien Jeannot de Moncey's attempt to capture Valencia in mid-1808. Napoleon had long realised the strategic importance of the key Mediterranean ports of Tarragona, Valencia and Alicante. Royal Navy supremacy allowed the free movement of victuals and equipment, providing a vital lifeline to the Spanish nation and her armies and in early 1810 Napoleon decided to slam shut this portal by attempting, for the second time, a *coup de main* on the key city of Valencia. However, like Moncey's earlier effort it failed; this second disappointment merely served to intensify Napoleon's determination to conquer the east coast. In mid-1810 General Luis Gabriele Suchet was allocated the task along with more resources and a realistic schedule. Suchet had been commanding the 3rd French Corps since the middle of the previous year and, after a shaky start, had shown promise and determination capturing firstly the fort and town of Lérida and subsequently that at Mequinenza. By early 1811 Suchet had added Tortosa to his conquests and now moved on to the first of the key objectives, the city of Tarragona. The movement of his siege train delayed the commencement of the operation but he arrived at the outskirts of the old Roman port on the 3rd May and progress was so swift that the Regency at Cadiz implored support from the Spanish Army of Valencia, while simultaneously considering options closer to home.

Requests for support were conveyed, via the Cortes, to Graham and in mid-June an expeditionary force was once again dispatched from Cadiz and Gibraltar, consisting of 1,200 men, under the command of Colonel John Skerrett. With Skerrett's force were two RA detachments from Cadiz and Gibraltar as follows:

RA Companies	Capt.	2nd Capt.	Lt.	ORs	Total	Distribution of Officers
Cadiz Detachment						
Campbell's Company	1			36	37	A. Hunt
Shenley's Company			1	16	17	T. O. Carter
Roberts's Company			1	1	2	W. B. Dundas
Total Cadiz	1		2	53	56	
Gibraltar Detachment						
Godby's Company			2	14	16	B. Robinson and R. J. Saunders
Dodd's Company			1		1	

Smyth's Company		14	14
Morrison's Company		13	13
Fead's Company		1	1
Total Gibraltar	2	54	56

Source: Laws and PRO.[14]

Escorted by the Royal Navy they arrived off the Catalan coast on the 26th June and Commodore Edward Codrington and Skerrett went ashore. They had clear orders not to deploy the force if they considered the Spanish position a lost cause. It was immediately apparent that the French were within days of capturing Tarragona; furthermore, the mission the Spanish commander, General Luis Gonzáles, Marquis of Campoverde, had allocated the British would, without doubt, have resulted in their loss. Meanwhile Skerrett demonstrated an overly eager determination to desist, which was noted with a degree of bewilderment by Codrington. Much to the disenchantment of the defenders, Codrington and Skerrett re-embarked and three days later Suchet had his prize and, with it, his elevation to the rank of marshal.

Skerrett's services were to be called upon again later in the year. Soult's frustration at not being able to fully subdue Andalusia ultimately focussed on the area around Cadiz, Gibraltar and Tarifa, which provided safe harbour to both regular and irregular forces, from land or sea operations. The first two locations were, thanks to British naval supremacy, considered impregnable but the latter was worthy of closer attention. Soult ordered a force of 12,000 men and a siege train of 16 guns to assemble on the perimeter of the French defences at Cadiz. Allied intelligence got wind early of the plan and decided to bolster the defences at Tarifa. In October Lieutenant General Colin Campbell, the Governor of Gibraltar, had sent an additional brigade under Skerrett to reinforce the handful of British companies that were already stationed in the place. Two days later the Spanish also sent another brigade from Cadiz, under General Francisco de Paula Copons, bringing the total allied defensive force up to 3,000 men. Lieutenant Michell, who had returned to the isolated and windswept fortress following the battle at Barrosa, had his small Gunner detachment but Duncan was ordered to shore up the artillery group and he duly dispatched Captain Hughes and an additional half company of men.

RA Companies	Capt.	2nd Capt.	Lt.	ORs[15]	Total	Distribution of Officers
Hughes's Company	1		1	40	42	P. J. Hughes, C. Manners
Dickson's Company			1		1	W. A. Raynes
Total	1		2	40	43	

Source: Laws and PRO.[16]

With Michell's Gunners this brought Hughes's strength up to that of a company. However a paucity of men was not his only defensive predicament.

The main problem was that the *enceinte* was too narrow to accommodate guns; Sánchez (the Spanish artillery commander) had a total of 26 pieces but only 12 were positioned inside the town. Two of the heavier guns were mounted in the towers, to the north-east, where the *enceinte* was wider and six 9-pounder field guns and four field mortars were positioned at various intervals along the walls. The balance of 14 guns were in the three batteries on the island and in the redoubt of Santa Catalina which protected the causeway to what was arguably the most defendable aspect of Tarifa. Copons and Skerrett had distributed their forces equally, each keeping two battalions in the town and one on the island.[17]

When Victor arrived to conduct a detailed reconnaissance on the 23rd December the vulnerability of the defensive structure was immediately apparent; also immediately apparent was the best mode of attack, for the hills which virtually overlooked the town from the north-east provided the perfect platform to commence proceedings. Skerrett's determination to hold the town was already beginning to waver and he proposed evacuation before the French had blasted a realistic breach in the eastern wall. Colonel Hugh Gough of the 87th, Major James King and Captain Smith (King was commanding the Battalion of Flank Companies and Smith was the senior Sapper), well aware of Skerrett's questionable resolve, were having none of it. Skerrett's track record at Tarragona was widely known and King sent word back to Campbell at Gibraltar of Skerrett's intentions and those of Copons who, in contrast, remained determined to hold the town. Campbell's furious reply and the withdrawal of the naval transports thwarted Skerrett's plans to cut and run.

Nevertheless, a combination of appalling weather, bad morale and questionable siege battery positions, which could be engaged from the sea, all took their toll on Victor's damp and demoralised gunners and sappers. His infantry, waiting in the wings, was equally dispirited and when their turn came to charge the breach they lacked the level of blind determination required to take the fortified structure by storm. Victor withdrew early in the New Year; the former drummer boy of an artillery regiment from Grenoble, who had earned his laurels in Italy at the height of the revolutionary wars, during the Prussian campaigns in 1806 and at the battle of Friedland in 1807, must have wondered where it had all gone wrong.

Notes

1. Although (brevet) Lt. Col. Campbell was still serving with the Spanish Army and the company was commanded by 2nd Capt. Hunt.

2. Oman, OHP, vol. IV, p.93 and Fortescue, vol. VIII, p.41 both list two brigades only: but Duncan's report in the PRO/WO 55/1195 pp.111–17 (referred to in Laws, LRA, p.197) and Henegan, vol. I, p.113 both state three brigades. As the former was the CRA and the latter one of the two lieutenant commissaries attached to the force this is unequivocal.

3. The details of the ORs may not be precise, though the total of ORs agrees with the figures quoted in the monthly return for Cadiz Garrison, dated 25th February 1811 – see PRO WO 55/1195 pp.13–17, PRO WO 10/848, 851, 855 & 856.

4. See Laws, LRA, p.199.
5. Duncan's report from Cadiz, dated 6th March 1811. PRO WO 55/1195 pp.111–17.
6. Henegan, vol. I, pp.112–13.
7. Duncan's report from Cadiz, dated 6th March 1811. PRO WO 55/1195 pp.111–17.
8. Fortescue, vol. VIII, p.54.
9. Henegan, vol. I, pp.116.
10. Duncan had also asked Gen. Dilkes to supply some infantry to support the guns and he instructed the Coldstream Guards to fall out and oblige; when it became clear that the two companies of the 2/47th had already been allocated the Coldstream Guards they remained with Wheatley's Brigade as Dilkes's Brigade had already moved to engage Ruffin on the Cerro de Puerco.
11. WD, vol. IV, pp.696–98. Graham to Liverpool from the Isla de Leon, dated 6th March 1811.
12. Duncan's report from Cadiz, dated 6th March 1811. PRO WO 55/1195 pp.111–17.
13. Laws, LRA, p.204. I have not been able to find this letter in the archives, or indeed any of Gardiner's letters from 23rd January 1809 until 27th October 1811.
14. Laws, LRA, p.150. PRO WO 10/847, 848, 850, 854, 856: PRO WO 17/1486 & 1797: PRO WO 55/1195 pp.155 and 161: PRO WO 55/1203 p.81.
15. The details of the ORs may not be precise, though the total of ORs agrees with the figures quoted in the monthly return for Cadiz Garrison dated 25th February 1811 – see PRO WO 55/1195 p.14, PRO WO 10/848, 851, 855 & 856.
16. Laws, LRA, p.151. PRO WO 55/1195 pp.215–17: PRO WO 10/855 and PRO WO 10/896.
17. Lipscombe, p.246.

CHAPTER 10

Ramsay's Breakout

Conditions throughout the winter, as bad as they were for the French, were little better for the British and Portuguese. On both sides of the mighty Tagus, water levels rose sharply covering much of the adjacent land in shallow water, leading to a corresponding increase in sickness among the men and horses. Ingilby was with Lawson's Company cantoned with the 6th Division at near Alenquer and suffered for three months from dysentery which cleared only when they moved to Ota, on slightly higher ground, the following January. 'A' Troop recorded the deaths of Gunner John McCarter on the 15th December, Driver James Smart six days later and Gunner John Middleton on New Year's Day along with the deaths of numerous troop horses due to glanders.[1] Dickson too was suffering and had been ordered to Lisbon for a change of air; he wrote to MacLeod that 'I am in so feeble a state that I can scarcely walk across the room'.[2] Indeed MacLeod's own sons, Lieutenant Colonel Charles MacLeod and Lieutenant Henry MacLeod, were both forced to return to England due to ill health.[3] However, not all predicaments and activities served to depress: Jenkinson recorded that they 'had races the other day, which afforded no small amusement, and which, as the French must have seen them will have given them a good idea of the merry way which we campaign. The country horses and ponies caused great sport ...'[4]

Wellington meanwhile was taking no chances: the bulk of his army were poised to strike at Masséna's units should the opportunity present, while, to the rear, work continued to improve the Lines.

> The lines are at this moment strengthening and the front clearing of everything that could afford the least protection to the enemy's light troops, and when you are told of a hill being scarped for six miles, of abattis two miles long, and of five hundred pieces of ordnance (exclusive of our field artillery) being mounted from right to left of our front lines, you will know how to estimate Ld Ws perseverance and determination.[5]

However, not everyone was making good use of the lull in the fighting; the Board of Ordnance remained remote and unresponsive to the urgent operational demands from theatre.

It should seem by your account that the Board of Ordnance are at length roused from their mischievous lethargy, which might have been productive of the most evil consequences, but like sluggards unexpectedly roused they have not yet quite opened their eyes, and can only make up their minds to send driblets of horses; of what use will three hundred horses be in the formation of a six and a nine pounder brigade? The latter of which will alone require one hundred and sixty of them. Three thousand would have been more to the purpose, and one thousand not a horse too many – but every act of theirs is the same; we having now been 18 months in the country without one article of clothing being sent to us, notwithstanding the most repeated representations upon that head to every person connected with that department – judge of the condition our men must be in, when I tell you that they have not slept without their accoutrements on for eight months – compassion alone for those who are suffering hardship should have called for more rigid attention to private and official applications, and in my opinion no one has been more culpable on that head than our friend Cleveland [Cleaveland], who has never deigned to reply to a single letter written to him by any one of our Captains.[6]

Nevertheless, as uncomfortable as the conditions were for the British and Portuguese troops and as frustrating as the failures of the Board of Ordnance may have been to the Gunners on the ground, their misery was nothing compared to the suffering and exasperations endured by Masséna's men only a few miles to their front. The damage and demoralisation, caused by back to back failures at Buçaco and in front of the Lines coupled with unprecedented levels of starvation and illness, led to a virtual total collapse of discipline. Bands of soldiers, some organised but many impromptu, roamed the Portuguese countryside in search of food and mercilessly extracted it from their hosts, many of whom responded by forming their own *ad hoc* groups and inflicting equally horrific acts of revenge on the smaller of these French detachments. By February 1811 Masséna realised that the situation was so bad that waiting indefinitely for additional reinforcements, supplies and fresh powder and ammunition was, despite Napoleon's intentions to the contrary, no longer a responsible option. Accordingly, he issued orders for a north-easterly retreat on the 3rd March.

It was not until the 6th that Wellington had the unequivocal confirmation that the French forces were withdrawing. The Light and 3rd divisions led the chase supported by Ross's and Bull's troops respectively. The French forces pulled back in the face of the allied advance but on the 11th March Ney, commanding the rearguard, made the first of a series of delaying actions to buy more time for Reynier's, Junot's and Drouet's formations.

They continued their retreat on the morning of the 11th, and were most closely pursued by us, and possessing as we did every possible advantage of the ground, we had an opportunity of following them at a canter, and annoying their columns of infantry and cavalry very considerably with Spherical case, and such was their alarm, that after they were driven from the first position they had taken to keep us in check they ran the whole way to Pombal ... Ld W made a most able disposition for the attack in the event of the enemy's not retiring in the night, which however they did, and joined by Bull's troop we pursued them so closely the next morning, that we again compelled them to halt a corps d'Armée, and take up a position to cover their retreat through Redinha ... It being of the utmost importance to push them there, Ld W very soon finished his reconnaissance, and directed the light division to dislodge them from the wood, whilst the third division moved round their left, and kept the main body of his army to attack their centre ... The light division performed their part nobly, and Ross's troop was posted with them ready to advance across the plain, as soon as the enemy should be compelled by the turning of their left flank to retire; their consternation as they discovered the third division was very great, and it was increased by the advance of the whole army in line, which was formed as if by magic, and the effect of which was majestic beyond description, nor was the rapid advance of the two troops of horse artillery, to cannonade and outflank their retiring columns less interesting, and they suffered considerably from our fire.

Having been compelled by night to halt, we proceeded on our route the next morning, and found the enemy again in position to cover the town of Condexa [Condeixa], and very soon discovered them moving on the road to Miranda de [do] Corvo ... Ld W arrived at his advanced post at about 8 o'clock, and having reconnoitred the enemy's position, directed two divisions of his army to cross the mountains and turn the enemy's left, whilst the light division moved on and attacked their right; the remaining two divisions of the army and the two troops of horse artillery, with the exception of two of Ross's guns which accompanied the columns moving on the enemy's left, were so placed in column as to make a rapid push at their centre, as soon as the flank movements should compel them to give way, and cede to us a height which commanded their future movements ...

General Picton's advance on their left was so rapid, and the attack of the light division on their right so furious, that they were obliged to abandon the hill in question with precipitation, the effect of which was beautiful, for their guns which were at one moment playing from the face of the hill which presented itself to us, were by Picton's division and two of Ross's guns getting so completely round their left flank, suddenly withdrawn and opened almost to their rear, which was followed by the rapid retreat of their infantry, and the no less rapid advance of ours and our artillery, which soon gained the height and played with the finest effect upon them whilst retiring in the utmost disorder ...[7]

Jenkinson's account of the attacks on Ney's rearguard gloss over some of the less than adequate leadership by Major General William Erskine in temporary command of the Light Division, actions which resulted in the unfortunate commander inheriting the equally unfortunate nickname *Arse Skin* by the men. Nevertheless, the two horse artillery troops had excelled themselves and they earned well deserved and particular praise from Wellington in his dispatch of the 14th March.[8] Dickson, in his periodic reports to MacLeod, credits the French with 'making a beautiful retreat and having his troops so well together that we make fewer prisoners than might be expected'.[9] The horse artillery had earned its spurs and proved its worth keeping up with the infantry in the fast moving pursuit of the French Army over difficult terrain but even Lieutenant George Belson in Ross's Troop admitted that some of the roads in bad weather would have required assistance from the infantry to pass. Belson's account also provided a more graphic description of the dreadfulness experienced in the vacated towns and villages during the chase. At Redinha they 'found vast numbers of their [French] dead and dying, consuming in the flames of the houses which they had set fire'. At Miranda do Corvo the French had destroyed 'a considerable quantity of ammunition and several baggage animals' and at Foz de Arouce there were 'messes all found on the fires which they left'.[10] However, neither described the horrors which had befallen the local inhabitants. Lawson's Brigade had followed hot on the heels of the leading divisions and was about two days behind but had caught up by the 18th March and even engaged the French at Ponte de Mucela. By the 23rd the brigade was at Meceira (Seia) and Ingilby takes up the story.

> Before the French had abandoned the positions of Sobral and Santarem they had suffered great privations, and their numbers had become much reduced. They now retraced their march, repulsed in their invasion, through a country exhausted of provisions and forage. The sick and dead were scattered on the roads and in their bivouacs, and the houses and hospitals in the villages and towns through which we pursued their columns were nearly all occupied, and some filled, with the dead and dying, the greatest part perishing from hunger and want. The horses in like manner died or became inefficient and were abandoned in great numbers, so that many of the tumbrils, with much other *materiel* of their Army, was obliged to be burnt or destroyed on the spot or fell into our hands. Since the affair at Redhina some guns had been discovered and dug up. The French set fire to the towns and villages and put to death numbers of the inhabitants, without regard to age or sex, and in return the peasants, watching every opportunity, fell upon their stragglers and sick and massacred them instantly, if no British or regular troops were at hand to protect them.[11]

As early as the 8th March, when Wellington was convinced beyond doubt that Masséna was withdrawing, he sent a force of 18,000 men under the command of Beresford to the vicinity of Elvas. They departed Abrantes on the 12th March unaware that Badajoz had fallen to the French the previous day; nevertheless, their task was more than just attempting to provide succour to General Rafael Menacho and the Spanish defenders. With Wellington in pursuit of the Army of Portugal, the back door was now open to Lisbon and Beresford's force was to slam shut any aspirations that Soult might have of using Mortier's 5th Corps in a dash for the city. Sending more than a third of his army was a necessary evil for Wellington and with Beresford's Corps were six brigades of guns (See Chapter 11). Framingham was earmarked to command this not insignificant artillery group but for now he remained with Howorth and Wellington's main body, and Major George Julias Hartmann of the KGA assumed the role in his absence. This decision rankled with Dickson but, in fact, he had no real cause for complaint as he was more junior than both Hawker and Lefebure who would therefore have had prior claim. For the balance of allied artillery two distinct groups now emerged. The first group was up with and supporting Wellington's main army and remained with them during the key battles that followed.

CRA: Brig. Gen. E. Howorth
Staff: Lt. Col. H. Framingham RA
Brigade Major: Maj. J. May RA

RHA Troops	Notes	Equipment
'A' Troop (Ross)	Attached to Light Division.	5 x light 6-pounders 1 x 5½-inch howitzer
'I' Troop (Bull)	Attached to 3rd Division for the advance.	5 x light 6-pounders 1 x 5½-inch howitzer
RA Companies	**Notes**	**Equipment**
Lawson's Company	Attached to 6th Division for the advance.	6 x 9-pounders
Thomson's Company	Attached to 1st Division for the advance.	6 x 6-pounders
Portuguese Artillery – Maj. Arentschildt KGA		
Da Cunha Preto's Company	1st Portuguese Regiment	9-pounders[12]
Rozières's Company	1st Portuguese Regiment	6-pounders
Pinto's Company	2nd Portuguese Regiment	6-pounders
De Sequeira's Company	2nd Portuguese Regiment	6-pounders
Rosado's Company	2nd Portuguese Regiment	6-pounders

Sources: Leslie, Laws, Teixeira Botelho, Vieira Borges and Chartrand.

The second artillery group were either employed on garrison duties or held as a form of mobile reserve which was to move (independently as companies and/or brigades) up and down the Portuguese–Spanish border with alacrity over the coming months.

RA and KGA Companies	Notes	Equipment
May's Company (Capt. Baynes)	January–March: Alverca do Ribetejo. April–May: Guarda. June: Alfaiates. July: Arronches. August–September: Carvallat. October–December: Sabugal.	Unknown
Bredin's Company	January–June: Alhandra. July: Oeiras (Lisbon). August: Oporto. September: Aldea del Obispo.	Unknown

	October–November: Guarda.	
	December: Gallegos.	
Glubb's Company	January–June: Torres Vedras.	Unknown
	July: Lisbon.	
	August: Oporto.	
	September–December: Vila da Ponte.	
Meadows's Company	Meadows died 4th September,	Unknown
	Elige assumed command.	
	January–March: Cabeća de Montachique.	
	April–June: Lisbon.	
	July–August: Elvas.	
	September–November: Vendada.	
	December: Celorico.	
Gesenius's Company KGA	In garrison at Lisbon.	Garrison guns

Sources: Laws and Dickson.

By 21st March Masséna's army were positioned from Celorico to Guarda and preparing to continue their easterly movement to the environs of Almeida and Ciudad Rodrigo but were exasperated to receive orders the following day to head south and not east. Admittedly Masséna's maps were bad and certainly he felt under pressure to minimise Napoleonic criticism by executing more than just a 'cut and run' operation but there is little doubt that the Old Fox's decision was an indication that he was past his prime; it was also a suggestion that he was aware that his army, from his own commanders down to the rank and file, blamed him for the failures of the previous months. He wanted to prove to them, and to Paris, that he still possessed the qualities that had earned him the accolade the 'cherished child of victory'. The decision was, however, an extraordinary error in judgement. In view of the state of his army, their poor morale, their lack of discipline, munitions, food, boots and clothing and their paucity of serviceable artillery and wagons, it was simply astonishing to propose a change in plan, which took the whole through a mountainous, thinly populated area full of defiles and devoid of provisions. So astonishing in fact that Ney refused to obey and was, accordingly, relieved of his 'beloved' command, an action which turned the soldiers of the 6th even more resolutely against the Prince of Essling. A few days into the movement and Masséna was quick to admit that the largely infertile land, which formed the watershed between the Coa and Zezere rivers, was not an area in which to linger overly long and he issued orders for a general withdrawal east to Plasencia. Wellington's pursuit had been slowed by his desire to wait for the newly formed 7th Division, the 'Mongrels', to join up but on the 3rd April the Anglo-Portuguese army caught and engaged Reynier at Sabugal as the latter established a defensive line in an attempt to buy time for the withdrawal of the 6th and 8th corps.[13] Ross outlined the action in a letter to his brother.

… we beat the enemy at Sabugal. The whole brunt of the action fell upon the Light Division, and their conduct was as usual admirable. There was a good deal of blundering in the affair, or the fate of the enemy would have been disastrous;

as it was, it has done much credit to the British army. Our loss has been trifling; not more than 150 killed and wounded – all of the Light Division; the enemy's not less than 1300, including about 150 prisoners. Two guns of Bull's were so closely engaged, that there was much reason to apprehend for their safety, having for some time only the support of a wing of the 95th and the 43rd Regiment, opposed to four guns within 600 yards, and nearly a whole corps of the French army, which they maintained till reinforced by the rest of the division, when the enemy were three times compelled to give way, but returned again; and at last, upon seeing the approach of the Third Division, they retired, leaving a 6-inch howitzer on the ground. On this occasion we had again an opportunity of doing considerable execution, and, with our usual good fortune, with little or no loss – Bull only having one man wounded slightly, and I only lost one horse, killed in the shafts of the gun, and his companion severely wounded, a cannon shot having passed through both.[14]

The 'blundering' Ross referred to was our old friend Erskine who set off (with the cavalry) before plans were entirely clear in the other commanders' minds and ended up behind the French and entirely out of touch, while Beckwith, commanding the main brigade in the Light Division, undercut his (river) crossing point. Both Ross and Bull had been task organised with the Light Division and crossed the Coa over a ford to keep up with the advancing infantry; the significance of this intimate support is explained by Ross's second captain.

The light division, three regiments of Cavalry and Bull's and Ross's troops passed the ford without opposition, to our great surprise, for the enemy might have annoyed us very considerably – no sooner however had they reached the heights than they found the woods filled with the enemy's tirailleurs, supported by artillery, and strong columns of infantry and cavalry. Two of our guns soon gained the heights and opened fire upon the enemy, and the advance of the 95th, 43rd and 52nd regiments was so rapid and irresistible, and the fire of the two advanced guns of Bull's troop and of two of ours on the height so destructive, that the enemy gave way in every part of their line, leaving one of the howitzers in our possession, which they were so unwilling to part with, that the hill on which it was posted was thrice taken and retaken, but finally relinquished by the enemy upon the appearance of Genl Picton's division, and they retreated with the utmost precipitation leaving about 160 dead bodies on the field.[15]

The French pulled back deep into Spain and by early April the 2nd Corps were at Ledesma, the 6th at Salamanca, the 8th at Toro and the 9th at San Muñoz; Wellington allocated the Light and 5th divisions (and some cavalry) to monitor Drouet, who lay closest to the border, and the 6th Division and Pack's Independent Portuguese Brigade (and much of the balance of cavalry) were sent to invest Almeida, while the 1st, 3rd, 7th divisions along with the balance of the Portuguese troops were placed in cantonments in and around the border. Wellington, confident that Masséna would, for a short while at least, remain static, set off to (Spanish) Estremadura to monitor operations with Beresford's Corps. The artillery, other than the two horse artillery troops, went into cantonment while Bull and Ross were kept busy at and in front of Almeida.

> Yesterday we invested Almeida, in which the enemy have left a garrison, but of what strength is not yet known. We came up with a column marching out of it of about four battalions, with the cavalry, and Bull had the satisfaction of kicking them all the way to Fort Conception [Concepcion]. My troop was kept in reserve, to watch what might come out of the fortress, with the Hussars [1st KGL]. We took almost ninety prisoners, and a very considerable number are killed and wounded.[16]

> There is not now a single Frenchman in Portugal except in the garrison of Almeida and should our line of operations be successful throughout, what a brilliant campaign Ld W will have made; the enemy are afraid to give us battle, and the invasion of the country has cost them at least twenty five thousand men.[17]

Jenkinson, ever praiseworthy of his commander-in-chief, was right about French losses and about the last of the French in Portugal but wrong about the French state of mind and about how well the campaign had been planned and executed. Wellington's options were now very limited, for without a siege train with which to prosecute operations against Badajoz in the south, or Almeida and Ciudad Rodrigo in the north, he was, to all intents and purposes, going nowhere fast. All too often it has been assumed that the Board of Ordnance had failed to provide Wellington with such a train in time for operations in early 1811, but his correspondence to Vice Admiral Berkeley on the 20th March would indicate otherwise.

> In order to get rid of at least 25 vessels, I propose to disembark the ordnance stores (with the exception of the battering train and its stores) and to place them all at S. Julian … I [will] keep the battering train on board, because, whenever we may want it, it will be convenient to transport it part of the way by sea, and the trouble and inconvenience of embarking and disembarking it would be very great, and the expense of its tonnage is not very great. I shall write to you officially respecting the ordnance store ships, as soon as Gen. Howorth shall have got his stores out of them.[18]

Wellington's failure to move, or at least consider moving, this battering train much earlier is perhaps an indication that events, once rolling, moved far more rapidly than he anticipated and secondly, that he was not being given, or indeed asking for, advice on such matters from his artillery commander. Despite the existence of this siege train, Wellington seemed entirely content, even after his whistle-stop tour to Beresford at Badajoz, to allow the siege to continue with a motley collection of antique guns collected by the industrious Dickson from the ramparts at Elvas. What though of the other ordnance stores to which Wellington refers in his letter? If by unloading these stores, 25 ships could be released from straining at their anchors in the Tagus estuary it begs a question as to what these ordnance stores actually consisted of. Could these at least have contained some of the clothing and accoutrements that Second Captain Jenkinson bemoaned had not been sent by the Board of Ordnance in their 'mischievous lethargy'? Likely so, and as these were clearly the responsibility of the CRA and his representative in Lisbon, Lieutenant Colonel George Fisher, perhaps the lethargy lay closer to home. Furthermore, there were suitable siege guns within some of the forts in and around Lisbon and yet no effort, or indeed any contingency plan, seems to have been drawn up to move these guns, by land or sea, to either Almeida or Elvas.[19] Ross commented in his letter of 16th April that 'Almeida is expected to fall without the operation of a siege' but 'Wellington, to make sure of it, has ordered the necessary artillery … to be brought up to Oporto; indeed,' he added, 'I believe it is already on the way.'[20] It was a fair assumption but it was incorrect for it was not until the 19th July that the siege train at Lisbon was brought to Oporto. The ultimate responsibility for this breakdown must lie with Wellington, but Howorth must also shoulder a substantial portion of blameworthiness.

Jenkinson was also wrong in his assumption that the fire had left the French belly; Masséna discovered in mid-April that Napoleon had already decided to replace him and yet his successor, Marshal Auguste-Frédéric Marmont, Duke of Ragusa, was not expected for a few weeks. It was enough time for the Old Fox to restore his reputation. Within two short weeks, Masséna's Corps was restored, clothed, rearmed and reinforced; Marshal Jean-Baptiste Bessières, Duke of Istria and commander of the French Army of the North, had provided two cavalry brigades, a horse artillery battery and, most significantly, 30 teams of gun horses.[21] On the 1st May the Army of Portugal was concentrated at Ciudad Rodrigo and the next day they divided into two columns and advanced west. Wellington had received intelligence that the French were stirring and had raced back from Badajoz, arriving back in the vicinity of Almeida on the 29th April. He conducted an immediate, and, by Wellington's standards, a fairly cursory reconnaissance of the ground and selected the area due east from Almeida between Fuentes de Oñoro and Fort Concepcion. The Light Division and cavalry fell back in the face of the French advance and the scene was set for a major confrontation. There were some hasty adjustments in the army and the artillery was organised as follows:

CRA: Brig. Gen. E. Howorth
Staff: Lt. Col. H. Framingham RA
Brigade Major: Maj. J. May RA

RHA Troops	Notes	Equipment
'A' Troop (Ross)	Attached to the cavalry.	5 x light 6-pounders 1 x 5½-inch howitzer
'I' Troop (Bull)	Attached to the cavalry.	5 x light 6-pounders 1 x 5½-inch howitzer
RA Companies[22]	Notes	Equipment
Lawson's Company	Attached to 1st Division.	6 x 9-pounders
Thomson's Company	Attached to 5th Division.	6 x 6-pounders

Portuguese Artillery – Maj. Arentschildt KGA[23]

Da Cunha Preto's Company	1st Portuguese Regiment. Attached to 5th Division.	9-pounders[24]
Rozières's Company	1st Portuguese Regiment. Attached to 6th Division.	6-pounders
De Sequeira's Company	2nd Portuguese Regiment. Attached to 3rd Division.	6-pounders
Rosado's Company	2nd Portuguese Regiment. Attached to 3rd Division.	6-pounders

Source (regarding attachments): Leslie, WD and notes from the QMG, Col. Murray.

Colonel George Murray (Wellington's very able Quarter Master General had also given clear instructions to the CRA: 'the officers of the artillery will place their guns in the most advantageous manner for annoying the enemy in his advance up the slopes to attack that position'.[25] 'That position' being the ridge between the Dos Casas and Turones streams. The allies enjoyed superiority in artillery rarely witnessed throughout the war, with 42 allied guns to 38 French. Ross and Ingilby describe what happened next.

Massena made an effort to restore the spirit of his army, after recruiting it at Salamanca, assembling every man he could lay hold of, and advanced for the avowed purpose of relieving Almeida and driving us across the Coa. On the 2nd he had his whole force assembled at Rodrigo, and advanced on the third. We fell back to the position behind the Dos Casas river, and in the evening of that day the village was sharply contested for, but after three attacks remained in our possession.[26]

May 3rd. In the afternoon the village of Fuentes d'Onore [de Oñoro], which is on the road from C. Rodrigo to Almeida, was briskly attacked by the French and defended by the Brigade of Highlanders, supported by our guns.[27] A small rivulet divides the village. After a sharp contest, each retained possession at night of that portion of it on their own side.

May 4th. Everything remained quiet; nevertheless the shallow stream which separated the advance posts was only a few paces across, and the troops of both Armies, by silent consent drank and filled their water canteens at opposite sides, but with their muskets loaded and leaning against the walls ready to be seized and fired at a moment. The French foiled in the attempt to carry the village of Fuentes d'Onore, were observed in the evening to be moving troops to their left, and to indicate an intention to advance by the road coming from Nave d'Aver [de Haver].[28]

At six on the morning of the 5th, he commenced the attack with his cavalry, in the open country upon our right, which compelled Lord Wellington to throw back his right from the heights near Nave de Avea [Haver] towards Freneda [Freineda] upon the Coa. Their great superiority in cavalry made this movement necessary;

notwithstanding which, the steady conduct of our infantry and the galling fire of our artillery enabled it to be done without their being able to make any impression. While this was going on upon the right, the village of Fuentes was five times carried by the enemy, and as often were they beat out of it at the point of the bayonet …[29]

Curiously, Ross makes no mention of another affair on the 5th which was, in time, to embody the spirit of the Royal Horse Artillery. No account of the battle of Fuentes de Oñoro is complete without an interpretation of Captain Norman Ramsay's daring breakout, having been surrounded and cut off by the advancing French cavalry. Ross does in fact mention the episode in an earlier letter to his brother in which he questions the competence of the French cavalry rather than compliments his brothers in arms. 'Their cavalry were all drunk, and fought like madmen; but notwithstanding this … they did not do all they ought. They charged through Bull's guns, who mounted his detachments and sabred [*sic*] a

5. The Battle of Fuentes de Oñoro ~ 5th May 1811

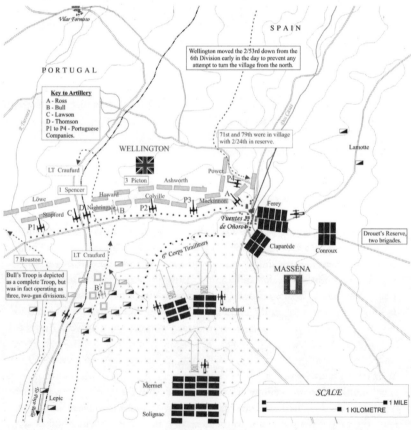

good many of them, and brought his guns off.'[30] Ingilby, who was just north of the action but most likely unsighted due to the rolling terrain, also records the achievement but credits the cavalry for setting the conditions for Ramsay's breakout. Cornet William Tomkinson with the 16th Light Dragoons dismisses the affair: 'the enemy's advance charged up the rising ground on which our horse artillery was posted, and passed two guns of Captain Bull's troop. Their advance was not well supported.'[31] Meanwhile Major Thomas Brotherton of the 14th Light Dragoons is quite clear that it was the actions of his squadron and a squadron of the Royals, who returned to drive off the French cavalry, which ultimately facilitated Ramsay's extraction.

> ... it was my squadron composed of a troop of the 14th and one of the Royals that charged the 13th Hussars to save his guns – and Lord Londonderry put himself at the head with me ... Ramsay, I found, could not see the head of the attacking column from where he stood and I sent an officer to him just before to warn him and see him cease loading his grape as I knew he had only seconds left at the scene.[32]

Jenkinson also credited the infantry for standing their ground. 'Their cavalry four to our one made the most desperate charges on our infantry and artillery, and but for the determined bravery of the former, and by the galloping fire of the latter would have destroyed all our brigades; as it was they galloped through Bull's guns, and compelled him to check them with his detachments, which he did to admiration.'[33] Captains John Kincaid, Jonathan Leach and Harry Smith, Lieutenant George Simmons and Rifleman Edward Costello, all members of the Light Division, prolific writers and in the thick of it during the orchestrated withdrawal, could hardly have failed to witness such gallantry, and yet none of them make any mention of Ramsay's exploits.[34] However, Lieutenant William Freer, a subaltern with William Napier's Company in the Light Division, does record the incident and provides a strong endorsement for Ramsay's actions on the day but hints, quite strongly, that the cavalry assisted the Horse Gunners in their breakout.

> We had not been long in this position before we observed the enemy forming columns in the wood opposite to that occupied by the sharpshooters, and on our right ... their cavalry collected in great force although played upon by some guns of Bull's Horse Artillery. The object of the latter formation was to take the guns, which they attempted by moving rapidly forward, following the cavalry to time, and had passed the guns and continued the charge against our horse, who falling back between the Lt Division and Genl Houston gave part of the latter Brigade an opportunity of giving them a volley, which had the effect of breaking them and causing them to retire in a confused manner ... The Royals behaved uncommonly well and made a severe example of a regiment of Horse Grenadiers. The Guns when passed by, by the enemy, succeeded in escaping by charging through them and joining the cavalry. The Division after these events formed squares of Regiments and shortly after, the whole retired.[35]

Wellington in his dispatch of the 8th May also makes no mention of Ramsay's individual action and recounts the overall activity as 'the enemy's efforts on the right of our position ... were confined to a cannonade and to some charges with his cavalry, upon the advanced posts'.[36] However, the fact that the commander-in-chief makes no mention of Ramsay is inconclusive, for not one word of Wellington's lengthy dispatch is devoted to the actions of his own artillery and not one officer or soldier of the artillery merits collective or individual recognition. This fact alone almost certainly contributed to subsequent events which culminated, several years later, in Ramsay's good friend, William Napier, penning the immortal words which elevated Ramsay's actions that day south of Fuentes de Oñoro as being 'wholly without a parallel in the annals of modern warfare'.[37]

> ... troopers were seen closing with disorder and tumult towards one point, where a thick dust arose, and where loud cries and the sparkling of blades and flashing of pistols indicated extraordinary occurrence. Suddenly the crowd became violently agitated, and English shout pealed high and clear, the mass was rent asunder, and Norman Ramsay burst forth sword in hand at the head of his battery, his horses, breathing fire, stretched like greyhounds across the plain, the guns bounded behind them like things of no weight, and the mounted gunners followed close, with heads bent low and pointed weapons in desperate career.[38]

Ramsay's escape was clearly both courageous and opportunistic but the elevation of this tale to a status which 'elicited the admiration of the whole world' merits further investigation.[39] Corresponding with Napier on the incident some years later, Brotherton recorded that, 'Homer himself could not have done more ample justice to our poor old friend Ramsay'.[40] However, there are three problems with this précis written 22 years after the event: the first is easy to dispel, it was not a battery but two guns; the second may be put down to poetic licence for in the same brigade as Napier were Leach, Kincaid and Costello none of whom saw fit to record the incident; the third is a harder sell, Ramsay would not have *burst forth* had it not been for the assistance of the 14th Light Dragoons and the Royals who turned to create the conditions for Ramsay and his detachments to escape.[41] Notwithstanding the role played by the cavalry or the infantry in assisting Ramsay, it still does not explain how or why this relatively minor action has gained such notoriety. It is also worthwhile considering, by way of comparison, an exploit which took place a few days later, and a few hundred miles to the south. During the closing stages of the battle at Albuera, the actions of General Jean-Dominique Bourgeat, an artillery officer, bought time for Soult's defeated French Army and all its supporting artillery to escape, an action which has largely gone unrecorded and which places Ramsay's achievements into some form of perspective.[42] The explanation, therefore, as to Ramsay's notoriety lies ultimately in Wellington's failure to recognise his Gunners in his post-battle dispatch.

To be fair, the cavalry too suffered from a lack of recognition in Wellington's subsequent report, a point not lost on Fortescue who stated that 'in future greater credit should be given to the four regiments of cavalry which took part in this battle, namely the Royals, The Fourteenth and Sixteenth Light Dragoons, and the 1st

Hussars of the German Legion. They, together with Bull's Battery of Horse Artillery, and not the infantry, are the real heroes of Fuentes de Oñoro.'[43] Bull's Troop aside, what contribution was made by the other allied guns? Ross and Jenkinson have very little to say about the exploits of 'A' Troop on either the 3rd or the 5th May; the former wrote that 'I had nothing to say to the affair, being on the left of the whole position';[44] while the latter officer wrote that 'Lawson's and Thomson's brigades, had to sustain a long and heavy cannonade from eight of the enemy's guns, 12 and 8 Prs. and 8 inch howitzers – but succeeded in silencing them'.[45] From this and his earlier comments about 'Bull's guns', we can conclude that 'A' Troop, surprising as it may seem, were probably not that busy but the other three British gun brigades certainly seem to have been keenly involved in the contest. Strangely there is very little about the four Portuguese brigades of guns. Private William Wheeler of the 51st was attached to the 'Mongrel Division' and he recounted that 'we only had two Portuguese Guns, one of these the enemy dismounted the first round they gave us, and the Portuguese very prudently scampered off with the other for fear it would share the same fate'.[46] No other mention of the Portuguese guns is readily apparent but it is clear that they played their part during the latter stages of the battle on the 5th May. Ensign John Cowell of the Coldstream Guards certainly saw Lawson's Company in action: 'at this moment part of Lawson's guns under Lane opened with grape on the French cavalry and mowed them down, destroying at the same time, many of our infantry, mixed up as they were in the *mêlée* with the French cavalry'.[47] Slightly later in the action Cowell noted that 'a shell passed through the tumbril of one of our guns that was in action in our front, and in its transient lit a portfire: the agility and rapidity with which the artillery-driver detached his horses from the shafts were admirable'.[48] At the culmination of the engagement Cowell witnessed and recorded the contribution made by Lawson's and Lane's guns.

> As the enemy began to withdraw from before us, their fire slackened; their guns first retired, then their tirailleurs retreated, and we rose from our earthy bed to witness some beautiful practice from Lane's portion of Lawson's troop [*sic*] of artillery. To cover their retreat, some heavy columns of the enemy's cavalry advanced to within six or seven hundred yards, and began closing up, bent, no doubt, upon mischief, when Lane opened three guns on them with spherical case-shot: the practice was excellent, the shells bursting within a hundred to a hundred and fifty yards from the head of their columns, creating chasms in their ranks, destroying and rolling over horses and riders, and drilling openings in their masses as if cut down with scythes.[49]

Lane also noted that 'a detachment was engaged at the combat of Fuentes Oñoro on the 3rd May and the whole brigade at that battle on the 5th May when Capt. G Thompson [Thomson] was wounded in the foot and Lieut. J. G. Martin ... was wounded by musketry and was with difficulty persuaded to go to the surgeon; there were various casualties among the men and horses'.[50] Wellington could not have failed to witness the involvement made by, in particular, Lawson's and Thomson's guns that day; that he chose to ignore mention in his dispatches is a clear indicator of the breakdown in relations between himself and Howorth, which were now in the terminal stages. The latter, perhaps inevitably, responded indignantly by penning his own version of events for the MGO (via MacLeod) and, in the process, embellished the proceedings surrounding Ramsay's 'breakout'.

I have the honor [*sic*] to acknowledge the receipt of your letter of the 7th ult: expressing The Master General's satisfaction at the public, and private accounts of the general good conduct of the Artillery under my command, and further desiring me to make known to Captains Bull and Ross, and the Officers and Men whose good fortune it has been to distinguish themselves … In this Army, unfortunately, it does not always follow that merit is noticed, for in Lord Wellington's Dispatches on the Battle of Fuentes de Oñoro, fought on the 5th ult., no mention, I am told, is made of the Artillery, and that one might consequently suppose he had none, or if he had, they had not deserved his notice. I have been told, for I have not seen the Gazette, His Lordship does mention something about the Enemies' [*sic*] Cannonade, but not a word of his own; upon this extraordinary occasion. I wish to mention to you, for Lord Mulgrave's information, the following circumstances, which happened relating to the Artillery in that affair.

The Battle commenced a little before 7 a.m. The Enemy having great superiority of Cavalry, continued advancing on our right, till they made direct charge on two guns, then in action, belonging to Captain Bull's Brigade, commanded by Captain Ramsay; notwithstanding these Guns were actually surrounded, and overwhelmed by the Enemies' [*sic*] Cavalry, still Captain Ramsay most adroitly limbered up, in spite of all impediments and interruption, made his Detachment draw their swords the moment they were mounted, and by acting as Cavalry, rescued themselves from this entanglement, and got fairly off without loss of man or horse.

Captain Lawson commanded a Nine Pounder Brigade, and Captain Thompson [Thomson] a Six Pounder; they were drawn up nearly in line together upon the Right, and in front of the Guards, from whence they kept up a heavy and severe fire, which checked the Enemies [*sic*] Cavalry, and destroyed many of their horses; I think I counted 60 dead after the Action. Captain Lawson's Brigade suffered much, having had five men killed, each by cannon shot, thirteen wounded, of who five lost their legs and arms by cannon shot; 27 horses were also killed and wounded. Captain Thompson was more fortunate, he had about three men wounded, two officers and seven horses, himself through the foot, Lt Martin [Lt John Martin from Glubb's Company, not mentioned was Lieutenant R. Woolcombe also injured] through the arm; his indeed is manifested in the Gazette, and is the *only notice* taken of them. Considering it therefore as a duty incumbent upon me, to mention the exemplary conduct of these officers on that occasion to the Master General, I hope that the humble source of this commendation, will not lessen the merits of Captains Lawson, Thompson and Ramsay, who have by their meritorious and distinguished conduct of the Battle of Fuentes, justly acquired my good opinion, although they have not been so fortunate as to be noticed to the Public, by higher and better authority.[51]

Howorth added a postscript a few days later. 'In my letter of the 19th ins., to you, I was guilty of a great omission in not mentioning Captain Bull's most admirable conduct at the battle of Fuentes de Oñoro, 5th May last, when he particularly distinguished himself by a skilful and well directed fire upon an advancing column of the enemy's infantry, which he checked most completely …'[52] Jenkinson, whose attitude towards Wellington bordered on hero worship, could not contain his anger but, in summing up, found the Board of Ordnance equally guilty of failing in their duties.

> You will be much surprised, when you read Ld Wellington's dispatch of the battle of Fuentes, not to find therein any mention of the artillery, at which we are justly most indignant, more particularly as we have had the pleasure of hearing their services extol'd [sic] in every society we have been in – if having to sustain a most destructive cannonade for many hours as Lawson and [Thomson] had, ultimately to silence the battery opposed to them, and to resist in various ways the most rigorous of charges of Cavalry do not form prominent features for public notice, it is useless to attempt to guess what can … that it is generated in the personal dislike of our chief, and that it is productive of contempt for, and oblivion of the Corps he commands – but that private pique should sway above public duty is not to be endured … yet I will not exonerate the Board of Ordnance for not enabling us to put our artillery upon that footing which could not but command respect, which can only be done by relinquishing that fatally obstinate attachment to guns of small calibre, when our enemy invariably opposes such heavy metal to them …[53]

On the field of battle, during those three difficult days, Wellington had 37,500 men under his command. Nearly 1,000 were Gunners and it is abundantly clear that their contribution, while not battle winning, was significant. Lawson's losses in killed and wounded represented over 13 per cent of his men; none of the infantry battalions, with the exception of the 71st and 79th who had been locked in the struggle for the village itself, had losses which exceeded this figure. The guards, alongside whom Lawson's men were fighting, suffered 6.7 per cent and 7.5 per cent losses for the Coldstream and 3rd Guards respectively. The inevitable and unequivocal conclusion to all this was that Wellington's failure to mention his Gunners was petty and unprofessional; they undoubtedly deserved better from their commander-in-chief. Ramsay was a brave man and by the time this tale had been woven into a fairytale legend he was long dead; that tale has long since inspired generations of Horse Gunners but it is time to recognise that other Gunner officers were perhaps more deserving of praise for their duty during the battle: namely Captain Henry Lane, who for the second time (the first at Buçaco) had demonstrated a level of bravery and professionalism which has escaped the selector's eye.

Notes

1. Whitehead, p.35.
2. Dickson, vol. III, p.337. Letter from Dickson to MacLeod from Lisbon, dated 19th January 1811.
3. Lt. Col. Charles MacLeod commanded the 43rd in the Light Division. He returned to the Peninsula later that year and died at Badajoz on 6th April 1812. There is a memorial plaque in the chapel of St. John the Baptist chapel, Westminster Abbey, with the following inscription: *To the memory of Lieut. Col. Charles MacLeod who fell at the siege of Badajoz, aged 26 years. This monument is erected by his brother officers.*
4. Jenkinson, letter from Valle near Santarem, dated 29th December 1810.
5. Ibid.
6. Ibid., from Valle near Santarem, dated 12th January 1811. Capt. Richard Francis Cleaveland RA (976) was Assistant Adjutant General RA at Woolwich.
7. Ibid., Pinensis (?), dated 22nd March 1811.
8. WD, vol. IV, p.668. Wellington to Lord Liverpool from Villa Seca, dated 14th March 1811.
9. Dickson, vol. III, p.362. Letter from Dickson to MacLeod, dated 21st March 1811.
10. Belson, entries 7–15th March 1811.
11. Ingilby, 23rd March 1811.
12. It is not known for sure that the one 9-pounder brigade was the one commanded by Da Cunha Preto.
13. Nicknamed the 'Mongrels' as the division included, *inter alia,* the Light Brigade of the King's German Legion, the Chasseurs Britanniques and the Brunswick Oels light infantry.
14. Ross, p.14. Letter from Ross to his brother (in the Engineers), dated 8th April 1811.
15. Jenkinson, letter from Vilar Formoso near Almeida, dated 8th April 1811.
16. Ross, p.14. Letter from Ross to his brother (in the Engineers), dated 8th April 1811.
17. Jenkinson, letter from Vilar Formoso near Almeida, dated 8th April 1811.
18. WD, vol. IV, p.683. Wellington to V. Adm. Berkeley from Arganil, dated 20th March 1811.
19. Although Wellington does offer some of the guns in Lisbon to Beresford to continue siege operations at Badajoz. WD, vol. IV, p.711. Wellington to Beresford from Celorico, dated 30th March 1811.
20. Ross, p.15. Letter from Ross to Dalrymple, dated 16th April 1811.
21. Although Bessières was to solicit Napoleonic rebuke for failing to provide Masséna more than the cavalry and a few horses.
22. Some of May's Company were in attendance on ammunition duty.
23. Two guns from Pinto's Company were left to support Pack in the investment of Almeida.
24. It is not certain that the one 9-pounder brigade was the one commanded by Da Cunha Preto.
25. WD, vol. IV, p.784. Extracts from instructions communicated by the QMG, heights near Fuentes de Oñoro, 3rd May 1811 at 10.00 a.m.
26. Ross, pp.16–17. Letter from Ross to Dalrymple, dated 13th May 1811.
27. This statement is not accurate; within the confines of the village were the light companies

from the brigades of Nightingale, Howard, Löwe, Mackinnon, Coville and Power.

28. Ingilby, 3rd May 1811.
29. Ross, pp.16–17. Letter from Ross to Dalrymple, dated 13th May 1811.
30. Ross, pp.15–16. Letter from Ross to George Ross, dated 9th May 1811.
31. Tomkinson, p.100.
32. Napier Papers, Bodleian Library, Oxford, MSS. Eng. lett. 41215 (d. 239), letter Brotherton to Napier, dated 28 March 1831. See also Brotherton's Memoir in Hamilton, pp.83–84.
33. Jenkinson, letter from position on the left of Dos Casas River, dated 9th May 1811.
34. Kincaid, *Random Shots for a Rifleman*, Leach, *Rough Sketches*, Smith, *Autobiography*, Simmons, *A British Rifle Man* and Costello, *Adventures of a Soldier*.
35. Freer, entry 5th May r/21. The Freer family provided the 43rd with three brothers and their young uncle. Uncle Gardner was killed during the French night attack at Talavera while serving as Gen. Stewart's Brigade Major. William's younger brother, Edward, was killed on La Rhune, aged 20, having joined 1/43rd on the eve of the Coa. The other brother, John, spent the war as a Gunner in Gibraltar and ended up as a Lieutenant General.
36. WD, vol. IV, p.796. Wellington to Liverpool from Vilar Formoso, dated 8th May 1811.
37. Browne, p.142.
38. Napier, vol. III, p.519.
39. Browne, p.142.
40. Napier Papers, Bodleian Library, Oxford, MSS. Eng. lett. 41215 (d. 239). Letter Brotherton to Napier, dated 28th March 1831.
41. See Oman, vol. IV, p.327. This fits in with other eyewitness accounts and explains why these exploits were not mentioned in any of the artillery eyewitness accounts and memoirs. Duncan's account makes no effort to research the facts and, quite rightly, receives criticism from Leslie, ch. IV, p.197. The other Light Division writer/source, Shaw-Kennedy, was not at the battle.
42. Dempsey, p.195. See also Ch. 11.
43. Fortescue, vol. VIII, p.175.
44. Ross, pp.15–16. Letter from Ross to George Ross, dated 9th May 1811.
45. Jenkinson to Sandham, Dos Casas River 9th May 1811.
46. Wheeler (ed. Liddell Hart), p.54.
47. Cowell, p.91.
48. Ibid., p.93.
49. Ibid., p.95.
50. Lane letters, p.15.
51. PRO WO 55/1195 pp.143–46. Letter Howorth to MacLeod, from Portalegre dated 19th June 1811.
52. Ibid. p.149. Letter Howorth to MacLeod.
53. Jenkinson, letter from L'Alameda [Almeida], dated 29th May 1811.

CHAPTER 11

Cleeves's Escape

For two days Masséna loitered to the east of the village of Fuentes de Oñoro fuelling the notion that he had not given up his quest to reach General Antoine-François Brennier and the French garrison at Almeida. In fact, the delay was for administrative reasons as the French decided to break the large convoy of provisions destined for Almeida and distribute this to the troops. Nevertheless, it left the two armies in a state of anxiety within pistol shot of each other and it was not until the 9th May that there were definitive signs of withdrawal. Lieutenant Ingilby recorded that 'in the afternoon the French seemed preparing to retire by withdrawing some of their troops from their front and other movements in their bivouac'. He added, curiously, that 'the remainder were paraded in clean white trousers, as if being reviewed'.[1] Masséna needed to get word through to Brennier, firstly to inform him of his failure to break through the allied line and secondly to instruct him to prepare the structure for demolition and to escape via the bridge at Barba de Puerco on the night of the 10th May where the escaping garrison would find elements of the 2nd Corps just to the east of the gorge. Three volunteers were enticed, through the offer of a 6,000-franc reward, to infiltrate the allied lines and get the message through; the first two, disguised as Spanish peasants, were caught and shot, but the third, Private Tillet of the 6e Léger, remained in uniform and succeeded in his mission.

Late yesterday evening [10th May] several rockets were seen sent up from the neighbourhood of the Agueda, and at midnight a loud explosion woke the whole camp. It turned out that the garrison at Almeida had employed themselves of late in mining the principal facings of the works, the rockets being signals from the French general [Masséna] of his inability to raise the blockade, they charged the mines and having matches to fire the trains, they suddenly sallied from the fortress, to the amount of 1,200 men, and instantly began their endeavours to escape through the investing force and effect a junction with the French army which had advanced to the Agueda at Punete de Ladrón near Barba del Puerco to favour their purpose. One half succeeded in getting across the river, the remainder were either killed or wounded and taken prisoner by our troops.

In fact nearer 1,000 Frenchmen slipped the noose prompting Wellington to call it 'the most disgraceful military event that has yet occurred to us'.[2] The ultimate responsibility for the defence of the defile lay with Erskine but Wellington had little time to dwell on the failings of this officer, or those under his command. Marmont, who had arrived at Ciudad Rodrigo on the 8th May, had assumed command of the Army of Portugal from a furious Masséna who only discovered his fate on the afternoon of the 10th May when Foy returned with a communiqué from Paris. Marmont was a gunner officer who had caught Napoleon's eye when they had served together at Toulon and had risen quickly through the ranks receiving his marshal's baton in 1809 at the age of only 34. He had commanded a corps with relative ease and with considerable acclaim and his arrival would have presented an additional preoccupation to Wellington who had his hands full trying to cajole the Portuguese government to take more responsibility for the reforming, re-equipping and re-supplying of the Portuguese Army and departments. Wellington had also decided to move the siege train, on board ships in the Tagus estuary, to Oporto and ordered Howorth accordingly. He was, however, less than happy that his orders to disembark the ordnance stores, and free up a number of ships, had not been executed by the artillery commander in Lisbon, Lieutenant Colonel Fisher. Howorth's response to this accusation infuriated the commander-in-chief:

> I have the honour to acknowledge the receipt of your letter of this day's date. I cannot but observe that, when you write to me to request that orders may be given to have a place put in such a state of repair as to make it capable of receiving stores, you should recollect that it is not in my power to give those orders, without knowing exactly what repairs are necessary; and you should take care, when you have no accurate knowledge upon the subject on which you write, to word your letter accordingly. Had you referred to the paper transmitted by Col.Fisher, you would have seen that the Colonel does not report any repairs to be absolutely necessary, excepting the bridge from the body of the place to the ravelin.[3]

Howorth and his staff should have known better, but to be fair, to both the CRA and his staff, he had lost his principal staff officer only two days prior. The Brigade Major RA, Major May, outlined the details in his monthly return to Woolwich: 'Major Downman, with Captain Walcott as adjutant, arrived here two days since, and Colonel Framingham immediately set out to take command of the British and German artillery in Alemtejo.'[4] May's letter also provided details of two additional companies which had arrived in theatre: Captain Harcourt Holcombe's and Captain Richard Raynsford's companies, which had both seen service earlier in the Peninsula under Sir John Moore. Both companies landed at the end of April and mustered, for the time being, in Lisbon awaiting further orders. On the same day that Wellington dictated his sharp response to Howorth, Beresford had received the confirmation he required that Soult was headed north to raise the allied siege of Badajoz.

Soult's army consisted of the 5th Corps complete and elements of the 1st and 4th corps (predominately cavalry from the latter two formations), providing a total of 25,000 which included 4,500 cavalry and eight batteries of guns.[5] Beresford's force was about 20,000 which included the 2nd and 4th divisions as well as Major General John Hamilton's Portuguese Division, Brigadier General Charles von Alten's German Legion Brigade and Brigadier General Richard Collins's Portuguese Brigade, two brigades of cavalry and six brigades of guns. Framingham was making best speed to assume command of the artillery but, as it turned out, he did not arrive in time. The artillery organisation was as follows:

CRA: Lt. Col. H. Framingham RA (Maj. G. J. Hartmann KGA)
Staff: Maj. J. Hawker RA and Maj. A. Dickson RA

RHA Troops	Notes	Equipment
'D' Troop (Lefebure)	Attached to the Cavalry Division.	4 x light 6-pounders
RA and KGA Companies	**Notes**	**Equipment**
Hawker's Company	Reserve.	4 x 9-pounder
2nd Cleeves's Company KGA (formerly Rettberg's).	Attached to 2nd Division	5 x light 6-pounders[6] 1 x 5½-inch howitzer
4th Sympher's Company KGA (formerly Cleeves's).	Attached to 4th Division	5 x light 6-pounders 1 x 5½-inch howitzer
Portuguese Artillery – Dickson		
Arriaga's Company	Attached to Hamilton's Division.	5 x 6-pounder 1 x 5½-inch howitzer
Braun's Company	Attached to Hamilton's Division.	5 x 9-pounder 1 x 5½-inch howitzer

Sources: Leslie, Laws, Duncan, Dickson (May), Unger and Teixeira Botelho.

Soult calculated that his force, outnumbering the Anglo-Portuguese, would be sufficient to persuade Beresford to raise the siege of Badajoz and withdraw back into Portugal. He was aware that the remnants of the Spanish Army of Estremadura were in the area, but he seems to have dismissed the notion that this severely depleted and demoralised force would make the slightest difference to the outcome of events. However, more significantly, Soult appears unaware, initially at least, of another force under General Joaquín Blake which had been dispatched from Cadiz and had landed at the mouth of the Guadiana on the 25th April and was making best speed along the river to Badajoz. This consisted of three divisions totalling 10,000 men and by the 12th May, Blake was 20 miles from the fortified city and in contact with Beresford. General Francisco Castaños, commanding the Spanish Army of Estremadura, had provided another 4,000 and, perhaps more crucially following the problems of allied command and control at Talavera and more recently at Barrosa, he had agreed to Beresford being the overall commander of the allied force of 34,000. The Spanish provided only a single battery, that of Lieutenant Colonel José Miranda, comprising six 4-pounder guns; Blake had been forced to leave his batteries for want of draught animals. Based on Wellington's memorandum, which he had penned during his brief visit during the initial stages of the first allied siege of Badajoz, Beresford had resolved, or at least had answers to, both the command and force balance issues of which the commander-in-chief had outlined in note; all that remained was to determine where to establish the defensive line to meet Soult. This decision too had been made by Wellington; with his legendary eye for ground, he had selected the small village of Albuera, 15 miles to the south of Badajoz.

Beresford, needing every available man, had decided on the 13th May to lift the siege of Badajoz completely and Dickson and the Gunners were busy removing the ordnance and stores and transporting them back to Elvas.

On the said night – the 12th – ground was broke accordingly for this purpose but – the approach of the enemy being ascertained with certainty – orders were given at one in the morning to discontinue working, and on the 13th I was directed to send away all the heavy ordnance stores to Elvas, and to use every exertion to save everything if possible. The numbers of pieces of heavy ordnance I had up were 29, with generally 400 rounds per piece; with exertion and not losing a moment, I had got everything in security by the morning of the 15th, and the same afternoon, I proceeded to Albuera where our army had taken up a position, and resumed command of my two brigades of field artillery.[7]

The position at Albuera is far from ideal; the ground is relatively flat thereby negating any significant advantage to the defender, but it is sufficiently rolling as to provide some degree of concealment for an attacker. The other problem was that Soult had three possible routes of advance on Badajoz and as Beresford was not sure of which route the French would take, he elected to cover the central axis at Albuera, but remained poised to react east or west as Soult's subsequent movement dictated. Beresford deployed the cavalry well forward to provide the earliest possible warning and by the night of the 14th May he had the verification he required and deployed astride the road at Albuera. The allied commander was, however, beginning to have doubts as to his decision to make a stand: his forces were still not up and he considered that Brigadier General Robert Long, his cavalry commander, had yielded the ground to the south-east far too readily and therefore not bought his commander more time to react and prepare. This hostility between the corps commander and his cavalry senior officer had been brewing since the action south of Campo Maior two months previously and culminated in Long's dismissal on the morning of the impending battle. Whinyates was with 'D' Troop RHA attached to the cavalry:

On the 13th May the cavalry, with our Troop of Horse Artillery which occupied Villa Franca, fell back by Almendralejo to Santa Marta. On the 15th we retired to Albuera, where we were joined by more Portuguese cavalry and baron Alten's Brigade of sharpshooters. Here we learnt that the army was marching to occupy a position near the village of Albuera, which stands within 300 yards of a stream flowing from the direction of Almendral and Torre [de Miguel], and falling into the Guadiana near Talavera Real. This rivulet flows through the valley from 1200 to 1600 yards broad, bounded on either side by rising ground of inconsiderable altitude and of easy acclivity. There is a stone bridge at Albuera, and close by, one of the many fords which everywhere traverse the streamlet. Our riflemen were posted in the village and on the banks of the stream, while the cavalry with our four Horse artillery guns (the two guns left in Lisbon had not yet joined) appuyed [covered?] their left on Albuera and extended in an almost parallel direction to the stream.[8]

In fact Whinyates's description glosses over the not inconsiderable difficulties of the allied deployment. Having determined that Soult was advancing via the Santa Marta–Badajoz road, Beresford deployed his army on the hypothesis that his opponent's aim would be to capture the village of Albuera and then storm the heights above. On the left were Hamilton's two Portuguese brigades supported by Collin's Independent Portuguese Brigade, Colonel Loftus Otway's Portuguese Cavalry Brigade and one of Dickson's Portuguese brigades of artillery under the command of Captain William Braun, which was equipped with six 9-pounder guns. In the centre, Alten's Brigade was in the village itself and, on the elevations to their rear, the three brigades of the 2nd Division were arrayed supported by both companies of KGA under the command of captains Andrew Cleeves and Augustus Sympher. Brigadier General William Lumley, who had replaced Long in command of the cavalry, was split with the 3rd Dragoon Guards, the 13th Light Dragoons and Lefebure's horse artillery located south of the village (near Dickson's second brigade of guns commanded by Sebastião José de Arriaga) and the balance to the rear of the 2nd Division. Still not in place by last light on the 15th May were all the Spanish and the 4th Division; the latter was supported by Hawker's four 9-pounders. Blake's troops were the first to arrive at around midnight and they moved to fill the allied right; however, in the dark and confusion they deployed too far forward and had to readjust their line at first light. The balance of the Spanish forces, a brigade under the command of General Carlos D'España, (from Castaños's Army of Estremadura) arrived at much the same time as Major General Lowry Cole's 4th Division at about 0700 hours.

First light was shortly before 0530 hours and the allied force was stood by their arms. It was a heavily overcast day and visibility was not good but the French cavalry could clearly be seen either side of the Badajoz road. The French troops were exhausted having marched through the night and when it was clear that Soult had no immediate intentions the allies used the time to readjust their lines and cook breakfast. Soult could not make out the allied deployment; Beresford had been directed by Wellington to keep his forces on the reverse slope, and with Hamilton's infantry covered by the woods and Alten's behind walls and in buildings within the village, it was difficult to determine the dispositions and strengths. The marshal could see Spanish troops but assumed these to be those of the 5th Army; he was firmly convinced that the 4th Army under Blake were still *en route*. He elected to demonstrate a feint against the village and with the 5th Corps complete, supported by the majority of the cavalry, to make a wide left flanking manoeuvre. The action commenced at 0800 hours with a French horse artillery battery on the west of the village.

> A Brigade of Horse Artillery, supported by Cavalry and Light Infantry, was drawn up about 600 yards in front of the bridge, and opened upon the troops defending the bridge and village. The Light 6-Pr. Brigade, German Artillery [Cleeves], of the 2nd Division, was posted on the right of Albuera with few Cavalry; the Light Division G.L. in the village, having at both bridges some Riflemen a little in front … As the Brigade 9-Prs. [Braun] was placed on the commanding spot within 700 yards of the place, and the French marched down a body direct to the village, I presume[d] a grand attack was expected on those Heights; but at the same time their largest force marched to their left … part of their cavalry crossed the small rivers a little above [south] the bridge, moving up the valley.[9]

> The wood through which the enemy advanced is pretty thick, and for a considerable time prevented us from discovering their intentions. Albuera is a small village, nearly in ruins, with the exception of the church and without inhabitants. The first appearance of the Enemy was the advance of seven or eight squadrons of cavalry, some light infantry, and a troop of horse artillery from the wood, toward the bridge at Albuera by the Seville road. They drove in our pickets on that side and formed in the plain commencing a fire of artillery towards the village, which was answered by some of my guns and those of the German artillery against the cavalry. At this moment I thought it was only a reconnaissance but soon afterwards a strong column of infantry was discovered advancing by the same road towards the bridge, and the brigade of General Stewart's division was sent to the village in consequence to support baron Alten. Soon afterwards another column was discovered moving through the wood to their left, apparently with a view of turning our flank, and the column approaching the bridge, having halted and beginning to return, proved that their effort would be directed on our right.[10]

Many on the allied side considered the action to the east of the village to be a feint but Beresford was less convinced and he moved not just Lieutenant Colonel John Colborne's Brigade up the village but also Brigadier General Archibald Campbell's Portuguese Brigade. It was a Brunswick Oel officer from Westphalia, serving on the Spanish staff, who was the first to notice and comprehend Soult's flanking intentions. Surprise on a Napoleonic battlefield was not easy to accomplish, but the vanguard of the French 5th Corps had made good use of the ground south of the village and had advanced some considerable distance before being spotted by Colonel Berthold von Schepeler. Beresford reacted accordingly and ordered the Spanish to swing *en potence* and face this new threat from the south but Blake was less easily convinced; with three French batteries now deployed to the east of the village, the Spanish commander was reluctant to expose his forces at right angles to this fire. In time, French intentions were patently clear and the Spanish divisions of generals José-Pascual Zayas, José Lardizabal and Francisco Ballesteros formed a line to face the advancing French with D'España's Brigade in reserve.

The heights which became the chief scene of action, were, however, occupied by some small corps of Spaniards, and when the design of the enemy was fully ascertained, our infantry made a counter-defensive movement in that direction. The French soon brought up some heavy guns and formed their troops under cover of some rising ground, which was at right angles to our first position and to the rivulet upon which Albuera stands. To meet this movement the Spanish infantry was formed on the first of the transverse heights, and the cavalry and Horse Artillery moved into a small plain on their right, and prolonged the alignment.[11]

Beresford also ordered Colborne's Brigade to move, from their new position on the outskirts of the village, to the right of the Spanish line and they were followed by the balance of the 2nd Division who remained in reserve. Cole also advanced the 4th Division to cover the Valverde road which ran due west out of Albuera. Major General Jean-Baptiste Girard's Division led that of Major General Honoré Gazan and they were supported by three field batteries, while Major General Marie-Victor Latour-Maubourg with the two brigades of dragoons and the light squadrons (which included the Polish Lancers) moved out further east supported by two horse artillery units. Dickson recalled that 'when the French column of infantry, supported by a strong corps of cavalry was marching … a thick shower of rain came on which much favoured their approach'.[12] Lieutenant Unger remembered it in much the same way: 'Many of our troops were immediately ordered to march to the right; a heavy rain came on, which prevented us for some time to perceive the disposition of the enemy.'[13] In fact the rain was so heavy that Brigadier General Jean-Pierre Maransin, commanding a brigade in the second division, recorded that it was not to the attacker's advantage. 'During this strategic manoeuvre to flank the enemy, a powerful cloudburst with the rain driven by fierce winds forced us to turn our backs towards the enemy and left us unable to take a step for a quarter of an hour, a circumstance that was to have a great influence on the start of the battle'.[14] This was the first of many torrential downpours that occurred and both the infantry and the Gunners had considerable problems preventing cartridges and charge bags from becoming inoperable through soaking.

As the allies frantically tried to readjust their defensive posture, Girard's leading division advanced in column towards the Spanish lines.[15] Neither Soult nor Girard could now be under any allusion that the Spanish 4th Army were indeed on the field, but with the rather pitiful performance by the Spanish at the battle of Gevora a few weeks earlier, the French commanders would not have been overly concerned. In fact, the defensive underbelly of the allied right was being furnished with very different troops from those of the Spanish 5th Army; Blake's 4th Army consisted of the most experienced and steady of (perhaps) all the Spanish forces and Girard was about to receive a nasty shock. The French two-brigade frontage of the leading division was about the same as Zayas's Spanish Division towards which it advanced but four times as deep. Girard's infantry columns moved into the attack and were met at about 75 yards with sustained and disciplined musketry from the Spanish lines, along the frontage, supported by well aimed canister from Miranda's battery to the left of Zayas's Division. The French were momentarily stunned by this display of professionalism and resolve by the Spaniards; their advancing columns began to slow and, as the hail of lead continued to tear into the French ranks, their momentum ceased altogether. Girard then made a fatal error; he gave the order for the columns to deploy into line. Such a manoeuvre was difficult enough out of effective range but in combat and under effective and sustained fire it was suicidal. Within minutes hundreds of the French officers and soldiers from the leading brigade were killed or wounded.

Miranda's men had served their colours well and many French participants recorded the accuracy and lethality of their fire. At about 1100 hours the first of the 2nd Division's reinforcements arrived and Major General Charles Stewart, realising that the Spaniards' right flank was exposed, ordered the first brigade to that section of the field accompanied by four of Cleeves's guns. To enable this reinforcing formation to engage the advancing French in the flank he ordered it to move south past the edge of the Spanish position and to deploy it in line so as to 'show a large front'. While Colborne's Brigade struggled to execute this complicated manoeuvre, Brigadier General Daniel Hoghton's Brigade closed behind the Spanish lines and for a time this additional firepower from an unexpected flank began to tell on the left-hand units of the 5th Corps. However, by extending Colborne's Brigade in line at a virtual right angle to that of the Spanish, Stewart had not only protected the allied right flank but had, in effect, exposed Colborne's men to an inevitable cavalry rejoinder. Soult's force enjoyed considerable numerical and serviceable superiority in cavalry; Latour-Maubourg was a most able commander and the ground perfectly suited to cavalry operations. The response, led by the Vistula Lancers, was swift, decisive and devastating. Cleeves, positioned with three guns and a howitzer in the middle of the brigade line, had little time to react before the French cavalry were amongst his guns; he struggled to get his horse teams forward and to limber up the guns and, for a while, three of his pieces were captured. His letter to Major George Hartmann (the acting CRA), four days after the battle, described the action:

> The enemy began the battle with a pretty heavy cannonade on our left, which the battery of artillery under my command opposed. The action getting warm on our centre and right, the first brigade of General Stewart's Division (Colonel Colborne's) was ordered to the scene of action with four guns of my battery, to the right of the head of the column, and the remaining two followed the rear. Getting near the enemy, I formed line, and came to action on the top of a hill, about eighty or ninety yards distance from the enemy's column (which I imagined was just going to deploy) to cover the formation of our infantry, which formed in the rear of my guns, making the hill nearly the centre of this front.
>
> The left of our line discharged a volley of musketry and charged the enemy, but were repulsed; the right did the same and would have been successful, had not, in this critical moment, our soldiers descried the enemy's cavalry, which tried *ventre à terre* to turn our right flank, and our line gave way.
>
> I then had no other chance left to cover our soldiers and save the guns (the men ran through our intervals which prevented our limbering up) but to stand

firm, and to fight our ground. We prevented the cavalry from breaking our centre; but finding no opposition on our right, they turned us, and cut and piked the gunners of the right division down. The left division limbered up, and both guns would have been saved; but the shaft horses of the right gun were wounded, and came down, and the leading driver of the left gun got shot from his horse. Corporal Henry Finke had presence of mind enough to quit his horse, to replace the driver, and then galloped boldly through the enemy's cavalry; his own horse, which ran alongside of him, secured him from the enemy's cuts and saved the gun, which I immediately made join the fight again. At this moment I was made prisoner, but had the good luck to escape unhurt.

Two guns were nearly immediately retaken; but the howitzer was carried off. Lieutenant Blumenbach was taken and wounded with the left division; Lieutenant Thiele and myself were taken with the right; the former badly wounded by the Polish lancers.[16]

The 2nd French Hussars made off with the howitzer but they were unable to secure the other two guns as French camp followers, who swarmed to that area of the field in the wake of the charge, cut the harnesses of the surviving draught horses and made off with them to the French rear.[17] The two guns were repossessed later in the battle. The small allied cavalry response was taken in the flank and driven back but, by now, the French cavalry were spread over a wide area and with the 2nd/31st having formed square on the allied right and the third brigade of the British 2nd Division in place, the French cavalry were recalled, bringing to a close one of the most decisive cavalry actions of the entire Napoleonic Wars.

Hoghton's and Brigadier General Alexander Abercromby's brigades were now ordered to conduct a passage of lines with the Spanish brigades to their front. This was a difficult enough manoeuvre at the best of times, but to order it to be carried it out in combat, in daylight and full view of the enemy, is example enough that Beresford was out of his depth. As luck would have it, at almost exactly the same time that Beresford ordered Stewart to conduct this relief in place, Maransin (who was now commanding the 2nd Division in the French 5th Corps) decided to conduct a similar manoeuvre moving through and relieving the shattered French 1st Division. Cleeves's other two guns and Hawker's four 9-pounder reserve guns had also been moved up in support of the 2nd Division, while Lefebure's horse artillery were on the allied right flank with the cavalry. The allied artillery took longer to come into action than the four French batteries that were concentrated on the rising ground to the south; indeed Lieutenant Charles Leslie of the 29th noted that 'this dreadful contest had continued for some time, when an officer of artillery – I believe a German – came up and said that he had brought two or three guns, but he could find no one to give him orders …'[18] Miranda's battery had withdrawn leaving only seven guns to reply to the 24 of the French, but this was merely a precursor to the most intensive infantry fire fights of the entire war.[19] Three battalions of the 28e Léger, supported by three from the 103e Ligne, faced off against (from left to right) the 48th, 57th and 29th battalions of Foot from Hoghton's Brigade, for a full hour, resulting in casualties on an unprecedented scale.

Surprisingly, the 2,000 casualties endured by the French during this single engagement were twice that suffered by the British, although as the French strengths were twice those of British in this part of the field, the ratio of one casualty to every two soldiers is applicable to both sides. Notwithstanding, with the French enjoying four times the number of well sited guns, such statistics are, at first glance, perplexing. Fortescue stated that 'the men stood like rocks, loading and firing into the mass before them, though frightfully punished not so much by French bullets as by grapeshot from the French cannon at very close range'.[20] However, this statement does not stand up to detailed scrutiny: firstly, the guns were not at close range, they were between 350 and 550 yards behind the front line of the French columns and, secondly, the two sets of infantry had closed to within 50 yards (in some cases even closer) of one another and although the French guns were on a slight rise it would not have been easy for the French gunners to engage the front of British lines with grape without inflicting considerable casualties to their own infantry. The few allied guns, however, had less restrictive fields of fire and were clearly able to fire shot, grape and spherical case with impunity into the mass of French to their front and

6. The Battle of Albuera - Situation at 1400 Hours, 16th May 1811

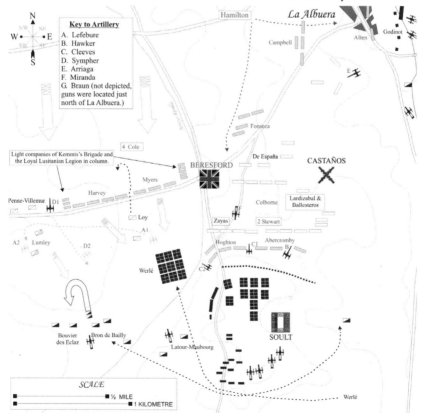

side. It was this very 'mass' which explains why the French suffered twice the casualties despite having twice the men. The sheer volume of grey-white smoke from the concentrated musket and cannon fire billowed low over the field and for the majority it would have been impossible to see the target let alone take aimed shots. The British were in two lines, while their counterparts were in densely formed columns; this resulted in it being far easier to score a hit or kill by firing into the general area of the French than vice versa. Furthermore, round shot was as likely to kill or injure half a dozen men, or more, as it continued its deadly path through the French ranks. Certainly, in the early stages of this contest, the fire from the French artillery took its toll but, as the two sides closed and visibility decreased dramatically, that advantage diminished.[21] However, what is perplexing is why the French gunners did not use their firepower to neutralise the allied guns, particularly the well situated brigade of Hawker's 9-pounders that was evidently inflicting huge damage on the static French columns.

Beresford was desperate to bring up additional troops to support the 2nd Division but, in view of the predominance of French cavalry, was reluctant to move the 4th Division who were holding the line of communication/withdrawal. The order to move Hamilton's Portuguese Division was delayed by an injury to the initial aide de camp bearing the order and by the second being unable to locate Hamilton who had moved closer to the village of Albuera in support of the Germans who were still embroiled in a stiff contest with Major General Deo-Gratias Godinot's infantry. Beresford then tried to personally move Carlos D'España's Brigade without having secured the brigade commander's permission and finally resorted to ordering Alten to abandon the village and 'come in haste to strengthen the centre'. Beresford's composure was, at this juncture, deserting him but it is curious that neither he (his staff), nor the Spanish, considered it sensible to move Miranda's battery of guns back up in support; although it is possible that their 4-pounder ammunition may have been expended. Soult, meanwhile, had now realised that Blake's Spaniards were on the field and that he was, therefore, outnumbered resulting in a decision, according to his subsequent dispatch to Napoleon, to hold the ground already captured and to move to a defensive posture. This may have sufficed while the battle continued in the centre but when the 4th Division began to form up in line on the allied right, the French commander realised he would have to deploy Major General François-Jean Werlé's nine-battalion reserve to counter. The decision to deploy the 4th Division was, as it turned out, decisive, but it was not made by the allied commander for when Hamilton could not be found and the Spanish could not be enticed to move, Beresford rode personally towards the village in search of the former. During his absence, which was for many minutes, Lieutenant Colonel Henry Hardinge took it upon himself to urge Cole to march his division in support of Hoghton's Brigade which was on the brink of collapse.

Once again the allies were outnumbered two to one: 2,600 allies to 5,600 French; but once again the French advanced to contact in column and once again the French were met by lines of muskets all able to bring fire to bear. Casualties were, once again, high on both sides. Sympher's Brigade of guns had moved with the 4th Division and was providing intimate fire support, while Lefebure's horse artillery was operating on the far left flank with the allied cavalry in protecting the division's flank and keeping the massed French cavalry at bay. At much the same time, Abercromby's Brigade, still relatively intact, executed a left flanking manoeuvre in the centre, against the massed flanks of the 5th Corps, and French resolve collapsed. Whinyates described the moment.

> ... at last the regular advance of Cole's, the steadfastness of the Portuguese, and the good countenance of the Walloon Guards turned the victory; the enemy gave way, and were successfully driven from the heights with immense loss. The advance and charge of the second Division against such masses of infantry and in such superiority of numbers was glorious, but it has been almost the annihilation of some regiments. Soult, however, though beaten, and most decisively so, carried off trophies. Three regiments lost their colours, or, more truly, the regiments being extinct, the colours remained in the hands of the enemy. We lost also one of the German artillery howitzers, the Brigade [Cleeves] having suffered in killed, wounded, and prisoners, forty five men. I am quite well and jolly, and did not get a scratch, although one of my guns was for a moment in the hands of the enemy, and I lost some men and horses.[22]

Dickson was adamant that when he was ordered (personally) by Beresford to withdraw, the commander considered the battle lost. 'The Marshal himself for a moment thought he was defeated, as I received an order to retreat with my artillery towards Val Verde [Valverde] and Baron Alten, absolutely by order, quitted the village.'[23] This was something Beresford hotly denied and it contributed to one of many areas of contention and controversy which dogged the aftermath of the bloodiest of all the Peninsular battles. Dickson added that, 'All this was, however, soon countermanded and rectified', for Alten had managed to retake the village with minor losses as the French had taken a considerable time to realise their opportunity and had only moved some light troops into the lower dwellings. Dickson also described the French withdrawal: 'the enemy gave way in their turn and were driven down with great slaughter, nor did they rally much until they had passed the rivulet when they retired into the wood'. What Dickson could not see from his position south of the village was what had initiated the French re-establishment of order. Brigadier General Bourgeat, the 5th Corps artillery commander, noted the fords blocked with fleeing infantry and that, as a result, the artillery was about to be cut off and lost. He immediately called forward the two reserve companies of artillery and deployed them, along with the 17 remaining from the corps artillery, in a long line parallel to the river. Their immediate fire was able to stem the allied pursuit and restore some composure to the demoralised French infantry. Once the fords were clear of infantry he pulled back the guns and supporting caissons by alternate companies, thereby ensuring that fire was maintained throughout the procedure. Lumley, the allied cavalry commander, was warmly criticised for not prosecuting the follow-up with sufficient vigour but, regardless, the actions of Bourgeat not only restored the situation for the French Army but also ensured that as many as eight artillery companies, and the associated caissons and carriages, were brought off without loss. This remarkable action of unsupported and relatively exposed artillery companies fighting off the follow-up of a victorious army has largely gone unrecognised.[24]

A victory it certainly was but there was little feeling of elation in the immediate aftermath of the French withdrawal:

> The field of battle was the most shocking spectacle that can be imagined. The dead actually amounting to thousands, were in heaps, and the scene was rendered more horrible by the Spaniards plundering and stripping the bodies, which consequently exposed the wounds in all their horror. Hundreds of wounded remained two days on the ground, unfed and undressed, and exposed to the burning sun – a situation infinitely more shocking than death itself; but the duties of humanity could not be extended at all.[25]

British (and KGL) losses (dead, wounded and missing) that day were 4,159, which represented 40 per cent of the total on the field: losses, in percentage/ratio terms, far worse than the first day of the battle of the Somme.[26] Portuguese losses were light in comparison at 4 per cent and Spanish losses ran to 10 per cent. French numbers were equally shocking at about 7,000, representing 30 per cent of Soult's total force. Allied artillery losses amounted to seven killed, 45 wounded and 31 missing, the latter nearly all coming from Cleeves's Company. Beresford, in his subsequent report to Wellington, acknowledged the contribution of his Gunners.

> I have every reason to speak favourably of the manner in which our artillery was served, and fought; and Major Hartmann, commanding the British, and Major Dickson, commanding the Portuguese, and the officers and men, are entitled to my thanks. The 4 guns of horse artillery, commanded by Capt. Le Fevre [Lefebure], did great execution on the enemy's cavalry; and one brigade of Spanish artillery (the only one on the field) I saw equally gallantly and well served.[27]

Wellington, conscious of the growing anger at the way the battle had been handled, felt compelled to amend Beresford's initial version of events. There is little doubt that Beresford's preliminary deployment and subsequent repositioning of forces, to counter Soult's flanking manoeuvre, were not well planned or executed but there is considerable doubt as to whether Beresford actually considered, as Dickson wrote, that he had been defeated. Dickson stated that the commander 'thought' this, but did not attribute this as a remark and so Dickson himself may have interpreted the commander's thoughts. Many on the field of battle that day, on both sides, would have entertained similar thoughts: Soult himself wrote after the event that 'everywhere victory was mine – but they did not know how to run!'[28]

Notes

1. Ingilby, 9th May 1811.
2. WD, vol. V, p.6. Wellington to Beresford from Vilar Formoso, dated 12th May 1811.
3. Ibid. p.10. Wellington to Howorth, Vilar Formoso, dated 14th May 1811.
4. Dickson, vol. III, pp.392–93. Letter from May to Baynes, Asst DAG RA, dated 14th May 1811.
5. Mortier had, much to his delight, been reassigned in March 1811 and command of the 5th Corps had been handed to Latour-Maubourg; however, at Albuera, in view of the large cavalry force, Soult had reassigned Latour-Maubourg to command the cavalry and temporary command of the 5th Corps had fallen to Gen. Girard, the senior divisional commander within the corps.
6. Contrary to what May wrote in his letter to Asst DAG RA, both KGA brigades had the 'standard' five guns and one howitzer. Although Unger's account and map of the battle (MD 228) list both brigades as having six 6-pounders, Dickson is quite clear (in the missing letter – see note 7) that when Cleeves's Brigade was overrun they were able to recapture their guns but not the howitzer, which was carried off by the French. Indeed in Ludlow Beamish, p.385, Cleeves's letter to Maj. Hartmann, explaining the circumstances of this loss, is reproduced and is referred to later in the main text of this chapter. Furthermore, Dickson wrote to both Napier (16th December 1830) and Beresford (19th March 1831) confirming the exact ordnance on the field on the 16th May 1811 and his reports following the battle and those made some 20 years later are consistent. The only area in which I disagree with Dickson is that of the Spanish guns; he lists these as 6-pounders but Spanish archives – Antonio Burriel, COS of the Spanish 4th Army – are quite clear in listing that Miranda's Brigade of guns were 4-pounders.
7. Dickson's 'missing' letter, Elvas, 22nd May 1811. In vol. III, Series 'C' of the Dickson Manuscripts, Leslie describes this letter as 'missing'; it was in fact in the possession of Mrs. Pat Burnaby (a descendent of Dickson) and was reproduced with Mrs. Burnaby's kind permission in the *RA Journal*, edited by Col. Desmond Vigors RA. In view of the paucity of other artillery eyewitness accounts of this battle, Dickson's letter is extremely valuable.
8. Whinyates, WCS, pp.59–61. Letter from E. Whinyates from bivouac near Solano, dated 22nd May 1811.
9. Unger, *Battle of Albuera.*
10. Dickson's 'missing' letter, Elvas, 22nd May 1811.
11. Whinyates, WCS, pp.59–61. Letter from E. Whinyates from bivouac near Solano, dated 22nd May 1811.
12. Dickson's 'missing' letter, Elvas, 22nd May 1811.
13. Unger, p.126.
14. Cambon, *Maransin*, p.82. See Dempsey, p.112.
15. They did not advance in mixed order (*ordre mixte*) as has been widely accepted in British accounts for the last hundred years, largely due to an error by Sir Charles Oman: Dempsey, pp.109–12.
16. Ludlow Beamish, pp.385–86. Letter from Cleeves to Hartmann from camp near Albuera, dated 20th May 1811.

17. Dempsey, p.137 – from Lapène, *Conquête*, pp.167–68. The howitzer was later recaptured by the British in Seville in 1812.

18. Leslie, LKH, p.222.

19. This assumes that Cleeves's remaining gun, removed during the French cavalry charge, was indeed back in action. Certainly, the other two guns, recaptured at a later stage, were not.

20. Fortescue, vol. XIV, p.200.

21. Hughes, HFI, pp.117–22. He provides a good account of the relative infantry strengths vis-à-vis effective muskets when comparing Line and Column. However, the artillery assessment is based on a statement that 'Fortescue and Oman both state that of the 3,000 casualties suffered by the French 1,000 were caused by the guns and 2,000 by British muskets'. He then goes on to explain how six (or seven) allied guns were embroiled in the contest and how many rounds they would have to have fired, etc. However, I can find no record of either Fortescue or Oman stating anything of the sort and, indeed, it would have been virtually impossible for either of them to have done so. What Oman does state is that 'the 5th Corps lost 3,000 men that day, and there can be no doubt that 2,000 of them fell during this murderous exchange of musketry' – Oman, vol. IV, p.387. However, this does not mean that the other 1,000 were killed by artillery fire, it merely means that they fell either during the earlier battle (against the Spanish and Colborne's Brigade) or later during the subsequent and final action on the French left.

22. Whinyates, WCS, pp.59–61. Letter from E. Whinyates from bivouac near Solano, dated 22nd May 1811.

23. Dickson's 'missing' letter, Elvas, 22nd May 1811.

24. See Dempsey, pp.195–97.

25. Whinyates, WCS, pp.59–61. Letter from E. Whinyates from bivouac near Solano, dated 22nd May 1811.

26. 27 Divisions went into the attack on 1st July 1916, numbering 750,000 men: 80 per cent were part of the British Expeditionary Force (600,000). 60,000 fell on the first day, representing 10 per cent of the total; although it must be remembered that the number killed (as opposed to wounded/missing) was far higher in the Somme statistics, due to the increased lethality of weapons a century on from Albuera. Indeed, half the 60,000 casualties fell in the first 90 minutes from 0730 to 0900 hours.

27. WD, vol. V, pp.36–39. Beresford to Wellington from Albuera, dated 18th May 1811.

28. Southey, vol. V, p.241.

CHAPTER 12

Dickson, the Die is Cast

Whether Albuera was a victory is a moot point; what is more certain is that following the battle, and that against Masséna at Fuentes de Oñoro, the tide slowly, but surely, began to turn. By the end of 1811 the French were no longer dictating either the pace or agenda of events. However, to enable Wellington and the allies to seize and hold the initiative they needed to besiege, capture and secure the key border fortresses of Ciudad Rodrigo and Badajoz. With these firmly in allied hands, the border with Portugal would be secured and operations to liberate Spain could commence. Wellington's experiences with siege warfare from the Maratha and Mysore wars in India coloured his early judgement in executing the art in the Peninsula; he quickly learned the error of that conclusion. The right tools and an able man to utilise those tools were also going to be essential; by the end of the year Wellington had both but not before the mighty walls of Badajoz had humbled his intentions on two occasions.

In early March 1811, when Wellington had been sure that Masséna was quitting Portugal, he had sent Beresford with nearly 20,000 men to Elvas to cover the southern corridor. They surprised Latour-Maubourg at Campo Maior at the end of the month and the allies reoccupied the town; they then began preparations to build a bridge across the Guadiana River and open communications between Elvas and Spanish Estremadura. Dickson, with one of his 6-pounder brigades, was up with the first infantry formations to cross the river and on the 7th April he received an order from Beresford's Quarter Master General, Colonel Benjamin D'Urban, to report to the marshal. 'On my arrival he desired me to make a return of stores necessary for the attack of Olivenza ... in case the enemy hold out. The only mode is to batter in breach, for which purpose I have demanded 6 24 Prs., and 2 9½ inch howitzers, the former with 300 rounds per gun'.[1] It was the break Dickson had been waiting for and, as if in answer to his prayers, the small French garrison obliged by staying put.

As soon as the enemies [*sic*] reply to the summons was received, the Marshal sent for me and desired me to proceed immediately … on the morning of the 15th [April] I began to batter a curtain close to a flank, and in four hours the breach was nearly practicable, and the French garrison so much alarmed that they surrendered at discretion, being about 460 in number … The enemy had 13 guns mounted in the place, but no calibre higher than a 12 Pr. They kept up a brisk fire upon us during our attack, but I only lost one artillery man killed with 3 wounded, and also a man of the 27th killed who was employed in repairing an embrasure.[2]

Five days later Wellington arrived at Elvas to give Beresford new orders; Richard Fletcher arrived at much the same time and the focus shifted to the far greater obstacle of Badajoz. Dickson's achievement at Olivenza would not have gone unmentioned and despite his disappointment at not being included in the direct discussions that ensued, he would have been elated at Wellington's instructions for the forthcoming siege, laid out in his Memorandum of 23rd April and personally addressed to Beresford, Fletcher and Dickson.[3] In fact, Dickson's exclusion from the initial engineer assessment was to act in his favour for Fletcher's plan, and the detail of the Memorandum outlined plans for attacks at three separate locations around the fortified city but most specifically on the Fort San Cristóbal located on the north bank of the River Guadiana. This, as it turned out, was an error. The weather delayed preparations but by the 8th May the investment was complete and Dickson, flushed with enthusiastic optimism, calculated 'that in about three weeks we ought to take the place'.[4]

Soult's appearance from the south less than a week later brought the first attempt on Badajoz to a rapid halt but, following Albuera, and in order to justify fighting that battle, it was equally quickly resumed.

On the 19th it being certain that they [Soult] were in full retreat, General Hamilton's division reinvested Badajoz, and I was ordered to proceed to Elvas to make again the preparations for the siege. On my arrival there the same day I found Lord Wellington just arrived, and learnt that two divisions – the 3rd and 7th – were on march from the North to reinforce us. As soon as they arrive Badajoz will be invested on both sides again. I am going on with my preparations, and Lord Wellington has told me I shall command the artillery for the siege. A company of British artillery [Raynsford's] is ordered from Lisbon to assist me.[5]

Two days before Dickson was to write to MacLeod declaring his meticulous preparations complete, Wellington had relieved Beresford of command and assumed responsibility for the siege. The strength of feeling against Beresford for his handling of affairs at Albuera forced the commander's hand and with General Hill on his way back to the Peninsula from sick leave the issue was, to all intents and purposes, taken care of: Beresford returned to Lisbon to resume his responsibility as liaison with the Portuguese political and military authorities. If Dickson was disconcerted at Beresford's rapid departure he certainly made no mention of it in his correspondence. The fact of the matter is that he was probably working flat out to assemble the train, the men to man it and the necessary ammunition. By the 29th May he declared 'our preparations are complete. My artillery marched, and Col. Fletcher breaks ground tomorrow.'[6] Dickson had assembled an impressive 30 24-pounder and four 16-pounder guns, along with four 10-inch and eight 8-inch howitzers (see Appendix 4). However, as Dickson was soon to discover, these guns were old and worn and certainly not up to the task of subduing a formidable structure like Badajoz.

> The ordnance employed at this siege, besides being of an excessively bad quality, was also totally inadequate in quantity to the reduction of such a fortress as Badajos, although every thing [*sic*] Elvas could supply was drawn from that garrison. The guns, it has to be stated, were of brass, false in their bore, and already worn from previous service; and the shot were of all shapes and diameters, giving a windage from 1-10th to half an inch. The howitzers used as mortars were defective equally with the guns: their chambers were all of unequal size, the shells did not fit the bore, and their beds were unsteady, so that the practice was necessarily vague and uncertain, and they proved of little service.[7]

Little surprise, therefore, that the guns started to fail at an alarming rate, prompting Picton to quip that Wellington 'instead of breaching, the operations appeared more like beseeching Badajoz'.[8] Furthermore, the structure of San Cristóbal was as formidable as the town itself and would not submit easily to battering or assault. The first attempt at assault was made during the night of 6th June; it was a complete failure. That on the 9th June was against the two breaches in the northern wall of the Cristóbal and fared no better. Wellington was to admit that 'we have not made a practicable breach in that [Cristóbal] outwork or in the body of the place'.[9] However, the same night he was to witness a level of resourcefulness which he had hitherto considered lacking in his artillery commanders. Attempts to prevent the garrison making repairs and clearing the ditch at the Cristóbal had failed because of the 'Portuguese grape and case, the iron and lead balls it was manufactured with being exceedingly small, so as to be of little or no use at 500 or 600 yards'.[10] When some 3-pounder shot arrived from Elvas, Dickson had it made up 'to be used as grape against the breach during the night, by putting eight or ten shot into a sand-bag, which formed powerful grape fire from the 24-pounders'[11]. Dickson's inventiveness had not gone unnoticed; nevertheless, Wellington was well aware that his own gamble had not paid off and with news of Marmont's move south to link up with Soult he had no choice but to call off the affair.[12] In his subsequent dispatch to Lord Liverpool he outlined the reasons for the failure and, most significantly, mentioned Dickson in the warmest of terms:

> The ordnance belonging to the garrison of Elvas is very ancient and incomplete ... although classed generally as 24 pounders, the guns were found to be of a calibre larger than the shot in the garrison of that weight. The fire from this ordnance was therefore very uncertain, and the carriages proved to be worse than we supposed they were; and both guns and carriages were rendered useless so frequently by the effect of our own fire ... Those who are accustomed to observe the effect of the fire of

artillery will be astonished to learn that fire was kept up from the 2nd to the 10th inst. from fourteen 24 pounders, upon the wall of the [Moorish] castle of Badajoz, constructed of rammed earth and loose stones ... and it had not at last effected a practicable breach. It was impossible to estimate the length of time which would elapse before a practicable breach could have been effected in this wall ...

I have every reason to be satisfied with the conduct of all officers and troops employed at the siege of Badajoz, whose labours and exertions deserved a very different result ... Lieut. Col. Framingham commanded the artillery, having under his orders Major Dickson, attached to the Portuguese service, who, during the absence of Lieut. Col. Framingham with the troops which were employed to cover the operations, conducted all the details of this important department. I have every reason to be satisfied with these officers, and most particularly major Dickson from whose activity, zeal, and intelligence, the British service has derived great advantage in different operations against Badajoz. Captain Cleves [Cleeves] of the Hanoverian artillery, conducted the department on the right of the Guadiana with great success. The service of the batteries was performed by detachments from the 1st, 2nd and 3rd regts. of Portuguese artillery, who conducted themselves remarkably well. They were aided by Capt. Rainsford's [Raynsford's] company of Royal artillery, who were indefatigable; some of them having never quitted their batteries.[13]

Such plaudits for the artillery from the pen of the commander-in-chief seemed unthinkable just a month prior; for Dickson they were the start of a process which saw him rise in a few short years to become the commander of the allied artillery, succeeding to what was a major general's command. Yet, had Framingham not been the regional artillery commander, the outcome for Dickson could have been very different.

Framingham has joined this army, and of course is general Commandant of the artillery, but Lord Wellington has desired that I shall continue to direct all arrangements for the siege, and to communicate immediately with him. I feel this as a very flattering circumstance, and at the same time the arrangement is fully to Framingham's satisfaction, whom I know spoke to me in the most handsomest manner of his Lordship. In short everything goes on as I could wish.[14]

Indeed so, but once it became apparent that Dickson's elevation was a more permanent fixture, not all the Gunner officers in theatre were happy with this arrangement. Bredin's Company was not attached to the army but had been left behind in the Lines, and subsequently the forts at Lisbon (Oeiras) when, in July, they were ordered by Wellington's staff to Oporto. Howorth was quite clear that Bredin, as a brevet Major and more senior captain than Dickson, could not serve under the latter's orders. Bredin, emboldened by the CRA's claim, made Dickson aware of his concerns at the first opportunity. Dickson, now with Wellington's ear, laid Bredin's objection before the commander and, emboldened by his support, wrote in response to Bredin's verbal objection.

As you gave it to me as your opinion last night that the two companies of British Artillery now at Oporto could not be under my orders in consequence of your being senior to me in the corps of Royal Artillery, I beg to state to you that you are entirely misinformed as to the footing on which I, as well as other British Officers in the Portuguese service, stand in this country. British rank, to make use of Sir David Dundasses [Dundas's] own words, remains dormant during the period Officers are so employed, but retaining the situation in their respective regiments they are to be promoted in their turn, their promotion being dependent on their good conduct in the Portuguese service equally as if they had always continued in the British. Under these circumstances it is obvious you have at present no right to consider me as an Officer belonging to the same corps as yourself, but as a Major of Portuguese service your senior in date of commission and in conformity of the practice of the allied army entitled to command as senior Officer when so directed. I know the order Colonel Framingham sent to Lisbon was to this effect being Lord Wellington's directions … I trust this matter will not create any misunderstanding between you and I, but as the difficulty must be cleared away if you will send me answer in writing stating your objections to this statement I will transmit the same to Lord Wellington for his determination.[15]

Bredin, electing for discretion rather than valour, did not respond but as a brevet Major he had a point and the episode serves to highlight the plight of Gunner officers with regard to promotion, brevet or otherwise. Around mid-May, following Fuentes de Oñoro and Albuera, the Prince Regent had instructed Wellington to make recommendations for brevet rank; Major Thomas Downman (former commander of 'B' Troop RHA) had arrived at much the same time and assumed the post of the CRA's principal staff officer – thereby releasing Framingham to join the artillery with Beresford's (now Hill's) Corps. Downman took up the cause on Ross's and Bull's behalf with General Stewart, who was in temporary command of the Light Division; he was assured that any oversight of their inclusion to the process of consideration was 'impossible'. Yet when the *Gazette* appeared, neither Ross nor Bull appeared; the former officer's frustration boiled over.

In it [the *Gazette*] there was not one individual promoted to Major within one year of our standing as Captains – some not within three, four, or five years, and I verily believe most of them little more than half our standing in the army. I trust I shall not justly be accused of assuming more than I ought, when I assert that we possess as much zeal as any of them; that our exertions must necessarily have been greater, from the nature and extent of our commands; that we have shared in all and every service that they have been engaged in; and that the conduct of our corps has in no instance fallen short of any merit that those to which they belong may lay claim to.

As it may excite your surprise that we did not receive any support from, or make any application through, our own Commanding Officer, it may be right that I explain the terms upon which Lord Wellington has long carried on duty with General Howorth, independent of the direct, unjust, and cruel insult offered to him and the corps by the total neglect of their distinguished services at Fuentes, [which] rendered such a step on our part impossible. Indeed, General Howorth would not demand an explanation wherein the honor [sic] and character of his regiment was so much concerned, but contented himself with sending a report of the case to the Master-General. We could not therefore expect him to exert himself for the interest of individuals. Upon his going to England, however, he offered to present any memorial to Lord Mulgrave we might wish, and recommended our correspondence that has taken place … to lay before his lordship; but for myself, I must own I don't entertain the least hope … After nearly seventeen years service, I find myself seventy steps from a Majority – a ladder which I shall in all probability be at least as many more in climbing, and I am refused a participation in the honor [sic] of brevet promotion with the rest of the army when equal pretensions can be brought forward … in addition to the claims that Bull and myself made upon Lord Wellington for the participation in the promotion, he was also spoken to on the subject by Sir William Erskine, who told me that he spoke in very handsome terms of both, but lamented that it was not in his power to do anything for us, which is quite conclusive in my mind that whilst on this service we have nothing to hope for.[16]

Dickson also felt he had a strong case for brevet promotion and he wrote to Beresford, submitting that application, in July.

Finding all the Officers under the rank of Lieut. Colonel that commanded corps at the battle of Albuera, or by the casualties of the service fell into command during the action, have received brevet promotion, I am therefore induced to address his Excellency on this subject with regard to myself and from the handsome testimony you were good enough to express on my services on that day, I feel every reason to hope that it may be considered I have also merited the same reward. Hoping this application may not be disapproved by you, and that you will have the goodness to recommend me to Lord Wellington or in such manner as you deem most proper.[17]

Hardinge, Beresford's Deputy Quarter Master General, replied instructing Dickson to resubmit his application 'so as to avoid the founding of your claim upon the promotion that has been given to Officers for the Battle of Albuera … *entre nous*, Albuera is a thread-bare subject, and as you have the weight of merit necessary to bear you successfully through your application express it according to the policy of the times, and touch but do not dwell upon Albuera'.[18] Dickson wasted no time in complying with Hardinge's suggestion and within days he had received a response which must have lifted his spirits enormously: 'your letter of the 19th was yesterday sent off to Lord Wellington with the Marshal's best recommendations, and there can be little doubt of its success'.[19] Downman meanwhile, had received a reply from Stewart which would have confirmed Ross's disappointment.

I have not failed to lay your letter of the 17th inst. before the Commander of the Forces, and I am directed by his Lordship to observe that the promotion to which he was directed to recommend was not to be confined solely to the Light Division, but the selection was to be made from the army generally. His Excellency took a larger proportion from the Light Division for the eminent services, and he is fully aware of the services that have been performed by Captains Bull and Ross. But their seniority in the army, compared with many officers in this country, cannot fairly at present bring them forward. I trust therefore, that the knowledge of the Commander of the Forces' good opinion of the zeal and abilities which the officers above have displayed will be as fully gratifying to them as if his Excellency had more power to recompense their several merits.[20]

As it turned out, Ross received his brevet promotion on the 31st December 1811 while Dickson had to wait until February the following year; however, such was the weight of patronage to Dickson's claim that he was made brevet lieutenant colonel a mere three months later. The whole system was nonsense and it was little wonder that it caused so much heat and light amongst Gunner officers; unquestionably, it was not helped by senior artillery commanders who failed to support those deserving cases and to petition for a change in policy with the Board of Ordnance. Howorth personified that lack of leadership and neither Wellington, nor the officers of the artillery, could have been other than overjoyed at his announced intention to return home to England due to ill health. Framingham assumed overall command in July 1811. In fact Wellington suffered an epidemic of applications to return home from across the force, 'some for their health, others on account of business, and others, I believe, for their pleasure'.[21] Howorth, on the surface at least, was returning for the initial reason; however, a letter from Framingham to Dickson some months later indicated that it may indeed have been motivation for the third. 'There are no letters from General Howorth. Report says that for a more speedy renovating of his health he has added to his establishment a blooming lass of sixteen. Much good may she do him'.[22] Sadly for Framingham, and the force, a replacement for Howorth was dispatched to Iberia at the end of the year; Major General Edward Borthwick had arrived in Lisbon at the end of November and assumed command a few weeks later.

A number of other changes had taken place with the arrival in May of two additional companies – Holcombe's and Raynsford's – and in August of 'E' Troop RHA commanded by Captain Robert Macdonald. By the end of the year the artillery organisation attached to the army was as follows:

CRA: Maj. Gen. E. Borthwick
Staff: Lt. Col. H. Framingham RA
Maj. E. Downman RA
Brigade Major: Maj. J. May RA
Adjutant: 2nd Capt. E. Y. Walcott RA

RHA Troops	Notes	Equipment[23]
'A' Troop (Ross)	Attached to Light Division. Received long 6-pounders in July 1811.	5 x long 6-pounders 1 x 5½-inch iron howitzer

'D' Troop (Lefebure)	Attached to 2nd Cavalry Division.	5 x long 6-pounders 1 x 5½-inch iron howitzer
'E' Troop (Macdonald)	Attached to 7th Division. Arrived 21st August 1811.	5 x long 6-pounders 1 x 5½-inch iron howitzer
'I' Troop (Bull)	Attached to 1st Cavalry Division.	5 x long 6-pounders 1 x 5½-inch iron howitzer
RA Companies	**Notes**	**Equipment**
Lawson's Company	Attached to 1st Division. Lawson was in England on sick leave and 2nd Capt. A. Thomson (1141) was in command.	5 x 9-pounders 1 x 5½-inch howitzer
Hawker's Company	Attached to 2nd Division.	5 x 9-pounders 1 x 5½-inch howitzer
Sympher's Company KGA	Attached to 4th Division.	5 x 9-pounders 1 x 5½-inch howitzer
Bredin's Company	Attached to 5th Division.	5 x light 6-pounders 1 x 5½-inch howitzer
Eligé's Company	Attached to 6th Division. Formerly Meadows's Company – this officer died at Castelo Branco on 4th September 1811.	5 x light 6-pounders 1 x 5½-inch howitzer
May's Company	2nd Capt. H. Baynes commanding. Located at Sabugal; in charge of reserve ammunition.	Nil
Portuguese Artillery		
Arriaga's Company	Dickson's (Artillery) Division – attached to Hamilton's Portuguese Division.	5 x light 6-pounders 1 x 5½-inch howitzer
Braun's Company	Dickson's (Artillery) Division – attached to Hamilton's Portuguese Division.	5 x light 6-pounders 1 x 5½-inch howitzer
Pinto's Company	Arentschildt's (Artillery) Division – attached to 3rd Division.	5 x 9-pounders[24] 1 x 5½-inch howitzer
De Sequeira's Company	Arentschildt's (Artillery) Division – attached to 3rd Division.	5 x light 6-pounders 1 x 5½-inch howitzer

Sources: Dickson, Laws, Leslie and Teixeira Botelho.

With Macdonald's Troop were two officers whose diaries provide a full and fascinating account of life on operations in Iberia: the troop's second captain Thomas Dyneley and one of the troop subalterns, Lieutenant William Swabey. The horse artillery troop had been stationed at Christchurch, on the south coast, when it received its orders for its first active service; they sailed on the 2nd August and arrived, due to inclement weather, on the 21st of the month. Within weeks the heat and rigours of campaigning were beginning to take their toll and Dyneley's fever, contracted while serving under General

Stewart at Maida and the siege of the Castle of Scylla, had manifested itself soon after his arrival.

> This is really too bad my dearest mother! a packet arrived yesterday, making the fifth since I left England, & only one letter from your party, & not a single line from that lazy fellow Robert [Macdonald]; he really is too bad. He would of course tell you that I had been unwell, & obliged to be left behind when the Troop marched. Perhaps it is quite as well I was, for they must have had a terrible time of it. The heat is beyond all imagination. I have already got ten of the troop back that have fallen sick upon the road, and obliged to come into hospital. As to myself, I feel completely recovered … my remaining here, keeps me in perpetual hot water, for I am in hourly expectation of an order to remain altogether, which order would most certainly drive me mad, if the troops were to get any of the blows [action] & I not there.[25]

For Swabey it was not just the heat that was causing him concern:

> On arriving at Villa Franca [Vila Franca de Xira], the scene between me and the Juiz de Fora [Justice of the Peace] must have been good, neither of us understanding a word the other said. I, however, contrived to get the billets, etc. There was much difficulty among the servants to-day, in consequence of their being unused to packing mules, and they were so late in, that we feared we would begin our march on an empty stomach, so their appearance at 5 o'clock was extremely gratifying. As to our quarters, fleas and bugs were the principal inhabitants, and so tormenting was their company that we did not regret a little fatigue, which supplied at last the place of an opiate.[26]

Meadows's Company were withdrawn from the Lines of Torres Vedras in April and a month later they joined up with guns and horses which had sailed from Portsmouth on the transport *Sybil.* Sergeant Charles Whitman was on board:

> We arrived in the Tagus the 28th May … our horses and men being formed into a light 6 pounder brigade, we were inspected by a Commanding Officer and ordered to march and join the Army as soon as possible.[27]

Within months Meadows was dead, having suffered a fatal heart attack; Whitman recalled that we 'marched at 3 o'clock in the morning to Castle la Branco [Castelo Branco] … our Captain was taken suddenly ill, with a pain in his hearty, and he died on the morning of the 27th inst. and was buried in the field'.[28] Captain John Eligé assumed command of the brigade and moved to Almeida where they were attached to the 6th Division.

Wellington had, in Dickson, earmarked his siege artillery commander but he now needed to resolve the issue of the tools. May, the Brigade Major RA, had written that 'in defensive warfare, we can, from our ships and depots established, do tolerably well without a Park (which we hitherto have never had) but in offensive operations

... a park is indispensible'.[29] In fact the long-awaited battering train had arrived at Lisbon as early as March 1811 but Wellington had decided not to use it, or to disclose its presence, for the first two attempts on Badajoz.[30] Indeed, he had issued orders to Vice Admiral Berkeley for the train to be moved to Oporto as early as the 14th May, even before he had resumed operations to take Badajoz following the battle at Albuera.[31] Fisher, the artillery commander in Lisbon, was instructed to place the necessary engineers' stores on board these ships. The stores and train, consisting of 78 heavy guns, mortars and howitzers, arrived at Oporto in mid-July and Wellington convened a meeting at his headquarters at Quinta São João (near Elvas) in order to issue his memorandum outlining the subsequent arrangements, responsibilities and timelines.[32] The Commissary General and engineers had a number of tasks but the lion's share fell to the artillery and Dickson in particular. Framingham forwarded the details to Dickson at the camp at Torre de Mouro (just north of Elvas) and while Dickson must have been delighted at his selection, the scale of the task would have been immediately apparent and somewhat daunting. The train, ammunition and stores were to be removed from the Royal Navy transports and reloaded on to barges and taken upriver to Lamego (actually to Peso da Régua), at which point they were to be transferred to carts and transported by road to Trancoso and finally to Almeida (although the memorandum states Ciudad Rodrigo). All of this, including time for Dickson to get to Oporto, was to be completed in 62 days! To assist him in this task Dickson was to receive the two companies of artillery at Lisbon – Glubb's and Bredin's.

Dickson, despite being racked with fever, made good time and arrived at Oporto (on schedule) on the 3rd August, the day after the two companies from Lisbon. He wrote a long and detailed letter to Wellington which concluded with an apology for 'entering so much into *minutia*' but it was Dickson's style and one of the principal reasons Wellington had selected him.

> On the 4th we commenced getting out the ordnance, etc. and have continued working with as much dispatch as possible. By the 6th day (9th August) I think we shall have the stores in boats, that is to say if the whole proportion of boats necessary can be got together, for in consequence of the state of the river, only one class [of boat] can be employed. The Douro is so low at present, that large boats cannot navigate part of the way to Peso de Régua, and small boats cannot pass the rapids above Vimiero [?] ... In the present state of the river, from all the information I can obtain, the boats will employ at least ten or eleven days to go up to Peso de Régua. I have found but one officer of civil department of ordnance here, which is a serious detriment to this operation being conducted with the system I would wish ... I am obliged to have made at least 300 ... strong blocks of wood about three or four feet long, with hooks and strong chains for the bullocks to draw the heavy guns ... In addition I am obliged to make 600 or 700 open boxes to place upon the bullock cars to carry shot and shells. The whole of the artificers I can collect from the arsenal and town are employed upon the foregoing works, which will require 8 or 9 days to compleat [*sic*]. The chief deficiency in this train is the want of block carriages for the conveyance of guns and mortars. There is no remedy but for the guns to go on their own carriages, and I dread much the consequences of this, that the carriages with the

guns mounted on them going over such roads as they must pass, will be so much shook as to be rendered unfit for the service required of them. For the 10 inch mortars there is absolutely no conveyance at all, except the sling and devil carriages, which it will be difficult to work bullocks in.[33]

With the Board of Ordnance's track record for inadequate provision being well known it begs the question as to why Fisher did not make a full inventory of the train as it lay on board ships at anchor in the Tagus estuary for at least four months. It left the enterprising Dickson a real challenge to construct carriages and tackle to maintain the tight schedule. Wellington had already decided that a subsequent operation against Badajoz was not feasible and now threw his entire weight behind a plan to attempt the capture of Ciudad Rodrigo before the year's close. The timetable he had laid down for the move of the train, plus an additional month to finalise the plans and secure the necessary siege stores, dictated commencement around mid-October. Such a scheme would certainly have resulted in the uniting of Marmont with (elements of) General Jean-Marie Dorsenne's Army of the North to break the siege but that amalgamation was preferable to a union of Marmont and Soult. However, Wellington was unaware that the Army of the North was poised to receive reinforcements of three divisions totalling 30,000 men.

Despite a recurrence of his debilitating fever Dickson succeeded in getting the train to Vila da Ponte (half way between Lamego and Trancoso) by the 20th September, although he owed a great deal to the CRA who dispatched May from his headquarters to cover for Dickson while he was bedridden. May, like Robe and Dickson, was a technical officer who thrived and excelled at the more scientific aspects of his trade; Dickson could not have wished for a more capable surrogate. Two days after Dickson reported his status at Vila da Ponte, Marmont moved with five divisions of infantry and one of cavalry while Dorsenne debouched with another four infantry divisions, including the two Guard divisions; the whole destined for Ciudad Rodrigo bringing to a rapid end any aspirations to capture the town before the winter.

A few weeks earlier Thomson's Brigade had been rendered ineffective through sickness and ordered back to Lisbon. Its place with the army was to be taken, much to Bredin's relief, by his company and Holcombe was ordered north to join the train. Dickson organised his charge into five divisions and one reserve as follows:

Commander Reserve Artillery: Maj. A. Dickson RA
Staff: Capt. W. Latham RA

Divisions of the Train	
1st Division	Lt. Bourchier (Glubb's Company)
2nd Division	Capt. Holcombe
3rd Division	2nd Capt. Power (Glubb's Company)
4th Division	Lt. Love (Glubb's Company)
5th Division	Capt. J. V. Miron, Portuguese Artillery
Reserve Division	Lt. Grimes (Holcombe's Company)

Source: Dickson.

Two distinct actions necessitate mention for they each, in contrasting manner, complete the story of the Gunners in the Peninsula in 1811. The first came soon after the battle at Albuera during the follow-up by allied forces, when, at Usagre on the 25th May, a cavalry action, supported by 'D' Troop, thwarted a rather abortive attempt by Soult to determine the strength of the force following him.

> On the 18th, we followed the French with cavalry and this Troop of Horse artillery, and continued to do so as far as Usagre, where we found 400 French cavalry, who retired. On the 25th, however, Latour Maubourg, with all the French Cavalry Division and some guns, marched from Villa Garcia [Villagarcia de la Torre] to attack us. In consequence of this temerity, he suffered a loss of at least 200 men. The French dragoons did not attempt to stand us, but the instant our jolly fellows came near them, they turned and were sabred in good style. Our guns were not innocent of mischief this day. We marched back here to cantonments yesterday (29 May), and hope to have some rest.[34]

However, further north, during Marmont's advance in September, events were less satisfactory.

> On the 25th [September] the enemy advanced, and his lordship disputed the ground retiring gradually from Pastores and La Encina, to the position at Fuenteguinaldo. In this advance the enememies [sic] cavalry and artillery were principally engaged, and on our side the cavalry, Portuguese artillery, and 3rd and 4th divisions of the infantry (Pictons and Coles). The principal feature in this was the enemy by a charge of cavalry gaining possession of 5 Portuguese 9 Prs. of Arentschildt's division (he is himself sick in Lisbon) which they were as quickly driven from the intrepid conduct by the 5th regiment of foot.[35]

Wellington, thanks to the charge by the 2nd Battalion the Northumberland Regiment, continued (for now) to be able to claim that he had never lost a gun in the field but as a result of the seemingly insignificant action on the 25th September, that was very nearly not the case. A month later, the Portuguese artillery gave a better account of themselves at Arroyomolinos when Hill inflicted a surprise attack on Girard's Division who had grown complacent having just driven back (west) a Spanish brigade under the Conde de Penne Villemur. There were two brigades of artillery with Hill's force; the first, Hawker's Brigade of 9-pounders, had to turn back on account of the roads, but the second was one of Dickson's previous charges under the command of Arriaga. He was delighted to recall that 'the Portuguese brigade of artillery was the 1st of my division, and I am happy to learn behaved well; it was one of those I had at Albuera'.[36] One of Girard's brigades was caught, completely unawares, forming up on the road to Merida. The brigade scattered, abandoning its baggage and artillery; a large number of prisoners were made, including General Bron, and Girard himself was lucky to have eluded the allied infantry.[37]

Fisher was, as we have seen, commanding the artillery garrison in Lisbon. Cleeves's German Artillery Company had joined him in June, following their considerable losses at the battle of Albuera and Thomson's Company had also been ordered back to Lisbon to recuperate after suffering a number of losses through almost constant campaigning. Gardiner had assumed command of Raynsford's Company as the latter commander had decided to resign on the 11th November; so Fisher's command was as follows:[38]

Artillery Commander Lisbon Garrison: Lt. Col. G. B. Fisher RA

RA and KGA Companies	Notes
Thomson's Company	Due to sickness the Company was ordered to Lisbon in September 1811 and replaced in the army by Bredin's Company.
Gardiner's Company	Formerly Raynsford's Company which arrived in May 1811.
Gesenius's Company KGA	In garrison at Lisbon.
Cleeves's Company KGA	In garrison at Lisbon recovering following the battle of Albuera.

Sources: Dickson, Laws, Leslie.

As the year drew to a close the mood among the Gunners would have been one of mixed feelings. Portugal had been liberated for a third time, three major battles had been fought and, to all intents and purposes, won; although Badajoz had eluded the allied army, they had managed to take the lesser prize of Olivenza and reoccupy Almeida and Campo Maior and, as the year faded, they had fought off Victor's designs on Tarifa. The siege train had arrived and been deployed; additional companies, equipment and horses had arrived and, including the companies in Cadiz and Gibraltar, there were 21 artillery companies and four horse artillery troops now in theatre. In addition to the death of poor old Meadows, Lieutenant Edmund Hawker, who had come forward from Lisbon (Raynsford's Company), was killed in action at Badajoz; lieutenants John Martin (Glubb's Company), Phillip Woolcombe (Dickson's Company) and Rodham Home (Robert's Company) had all died of natural causes; while Lieutenant William Johnson (Thomson's Company) had died while trying to cross a ford in June. Dickson would have been elated at his newfound status, while Ross would have been less sanguine about his prospects, although he would have been equally unaware that brevet rank was just around the corner. Framingham would undoubtedly have been disappointed that his overall command had been cut short by the arrival of Borthwick and there would have been hopes that this change of personalities would repair the recent rift with the commander-in-chief. Jenkinson was less convinced:

My expectations of any thing [*sic*] General Borthwick may effect for us, are not very sanguine, and I must confess I pity him from the bottom of my heart, for I am convinced that were an angel to come down from Heaven he would not please Lord W, or remove from his mind, that rancorous hatred of our corps.[39]

As it turned out, his premonition was not far from the mark.

Notes

1. Dickson, vol. III, p.377.
2. Ibid., p.383.
3. WD, vol. IV, pp.765–66.
4. Dickson, vol. III, p.390. Dickson to MacLeod, dated 7th May 1811.
5. Dickson's 'missing' letter, Elvas, 22nd May 1811.
6. Dickson, vol. III, p.394. Letter from Dickson to MacLeod from Elvas, dated 29th May 1811.
7. Jones, vol. I, p.71.
8. Robinson, vol. II, p.26.
9. WD, vol. V, p.80. Wellington to Stuart from Quinta de Granicha, dated 10th June 1811.
10. Jones, vol. I, p.59.
11. Ibid., p.60.
12. Marshal Marmont was the replacement commander for the French Army of Portugal following the removal of Masséna.
13. WD, vol. V, pp.88–94. Wellington to Liverpool from Quinta de Granicha, dated 13th June 1811.
14. Dickson, vol. III, p.394. Letter from Dickson to MacLeod, dated 29th May 1811.
15. Dickson, vol. III, p.437. Letter from Dickson to Bredin from Oporto, dated 4th August 1811.
16. Ross, pp.19–21. Letter from Ross to Downman from Las Agallas, dated 31st August 1811.
17. Dickson, vol. III, p.437. Letter from Dickson to Beresford from Torre de Mouro, dated 9th July 1811.
18. Ibid., pp.415–16. Letter from Hardinge to Dickson from Cintra, dated 17th July 1811.
19. Ibid., pp.422–23. Letter from Hardinge to Dickson from Cintra, dated 24th July 1811. See also WD, vol. V, p.188, Wellington to Beresford from Portalegre, dated 26th July 1811, in which he writes: 'My dear Beresford, I concur entirely with you about Dickson's merits and I will endeavour to get for him the rank of Major.' Also see Dickson, vol. III, p.444, letter from Hardinge to Dickson from Cintra, dated 14th August 1811.
20. Ross, p.22. Letter from Stewart to Downman from Elvas, dated 29th May 1811.
21. WD, vol. V, p.185. Wellington to Torrens (Military Secretary) from Portalegre, dated 25th July 1811.
22. Dickson, vol. III, p.486. Letter from Framingham to Dickson from Freineda, dated 20th October 1811.
23. The iron howitzers arrived in September 1811.
24. It is not clear which officer was brigaded with the 9-pounder guns and which with the 6-pounder guns.
25. Dyneley. letter from Lisbon, dated 26th September 1811.
26. Swabey (ed. Whinyates), p.27. Letter dated 27th September 1811.
27. Whitman, p.4.

28. Ibid., p.15, entry dated 25th August. In fact Meadows died on the 4th September 1811. Whitman wrote his journal in 1853 and so many of details are not that accurate.

29. Dickson, vol. V, pp.392–93. Letter from May to Baynes (assistant DAG RA, Woolwich) from Vilar Formoso, dated 14th May 1811.

30. WD, vol. IV, p.685. Letter from Wellington to V. Adm. Berkeley from Arganil, dated 20th March 1811. There were many French prisoners in Lisbon awaiting transportation back to England. Oman (vol. IV, p.549, footnote 2) is mistaken in assuming that the 19th July 1811 Memorandum indicated the arrival of the siege train into theatre and his comment that it 'would have been invaluable in May for the breaching of Badajoz' is therefore invalid.

31. Ibid., vol. V, p.10. Letter from Wellington to V. Adm. Berkeley from Vilar Formoso, dated 14th May 1811.

32. Ibid., pp.168–69. Source Jones: the train consisted of 34 x iron 24-pounders (644), 4 x iron 18-pounders (440), 8 x iron 10-inch mortars (525), 20 x iron 5½-inch howitzers (348), 10 x brass 5½-inch howitzers (348) and 2 x brass 8-inch howitzers (215). Figures in brackets indicate the ammunition for each piece of ordnance.

33. Dickson, vol. IV, pp.438–39. Letter from Dickson to Wellington, dated 6th August 1811. The sling cart and devil cart were used for moving heavy guns. The barrels were, as the name suggests, slung under the axle; to achieve this, the two wheels were around 7 feet in diameter. The sling wagon was even larger and had four wheels and was used to transport heavy ordnance over long distances.

34. Whinyates, WCS, p.62.

35. Dickson, vol. III, pp.471–3. Letter from May to Dickson, from Quadrazaes, dated 29th September 1811.

36. Dickson, vol. III, p.503. Letter from Dickson to MacLeod from Villa da Ponte, dated 15th November 1811.

37. The artillery consisted of 1 x 8-pounder, 1 x 4-pounder and 1 x 6-inch howitzer.

38. Raynsford's resignation was an acrimonious affair instigated by accusations of questionable courage at the siege of Badajoz by an unknown officer of the engineers. The CRA refused to support his case and so he considered resignation his only option. See PRO WO 55/1195 pp.193–99.

39. Jenkinson, letter from Puebla de Azara, dated 3rd December 1811.

CHAPTER 13

Borthwick, the Walking Target

Wellington's frustration at the failure to secure Badajoz the previous year was principally aimed at his lack of engineers; following his decision to lift the siege, he is rumoured to have muttered that 'next time he would be his own engineer'.[1] The number of trained officers of the Royal Engineers with Wellington's army was fewer than 35 and there was about the same number of Royal Military Artificers (the forebears of the Royal Sappers and Miners).

> Indeed, as a result of general experience, it may be assumed, that should an army, unprovided [sic] with sappers and miners, and the necessary materials and means to render their services efficient, be opposed by a place fortified according to the modern system, so as to have its walls completely covered, all the usual and known efforts to reduce it would prove unavailing; no period of time, nor sacrifice of men would purchase success, and the prudent plan would be to decline the attempt.[2]

Undoubtedly the questionable quality of the guns employed in the 1811 siege played a significant part and yet Wellington, as we have seen, had received the siege train from England as early as March and could therefore have employed it had he chosen so to do; furthermore, a corresponding lack of trained artillerymen was not an issue, particularly by 1811. The fact was that the British Army in the early 19th century was wholly unskilled in the art of siege warfare; true, Wellington had some experience from India, but this was against forts that were not built or converted to the *modern system*.

Learning on the job was not an option, for the one thing Wellington would not have, once the siege opened, was time. However, the one thing that Marmont's operations, in concert with those of the Army of the North, provided Wellington with was that very time. In the autumn of 1811, once the French commander had dispensed with the option of capturing Ciudad Rodrigo, Wellington now had the breathing space both the Engineers and Gunners required to prepare and train. Dickson had arranged the train into five divisions and a reserve division; and the officers and gunners attached to these divisions now began to conduct training on their respective equipment and on the conduct of siege warfare generally. Likewise, the few Military Artificers were engaged in instructing infantrymen from the line in making the requisite engineer stores such as gabions, ladders, fascines and wool sacks. In addition the route from Vila da Ponte to Almeida was reconnoitred in detail, repaired and prepared in anticipation. This task was given to Lieutenant William von Göben of the KGA; this is an extract from a very full report he furnished following his reconnaissance.

> I have the honour to report to you, that according to your orders I went along the road newly made, by Trancoso to Almeida, for the use of the battering train. The road I found to be good, as far as a league and a half this side of Trancoso, with exception of a few places damaged by the rain, which are easily repaired, but the last league and a half to Trancoso is hilly, in very bad repair, and according to the report of the *Capitão Mor* never was well repaired from the beginning, for want of tools … The road from the hill half a league on this side Vendada to Valverde is very hilly and bad, but can be ameliorated by leading it off to the right or left. Principally difficult to pass is the hill close to Carvalhal, going down to the river Ribeiro de Pinhel; two very steep places on this hill and a short turn to the right under the steepest of it, is at present unpassable [*sic*] … The bridge over the Coa is built up again of wood, and passable for guns … From Pinhel to opposite Santa Euphemia the road leads over some little hills to the right of Valbom; it is in several places destroyed by water, but easily repaired. The *Capitão Mor* of Pinhel was with me, and I showed him all the places wanting to be mended.[3]

It was a thorough inspection and an equally meticulous report and Dickson ensured that the requisite Portuguese labour was employed to effect repairs as quickly as possible. Also hard at work were three regiments of Portuguese militia and 400 British soldiers in repairing and reinstating Almeida. As early as mid-October 1811 Dickson was beginning to speculate that the battering train would remain at Vila da Ponte for the winter when, on the 14th November, Wellington wrote to Dickson:

> I believe that our train and stores, and the means of moving them, are in the following situation. The engineer stores, with the carts and bullocks, ready to move; the gun bullocks at Lamego, but the guns at Villa da Ponte, but the carts etc., employed by the Commissary Gen. I beg that you will order what there are the means of moving to proceed by regular easy stages to Almeida …[4]

Dickson corralled the bullocks from their respective pastures and began the process of transferring the huge train and associated ammunition and stores to Almeida. By the 21st November the six divisions had departed with all the ordnance and half the ammunition; 1,100 beasts hauled the great convoy over the demanding terrain. Dickson calculated that there were 3,000 cart loads of artillery stores and this was in addition to the 1,600 barrels of powder which were still at Peso da Régua which he could not transport for want of tarpaulins to protect the barrels from the autumn rains which had already commenced. By the 28th November all the ordnance had arrived at Almeida and, in an attempt to maintain security of future intentions, they were taken into the town under the pretence of being necessary to replace the guns spiked by Brennier and his men when he vacated the structure in May. Wellington had also instructed Dickson to repair these damaged pieces as best he could. There were a total of 92 in all; the rest were irreparable having been destroyed by having shot fired against the chase. It was an added distraction but Dickson got on with it in his characteristically industrious manner. The barrels had to be heated red hot and then the vents re-drilled but Dickson was to discover that the majority of the vents required new copper bushes and these had to be ordered and made to specification in Lisbon.

> As it appears that on unspiking the ordnance in Almeida the greatest part will require new bushing, Lord Wellington begs you will have the goodness to order a proportion of copper bushes to be immediately made in the foundry at Lisbon agreeable to enclosed return, and that they may be sent to Almeida as quick as possible. Also he requests your Excellency to give orders that civil artificer Joseph Holden, Ordnance department, who is ordered up for the said service may be supplied from the arsenal with such tools as he deems necessary … When the bushes are ready, Artificer Holden will accompany them to Almeida, if General Roza will acquaint Colonel Fisher when they are finished.[5]

Clearing the barrels of the spiked guns was another challenge, for the French had stuffed them with 'high shot, plaster, loaded shells, cartridges, spike nails etc.'; several Dickson had to leave to chance, pointing the muzzle at an earth bank and heating them, hoping for the best! Holcombe's gunners caused Dickson no end of frustration as they broke one of the drills in one of the 24-pounders earning the accolade 'bungling rascals' but he was hopeful they would improve. Of a greater concern was the transport of the artillery stores; he confessed in mid-December that 'unless I have much greater assistance, it will take a length of time to convey all the stores to this place'. Dickson worked in concert with the Commissary General's representative, Mr. Boyes, to turn the carts around as quickly as possible but, as it turned out, the stores had not all been delivered by the time Wellington decided to capitalise on a strategic development which delivered a tactical window of opportunity.

In October 1811 Napoleon began withdrawing troops from the French armies in Iberia for his impending Russian campaign; these numbers were not that substantial on their own but when Napoleon decided, at much the same time, to reinforce Suchet's success on the east coast the cupboard began to look rather bare. The east coast operation had been instigated by Napoleon at the end of 1810 in order to capture and deny the significant Mediterranean ports of Valencia, Alicante and Cartagena which, by this stage of the war, were maintaining the Spanish nation and her armies. Early successes by Suchet at Tortosa and Tarragona met with emphatic Napoleonic approval and, at the end of October 1811, with the battle (and siege) at

Saguntum fought and won, Napoleon directed that additional troops would be needed in the region for the final push to capture Valencia and then move on Alicante. His initial intention, to provide these men entirely from Joseph's Army of the Centre was quickly dismissed as his brother only had 15,000 men and to significantly reduce this force, which held the nation's capital, would not be wise; so he turned to Marmont for assistance. The divisions of Foy, Jacques-Thomas Sarrut and Louis-Pierre Montbrun were dispatched east to link up with General D'Armagnac (from the Army of the Centre), who was already at Albacete, and then move to assist Suchet. At a stroke Marmont lost a third of his force and, with the Army of the North having provided the lion's share of the troops destined for Russia, Marmont's options for both defence and reinforcement in his sector of responsibility had been severely curtailed.

When the remnants of Marmont's command moved into winter quarters, Wellington seized the opportunity and wrote to Dickson on the 1st January to 'hurry it on' as 'the operation will be undertaken immediately'.[6] The same day the commander-in-chief issued his Instructions to General Officers commanding divisions for the siege; the 1st, 3rd, 4th and Light divisions had been selected and they now moved from their cantonments to concentration areas close to 'the ground'. These four divisions were to provide the cordon as well as take it in turns to conduct operations; the weather was bitter and so each division was to be active for a 24-hour period and then relieved. Each division was also to earmark 20 miners and 30 artificers to be allocated on a daily basis to Fletcher and the engineers. In addition, Sympher's Brigade of 9-pounders was to be brought up onto the ground but then his gunners, along with those from Ross's Troop and Lawson's Company, were to assist Glubb's and Holcombe's men in preparing the batteries and manning the guns. Meanwhile the 5th, 6th and 7th divisions were brought up (slightly later) to around Almeida and Fuenteguinaldo to cover any move by Marmont to lift the siege. Their brigades of artillery, commanded respectively by Bredin, Eligé and Macdonald, moved and stayed with the divisions as did Lefebure and Bull with their cavalry divisions.[7] The gunners from Arentschildt's Portuguese artillery were manning the guns at Almeida.

The artillery and engineer parks were established, along with the troop cantonments for the siege, at Gallegos 10 miles east of Ciudad Rodrigo and 16 miles from Almeida. Dickson immediately set about transferring ammunition and stores to the park; in addition to all the artillery ammunition and stores that had been transferred from Oporto, there were now all the engineers' stores which had been manufactured by the infantry under the supervision of the engineers. A total of 2,500 fascines – 6 feet long, 1 foot thick; 2,000 gabions – 3 feet high, 2 feet 3 inches in diameter; another 30 gabions – 5 feet 6 inches high, 4 feet 8 inches in diameter; 1,800 tracing fascines – 4 feet long by 6 inches thick; 400 splinter-proof timbers – 12–14 feet long and 8–10 inches thick; 200 sleepers for platforms – 15 feet long and 6 x 4 inches square; 7,000 fascine pickets – 3 and 4 feet in length.[8] Such was the scale of this logistical operation that even Wellington himself got involved in the detail:

Ninety cars now at Freineda & sixty-six expected from Brigadier Alava to be sent on the 2nd to Almeida to be loaded, 106 with Engineer's stores and 50 with small stores of the Artillery; to carry these articles on the 3rd to Gallegos; return on the

4th to Almeida, and load with powder and shot, return on the 5th to Gallegos and lay down the powder and shot, and to be reloaded with Engineers' stores to proceed to Ciudad Rodrigo on the 6th.

The guns did not move until the 9th January for the bullocks had to be brought back from pasture at Viseu, over 60 miles away, a clear indicator that events had moved rather more quickly than Dickson, at least, had anticipated. Being wrenched from the winter cantonments must have also been a rude shock to the rest of the force; Jenkinson recounted his personal difficulty and gave a relatively shrewd assessment of the situation to his friend Captain Sandham at Woolwich.

My predictions respecting the preparations for the siege being earnest ones, were it should seem well founded, for the 1st, 3rd, and 4th and light divisions quitted their cantonments on the 5th inst, and such a day as we had for our march I never did and hope I shall never see again, for all the horrors of winter were marshal'd against us, which was a severe trial to me after my illness, as will also a tertian residence in the trenches; however I must hope for the best ... Do not be too sanguine respecting the result of the siege, for it is undertaken as much with a view of diverting Marmont from his present purpose of aiding in the conquest of Valencia, as with that of taking this place – should he however consider the subjugation of that province of such consequence as to pursue his operations against it, notwithstanding our attack on Ciudad Rodrigo, then shall we vigorously finish the siege, and I should hope, with our present means very soon reduce it ... our long preparations for this siege is a point very much in our favour ...[9]

The weather was so abysmal that the timetable laid down in Wellington's letter to Dickson could not be adhered to as the animals were unable to move through the heavy snow but, by the 6th January, Wellington's headquarters had moved to Gallegos and he, with Fletcher and other members of staff, made a reconnaissance of the town. The decision was made to attack the town from the north-west by establishing batteries on the two hills known as the Greater and Lesser Teson. This had been the same mode of attack adopted by Ney in 1810 but, since then, the French had strengthened the area by the construction of the redoubt Renaud on the Greater Teson, equipped with two guns and a howitzer, and by strengthening and fortifying the Convent of San Francisco and placing a large amount of artillery within the ruins to engage activity on both Tesons. The breaches made during Ney's siege had been well repaired but were undoubtedly a weak point. Wellington's plan was to capture the redoubt in a preliminary operation, build parallels and batteries as quickly as possible from behind the Greater Teson and, under the cover of the fire from these batteries, sap forward to the Lesser Teson to establish the breaching battery; then capture the two convents of San Francisco and Santa Cruz from which two of the (five) assault groups would be launched.

Within the town General Jean-Léonard Barrié was in command of a relatively smali force of about 2,000 men; it had been deliberately kept low to reduce the burden of re-supplying the garrison. In contrast, the number of guns was exceptionally high, including 153 heavy guns most of which constituted the Army of Portugal's siege train left there by Masséna when he commenced his third invasion of Portugal in September 1810. The day after the reconnaissance, Wellington wrote to Lord Liverpool, but he was not prepared to predict the outcome or the timescale of the endeavour. 'I can scarcely venture to calculate the time which this operation will take, but I should think not less than 24 or 25 days. If we don't succeed … I hope we save Valencia … if we do succeed, we shall make a fine campaign in the spring.'[10] The next morning, the four infantry divisions, already beginning to suffer badly from exposure, established the cordon and the operation commenced.

The preliminary operation to capture the Renaud redoubt took place at 2000 hours that evening and provided the perfect start; within minutes ten companies from the Light Division under Colonel John Colborne had captured the structure and work began immediately on a communication trench.[11] Wellington instructed Dickson of this success and hastened forward the guns, noting that the chief engineer would be ready for them as early as the 11th January.[12] The next night work commenced on the first parallel and the first three batteries; the distance from the parallel was about 600 yards and the batteries were each traced for 11 guns. The French responded furiously by pouring fire on the working parties and the captured redoubt. Early into the second night, the engineer on duty, Captain George Ross, was killed early in the night by grape shot from the San Francisco convent; Hew Ross would have had little time to mourn the loss of his last surviving brother.[13]

Work continued over the next two nights with a workforce of over 1,000 men provided by the duty division.[14] The infantry hated this work but with no sapper workforce there was no other option and for many the weather was so cold that the opportunity to keep warm through physical exertion was preferable to guard duty where many were found frozen to death at their posts the following morning. During the night of the 11th January the French moved a howitzer into the garden of the San Francisco convent which directly enfiladed Battery 1 and caused many casualties. The guns within the town had also 'now attained the range [of the batteries] so accurately, and threw shells so incessantly and with such long fuses, that half the time and attention of the workmen were directed to self preservation'.[15] These developments, coupled with the bitterly cold weather, were a concern for Wellington but on the 13th January two additional pieces of news occupied his mind. Firstly, it was now clear that the large amount of 24-pounder ammunition which was still at Vila da Ponte could not be brought up in time and, secondly, Marmont's return to Salamanca along with news that a number of his divisions were on the march towards the Douro valley could only mean one thing. However, in fact, Marmont first got to hear about the siege on the 15th January and the movement of the French divisions had been pre-planned in accordance with Napoleon's instructions in December of the previous year; in consequence Wellington's concerns were unfounded. Nevertheless, based on the situation as he saw it, Wellington, following consultation with Fletcher, decided to speed up the siege and to use the batteries on the Greater Teson to batter a breach rather than, as previously planned, engage the French defences.

The guns had arrived in the park on schedule and consisted of 34 24-pounders and four 18-pounders; the heavy mortars and howitzers were conspicuous by their absence. Wellington had made this decision for humanitarian reasons; after all, the town was Spanish and collateral damage under such circumstances would have been unacceptable. It was a standpoint that Wellington altered as the war progressed. Major May had firm views on the subject:

> The reason why mortars were not allowed to be made use of at Ciudad Rodrigo and Badajoz, was from a motive of humanity, these towns being inhabited by Spaniards, our allies. But though a proportion of mortars and howitzers should in all cases form a constituent part of a battering train, yet when a place be sufficiently garrisoned, it is not against the town but only for the destruction of the enemy's artillery, to prevent the breach being retrenched, and to clear all impediments as to fire in going to the assault, that their powerful effects should be employed.[16]

May was undoubtedly correct in this assessment but it was, of course, written in retrospect and highlighted the lack of knowledge about the conduct of siege warfare

7. The Siege of Ciudad Rodrigo - 8th–19th January 1812

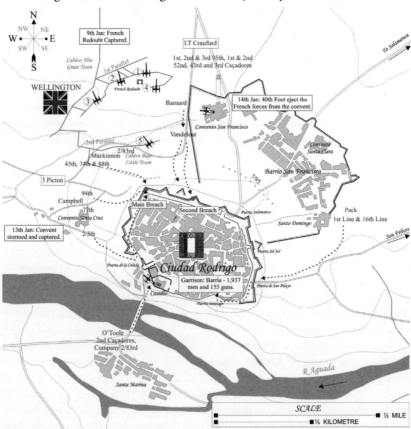

in the Royal Artillery at the time. A few weeks later at Badajoz, howitzers were used to enfilade the areas in front of the breaches and to neutralise the outlying structures, exclusively manned by the French defenders. Wellington's decision to use the first parallel batteries as principal breaching batteries against the walls instead of the enemy's defences had, in point of fact, given rise to a new concept of conducting sieges. Hitherto, siege warfare doctrinally had largely been the domain of the French and as May concluded, 'it therefore becomes interesting to inquire why they [the French] should be blindly and implicitly followed, since it is evident that the British, without suspecting it, by striking out methods of their own, have arrived at ameliorations in their service, and indeed in most of the mechanical arts, superior to their ingenious and warlike neighbours'.[17] Of course, Wellington's overriding desire for speed was driven by the size of his army, and yet a siege not conducted in the regular manner was bound, as we shall see, to be more expensive in human terms both during the preparations and during the final assault. Losses he could ill afford but were a necessary evil nonetheless.

To man the 38 guns a total of 541 officers and men were brought up; this, as it turned out, was not enough to cover the reliefs and replace casualties and so for the last two days of the siege it was necessary to use men from Ross's, Lawson's and Sympher's companies. Twenty-seven guns were placed into the first three batteries during the night of the 13th January (see Appendix 4) and, with the exception of two 18-pounders directed at the San Francisco, the balance began to batter the walls at the salient point between the north and west walls. That night the 40th stormed the convent and took the San Francisco and held it for the rest of the siege.

The batteries consisting of thirty four 24 prs. and four 18 prs. opened on the morning of the 13th and one day's fire proved that the hopes of Coll. Fletcher and Maj Dixon [Dickson] were well founded, and on the morning of the 19th the breach was declared practicable and capable of admitting fifty men abreast, and a battery of seven guns which had been opened in the 17th had made another, which though not so wide was equally easy to ascend.

Having stormed the suburbs on the night of the 16th we had three points of assembly and about 6 o'clock in the evening of the 19th the three columns assembled there and advanced to the wall and breaches, the former of which were scaled in two places and the latter stormed and secured in less than an hour – every effort to annoy our troops was made by the enemy, such as separating the breach by a ditch from the parapet and placing rows of shells along it, and pointing any gun towards it which could possibly be brought to bear on it – but all was in vain, for they were assailed by troops accustomed to victory and were determined to carry their point, which the French garrison soon discovered and fled in every direction and thus have we achieved that work in eleven days which occupied the French army of 63,000 men 32 days.[18]

Dyneley with 'E' Troop was also present at the siege, having convinced Borthwick, and subsequently Wellington, to allow him based on a rather spurious letter from the Lord High Chancellor of England. He was injured on the 15th January in one of the batteries and then seems to have involved himself at the main breach during the assault and earned himself a mention in Wellington's subsequent dispatch.

> I got a thump on the head from the splinter of a shell on the 15th, which brought me to the ground. I bled a good deal at the time and, having near two miles to walk to hospital, I became a little sick; however, I soon got the wound dressed, borrowed a horse and was back at the guns in less than an hour and a half … I do assure you the duty has been pretty severe, 24 hours on and 24 hours off, and we crowned it all with a most brilliant storm. I went down with our troops merely intending to see them make the start, but when there I thought I might as well see the whole of the fun, and made one of the party to enter the breach and certainly it was a very fine thing.[19]

Describing the storming of a breach as 'fun' and a 'very fine thing' is, of course, utter nonsense and his recollection of time was clearly flawed, but it does seem extraordinary how Dyneley was able to set his own agenda during the course of the siege and assault. Ingilby was commanding the field howitzer in Battery 5.

> I marched with the howitzer to assist in the batteries before C. Rodrigo. After the necessary preparations, and two breaches being practicable, at a quarter before eight o'clock in the evening the assault was begun. There was a severe contest for about three quarters of an hour at the breaches, but the troops succeeded in forcing them, and the 3rd Division having scaled the walls at other points, the place fell and the garrison were made prisoners of war. Generals Craufurd and McKinnon [Mackinnon] were both killed.[20]

From the Gunners' perspective the operation at Ciudad Rodrigo had been an undoubted success: 8,950 rounds of 24-pounder and 565 rounds of 18-pounder shot had been expended using 834 (90-pound) barrels of powder. Two gunners were killed and two officers and 27 NCOs and gunners were wounded, although three of this latter group were to die subsequently; but these figures were small compared to the overall losses during the final assault.[21] Borthwick submitted his post-siege report to MacLeod the following day:

> The siege of Ciudad Rodrigo terminated last night, by the place being successfully stormed in three parts of it, in two of which practicable breaches had been made; the first by four days firing from our front Batteries at a distance of 560 yards, the second by little more than one day's firing from a Battery not one hundred yards from the place.[22]

The behaviour of the allied troops following the capture of the town was, however, a low point in the whole affair; Dyneley made an interesting, if unsubstantiated, observation:

> The enemy soon left the ramparts and the scene of plunder, which took place afterwards, was dreadful to a degree. The poor wounded on both sides were

entirely stript [*sic*] in less than half an hour; fellows got drunk, and by 12 o'clock half the town was in flames. I am not far wrong when I say more than half our killed were killed by our own people; however, this is only for your own private ears, it is too disgraceful for the English name to relate. We lost General Mackinnon, blown-up; General Craufurd was mortally and General Vandeleur slightly wounded … The fire upon our batteries was really so hot that it was almost impossible for the men to stand to their guns. The Commandant of French Artillery says himself that he threw 1000 shells into our batteries, and I must do justice to say, artillery could not have been better served.[23]

Wellington certainly thought so, and in his subsequent dispatch to Lord Liverpool the Gunners were given a very satisfactory mention:

Major Dickson of the Royal artillery, attached to the Portuguese artillery, has for some time had the direction of the heavy train attached to this army, and had conducted the intricate details of the late operation, as he did those of the two sieges at Badajoz in the last summer, much to my satisfaction. The rapid execution produced from the well directed fire kept up from the batteries affords the best proof of the merits of the officers and men of the Royal artillery, and of the Portuguese artillery, employed on this occasion; but I must particularly mention Brigade major May, and Capts. Holcombe, Power, Dyneley, and Dundas, of the Royal artillery, and Capts. Da Cunha and Da Costa, and Lieut. Silva of the 1st regt of Portuguese artillery.

This was very satisfactory unless of course you were the commander of the artillery and, despite being wounded, you were overlooked, quite deliberately, in the commander's report. Jenkinson had predicted that Borthwick would not cut the right figure with Wellington: 'General Borthwick is expected today … they tell me he is lame, if so appearances will be against him.'[24] William Swabey was more practical, but no less unflattering, in his character assessment of the new CRA:

The arm of the service to which I belonged was then commanded by a gallant old gentleman, rather corpulent indeed, but of an indomitable spirit. When the relief from the trenches and batteries takes place, as all frequenters of such places can testify, the party relieved run off as fast as they can to get under cover; this gallant old veteran, however, neither could nor would run, so there he strode along in all his glory with shot and shell, musket and rifle, blazing at him, which occasioned Lord Wellington to designate him 'the walking target'. [25]

Within weeks Borthwick was invalided home and Framingham once again became the CRA, at least until August 1812. It was one less thing that Wellington would have to worry himself about when he tackled the second and more difficult 'key' to the south. However, falling out with his artillery commanders was now becoming a bit of a habit and there was more than a slight suspicion that Borthwick had not been given a fair crack at the whip.

You will no doubt, be a little surprised at the strange trap for the reputations of our senior officers [which] the service of this country has been. It was but very lately that General Howorth felt himself under the necessity to withdraw, and ... owing to some difference of opinion (we suppose) between Lord Wellington and General Borthwick, he has also left the army for England, and is succeeded by Lieut.-Colonel Framingham, the very officer Lord Wellington applied to have superseded, when in command, previous to Borthwick's coming out. This will surely work some changes in our regiment. Report says that Lord Wellington told Borthwick that he wanted an active officer to fill so important a situation as Chief of Artillery, and recommended him to go home. This may be exaggerated, but we really believe there is some truth in it. We have to regret in his departure the loss of an officer who was held in much esteem by his corps, and lament that his character was not better known by our Chief, from whom, I fear, he has not had a fair trial.[26]

The speed of capture of Ciudad Rodrigo surprised Wellington himself and credit must be given to the Spanish guerrilla force operating in the area under Julian Sanchez for its ruthless efficiency in preventing any timely communiqués reaching either Marmont or General Paul Thiébault (the garrison commander) at Salamanca. However, Marmont's predicament was such that, even with timely intelligence, he simply could not mass sufficient numbers to move on Wellington's six divisions. The very wet weather at the end of January and for the first week of February assisted the allied cause but long before Marmont gave up hope of moving in strength towards Ciudad Rodrigo, Wellington had already issued orders to Dickson to start moving the huge train back the way it had come. Hew Ross wrote to Sir Hew Dalrymple and provided an update on events.

The official accounts of the fall of Ciudad Rodrigo, with all the circumstances attending to it, must have long since reached you. It is therefore, unnecessary for me to say anything on that subject, beyond stating that I understand the breaches are thoroughly repaired, and two outworks which are constructing ... are in a great state of forwardness. At present the 5th Division occupy the place, and assist in the arrangements for its defence; but a special garrison from Castanos' army are to be put in it under a Spanish governor ... In it was found an ample store of ammunition and every other requisite for its supply, together with what is said to have been Massena's battering train ... a great part of which ... is now moving with exertion to Almeida; and I am concerned to add that my unfortunate troop is likely to be sacrificed in the performance of that labour ... The battering artillery has already been put in motion, and to judge from appearance, we shall very shortly make another attempt on Badajos.[27]

In prosecuting the battering and capture of the first 'key', both Wellington and Dickson had learned a great deal about the movement of heavy ordnance and associated ancillaries. The speed of capture of the second 'key' was, undoubtedly, a significant factor but there is evidence to suggest that, when it came to furnishing a battering train, corners were cut. Over the period of the 26th–28th January, Wellington instructed Dickson to send, by way of the land route (Almeida – Vila Vehla de Ródão – Elvas), 16 of the 24-pounder howitzers along with 26 of the 24-pounder gun carriages, and, by way of the water/land route (Almeida – Oporto – Alcácer do Sal – Elvas), 16 of the 24-pounder guns on block carriages. In tandem, Admiral Berkeley was tasked to procure an additional 20 24-pounders, likely carronades, from his fleet and, if these were not available, 18-pounders of these dimensions, a decision based on Fletcher's advice to Wellington, informing the commander that 'if 24-pounders were not available then 18-pounders would answer'.[28] This is an interesting development which suggests that Fletcher's opinion outweighed that of the artillery expert on matters which undoubtedly involved both technical corps. Indeed, Major John Jones RE, Fletcher's Brigade Major, in his work *The Journal of Sieges* has a footnote (most likely written by either Dickson or May) which states that 'the difference of effect produced by the concussion of a 24-pounder or an 18-pounder shot striking a wall, particularly at a distance of four or five hundred yards, is far greater than would be conceived ... no engineer should ever be satisfied with 18-pounder guns for breaching, when he can by any possibility procure 24-pounders'.[29]

Wellington refers to the letter sent to Berkeley in his correspondence to Dickson of the 29th January and in the same he also writes, 'I write to Major Tulloh [artillery commander in Elvas] to find out if there are any 24 pounder or 18 pounder Carron guns 9 feet long at Elvas'.[30] Three points emerge from these exchanges: firstly, Dickson had only recently left Elvas and surely knew the siege ordnance well, so why he was not consulted is a mystery; secondly, why was an inventory of available naval ordnance not known following the sieges the year previously when Dickson was scrabbling around trying to establish a suitable train for the first attempts on Badajoz; and, finally, what was our friend George Fisher doing throughout this time – he was, after all, the artillery commander at Lisbon, hardly an arduous task and one for which the knowledge of available ordnance in Lisbon (and the off shore fleet) and in Almeida and Elvas would surely have been an integral part of his job description. It all smacks of incompetence; and, inevitably, there were no 24-pounders to be had and, as luck would have it, the 18-pounder guns were not quite what Wellington expected or Dickson had hoped for.

> I inspected two 18 Pr. Carron guns, 8' 8" long on the wharf at the Naval Arsenal [Lisbon] that were pointed out to me as Russian guns the same as those you have embarked in compliance with Wellington's requisition. They are very rough in the bore; their calibre is greater than 18 Pr. And on the whole I do not hesitate to say that these guns are not in conformity to the spirit of Lord W's wish who is desirous to have ordinance of the late English construction such as are being used on board His Majesty's ships of war ... the windage of these Russian guns is upwards of 4/10 inch which is too great for the necessary precision in our service ...[31]

Dickson wrote repeatedly to Admiral Berkeley and Captain Hardy on the matter over the next few days but received no answer and, somewhat frustrated, he wrote on the 18th February to Wellington and ordered the Russian guns to proceed to Alcácer. A few days later he received a reply:

I received only this evening your letter of the 18th. I don't know what answer you were to expect from me upon the subject of the Russian 18 Prs. I wrote to the Admiral to express my disappointment, but there was no use in writing to you. You could not mend the matter, & there was no use in discussing with you by letter the resources which occurred to my mind, to extricate us from the scrape into which we had got notwithstanding all the pains I had taken to avoid it in consequence of the busy meddling folly of those to whom I had been inclined to trust on this occasion. I do not know if the Admiral will send you English guns or not. If he should not we must separate carefully & mark the English, Russian & the Portuguese shot, & we must use those of each nation in different batteries. The artillery officers must then calculate upon the windage of different descriptions of shot in their charges, & the direction & elevation of their guns: and as the shot in each battery will always be the same there will not be much difficulty in managing these pieces, as we experienced in the last siege, under similar circumstances. I hope however, that if the Admiral has them he will send English 18 Prs.[32]

Then, on the 27th February, Wellington informed Dickson that Berkeley had indeed found ten 18-pounders of English origin but Dickson considered the problems of having ten English and ten Russian 18-pounders with different calibres more trouble than it was worth and promptly suggested to Wellington that he persevere with the Russian guns. Dickson's concerns were based on the difference in the size of bore and *ipso facto* of the shot of these guns. The calibre of a Russian 18-pounder was 5.45 inches in diameter, while the English guns were smaller at 5.29 inches; with English shot at 5.04 inches this resulted in windage with the Russian guns at .41 inch compared to .25 inch for the English guns. Although these tolerances seem small the reduced velocity of the Russian guns firing English shot would have been significant. Dickson had received 1,800 Russian 18-pounder shot with the guns but this would not be sufficient; however, he was well aware that Portuguese 18-pounder shot was larger than English and slightly smaller than Russian shot and had managed to secure about 6,000 of the Portuguese shot which he considered would suffice.

Thus the third siege of Badajoz was destined to be conducted with a majority of guns of aged Russian origin, with significant windage and correspondingly reduced velocity, and of a calibre which alone would have precluded them as the weapon of choice. With everything resting on a rapid conclusion to capturing the second 'key' in the first phase of the impending Salamanca campaign and in the full knowledge, based on the previous failures, of the formidable task that lay ahead of them, it is hard not to find considerable fault with Wellington's judgement and the support he received from his technical arms in that decision making process. These were not decisions made in the heat of battle but basic operational staff work which should have been second nature to officers three years into the campaign. Not the best backdrop to events that were about to unfold.

The infantry and cavalry of the Anglo-Portuguese army moved some time after the guns in order to maintain deception. From the 19th February onwards the divisions began to move south, one after the other, and they were followed on the

5th March by Wellington who had remained throughout at his headquarters at Freineda. He reached his new headquarters at Elvas on the 12th March and, two days later, with all the forces in place, the guns and ammunition prepared, the engineer stores procured and manufactured and the pontoon bridge arranged and loaded, the order was given to commence operations. The bridge was laid across the Guadiana 4 miles from Badajoz and the investing troops crossed, consisting of the 3rd, 4th and Light divisions, and they proceeded to encircle the town. A few hours later the covering force, consisting of the cavalry, the 1st, 6th and 7th divisions under Graham, headed south on the road to Seville while a second force, consisting of the 2nd and Hamilton's divisions and the balance of the cavalry under Hill, marched along the north bank of the Guadiana towards Merida. The reserve consisting of the 5th Division and the independent Portuguese brigades of Denis Pack and Thomas Bradford were still *en route* and expected in the area within days.

Brigadier General Armand Phillipon was still commanding the French garrison but his force was now 5,000 men, more than twice the size of the previous year. In addition the defenders had considerably strengthened the overall defences: the glacis and counterscarp of the Fort San Cristóbal had been raised and the rear (southern) face and main entrance reinforced; the castle had an interior retrenchment and more guns on the ramparts; to the south they had finished one ravelin and strengthened two others; they had countermined the three walls to the right front; and they had dammed the small river to the east of the town, flooding a large area. Notwithstanding the speed with which Wellington's men had captured Ciudad Rodrigo, Phillipon and his men were confident that such a fate would not befall them and that support from Soult, Marmont, or both, would force the allies to lift the siege for a third time. Wellington, ever mindful of this eventuality, agreed with Fletcher's advice to leave the San Cristóbal and concentrate on the small Fort Picurina and, once that had been captured, the bastions of Trinidad and Santa Maria and the curtain in between.

Assisting Dickson were Holcombe's, Gardiner's (commanding Raynsford's former Company) and Glubb's companies of artillery and a detachment from von Rettberg's KGA Company which had come up with the ordnance from Lisbon. These British and German gunners were assisted by 566 Portuguese artillerymen. Dickson established three shifts, each with 161 men, as follows:[33]

First	Second	Third
Maj. H. F. Holcombe	Capt. R. W. Gardiner	Capt. C. von Rettberg KGA
2nd Capt. W. B. Dundas	2nd Capt. C. C. Dansey	2nd Capt. W. G. Power
Lt. R. Grimes	Lt. G. B. Willis	Capt. L. Daniel KGA
Lt. H. Thiele	Lt. F. Weston	Lt. D. M. Bourchier
Lt. W. von Göben KGA	Lt. E. Lüchow KGA	Lt. J. J. Connel
		Lt. J. Love

At dusk on the 17th March Fletcher traced out the first parallel opposite the small fort Picurina to house batteries 1 and 2. Two nights later the garrison executed a sortie to disrupt the works; losses were slight, although Fletcher was badly wounded and forced to conduct the rest of the siege from his sick bed. Phillipon's men, clearly well briefed, made off with about 200 of the entrenching tools. However, that night the allies expanded, unperturbed, the first parallel opposite the lunette San Roque. On the night of the 22nd–23rd March the first two batteries were armed and the following night batteries 3 to 6 were also equipped with their guns (see Appendix 4). The wet weather hampered operations and it was not until the 25th March that all the batteries opened against the Picurina, San Roque and main walls of the fortress. Wellington ordered the Picurina to be stormed that night; it was taken with little difficulty and relatively heavy loss but its rapid capture enabled the next set of parallels to commence and for the siege to enter the second phase.

Batteries 1 and 2 were now superfluous but the other four batteries continued to fire keeping the defenders' heads down at the San Roque and bastions of San Pedro

8. The Siege of Badajoz ~ 16th March–6th April 1812

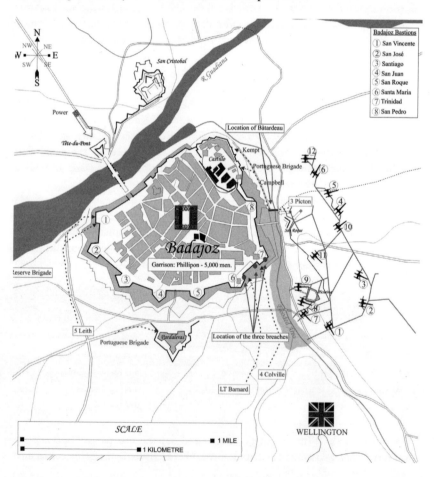

and Trinidad. The first of the breaching batteries was armed on the 29th March and the second the next night; these opened against the Santa Maria and Trinidad bastions respectively. The former was armed with eight 18-pounders and the latter with 12 24-pounders and yet, interestingly, both appear to have battered suitable breaches in about the same timeframe, albeit the one at the Santa Maria bastion was smaller. The assault was scheduled for the night of the 5th April but postponed by Wellington when it was clear that the defenders had retrenched the areas to the rear of the breaches and so a third breach was ordered between the two in the curtain. The guns in batteries 7 and 9 obliged and the assault was delivered that night. Lieutenant William Bent described the event in a letter to his sister Fanny.

> Our batteries were constructed almost under the walls. Between our batteries and the town, the French had contrived to let in water from the Guadiana … to such a degree as almost to render our approach to storm the town impossible. The breaches were reported practicable on the 6th of April; and that night Lord Wellington ordered the 3rd Division to scale the walls of the Citadel; the Light Division [and the 4th Division] to storm the breaches; and the 5th Division to storm the fort, which was on the outside of the town, and after that to scale the walls of the town near a gate … As soon as our Batteries had ceased firing & the French found the storming part was advancing, they placed Chevaux-de-Frises [*sic*] on the top of the breaches … 3000 men were on the top defending the breaches and firing down on our poor fellows who were in the ditch trying to get up. The French threw down all sorts of combustibles, shells, barrels of gunpowder, hand grenades etc. with lighted matches in them … The attack began at 10 0'clock & the place was not taken until 1, which was done by the 3rd Div under Gen Picton scaling the citadel and placing 3000 [men] in it, and the 5th Div scaling the town, which obliged the French to withdraw from the breaches and to give themselves up as prisoners … Poor Latham fell among the rest, prompted by a violent military zeal to enter with the storming party.[34]

Second Captain William Latham and Lieutenant John Connel were killed in action along with 27 gunners, and Second Captain William Dundas and lieutenants Robert Grimes, William von Göben, James Love and Ernest Thile were injured in addition to 55 NCOs and gunners. These losses compared to the infantry losses of 800 killed and nearly 3,000 wounded are small but were felt just as keenly. Dickson wrote to Latham's father, while Framingham wrote to Connel's; their contrasting styles speak volumes:

> It is with great regret that the painful task devolves on me of disclosing to you the death of your son captain Latham. He fell nobly in the great breach at the assault of this place on the night of the 6th inst., being in the immediate command of detachments of artillery that accompanied the several columns to the assault. It is impossible for me to express in words anything that can serve to alleviate such a loss, but at a hereafter period when the first weight of sorrow is abated, it will be consolatory and gratifying reflection in knowing that he died possessing universal

admiration and esteem … the fatal wound that deprived him at once of life. He was found on the spot where he fell, and was entered yesterday with as much decency as in my power, followed to the grave by his brother Officers.[35]

It is with the deepest concerns I inform you of the death of Lieutenant Connel of the Royal Artillery, he was killed in the batteries, when nobly fighting his guns, by a cannon shot which went through him …[36]

The cost of taking Badajoz was high but with Soult closing on the town the decision to assault the breaches was understandable, and with the second 'key' in Wellington's hands he now held all the aces. The greatest sacrifice had, for the second time, befallen the infantry but that did not stop him mentioning the artillery, and Dickson in particular, in the most favourable manner.

Major Dickson conducted the details of the artillery service during the siege, as well as upon former occasions, under the general superintendence of Col. Framingham, who, since the absence of Major Gen. Borthwick, has commanded the artillery with the army. I cannot sufficiently applaud the officers and soldiers of the Royal and Portuguese artillery during the siege; particularly Lieut. Col. Robe who opened the breaching batteries; Major May, Capt. Gardiner, Major Holcombe, and Lieut. Bourchier of the Royal artillery; Capt. de [von] Rettberg of the German, and Major Tulloh of the Portuguese artillery. Adverting to the extent of the details of the ordnance department during this siege, to the difficulties of the weather, etc., with which Major Dickson had to contend, I must mention him most particularly to your Lordship.[37]

Exactly one year earlier, when he found himself in charge of Portuguese guns and not an integral part of the main army, Dickson had yearned for action and recognition. No one, least of all himself, could have ever predicted the speed with which his star would rise. It had been, quite simply, meteoric; such is war. Lieutenant Colonel William Robe had returned to Iberia the year previously in a more or less advisory capacity and it is interesting to note that Robe, Dickson and May, probably the best technical gunnery officers in their peer group, found themselves working together for the greater good of the Royal Artillery and Wellington's allied army. It could not have been better timed.

Notes

1. Burgoyne, p.135.
2. Jones, vol. I, p.xvii.
3. WD, vol. V, pp.488–90. Letter from von Göben to Dickson from Vila da Ponte, dated 25th October 1811. A league was a measure of land distance which equated to the distance a person or horse could walk in an hour; this was generally considered (on

land) to be about 3 miles. The entire distance of the route was about 50 miles, about 16.6 leagues. Interestingly, von Göben estimated about 13 leagues (in his report), which perhaps highlights the imprecise nature of this system and the difficulty of judging distance over hilly terrain.

4. Ibid. p.365. Wellington to Dickson from Freineda, dated 14th November 1811.

5. Ibid., p.512. Dickson to Beresford from Freineda, dated 4th December 1811.

6. Dickson, vol. IV, p.562. Letter from Dickson to MacLeod from Freineda, dated 1 January 1812.

7. WD, vol. V. pp.450–51. See also Fortescue, vol. VIII, p.350; and Dickson, vol. IV, pp.566–67.

8. Jones, vol. I, p.90.

9. Jenkinson, letter from El Badon [El Bodón], dated 7th January 1812.

10. WD, vol. V, p.461. Wellington to Liverpool from Gallegos, dated 7th January 1812.

11. Four companies executed the attack; two from the 52nd and two from the 43rd.

12. WD, vol. V, p.462. Wellington to Dickson from Gallegos, dated 9th January 1812.

13. Jones, vol. I, p.107. Ross, p.24. Note: of his three other brothers, the eldest, a clergyman of the Church of England, was lost in a ship which was supposed to have foundered in the West Indies. The second died in London. The youngest died of yellow fever while serving as a midshipman in the West Indies.

14. The rotation was conducted in the order, Light, 1st, 3rd, 4th.

15. Jones, vol. I, p.110.

16. May, p.19.

17. Ibid., p.8.

18. Jenkinson, letter from El Badon [El Bodón], dated 20th January 1812.

19. Dyneley, letter to Douglas from Fuentes d'Onore [de Oñoro], dated 22nd January 1812.

20. Ingilby, 19th January 1812.

21. Overall allied losses were nine officers and 186 other ranks killed, and 70 officers and 846 other ranks wounded. Source Oman.

22. PRO WO 55/1195. Letter from Borthwick to MacLeod from Gallegos, dated 20th January 1812.

23. Dyneley, letter to Douglas from Fuentes d'Onore [de Oñoro], dated 22nd January 1812.

24. Jenkinson, letter from Puebla de Azaba, dated 1st January 1812.

25. Swabey (ed. Whinyates), p.27. Letter dated 15th January 1812.

26. Ross, pp.26–27. Letter from Ross to Dalrymple from a camp before Badajoz, dated 27th March 1812.

27. Ibid., pp.19–21. Letter from Ross to Dalrymple from El Bodón, dated 29th January 1812.

28. WD, vol. V, p.490. Wellington to Dickson from Gallegos, dated 29th January 1812.

29. Jones, vol. I, p.145. Dickson and May are credited in the preface of this work as having provided the 'additional artillery details'.

30. WD, vol. V, p.490. Wellington to Dickson from Gallegos, dated 29th January 1812.

31. Dickson, vol. IV, p.586. Letter from Dickson to Berkeley from Lisbon, dated 12th February 1812.

32. Ibid., pp.597–98.
33. Ibid., pp.613–14.
34. James Clavell Library MD 632. Letter from Lt. William Henry Bent to his sister Fanny from Vila Franca, dated 26th April 1812.
35. Dickson, vol. IV, p.586. Letter from Dickson to Dr. Latham from Badajoz, dated 8th April 1812.
36. James Clavell Library, MD 869. Letter from Framingham to Mr. Sealey (Connel's father) from Badajoz, dated 28th March 1812.
37. WD, vol. V, pp.576–82. Wellington to Liverpool, from Badajoz, dated 7th April 1812.

CHAPTER 14

Douglas's Close Support

With Ciudad Rodrigo and Badajoz in allied hands Wellington had three operational aims in order to stabilise the situation and set the conditions for his main campaign. Firstly, he needed to spoil any possible intentions of Soult moving against Badajoz, or moving north to link up with the Army of Portugal; secondly, he needed to prevent any possibility of the Army of Portugal moving south to link up with elements of the Army of the South, and finally, he needed to thwart Marmont's intentions of invading Portugal from the north. The continued presence of Hill's and Graham's corps-sized covering forces, coupled with the news of the fall of Badajoz and that of the movement of three Spanish divisions towards Soult's vice regal hub at Seville, was enough to convince the commander of the Army of the South to abandon any aspirations of an early recapture of Badajoz or to move against the allied forces positioned there.[1] With Marmont's move into northern Portugal in early April, the likelihood of a successful link-up with the Army of the South was greatly diminished: Wellington's main aim therefore, once Badajoz was secure, was to move north and counter Marmont.

Marmont's three divisions, which had moved in support of Suchet's operations on the east coast, had been returned to his command in late January. Despite this, Major General Jean-Pierre Bonnet, as per Napoleonic instruction, remained in the Asturias and Marmont considered it prudent to leave Foy's infantry and Montbrun's cavalry to the south, maintaining his lines of communication. In addition, his garrison commitments were widespread, leaving him a mere four infantry divisions and a light cavalry brigade to prosecute the fourth invasion of Portugal. With only 25,000 men and no siege artillery his options were limited. Ciudad Rodrigo was by-passed on the 30th March and an optimistic attempt to capture Almeida by *coup de main* failed two days later. He then moved south into Portugal, evicting Lecor's Portuguese Brigade from Castelo Branco, and was preparing to move on Trant's Portuguese Brigade at Guarda when news arrived that Wellington's force was moving north. Marmont pulled back to Sabugal and waited for better intelligence as to Wellington's strength and intentions and was very nearly caught off-guard as Wellington's 40,000 men closed with speed and determination forcing the French force back across the border.

With Napoleon now embroiled in planning for the Russian campaign, overall command and control had, for the first time, been vested in his brother King Joseph, who received Marshal Jean-Baptiste Jourdan to assist and 'guide' him in the process. Joseph's orders to Soult and Marmont to unite against Wellington were ignored by the former and dismissed, with judicious reasoning, by the latter. Through captured communiqués Wellington was able to capitalise on this difference of opinion and, while he prepared to strike against Marmont in strength, he decided to complicate any future intentions to link up the two French armies by capturing the vital bridge crossing at Almaraz. Wellington wrote to Hill on the 24th April and allocated the mission to his force.

> I think you might avail yourself of this opportunity to strike your blow at Almaraz. I think that one of your British brigades & two Portuguese brigades, or one and a half British, & one strong Portuguese brigade would do your business as to the French in that neighbourhood. All the iron howitzers are now in Elvas, and you might employ to draw six of them [with] the mules attached to one of General Hamilton's brigades of Portuguese artillery. If Dickson has got the ammunition carriages prepared for the brigades of howitzers which I proposed should be in reserve of the Artillery, you might get the mule carts to carry the quantity of shot & of howitzer & spherical shells which you might think it expedient to take. See Dickson in regard to this equipment & settle the whole with him. You had better take him on this expedition with you.[2]

Dickson must have been elated, but that euphoria would certainly have been surpassed when, a few days later, news came through that the Prince Regent (on behalf of His Majesty) had agreed to his brevet promotion to lieutenant colonel with commissioning dated of the 27th April.[3] Dickson decided to take a brigade of six 24-pounder iron howitzers, which he had recently established using resources from Arriaga's Portuguese Company, supplemented by some manpower from Glubb's Company and a half brigade of 9-pounders from Captain Stewart Maxwell's Company.[4] However, Dickson was soon to discover that these heavy guns, and the heavy howitzers, were not able to move through the hills in support of the infantry on the main objective and their contribution was restricted to the deception operation on Fort Miravete. With the main force attacking Fort Napoleon, Lieutenant James Love, one sergeant and 20 gunners were to accompany the attacking column to destroy or employ the enemy's artillery as the opportunity presented.

> … Fort Napoleon was entered by escalade; Lieutenant Love of the artillery immediately turned the guns on the fugitives who by an unaccountable oversight cut the bridge of boats on the side to which they retreated and left it to swing

round to the other by which means our passage was not interrupted and we crossed over and took possession of Fort Ragusa which with the ordnance, Fort Napoleon and the bridge were all destroyed.[5]

A total of 18 pieces of French ordnance were captured in this most successful raid but unfortunately during the destruction of Fort Ragusa, Lieutenant Thiele of the KGA, who undertook to light the portfire, was killed in the resulting explosion. Jenkinson noted that 'every person speaks in the highest terms of the conduct of Lieuts Love and Thiele, the two officers who accompanied the columns – the former is left to enjoy the fame he has acquired, but the latter was unfortunately blown up whilst destroying the works'.[6] The operational advantage to the allies furnished by the destruction of this vital French north–south crossing point was considerably enhanced a few days later when Colonel Henry Sturgeon and Major Alexander Todd of the Royal Staff Corps repaired the bridge at Alcántara, thereby re-opening short notice reinforcement capability to, or from, Wellington's main force in the north, that of the Spanish Army of Estremadura under Castaños in the centre and Hill's Corps to the south. All was now ready for the advance upon the Tormes.

Two additional companies of artillery had arrived in theatre in April 1812; Captain Henry Stone's Company (Stone did not deploy) remained in Lisbon to enhance the garrison there under Fisher, while the other, Captain Robert Douglas's Company, was allocated to the main army. Lieutenant Colonel Charles Waller RA had arrived in theatre in April and Framingham considered him ideal to assume the post of CRA with the detached corps. Framingham, despite his previous kind intentions and manner towards Dickson, cannot have been anything other than annoyed at the overt manner with which Wellington had tried to elevate the relatively junior officer and it had been his intention of leaving Dickson with Hill's Corps and then placing him under Waller. Wellington, however, had other ideas and he wrote to Hill instructing him that Dickson's and his reserve brigade of 24-pounder howitzers 'must be ready to cross the bridge at Alcántara on the day Sturgeon will have it prepared'.[7] In consequence, Dickson's and Arriaga's brigades and heavy howitzers, were included in the main army.

CRA: Lt. Col. H. Framingham RA
Staff: Lt. Col. W. Robe RA, Lt. Col. A. Dickson RA and Lt. Col. J. May RA[8]
Maj. J. H. Carncross
Brigade Major: Maj. E. Downman RA and Lt. L. Woodyear RA

RHA Troops	Notes	Equipment
'A' Troop (Ross)	Attached to Light Division.	5 x long 6-pounders 1 x 5½-inch iron howitzer
'E' Troop (Macdonald)	Attached to 7th Division.	5 x long 6-pounders 1 x 5½-inch iron howitzer
'I' Troop (Bull)	Attached to 1st Cavalry Division.	5 x long 6-pounders 1 x 5½-inch iron howitzer

RA Companies	Notes	Equipment[9]
Gardiner's Company	Attached to 1st Division.	5 x 9-pounders 1 x 5½-inch iron howitzer
Douglas's Company	Attached to 3rd Division.	5 x 9-pounders 1 x 5½-inch howitzer
Sympher's Company KGA	Attached to 4th Division.	5 x 9-pounders 1 x 5½-inch howitzer
Lawson's Company	Attached to 5th Division – 9-pounders handed over to Gardiner in May.	5 x 6-pounders 1 x 5½-inch iron howitzer
Eligé's Company	Attached to 6th Division Commanded by 2nd Capt. Greene – Eligé was KIA at the Salamanca sieges.	5 x light 6-pounders 1 x 5½-inch iron howitzer
Arriaga's Company	Reserve: Dickson's Portuguese (Artillery) Division.	6 x 24-pounder howitzers
Glubb's Company	Reserve: Commanded by 2nd Capt. Power – Glubb was in England.	4 x 18-pounders
May's Company	Commanded by 2nd Capt. H Baynes – in charge of reserve ammunition.	Nil
With General Hill's Corps (CRA: Lt. Col. C. Waller RA)		
'D' Troop (Lefebure)	Attached to 2nd Division.	5 x long 6-pounders 1 x 5½-inch iron howitzer
Maxwell's Company	Attached to 2nd Division. Formerly Hawker's Company.	5 x 9-pounders 1 x 5½-inch howitzer
Da Cunha Preto's Company	Dickson's (Artillery) Division – attached to Hamilton's Portuguese Division.	5 x light 6-pounders 1 x 5½-inch howitzer
Braun's Company	Dickson's (Artillery) Division – attached to Hamilton's Portuguese Division.	5 x light 9-pounders 1 x 5½-inch howitzer

Sources: Dickson, Laws and Leslie.

Wellington commenced his offensive movement, the first since Talavera, on the 13th June by crossing the River Agueda and marching on Salamanca.

Our march from the Agueda to the Tormes, was until we approached the latter river, wholly without interest, except to the person present, to whom the arrival at the same moment of our three columns on the plain, between the forests we had been four days marching in, and the heights overlooking Salamanca, was a most magnificent and cheering sight, for never was such a force seen in higher spirits, or in more close and compact order of battle; and never was an army better supplied, or with a fairer prospect of continuing to be so.

The enemy were soon dispossessed of the hills which command a view of the town, river and surrounding country ... we made no attempt to force that day, but defer'd [*sic*] it until the next, when Marmont's retreat during the night with the small force he had there, enabled us to pass the river both above and below the town, without opposition, the bridge being still commanded by a fort in which the enemy left a garrison of five or six hundred men. This fort was immediately invested and well reconnoitred …[10]

That reconnaissance revealed that there were in fact three convents which had been strengthened and the buildings to their front and sides destroyed. Major General Henry Clinton's 6th Division invested the forts while the rest of the army established bivouacs around the outskirts of the city. Lieutenant Colonel John Fox Burgoyne was the senior engineer while the task of coordinating the artillery was delegated, in Dickson's absence, to Lieutenant Colonel John May. The only siege guns up with the force were the four 18-pounders which May supplemented with an additional three 5½-inch howitzers from the field batteries. It was a woefully inadequate train and there is no hiding the fact that the responsibility for this failure lay with Framingham as there were copious amounts of heavy artillery at both Ciudad Rodrigo and Almeida. Wellington did not shy away from taking his share of the blame.

> The enemy had been employed for nearly three years in constructing these works, but with increased activity for the last eight or nine months. A large expense had been incurred; and these works, sufficiently garrisoned by about 800 men, and armed with 30 pieces of artillery, were of a nature to render it quite impossible to take them, excepting by regular attack … I was mistaken in my estimate of the extent of the means which would be necessary to subdue these forts; and I was obliged to send to the rear for a fresh supply of ammunition. This necessity occasioned a delay of six days.[11]

Capturing the forts at Salamanca was, therefore, to be anything but swift and trouble-free. Ingilby was now with Gardiner's Brigade of guns and had come forward with the howitzer.

> The forts were immediately invested, and in the night of the 18th we used the greatest exertions to construct two batteries, one to be directed against each fort. There was a great scarcity of tools and the ground excessively hard, but notwithstanding at sunrise we commenced the fire, but the shots from the forts shattered our incomplete and flimsy batteries, constructed out of the rubbish and ruins of the levelled houses; and … caught fire from the muzzles of the howitzers and proved very inconvenient, and, which eventually contributed to aid the enemy's fire, rendered our battery, at least for the howitzers, nearly untenable. Notwithstanding, after a few hours we succeeded in battering down the side wall of the convent, which fell, accompanied by the cheers of the gunners, but it was useless, and failed to fill up the ditch, or even offer any appearance of facilitating an assault. Captain Eligé was killed on the spot, and the gunners suffered severely. Kneeling and placing myself at an embrasure to watch the effects of a shot … I gave the order without turning 'Fire' for the howitzer on my left hand, by mistake

the non-commissioned officer fired the piece which was exactly behind me and close to my head … completely stunned by the violence of the concussion I fell, of course, as if shot, but soon recovered no other mischief seemed done than by fire singeing my hair and tarnishing my epaulet on my right shoulder and … both my ears gushed out with blood instantly. Presently after the Commander-in-Chief came into the battery and addressing some questions to me, I found myself too completely deafened to hear a syllable.[12]

Dickson arrived with his six iron howitzers on the 20th June and these were immediately deployed to the two batteries but, by the end of the day, only 60 18-pounder shot and 160 24-pounder howitzer shot remained. The same day Marmont advanced towards the city and the siege was put on hold with one brigade of the 6th Division returning to the army while the other manned the trenches. During the night of the 22nd/23rd June, Marmont withdrew and Wellington, eager to capture the city ordered an immediate resumption of the battering and an attempt to be made by the infantry that evening. Captain Charles Dansey, serving as Gardiner's second captain, summed up the situation in a letter to his uncle:

… on the 19th our batteries opened but I am sorry to say with little effect and considerable loss on our side. I believe the strength of the place had been somewhat undervalued, and our means for its reduction consequently insufficient. They went on however & on the night of the 23rd an attempt was made to escalade it, it was disastrous, & unsuccessful. General Bowes was killed, & we had about 90 men and several officers killed & wounded in this affair.[13]

The re-supply ammunition arrived from Almeida on the 26th June and the second battery, commanded by Captain Charles Cornwallis Michell, was ordered to fire heated shot onto the roof of the San Vincente convent; a battery had also been constructed by the hospital of San Bernardo, under the command of Captain William Greene, and armed with two long 6-pounders and a brass 5½-inch howitzer with the task of keeping the French counter-battery fire in check – as best they could. The heated shot had an immediate effect and by the evening the San Vincente was on fire in several places. Young Second Lieutenant Henry Hough, who had arrived as part of the battle casualty replacements sent out in April, had joined May's Company only the month prior and now found himself at the forefront of the action.

About 8 o Cl. Friday evening [26th] we set the roof of the left wing of the fort on fire, which burnt for nearly 4 hours and then was extinguished, the French batteries playing upon us all the time, their riflemen very troublesome indeed. Kept up firing all night, they returning us shot for shot, and shell for shell, with plenty of grape into the bargain but, thank God with not much effect. Near about 7 o Cl. Saturday morning we got it in flames again … and sending plenty more red-hot into the same spot, soon made a fine blaze, and made them abandon their batteries and send out a flag of truce. Their offers of giving up two forts, provided we wou'd [sic] let them quiet 2 hours, Lord Wellington would not listen to. The officer returned and we rattled away again as hard as we could lick at them. This made them send out a second flag, which was also refused, and we gave them another taste of the red-hot, the 6th Division (Clinton) storming the breaches at the same moment.[14]

Sergeant Charles Whitman was part of Eligé's Company and in his journal he summed the action. 'In this affair we took 400 effective prisoners, several wounded, quantities of ammunition of every description with quantities of stores and provisions, we rested here one day, after all this fatigue.'[15] With the forts having fallen there was little point in Marmont lingering on the Tormes and he issued immediate orders for his force to fall back towards Valladolid and his reinforcements. Wellington was in no hurry to follow; the first part of his campaign plan was complete and he allowed his force the opportunity to recuperate for 24 hours. Hough, however, was too tired to partake of the revelry; he wrote, 'A general illumination and dances took place in the evening, but I was too fag'd [sic] to enjoy the amusements'.[16]

On the 7th July Bonnet's Division linked up with Marmont but hopes of receiving additional reinforcements from the Army of the Centre were dashed when Jourdan announced his intention of keeping the command intact to fend off any attempt on the capital by Hill. Furthermore, the 10,000 expected from the Army of the North had been reduced to a brigade of light cavalry and some field guns; the commander General Louis-Marie Caffarelli could simply spare no more as he found his area of responsibility under constant threat from resurgent guerrilla operations and from the activities of the Royal Navy along the Cantabrian coast. Nonetheless, by mid-July, Marmont had gathered a force of just under 50,000 and resumed the offensive. An extraordinary series of moves and counter-moves took place by the two armies in the ground between the Tormes and Douro and both Ross's and Bull's troops were heavily involved in the numerous low-level actions between the vanguards of both forces. The Troop Records of 'A' Troop RHA record in magnificent detail the (largely) cavalry-on-cavalry combat at Castrejón on the 18th July:

At daybreak this morning ... the Troop, being all ready moved off at a gallop to this Regiment [11th Light Dragoons] leaving the [Light] Division on the ground descending to the low ground. The enemy commenced a heavy cannonade on the Troop. Subdivisions 1, 2, 3 & 4 crossed a small rivulet leaving 5 & 6. Lieut Belson, in the valley, moved rapidly to the relief of 4 guns of Major Bull's Troop whose ammunition were expended, [and] took up the position. Major Ross directing the fire against the enemies 8 guns, Trumpeter Virgin by his side. A gun shot struck the Trumpeter's horse on the off side behind Virgin's right thigh, [it] passed thro' his body, carried away his sword and nose bag on the near side. The horse drops dead. The Trumpeter, under heavy fire, stripped his horse of all his appointments, carried them to the wagons, saddled another horse and came up to us again ... Expending all our ammunition in this position, limbered up and moved off. A gun shot struck the back of Corpl [Corporal] Adams horse in front of the saddle and dropt [sic] him but after a time he recovers from the stun he had received, but not [enough] to carry the Corporal. During this time Lieut Belson with his guns are charged with [by] the enemies [sic] cavalry with determined fury, he drops his detachments rear to cover them. Lieut Belson is wounded by a sabre. The enemy's right flank pushing forward to cut off the Light Division, their cavalry repeatedly charging. Troop having changed the gun limbers for those of the wagon[s], galloped up to them covered by the 12 Lt Dragoons and came into action at 200 yards with common case and put a stop to them. Gunner Bessford is wounded. The Light Division then inclines to the left, the Troop keeps to the road ... a gun shot struck and broke one of Dvr Reid's horses legs of No 2 gun. Halted, changed and destroyed the disabled horse and marched on ... Troop then joined the Division ... this was a smart day's work.[17]

A smart day's work it most certainly was, producing an action which encapsulates absolutely both the *raison d'être* and *esprit de corps* of the Royal Horse Artillery. This bilateral manoeuvring culminated in a parallel march of both armies, within sight of each other, towards Salamanca on the 21st July. Both sides occasionally exchanged a cannonade as they marched methodically in the July heat back towards the Tormes and the city of Salamanca.

> The French continued their movements which caused the Armies to march in two parallel lines. Lord Wellington gradually refused [battle], or fell back by his right, in order to preserve his communications with his rear from whence we drew all our supplies, and which was threatened by the French General. We re-passed the Tormes and occupied a position at night upon the heights on the left bank under arms. The night was remarkably dark, with heavy rain, accompanied with tremendous thunder and lightning, and one loud explosion of thunder so frightened the horses of the cavalry that from Colonel Ponsonby's regiment 50 broke away from the men as they lay bivouacked with the reins in their hands, and caused considerable confusion. Our bridles were off for the horses to feed and they made violent rush, but being yoked in the guns were easily stopped.[18]

In Ross's Troop Gunner Reeves lost the sight in his right eye, an injury attributed to the lightning, as the officers and men fought to regain control of their horses and, once done, the men 'stood to horses heads' until dawn.[19] Dawn, when it came, heralded a cloudless sky, the heat of the early morning sun providing a welcome relief to the men of both armies but the mood quickly turned to one of anticipation at the prospect of battle. Dansey was with the 1st Division just south of Carbajosa de la Sagrada and he recalled that 'On the morning of the 22nd an attack was decidedly expected, & we hailed the dawn of the day most confidently expecting that it would be numbered amongst those which have already shed such lustre on the British army in the Peninsula'.[20] Words clearly penned in hindsight for Wellington's intention, at the break of day, was to continue his westerly movement and try to break clean from Marmont's pursuit; it was only later, when the merest glimpse of an opportunity presented itself to Wellington's trained eye, that the army were unleashed to secure, arguably, their greatest victory of the war.

Only the 7th and 4th divisions were deployed; the former, supported by the guns of Macdonald's Horse Artillery Troop, was on the ridgeline looking east across the valley and the latter, supported by Sympher's KGA, was anchored on a small hill known as the Lesser Arapil. The balance of the army was out of sight a mile to their rear except the 3rd Division and D'Urban's Portuguese Cavalry Brigade which were still north of the Tormes. The latter officer had recently assumed command of this brigade of Portuguese cavalry having previously been Beresford's Quarter Master General. Wellington was on the ridge with Lieutenant General Sir John Hope and could clearly see Marmont and Foy through his glass across the valley. He instructed Hope to send out a strong skirmish line to deny the French intelligence of the army's location and *ipso facto* future intentions. As the battalions of the 68th and 2nd Caçadores advanced across the valley floor they slightly over-extended the movement prompting Foy to respond by sending out his own light infantry to drive them back. However, while this action was playing out, Marmont had moved south; he had sighted a second larger hill in the half light of the dawn and had already put troops in motion to capture the feature. Wellington spotted the movement and the tactical significance of the Greater Arapil too late and, despite an attempt by the 7th Caçadores to counter, the three battalions of the 120e Ligne were already firm. Marmont had scored the first point of the day.

Downman, who was on the artillery staff, witnessed events as they unfolded.

A cannonade was going on during these movements and His Lordship closed up his army & strengthened his right by ordering up the 3rd Division from Salamanca, which came up almost concealed and immediately on the enemy's left. The 5th and 6th with the 4th formed the first line. 1st Division, General Pack's and Bradford's brigades with Don Carlos's troops the support. The Light and 7th continuing on the left and the centre supported by a most commanding height on which Captain Macdonald's Troop was posted ... the two brigades of heavy cavalry were also on the right and General Alten's brigade ... General Anson's centre and left. Marmont was galloping along the front repeatedly, moving his immense quantity of artillery, with very heavy columns of infantry and cavalry to our right.[21]

Each of Marmont's infantry and cavalry divisions had their own integral artillery battery and he held four batteries as an army reserve, providing a total of 78 guns. Captain William Greenshields Power, with the four 18-pounders, was already on the road to Ciudad Rodrigo but the remaining nine brigades, supplemented by six guns of De España's Division, furnished the allies with a respectable 60 guns in reply. Dyneley was with 'E' Troop on the lower ground, to the east of the Lesser Arapil, when he received orders to redeploy onto the feature itself.

On the day of the battle after a very few minutes fighting, an order from his Lordship came desiring me to get my guns upon a height to receive an attack the enemy were about to make. The order I received had certainly a very awkward signification: 'His Lordship desires you will get your guns up that height and wishes you to defend it as long as you have a man left to your guns. In the event of you being obliged to retire, you will spike your guns and leave them and the

General officer commanding has most positive orders that he supports you to the last; in fact', his Lordship says, 'he must have the hill kept'.

From these orders I made sure of an 'ex' or 'dis' – tinguish. I got my guns up with the assistance of a company of the 40th regiment, unloaded my limbers and sent them to my gunners' horses to the rear, as I thought, if we have to run for it, my men should get away as fast as the infantry ...[22]

As the morning wore on, both sides held their ground and an artillery duel commenced and although the atmosphere was tense the likelihood of a general action appeared to ebb. Around midday that all changed. Marmont, impatient to cut off Wellington's line of retreat, dispatched Major General Jean-Guillaume Thomières and Major General Jean-Baptiste Curto to move west and get in behind the allied left flank. At much the same time that he issued these orders Marmont was injured by one of Dyneley's shells as he was descending the heights and command passed to General Bonnet.[23] Nevertheless, the seeds of French failure had been sown and the errors of Marmont's instructions were soon apparent to Wellington.

The opportunity which Lord W. was watching for with the greatest anxiety & hopes that it would occur, happened, and an immediate attack was ordered. The 3rd Division moved rather upon their left flank ...[24]

No sooner was Pakenham in motion towards the heights than the ridge he was about to assail was crowned with twenty pieces of cannon, while in the rear of this battery was seen Thomières' division endeavouring to regain its place in the combat. A flat space, one thousand yards in breadth, was to be crossed before Pakenham could reach the heights. The French batteries opened a heavy fire, while our two brigades of artillery, commanded by Captain Douglas posted on the rising ground behind the 3rd Division, replied to them with much warmth. Pakenham's men might thus be said to be within two fires – that of their own guns firing over their heads, while the French balls passed through their very ranks, ploughing up the ground in every direction; but the veteran troops which composed the 3rd Division were not to be shaken by this.[25]

There are very few examples of the artillery firing over the heads of the infantry during the entire war and none, hitherto, under such trying circumstances as Robert Douglas and his men experienced that afternoon during the advance to contact of the 'Fighting' 3rd Division. The Connaught Rangers most certainly were veteran troops by this stage of the Peninsular campaigns, but Douglas's men, having only arrived four months earlier, were fighting their first battle and, by all accounts, according to Lieutenant William Grattan of the 88th Foot, doing a very fine job. Thomières's and Curto's dispositions clearly indicated that they had no inkling of the 3rd Division's flanking manoeuvre and had not expected an attack from this quarter. Both French commanders tried to redeploy their men to meet the threat but they were soon under artillery fire and unable to regain their composure; when Pakenham released his infantry French resistance collapsed. Within a few minutes

Thomières was dead, about 2,000 French were either killed or captured and one of the French batteries captured complete. To make matters worse, to their rear, Wellington had just released the 4th and 5th divisions and two independent Portuguese brigades who were now closing with speed against Maucune's, Clausel's and Bonnet's divisions.

> The hill we attacked was exactly the same height and size as our own and distant 700 yards. As soon as the enemy discovered we were advancing, they got four guns up, but our fire obliged them to retire before they had fired four rounds. Our infantry, two Portuguese regiments [Pack], then stormed the hill which the French let them get to the top of before they opened much musketry.[26]

Pack's attack failed and the battle, in this part of the field, lay in the balance for a short while until Wellington deployed the 6th Division to support Cole's 4th

9. The Battle of Salamanca - Early Afternoon, 22nd July 1812

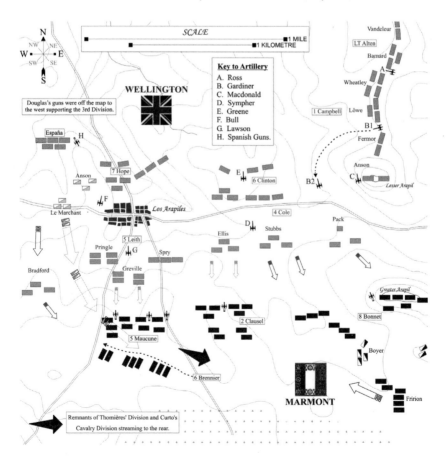

Division and the French counter-attack was brought to an abrupt halt. However, to the west, the 3rd and 5th divisions and Bradford's Portuguese Brigade were rolling up the remnants of Thomières's Division, and the divisions of Maucune and Brennier, which had been destroyed during a most magnificent charge by Major General John Gaspard Le Marchant's heavy cavalry. By about 1700 hours the French Army was falling back at every point and they sought refuge behind the division of Ferey, which had been brought up to join the fray but which now found itself, along with some of the more intact battalions from Sarrut's Division, providing cohesion to the otherwise disorganised main body. Major General Bertrand Clausel, who was now in command of the army, with both Marmont and Bonnet injured, ordered Foy to move towards the fords over the Tormes and provide flank protection to the army as it retired. Wellington, accordingly, ordered the Light Division and 1st Division to follow up and Ross's Troop finally got some action.

> About 6 o'clock we limbered up to the right and galloped off some distance when an order was given to change left in front by right flank, this done we formed line for action at 500 yards, firing 7 or 8 rounds a gun. Limbered up to front advancing at the gallop … continued this until 12 o'clock [midnight] being on the threshing floor of the Huerta. His Grace the Commander in Chief ordered halt, found water for the horses and barley to feed with. Halted two hours and resumed the pursuit. At 4 o'clock came into action at 400 yards on the enemies [sic] rear as they were fording the Tormes.[27]

The 1st Division were slower off the mark and never really got into their stride; Ingilby recalled that 'the Light and 1st divisions advanced to attack their right, but the retreat had become general and night put a stop to the pursuit. We bivouacked on the ground.'[28] Throughout the battle Dickson, with the brigade of 24-pounder howitzers, had been a mere onlooker to events and could not subsequently hide his frustration.

> The only artillery I had in the field was a brigade of iron howitzers, and as I was stationed on the left of our line was but little engaged, and then only for a short time of artillery fire. The greatest part of the time I was therefore a mere spectator. I was ready however, to join in the pursuit which had been continued as far as this, and I conclude will still be made further.[29]

The pursuit was unrelenting but hopes of capturing large numbers of the retreating French were, to an extent, undone by the Spanish commander's decision to abandon the bridge over the Tormes at Alba and the adjacent castle which dominates the crossing. During the night the majority of the beaten army crossed the bridge and the ford south of Huerta and by dawn on the 23rd, except for a few isolated detachments and some of the wounded, the French were firm on the east bank where they tried to regain some semblance of order. The 1st Division soon resumed the hunt and, near the small village of Nava de Sotrobal, Ingilby soon found himself at the forefront of the action.

At daylight, in the morning, we began our march, but having received no orders in the night and without intelligence of the route the French had taken, the General was at first uncertain which road to pursue with his Division. About 10 o'clock in the morning we came up with our most advanced troops, the Brigade of German Heavy Cavalry that had just executed a bold charge and obliged 150 infantry of the rear-guard of the French to lay down their arms [Garcihernández]. The cavalry had several officers and many of the dragoons killed, but acquired a great reputation. A squadron of Light Dragoons, followed by the infantry, continued the pursuit. We kept pace with the dragoons, mounting the gunners of the gun-carriages and, outstripping the infantry, came up with their rear-guard again. The French squadrons threatened to charge, the Commander-in-Chief dismounted, threw himself amongst our guns, and directed our fire personally. Had the French known the circumstance, it was not difficult to have captured him, but they stopped short at grape shot distance, and in the meanwhile our infantry and more squadrons arrived.[30]

May had been up at the front with Wellington's staff during the pursuit and at Garcihernández had been tasked to take orders to the short-sighted Major General Eberhardt Otto von Bock releasing him to attack the unsupported infantry of the French rearguard. Bock asked May if he would be 'good enough to show us the enemy'; he obliged and received two musket balls in his thigh as he rode in execution of his accord. When afterwards relating the story, May would add 'That was what I got by playing dragoon, and leading the Germans'.[31] Dansey, the second in command of the brigade of guns attached to the 1st Division, also recalled the action but, interestingly, makes no mention of Wellington's presence or indeed of his assistance in directing the guns.

The main column was in full march by the villages Coca [de Alba] & Nava de Sotrobalo [Sotrobal], our guns advanced with the cavalry and as we approached the latter village the skirmishers suddenly galloped in and a large body of French cavalry immediately appeared in our line; on an eminence in our front; and sounded the charge, I certainly expected we should either have been killed, wounded, or prisoners, but however we came into action as quick as we could, and after a few rounds they thought fit to retire and we continued our salute until they were out of reach.[32]

Both Bull's and Ross's troops were in action supporting the cavalry and Light Division, the latter officer recalling on the 24th July that they came 'up with the enemy, who retired *en masse*, covering their rear with 22 squadrons of cavalry. Our force too small, and without infantry, they go off unmolested.'[33] That the pursuit of Marmont's army had been mishandled there can be no dispute and yet the scale of the operation was far greater than might be perceived. Even Lawson, in support of the 5th Division, recalled that on the 23rd he and lieutenants James Sinclair and James Johnston, 'expended 259 rounds of six Pr. Ammunition & 24 of howitzer'.[34] Despite the follow-up and the relatively minor successes that accompanied the various manoeuvres, there is no doubt that the French had regained their composure and had withdrawn with great speed and purpose to the security of their base at Valladolid. Nevertheless, the scale of the victory at Salamanca and the losses to the French higher command were significant. The CRA's post-battle report was understandably upbeat.

> It is with the greatest gratification I report the very highest meritorious conduct of the Corps; the professional ability and skill displayed by the officers, with the determined bravery and firm countenance of the non Commissioned Officers, Gunners and Drivers surmounted every difficulty, and I trust will not be unnoticed by His Excellency the Commander of the Forces.[35]

Salamanca was not an artillery battle *per se* but the Gunners had certainly played their part and in Wellington's post-battle dispatch he acknowledged that 'The Royal and German Artillery, under Lieut. Col. Framingham, distinguished themselves by the accuracy of their fire wherever it was possible to use them; and they advanced to the attack of the enemy's position with the same gallantry as the other troops.'[36] Framingham had developed a working relationship with the commander-in-chief and was not frightened to speak his mind but the fact remained that Wellington did not find that his latest artillery commander possessed the level of initiative or positive attitude he was seeking.

> Colonel Framingham who commanded the artillery at the battle of Salamanca and who is well spoken of by everyone, but at times I believe is slow, was once with Lord Wellington at an audience when things went wrong and Lord Wellington got irate and told him pretty nearly that his friend concerning whom he was enquiring 'might go to hell'. Colonel Framingham came muttering out: 'I'll go Sir to the Quartermaster-General for a route', which Wellington heard and laughed well.[37]

Artillery losses in the siege and battle were remarkably small. Captain John Eligé had died capturing the Salamanca forts and Lieutenant Colonel John May was twice wounded in the thigh at Garcihernández. A far greater toll had befallen the artillery mounts and whichever decision Wellington chose to pursue over the comings days, a continued pursuit of Marmont or a move on Madrid, would require numerous replacements. Wellington emphasised this point in his dispatch; he also touched on the need for more 9-pounder guns in his inventory.

> I request your Lordship to send us out remount horses for the cavalry and artillery. These daily marches, skirmishes, battles, etc., consume an immense number of them; and we can get none here to suit our purpose ... our cavalry must be kept up, or we cannot stay in the plains. I should also wish to be able to equip some more artillery of a larger calibre; as it is not agreeable to be cannonaded for hours together, and not to be able to answer with even one gun.[38]

The paucity of suitable mounts, and the clear priority to maximise the allied cavalry to counter the large numbers of French of that arm, was to have significant consequences in influencing the quantity of artillery Wellington was to take with him in subsequent operations. His sentiments regarding the heavier 9-pounder guns were, at this time, liberally expressed across the Royal Artillery but it was to be some months before more of the field brigades were equipped with the heavier guns. Alas the horse artillery was to have to wait until the war in the Peninsula and southern France had concluded before they were to receive the larger calibre guns.

Notes

1. The three Spanish divisions were those of Penne Villemur, Morillo and Ballesteros.
2. WD, vol. V. pp.608–09. Wellington to Hill from Alfaiates, dated 24th April 1812.
3. Dickson, vol. IV, p.654.
4. Ibid., pp.625–26, 628 and 641–42.
5. Swabey (ed. Whinyates), p.101.
6. Jenkinson, letter from Puebla de Azaba, dated 28th May 1812.
7. WD, vol. V. p.675. Wellington to Hill from Fuenteguinaldo, dated 28th May 1812.
8. May had been promoted brevet Lt. Col. on 27th April 1812, along with Dickson, Alexander Tulloh and Harcourt Holcombe. At around this time May was selected as Assistant Adjutant G1 with the Army HQ.
9. By this stage some of the field brigades had also been equipped with the 5½-inch iron howitzers: Dickson, vol. IV. p.730.
10. Jenkinson, letter from camp before Salamanca, dated 26th June 1812.
11. WD, vol. V. pp.726–28. Wellington to Liverpool from Fuentelapeña, dated 30th June 1812.
12. Ingilby, 16th June 1812.
13. Dansey (ed. Glover), letter from Medina del Campo, dated 3rd July 1812.
14. Hough, entries dated 26th and 27th June 1812.
15. Whitman, entry dated 27th June 1812.
16. Hough, entry dated 27th June 1812.
17. Whitehead (ed.), entry dated 18th July 1812.
18. Ingilby, 21st July 1812.
19. The order 'Stand To Horses Heads' is a variation on Stand To Arms – in other words be prepared for an attack, usually undertaken at last and first light – horses heads indicating that the men were stood next to their horses, bridle in hand.
20. Dansey (ed. Glover), date of letter unknown.
21. Downman, 22nd July 1812.
22. Dyneley, letter from Nava de Setrobal, dated 25th July 1812.
23. Marmont records (Memoirs, vol. VII, p.116) that just prior to Waterloo he had visited a British horse artillery battery and met Quartermaster Sergeant J. Wightman who had laid the gun which had fired the shot causing his wound on 22nd July 1812. Marmont recalled 'I gave this under officer a good reception. Since then I saw the same man at Woolwich where he was a storekeeper when I was there in 1830, to visit that magnificent arsenal. Then, however, he had only one arm, having lost the other at

Waterloo. In condoling with him I said, "my good fellow, each has his turn."'

24. Downman, 22nd July 1812.

25. Grattan, p.243. There was just a single brigade of guns with Douglas.

26. Dyneley, letter from Nava de Setrobal, dated 25th July 1812.

27. Whitehead (ed.), entry 22nd July 1812.

28. Ingilby, 22nd July 1812.

29. Dickson, vol. IV, pp.681–82.

30. Ingilby, 23rd July 1812.

31. Ludlow Beamish, vol. II, p.82.

32. Dansey (ed. Glover), letter dated 5th August 1812.

33. Ross, p.30, dated 24th July 1812.

34. Lawson, dated 24th July 1812. J. W. Johnston (1193) and James Sinclair (1207); the latter officer belonged to Ilbert's Company (at Woolwich) and was attached to Lawson's Company at this time.

35. Duncan, vol. II, p.326.

36. WD, vol. V, p.757. Wellington to Bathurst, 24th July 1812.

37. Larpent, p.185.

38. Ibid.

CHAPTER 15

Dyneley's Capture and Wellington's Failure

Wellington's initial intentions to pursue Clausel's beaten army were ultimately undone by French discord within their higher command. Joseph had in fact left Madrid on the day of the battle of Salamanca, intent on reinforcing the Army of Portugal with 14,000 men. However, news of the defeat stopped him in his tracks and he decided to return to the capital in preference to moving to link up with Clausel. Weeks earlier, Joseph had issued orders to Soult to abandon a large part of Andalusia and fall back to Toledo; true to form, the Duke of Dalmatia had failed to comply but, instead, offered an alternative plan. Joseph, in a state of utter desperation, rebuked Soult and steadfastly reiterated his order but it was to be some weeks before the Army of the South began a withdrawal. With the two French armies at his front now retreating in different directions, Wellington faced a dilemma: split his force and pursue both Clausel and Joseph, or concentrate his force and follow one or the other. In the end he elected to undertake both options, to a degree, by forcing Clausel back beyond Valladolid and then pursuing Joseph and driving him out of Madrid.

On the 7th August D'Urban's Portuguese cavalry and the German Dragoons, under Colonel Charles de Jonquières, supported by a single KGL battalion and Macdonald's Horse Artillery Troop, moved from Segovia and began the advance towards Madrid. Colonel Marie-Antone Reiset's Brigade of Dragoons was all that opposed the group until they reached Majadahonda four days later where Reiset was joined by General Anne-François-Charles Treillard and the small allied vanguard was fixed, dispersed and exposed. Dyneley was at the front with the cavalry of the KGL.

> … at daylight the next morning, 11th, discovered the enemy's cavalry drawn up about half a league ahead of us; we advanced and they retired over near two leagues

243

of ground, the Col [from the KGL] constantly asking me if they were in range. No, no, no Sir, and I asked him if he would let one of his Regts accompany my guns to the top of a hill, the cavalry were then going down, in which he immediately acquiesced, and off we set at a trot: from that to a gallop, and then to speed, and reached the hill just as they [the French] had got to the bottom, opened my fire, and put them to flight in style and the made for the town of [Las] Rozas … Soon after this Macdonald came up with his two guns, and took command of the whole.[1]

'E' Troop fired a few rounds and it appeared that the French, as they had done during the preceding days, had given ground and the entire group entered Majadahonda, cooked breakfast and began to get some rest. Their respite was brief and rudely interrupted.

A Portuguese officer put his head into the window, frightened out of his life, and stuttered out, 'Molto grande feroce cavaleria Francese, vene vene per la Fenestra, Sigr Capitano con sua canone, Molto brave, brave, brave', this my dearest mother, is not my language, nor a word spelt right, but I give it to you as it struck the drum of my ear at the time … not a soul knew Macdonald's house … as soon as I got two guns ready, my friend Harding [Hardinge] and I went away with them at score to the front and directed the rest to follow me … We had no sooner gained the ground, from whence we opened our fire, then I saw how the thing was to go with us. The Portuguese wavered, and I turned to Harding and said, 'they'll most certainly turn our right flank, I hope the guns on the right will be able to get away'. By this time, the French cavalry gained march upon us … we, of course, limbered up and away we went at speed … we had galloped about 3 or 4 hundred yards, the confusion became very great … I was at the time galloping about half a dozen yards in the rear of the last gun … when my horse making a trip … I came head over heels … I was hurt a little and had one of my shoes nearly torn off my foot.[2]

The French were advancing on three axes and although outnumbered three to one, D'Urban had ordered his cavalry to charge but they had pulled up 20 paces from the advancing French and fled in panic back onto the four guns. The detachment of King's German Cavalry, under the command of Lieutenant Augustus Kuhls, fought bravely but was soon overwhelmed. Dyneley continued:

How I escaped being rode over I know not, for the dust was so great it was impossible to see a yard before you, however as soon as I got upon my feet and had run about fifty yards, I found the cavalry had got in upon one of our right guns, and saw them cut the drivers from their horses. I thought I had no business there and ran on, when I came upon the second right gun, which the French had been at: the three drivers were lying dead by their horses' sides. I then made away to the right, and still kept running on, when I discovered then one [gun] I had left was not in the hands of the enemy, but had been upset, and my poor fellows (my friend Bombardier Morgan at their head) had dismounted to right it. I made towards them but before I had run yards, I heard a terrible shriek of 'Advance, advance, Alanate Ah Trater Englese', I looked behind me and discovered about four squadrons not more than fifty yards in my rear – the officer commanding them rode at me and made a cut at me, but I made my bow and escaped. As soon as he could pull his horse up, he came at me again. When I saw this I sung out 'Officiale Englese Prisionere' and he came up to me brandishing his sword over my head, saying 'Darre me sua Spada, Dare me sua Spada' and all I had to say upon the subject was 'Si, Si, Si'.[3]

Dyneley was then subject to the emotions of capture and the humiliation of plunder as different groups relieved him of his money, his watch, his silver pencil case, pocket comb and lip-salve box. The fall from his horse at speed had left Dyneley worse for wear and Bombardier Morgan had to assist his troop officer as his French guards repeatedly drove him on with the butt end of their muskets. His captivity improved as the days passed and on the 13th August he was introduced to the English wife of General Chassie and the following day called to dine with the French divisional commander, D'Armagnac. Bombardier Morgan stayed with Dyneley throughout pretending to be his batman and, while Dyneley regained his strength, the two planned their breakout; after a couple of false starts, the two sneaked out through the French artillery park and made good their escape. On the 18th August the pair reached Madrid and Dyneley reported to Wellington's staff.

Col. Gordon took me into him, and most exceedingly glad he was to see me, got me a chair and seated me close by him – 'by the bye', says his Lordship, 'you cannot have had anything to eat lately; order dinner directly for him, and see that he has a comfortable bed instantly, he appears so much fatigued'. I said if his Lordship would allow me to ask for some tea, I should prefer it to dinner … he then entered into conversation and I told him everything I knew as to their strength, their route etc. etc. This being finished, he said he was going to send letters to England, and desired me to go into the Secretary's room, and let my friends know I had returned, in fact nothing could have been more kind than he was. This at once shewed [sic] me that he was not displeased with our conduct.[4]

Wellington might have been less accommodating had 'E' Troop's guns not been recovered. As at El Bodón, the previous year, when the five Portuguese guns were almost immediately recaptured, those of Macdonald's Troop were also repossessed later in the day when Brigadier General William Ponsonby's (formerly Le Marchant's) Cavalry Brigade and the forward elements of the 7th Division arrived and drove the French back towards the capital. At this point in the war the myth that Wellington never lost a gun in battle remains credible. The troop had lost six men killed, six wounded and 12 missing; however their guns were hardly damaged, and although the carriages needed replacement, it could have been far worse.

The following day Wellington entered Madrid and was received, along with the rest of the army, with the warmest welcome. Ross recorded 'the joy and acclamations of the inhabitants of Madrid on their release from French power is not to be described, and their attention and hospitality to the British cannot be excelled'.[5] It must have been a proud and emotional moment and one that lieutenants Hough and Ingilby would remember for the rest of their lives.

> Lord Wellington entered Madrid at the head of the 7th division with Don Carlos [de España] on his right and Don Julian [Sánchez] on his left, followed by several English Generals, and a very large staff. The manner in which the inhabitants received him was beyond believe [*sic*]. He was surrounded and nearly dragged from his horse and 'Viva! Viva! Viva los Engloises!!' was only to be heard. In the evening illuminations, music and dancing.[6]

> Lord Wellington and the advanced troops entered on the 12th. The Divisions of Infantry were bivouacked on the skirts of the suburbs, but many of the officers had billets in the capital. We were quartered (the officers) [Gardiner's Company] in the house of a Juramentado or one who had taken the oath of allegiance to Joseph Bonaparte, he was a general, and had besides entered into the service of the French.[7]

Joseph had withdrawn south-east of the city towards Ocaña and the road to Valencia but he had left behind 2,000 men under General Guillame Lafon-Blaniac, the governor of La Mancha, in Fort La China within the El Retiro entrenchment just outside the eastern gates to the city. This structure had been purpose built to control the city and house the main arsenal, huge amounts of small arms and ammunition as well as the Spanish guns captured at the battles of Uclés, Almonacid and Ocaña. Ross described the capitulation by Lafon-Blaniac.

> Aug 13th – Lord Wellington fixes head-quarters in the Palacio del Rey. Reconnoitres the Retiro and La China. Col Burgoyne is sent to communicate with the Governor, who refuses to surrender, and, in consequence, the outer wall which surrounds the La China Fort at a distance and connects with the Retiro, is broken at several places after dark. The pipes conveying the principal water supply to the fort cut off; and as the troops occupying the Retiro are in danger of being cut off from any relief, the Governor withdraws them within the works of La China …
>
> Aug 14th – The 7th and 3rd Divisions ordered for the assault in the morning; but the Governor offering to surrender, a capitulation is drawn up … Two thousand and upwards effective men are marched off at four o'clock in the evening, and there are 300 or 400 sick, unfit to move, 203 pieces of artillery (principally French) nearly 20,000 stand of arms (nine of the English) and clothing for 10,000 men, besides an immense quantity of ammunition, timber iron, and every stores, and two eagles found in the place.[8]

Some heavy guns were also being moved into place to assist the infantry in their planned assault although it is unclear who was manning the guns and where the heavy ordnance had been found within the city. Dickson was following the army with the reserve artillery which included the three 18-pounders of Glubb's Company (commanded by Captain Power) but he received orders to hold the guns at the pass over the Guadarrama on the 15th August and await further orders. With the capitulation the day prior it was, to all intents and purposes, academic and, with the city rid of the final vestiges of French rule, the officers of Wellington's army had other things on their minds. Ross completed his entry of the 14th August with 'Go to the Opera'; after so many months campaigning in remote and inhospitable terrain the allure of Madrid must have seemed like a distant dream. Some even suggested that 'Madrid, to speak plain, is … far superior to London'[9] and Dansey wrote that he 'never saw [such] a handsome town, the streets are wide and spacious, and every house is like a palace'.[10] Wellington was in no hurry to cut short their fun as he was waiting for confirmation of Soult's intentions in Andalusia and it was not until the end of the month that he received the information he sought. Soult, having delayed evacuation from the southern region until the last possible moment, had negated the possibility of falling back on Toledo and elected instead to withdraw east towards Valencia.

> According to accounts which I have received from Gen. J. O'Donnell, commanding the Spanish Army of Murcia, of the 25th and 27th inst., I learn that The King has decidedly marched to Valencia … The reports still continue to prevail of the intentions of Soult to evacuate Andalusia … there is reason to believe that such design is being entertained … Lieut. Gen. Sir R. Hill had no intelligence that the march was commenced on 23rd inst., when I last heard from him; but there is every appearance of it … I propose to return to this part of the country, as soon as I have settled matters to my satisfaction to the right of the Duero; and I hope I shall be here, and shall be joined by the troops under Sir R. Hill before Soult can have made much progress to form his junction with the King. With a view to Sir R. Hill's march, we are employed in repairing the bridge at Almaraz.[11]

While Wellington's main army had been engaged against Marmont and Joseph in the centre of the country, Hill and his corps had not been idle in the south. Things did not start well with the rather questionable cavalry performance at Maguilla on the 11th June which prompted Wellington to write to Hill in the most derisive manner about the cavalry's performance and agreeing to the need for an inquiry. Matters improved, however, when Hill's force successfully checked the advance of Drouet's two divisions at Albuera in late June and early July. Hill then took the fight to Drouet, forcing the French commander to fall back on his lines of communication with Andalusia. Later in the month the French began to move north in response to orders from Madrid to concentrate, resulting in an engagement on the 24th July at Ribera (del Fresno) at which 'D' Troop distinguished itself.

> On the morning of the 24th, two regiments of French dragoons and one regiment of Chasseurs, under General Lallemand, drove in the Portuguese picquet from Hinojosa to Ribera, where four squadrons of Portuguese cavalry were stationed under Colonel Campbell. His force being so inferior to the enemy, Campbell retired upon Villa Franca, from where General Long's Brigade advanced, accompanied by 'D' Troop. The enemy withdrew beyond the defile of Ribera,

through which Long advanced, and, pushing his squadrons round the town, attacked the enemy with spirit, while the Artillery fired with great effect from some high ground, and near the river on the Villa Franca side of the defile. The French gave way and retired rapidly on Hinojosa.[12]

General Long warmly congratulated captains Lefebure and Whinyates in his dispatch, complimenting the troop on its movement and accuracy of fire. Even General François-Antoine Lallemand commented during the subsequent cessation of hostilities on the efficiency of the guns and sent the following message to Whinyates who was commanding the guns near the river: 'Tell that brave man that if it had not been for him I should have beaten your cavalry; but that, meeting me in every movement with his fire, he never would allow me to form for the attack. Say that I shall mention his name in my orders as having been the cause of our defeat, and not your cavalry. Be sure you tell him this, promise to give him my message'.[13] In addition to 'D' Troop and two brigades of artillery from the Portuguese Army, Hill also had Maxwell's Company who were brigaded with 9-pounders. In July 1812, William Webber returned to the Peninsula as the second captain of the company, having last seen service in theatre with 'C' Troop during Moore's campaign and retreat in 1808–09. Wellington's orders for Hill to move north and link up had not reached the corps commander by the start of September but Webber was well aware that instructions were imminent.

No orders for marching, which we know not how to account for unless Gen Hill is waiting for Lord Wellington's further directions. A Spanish Sergeant, deserter from the French army, came in today and gave information that Soult is retiring in great haste, abandoning his sick, destroying most of his carriages and marching for Valencia. His army, very sickly and much dispersed. If half this is true it is enough. The Spaniards positively assure us that our English force is in Cordoba – if so this must be Col Skerrett's, who may have followed the rear of Soult's army.[14]

On the 31st August, with no definite intelligence as to Soult's exact future intentions but satisfied that Hill was finally on the move, Wellington felt compelled to commence his autumn campaign by advancing north to re-engage the Army of Portugal who had grown in confidence, evicted the Galician Division from Valladolid and begun to pose a threat to Wellington's left flank and lines of communication. To counter Clausel he took the 1st, 5th, 6th and 7th divisions, Pack's and Bradford's Portuguese brigades, and Bock and Ponsonby's brigades of heavy dragoons. The divisions had their integral artillery brigades (see Chapter 14), Bull's Troop went in support of the cavalry and Dickson brought up the reserve artillery consisting of three 18-pounders under Captain Power and five iron 24-pounder howitzers under Captain Arriaga with fewer than 3,000 rounds of various descriptions. The 3rd and Light divisions were left in Madrid, the 4th Division at Escorial and De España's Spanish Division at Segovia. These divisions, and their direct support artillery brigades, had suffered heavily during the preceding campaigns and their exclusion from the pursuit force provided some badly needed relief. However, Wellington's decision to leave half his infantry divisions around Madrid is interesting, for by the time Hill's force had joined them from the south this force numbered in excess of 40,000, while that taken by Wellington in pursuit of Clausel totalled less than 30,000. As events unfolded, it was to prove an error.

A more critical error, however, was the composition of the artillery train. Although Framingham was still the CRA, Robe was designated the commander of the artillery for the pursuit force and Dickson was in charge of the reserve. All three officers would have had a hand in the decision-making process and there is no evidence that their hands were tied in the matter by the commander-in-chief's decree. In point of fact the decisions on both the force balance and heavy artillery were predicated on the belief that Soult would move north and not east and that the combined forces of Soult, Joseph and (potentially) Suchet would therefore make an attempt on the capital. Notwithstanding, the British siege train was, at this juncture, split between Elvas in the south and Almeida/Ciudad Rodrigo in the north, with the bulk at the latter locations.[15] Wellington's decision not to risk losing these assets was understandable: also at Ciudad Rodrigo were the remnants of the Army of Portugal's siege train captured that January consisting of nearly 50 pieces of ordnance, while within the confines of the Retiro were other (modern French) siege guns. The decision not to bring forward and take some of this equipment is less easily dismissed and Wellington, his staff, and the artillery and engineer commands must all take their share of blame in this seemingly astonishing oversight.

The advance from Madrid commenced on the 1st September and, as the allies closed on Clausel's force at Valladolid, the Army of Portugal fell back to Burgos. Since 1808 the French had rebuilt and strengthened the old medieval castle and established a large logistic base there. The garrison was commanded by Brigadier General Jean-Louis Dubreton and consisted of 2,000 men and nine heavy guns. The allies closed in on the city on the 18th September prompting Clausel to evacuate the municipality and fall back many miles on the road towards the River Ebro. Robe was up with the leading elements of Wellington's force and quickly recognised that the castle was a far more formidable structure than they had hitherto realised. He wrote to Dickson who was sick and convalescing at Valladolid.

> We are within two leagues of Burgos whither we expect to march and attack the enemy if he stands this morning. He seems disposed to dispute the ground and yields it only as we advance, yet he has not yet stood for close attack. We have had a view of the castle which appears a more tough job than we might have supposed. It stands on a knoll above the town and is separated from the remaining part of the height by a deep valley and there is a hornwork unfinished on the height which appears the only approach.[16]

Dickson's reserve had continued without him and on the 19th September the park was established at Villatoro and Captain Hugh Carncross was sent from Robe's staff to look after matters in the interim. The investment was complete the same day and things started well with a successful storming of the hornwork, despite losses being greater than hoped in this preliminary operation. Work began immediately on the approaches and batteries and the first battery of two 18-pounders and three howitzers was complete and armed on the night of the 22nd September and prepared but Wellington, acutely aware of his inadequate train, his lack of ammunition and perhaps encouraged by the success in storming the hornwork, decided to attempt another attack by escalade. Four hundred men under the command of Major Andrew Lawrie (79th Foot) attempted the storm but were quickly pinned down and subjected to heavy and accurate fire from the city's ramparts, Lawrie was killed and the attempt called off with the worthless waste of 160 lives. Wellington and his engineer commander, John Fox Burgoyne, accepted that their only option was to sap to the outer wall and destroy the defences by use of mines. Dickson had, by now, arrived and the second battery position was also complete. The two guns were moved from Battery 1 into the new battery and all the howitzers were now placed into the first battery and they opened on the 25th September in an attempt to destroy the palisades on the outer wall 'but without much success, it being found that from the want of precision in the howitzers with round shot, a greater expenditure of ammunition would be required …'.[17]

At this point it must have been abundantly apparent that the structure at Burgos was not going to succumb. About 10 per cent of the howitzer ammunition had been employed in trying to knock down the palisades at a range of about 350 yards; if they were unsuccessful in dislodging wooden stakes at such a short range it was evident for all that against stone and masonry they would be virtually futile. This should not have come as a surprise to men like Dickson and Robe yet there is no evidence that they expressed any such sentiment to Wellington; instead Dickson's notes highlight a preoccupation with duty rosters and relief procedures. Lieutenant Colonel John Jones was Burgoyne's second in command and his record of events reinforced the state of the besieging infantry morale following the failure of the second attempt at escalade.

At midnight, a storming party of 300 men having paraded in the lower trenches … the mine was sprung. The explosion made very little report, but brought the wall down. The earth of the rampart behind the ruined escarp remained very steep … the breach, however, was not such as a charge of 1080 lbs. of powder … ought to have produced … The night being dark, and the circumstances of the case novel, the officer commanding the first division of the storming party erred in direction of the breach, and reached the escarp wall too much to his right; where finding the masonry uninjured, he returned his party into the parallel … and was ordered to retire … during the interval, the garrison had formed under arms and a considerable force had moved to the breach, so as to preclude all hope of success in a second attempt, no further effort was made.[18]

Over the next few days the guns and howitzers tried to batter a new breach on the west wall and level the supporting palisades; on the night of the 4th October a second mine was sprung and the subsequent assault successful in that the storming parties established a lodgement driving the French back behind their retrenched defences. However, this encroachment was short lived, for the next day a vigorous sortie drove the British infantry back off the breach and the defenders quickly re-established the outer defensive line. Dickson tried to replicate the success at the Salamanca forts by firing heated shot at the church of Santa Maria la Blanca but this had mixed results and by the close of play on the 10th October there were only 42 rounds of 24-pounder shot remaining. The shortage of ammunition was a critical factor and the levels of 18-pounder ammunition would have been equally alarming had it not been for the policy of rewarding soldiers for bringing in 'fired' French shot or, more boldly perhaps, in recovering 'English shot dug out of the breach'. The French 16-pounder ammunition could be used; the windage was greater and the energy correspondingly reduced, but it added in excess of 400 badly needed shot to the magazine. Powder was also in short supply and as early as the 26th September Wellington had written to Admiral Sir Home Riggs Popham, who was operating off the Cantabrian coast (in conjunction with the many guerrilla bands), and requested support. Ten days later 40 barrels duly arrived at the artillery park but it seems extraordinary that some naval 24-pounders were not also requested at the same time. Two guns were indeed dispatched on the 9th October but they were still 50 miles from Burgos when Wellington lifted the siege; they could have made a large difference if they had been requested at the same time as the powder.

Amidst rumours of French stirrings to the north, Wellington was determined to have one last attempt to capture the fortress but two failed assaults, a lack of infantry ammunition, the paucity of trained sappers and miners, the woefully inadequate train of artillery and the relative successes of the French sorties had served to erode infantry morale. The attack, when delivered, was not pressed home with the unbridled courage and determination of the year's earlier sieges:

> The Engineers boldly carried the sap commenced at that part of the 3rd line in our possession to within 6 feet of the 2nd line. Mines were made and charged. The field guns were placed in battery at different posts on the opposite side of the Citadel to that attacked, and by their fire annoyed and distracted the attention of the fort from the troops in the trenches, and things being finally arranged, a signal was given and the mines being sprung, the troops rushed forward to possess themselves of the breaches and to assault the works. For a while they were successful, but eventually they were repulsed, leaving some of their dead on the parapet of the 3rd line, a proof of the courage of the troops who advanced at open day across a space swept by the grape and musketry of the garrison from behind their walls and entrenchments. This was the last serious effort made to possess ourselves of the fort by assault, and, as from the first the troops had seen the inadequacy of our means in artillery, the operations were not begun, or carried on, with that same spirit as at C. Rodrigo or Badajos, which seemed to cause some discontent at the troops in the mind of the Commander-in-Chief.[19]

The siege was raised at 0500 hours on the 22nd October; Ross, who was still in Madrid, had written the following three days earlier:

> Perhaps while I am writing the place may be ours, but I confess I am not very sanguine; and even should you have later accounts from thence than this will

convey, I am sure you will excuse me for giving you the foregoing extract, which will at least show you the poverty of means our corps have had to work with; and even if his Lordship should deal with us in his usual cold manner in his report of the affair, I trust that you will believe that those who have been employed in it have not been wanting in zeal and exertion.[20]

Ross's support of his brother officers and men was commendable; artillery losses were 16 killed (including Lieutenant Felizardo Xavier Pereira of the Portuguese Artillery) and 46 wounded including Power, Dansey and Elgee, but his assessment of Wellington's report on the matter was, on this occasion, a touch harsh. In his subsequent dispatch the commander-in-chief praised his technical staff and accepted full responsibility for the failure.

> The officers at the head of the Artillery and Engineer departments, Lieut. Col. Robe and Lieut. Col. Burgoyne, and Lieut. Col. Dickson, who commands the reserve artillery, rendered me every assistance, and the failure of success is not to be attributed to them. By their activity we carried off every thing in the course of one night, excepting 3 18 pounders destroyed by the enemy's fire, and the 8 pieces of cannon which we had taken from the enemy on the night of the 19th ult., in the storm of the horn work, not having cattle to move them.[21]

At the commencement of the withdrawal Wellington's army was unbalanced and vulnerable, the weather had turned and morale had been badly affected by the failure under the walls of Burgos. Discipline began to unravel at an alarming rate and comparisons with Moore's force in 1809 were immediately apparent.

> The effects of the privations during the siege, the wet weather and these forced marches caused some relaxation in the discipline of the Army. The soldiers in many instances broke into wine cellars and, many drinking to excess, became incapable of proceeding and fell into the hands of the advance-guard of the French.[22]

> Our halt here [Dueñas] has restored order to the army. Our march from Ribena [Rubena] and Burgos to Duenas was a sad scene. I am sorry to say I again witnessed the disorganisation and excesses that occasioned such trouble and mortification to Sir John Moore in Galicia. In other respects the movements of our retreat have been a masterpiece of skill.[23]

> At 4 o Cl. a.m. went to the front with orders to Capt. Macdonald's Troop; returned to the camp and at 7 marched for Dueñas 4 long leagues, the French quite close on our rear. Major Bull's Troop H.A. and the cavalry skirmish all day. Our loss both this and yesterday was rather severe, the enemy having a great superiority in cavalry.[24]

To the south, Hill had been ordered to fall back on Salamanca from his position along the River Tagus. For the inhabitants of Madrid the prospect of once again being under the French heel was too much to bear.

I did not go to Madrid, unwilling to witness such sad scenes, but Maxwell was there and gave me an account of them. Those who had been most conspicuous in their attentions to the British army and most forward in rejoicing at their entrance, were obliged to quit it from fear of death. For the French would have been made acquainted with every one and not one would have escaped punishment of some kind. The Retiro was ordered to be blown up and our engineers are employed in mining it. All the gun, carriages etc. in it are to be destroyed and the explosion is expected to take place tomorrow morning. Soult sent a message by a Spaniard a few days ago to Madrid saying he should dine there on the 1st November, and so I think he will.[25]

We arrived at the Madrid bridge where we met Captain Cleeves, of the German Legion Artillery, who having the day before destroyed the greater part of the Retiro and all the battering train had returned anxious, before the French came, to blow up one mine which had failed. I volunteered going with him. When we went into the mine I could not but notice a want of caution in the way the train was laid, but nevertheless agreed to do the job with him. He, anxious to perform his duty without assistance, sent me to see if the coast was clear, and put the match to the train, when to my dismay the whole exploded before he was out of the building, and so persuaded was I that he had perished, that I dismounted from my horse and took a shovel to dig him out, when, making my way in the dark through the smoke that almost suffocated me, to my astonishment, he came out, with no other injury than being well burnt.[26]

By the 8th November Wellington's army was complete at Salamanca and had a defensive screen along the line of the River Tormes. The rigours of the retreat were experienced by all, regardless of rank:

This day a curious circumstance occurred at the Head Quarters of Earl Wellington as follows; the troops went into the village to procure wood, and after unroofing [sic] several houses they came to the house where Earl Wellington slept (not knowing it was his quarters) and began very deliberately to unroof [sic] the house. My Lord hearing the noise came out, and perceiving what they were about, begged of them to go to some other place and 'for God's sake let him have the roof for one more night' ... shortly after seeing his head servant, a black man, on top of the house getting wood, called to him by his name and said 'What are you about?' 'Oh, nothing master, My Lord, only getting a piece of wood to cook dinner with'. He had on one of his Lordships old cock'd hats with the feather around it: in the near time The Prince of Orange [one of Wellington's ADCs] came up to his Lordship and seeing the black [man] with my Lord's hat on exclaimed 'By God, now Lord we have got a black general at last', at which his Lordship and attendant laughed heartily.[27]

The French were hot on Wellington's heels and Soult, Joseph and Jourdan all agreed to wait for the arrival of the French armies of the South, Centre and Portugal before forcing battle. On the 10th November, while the French were concentrating, Soult decided to test Wellington's resolve at Alba de Tormes; probing and general actions continued at the bridgehead and along the river for the next few days. The allied troops holding the town, castle and the west bank came from Hamilton's Portuguese Division supported by João Da Cunha Preto's and William Braun's brigades of artillery, and from the 2nd Division supported by Maxwell's Brigade of guns and the cavalry supported by 'D' Troop, which was by this time under the command of Whinyates, Lefebure having died of fever at Madrid on the 22nd October.

November 10: Several bodies of cavalry were seen moving opposite us this morning. At 3 in the afternoon the enemy invested and cannonaded the castle of Alba …

November 11: All our cavalry left us for the fords. The enemy in great force are very visible with a glass and we expect something to be done before night … At 1 o'clock Trotter was ordered with two guns to attach himself to Colonel Ashworth's Brigade of Portuguese Infantry and at 3 they marched to a ford higher up the river …

November 14: At 9 a.m. heard that the enemy had been crossing the river without opposition since daylight. The [Spanish] garrison of Alba de Tormes abandoned it about half past nine, after crossing the bridge, the mine was sprung and the entire centre of it was completely destroyed. At 10 we were ordered to march … we went to the Arapiles and from thence to the left of Lord Wellington's intended position … After remaining on the ground about 2 hours, at 3 o'clock we marched for another part of the position … to take up ground on top of the hill where the Horse Artillery (Captain Whinyates' Troop) were already posted and had commenced firing … On reaching the place marked out for our brigade we had orders to fire on a large body of French cavalry in our front and distant about 1,500 yards. Our fire with round shot and spherical case had great effect and after sustaining considerable loss from a discharge of 55 rounds, they retired in good order. I never saw troops more steady, for although the round shot made interval in their ranks, there was not the least appearance of confusion. Lord Wellington and staff were behind some rocks and close to our right hand gun, noticing the effect of our fire. The guns of the Horse Artillery were of too small a calibre for such a range and ceased firing when we commenced.[28]

The greater reach and effect of Maxwell's 9-pounder guns will undoubtedly have left an impression on Wellington but, for now, he had more pressing issues on his mind. His force was split between their positions north of Salamanca at San Cristóbal and those to the south astride the Arapiles and the combined French armies were trying to outflank his force from the south. Wellington collected his army on the southern position and the next day offered battle to Soult who, acutely aware of outcome of the last encounter on this ground, declined. Soon after midday, Wellington realised he could linger no longer and ordered an immediate retreat on Ciudad Rodrigo. Ingilby recalled that 'the weather was cold and the rain fell very heavy, accompanied with strong winds'.[29] The retreat was yet another Peninsular chapter of hardship, excesses, aggressive pursuit and equally forceful rearguard actions; by the 17th November the Light Division was at San Muñoz:

> Engaged this day. The Division is surrounded by the enemy's cavalry and headed by their horse artillery. 5 or 6 miles at times thro' a long dreary wood and bad roads … On approaching the end of the wood the enemy pressed our rear. The Troop came into action on a body of cavalry. Genl. Sir E. Paget taken prisoner by another body of cavalry on our right. The Division formed square, troop limber up, the whole move off. The infantry takes the mountain to the right retiring, Troop keeps the road between the two mountains, in the valley is a river midsize deep for the ammunition wagons and baggage mules were fording. The enemy brought 8 guns into action on them. Killed a horse belonging to Col Sir H D Ross and a mule belonging to Lt Belson. The wife of Gunner John Butcher seated on her pony with her little baggage when a gunshot struck the pony's head from his neck, down she drops, she carries away her baggage in safety. The Troop has not reached the ford, Captain Macdonald's Troop now comes into action above our guns. Troop forded the river under the crossfire of the enemy and as the Light Division had made a long circuit round the mountains closely pressed with a body of cavalry and guns. Troop hastened to them and came into action while they forded the river and checked the enemy's advance. Captain Macdonald severely wounded. Night put an end to the affair.[30]

Within hours the French had broken off the pursuit and Wellington's army were able to continue their retreat unmolested; but racked with fever, exhaustion and half starved, many men were unable to continue and died where they lay. In fact many of the men had been sick for weeks; there had been a general fever which had permeated Hill's men as they waited along the valley of the Tagus, while that of the main army had been brought about through general fatigue of campaigning without halt. Over the next few weeks the army moved into their winter cantonments and at the end of the year the artillery was as follows:

CRA: Lt. Col. G. B. Fisher RA
Staff: Lt. Col. W. Robe RA (injured)
Brigade Major: Lt. Col. J. May RA
Horse Artillery: Maj. T. Downman RA
Field Artillery: Maj. J. H. Carncross RA
Reserve Artillery: Lt. Col. A. Dickson RA
Adjutant: Lt. A. Woodyear RA

RHA Troops	Notes	Equipment
'A' Troop (Ross)	Attached to the Light Division. Cantoned at Aldea del Obispo, Spain.	5 x long 6-pounders 1 x 5½-inch iron howitzer
'D' Troop (Bean)	Attached to 2nd Cavalry Division. Cantoned at Zarza la Mayor, Spain.	5 x long 6-pounders 1 x 5½-inch iron howitzer

Lefebure had died at Madrid 23rd October
1812 – Bean did not join until March 1813.

'E' Troop (Macdonald)	Attached to 7th Division. Cantoned at Sampaio, Portugal.	5 x long 6-pounders 1 x 5½-inch iron howitzer
'I' Troop (Bull)	Attached to 1st Cavalry Division. Cantoned at Midões, Portugal.	5 x long 6-pounders 1 x 5½-inch iron howitzer
RA Companies	**Notes**	**Equipment**
Gardiner's Company	Attached to 1st Division. Cantoned at Pena Verde, Portugal.	5 x 9-pounders 1 x 5½-inch iron howitzer
Maxwell's Company	Attached to 2nd Division. Cantoned at Alcains, Portugal.	5 x 9-pounders 1 x 5½-inch howitzer
Douglas's Company	Attached to 3rd Division. Cantoned at Sernancelhe, Portugal.	5 x 9-pounders 1 x 5½-inch howitzer
Sympher's Company KGA	Attached to 4th Division. Cantoned along the Douro, Portugal.	5 x 9-pounders 1 x 5½-inch howitzer
Lawson's Company	Attached to 5th Division. Cantoned at Mondim, Portugal.	5 x 6-pounders 1 x 5½-inch iron howitzer
Brandreth's Company	Attached to 6th Division. Cantoned at Torrozelo, Portugal. Eligé KIA at the Salamanca siege.	5 x light 6-pounders 1 x 5½-inch iron howitzer
Glubb's Company	Reserve: Commanded by 2nd Capt. Power. Cantonment unknown.	4 x 18-pounders
Dickson's Company	Reserve: Commanded by 2nd Capt. R. H. Birch, moved from Cadiz in October. Cantoned at Valle de Mula, Portugal.	5 x 9-pounders 1 x 5½-inch iron howitzer
Stone's Company[31]	Reserve: Commanded by 2nd Capt. J. M. Parker, joined army in November. Cantoned at Covilhá, Portugal.	5 x 9-pounders 1 x 5½-inch iron howitzer
May's Company	Commanded by 2nd Capt. H. Baynes – in charge of reserve ammunition. Cantoned at Covilhá, Portugal	Nil
Owen's Company	Reserve. Cantoned at Coimbra, Portugal.	Nil
Arriaga's Company	Reserve. Cantoned along the Douro, Portugal.	24-pounder howitzers, left at Almeida
Rozierres's Company	Reserve. Cantoned along the Douro, Portugal.	Light 6-pounders, left at Almeida
Da Cunha Preto's Company	Attached to Hamilton's Portuguese Division. Under Lt. Col. Tulloh – moved to Elvas. Refitting at Elvas	
Braun's Company	Attached to Hamilton's Portuguese Division Under Lt. Col. Tulloh – moved to Elvas. Refitting at Elvas	

Sources: Dickson, Laws, Leslie, Vigors and Teixeira Botelho.

Macdonald was 'wounded in the thigh with a shell, which laid it open to the bone' but he was not the only senior artillery officer to be injured during the retreat.[32]

Robe had also received a severe leg wound at Cabezón on the 17th October during the retreat from Burgos. This latter injury was of considerable inconvenience to Wellington as he was rather hoping to supersede Framingham (for the second time) as CRA and a combination of Robe and Dickson suited his purposes. Rather than risk another 'unknown' from the aged ranks of the senior artillery officers appointed by the Board of Ordnance, Wellington opted for Lieutenant Colonel George Bulteel Fisher who had been commanding the artillery in Lisbon since early 1809 and he wrote to the Earl of Mulgrave on the matter.

> I enclose a letter which I have received from Col. Robe from which you will see that his wound is of a nature to prevent, for the present at least, the services in this country ... As it is possible that Col. Robe may return, and I may have reason to be satisfied with the intelligence and zeal of Col. Fisher, I am not desirous that that officer should be superseded. His health is not very good, but I hope he will last out.[33]

Henegan, who was commanding the Field Train, had daily contact with Fisher, a superior officer he considered 'had seen but little service beyond the routine of garrison duty at Lisbon; where he was much liked and respected for his many kind and gentlemanly qualities – to these, however, nature had not added the requisites for a rough and ready soldier'.[34] Fisher, a man with a creative temperament and undoubted artistic ability, was happily ensconced in Lisbon and was far from contented at the prospect of joining the field army. He expressed his concerns to Robe in early November.

> Since I wrote you my private letter saying I thought it necessary to put myself under the hands of a physician in Belem ... the charge you mention may want a great deal of my personal looking into and attention, and if my health should prevent my doing this and I have not people under me I can look to, everything must go to rack and ruin. I must leave this matter to your good judgement what I am fitted for best, whether for this or with some division of the army, and if I should be *hors de combat*, which service might suffer most by such a circumstance.[35]

Fisher's concerns as to his suitability were well placed but not for health reasons; his temperament was entirely unsuited to working on the staff for a commander like Wellington and within weeks it was clear that the commander-in-chief was not happy.

> Fisher who has done the Corps more good in four months than his predecessors could contrive in four years & who promised to represent & command us ably as we could desire, is another sacrifice to his abominable intemperance & disregard of all consideration of feeling etc. etc. His dismissal literally arose (as well as we can learn) from his not being able to tell him at what place so many remount horses would be on such a day on their march from Lisbon, and in what exact number. He was then asked some details about the Portuguese Artillery, about who he professed candidly to know nothing as he had only then for the first time known

that he had anything to say to them. His Lordship in a rage said 'Sir, you know nothing', so when Fisher got home he wrote a letter asking for leave which Lord W. answered in his own hand – a letter that gratified Fisher which is enough, but not considered by his friends at all reconciling or satisfactory.[36]

Fisher's letter to Macleod informing him of his decision to resign the command of the artillery was full of emotion.

> Under these circumstances it has been extremely unfortunate that I should have seemed to have lost the confidence of the Commander of the Forces, at a time when everything was accomplished, and without feeling any consciousness on my part having merited a distrust and mode of treatment painful and distressing to my feelings – such, however, being the case, and at the same time feeling my state of health perfectly unequal to struggle not only with the unavoidable fatigues of a campaign but to bear up against that want of countenance and support which I felt necessary to one in the highly arduous and responsible situation I found myself placed in, I came to the resolution of retiring from a command which however flattering with the promises held out at the commencement, has become painful and distressing to the greatest degree.[37]

Lieutenant Colonel Charles Waller was now the most senior officer of the artillery in theatre and must have considered his claim to the artillery commander's post all but sealed. However, his rather arrogant, know-it-all manner was acknowledged across the force; William Swabey had recorded, as early as May the previous year, Waller's opinionated manner.

> I may be pardoned for predicting that his [Waller's] plans for the improvement of the corps here will not be attended with success, and I think him a little presumptuous in forming any, especially as they are directly opposed to what experience points out in this country. They are the more objectionable as being in direct opposition to Lord Wellington's to conciliate whom is the only road to popularity, and by no means incompatible with independence of thought and feeling.[38]

'Chas' Waller, far from fulfilling his yearning ambition, found himself consigned to the rather dull and mundane administrative command at Lisbon, with the following artillery units:

Artillery Commander Lisbon Garrison: Lt. Col. C. Waller RA
Adjutant: Lt. Litchfield RA

RA and KGA Companies	Notes
Bredin's Company	In garrison at Fort São Julião, Lisbon.
Morrison's Company	In garrison at Lisbon, arrived 24th October 1812.
Von Rettberg's Company KGA	In garrison at Lisbon – detachment at Badajoz.
Cleeves's Company KGA	In garrison at Lisbon.

Cadiz Garrison

Hughes's Company	Isla de Leon, Cadiz.
Shenley's Company	Cadiz.
Roberts's Company	Isla de Leon, Cadiz.

Sources: Dickson, Laws and Leslie.

Fisher's relief led to Waller's disappointment and ultimately to Dickson's joy; for finally Wellington was to have *his* man.

Notes

1. Dyneley, letter from Madrid, dated 21st August 1812.
2. Ibid.
3. Ibid.
4. Ibid.
5. Ross, p.30, dated 12th August 1812.
6. Hough, entry dated 12th August 1812.
7. Ingilby, 14th August 1812.
8. Ross, pp.13–14, dated 13th and 14th August 1812. The two eagles are those of the 51e Ligne and the 13e Dragoons and remain to this day in the Royal Chelsea Hospital, London.
9. Hough, entry dated 14th August 1812.
10. Dansey (ed. Glover), letter dated 21st August 1812.
11. WD, vol. VI, pp.48–49. Wellington to Bathurst from Madrid, dated 30th August 1812.
12. Whinyates, WCS, p.63. 'D' Troop at Ribera.
13. Ibid., p.64.
14. Webber (ed. Wollocombe), p.46, dated 4th September 1812.
15. The train at Almeida and Ciudad Rodrigo consisted of 18 x 24-pounder guns, 4 x 18-pounder guns, 8 x 10-inch mortars, 4 x 24-pounder (iron) howitzers, 10 x 5½-inch howitzers and 2 x 8-inch howitzers: at Elvas there were 16 x 24-pounder guns, 10 x 24-pounder (iron) howitzers and the 20 x (Russian) 18-pounder guns.
16. Dickson, vol. IV, pp.742–43. Letter from Robe to Dickson from Frandovínez, dated 18th September 1812.
17. Jones, vol. I, p.289. Entry for 25th September 1812.
18. Ibid., pp.305–07.
19. Ingilby, 18th October 1812.
20. Ross, p.34. Letter from Ross to Dalrymple Ross from Madrid, dated 18th October 1812.
21. WD, vol. VI, p.135. Wellington to Bathurst from Cabezón, dated 26th October 1812.
22. Ingilby, 23rd October 1812.
23. Gardiner, letter FB 25, from camp before Tordesillas, dated 4th November 1812.

24. Hough, entry dated 24th October 1812.

25. Webber (ed. Wollocombe), p.102, dated 30th October 1812.

26. Swabey (ed. Whinyates), dated 3rd November 1812. Swabey clearly has confused the date as the allies evacuated Madrid on the 31st October and the French entered the next day.

27. Whitman, p.66, dated 8th November 1812.

28. Webber (ed. Wollocombe), pp.110–111, entries for 11–14th November 1812.

29. Ingilby, 15th October 1812.

30. Whitehead (ed), entry for 18th November 1812, San Muñoz camp. (Date should have read 17th November 1812.)

31. Captain Stone was attached to the British Embassy in Persia.

32. Belson, dated 17th November 1812.

33. WD, vol. VI, p.251. Wellington to Mulgrave from Freineda, dated 27th January 1813.

34. Henegan, vol. I, p.163.

35. Dickson, vol. IV, pp.781–82. Letter from Fisher to Robe from Lisbon, dated 3rd November 1812.

36. Letter from 2nd Capt. Cairnes RA, who was commanding Dickson's Company written to his step-father, Major General William Cuppage RA, from Itero del Castillo, dated 11th June 1813. Listed in Dickson, vol. V, pp.902–05.

37. PRO WO 55/1195. Letter Fisher to MacLeod dated 11th May 1813.

38. Swabey (ed. Whinyates), dated 12th May 1811.

CHAPTER 16

Holcombe's Opportunity

In the east of Spain, Tarragona had fallen to Suchet's forces by the end of June 1811 and, with Tortosa in French hands, following the siege at the start of the year, the road to the region of Valencia was now open. With each conquest Suchet's army began to dwindle, as he was committed to leaving elements of his force to garrison these captured fortifications and municipalities. Furthermore, the movement of his siege train south along the coast road was subject to frequent attacks by Spanish guerrillas from the mountains and coastal bombardment by Royal Navy ships in the Mediterranean. Consequently, his army did not reach its next objective for a full three months. At the end of September they arrived at the walls of the fort at Saguntum; a structure which had held up Hannibal during the 2nd Punic Wars. It boasted no 'modern' Vauban defences but was to prove a difficult nut to crack. Indeed, Suchet failed to capture the fort by conventional means; in the end the garrison surrendered the day after they witnessed their Army of Valencia beaten on the plains south of the fort. The city of Valencia fell in early January 1812 and Suchet, now behind schedule, began planning for the final push to capture Alicante. Napoleon was also planning; his objective was Moscow, but he had nevertheless been impressed with Suchet's achievements, which shone like a beacon in a sea of subordinate mediocrity. Accordingly, the Emperor ordered another 15,000 men to be redirected from the other French armies in Spain to assist operations on the east coast which was, by now, the French main effort in Iberia. The majority of these reinforcements came from Marmont's Army of Portugal, thereby creating the opportunity which Wellington had capitalised upon so adroitly at the commencement of the Salamanca campaign.

That campaign had commenced, as we have seen, with the capture of Ciudad Rodrigo and then Badajoz before a series of diversionary and preliminary operations were executed, or instigated, to coincide with the allied advance to Salamanca. One such operation was the landing of an Anglo-Sicilian expeditionary force, supplemented by two Spanish divisions under British officers Philip Keating Roche and Samuel Ford Whittingham, based at Alicante and Majorca respectively. This expeditionary force was expected to concentrate on the Spanish mainland some time in June; however, Lord William Bentinck, the British commander in Sicily, grew increasingly alarmed at the recent intrigues of the Queen of Sicily and began to get cold feet, pontificated and consequently missed the prescribed deployment timeline. It was the end of July before the force finally arrived off the coast of Catalonia and, at 14,000 men (including the Spanish), the numbers were less than previously expected. However, the force commander, General Frederick Maitland, was unable to agree terms with the Spanish commanders in the region and immediately re-embarked, setting sail for Alicante where he and his force arrived on the 7th August 1812. He was greeted with the news that the combined 2nd and 3rd Spanish armies under General Joseph O'Donnell had, contrary to Wellington's orders, attacked Suchet's forces and been heavily defeated at Castalla.

Thus events on the east coast had not started well for the allies and it was to be some months before they were able to take the fight to the French, by which time the battle at Salamanca had been fought and won and Madrid had been liberated; prompting Soult to finally concede that his position in Andalusia was untenable, activating his easterly withdrawal. General Juan de la Cruz Mourgeon and Colonel Skerrett followed in his wake and secured Seville in late August. Lieutenant Spencer Brett RA (P. Campbell's Company) was attached to Skerrett's *ad hoc* group and was killed in action during operations to secure the city. Wellington issued swift orders for an additional force of about 4,000 men to move from Cadiz to Seville and protect this key acquisition. This group included Dickson's Company (commanded by Cairnes) and Owen's Company, both under the overall command of (brevet) Lieutenant Colonel Alexander Duncan.[1] At the end of the month Duncan, Cairnes, Cator (Owen's Company) and Francis Bedingfeld (Hughes's Company) were inspecting the French powder mill in the city when it exploded:

I am extremely sorry to have to report to you, the lamented and melancholy death of Lt. Colonel Duncan on the 29th September, at Seville – he went on that day accompanied by Captains Bedingfield [Bedingfeld] and Cairnes, to see a powder mill about a league from the town; one of the workmen said there was no danger, and that he knew how to put the machinery into motion; it had scarcely commenced its movements, when the whole blew up; the Colonel was found about six yards from where he stood, in a small yard, and died almost instantaneously. Captain Cairnes is a good deal burnt, but out of any danger, and may be able to follow his Company in three or four weeks. Captain Bedingfield was a little scorched and will be able to return here in a few days.[2]

Duncan's untimely loss was a cruel reminder of the ever-present danger of serving the guns and working with the 'black' powder.

The artillery commander for Maitland's Force was Major John Williamson but when (brevet) Lieutenant Colonel Harcourt Holcombe arrived with his company, he assumed the post with Second Captain Tom Scott as his adjutant. Williamson had commanded the artillery in Sicily and this change of artillery commander and chief advisor did not meet with Maitland's approval, nor was it met with much enthusiasm by many of the other artillery officers in the force. Williamson could not hide his disappointment in his return to Macleod: 'I must reconcile myself, as well as I can, to serve under Lt. Colonel Holcombe, however unpleasant it may be to my feelings.'[3] The artillery which landed with the initial formations in August 1812 consisted of the following:[4]

CRA: Lt. Col. H. F. Holcombe RA
Staff: Maj. J. S. Williamson RA
Adjutant: Lieutenant T. Scott RA

RA Companies	Notes	Equipment
Thomson's Company	From Lisbon, via Port Mahon.	5 x long 6-pounders 1 x 5½-inch howitzer
Holcombe's Company	From Lisbon, via Port Mahon (commanded by 2nd Capt. Arabin).	5 x long 6-pounders 1 x 5½-inch howitzer
Williamson's Company	From Messina, Sicily.	5 x long 6-pounders 1 x 5½-inch howitzer
T. Cox's Company – Portuguese Artillery	Joined the force at Port Mahon.	
A. Penedo's Company – Portuguese Artillery.	Joined the force at Port Mahon.	

Sources: Dickson, Laws, Woollcombe and Scott.

With Holcombe elevated to CRA, Thompson's second in command, Second Captain Charles Gilmore, assumed temporary command of Holcombe's Brigade, as Holcombe's own second in command, Second Captain William Dundas, had been badly wounded and had lost an arm at Badajoz in April 1812, and his senior subaltern, Lieutenant Tom Cox, was commanding one of the Portuguese artillery companies. Also included in the force were some 50 gunners of the Royal Marine Artillery under Lieutenant R. P. Campbell who had been sent to Sicily (from Cadiz) in June 1812 to assist in manning the guns of the Anglo-Sicilian gunboats. Interestingly, they were equipped with some of Congreve's rockets and 50 British and Portuguese gunners were allocated to this Rocket Brigade.[5] In addition, Roche's Spanish Division had six light mountain guns mounted on mules, although Whittingham does not appear to have been similarly equipped.[6]

Initially when the force landed there was a relaxed air predicated on the firm belief that Soult would not abandon his vice regal status in Andalusia and that Joseph would not venture so far to the east. Scott, the force adjutant, somewhat bemused by the early change in CRA, soon put the interruption behind him and wasted little time in getting acquainted with some of the local girls. On the 27th August the officers of HMS *Malta* decided to host a ball in the Town Hall which presented Scott the perfect opportunity:

Went about half past 10, and upon entering the room was struck with the motley group; had eyes enough to see two or three very pretty women, who were dancing Spanish country dances, in figures infinitely prettier than ours; the music was bad and their tunes nothing remarkable ... Another, who danced a Waltz in very good style, was very pretty and by her various gestures and attitudes pretty plainly showed she was very well made. A fat lady amazed me with her activity and she certainly kicked out in uncommon touches. One man who danced with her took her in his arms and made her leave the ground two feet at least ... A violent commotion was at one time raised by some females entering, who were not invited and whose reputations were supposed to be a little worse for wear ... There are some beautiful creatures in town, but I conjecture they are not exactly *bon ton*. I was rather glad I went however.[7]

This levity was brought to an abrupt halt when it became apparent that Soult's and Joseph's armies were both moving east and appeared on a collision course with Maitland's small force and the remnants of the 2nd and 3rd Spanish armies, who were hastily trying to reorganise. The next month was, therefore, one of considerable uncertainty. However, as it transpired, Joseph went firm with Suchet's forces in the north of the region of Valencia while Soult had marched eastwards but remained in the interior and therefore gave Alicante a wide berth. Ballesteros should have been pursuing him with his division from the Spanish 4th Army, but instead had been arrested after refusing to soldier under 'the foreigner' Wellington, when the latter was elevated (following the liberation of Madrid) to Generalissimo of the Spanish Army. To make matters worse for the expeditionary force, Maitland resigned on 1st October due to ill health and was replaced. The fact of the matter was that Maitland was losing his nerve so his resignation was received with no little relief at Wellington's headquarters. However, the force was to have five commanders in as many months before Lieutenant General Sir John Murray returned to the Peninsula to assume command of the expeditionary force; a decision that cannot have overly pleased the commander-in-chief who well remembered Murray's questionable performance both in India and commanding the flanking force at the recapture of Oporto in May 1809.

Wellington's retreat from the humiliating failure at Burgos had not only drawn the Army of Portugal and elements of the Army of the North in his wake, it also provided the grounds for the French armies of the Centre and South to move west from Valencia in order to drive Hill's Corps from south of the capital and push the allies back across the Portuguese border. Significantly, and somewhat fortuitously, the presence of the allied concentration in and around Alicante prevented Suchet from joining Soult and Joseph.

Lord Wellington is convinced that the hovering on the coast for so long a time of the Alicante expedition was of essential use in distracting the attention of the enemy, and that, considering the paucity of force (the real evil), everything that could be expected was done.[8]

When Napoleon had assembled his Russian invasion force he had withdrawn formations across Iberia. Suchet had felt this loss most keenly. He had lost all his

Polish battalions and two of his trusted divisions and by mid-October, when Joseph and Soult had moved west, he had also lost his support and flank protection. His ability to take the battle to the allies was, for the time being, at an end. To his front Whittingham's Division had established a screening force in the interior between Alicante and Valencia.

> The Majorca division has the honour of occupying all the outposts of the army. I am just returned from them, and avail myself of the opportunity of a vessel going to Cadiz to let you know what is going on. We have had since our arrival a great number of affairs of posts, in all of which my troops have been successful; and have in consequence begun to form a character which I hope and trust will soon be established. My force at present is rather more than 6,000 men; but I expect another battalion from Minorca in a few days, which will complete my force to 7,000 men ... On the 18th, the French of the army of Suchet fell back from Sax, Villena, and Biar, upon Fuente la Higuera; and from Alcoy upon Concentayna, Albayda, and San Felipe [now Xàtiva]. In consequence of this movement, my advanced posts are now at Sax, Biar, and Alcoy.[9]

It would appear that Captain Frederic Arabin's Brigade of guns (Holcombe's Company) were in support of Whittingham while the balance of the Royal Artillery were cantoned around Alicante and Cox's Portuguese Company were manning the garrison guns in Alicante Castle. By early December the force had been reinforced including an additional two companies of artillery.

> Was very much surprised after breakfast to see a large fleet of transports etc. off to the eastward and the breeze springing up favourable soon signalised and proved to be the [HMS] *Thames* with a reinforcement of English and Sicilian Troops, but no Lord William (Bentinck) ... General Campbell and many of the staff arriving in the *Mermaid*. Lacy's Company arrived and another Company of Sicilian Artillery, this has put us alive for a day or two.[10]

Bentinck's non-arrival was a surprise as it was anticipated, across the force, that Lord William would come to assume overall command but Lieutenant Robert Woollcombe considered this a gracious release as he undoubtedly would have been accompanied by Lady William, who, in his opinion, 'was always the politician and may be coming to take command of the army. The command of its commander has long been vested in her hands. Nothing like a petticoat government; it ensures the good opinion of all the Amazons engaged in the contest, which at present are not a few.'[11]

In September Scott had received news of his promotion to second captain enabling him to assume the post of Brigade Major to the artillery but his relations with the CRA were not that harmonious. Indeed, it was readily apparent that Holcombe was not that popular:

> Read Col H's orders, no small quantity and rather of an extraordinary nature. Heard of his terrible falsehoods with respect to the relief of Thompson – a such

underhand, shameful way of proceeding; and of course astonished us all at his barefacedness.[12]

The arrival of Murray, as commander of the force, on 25 February 1813 seemed to stir both the army staff and Holcombe into some form of activity with the CRA issuing orders for the artillery to deploy to a number of locations at the front line. However, Scott did not agree with either set of decisions:

> The Battalion of Rolls-Dillon marched for Agost. Sax ordered to be occupied by part of the 20th [Light Dragoons] and some Calabrese, Elda Novelda etc; thereby forming a line in advance, which in my humble opinion ought to have been done long ago, as it gives us much more country and takes away from that of the enemy. Charley's brigade [Williamson's Company] ordered to Venta de Chevian, Bayly [Thompson's Company] with two mountaineers [i.e. mountain guns] to Elda, as also Hill [Lacy's Company]. Woollcombe [Thomson's Company] to Castalla and Townsend [Holcombe's Company] to Venta de Tibi. Very great errors in my opinion, diminishing the commands and frittering the (guns) away in such small numbers.[13]

Scott had a point; after all, battalion guns had been done away with at the back end of the previous century and there seemed little to be gained and much potentially to lose by such tactics. However, Holcombe's hands were somewhat tied by Murray's rather extraordinary plans to advance on four separate axes against the exposed French brigade at Alcoy. The link-up, not surprisingly, failed and the relieved French force was able to slip the noose. Murray now seemed devoid of ideas for any subsequent manoeuvres and instead ordered Whittingham to advance and probe the French lines. Arabin was also ordered from Alicante with two mountain guns to Alcoy and he arrived just in time to support Whittingham's forces in a skirmish with some of Major General Pierre-Joseph Habert's troops.

> Our advance through the wood was most brilliant and as soon as we had cleared it, our guns were instantly in position; and the two first shots directed by Captain Arabin plunged into the centre of the French line, and created considerable confusion. I forthwith ordered a general advance of all the troops under my command; nor was there any further check till we had conducted the French through the pass of Albaida.[14]

The French now fell back across the front but Murray again dithered and then announced his intention to take Valencia by a combined land and amphibious assault. At much the same time, Lord Bentinck was growing increasingly concerned about events back in Sicily and had requested the return of 2,000 men of the Anglo-Sicilian force. While this was being staffed Murray seemed paralysed into complete inactivity and for a whole month the Spanish brigade of Brigadier General Fernando Miyares lay tantalisingly exposed to Suchet's front. The French commander was undoubtedly puzzled by this apparent apathy but eventually he could no longer resist the temptation, and in early April gave orders for an attack. Harispe's Division surprised Miyares's men when a combined infantry and cavalry attack broke the Spanish squares and the rampant French cavalry followed up, wreaking havoc among the unfortunate infantrymen as they fled the scene. Murray's force meanwhile had spent the intervening period establishing their defences in and around Castalla, and Suchet now moved his divisions in that direction and captured a Spanish battalion that had been needlessly left in the castle at Villena.

Castalla itself is an old Moorish town, with a castle, which at the period of our arrival was in ruins – large breaches having been effected in the walls, and the interior entirely dismantled. It stands upon the ridge of a low hill, which, stretching way both to the right and left, becomes connected with other ranges of greater attitude and ruggedness … Moreover, there was a pass through the heart of these perfectly level and accessible to wheel carriages, which, in the event of battle, it was obvious would become an object of a very serious attack.[15]

Suchet's combined army amounted to about 18,000 men, 1,200 cavalry and 26 guns. The pass of Biar, as it is known, was exactly the direction that Suchet's forces would take to enter the valley of Villena; and Murray had placed his DAG, Colonel Frederick Adam, with a small light brigade supported by Arabin and four mountain guns to cover the pass.[16] In addition, there were five brigades of guns up with the main force and deployed at Castalla as follows:[17]

CRA: Lt. Col. H. F. Holcombe RA

Staff: Maj. J.S. Williamson RA

Brigade Major: Second Capt. T. Scott RA and Lt. W. Furneaux RA

RA Companies	Notes	Equipment
Thomson's Company	Half brigade with Mackenzie's Division.	6-pounders
Williamson's Company	Supporting Clinton's Division. Commanded by 2nd Capt. C. Gilmore.	5 x 6-pounders 1 x 5½-inch howitzer
Lacy's Company	Supporting Mackenzie's Division.	6-pounders
T. Cox's Portuguese Company	With Roche's Division (unconfirmed).	6-pounders
Garcia's Sicilian Company	Supporting Adam's Brigade and Whittingham's Division.	4- & 6-pounders
Arabin's Half Brigade	Supporting Adam's Brigade.	4 x 4-pounders
Patten's Flying Detachment	Supporting the cavalry.	2 x 6-pounders

Sources: Scott, Oman, Dickson, Woollcombe and WD.

The delaying action fought by Adam and his small brigade was a most creditable affair.

We made a stout resistance; but the odds were fearfully against us, and we lost ground continually, multitudes dropping both from our ranks, and the ranks of the French, never to rise again. At length they won the crest of the hill, upon which our two mountain guns, after having been fought with incredible courage to the last, were abandoned. When the enemy saw that they had taken our cannon, they raised a shout of triumph; and pouring down the slope made as if they would have destroyed us at a single rush.[18]

Murray in his subsequent dispatch described the action and the pivotal part played by Arabin and his four mountain guns.

The advance consists only of the 2nd batt. 27th regiment, commanded by Lieut. Colonel Reeves; the 1st Italian regiment, commanded by Lieut. Colonel Burke; the Calabrian Free corps, commanded by Major Carey; one rifle company of the 3rd and 8th batts. King's German Legion, commanded by Captains Luedor and Brauns of those corps; and a troop of foreign hussars, under the orders of Captain Jacks, of the 20th dragoons, with four mountain guns, in charge of Captain Arabin, Royal artillery. The enemy attacked this corps with from 5000 to 6000 men, and for five hours (and then only in consequence of orders) succeeded in possessing himself of the pass … in retiring from Biar, two of the mountain guns fell into the hands of the enemy; they were disabled, and Colonel Adam very judiciously directed Captain Arabin, who then commanded the brigade, to fight them to the last, and then to leave them to their fate. Captain Arabin obeyed his orders, and fought them till it was quite impossible to get them off, had such been Colonel Adams's desire.[19]

Suchet's forces emerged from the defile late in the day but there was still enough daylight for the French commander to reconnoitre the allied position. Suchet was dubious, the position was strong, and there were many more redcoats that he had hoped; furthermore, his possible withdrawal routes were limited and vulnerable. Despite these concerns his lieutenants, flushed with the confidence of their recent victories, managed to convince him that the *ad hoc* multinational force would not stand. The next morning he issued his orders. They would screen the main force from the road leading to Castalla while executing a right flanking manoeuvre to get around the town from the south. The fighting was fierce across a frontage of over a mile and at several points the French infantry reached the crest but each time they were counter-attacked by the allies and driven down. Brigadier General Louis-Benoit Robert's infantry tried to hold their ground, and in some places attempted to deploy into line, but they were not able to make the movement under such heavy fire, their momentum waned and a series of bayonet charges finally broke their resolve. Woollcombe recalled the incident and the squandered opportunities that followed:

At about half past one o'clock the attack commenced. The grenadiers of the 3rd Battalion, 3rd Regiment first ascended the hill and were followed by another strong column. They advanced with that determination that had they not had British troops in their front the hill would certainly have been carried. Already had they gained the summit and successively cheered when the 27th Regiment, led on by Colonels Adams and Reeves, charged them with the bayonet. Hundreds were killed on the spot and the remainder driven down the hill headlong, and received at the bottom by a detachment of cavalry ... On their observing their right repulsed they retired towards Onil, and an opportunity now offered for our cavalry to act. But this the Commander-in-Chief did not observe or would not avail himself of. Never perhaps during the present war was there such an opportunity as the present moment for a Commander-in-Chief to have displayed his abilities. But Sir John Murray did not take advantage of it, and surely he must have had good reasons for the cautious movement that followed. The forward two lines, with nine guns in their front, had advanced towards their columns, which were then in full retreat towards the pass [of Biar]. The consequence was that the artillery commenced a cannonade which at first did considerable execution, but the enemy retired so fast, and we advanced so slow, that they were soon out of range.[20]

Murray's victory was beyond doubt but he did outnumber Suchet's force by 5,000 men, his defensive position was strong and his pursuit of the defeated French was bungled; however in his favour, his force was a multinational mix and he had only been in command for a couple of months. In his post-battle dispatch he recalled the contribution made by the artillery.

Lieut. Colonel Holcombe, and under his orders, Major Williamson, conduct the artillery branch of the service in a manner highly creditable. The different brigades of guns, under Captains Lacy, Thomson, and Gilmour, (and Garcia of the Sicilian army,) and Lieut. Patton, of the flying artillery, were extremely useful, and most gallantly served; and the Portuguese artillery supported the reputation their countrymen have acquired.[21]

Suchet was fortunate to escape relatively intact; a better allied commander could have extracted a heavy toll for his temerity. Murray's real test was yet to come, but for now, the opening moves on the east coast had been completed, and though they cannot claim to have laid the foundations for Wellington's subsequent campaign for 1813, they certainly maintained their aim as an additional distraction and irritation to the French.

Notes

1. WD, vol. VI. pp.65–66, Wellington to Maj. Gen. Cooke from Valladolid, dated 9th September 1812.
2. PRO WO 55/1195. Birch to MacLeod from Isla de Leon, dated 2nd October 1812.
3. Ibid.. Letter Williamson to MacLeod from Alicante, dated 19th October 1812.
4. In addition, P. Campbell's Company were sent from Cadiz to Cartagena as early as January 1812 to assist in the establishment of the stores and ammunition base for the expeditionary force and operations on the east coast.

5. Woollcombe (ed. Ward), p.166; entry dated 9th August 1812.
6. Sañudo, database entry for battle of Castalla.
7. Scott, vol. II, entry dated 27th August 1812.
8. Frazer (ed. Sabine), letter from Lisbon, dated 19th December 1812.
9. Whittingham, letter from Mutxamel, dated 20th October 1812.
10. Scott, vol. II, entry dated 2nd December 1812.
11. Woollcombe (ed. Ward), p.171; entry dated 22nd August 1812.
12. Scott, vol. II, entry dated 7th February 1813.
13. Ibid., entry dated 12th March 1813.
14. Whittingham, undated letter refers to the incident on the 15th March 1813. Curiously, on the 8th April, 1847, the eldest son of Sir Samuel Ford Whittingham married Eliza, the eldest daughter of Col. Arabin.
15. Landsheit (ed. Gleig), p.197.
16. Lt. Col. Lord Frederick Bentinck, brother of Lord William Bentinck, had initially commanded the advance guard until he was replaced (due to inefficiency) by Col. Frederick Adam.
17. The exact task organisation and equipment of the artillery force is difficult to conclude but in addition to the five brigades of guns there was also a 'flying detachment' under Lt. William Patten RA (1262), which acted in support of the cavalry.
18. Landsheit (ed. Gleig), p.196.
19. WD, vol. VI, pp.467–70. Report by Murray to Wellington, dated 14th April 1813.
20. Woollcombe (ed. Ward), p.177; entry dated 13th April 1813.
21. WD, vol. VI, pp.467–70. Report by Murray to Wellington, dated 14th April 1813.

CHAPTER 17

Ramsay's Arrest

As 1813 dawned there were many in Wellington's force, and at home, who lamented the disappointments and hardships of the previous year. Wellington's reprimand to the army and the censure of his officers had done little for morale, but not all officers viewed events, past, present or future, with quite the same pessimism. Major Gardiner had a very different perspective on things, and on his commander-in-chief:

> There are not wanting blockheads here to magnify our evils though, from the cheering side of the picture they turn: Cadiz freed, ten or twelve of the enemy's most important arsenals destroyed, 1,000 pieces of cannon and 20,000 prisoners taken ... I every day see more and more to admire and look up to in Lord Wellington. He saves us in such difficulties, the errors and stupidity of some of the staff and general officers would be so fatal if it were not for him, that one feels that sort of gratitude towards him that we owe people, who rescue us from a terrible fate. As to the nonsense one hears about our present retreat, don't listen to it. We have not been compelled to pass the Agueda, it is a movement that comes with the course of things and we are only preparing for future operations, more brilliant if possible than his former achievements.[1]

Within two months of penning this letter Gardiner was informed that he was to assume command of Macdonald's Troop of the horse artillery, that officer having been invalided home. However, Gardiner's sanguinity did not extend to all the officers in the artillery; many were troubled by the ongoing difficulties between Wellington and his artillery commander and enraged by the continued discrimination of brevet promotion across the arms. Wellington's decision to accept Fisher was largely predicated on the principle of 'better the devil you know' coupled with his determination to block the MGO's nominated replacement, Colonel Sir George Wood. May would have welcomed Wood's arrival: 'indeed I shall be most happy if this appointment completely settles the point with no probability of change.'[2] But Cairnes, commanding Dickson's Company, was less sure for he was quite clear that 'Sir George Wood is too fat, depend on it. He could not have galloped 60 miles on these roads with the Marquis the day before yesterday.'[3] Cairnes's opinion was undoubtedly correct but May's position had an altogether different foundation. Indeed, Robe had written in December 1812 to MacLeod outlining the problems of Dickson's Portuguese rank, for having obtained brevet lieutenant colonel he would, in time, become a Portuguese colonel and this would 'have given him the right to command, although he could not do so regimentally'.[4] It was, in short, a real mess and a right muddle.

When Fisher resigned in May 1813 Wellington summoned Dickson and Lieutenant Colonel Hartmann of the KGL to his headquarters:

> He first of all asked me which was senior, Colonel Hartmann or myself. On my informing him I was, he then said, 'How are you in rank as to Colonel Waller?' I explained that he was considerably senior to me both in army and regimental rank. His Lordship then said, 'Colonel Dickson will take the command of all the Artillery in the field, both British and Portuguese, and Colonel Waller and General Roza, as Commandants of the Artillery of the two nations will remain at Lisbon for the purpose of forwarding supplies, &c.[5]

In fact, there were four officers in theatre more senior than Dickson.[6] Wellington's interference in such matters, coupled with obvious judgements of sympathy from fellow Gunner officers towards the genteel and popular Fisher, were bound to make Dickson's task a difficult one. Major Augustus Frazer, who had arrived at the end of 1812 and was now commanding the Royal Horse Artillery, recalled that Dickson had been his second in command during the ill-fated Buenos Aires operation and quickly admitted that Dickson 'is a man of great abilities and quickness, and without fear of anyone'.[7] However he was unconvinced that such meddling on the part of the commander-in-chief would settle the matter; he feared that 'we shall have a jumble, and that the public service may suffer'[8] and added that he hoped 'Dickson's reign may be long, for the sake of the service, but times are slippery'.[9] In short Dickson's appointment created a sensation and one man, above all others, had greater reason to seek redress. Waller was furious; he knew as well as anyone that once Wellington's army moved east the *raison d'être* for retaining Lisbon as the logistic base of the army would cease and his post with it. He would inevitably be recalled. He wrote to some of his friends for advice who, in turn, counselled him to 'think of the good of the service', and on this guidance he 'tamely referred his case to England' but he knew, only too well, that a *volte-face* was unlikely.

Of course, the situation for Dickson was exceedingly awkward and he wrote what must have been a very difficult letter to Charles Waller. Inwardly he must have felt elated at his endorsement and good fortune, but outwardly Dickson remained attuned to the sensitivity of his situation as Henegan, the Assistant Commissary, recalled:

… he appeared in an old and very shabby Portuguese uniform – which he wears in virtue of his rank in the Portuguese service. This dress he never changed during the whole campaign, and by this admirable display of tact – which by the undiscerning might have passed even without notice – escaped the feelings of jealous envy that would have rankled in the hearts of many, had he worn the British uniform while in command of senior Officers.[10]

Sensationalistic emotions aside, Dickson was not a man who was about to let slip such an opportunity from his grasp and his brother officers, realising Dickson's obvious abilities, rallied to his cause. Wellington finally had *his* man and from now until the end of the war the relationship between the commander-in-chief and his senior artillery advisor was not an issue.

The other concern, that of brevet promotion for second captains of the artillery (and engineers) who, unlike their infantry and cavalry counterparts, were ineligible for brevet promotion based upon distinguished operational conduct, was also about to be challenged. Jenkinson had no doubts that the opposition to their advancement lay with his own corps. Cairnes was of the same opinion. 'The work in the Peninsula is hard & unceasing, but great men in London don't feel it. Lord Mulgrave is resolved to do nothing.'[11] Many officers, like William Swabey, considered this particularly galling for he was clear that Wellington's recent censure of his officers was 'too just' but that 'this falling off has not … reached the officers of artillery, who are doubtless more soldiers by profession than any other part of the army'.[12] In the end this discrimination was simply too much to bear. Every one of the (in-theatre) second captains wrote a Memorial to their commander-in-chief which was strongly supported by Fisher:

In presuming to request your Lordship to lay the enclosed Memorial before H.R.H. The Prince Regent of England, the Second Captains of the R.A. serving under your Lordship's command in this country, would not presume to take that liberty were it not for Your Lordship's well-known attention to any cases of hardship which may be considered as existing in the Army under your command.

The Memorial which they have the honor [*sic*] to enclose is not founded on Your Lordship's supposed approbation of the Services of any of those who have signed it; but upon the mention of some of them in Your Lordship's Public Dispatches after the captures of C. Rodrigo & Badajoz, & some subsequent events of the late brilliant campaign.

The Second Captains of the R.A. who were thought by Your Lordship to have distinguished themselves in those operations, were classed with First Captains of their own Regiment and younger Captains of others, who received that Brevet promotion which on account of their Regimental rank was denied to them. Trusting therefore that Your Lordship will see how grating it must be to the feelings of any soldiers to find themselves without a hope of reward whatever may be the nature of their services & however much they may be considered to merit the approbation of the Officers they are serving under, they anxiously hope that your Lordship will lend the powerful aid of your recommendation to their case, that should any of them be fortunate enough in the ensuing campaign to be publicly mentioned by Your Lordship, it may obtain for them that Brevet promotion which has hitherto been alone withheld from them.

We have the honour, &c. (signed)

E. C. Whinyates	R. M. Cairnes	A. Thompson	W. N. Ramsay
T. Dyneley	B. Wills	G. Jenkinson	J. B. Parker
E. T. Mitchell	W. G. Power	W. Cator	W. Webber[13]
W. Greene	C. C. Dansey	A. Macdonald	

Wellington promptly passed, and strongly supported, the Memorial to the Prince Regent via the Duke of York at Horse Guards. A few weeks later a most satisfactory response arrived from the Duke of York's military secretary which concluded that:

Upon a consideration of the whole case however His Royal Highness will submit the Memorial for the gracious & favourable consideration of the Prince Regent, in order that your Lordship may in future be enabled to recommend for brevet rank such second Captains of Engineers and Artillery whose conduct shall merit your notice & protection.[14]

Jenkinson and his peers were delighted; the longstanding and contentious issue of brevet promotion for distinguished service had at last been resolved.

Hail our triumph over the Ordnance, and congratulate us. The second captains of the artillery serving in the Peninsula have petitioned the Prince Regent for a removal of that worse, that more unjust, and more iniquitous than Papal ban they laboured under, and their prayers have been heard – if there is faith in man we are now emancipated, we are Captains in the army – and for this we are indebted to Colonel Fisher and Lord Wellington.[15]

In fact, despite Frazer's reference to 'slippery times' the state of the artillery in the force had never been better. Since Salamanca another troop of horse artillery and five additional foot companies had been dispatched from England or released from Cadiz. Enough 9-pounders had arrived to equip four additional brigades and the less successful iron 24-pounder howitzers had been withdrawn and replaced with the more reliable brass heavy 5½-inch pieces. This decision had been taken by Wellington personally but certainly met with Dickson's approval:

He [Wellington] had ordered the 24 Prs. to be sent back to England which I am not sorry for; indeed we have suffered too much already by having been obliged to use inapplicable ordnance. I allude to the iron howitzers, which although excellent howitzers, are miserable guns, for in the latter capacity often have we been obliged to employ them, and I need not observe that their shot go every where but where they ought to do. Besides if more guns are necessary the remains of our two battering trains are in Almeida and Elvas, from either of which places as many good English 24 Prs. might be furnished as we could want.[16]

The siege train at Elvas was ordered north at the end of April, with the aim of concentrating all the heavy guns in a single location so that they were poised to move in support of the force as required or, relatively easily, returned (via the Douro) to Oporto and shipped to the Cantabrian or Mediterranean coast. Integral to the army, and moving with it, were to be two companies of artillery, each with three 18-pounder guns, and suitable sling and firing carriages were constructed to transport this heavy ordnance. Also requiring transport was the pontoon train which lay at Lisbon; it was a vital tool in the execution of Wellington's campaign plan and, although the responsibility for the train lay with the Engineer Commissariat, the task of getting it ready to move fell to the artillery. The large train, consisting of 44 carriages, took priority over the equipping of the brigades and Cairnes was none too pleased to discover that his entire driver establishment was being redirected to move the train.

> I have received a damper which altho' perhaps considered by His Lordship unavoidable & essential to the service, has mortified and vexed me beyond all possible expression, that of having all my Driver Establishment in Toto transferred to the Pontoon train, and my Brigade remounted by horses coming from Lisbon (which horses are to be tomorrow night within 2 leagues of this place). His Lordship was, I hear, pleased to express his regret at knocking up my Brigade.[17]

It was a particular blow to Cairnes who was a highly professional officer and one who harboured strong views on the Corps of Drivers and how they should be integrated within the sub unit to best effect. He was clear that the divided allegiance and a lack of accountability and ownership of these men was detrimental to the collective good. He had written much on the subject and felt keenly that 'by being with a Brigade, there is some hope of instilling into them the idea that they are soldiers and, when they find themselves looked after and treated precisely as the Gunners of the Brigade, they certainly evince a difference'.[18] For now, Cairnes had to wait for the replacement mounts and drivers to arrive in Lisbon. Two weeks later Cairnes's despondency lifted: the drivers and mounts had arrived and the company was re-designated a brigade of guns and was placed in direct support of the 7th Division.

By early May the Anglo-Portuguese army had never been stronger or better equipped. Of infantry there were 56 British and 53 Portuguese battalions; of cavalry, 18 British and four Portuguese regiments with in excess of 8,000 mounts, but the increases in artillery were particularly significant, with 18 brigades of guns and three additional artillery companies for ammunition support and manpower. The army now boasted 102 guns and howitzers, still well below the (desired) Napoleonic maxim of five guns per 1,000 infantry but, nevertheless, a far cry from the situation Robe had faced on the shores of Portugal in the summer of 1808. The situation and organisation were as follows:

CRA: Col. A. Dickson RA
Staff: Lt. Col. J. May RA
Brigade Major: Maj. L. Woodyear RA
Command of the Horse Artillery: Maj. A. S. Frazer RHA

RHA Troops	Notes	Equipment
'A' Troop (Ross)	Attached to the Light Division.	3 x 6-pounders 2 x heavy 6-pounders 1 x 5½-inch howitzer
'D' Troop (Bean)	Attached to 2nd Cavalry Division. Bean did not join until March 1813.	3 x 6-pounders 2 x heavy 6-pounders 1 x 5½-inch howitzer
'E' Troop (Gardiner)	Attached to Hussar Brigade. Gardiner assumed command January 1813.	5 x 6-pounders (1 x long) 1 x 5½-inch howitzer
'I' Troop (Bull)	Attached to 1st Cavalry Division. 2nd Capt. Ramsay in command.	3 x 6-pounders 2 x heavy 6-pounders 1 x 5½-inch howitzer
'F' Troop (Webber Smith)	Attached to the Reserve.	5 x 9-pounders 1 x 5½-inch howitzer

RA Companies	Notes	Equipment
Du Bourdieu's Company	Attached to 1st Division. Formerly Gardiner's Company.	5 x 9-pounders 1 x 5½-inch howitzer
Maxwell's Company	Attached to 2nd Division.	5 x 9-pounders 1 x 5½-inch howitzer
Douglas's Company	Attached to 3rd Division.	5 x 9-pounders 1 x 5½-inch howitzer
Sympher's Company KGA	Attached to 4th Division.	5 x 9-pounders 1 x 5½-inch howitzer
Lawson's Company	Attached to 5th Division.	5 x heavy 6-pounders 1 x 5½-inch howitzer
Brandreth's Company	Attached to the 6th Division.	5 x heavy 6-pounders 1 x 5½-inch howitzer
Dickson's Company	Attached to 7th Division. Commanded by 2nd Capt. Cairnes.	5 x 9-pounders 1 x 5½-inch howitzer
Da Cunha Preto's Portuguese Company	Under Lt. Col. Tulloh. Attached to Gen. Hill's Corps (Da Costa).	5 x light 6-pounders 1 x 5½-inch howitzer
(C. C.) Mitchell's Portuguese Company	Attached to Gen. Hill's Corps (A. Campbell). Under Lt. Col. Tulloh.	5 x 9-pounders 1 x 5½-inch howitzer
Reserve Artillery: Commanded by Lt. Col. G. J. Hartmann KGA ('F' Troop RHA also in reserve)		
Parker's Company	Formerly Stone's Company – Parker in acting command awaiting Mitchell.	5 x 9-pounders 1 x 5½-inch howitzer
Arriaga's Portuguese Company[19]		5 x 9-pounders 1 x 5½-inch howitzer
Glubb's Company	Commanded by 2nd Capt. Power.	3 x 18-pounders

Morrison's Company		3 x 18-pounders
Owen's Company	Capt. Owen joined the staff and his men were allocated to the other companies.	Nil
May's Company	Reserve ammunition: Command Lt. Elgee	Nil
Hutchesson's Company	Reserve ammunition: Arrived March. 1813	Nil

Sources: Dickson, Laws, Leslie and Teixeira Botelho.

With Macdonald and Bull convalescing, their troops were under the respective commands of Gardiner and Ramsay. Captain George Bean had arrived to assume command of 'D' Troop from Lefebure who had died in October. Captain James Webber Smith had arrived and was commanding the only horse artillery troop with 9-pounders – albeit on 6-pounder carriages. Captain Saumarez Du Bourdieu had also deployed to assume command of Gardiner's Company; John (Boteler) Parker's, William Morrison's and Thomas Hutchesson's companies had arrived from England and those of Dickson (under Cairnes) and Humphrey Owen had been redirected from Cadiz. The Portuguese artillery had been retained at three brigades, two of which were attached to Hill's Corps under the watchful eye of Lieutenant Colonel Alexander Tulloh RA. Many new mounts had been transported as early as April 1813 and as Sergeant Whitehead recalled when 'A' Troop lined up on the 16th May: 'Parade this morning in heavy marching order, Light Division reviewed on the plains of Espeja, returned home after the review: I never saw the Troop look better …'[20]

Webber was in full agreement with the horse artillery sergeant and provided more reasons as to why the army was in such good condition.

Our army was never more healthy, indeed I should think troops in England can not be in a better state. Marching to a certain degree agrees with most men if the weather is favourable and they are well supplied … The soldiers have tents and although they are much crowded (one being allowed for 20 men) the nights are sufficiently cool to prevent their feeling any ill effects from that cause. During the last campaign they had none and it was very trying to the strongest constitution to lie down, after a long march, exposed to the mists or dampness of the night air.[21]

Tents were but one improvement, Jenkinson noted another:

Lord Wellington has determined to abolish the camp kettles of the army, and to substitute the little tin ones … every tenth man carrying in his turn as a fatigue a somewhat larger one for the use of the company; a regulation that will attend many advantages, but particularly that of enabling the company's bat mules to the conveyance of tents … by the abolition of camp kettles the operation of cooking will be much more rapid and more convenient and comfortable to the soldier, and the movements of the army thereby materially facilitated.[22]

Within days of Dickson assuming the mantle as CRA, with the men trained and equipped, the horses well fed on spring grass, the commissariat wagons full to brimming, and the slow-moving pontoon bridge ready to roll, the advance began. The army was split on two routes: Hill was commanding the group in the south, consisting of the Light Division, De España's and General Pablo Morillo's Spanish divisions, Silveira's Portuguese Division and the 2nd Cavalry Group, while the balance moved on a more northerly route. Moreover, Hill's group set off a week earlier, enabling Wellington to remain in intimate contact with both groups as they progressed and ensured their junction, at Toro, by early June. Hill's group experienced the most resistance, as General Villatte seemed somewhat oblivious to the strength of force approaching Salamanca, as Dickson recalled:

> General Fane, commanding Sir R. Hill's Cavalry, passed the river in a moment, and came up with the French before they had got three miles from Salamanca. They were retiring in squares by the Arévalo road ... on overtaking them the Horse Artillery opened upon their squares with considerable execution, and the pursuit was thus continued for five or six miles, the Horse Artillery cannonading them from every point they could.[23]

Brereton, a subaltern in Bean's Troop, recalled that during the action 'a remarkable circumstance occurred for which Lord Fitzroy Somerset and the Duke of Wellington will vouch, and have spoken of since. Sixteen men were killed by one shot. They fell like a pack of cards, one partly over another in a line.'[24] This was Augustus Frazer's first Peninsular action, but he was not elated as 'there was not even the false emotion of honour where there was no danger, and to slaughter flying enemies, though duty requires it, is nevertheless shocking'.[25] Riding among the French dead and injured at Aldealengua Frazer noted upwards of 80 dead on the road: 'few, if any, were killed or wounded *but* by the fire of the horse artillery'.[26] With six French caissons also captured it was a good start to the campaign and while the locals were relieved, their '*vivas*' were somewhat subdued – they had seen it all before. The advance continued to the north of the Douro, and when General Pedro Agustín Girón's Spanish 4th Army joined the advance at Medina de Ríoseco, the allied army was now advancing on four routes; it was about this time that a number of Gunner field officers arrived to superintend pairs of brigades.

> Major Dyer superintends the Artillery of the 1st and 6th Divisions; Major Carncross that of Sir R. Hill's Corps consisting of Maxwell's Brigade and Bean's Troop. Major Buckner has the Brigades of the 3rd and 5th, so that the 4th and 7th Divisions remain (poor fellows) without a Field Officer, and no doubt we shall go headlong to destruction in consequence.[27]

What was quickly apparent, however, was that 'in consequence of Dyer's absurd interference in the private economy of his Brigades, Dickson has defined very clearly what is expected from these Inspecting Field Officers'.[28] The advance continued unabated and as the lead elements bypassed Burgos to the north, the

French were compelled to destroy the defences and retreat from its confines. Wellington, Fletcher and Dickson made a quick detour to confirm that the *bête noir* of the previous campaign had indeed been rendered indefensible.

> I went over all the works of the Castle. The lines are blown in many places; the castle itself is entirely destroyed and the explosion killed and wounded a number of French troops which were encamped around. I could find nothing except a few shot and broken iron guns ... Frazer and May were with me. The whole army are moving towards the Ebro, which I think we shall cross in a day or two, and take the French in again.[29]

All four groups closed on the mighty Ebro River with its steep banks. For the Gunners, getting down and then up the other side was a real test of skill and stamina. Webber, with his 9-pounders, recalled the experience.

> We now began the descent of the hill and to prepare for the accidents and disasters to our carriages. Although the road was paved and rather broad, it would have been impossible to have moved without infantry to hold the drag ropes. General Stewart gave us two companies of the 71st and by great care we succeeded in reaching the valley without any accident. Had we locked our wheels, as is the plan in some Brigades, I think not a carriage would have escaped injury and several might have been totally disabled.
>
> I never saw anything so tremendous as this pass, so steep that even with the assistance we had, the wheel horses frequently fell on their hocks and it was with the greatest difficulty we prevented the carriages from running over the side of the pavement – in which case they would have precipitated (in some parts) 30 or 40 feet, and horses and drivers must have been killed.[30]

Within two days the columns had advanced to the high ground surrounding the plains of Vitoria; Ross recollected that Wellington's army were 'in possession of all the passes looking into the plains of Vitoria, and this evening the whole of the Army will be close up, ready to pour into it, which we expect to take place tomorrow'.[31] In fact the 6th Division had been left at Medina de Pomar to provide rear security and they, along with Brandreth's Brigade of guns, were to miss the battle. Wellington's plans were for a three-pronged attack. Graham with a force of 20,000 men was to move on the allied left flank and capture the bridges north of Vitoria, and the key town of Gamarra Mayor, thereby severing the Bayonne road and the principal French escape route. To the south, Hill with another 20,000 men, including the 2nd Division, Silveira's Portuguese Division and Morillo's Spanish Division, was to capture the heights known as Altaras de Puebla, force the passage of the River Zadorra and menace the French left wing while Wellington advanced with the balance through the centre along the axis of the Burgos to Vitoria road. With Graham's force were Du Bourdieu's and Lawson's guns in support of the 1st and 5th divisions respectively and Bull's Troop of horse artillery with the cavalry.

On the 20th June, the massive French baggage train had started to withdraw along the Bayonne road (*Grande Chaussée*) but Joseph realised he needed to buy more time and, after conferring with Jourdan, decided to make a stand in front of Vitoria. His combined force consisted of three armies: the Army of the South under the command of Gazan; the Army of the Centre commanded by Drouet; and the Army of Portugal under General Honoré-Charles Reille. His total force numbered 57,000 men; it was relatively weak in cavalry but in artillery it boasted 21 batteries and more than 120 guns. Gazan, commanding the largest of the three armies, established the first line of defence across the main road; behind that was Drouet while Reille was providing flank protection to the north and along the Bayonne road. Missing, but *en route*, was the French Army of the North commanded by Clausel with 20,000 men.

On the 20th June Jourdan, racked with fever, was confined to his bed in Vitoria; when he visited the field early the following day he immediately realised the shortcomings of the French deployment and set about rectifying the situation. Wellington had also recognised the deficiencies in the French dispositions and the opportunities afforded by the terrain. The dominating ground in the west would mask allied intentions until the last minute but, more significantly, the River Zadorra, which bends and twists initially south to north and then swings sharply west to east before again turning north, had no fewer than 11 bridges along the stretch. Very few of these crossings were covered by the French forces and of those that were not, astonishingly, none had been destroyed or blocked.[32] Reille had been holding the line of the river two days prior but had pulled back to behind Vitoria on Joseph's order. Jourdan knew, only too well, that a man of Wellington's calibre would not hesitate to exploit this oversight but as he contemplated readjustment, reports began to arrive of allied movement to the south.

Wellington's plan was, by Peninsular standards, quite ambitious as he had split his force into four separate columns, spread over a wide distance, which needed to arrive simultaneously at their selected point of attack. Swabey was with Gardiner's Troop of horse artillery attached to Brigadier General Colquhoun Grant's Hussar Brigade of cavalry in the centre:

> Lord Wellington expected Sir Thomas Graham with the 1st and 5th divisions to make his appearance and act against the enemy's right and to completely cut off his retreat. Finding he did not appear [at the allotted time], Lord Wellington ordered General Hill to make his false attack a real one, and Sir Thomas Picton with the 3rd division to force the passage of the bridge on the enemy's right, and thus turn that flank. At the same time the light division was to cross at the second bridge on the right and attack the front. As soon as the 3rd division had crossed, Major Gardiner's troop of Horse Artillery (which had left the cavalry because that arm on account of the unevenness of the ground could not act) was to pass at one of the centre bridges commanded by the enemy's artillery, and support the light division. The 7th division followed the 3rd, the 6th was not up. The 4th division under Sir Lowry Cole was to force the bridge on the great Vitoria road which was completely commanded by numerous artillery. On Sir Thomas Picton's forcing his bridge the [French] right gave

way and all advanced; the enemy's centre and left still however made an obstinate resistance, and having every advantage of ground their artillery did great execution … the moment the enemy's right, which we had helped along with a few shots, gave way, we crossed. At that moment I strongly recommended Gardiner not to follow Ross and the light division over the immense hill, but to go round it. In doing this we got to the high road and found the French centre resting there still unforced. Webber Smith's, two of Ross's and Sympher's guns all firing on it, though the ground was such that we were all commanded by their artillery … in about a quarter of an hour the 4th and light divisions forced the centre. The troop immediately limbered up and, taking the lead of all artillery, we pushed through the village. At this moment, as Harding [Hardinge] has since told me, Lord Wellington turned to Dickson and asked 'what artillery it was?' and when informed, he said, 'That is something like Horse Artillery'.[33]

Sergeant Whitehead was with 'A' Troop and describes the action with the Light Division:

At two o'clock this morning we moved off clearing out of a wood. At day break, on the road to Vittoria, His Grace the Commander in Chief, [was] sitting on the steps of a church, writing dispatches for the movements. The General of division received his, Col Sir H D Ross received his. Troop moved onto the banks of the River Zadorra – halted till heard a cannonade on our left, we then advanced rapidly. Came into action 450 yards distance; guns very close intervals on account of the ground. We soon had a return of gun shot, one of which twisted Serjeant Unsworth's helmet off his head, on to his shoulders without any other injury. This was to cover the ford where the 4th Division passed on our right and the bridge on our left over which the Light Division passed.[34]

Sergeant William Unsworth was clearly a lucky man; in fact he was the oldest of four brothers serving the 5th gun in the troop that day; gun number 9 was acting Bombardier Israel Unsworth, at number 10 was acting Bombardier John Unsworth, and their younger brother, Gunner Abel Unsworth, was gun number 2. In the words of Sergeant Thomas Whitehead it was, 'quite a singular instance'.[35] 'A' Troop's second captain described the effects of these opening moves:

This answered a merveille [du jour], for the enemy believed Sir R. Hill's attack to be what it was not, and reinforced their left with the whole of their second line, when the light and 4th divisions made a rapid movement to aid the 7th and 3rd divisions in the attack of the enemy's right, which also being aided by Sir Thos [Thomas] Graham's appearance in the rear of it, they abandoned their first line, on which we had sixty pieces of artillery placed before noon …[36]

The difficulties presented by the terrain alluded to by Swabey had a significant impact on the intimate support for the infantry by both cavalry and artillery. Indeed the lack of suitable roads resulted in the bulk of the artillery remaining in the centre and moving east along the main road and therefore not providing direct support to their allocated formations. This, as it turned out, was not a significant concern for once the infantry had crossed the river, the (centre) divisions moved together to push back the French defensive lines. Dickson recorded that:

The nature of the country, and want of roads, was the means of throwing a large proportion of the Artillery together away from their Divisions, which I availed myself of, and by employing them in masses it had a famous effect. This was adjoining to the great road to Vitoria and the French brought all the artillery they could to oppose our advance so that the cannonade on one spot was very vigorous. In none of our Peninsular battles have we ever brought so much cannon into play, and it was so well directed that the French were generally obliged to retire 'eer the

10. The Battle of Vitoria ~ 21st June 1813

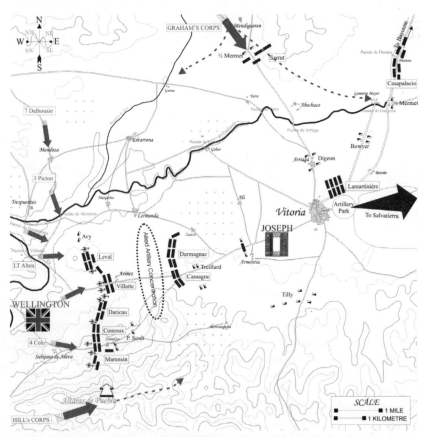

This map depicts the situation prior to the collapse of the French first line. Allied gun positions were constantly changing in this fluid battle but the approximate location of the allied artillery concentration against the French second line is shown.

Infantry could get at them. There were few or no instances of the bayonet being used during the day.[37]

Seventy-five allied guns were, at one stage, concentrated engaging the French second line of defences and Dickson had under his immediate command about half these guns and 'dreadful indeed was then the struggle between the contending armies; it was for one hour a battle of artillery, but at no moment was the victory doubtful …'.[38] Once the initial French defensive line had been breached and their right flank turned, the determination of their defence wavered. In fact the flanking manoeuvre by Graham's men had not physically cut the Bayonne *Chaussée* although they did command large sections of it by fire from the west bank. Nevertheless, that was enough to convince Jourdan that withdrawal north was not a sagacious option and orders were given to pull back on the Salvatierra road to the east. By the time these orders had been disseminated it was too late: three armies converging on the same spot at much the same time, preceded by the second half of the huge baggage train and carriages carrying the camp followers and wagons of wounded, produced a theatrical pandemonium of unprecedented proportion. At this spot the baggage was discarded; huge paintings, tapestries, gold coins, silver tableware and all manner of other trappings of regal plunder added to the drama. Also abandoned in and in front of the town, lay the remnants of the French artillery: 151 guns and howitzers, 415 caissons, 14,249 rounds of gun and 1,973,400 of small arms cartridges, 40,688 pounds of powder and a number of forge wagons.[39] In the words of Napier, 'It was the wreck of a nation!'

Dickson's post-battle report to the MGO would not have been too difficult to pen:

> I have to report for the information of the Master General that the Marquess of Wellington on the 21st inst. attacked the French army under the immediate command of Joseph Napoleon in position in front of Vitoria, and after a series of successful operations which lasted for great part of the day, the battle was concluded by the French army being totally routed with the loss of the whole of its artillery, ammunition, carriages, military chest, and baggage. As the details of this important event will be fully given in Lord Wellingtons Dispatches I will not intrude upon your time by entering into them, but keep myself to the object of this letter which is to make known to Lord Mulgrave how much I have reason to be satisfied with the conduct of the Officers and Men of the Royal Artillery on this occasion. Their skill and bravery was highly conspicuous, as were their exertions in bringing forward the Artillery through a difficult and intersected country, both during the attack and the pursuit; in short I can safely assert that Artillery could not be better served, and to the credit of the Officers I have to add that from the beginning of the day to the last moment of the pursuit it was always to be found where it was wanted.

The MGO thought so too and in a quite uncharacteristic show of intimate support wrote directly to the CRA and informed him that the Prince Regent had agreed to a series of allowances for the officers of the artillery in recognition of their good service. He continued:

In notifying to you His Royal Highness gracious liberality, I am happy to avail myself of the opportunity of expressing the high sense which I entertain of the distinguished part which the Royal Artillery has borne (on every occasion) in the glorious events which have rendered the War in the Peninsula the brightest Epoch in the Military History of Great Britain. I beg you to express to the several officers whose names you transmitted to me, my sincere congratulations, upon the honourable remuneration which their services have received from the gracious consideration of His Royal Highness, the Prince Regent.[40]

In view of the extensive use of the artillery during the battle and the fact that every brigade of guns (except Brandreth's) had fired in anger, their casualties were light. Twelve killed and 55 wounded, with two missing: the wounded included May who received a severe contusion in the stomach from a musket ball, Swabey who was shot in the knee and Lieutenant Lumley Woodyear, struck in the shoulder by a spent cannon shot. Woodyear was to die two months later from the effects of the wound. On the strength of their contributions, majors Frazer and Ross were made brevet lieutenant colonel and Jenkinson became the first second captain to pin on his brevet major since the earlier petition. Their elation would have been eclipsed by that of Dickson who could not have hoped for a better start to his tenure of command. Robe, who had been invalided back to England following his injury during the retreat from Burgos the year prior, wrote in glowing and honest terms to the man he considered had jumped the queue.

> I congratulate you and all the Corps on the glorious success you have obtained at Vitoria … You are a fortunate fellow, Dickson, & I have told Frazer that I envy you. I feel that it is not the despicable passion bearing that name that I possess but I do envy you in the singular good fortune of having at such a time your artillery in your own power & being able to give the weapon its full force. Your manner of using it is your own right & I do not envy that but heartily rejoice at your success.[41]

Robe would unboundedly have wondered where he would be now if he had been endowed with so much artillery, and so many well-equipped brigades, at the earlier stages of the campaign.

The Army's Judge Advocate General, Francis Seymour Larpent, noted that, 'In the pursuit after Vitoria, in the bad roads, Lord Wellington saw a French column making a stand, as if to halt for the night. "Now Dickson," said he, "if we had but some Artillery up!" "They are close by, my Lord."'[42] was Dickson's reply and within minutes Ross's Troop came over the brow of the hill and were rapidly into action. Ross recalled the moment his troop captured the only two guns that the French had managed to take with them following Vitoria: 'and to-day we have taken the only two they have remaining – the last within a league of Pamplona'.[43]

> … about ten in the morning about five thousand of the enemy's infantry, and a few squadrons of cavalry were found in position across the high road leading to Pampluna [Pamplona], and here, one gun and a howitzer, all that they had saved

from the wreck of Vittoria, were placed. The light division under Charles Alten, in their usual gallant style, soon dislodged the enemy, and the hussars and horse artillery dashing after them with rapidity, deprived the beaten army of their last gun. The loss of the French was considerable … The British horse artillery, closing up, poured a terrific fire into the ranks of these unfortunate men, scarce a shot missed its aim; one single ball was seen at once to deprive five infantry soldiers of both legs, taking the first under the hip, and the fifth under the chin! So great in deed was the torture experienced by these poor creatures, that, as the hussars rode by, they implored them as countrymen [the German Nassau regiments were forming the French rearguard], to put an end to their torments by at once depriving them of life. This could not, of course, be complied with and the whole road presented a frightful spectacle of mutilated human beings in the most excruciating endurance.[44]

It seemed, on the surface, that the friction between Wellington and his Gunners had finally been overcome; however, any such mawkish thought was entirely premature. During the pursuit of the French an incident occurred on the 23rd June, which resulted in Captain Norman Ramsay being placed under arrest by the commander-in-chief. The circumstances of this affair, in themselves relatively inconsequential, do provide an intriguing insight into both men. They also demonstrate a petulant streak in Wellington's persona, which had manifested itself on more than one occasion in the past. Ramsay was an extraordinarily popular man and Duncan, in his history, has summed this up perfectly.

If there is one name more familiar than any other to the Artillerymen, it is that of Norman Ramsay. From public orders and the pages of history his gallantry and professional skill may be learnt; but it is from the pages of private correspondence that one ascertains how loveable he was. He joined the Regiment in 1798, and he fell at Waterloo; and yet in that short space of seventeen years he had gained the love of his brother officers without exception, the devotion of his men, and the admiration of all … But there was more: he possessed that professional enthusiasm, which hallows the dullest of tasks, and gilds the severest hardship. His pride in his troop made its men strive to be worthy of his good opinion; and it is in this way that a commander can with certainty generate *esprit de corps* among his men.[45]

Even Wellington was well known to have a liking for Ramsay, which makes the story of his arrest all the more extraordinary. The account of this bizarre affair by Augustus Frazer is a good basis, as he was the man Wellington tasked to place Ramsay under arrest.

After moving forward on the 22nd June, towards the evening, Lord W. spoke to Ramsay as he passed, desired him to take his troop for the night to a village then near; adding that, if there were orders for the troop in the course of the night, he would send them. The night passed away, no orders were received. At 5 next morning, an assistant-quarter-master general (Captain Campbell) came to Ramsay, and asked if he had any orders. Being answered in the negative, he said, 'You will then immediately march and rejoin the brigade to which you belong.' Accordingly, the troop marched; and soon afterwards a written order was received by Ramsay from General Murray, the Quarter-master General of the Army, also ordering 'Captain Ramsay's troop to rejoin General Anson's brigade.' While the troop was doing this, and was halting for the moment, whilst Ramsay having the quarter-master general's order had ridden to discover the road in one direction, and Captain Cator, with a copy of the order, had gone for the same purpose in another, Lord Wellington came up, called repeatedly for Ramsay, then for Cator; neither at the moment was on the spot. His lordship then called for Dickson, whose horse being unable at the instant to clear a wide ditch over which we had just passed, I rode up to mention the circumstance to Lord Wellington, who ordered me to put Captain Ramsay in arrest, and to give the command of the troop to Captain Cator. This I accordingly did, having soon found Cator, and soon after Ramsay, whom I sent two or three people to look after. It appears that Lord Wellington had intended that Ramsay's troop should not have moved that morning till he himself sent orders, and his lordship declared that he had told Ramsay so; this Ramsay affirms he never heard or understood, and his lordship's words, repeated by Ramsay, young Macleod, and by a sergeant and corporal, all at hand when his lordship spoke to Ramsay, are precisely the same, and do not convey such a meaning.[46]

Lord Fitzroy Somerset and Dickson appealed to Wellington but he was not to be swayed; two days later Graham wrote urgently on the matter which merely served to annoy the commander-in-chief. 'Lord Wellington would listen to no reason or explanation, and as Major Frazer informed me, raved like a madman to Colonel Dickson, applying to Ramsay every ungentlemanly and vile epithet that ever disgraced Billingsgate.'[47] On the surface it seemed to be just a simple misunderstanding, the results of which were inconsequential. Neither Murray nor Captain Campbell seem to have been aware of Wellington's order or intentions with regard to Ramsay's Troop and nor do they appear to have been questioned following the arrest. Ramsay himself never put pen to paper about the unpleasant incident but a man who did was Second Captain William Cator who was serving with 'I' Troop as his own company (Owen's Company) was being used to make good the manning deficiencies across the force. His notes, clearly written after Ramsay's death, provide a very different motive for Wellington's actions:

Memo: of circumstances attending the placing of the late Major Norman Ramsay under arrest by the Duke of Wellington, two days after the Battle of Vittoria in 1813.

It was intended to make a movement across difficult country from the vicinity of Salvatierra, to intercept a French column from Bilbao on the Bayonne road, so as to cut that column off from reinforcing San Sebastian.

1st. The troop of horse artillery commanded by Captain Ramsay, to which I was attached as second captain, marched the day after the battle to Salvatierra with General Anson's Brigade of Cavalry, to which the troop was attached.

2nd. In the afternoon of that day, Captain Ramsay was outside the town, when the Duke of Wellington returning from the front after reconnoitering, desired Ramsay to put his troop up at Salvatierra and as Captain Ramsay understood, told him he would send him orders.

3rd. On the following morning early, one of the Quarter Master General's Department, Captain Campbell, came into the room before the officers were out of their beds, all of them being in one room – Captain Campbell asked if Captain Ramsay had received any order – he answered no! 'Not any' he again asked? None was the reply. Captain Campbell then said, 'Well then you had better saddle your horses (was his expression) and join General Victor Alten's Brigade of Cavalry' – which Captain Ramsay carried out.

4th. Captain Ramsay marched about two leagues to a small village, when it was found a Bridge had been destroyed by the French, and went forward himself to ascertain how he was to get over the small river.

5th. The Duke at this time came up and was exceedingly angry – he found his general arrangements had not been carried out as he wished. Corps he had intended to move from Salvatierra to the Bayonne road were moving on the Pamplona road, and to add to his disappointment, when he reached Captain Ramsay's Troop he found the Bridge, above alluded to, destroyed – he then put Captain Ramsay under arrest and directed Captain Cator to take charge of the Troop.

6th. Captain Cator was directed to put the Troop up in the village where the bridge was destroyed.

7th. The following morning Captain Cator considered he was forgotten, having received no orders, and having ascertained what was going on, he marched about 8 o'clock a.m., contrary to the advice of Captain Ramsay, to the Bayonne road, which he reached about 1o'clock.

8th. Captain Ramsay was, I should say, some three weeks or so, under arrest; great interest was made to soften the Duke of Wellington without effect. At last the late Sir Frederick Ponsonby wrote a private note to the Duke to solicit his release. The Duke wrote on a leaf of the note turned down. 'I never accused Captain Ramsay of intentional neglect of duty, but it is sometimes necessary to make examples.'[48]

This (hitherto unpublished) account provides a much altered picture of Wellington at the pertinent point in time. There is no doubt that Wellington was furious at the missed opportunities following the battle and he was clearly enraged that his 'general arrangements' for the pursuit of the French, issued in subsequent orders, were not being executed properly. The broken bridge was perhaps the final straw but what is less clear from this account is the detail of the orders given to Ramsay by Wellington himself and by Campbell the following morning. Colonel Francis Whinyates, the editor of Swabey's marvellous diary, provides more substantiation in the form of two reports by Cator and (Henry) Blachley, who was the senior subaltern in the troop at the time. These were provided to Whinyates by Cator's son many years after the affair. They confirm that Wellington gave direct orders to Ramsay to remain in the designated spot until he received *personal* orders from him.

Early next morning one of the Quarter-Master-General's Staff, I forgot his name but he was a prig, came up with orders for Ramsay to move to Pamplona. Ramsay, who was a very lazy man, and only the gallant and brilliant soldier when under fire, was in bed in his tent. My father [Cator] went to him with the Staff Officer who gave him his orders. Ramsay asked, 'Am I to take this order as from Lost Wellington, for he gave me positive orders not to move without personal orders from himself'. The reply was. 'This order is from Lord Wellington', upon which with much hesitation Ramsay prepared and marched.[49]

If this is to be believed, and it must be remembered it is an account recalled by Cator's son many years after the event, then clearly the actions of Captain Campbell should have been investigated. Under the circumstances, Wellington's initial reaction was explicable but, once he had recovered from his fit of pique and the full circumstances became known, he should have rescinded his instruction and the episode would, likely, never have been recorded at all. It is an undeniable personal failing of Wellington that he did not, and the similarities with this episode and his treatment of Lieutenant Colonel Charles Bevan in 1811, following Brennier's breakout from Almeida, are all too apparent.[50]

What is curious about Cator's memorandum is that it was clearly written after Waterloo and personally signed by Wellington himself. Perhaps it was produced in answer to a board of inquiry, although I can find no record to support this hypothesis. One thing was certain, there were many Gunners who considered the Duke's actions beyond the pale and they could never bring themselves to forgive him for this error in judgement.

The next morning I was breakfasting with Norman Ramsay, and the officers of his troop, now commanded by another, when General Vandeleur arrived. Upon entering the room, he went up to Ramsay, and grasping his hand with a brother soldier's warmth, said:

'The object of my visit, Captain Ramsay, is to inspect your troop'.

'My troop, General, is mine no longer', answered poor Ramsay, with deep emotion.

'I am glad to say you are mistaken, Captain Ramsay', rejoined the General, 'for I am the bearer of orders from head-quarters that authorise me, as I before said, to inspect your troop. The command of it is restored to you.'

Ramsay, overcome by his feelings, turned away and wept ...[51]

Notes

1. Gardiner, letter from Alameda [Almeida], dated 23rd November 1812.
2. Dickson, vol. V. Letter from May to Blomefield, dated 3rd February 1813.
3. Ibid. Letter from Cairnes to Cuppage, dated 28th January 1813.
4. Dickson, vol. IV, p.788. Letter from Robe to MacLeod, dated 18th December 1812.

5. Dickson, vol. V, pp.890–92. Dickson to MacLeod, dated 25th May 1813.

6. Based on regimental seniority, there were actually 13 officers more senior.

7. Frazer (ed. Sabine), letter dated 8th May 1813.

8. Ibid.

9. Frazer (ed. Sabine), letter dated 16th May 1813.

10. Henegan, vol. I, p.165.

11. Dickson, vol. V, pp.832–33. Letter from Cairnes to Cuppage, dated 28th January 1813.

12. Swabey (ed. Whinyates), p.166.

13. Dickson, vol. V, pp.841–42. To Wellington, dated February 1813.

14. Dickson, vol. V, p.849. Torrens (Military Secretary) to the Duke of York, dated 3rd March 1813.

15. Jenkinson, Aldea de Obispo, dated 31st March 1813.

16. Dickson, vol. V, pp.835–36. Dickson to MacLeod, dated 30th January 1813.

17. Ibid. Letter from Cairnes to Cuppage, dated 12th May 1813.

18. Ibid. Letter from Cairnes to Cuppage, dated 30th May 1813.

19. Oman repeatedly states that Arriaga's Portuguese Brigade was equipped with 18-pounders; this is incorrect.

20. Whitehead, entry for 16th May 1813.

21. Webber (ed. Wollocombe), p.167.

22. Jenkinson, Aldea de Obispo, dated 3rd March 1813.

23. Dickson, vol. V, pp.898–900. Letter from Dickson to MacLeod, dated 6th June 1813. The guns that executed this destruction belonged to Bean and not Gardiner as reported by Oman, although the latter's guns were up with the Hussar Brigade at the time.

24. Brereton Papers, p.v.

25. Frazer (ed. Sabine), letter dated 27th May 1813.

26. Ibid.

27. Dickson, vol. V, pp.902–05. Letter from Cairnes to Cuppage, dated 11th June 1813.

28. Ibid.

29. Dickson, vol. V. pp.908–09. Letter from Dickson to MacLeod, dated 13th June 1813.

30. Webber (ed. Wollocombe), p.170.

31. Ross, p.39. Letter dated 20th June 1813.

32. Fortescue, vol. IX, p.164, dismisses the fact that the Zadorra is a significant obstacle; that may be correct for the infantry but Gardiner's guns would most certainly not have been able to cross in support of the 3rd Division had the bridge at Mendoza been destroyed.

33. Swabey (ed. Whinyates), entry dated 21st June 1813.

34. Whitehead, entry for 21st June 1813.

35. Ibid. These are clearly the old gun numbers.

36. Jenkinson, letter dated 29th June 1813.

37. Dickson, vol. V. pp.916–17. Letter from Dickson to MacLeod, dated 23rd June 1813.

38. Jenkinson, letter dated 29th June 1813. The 75 guns included the 12 British and Portuguese brigades not attached to Graham's Corps and three Spanish guns of Morillo. The guns in support of the 3rd and 7th divisions also joined the mass battery.

39. WD, vol. VI, pp.539–43. Wellington's official post-battle dispatch to Bathurst, dated 22nd June 1813.

40. Dickson, vol. V, pp.930–31. Letter from Mulgrave to Dickson, dated 16th July 1813.

41. Dickson, vol. V, pp.927– 29. Letter from Robe to Dickson, dated 4th July 1813.

42. Larpent's Journal, p.142.

43. Ross, p.40. Letter dated 24th June 1812.

44. Ludlow Beamish, vol. II, p.220. Browne gives a more detailed account of this affair but provides no primary sources; in view of the author's track record for inaccuracy this tale is therefore not included.

45. Duncan, vol. II, p.357.

46. Frazer (ed. Sabine), letter dated 8th July 1813.

47. Swabey (ed. Whinyates), p. 211, entry dated 22nd July 1813.

48. Unpublished notes found in Brereton's Box MD 2405. This document is signed by Wellington and has the additional footnote: This document I found among the late Sir William Brereton's papers. *Signed:* Major W. R. Brereton [his nephew and executor]. He adds: 'and it may interest your Royal Highness to have it'.

49. Swabey (ed. Whinyates), p.211. Note by Whinyates after the entry dated 22nd July 1813.

50. Lt. Col. Charles Bevan was the commanding officer of the 4th Foot held responsible for the dramatic night escape of the French garrison from Almeida. See Hunter, A., *Wellington's Scapegoat, The Tragedy of Lieutenant Colonel Charles Bevan* (Barnsley, 2003).

51. Henegan, vol. II, p.23.

CHAPTER 18

Williamson's Fury

The day after the battle at Castalla, but unaware of the contest or the outcome, Wellington penned his Memorandum for Operations on the East Coast. It contained three prime objectives: to capture the 'open part' of the land, or regional area, up to the city of Valencia; to establish a presence (from the coast) north of the River Ebro and open communication with the Spanish Army of Catalonia; and lastly to 'oblige' the enemy to withdraw from the lands south of the River Ebro.[1] No particular priority was applied to these tasks but Wellington strongly suggested that an attack by 10,000 men on Tarragona (from the sea) would satisfy the first two objectives in a single operation. Wellington's hope was that such an operation would entice Suchet north with speed, thus opening opportunities for the 2nd and 3rd Spanish armies to exploit in the region of Valencia. Alternatively, similar opportunities would avail themselves to the Spanish armies and irregulars in that neighbourhood if Suchet held firm in Valencia and ordered General Charles Decaen, commanding the French Army of Catalonia, to intervene.

Suchet had been grateful that Murray's follow-up after the battle at Castalla had been so feeble and, as a consequence, he had been able to extract his ever dwindling force virtually intact and re-establish a defensive line north of the River Xucar. He was unaware that Murray's force was about to be reduced by the troops required by Bentinck to keep the lid on the simmering pot of Sicily. However, since Joseph O'Donnell's disastrous attempt against the French at Castalla the year prior, the Spanish 2nd and 3rd armies had been rejuvenated and were now under the commands of the more able General Vincente María Cañas, 6th Duke Del Parque and General Francisco Javier Elío respectively. Wellington wove these formations into his plan and, by so doing, removed the convenient excuse that Murray furnished of lacking sufficient forces to take the fight to the French. The Memorandum for Operations on the East Coast was characteristically thorough, running to 29 points, but one final proviso was forwarded to Murray two days later, emphasising that he had free rein on the composition of his expeditionary force to Tarragona. If there were sufficient naval transports Murray retained the option of taking Whittingham's very capable division. Wellington finished this letter responding to Murray's rather excessive demand for additional artillery:

> Of all your wants that of artillery-men appears most extraordinary. Besides the artillery-men who came with the corps from Sicily, which, as the corps came to carry on a siege, I conclude cannot be inconsiderable in number, you have two companies of British and two of Portuguese artillery belonging to this army; I believe the very same men, in the same numbers, that took Badajoz for us last spring. It would, however, be desirable, now that communication is quite secure, to send me a regular return of your force. I cannot let you have the artillery-men at Cartagena [P. Campbell's Company], as I have nothing else to take care of our stores, etc., there; but if 4 companies, besides those belonging to Sicily, are not enough, I will try and send more from this army.[2]

In fact Murray had already complained to Wellington about his artillery commander as early as the 25th March and the commander-in-chief, somewhat surprised by the complaint as 'we had found him here a very capable officer and was promoted ... by brevet for his conduct at two sieges', nevertheless discussed the matter with Fisher and agreed to replace him. The truth of the matter was that Holcombe was universally disliked, largely originating from his rather arrogant nature and accompanying lack of consideration. Scott had made his feelings towards the CRA very clear but he was, nevertheless, of a mind that 'the way of removing Holcombe does not appear ... exactly just, as it is finished with very little ceremony'.[3] Holcombe was clearly furious at his removal but had the presence of mind to write to all the artillery officers in the (east coast) force and inform them that it had been at his own application. However, his frustration clearly boiled over soon after arriving back in Lisbon and his subsequent behaviour clearly incensed Erasmus Weld, the Commissary and Paymaster of the Field Train Department, who wrote to Dickson on other matters but made his position absolutely clear with regard to Holcombe.

> Perhaps Colonel H. will now be quiet. May's letter was certainly a tickler & such he deserved richly. All of us were delighted at it, as we hate him & we regret that he ever had the command here. He takes delight in annoying the Field Train Department. In one instance he has carried it too far & when he throws off the Commanding Officer he will not fail to meet with that treatment that his conduct so merits. Believe me, I fear him not, nor do I respect him, on the contrary I hate him, & so do we all & glad shall we be when separation takes place.[4]

Patrick Campbell's Company was sent to replace that of Holcombe providing an opportunity for John Williamson to resume his post as the force CRA. With Scott as his Brigade Major they set about strengthening the redoubts along the defensive lines facing the French amidst rumours of an impending campaign to the north.

However, firm orders were not received until the 26th May when Scott recorded that 'the mystery at an end, and we jolly fellows about to retrace our steps to Alicante, and from there to future glory'.[5] The following day, after a hasty passage of lines with the Spanish, Murray's forces marched for the coast.

> Williamson marched the brigades off about 8 o'clock, and we ourselves at half past. No mercy of consideration for one's hind parts has the Major, for he jolted us in the short time of two hours and a half; and after refreshing with a wash, commenced work by getting everything prepared for the embarkation of our guns ... Packed off Charly [Gilmour – commanding Williamson's Company] with three guns on board the *Malta*, Thompson [Thomson] with three on board the *Fame*. Two with Woolcombe [Woollcombe] to *Brune* and two with John [Lieutenant John Scott – cousin of diarist] to *Bristol*, besides the reserve and 150 animals.[6]

Over the next three hours the balance of guns were loaded by division and early on Monday 31st May the fleet got under way. The exact composition of the artillery force is difficult to establish with any degree of certainty. There were three brigades of guns, all formed on Williamson's, Thomson's and Richard Lacy's companies; the balance of companies appear to have provided men to man the siege guns although these were built on the nucleus of Campbell's Company and Cox's Portuguese Company. It is clear, however, that additional Portuguese gunners from Maximiano Penedo's Company and Sicilian gunners from Garzia's Company were also taken to assist with the siege train. In addition there was a detachment of German gunners from Captain Bernhardt Busmann's Company of the KGA.[7] The number of siege guns is also difficult to establish; the force had certainly come equipped with a train from Sicily and it is clear that additional guns were sent from Lisbon or Cartagena in the interim. Between 25 and 30 pieces of ordnance is a fair estimate although Fortescue does refer, quoting Rear Admiral Benjamin Hallowell, to 'forty siege pieces', but he may have been including additional naval guns which were used and manned by naval gunners during the operation.[8]

CRA: Maj. J. S. Williamson RA
Brigade Major: Lt. T. Scott RA

RA Companies	Notes	Equipment
Thomson's Company	Half brigade under 2nd Capt. Arabin supporting the Advance Guard.	5 x 6-pounders 1 x 5½-inch howitzer
Williamson's Company	2nd Capt. Gilmour commanding.	6-pounders
Lacy's Company	Supporting Mackenzie's Division.	6-pounders
A. Campbell's Company	From Lisbon, April 1813 to replace Holcombe's Company.	Siege
T. Cox's Company – Portuguese Artillery		Siege

Sources: Oman, Teixeira Botelho and Scott.

Murray's force, including (most of) Whittingham's Division, numbered in excess of 15,000 men. The weather was kind and the winds were favourable, resulting in the journey to Salou Bay, just south of Tarragona, taking less than two days. Corporal Joseph Coates, in the Corps of RA Drivers, attached to Williamson's Company, was by his own admission 'a poor sailor' but he had 'never enjoyed a voyage more than this after such hardships' following the battle at Castalla.[9] Scott was similarly sanguine, noting that 'we must improve that fortune which has wafted us so quickly hither by our activity. Lord William certainly embarked [from Palermo] on the 21st [June] and may be hourly expected, which adds fresh life to our new bright hopes; and we may look forward to an appellation more worthy of Britons, than the newspapers have deigned to give.'[10]

The force began to disembark early on the 3rd June and Murray dispatched a force consisting of two battalions and two 6-pounder guns under the command of Second Captain Arabin to move and capture the small fort of San Felipe, which dominated the pass at Balaguer, thereby preventing French reinforcements from the south. The balance of the force, including 'twenty-two pieces of cannon and nearly two hundred horses and mules' was ashore before mid-afternoon.[11] General Francisco Copons, commanding the Spanish Army in Catalonia, had, as instructed by Wellington, made early contact with Murray, increasing the allied force to 25,000 men. The French defenders in Tarragona numbered little more than 1,500 men and many felt that their fate was sealed by the size of the attacking force and their not inconsiderable siege train. Little had been undertaken by the French to repair or enhance the structure since they had captured it in 1811 and the garrison commander, Brigadier General Antoine Bertoletti, considered withdrawing from the Fort Royal and San Carlos bastion to the west of the town but reconsidered as these two structures, and their guns, covered the harbour.

Down the coast, at the Fort San Felipe, the small allied force under Colonel William Prevost (67th Foot) was encountering difficulty with the rugged terrain. On the first day, Arabin engaged the works with some shrapnel shells at a range of 700 yards to buy time for more support to be brought up by the naval gunners. On the 4th June, two 12-pounders and a howitzer arrived and two new battery positions were marked out just 300 yards from the structure. However, it was not until the evening of the 6th that five 24-pounders and two mortars were in position; these guns had been sent by Captain Peyton RN from the *Stromboli*.[12] They opened early on the 7th June, and, according to Scott, when Captain Arabin's second round exploded the fort's magazine, the commander surrendered.[13]

However, events had not progressed quite so well at the main objective. On the 5th June Scott recorded that 'this day we made some advance and in the evening threw four 8-in Howitzers into a battery on the sea beach, about 900 yards from the body of the place and another battery of two 24s near the main road'.[14] Murray had ordered these batteries to be constructed when he noted the French repairing and strengthening Fort Royal and the San Carlos bastion. A third battery was also ordered slightly further north along the main road and two 24-pounders, under the command of Cox, were established there on the night of the 6th June. Hallowell's naval guns had supported the construction of all three batteries. However, the results were mixed and with Murray seemingly paranoid about French reinforcements arriving at any time, tempers began to fray.

> Skelton's [Campbell's second captain] fire from the Howitzers as well as Cox's from the advance appeared to do much damage to the work, but this very piddling work, and every one crying: 'Why haven't you got more guns up?' However, what officers of the line generally know about sieges is regulated by the quantity of noise and fire they hear and see, without reflecting upon the nature of the ground, the situation or the place or the difficulties to be overcome, and conceive it as easy work for the Engineers and Artillery to proceed in their duty, as the common routine of Infantry parades.[15]

Four additional 24-pounders were placed in Battery 3 (see Appendix 4) but it was now readily apparent to the entire force, allies included, that Murray was out of his depth and increasingly fixated in the belief that Suchet or Decaen, or both, were poised to fall on his force like the Sword of Damocles. Hallowell and major generals William Clinton and John Mackenzie were almost beside themselves with rage at the conduct of the siege and by being kept in the dark as to Murray's intentions.[16] Rather than lose men needlessly dragging heavy ordnance in broad daylight, at right angles to the enemy's defences, they would far rather have been given permission to take the outworks by force. On the 7th June the senior engineer officer, Major John Thackeray, reported that the outworks were ready to be taken but added, rather strangely, that 'if the fort were escaladed and occupied, the ground gained would be of no immediate use for the attack upon the Upper city, whose most accessible front might be more easily battered from the slopes of the Olivo hill'.[17] It was an extraordinary admission and Scott recorded the next day the 'terrible invectives thrown against our sister corps; cannot help concurring in opinion that they are rather slack in our present situation, a little more activity would be highly commendable'.[18]

Murray pounced on the declaration, deferred the attack, and accepted Thackeray's plan to open a new angle of attack from the Olivo hill onto the north walls and bastions of San Pablo, despite the caveat that to so do would take another two weeks. The decision was also made to land more of the siege train and stores along with the balance of field equipments and work began in earnest on the two new batteries. Within two days the first of the ordnance was in place and by dusk on the 10th June it opened. The same day Murray had received reports of French forces advancing from both the south and north towards Tarragona but he seemed to take the news in his stride and the next day he rode out, north of the city, to Copons's position and discussed his defensive plans and his intentions to support him should the situation require. Orders were given to storm that night:

> At night the 10th Regiment with three companies of the Levy [Italians], headed by general M'Kenzie were paraded for the purpose of storming the outwork, and a strong diversion was to have been made by the division under Gen Clinton, as well as from Whittingham's Corps. 10 was the hour fixed, and every one in

anxious expectation of seeing it, when at ½ past 9 an order arrived to postpone it till 11. This was far from being relished, but how dreadfully disappointed and vexed was every one in half an hour after to find it was not to take place. A murmur passed along the troops, and every one expressed themselves in strong language against this horrid decision of Sir John [Murray], and no one more so than Gen M'Kenzie, who was all anxiety to gain a name in the Annals of Military History and lead the panting troops to victory. 'Shame – Shame' was echoed on every side and the discontent was evident thro'out … I was employed till 11 o'clock forwarding ammunition to Lacy [Batteries 4 and 5] & had retired to the Marquee for rest, when Kenah [Capt Thomas Kenah, 58th Foot] came down and informed me that we were all to embark tomorrow. Good God! How was I thunderstruck![19]

Murray had clearly lost his nerve and ordered that the force was to complete embarkation by dusk on the 12th June. Williamson was told at midnight to bring off all the guns but he protested in the strongest terms that no provision had been made for such a hasty withdrawal and that there was no hope of getting the guns in batteries 4 and 5 off before daybreak, thus exposing the working parties and the equipment to the mercy of the garrison guns. He pleaded for an additional 24 hours and, at length, Murray acceded. Thus placated, Williamson concentrated on getting the guns in batteries 1–3 during the first night, leaving those on the Olivo hill until the following night. However, Murray, on being apprised of the situation early on the 12th June, ordered the guns to be abandoned and spiked; Williamson again protested to Murray, Hallowell remonstrated at the hastiness of the departure and many of the general officers pressed him to engage the small French force which had appeared on the Barcelona road in order to buy sufficient time to conduct a controlled withdrawal. However, Murray's mind was, by now, clearly in the terminal stages of meltdown, for he passed Clinton no fewer than seven different and contradictory orders in the space of an hour; the fifth ordered that the guns on the Olivo were to be spiked, the sixth countermanded this and tasked Whittingham to assume control of the Olivo from Clinton and facilitate the withdrawal of the guns that night but the seventh countermanded the sixth and reiterated that the guns were to be destroyed.

Fortunately, Hallowell kept his nerve and ordered his men to continue loading well beyond midday and at 1500 hours Murray allowed some of the cavalry and Thomson's and Williamson's brigades to move round to the anchorage at Col de Balaguer. The fleet and transports weighed anchor in mid-afternoon, leaving 18 (spiked) guns in the Olivo batteries but more significantly abandoning Copons's Spaniards to their fate. Murray, contrary to Wellington's orders that should he fail at Tarragona, he was to return to Valencia with haste, now decided to loiter with the entire force just off shore. He then began to dream up all sorts of new schemes of operation. Lord William Bentinck landed on the 17th June and, having listened to various renditions of events in abject horror, assumed command of the force and set sail immediately for Alicante. Regrettably, this most lamentable episode in the British Army's involvement in Iberia did not end here,

Colonel Sir Augustus Frazer. (RAI)

Major General Sir Hoylett Framingham. (RAI)

Major General Sir George Bulteel Fisher. (RAI)

Major General Sir John May. (RAI)

General Alexander Cavalie Mercer. (RAI)

Second Captain Richard Bogue. (RAI)

Captain Charles Sillery. (RAI)

Lieutenant General Sir Thomas Downman. (RAI)

Captain William Webber. (RAI)

General Sir Edward Whinyates. (RAI)

Second Captain William Swabey. (RAI)

Colonel Charles Dansey. (RAI)

Major Henry Baynes. (RAI)

Major Robert Ord. (RAI)

Major General John Boteler Parker. (RAI)

Lieutenant Henry Mussenden Leathes. (RAI)

Lieutenant William Lempriere. (RAI)

Lieutenant General Sir Burke Cuppage. (RAI)

Second Captain George Silvester Maule. (RAI)

Second Captain John Edmund Maunsell. (RAI)

Colonel William Robe. (Author's Collection)

Lieutenant William Robe. (Author's Collection)

The tombstone of Major (William) Norman Ramsay at Musselburgh, Edinburgh. (Author's Collection)

A drawing of the headstone of Lieutenant General Sir Edward Howorth at Banstead Church, Surrey. (RAI)

The Dickson Memorial (**LEFT**) was raised in 1847 to Sir Alexander Dickson and erected in the Repository, Woolwich before being moved in 1911 to Front Parade, Woolwich (**CENTRE**) and the again to the Royal School of Artillery, Larkhill in 2007 (**RIGHT**) when the Regiment relocated from its home at Woolwich after 291 years. (RAI and author's collection)

Dickson, aged 21. (RAI)

Dickson in the uniform of a Portuguese Artillery Officer. (RAI)

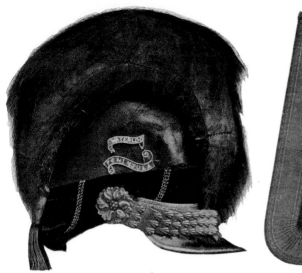

RHA Headdress worn in the Peninsula and at Waterloo. (RAI)

A Royal Artillery Sabretache. (RAI)

Coat of Arms of the Board of Ordnance. (RAI)

for Murray's subsequent court martial was bungled and the Spanish evidence excluded, enabling the defendant to 'fabricate falsehoods', which resulted in him being acquitted of everything but an 'error of judgement'. That error was predicated on his leaving the guns and stores at the town. Britain's foremost military historian concluded that Murray should be pilloried by history as 'a cowardly and dishonourable man, unworthy to hold the Sovereign's commission or to wear the red coat of a British soldier'.[20] Williamson, forced to abandon his colours, would undeniably have concurred.

Wellington was understandably disappointed and unquestionably concerned in the immediate aftermath of Murray's withdrawal and wrote to him on the 1st July.

> … I confess that which weighs most on my mind in all this is the loss of your artillery and stores, of which you think the least. 1st: They are very important trophies to the enemy, of which he will make good use … 2dly; The loss of them entirely cripples our operations on the Eastern coast during the Campaign, and prevents the army of the Eastern coast from taking all advantage which they make take of our success in this quarter [i.e. Vitoria], which it is probable will be followed by Suchet's throwing his army on our right flank.[21]

In fact Suchet was in no position to undertake such an ambitious manoeuvre but the reasons for Murray's behaviour confused Wellington and he concluded by stating that the 'consequences are not so important as the facts themselves'. He had written to Lord Bentinck the same day expressing his surprise at Murray's actions and his frustration at the lack of specific information to enable him to formulate an opinion. His 13th clause in his original memorandum to Murray in which he made it abundantly clear that he would 'forgive anything, excepting that one of the corps should be beaten or dispersed' would, no doubt, have been the reason for his hesitation in writing in far stronger terms.[22] It was a clause which, unsurprisingly, Murray referred to many times in the course of his subsequent court martial.

After a difficult passage the transports arrived at Alicante on the 28th June and the disembarking troops were welcomed back to the jibes of their comrades and the well deserved ridicule of their allies.[23] Scott, along with many of the participants, was concerned that they 'should go into Winter Quarters with disgrace, disgust, hooted, hissed and despised'.[24] Within days of arrival, Bentinck had dispelled any possibility of such indolence. News of the significant French failure at Vitoria had forced Suchet to withdraw back towards Valencia: it had changed the dynamics of the war and significantly influenced French plans on the east coast. The loss of Saragossa to Spanish irregular forces and Clausel's withdrawal north over the Pyrenees a few days later left Suchet no choice but to follow north or risk isolation and capture. Bentinck readied his force to commence an aggressive pursuit; a new siege train was assembled (from the remnants of the previous expedition and from the guns at Alicante) and Lacy's Company exchanged their 6-pounder guns for the heavier 9-pounder, which had arrived in the interim.[25] The Spanish 2nd and 3rd armies, under Elio and Del Parque respectively, were similarly energised and the three allied groups had begun their northerly movement by the 7th July.

Bentinck was under the firm impression that Suchet, thus pressed, would withdraw and abandon southern Catalonia. Indeed, earlier reports had already suggested that the French had abandoned Tarragona and Clinton's Division was accordingly loaded on the naval transports, which were shadowing the advance, and moved directly to the city along with the siege train and many Gunners who had also been loaded in anticipation. Suchet's force was concentrated just north of Tarragona but he still held the city in strength and he had placed garrisons at Valencia, Saguntum, Peñiscola and Tortosa. Clinton landed his division south of the city and moved to the Col de Balaguer to cut off any attempt by the small garrisons to escape. Leaving Elio to deal with the French garrisons south of the River Ebro, Bentinck and Del Parque headed north and by the 3rd August both formations had crossed the formidable obstacle of the Ebro and concentrated to the south of Tarragona. Suchet, supported by 8,000 men from Decaen's Army of Catalonia, then temporarily pushed the allies back and destroyed the fortifications at Tarragona before withdrawing north towards Barcelona.

Bentinck once again moved north in the French wake and, confident that Suchet would not venture south again in strength, established Adam's vanguard brigade at the pass at Ordal on the road midway between Tarragona and Barcelona. Elio was still ensconced in mopping up operations with the isolated French garrisons and Del Parque was summed by Wellington to make best speed west to Tudela. At much the same time, Bentinck became preoccupied by reports of legislative bungling and riotous activities in Sicily and submitted a request to Wellington to be allowed to return there. However, on the 13th September, before he departed, Suchet attacked Adam's small force at Ordal. Arabin had a (full) brigade of 6-pounder guns in support of the vanguard and they had been placed in hastily prepared redoubts straddling the road. The small allied force had received some advance warning of French intentions but their greatest problem was that the balance of Bentinck's force was more than a day's march to the south. Very early in the fight Adam was wounded and Lieutenant Colonel George Reeves assumed command but during the second concerted French attack the Spanish fell back in the centre and Reeves ordered Arabin to withdraw the guns. 'The word was hardly out of his mouth before he too fell wounded; the next senior officer, Lieutenant Colonel Carey, was far away on the left, and the allies were left for a time without a commander. In a few minutes the Spaniards rallied. Arabin brought up his guns to their assistance, and Sarsfield's gallant battalions, charging with the bayonet, bore back the victorious French ...'[26]

The vanguard was helpless against the third French assault and Arabin withdrew the guns for a second time from the forward redoubts and made best speed south. Four guns were escorted by a few survivors of the 27th and some 50 Spanish cavalry and the other two by De Roll's Sicilian infantry and a squadron of KGL cavalry. The first group of four guns had travelled south at speed and must have considered their extraction to have been a success when, at that moment, French hussars were seen closing at speed. The ensuing panic by the fleeing Spanish prevented the gunners unlimbering the guns and the four pieces were captured.

The two guns to which we were attached, after keeping up their fire until the French were close upon them, limbered up and moved to the rear. Repeatedly the enemy formed as if to charge them; but the bold front which our squadron presented struck them with awe, and they held back. Away, therefore, we went, till we had come within a short distance of the bridge, which to our horror and amazement … was on fire. The fascines that filled up the space between the double layer of boards was blazing terribly and the smoke gathering in a cloud overhead … What then were we to do? With our tumbrils [sic] full of ammunition and our heavy pieces, could we venture to pass between two volumes of flame, or were we to halt on this side and die with our arms in our hands, or be taken? Captain Jacks, fortunately for us, was a man of decision, and the officer commanding the artillery proved equally intrepid. 'Dash at it, men' was the cry, and we did dash at it. With the very flames curling up on both sides, and the smoke meeting in an arch over our heads, we galloped across bearing off our guns, tumbrils, and all our people safely. Yet scarcely were we across when a loud crash gave notice that the planks had failed. The bridge was broken, and multitudes of those who were crossing at the moment perished in the ruins.[27]

Bentinck took full responsibility for the incident and accepted that his dispositions lacked mutual support for no cogent reason. Once again, that would have been scant comfort for Williamson who had to suffer the indignation of losing four more guns. Adam himself also came in for considerable criticism but he was at pains to point out that Arabin and his men did all that was expected of them and that 'the brigade which during the campaign served under his orders behaved in a manner worthy of its former reputation'.[28] Bentinck left the Peninsula a few days later and Clinton assumed command of the force. His only operation was an ill-timed attempt to capture Barcelona in January the following year which brought the final curtain down on the activities of the Anglo-Sicilian force on the east coast. Wellington said of Clinton that he 'Did nothing in particular – and did it pretty well'. He can, at least, claim to have lost no guns while in command of the force.

Williamson set about reorganising his artillery but was suffering badly from a lack of RA Drivers. The Spanish replacements were, in his opinion, 'not really worth the bread they eat; they are idle and lazy and good words and example has little effect upon them'.[29] Had it not been for the Portuguese gunners who undertook the role, his brigades could not have been effectively fielded. By early November his own company, and that of Lacy, were equipped with 9-pounder guns, Thomson's and the Portuguese had 6-pounders, two guns were attached to the cavalry and two were in reserve. During the winter a small rocket brigade was also established and this was also attached to the advanced brigade just outside Barcelona. He remained CRA of the Anglo-Sicilian force until the war came to an end and his companies dispersed between March and June 1814. He knew full well that his chance had come and gone; Holcombe, Murray and Bentinck had inadvertently conspired to tarnish any further chance of field command and distinction.

Notes

1. WD, vol. VI, pp.426–29.
2. WD, vol. VI, p.430.
3. Scott, entry dated 27th April 1813.
4. Dickson, vol. V. p.906. Letter from Weld to Dickson, dated 12th June 1813.
5. Scott, entry dated 26th May 1813.
6. Ibid., entry dated 27th May 1813.
7. Ludlow Beamish, vol. II, p.158.
8. Fortescue, vol. IX, p.65
9. Coates, p.3.
10. Scott, entry dated 2nd June 1813.
11. Fortescue, vol. IX, p.52.
12. Ibid., p.55.
13. Scott, entry dated 17th June 1813. In fact it was a mortar round that ignited the magazine and despite Scott reporting that this was Arabin's second round, it is unlikely to have been so.
14. Ibid., entry dated 5th June 1813.
15. Ibid., entry dated 17th June 1813.
16. These two officers should not be confused with Gen. Henry Clinton, William's brother, commanding the 6th Division with Wellington's main army, and with Gen. John Randoll Mackenzie, who fell at Talavera.
17. Oman, vol. VI, p.497.
18. Scott, entry dated 8th June 1813.
19. Ibid., entry dated 11th June 1813.
20. Fortescue, vol. IX, p.73.
21. WD, vol. VI, p.569. Wellington to Murray, dated 1st July 1813.
22. Ibid., pp.426–29.
23. Landsheit (ed. Gleig), p.207.
24. Scott, entry dated 13th June 1813.
25. Ibid., dated 1st July 1813.
26. Fortescue, vol. IX, p.378.
27. Landsheit (ed. Gleig), p.247.
28. Lane letters, p.17.
29. Dickson, vol. V. pp.1094–95. Letter from Williamson to Dickson from Tarragona, dated 5th November 1813.

CHAPTER 19

Curtain of Fire

Following the decisive defeat of Joseph's army at Vitoria Wellington was drawn into dividing his army. The 3rd, 4th, 7th and Light divisions continued the pursuit of the French main body eastwards towards Pamplona, while Graham was sent with the 1st Division, two Portuguese infantry brigades and a cavalry brigade north in pursuit of General Antoine-Louis Maucune and the large convoy which had been dispatched just prior to the battle.[1] They were joined a few days later by Giron's 4th Spanish Army. Finally, Wellington was compelled to leave the 5th Division and a cavalry brigade to hold Vitoria, bury the dead, tend to the wounded and to sweep up the significant quantity of spoils, including 151 guns and 415 caissons. They were rapidly relieved by the 6th Division that had been covering the rear of the allied army. Clausel, commanding the Army of Aragon, closed on Vitoria from the south unaware of the catastrophic defeat suffered by Joseph and the French armies of Portugal, Centre and North but soon beat a hasty retreat and, hounded by Spanish irregular forces, withdrew first to Saragossa and then north over the Pyrenees to the relative safety of France.

Dickson sent Bull's and Webber Smith's horse artillery troops along with Du Bourdieu's and Arriaga's 9-pounder brigades north with Graham. They were joined by Lawson's Brigade a few days later when the 5th Division moved north in support of this force. Other than Brandreth's Brigade, which was with the 6th Division at Vitoria, the balance of artillery moved with Wellington's main body. Hartmann commanded the artillery group with Graham's Corps while Dickson remained with the army.

Wellington now faced a dilemma. The strategic-political posturing in central Europe, following the battles of Lützen and Bautzen and the consequent Armistice of Plässwitz, presented the possibility of peace between France, Prussia and Russia and the collapse of the 6th Coalition. An invasion of France under such circumstances would not have been wise. Furthermore, the French had left significant garrisons at both San Sebastian and Pamplona. With Bentinck under clear orders to keep Suchet occupied on the east coast 'at all costs', Wellington set about driving the French back over the River Bidassoa and the Pyrenees and laying siege to the two fortresses. The previous winter Wellington had requested an enhancement to the in-theatre battering train for operations in 1813 and this had arrived at La Coruña in early May.[2] In late June he issued orders for the train to be brought forward initially to Santander and then to Deba; Frazer was dispatched to collect the guns and ammunition and move the whole to Pamplona. Frazer was with Wellington's main army at the fortress and, like many other officers, remained puzzled as to why the army was not pursuing the defeated French and pushing on to Paris. His orders to move to the Biscay coast and take responsibility for the siege train cannot have been well received. 'Strange times these', he noted. 'Off to Santander to bring up the guns for the siege of Pampeluna [Pamplona].'[3]

In early July Wellington decided to blockade Pamplona and concentrate his efforts on besieging San Sebastian. He wrote to Dickson accordingly:

> From what I have heard of San Sebastian, I am inclined to form the siege of that place: and I should be very much obliged to you if you will send an officer to Bilbao, to order the train from there to Pasages [Pasajes, now called Pasaia]. Send the enclosed letter with this officer to be delivered to Sir G. Collier; and desire Major Frazer to communicate with Sir George in regard to the convoy from the train from Bilbao to Pasages, and to it maritime security while there; as it will actually be within sight of the French posts.[4]

Unloading such a vast train so close to the large French garrison at San Sebastian was certainly a risk; however, that peril was exacerbated by the lack of Royal Naval support in the region. Since the commencement of the War of 1812 against America, the Admiralty had been more concerned with the blockade of the east coast of America than the littoral waters of Iberia. Early Royal Navy failures and news of Napoleon's disastrous Russian campaign convinced Lord Melville, the First Sea Lord, of the need to send yet more ships of the line to support the flagging campaign across the Atlantic. The situation became so critical that in March 1813 some American privateers captured and destroyed ships off the Portuguese coast. Wellington quickly realised the enormity of losing naval supremacy around Iberia; he had plans to move his logistic base from Lisbon to Santander and yet he could not be sure of maritime security from Cadiz to La Coruña let alone along the Cantabrian coast. Relationships between Wellington and Melville, and between the two services, plummeted and were not helped by the fact that, in recent years, the tables had now been turned. The gloriously triumphant Royal Navy had long since treated the consistent failures of the redcoats with contempt; such a transformation of fortunes was bound to rankle.

The French took full advantage of the diminished allied naval ascendancy to commence movement of supplies and equipment from the west coast of France to the garrison at San Sebastian. This certainly influenced Wellington's decision to tackle San Sebastian before Pamplona but it was the significant lack of bullocks which caused him to risk the unloading of the train relatively close to the intended target.[5]

The train consisted of the six 18-pounders which had moved with the main army (with Morrison's and Glubb's companies) and the new train from England which had been moved from La Coruña consisting of 28 pieces of ordnance. In addition, Admiral Sir George R. Collier agreed to provide six additional 24-pounder guns from HMS *Surveillante* and a detachment of 50 naval gunners. These men embraced their task with courage and determination and were warmly received, dispelling any suggestion of service animosity among the rank and file.

With Hill's Division pushing back the French from the Baztan and across the pass at Maya and Major General John Byng achieving similar success to the east at the pass of Roncesvalles, Wellington turned his full attention to San Sebastian. He arrived at the fort on the 11th July and on the same day the 18-pounders arrived from Vitoria and the train began disembarkation at Pasajes. Frazer was busy trying to find suitable routes to move the heavy guns up onto the Chofre sand hill which overlooked the fortress.

> A good deal of running about yesterday, and a famous fatiguing work over the mountains, to discover a road (not yet found) for transporting a couple of 24-pounders, which I want to get on a height commanding, though at a distance, the castle of St. Sebastian and a battery called the Mirador which we must silence. Webber Smith, who is active, has offered his services to assist. The mule road from Passages [Pasajes] to this place is bad, and is partly on the edge of a rocky precipice, over the rocky shore of the harbour.[6]

Wellington, Dickson and Major Charles Smith RE completed a reconnaissance on the 12th July and confirmed the plan of attack.

> To open trenches in the Chofre sand hills to the north of the Urumea and to construct batteries to batter the exposed town wall facing that river, and as a preliminary to drive the enemy from the Convent and redoubt of San Bartolomé, where they had established a strong post about 800 yards in front of the town, which being effected, to raise batteries in that situation to aid the main attack, and to oblige the enemy to withdraw from the circular work on the causeway.[7]

The exposed town wall was, unsurprisingly given the surrounding terrain, the same spot selected by the Duke of Berwick in 1719 when Britain and France had been allies in the War of the Quadruple Alliance against Spain. The Chofre sand hills which faced the eastern wall were, equally unsurprisingly, covered by fire from no fewer than three strong and well-positioned batteries within the fort and adjoining castle. However, it was soon to become apparent that the plan had two significant flaws. Firstly, the lower part of the wall could only be battered during low tide; secondly, the approaches were similarly subject to the mercies of the tide and would necessitate a long and exposed approach. Furthermore, the French garrison commander, Brigadier General Louis-Emmanuel Rey, was a very different character to his Spanish counterpart from the 1719 siege who had happily capitulated once the walls were breached. Frazer noted that the French had 'some good head in the fortress: we must feel for it. He fires and takes his measures with judgement …'.[8] Frazer was having a devil of a time getting the ordnance into place but was eased in his plight by the assistance of the infantry and the local women.

> The roads are detestable. The night before last, we lost Webber-Smith's howitzer in the river Urumea, and last night one of Captain Du Bourdieu's 9-pounders and five horses were drowned. The two guns have not yet been got out; we must try again. Yesterday we have no working party of infantry, so I was obliged to run about, first here and then there, until I got a brigade of infantry placed at my disposal. General Spry's [Portuguese] brigade has been so placed, and is amusing itself with dragging 24-pounders up a slippery mountain … Our batteries will open against the castle and town in a couple of days, but without cars, or mules, or oxen, one looks at the carriages and piles of shot with something like wonder how they are to be moved. I am at my wits' end, or nearly so, with the ladies here: they are everything and do everything, and are supreme; they row, unload vessels, bring shot on shore, yet I have been a week begging, praying, and urging in vain, that they receive rations and some remuneration.[9]

Dickson assumed command of the artillery operation from Hartmann. He had the 43 officers and 526 NCOs and gunners to man the 39 pieces of ordnance. These men had been provided from Webber Smith's Troop of horse artillery, Du Bourdieu's, Lawson's, Morrison's, Glubb's and Parker's companies from the Royal Artillery, Arriaga's Portuguese gunners and 50 naval gunners.[10] Hartmann was placed in charge of the operation on the left (south of the town) and May had responsibility for the right attack. Four of the 18-pounders and two 8-inch howitzers were moved into place for the left attack during the night of the 13th July (see Appendix 4) and they opened early on the 14th against the convent of San Bartolomé. The same morning, Wellington set off to rejoin the army, leaving Graham and General John Oswald's 5th Division to complete the task.

The clearance of the French defences at the San Bartolomé convent at the end of the isthmus leading to the fort was a crucial preliminary operation as the French redoubts had arcs of fire covering the eastern approaches as well as those from the south. An attempt had been made by Hartmann to clear the structure using Arriaga's guns on the 7th July but 'our Portuguese friends brought only three guns into play, frequently missed the whole building, and fired shot not half heated'.[11] The 18-pounders commenced firing heated shot directly into the structure while the heavy howitzers kept the heads of the defenders down enabling work on new batteries to continue. The cannonade from the town was largely ineffective as the convent and other buildings along the isthmus blocked their view and line of fire. The two batteries continued through the next day and Webber Smith's Troop of 9-pounder guns and a heavy 5½-inch howitzer was moved up to a position on the east of the river to engage the structure from the rear flank. Despite an attempt by the 8th Caçadores to dislodge the defenders on the 15th July, they were to hold out for two more days until a more concerted effort had been made by Pack's Portuguese Brigade. Work began immediately on the construction of two batteries (3 and 4) to enfilade the eastern walls and heavy guns and howitzers were moved to the top of Monte Ulía to neutralise the Mirador Battery. The breaching batteries (13 and 14) were also commenced in the sand hills.

The sandy stratum was a blessing, allowing the rapid and relatively easy construction of the batteries, but it played havoc with the firm anchorage of the heavy guns and with the 'soles' of the embrasures. The breaching batteries opened at 1000 hours on the 20th July and they soon received a very warm and accurate reception from the French. Lieutenant Richard Hardinge recalled that 'Du Bourdieu and myself with the Company to man 9 guns of the breaching battery … from several delays did not open till 10 a.m. At 12 D [Du Bourdieu] was cut down. Lost before evening. Bombrs. Miller and Smyth killed. Gunner Johnstone do. and Smith and Todd wounded.'[12] Du Bourdieu was buried the following evening in the cemetery of the captured convent of San Bartholomé.[13] The breaching batteries were working at the maximum effective range but they were having an effect on the walls and on the town itself.

11. The First Siege of San Sebastian ~ 11–25th July 1813

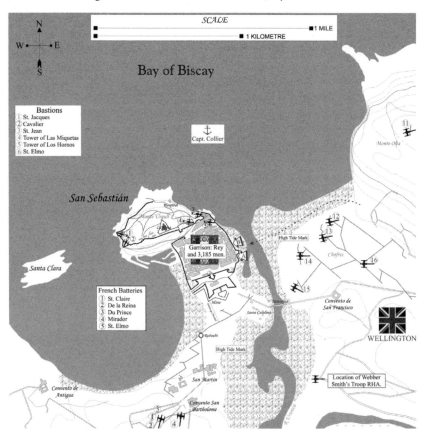

Great part of the town is ruined by our fire. The crashing of houses, and roaring of guns on all sides, make a horrible din. How dreadful must at this moment be the feelings of the poor inhabitants, and indeed, those of the garrison! We who witness these horrid scenes do not feel them as we ought: the habit of continually seeing shocking sights takes away every finer feeling; 'tis well that it does.[14]

The bombardment continued for two more days until the 23rd July when a large slab of the curtain fell outwards on to the mud flats. Graham, having received intelligence from some locals that the curtain was narrower to the north, issued orders to Dickson after consultation with Fletcher (who had arrived on the 15th July), to batter a third breach (point C). The efficacy of this secondary breach along the same wall is certainly open to question, all the more so because that very evening the working parties digging parallels north along the isthmus came across a draining ditch which advanced all the way north and under the counterscarp of the hornwork. Thirty barrels of gunpowder were inserted and the entrance sandbagged; the resultant explosion during the first assault was far more effective than anticipated. It is curious that Jones (in his extremely detailed *Journal of Sieges*) makes scant mention of the discovery of the drainage channel but Burgoyne, Fletcher's deputy, considers the discovery so significant that the entire plan of attack should have been altered to exploit the advantage.[15]

Firing continued during the 23rd July to create the new breach and to harass the defenders and prevent them repairing or retrenching the existing gaps. The Royal Navy gunners were manning the short 24-pounder guns in Battery 14 alongside their counterparts of the Royal Artillery; spirits had been high but that was all about to change.

The French had, in San Sebastian, four immense mortars, from which they threw shells of fourteen inches in diameter – hitherto none of these monsters had found their way to the batteries, but as they passed over our heads, the heavy rush they made through the air, and the terrific noise of their explosion, made us distinctly recognise them, amidst the thundering of the other guns. The tars had christened them 'the babies', and as each 'baby', with its own peculiar cry, ranged beyond the mark of our battery, the sailors cut capers at their escape, and the fiddle played.

It was about eleven o'clock on the morning of the 23rd, when one of those awful shells, thrown with fatal precision, appeared in the air, descending like a mighty destroyer, in the direct line of the sailors' battery. The monster alighted on the back of a poor fellow, who had thrown himself on his face as the only chance of escape, and exploding at the same instant, killed, or dreadfully mutilated seventeen of these noble-spirited champions of England's wooden walls.[16]

Preparations had been made for the assault to go in on both breaches early on the 24th July. During the day of the 23rd, while Dickson's Gunners were busy making a second practicable breach, the French mounted an additional pair of field guns behind the demi-lune. These pieces would create havoc to the assaulting troops on entering the lower breach. They were not the only guns giving Graham cause for concern: there was a light gun on the left wing of the hornwork; two casemated guns facing the breach approaches; two field guns in a ditch south of the hornwork again facing the breach approaches; a gun behind the Tower of Los Hornos; and two guns in the St. Elmo Battery enfilading the eastern curtain. Dickson gave his assurance to Graham that the Gunners would neutralise these pieces and keep the parapets clear of French.[17]

The next morning the assaulting parties were in place waiting for the tide to ebb sufficiently to allow them to cross the estuary when Graham called off the attack. The houses adjacent to the breach were ablaze and the ferocity and proximity of the flames was considered to be a considerable hindrance to the troops once inside the breach. Rey immediately set about using the extra time to enhance the already considerable distractions. The next low tide was at 1600 hours but the decision was made to delay the attack until an hour after daylight the next day. As it transpired, things did not go according to plan.

The assault was made, but stupidly an hour before, instead of after daybreak. Lieutenant Jones of the Engineers, with an officer and nine men of the Royals, led the way, and gained with no loss the top of the breach (the large one). This party was followed by two companies of the Royals, which reached the foot of the breach, and were faced to their left, so as to front it in good order; but the enemy at this time commencing a roll of musketry, the men, panic-struck, turned, could never be rallied, and sustained loss in running back.[18]

The assaulting troops stumbled over the slippery seaweed-clad rocks, detritus and numerous deep pools which afforded no warning in the half light. Ironically, the mine was fired at much the same time as the main assault was delivered but the follow-up attack in this sector by the Portuguese troops was more of a feint and the opportunity passed. After half an hour of trying, the impetus long sapped, the order was given to pull back from both locations. The assault had incontrovertibly failed with the commander, the infantry, the Engineers and the Gunners all having to take their share of responsibility for the disappointment.

As the day dawned, we discovered with our glasses bodies both of officers and men in the breach, and under the demi-bastion and returning wall. We then began to suspect what we soon found to be the case; the assault had been made and failed. In a little while one or two of the enemy appeared on the breach, and one sergeant, with a gasconading humanity, ran down among the wounded, raising some, and speaking to others. We stopped our fire, which till then had been continued occasionally over the breach. More of the enemy appeared: a kind of parley took place between them and three of our people at the head of the trenches: when a white flag was hoisted, by what authority I know not.[19]

Under the walls of the fortress and strewed along the strand, lay our wounded officers and soldiers. The shells from our batteries bursting over the walls of the fortress, fell upon these poor defenceless creatures, killing and wounding the already wounded, while the shots also rebounded from the walls among them. The spectacle of so much suffering was not to be endured even by their enemies, and a noble spirited young French officer stepping forward to make known their distressing situation, sought the dangerous and conspicuous position on the breach, as the best means to acquaint us with the fatal effect of our guns on our own wounded countrymen.[20]

Major William Gomm, serving on the staff as Assistant Quarter Master General, considered both the Gunners and Engineers to have been deficient in their planning and execution.

I am afraid our success at Ciudad Rodrigo and Badajoz, owing to the almost miraculous efforts of the troops, has stopped the progress of science among our engineers ... our soldiers have on all occasions stood fire so well that our artillery have become as summary in their processes as our engineers. Provided that they have made a hole in the wall, by which we can claw up, they care not about destroying defences. In fact, we have been called upon hitherto to ensure the success of our sieges by the sacrifice of lives. Our Chief Engineers and Commandants of Artillery remind me of Burke's 'Revolutionary Philosophers' and their 'dispositions which make them indifferent to the cause of humanity; they think no more of men than of mice in an air pump'.[21]

Such criticism merits scrutiny. Gomm's regiment was the 9th Foot and he had just seen many good friends and fine soldiers thinned from its ranks as a result of the failed assault, but his accusation of indifference against the technical arms is not entirely appropriate. Leaving aside the first two sieges of Badajoz in 1811, as these were conducted without a proper siege train, the sieges of Ciudad Rodrigo and Badajoz the following year were conducted in what has been termed an irregular manner. May, who had responsibility for the artillery of the right attack at San Sebastian, wrote about the three sieges some time later and concluded that the British had hit on a new method of siege warfare superior to that of the French (Chapter 13).[22] This irregular manner was, to all intents and purposes, the breaching of the walls from the first parallel and the storming at the first opportunity to prevent the defenders retrenching the breaches or preparing all manner of other devices to deny and delay the attackers. It was, potentially, going to be more costly in lives and the decision to adopt it was taken at the first two sieges for sound operational reasons. The army of Marmont at the former and Soult at the latter were within a few days' march of coming to the aid of the defenders. Time was clearly critical and the decision to adopt an irregular method was undeniably made by Wellington himself.

It is debateable as to whether speed was so critical at San Sebastian. An attempt (by land) to succour Rey's garrison was unlikely, yet Wellington realised that the next phase of the campaign lay in the balance. If events in central Europe settled favourably, the opportunity to strike across the Pyrenees could manifest itself with speed and the rapidity of exploiting that window would be decisive. While not the commander on the ground for the siege at San Sebastian, Wellington was nevertheless aware of the plan and clearly satisfied with the proposal to execute another irregular operation. In fairness to Dickson, he arrived some days after the initial plans were discussed, but he appears to have made very few changes and yet it should have been readily apparent that the structure was a formidable obstacle and that the available train was barely adequate. His assurance that the French guns on both sides of the breaches could be neutralised or silenced was not honoured, partly due to the fact that the attack was made in the dark. Fletcher too arrived much later and he seems to have accepted Smith's plan without modification, although in his mitigation it was a plan which had been discussed and agreed with Wellington some days earlier. The discovery of the drainage ditch could certainly have been exploited to greater effect, allowing the infantry in this quarter to gain ingress while, perhaps, making the attack on the breaches a feint. Of course all of this is fine in hindsight but there are clear and evident disadvantages in making too many comparisons: the fortresses at Ciudad Rodrigo, Badajoz and San Sebastian were very different; the determination and innovativeness of the French commanders more so; and the available siege trains and ammunition not standard. The Gunners must take their share of the blame for the failures in the first siege but, at the end of it all, the principal reason for the failure stemmed from a poor all-arms plan and a questionable resolve on the part of the very brave men who made the assault. Ross, who witnessed the attack, was quite clear as to the nucleus of the failure:

> The assault was made at daybreak, and to commence by signal from Sir Richard Fletcher. Some say the signal was given (and possibly it might be so) too soon; the troops, however, went on, and Captain Jones of the Engineers, followed by the greater part of the grenadiers of the Royals, carried the breach and entered the place. Support, however, hung back, and the reason assigned for it is publicly talked of to be this: that General Oswald – who was directing the attack, and at the head of the trench – called out at an unlucky moment to Sir Thomas Graham, who stood a little way from him, 'It won't do, it won't do; shall we call them back?' or some words to that effect, which naturally being overheard by all near, checked ardour, and lost the time which ought to have been taken advantage of whilst the enemy was alarmed and the breach in our possession.[23]

Early on the 25th July Wellington received news of the failure and he rode to the outskirts of the town for a first hand report. He gave instructions to Dickson and Fletcher to think again and for more guns and ammunition to be collected once they arrived from England. Soon after noon he rode back to his headquarters at Lesaka and was met on the road with news that Soult, who was now commanding the French armies on the border, appeared to be moving on the passes at Maya and Roncesvalles. He wrote immediately to Graham to lift the siege, maintain a (land) blockade and ship the guns from Pasajes and move the balance of his division north towards the Bidassoa. For now, the capture of San Sebastian was on hold.

The battle of the Pyrenees lasted ten days. Soult's attempt to force the passes and relieve Pamplona had failed but, for now, the outcome of events in central Europe remained uncertain and Wellington turned his attention back to the capture of San

Sebastian and Pamplona. The re-embarkation of all the guns and stores had only just been completed by the 30th July but Wellington was quite clear that until new ordnance and ammunition should arrive from England the siege would not resume.

> I went to the siege on the 25th, and having conferred with Lieut. Gen. Sir T. Graham and the officers of the engineers and artillery, it appeared to me that it would be necessary to increase the facilities of the attack before it should be repeated. But, upon adverting to the state of our ammunition, I found that we had not a sufficiency to do anything effectual till that should arrive for which I had written on the 26th June, which I had reason to believe was embarked at Portsmouth, and to expect every hour. I therefore desired that the siege should for the moment be converted into a blockade ...[24]

Wellington wrote again to the Admiralty asking to increase the naval force to assist the blockade and, until the train and stores should arrive, he ordered the Commissary General to prepare the landing boats and wharf, the Engineers (based on Fletcher's revised plan) to commence digging on the new works and repair and enhance the road from Pasajes, and the Gunners to re-land sufficient guns and ammunition to protect and support these initiatives. In addition, May was ordered to Wellington's headquarters to 'arrange the ammunition concerns of the army'.[25]

Dickson had other problems on his mind. The vents on the iron 24-pounders were deteriorating:

> Our guns here have gone the same way as Badajoz. Of 14, 24 Prs., four are unserviceable, and two much enlarged in the vents, and this with four or five days firing during the day only, and a few occasional rounds of grape shot in the night. The matter resolves itself to this therefore, that Iron guns must not be fired more than a certain number of times a day, and in long summer days must be allowed to stand still part of the day. It remains to be proved, however, what number of rounds may be forced without injury, until which in all vigorous operations, particularly of breaching, when haste is an object, guns will be liable to give way, and a new operation will require new guns. I consider the metal softens and scores the vent, and it widens into the most irregular shapes ...[26]

Notwithstanding these obvious problems with iron siege guns, May was quite clear in his assessment that iron guns remained infinitely better than brass ones as 'their bore would remain unchanged even after 2 or 3000 rounds'.[27] Vents could be repaired, as indeed they were following Badajoz, but a damaged or worn bore rendered the piece unserviceable or frustratingly unreliable in the prosecution of precision siege work.

On the 19th August transports *Globe, Northumberland, Three Sisters* and *Friendship* arrived off the Cantabrian port of Pasajes and two days later transports *Eliza, Christiana, Ajax* and *Goodstatesman* sailed into the straits. On board were a replacement train, identical to that which had arrived in May (see note 2) but also a number of pieces of ordnance destined for garrison service at Cuxhaven and considerable quantities of ammunition and stores. Dickson now had a most formidable train consisting of 56 24-pounder guns, 14 18-pounder guns, 16 10-inch mortars, 18 8-inch howitzers, 12 68-pounder carronades and one 12-inch (Spanish) mortar: a total of 117 pieces of ordnance as well as over 60,000 round shot, 3,500 case and grape, over 20,000 spherical case, over 6,000 common case, a number of carcasses for the mortars and over 8,000 barrels of powder. There had been some problems with the initial preparations to assemble the train in England, and furthermore the heavy guns originally destined for Cuxhaven were still attached to garrison carriages and were to be of little use at San Sebastian; nevertheless, the Board of Ordnance had certainly risen to the task and they should, along with MacLeod and his staff at Woolwich, receive plaudit for their achievements.

Graham, eager to get on with the siege and restore reputations, was less sanguine. 'It is too provoking to think of such mistakes and delays at home, where they have nothing else to do or think of, but the execution of demands made at an early enough period to give full time for preparation.'[28] Dickson too was equally anxious to recommence operations but with such a large train he needed more Gunners. Accordingly, Douglas and Sympher were ordered to move their guns to Tolosa and move with their companies to San Sebastian. He now had 761 artillery officers, NCOs and gunners, including 80 naval gunners (Dickson noted that the naval contribution diminished after the first three days), to transport, prepare and serve the considerable train. Nevertheless, the disembarkation and movement was proving a real challenge and once again the lack of naval manpower impinged on operations; Wellington wrote in strong terms to Lord Melville, more in frustration than expectation.

> The soldiers are obliged to work in the transports, and unload the vessels, because no seaman can be furnished. We have been obliged to use the harbour boats of Passages, navigated by women, in landing ordnance and stores, because there is no naval force to supply us with the assistance that we have required in boats. These harbour boats being light, and of weak construction, have, many of them, been destroyed, and there will be great delay from want of boats in further operations of the siege. The soldiers have to load and unload the boats, the women who navigate them being unequal to the labour …[29]

Both Fletcher and Dickson had agreed to continue, in outline, with a main breaching attack from the right but to expand the left attack with a number of batteries concentrating on countering the French defences which would be sapped forward to within a few hundred yards of the southern walls. Hartmann once again assumed responsibility for the left attack and Frazer that of the right, with field officers allocated to each battery on the right (Webber Smith, Buckner, Dyer and Sympher). A total of 63 pieces of ordnance were to be used for both attacks and by first light on the 26th August 57 pieces (42 on the right and 15 on the left) were ready; an opening round from Battery 11 at 0800 hours commenced the second siege in earnest (see Appendix 4).[30] The breaching batteries were directed to complete the destruction of the two towers and the walls to the left, up to the demi-bastion of St. Jean and to bring down the curtain above it, from the demi-bastion to the right-hand tower. By the end of the first day the achievements of the right attack were considered 'most satisfactory' but those on the left required an adjustment to the plan and the construction of Battery 7 was commenced.

That night a boat squadron from HMS *Surveillante*, under the command of Lieutenant James Arbuthnott RN (younger brother of William Arbuthnott RA), assisted by an infantry detachment from the 9th Foot, surprised the small French garrison on the island of Santa Clara. The decision was taken to mount a battery here to enfilade the rear of the castle and its defences. The first attempt to move guns into Battery 7 during the night of the 27th August was thwarted by the state of the tracks along the isthmus and the three 24-pounders were not in place until the following night. By the 29th August the situation was as follows: the breaching batteries had battered a practicable breach and the Tower of Las Miquetas, which had proved a most obstinate target, was finally levelled along with the gun housed behind it. Also destroyed was the gun at the Tower of Los Hornos and Dickson now directed a number of guns to fire against the east face of the hornwork to try and render ineffective some of the mines the French were known to have placed there. A gun and howitzer were moved and installed that night onto Santa Clara island. Battery 7 was found to be a most useful addition and the three 24-pounders housed there, along with Battery 6, began to batter the south face of the demi-bastion and the high curtain with evident anxiety to the defenders.

However, Dickson was growing increasingly concerned about the likelihood of a sortie to destroy these guns and indeed those of the two main breaching batteries at 14 and 15.

One of the infantry brigades having been withdrawn, it became a source of uneasiness lest the garrison should make a sortie during the night, and spike the guns of No. 7. In order, therefore, to guard against such misfortune, the artillery officers took some measures for their security by fastening an iron plate over the vents, locked on by a chain, which would have occasioned some delay in spiking them, even if attempted by experienced artillerymen. They also resorted to similar measures for the safety of the breaching batteries on the right, which being almost unsupported by a parallel, and having only a small guard for their protection, were very much exposed to danger, should the garrison show any enterprise; for, the Urumea being perfectly fordable at low water, to cross and spike the guns and return back would only have been the work of a few minutes.[31]

Macdonald had, under his own accord, waded across the Urumea at night to the foot of the breach and determined that the river itself offered scant protection to the batteries.[32] In addition, the fire of the howitzers, carronades and mortars was kept up, day and night, to harass the defenders and hinder their attempts at retrenchment and the construction of other defensive enhancements. Nevertheless, the officers of the 5th Division were (largely) of the opinion that the second plan was merely a repetition of the first and equally unlikely to succeed. They had bitterly resented earlier suggestions of a lack of zeal and were in no way prepared to incur a second failure through, as they saw it, the shortcomings of the artillery and engineers. Graham wrote to Wellington on the subject on the 22nd August and received the following by return. 'It is impossible to stop people's mouths, if they are so indiscreet as to deliver their opinions on such a matter as to the practicability of storming a breach, where those opinions can be of no use, excepting to render success so unattainable by the inferior officers and troops who hear opinions.'[33] Wellington considered relieving the 5th Division of the task but then decided to ask the three nearest divisions for volunteers to supplement the forlorn hope and leading assault groups. General Sir James Leith, who himself had only arrived back in theatre on the 28th August to assume command of the operation from Graham, was infuriated by this snub. He selected Brigadier General Frederick Robinson's Brigade to lead the assault using the 750 volunteers in supporting roles only; Andrew Hay's and William Spry's brigades were in reserve and the 5th Caçadores (from Bradford's Brigade) were used to provide intimate infantry fire support. The balance of this brigade was allocated the smaller breach

12. The Second Siege of San Sebastian ~ 6th August–8th September 1813

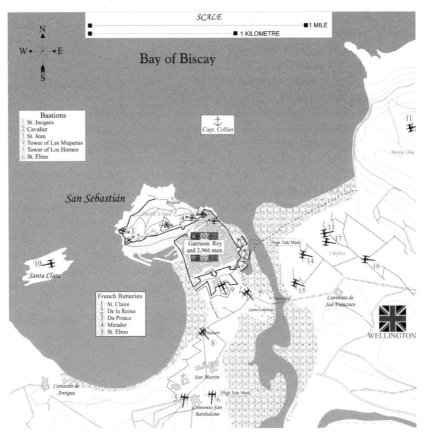

to the north of the Tower of Las Miquetas (point C). Their approach was across the Urumea while the other three brigades were to approach along the isthmus.

Soult, who was in constant contact with Rey, felt committed to make an attempt to relieve the garrison and force the allies to lift the siege. On the 31st August, under cover of a heavy morning haze, Soult crossed the Bidassoa. Wellington returned with haste to his army to counter the threat and left instructions for Leith. The breaches had been declared practicable during the afternoon of the 30th August and it was decided to assault the next day; with low tide at noon, H Hour was set for 1100 hours. During the preceding 24 hours the Gunners bombarded the fort, castle and defences from every angle. Frazer recorded that 'the wood and rubbish of the right breach of the former siege is in flames, and a mine near it blew up'.[34] Later that day he added 'five little mines have this moment blown up near the hospital in the town; one of our shells found them out'.[35] At 0200 hours the engineers prepared and blew three charges to bring down the sea wall between the left salient angle of the hornwork and the trenches in front of Battery 7. Once blown they set about constructing gabions (6 feet high and 3 feet wide) to screen the advancing troops from grape and canister. The preliminary bombardment had also cut the train to the huge mine at the main breach, although this was only discovered *ex post facto*. Not so fortunate were the sergeant and 12 men earmarked to cut the *saucisson* on the large mine at the end of the hornwork; all of them perished but the main group had already passed and casualties were lighter than they might have been.

The assault was delivered as planned but the strength of the structure and the many unseen traps and pitfalls prevented tangible progress; after half an hour, despite repeated attempts to gain lodgement, the attack was beginning to lose momentum. Leith was standing on the beach under the damaged sea wall; Major General John Oswald and Fletcher were next to him. Soon after the attack commenced Fletcher was shot through the neck and died instantly; a few moments later Oswald was struck in the face and taken to the rear. At 1135 hours an observer noted that 'much firing ... the troops do not advance ... though the bugles keep sounding the advance'.[36] At exactly this time, Bradford's Portuguese began their advance to the other breach across the estuary and were at the base of the structure within ten minutes, catching the French gunners off guard and denying them the opportunity to wreak disproportionate havoc on the Portuguese infantry. They too found the area behind the breach to be traversed; their position was slightly higher than that of the defenders but the likelihood of success in this quarter was equally remote. The situation was bleak indeed but it was at this point that Graham and Dickson made a decision that was to alter events.

In this almost desperate state of affairs, Sir Thos. Graham, having consulted with Lieutenant-Colonel Dickson, ordered that the whole artillery of the breaching batteries of the Chofre sand–hills should, as far as possible, be brought to bear on the high curtain above the breach in the demi-bastions, and in a few minutes the fire of 47 guns, howitzers, and carronades, was directed with such effect on the traverse, that the garrison (who, encouraged by the success of their efforts, had recently become more bold and forward,) were obliged to retire from its effects behind more distant cover, and to slacken their musketry fire. The artillery from five days continued firing, knew the range precisely, and the practice against the high curtain was admirable; for although the shot passed immediately over the troops on the face and foot of the breach, and swept amongst the defenders of the curtain, it occasioned no casualties among the assailants.[37]

This hitherto untried artillery close support continued until about 1235 hours and the slaughter among the tightly packed defenders was terrible. Frazer noted that at 1240 hours 'men were going down from the old breach into the town. It will do; they wave their hats from the terre-pleine of the castle.'[38] The momentum regained, the attacks pushed home and British soldiers occupied the hornwork (which the French abandoned when their line of retreat was threatened) and the high curtain at the main breach, and then found ingress at the smaller breach by some of the Light Division's soldiers, from the group of volunteers. Frazer, from his vantage point of the sand hill, noted at 1325 hours that 'firing in the town continues and increases'; 50 minutes later he noticed that it began to dwindle. The fight for the town was all but won. Rey retreated with 1,000 men into the castle and such was the confusion that he was able to make good his escape but he was bombarded into submission eight days later (see Appendix 4 for artillery plan and execution). Frazer's final note in his meticulous minutes was made at 1530 hours: 'great fire in the town; as dark as it is generally at half-past six. Nothing of the town can be seen from excessive smoke.'[39]

Major Gomm had witnessed both sieges; his diary entry of 4th September 1813 makes no attempt to reconcile his differences with the technical arms but he does present views of both the excesses committed by the force following the capture of the town and the subsequent fire which devastated large parts of the municipality. They are worthy of examination:

> The day closed, as it has always done since the first town was taken, in riot and tumult: and although many of the excesses committed at Badajoz were avoided here, St. Sebastian is a more melancholy story than either Badajoz or Rodrigo. For with the exception of ten or twelve fortunate buildings, there is nothing left of St. Sebastian but the blackened walls of its houses, and these are falling every instant with a tremendous crash. How the fire was started was uncertain – I think there is little doubt of its having been done intentionally by the enemy ... Never surely was there a more complete picture of desolation than the place presents.[40]

Leaving aside the debate as to whether the excesses of the troops exceeded those witnessed at Badajoz (although I agree with Oman wholeheartedly that they did not) the question of exactly how the fires started is relevant to Wellington's Gunners. The Manifesto, issued by the Constitutional Town Hall in 1814, apart from accusing Wellington of having ordered the town destroyed for reasons of commercial jealousy, most certainly lays the blame for the fires on the allied artillery.

... the live fire of the allies; and the damages that were caused by the grenades and other projectiles that accidentally, or targeted, fell on the City, they increased its miseries ... When houses were set on fire they set light to those adjacent ones ...[41]

It will be recalled that Wellington did not sanction the use of mortars and howitzers at Ciudad Rodrigo for fear of the collateral damage the projectiles would inflict on the civilian population. Dickson, having taken up his *unofficial* appointment as Wellington's siege commander months earlier, was not about to argue the point. However, 18 months later he felt compelled to request their use, as by accepted convention, at San Sebastian and he wrote accordingly to Graham who, in turn, submitted the idea to Wellington. His response is illuminating.

I am certain that the use of mortars and howitzers in a siege for the purposes of what [Colonel Dickson] calls *general annoyance*, answers no purpose whatsoever against a Spanish place occupied by French troops, excepting against the inhabitants of the place; and eventually, when we shall get the place, against ourselves, and the convenience we should derive from having the houses of the place in perfect state of repair. If [Colonel Dickson] intended to use his mortars and howitzers against any particular work occupied by the enemy ... their use *might* answer his purpose. I say *might*, because I recollect that at the siege of Ciudad Rodrigo, our trenches were bombarded by 11 or 13 large mortars and howitzers for 10 days ... which occasioned us but little loss ... and I may say did not impede our progress for one moment ... If this effect of the bombardment is a matter of doubt, it remains to be stated by [Colonel Dickson] what advantage will be derived from a general bombardment of the town ... he will not forget ... the increased difficulties of storming it, in consequence of the fire in the neighbourhood. If the general bombardment should set fire to the town, which it probably will, then the attack of the enemy's entrenchment will become impracticable.[42]

Wellington accepts, in the same letter, that the use of such ordnance at Badajoz was due entirely to the paucity of other suitable siege guns but, intriguingly, concludes that these are his opinions and that should Dickson decide to go ahead he should do so from the right attack as this would save on transport and labour. Wellington's views on the effectiveness of mortars and howitzers in siege tactics of the day certainly fly in the face of hard evidence of the era but his sensitivity to collateral damage and the dangers of secondary conflagration are both commendable and, in this instance, prophetic. There can be little doubt that the artillery shells caused the fires which started at the back of the breaches, but what is less clear is how they spread; whether the French did indeed set additional fires as they retreated; or why the allies seem to have made little attempt to fight the fires once the town was in allied hands. Major General Andrew Hay, who by mid-afternoon, was in overall command, stated that the fighting at the north of the town leading to the castle lasted until late in the afternoon, that there was some looting ongoing but that the fires were already well established across the town, fuelled by strong winds, and that his first priority was the powder magazine and the hospital. However, as regrettable as the fires were, they cannot be attributed to deliberate negligence on the part of the artillery, or indeed to any part of the allied army.

The decision to use the artillery to fire at the defenders at the top of the curtain in an attempt to buy protection and time for the attackers at the base of the structure was, quite simply, audacious and unique. Graham, certainly not an artillery expert, had the foresight to discuss the possibility of bringing fire down from the breaching batteries to support the, by now, flagging assault. Dickson, in an equally visionary moment, agreed to the idea and issued orders accordingly. He later wrote:

> The great body of our cannon, howitzers, and carronades fired upon the great curtain and behind it – over the heads of our own men with a vigour and accuracy probably unprecedented in the annals of artillery. It was the admiration and surprise of Sir Thomas Graham, and Marshal Beresford, and all who beheld it. No one could say there was a single error to the disadvantage of our own people; and the force of the fire entirely prevented the enemy making any effort along the rampart to drive us from the breach … In short, on this occasion, our artillery was served in such a manner that I would not have believed it, had I not seen it.[43]

This was a *curtain of fire* and, without doubt, the forerunner of the creeping barrage which provided the infantry a screen of artillery cover during an attack and featured so predominantly on the static European battlefields of the Great War 100 years later. Graham was effusive in his praise for the success of the suggestion, and the accuracy of its delivery, in his post-siege dispatch to Wellington. 'A heavy fire of artillery was directed against it; passing a few feet only over the heads of our troops on the breach, and was kept up with a precision of practice beyond all example.'[44] He went on to praise Dickson who had conducted every aspect of the artillery with 'the greatest ability'. Morrison, Power and Parker were singled out for mention in a subsequent dispatch. Dickson had every reason to be pleased and not a little relieved at the outcome of the second attempt on the city. With only 19 killed and 75 wounded in action, the artillery returns appear conspicuously small against those losses endured by the infantry. It was ever thus, and Dickson and his men could take comfort that their day's duty had saved many infantrymen's lives and turned defeat into victory.

Notes

1. The passage of orders for Graham's Corps was bungled leading to some of the formations having to counter-march and it was during this episode that Capt. Ramsay was arrested.
2. This consisted of 28 pieces of ordnance: 14 x iron 24-pounder guns, 4 x iron 68-pounder carronades, 4 x iron 10-inch mortars and 6 x brass 8-inch howitzers.
3. Frazer (ed. Sabine), letter dated 25th June 1813, above Pamplona.
4. WD, vol. VI, p.584. Wellington to Dickson from Lantz, dated 4th July 1813.

5. His overriding reason, however, was Murray's disaster at Tarragona (Chapter 18) and the possibility of Clausel linking up with Suchet to prosecute operations against a siege of Pamplona.

6. Frazer (ed. Sabine), letter dated 11th July 1813 at 6 a.m.

7. Dickson, vol. V, p.959.

8. Frazer, letter dated 19th July 1813.

9. Ibid., letter from Pasajes, dated 16th July 1813.

10. Elements of May's Company were also in location responsible for the ammunition and Bull's Troop was at Hernani with the cavalry. For a list of the officers at the siege see Dickson, vol. V, pp.963–65.

11. Frazer (ed. Sabine), letter dated 8th July 1813, at 6 a.m.

12. Dickson, vol. V, p.957. R. Hardinge's diary; elements of this diary were included in vol. V of Dickson.

13. All the British officers killed in the siege were buried here. It was dug up at the end of the 19th century and the remains moved to a single grave over which a solitary monument was erected. Sadly that monument bears no individual names and is now in a dreadful state of repair.

14. Frazer (ed. Sabine), letter dated 23rd July from Pasajes.

15. Burgoyne, vol. I, p.271.

16. Henegan, vol. II, p.28.

17. Jones, vol. II, p.39.

18. Frazer (ed. Sabine), letter dated 26th July 1813.

19. Ibid.

20. Henegan, vol. II, p.34.

21. See Oman, vol. VI. pp.581–82 (quoting Gomm).

22. May, p.8.

23. Ross, pp.49–51. Letter from Ross to Dalrymple Ross, dated 31st October 1813.

24. WD, vol. VI, pp.636–44. Wellington to Bathurst from San Estevan, dated 1st August 1813.

25. Ibid., pp.646–47. Wellington to Graham from Lesaka, dated 4th August 1813.

26. Dickson, vol. V. pp.997–98.

27. May, p.13. Henegan states that some of these guns had also suffered 'muzzle droop' but I can find no evidence of this and it is not supported by Dickson: Henegan, vol. II, p.41.

28. Duncan, vol. II, p.367, quoting Graham's correspondence dated 7th August 1813. Napier's assertion that 'with characteristic negligence this enormous armament had been sent out from England with no more shot and shells than would suffice for one day's consumption' was typically absurd.

29. Oman, from WD, vol. XII, pp.18–19, Wellington to Lord Melville.

30. Frazer and Burgoyne list 0800 hours as the first round, Jones states 0900 hours.

31. Jones, vol. II, pp.68–69.

32. Macdonald and Brereton, both with Bean's Troop at Pamplona, had asked permission to join the siege. Brereton notes p.v. Macdonald may have made this sortie during the first siege as both he and Brereton returned to 'D' Troop and the 3rd Division at the end of July.

33. WD, vol. VI, pp.704–06. Wellington to Graham from Lesaka, dated 23rd August 1813.

34. Frazer (ed. Sabine), letter dated 30th August 1813 at half past 9 a.m.

35. Ibid., at three-quarters past 4 p.m.

36. Oman, vol. VII. p.24.

37. Jones, vol. II, pp.77–78.

38. Frazer (ed. Sabine), minutes taken during the Assault, 31st August 1813.

39. Ibid.

40. See Oman, vol. VII, p.32 (quoting Gomm).

41. *Manifestó que el Ayuntamiento Constitucional, Cabildo Eclesiástico, Ilustre Consulado y Vecinos de la Cuidad de San Sebastián presentan a la naciůn sobre la conducta de las Tropas británicas y Portugueses en dicha plaza el 31 de Agosto de 1813 y días sucesivos* (San Sebastián, 1814). Notes from p.2 and p.6.

42. WD, vol. VI, pp.704–06. Wellington to Graham from Lesaka, dated 23rd August 1813.

43. Duncan, vol. II. p.369 – quoting Dickson; however, this letter does not appear in Dickson.

44. WD, vol. VI, pp.727–30. Graham to Wellington from Oiartzun, dated 1st September 1813.

CHAPTER 20

Waller's Remonstrance

During the period 1811–12 many of Napoleon's more capable Peninsular commanders had been re-directed to central European appointments for political, personal and military reasons. Soult, Marmont, Ney, Reynier, Victor, Bessières, Latour Maubourg, Sebastiani and Kellermann were all part of Napoleon's army embroiled in the growing contest in Saxony. As far as Napoleon was concerned the failures in Spain were a direct result of his brother's poor leadership and that of his principal advisor, Jourdan. The unfortunate sibling was not only held responsible but placed under some form of arrest; Jourdan was recalled in disgrace and Soult was sent back to assume command of the armies of Spain and remedy the situation. For the first time since Napoleon departed from Valladolid in January 1809, there was a single commander-in-chief; Soult, who had long desired such an opportunity, had every intention of making best use of his chance and the situation.

The Duke of Dalmatia had arrived at Bayonne on the 12th July 1813 and three days later issued his orders for the reorganisation of his army. Guided by Napoleonic instructions from Dresden, Soult established three corps of the Right, Left and Centre under generals Reille, Clausel and Drouet respectively. These titles soon became irrelevant for, in the forthcoming campaign, Drouet found himself on the French right, Clausel in the centre and Reille on the left. His logistic base was centred on Bayonne and, from the large stores and arsenal, he was able to re-supply his army with both provisions and guns, but his chronic shortage of wheeled vehicles and animals to move the few carts and caissons was to have a significant impact on his future plans.

Wellington had wasted little time in moving his logistic base from Lisbon to Santander; despite the shortage of Royal Navy vessels to protect the sea lines of communication, the new base was closer to Britain and her ports, closer to the army and pivotal for Wellington's plans for the invasion of French territory. One minor consequence of this decision was that many of the officers and much of the infrastructure established in the Portuguese capital were now superfluous to requirements. That which was not needed on the Cantabrian coast was to be sent home. This was all too much for Waller who had predicted such an eventuality some months previously. In early July, having received orders to make his reports to Dickson, and despite having previously agreed to keep silent 'in the interests of the Service', Waller could contain himself no longer and wrote to Wellington.

> I waited until I had reported to England Col. Fisher's resignation, and your Lordship's order in consequence.
>
> My Lord, you will, I am sure have expected that I should remonstrate against a proceeding, passing a censure upon me, perfectly unconscious as I am, of having merited it by any act of mine, since I had the honour to be placed under your Lordship's command.
>
> It is unnecessary for one to take up your Lordship's time in adverting to the humiliating circumstance of my being placed, if not directly, yet indirectly under a Junior; and I put it to your Lordship's candour, if when you was [sic] a Lieut. Colonel of a Regiment, you would not have felt it compromising your honour, not to notice a Captain of your Regiment, being put over you in command.
>
> After Twenty Five Years Service, I trust your Lordship will see how necessary it is for me to give some explanation, in the event of my returning to England, which I trust your Lordship will not object to, unless I am allowed to command in the Army, which under the present circumstances my Rank entitles me to.[1]

One can only imagine just how furious the commander-in-chief would have been to have received such an ill-judged letter from a relatively junior officer. The response from the pen of Wellington's military secretary captures the mood:

> In acknowledging the receipt of your letter of the 1st Inst. to the Marquis of Wellington, I am directed by his Lordship to express to you his astonishment that any Officer should have written him such a letter. He desires me to inform you, that you may go to England, or anywhere else you please; but he never can consent to your taking the command of the Artillery of the Army, serving under his orders.[2]

Dickson would, undoubtedly, have heard rumour of Waller's injudicious correspondence but he would not have allowed it to have concerned him unduly. Indeed, the consensus view across the artillery was one of support for the CRA. Cairnes considered that 'Lord W's letter to him [Waller] was what he richly deserved' and Frazer, in one of his letters home, dispelled any concerns of serving under a more junior officer.[3]

> You fancied I was unwilling to serve under Dickson, quite the reverse: I like him, always did, and have no feelings of the kind. Moreover, I should have served cheerfully under anyone. I did not come to this country to make difficulties, or objections to anything or anyone; and having long since made up my mind, and taken my line of conduct, have no intention of changing the one or swerving from the other. Both seem to me to be right, and that is enough.[4]

Not enough, however, was the recognition of services following the battle of Vitoria. A number of captains and second captains felt that their contributions had been marginalised or overlooked in the post-battle dispatches and subsequent selection for brevet rank. There was a widely held view that Wellington had, out of ignorance rather than design, bestowed disproportionate laurels upon the CRA, his staff and the horse artillery. Cairnes, robustly supported by Lieutenant General George Ramsay, Lord Dalhousie, his divisional commander, felt particularly aggrieved.

> The Commanding Officer of Artillery of an Army has less probably to say to the placing of the guns in a general action than any subaltern of a Corps. A Brigade of Artillery is attached to each Division of cavalry or Infantry: the remaining Brigades are in reserve under a Field Officer. With these the Commanding Officer *may* interfere, but with the Divisional Artillery he *cannot* without telling the General Officer Commanding that he knows nothing of the matter … I am probably one of the last men under his command to detract from his great merit, or from anything that might conduce to his advantage, but his Lordship must be either grossly ignorant of the matter in which his Artillery are directed & disposed in the field, or he must be wantonly unjust to those who *earned* the credit, as they would (assuredly) have *received the blame*, had anything gone wrong.[5]

Douglas, meanwhile, had used the influence of his father, Major General Douglas, Commandant of the Corps of RA Drivers, to request that Borthwick raise his case directly with Dickson. Douglas's support to the 'Fighting' 3rd Division at Salamanca under Pakenham and at Vitoria under Picton was well known and Borthwick's case highlighted that Ross had benefited with a second brevet promotion and that Jenkinson, not even commanding a brigade of guns, had been gazetted to the rank of major. Captain Alexander Tulloh was more concerned that he was to miss out on the not insignificant pension which the MGO had bestowed on the artillery officers in command positions at Vitoria.[6] His concerns were well placed for his name had indeed been omitted from the return submitted by artillery headquarters on the basis that he had been commanding two brigades of Portuguese artillery. However, Cairnes felt the 'substitute' to be 'a most detestable and despicable one, and such as *no Soldier* should accept'. He judged that the only honourable reward was that of rank and command.[7] In fact Cairnes was not alone in considering the award abhorrent; Wellington was furious at the scheme, which he considered divisive to the army's unity of command. It was, by a cruel twist of fate, to have a significant influence on his post-Waterloo correspondence with the MGO two years hence.[8]

For now, Wellington had far more important things on his mind. His forces were split three ways: conducting the siege at San Sebastian; executing the blockade at Pamplona and the associated approaches from the peak of La Rhune to the sea; and, finally, covering the three key passes over the western Pyrenees. The entire area was known as the 'quadrilateral' from Bayonne to St. Jean-Pied-de-Port in the north and San Sebastian to Pamplona in the south. In early to mid-July Wellington, conscious of the low morale of the French forces, had concentrated on pushing them back from the passes.

On the 7th [July] Head Quarters moved to Irurita and an arrangement was made for driving the enemy from the pass of Maya which is a very strong pass near the frontier. The 2nd and Portuguese Divisions with the 6 Prs. were to advance up the valley, whilst the 7th Division moved from San Estevān through the mountains to take the enemy in the flank ... There was some skirmishing in the pass, in possession of which they remained all night but retired in the morning following, and they have now left Spain. This force was three Divisions, but without artillery, under Gazan. Our guns opened once or twice and I believe surprised them much. It always occasioned their moving off.[9]

The only guns that moved into the inhospitable terrain of the Baztan to assist in pressing the French were the 6-pounders of Da Cunha Preto's Company and Ross's Troop. Jenkinson recalled that 'we have in truth had difficulties to encounter to get here, however we have overcome them without any serious injury and when Lord Wellington saw us nearly through them, he expressed himself well pleased – no artillery ever traversed this road before'.[10] The equipment, however, was badly shaken; Sergeant Whitehead recalled that 'the roads were like stairs [we] have to take up and let down our guns by hand. A number of wheels [were] broken in the pass of Valett [Velate].'[11] The plight of Ross's Troop was not helped by the fact that when the French had been driven back, Wellington readjusted his defensive line and moved the Light and 7th divisions to close a weak point at the pass of Vera. The movement of guns over this sort of terrain was a herculean task, for a single brigade of guns with all the accompanying vehicles and appurtenances spanned a considerable distance. Lieutenant George Robert Gleig with the 85th Regiment provides an excellent description.

> On these occasions, no part of the spectacle is more imposing than the march of the artillery. Of this species of force, six, sometimes eight pieces, form a brigade, each gun is dragged by six or eight horses; by six, if the brigade is intended to act with the infantry, by eight, if it belongs to what is called the flying artillery. In the former case, eight gunners march on foot beside each field piece, whilst three drivers ride *a la postilion*; in the latter, the gunners are all mounted and accoutred like yeomanry cavalry. Then the tumbrils and ammunition-waggons, with their train of horses and attendants, follow in the rear of the guns, and the whole procession covers perhaps as much ground as is covered by two moderately strong battalions in marching order.[12]

The arrival at Pamplona on the 16th July of O'Donnell's Spanish Army of Reserve of Andalucía released the 3rd, 4th and 6th divisions who had, up until that point, established the blockade. With the 5th Division tasked with the capture of San Sebastian, Wellington deployed the remaining divisions, along with the independent Portuguese infantry brigades, General Manuel Freire's six Spanish infantry divisions and the two cavalry divisions to cover the two approaches. The allocation of artillery was complicated by the ongoing siege at San Sebastian and the unfavourable terrain, particularly in the Pyrenees above Pamplona, which prevented (in some instances) the guns moving in direct support to their divisions. The situation at first light on the 25th July was as follows:

Acting CRA: Lt. Col. J. May RA
Brigade Major: Maj. L. Woodyear RA (Sick)

RHA Troops	Notes	Equipment
'A' Troop (Ross)	Attached to the Light Division *en route* to Lanz.	3 x 6-pounders 2 x heavy 6-pounders 1 x 5½-inch howitzer
'D' Troop (Bean)	Attached to the cavalry at Pamplona and subsequently attached to 3rd Division.	3 x 6-pounders 2 x heavy 6-pounders 1 x 5½-inch howitzer
'E' Troop (Gardiner)	Attached to the cavalry on allied left wing.	5 x 6-pounders (1 x long) 1 x 5½-inch howitzer
'I' Troop (Bull)	Ramsay in command Attached to the cavalry on allied left wing.	3 x 6-pounders 2 x heavy 6-pounders 1 x 5½-inch howitzer
'F' Troop (Webber Smith)	Attached to the Reserve and second siege of San Sebastian.	5 x 9-pounders 1 x 5½-inch howitzer
RA Companies	**Notes**	**Equipment**
Du Bourdieu's Company	Attached to 1st Division on allied left – involved at San Sebastian.	5 x 9-pounders 1 x 5½-inch howitzer
Maxwell's Company	Attached to 2nd Division but located at Pamplona and Lanz.	5 x 9-pounders 1 x 5½-inch howitzer
Douglas's Company	Attached to and with 3rd Division.	5 x 9-pounders 1 x 5½-inch howitzer
Sympher's Company KGA	Attached to 4th Division but located at Zabaldica.	5 x 9-pounders 1 x 5½-inch howitzer
Lawson's Company	Attached to 5th Division at San Sebastian.	5 x heavy 6-pounders 1 x 5½-inch howitzer
Brandreth's Company	Attached to 6th Division but located at Ostiz.	5 x heavy 6-pounders 1 x 5½-inch howitzer
Dickson's Company	Cairnes in command Attached to 7th Division.	5 x 9-pounders 1 x 5½-inch howitzer
Da Cunha Preto's Portuguese Company	Attached to and up with Gen. Hill's Corps (Da Costa's Brigade) under Lt. Col. Tulloh.	5 x light 6-pounders 1 x 5½-inch howitzer
(C. C.) Michell's Portuguese Company	Attached to and up with Gen. Hill's Corps (Ashworth's Brigade) under Lt. Col. Tulloh.	5 x 9-pounders 1 x 5½-inch howitzer

Sources: Dickson, Ross, Jenkinson, Cairnes, Beatson and Brereton.

Soult, having been informed by communiqué on the 15th July from the governor at San Sebastian that he was confident of holding out for at least another two weeks, decided to attack through the passes and relieve Pamplona before getting in behind the allies and moving on to liberate San Sebastian. He made a weak feint on the allied left with a bridging operation at Behobia but it was soon clear to Wellington that the main effort was to be made through the passes north of Pamplona. He sent word to Cole and Hill, at Roncesvalles and Maya respectively, to defend the passes to the utmost and prevent any turning movement at all costs. The only allied guns that were up with the forward troops at this stage were the two Portuguese artillery companies both at Maya; there were no guns at Roncesvalles. On the 25th July the French advance commenced with Reille (eight mountain guns) and Clausel attacking through Roncesvalles and Drouet through the pass at Maya.

> The attack was made on the 25th ulto. whilst Lord Wellington was at St. Sebastian, and was directed against the passes of Maya, Espeja and Roncesvalles, and had Lord Wellington been present, the enemy would in my humble opinion never have been able to dislodge our troops; but the ground was so ill occupied and the attack so unexpected, that the enemy had gained the summit of the mountains before the troops destined for their defence knew they were attacked. Nor was Sir Rowland [Hill] aware that his position had been assailed until his corps had been driven from it, though not without having made a defence which so appalled the enemy as to deter them from pursuit that day.[13]

During the attack and subsequent retreat at Maya, Da Cunha was forced to abandon three of his guns and one howitzer and subsequently one of Captain Charles Cornwallis Michell's 9-pounder guns was also lost along with a number of support vehicles. Tulloh explained the circumstances in a letter to Dickson.

> I was not present, but from every circumstance I can assure you that no blame is to be attached to him [Da Cunha] or his officers. The guns were taken up the mountain in pieces, placed in situations by hand where the animals could not go to them, left firing case shot to the last moment, and consequently could not be saved.
>
> On our retreat we were pushed so hard by the enemy and in one of the darkest nights possible, that Sir Rowland Hill ordered me to get rid of and destroy every encumbrance. We left (destroyed) the forage cart and 3 cars of the 9 Pr. Brigade, and the ground on the edge of a precipice of some 300 feet gave way under a 9 Pr. gun, which went down, and of course was lost. The shaft animals with it.[14]

Wellington was furious about the loss and clearly blamed Major General William Stewart, who had recently assumed command of the 2nd Division, and to a lesser extent Major General Sir William Pringle, who had just taken command of one of the brigades in that division:

> … I feel very unwilling to draw the attention of the Sec. of State, again, to the loss of the guns in the Puerto de Maya, in order to show that they were lost going to a position to which you had ordered them by the very same road, and under the very same circumstances, under which I stated they were lost retiring to Elizondo. I was

very sorry to have lost those guns, as they were the only guns that have ever been lost by troops acting under my command; but I attributed their loss then, as I do now, to unfortunate accident to which the best arrangements must be liable, and above all, to that most unfortunate accident of your being absent when the attack was made, and [General Pringle], who commanded, having been with the division only two days.[15]

The passes lost, Wellington was thus forced to reorganise his divisions to establish a defensive line north of Pamplona at Sorauren. Amidst considerable confusion and with the 4th Division falling back on the 3rd, he issued orders for the 2nd, 6th and 7th divisions, along with elements of O'Donnell's Spanish troops around Pamplona, to move with all haste to the position. Ross's, Webber Smith's and Ramsay's troops of horse artillery were also ordered to the area; none were to make it in time for the subsequent actions at Sorauren, however; the order to move had caused real problems for 'A' Troop.

We were placed in a very awkward situation by our right being turned, for we had at least fifteen leagues to traverse and but one road by which we could retire … so pressed were we therefore on our march that we had no time allowed us to repair our damage but orders to destroy all we could not get on, and our howitzer having nine pound wheels, with only one spare, we were compelled to inter it with full military honours, two wheels having been irreparably demolished in the space of one mile …[16]

The French advance was also hindered by the difficulty of moving large formations through the challenging terrain and only Clausel was up on the 27th July; Reille's divisions began to appear on the Zabaldica road late in the afternoon and Foy's Division was sent immediately to hold the heights of Huarte. Drouet's divisions had been held up at Maya but they were not making best speed to link up nor were they pressing the 2nd Division to their front with the requisite urgency to prevent Hill's men breaking clean and heading south, as directed by Wellington. The French attack was expected early on the 28th July but instead Soult frittered away the time readjusting his forces. He brought four howitzers forward and positioned them near Zabaldica, but otherwise no guns were deployed other than two light 4-pounders by Clausel near Sorauren. This delay played into Wellington's hands and by midday the 3rd, 4th and 6th divisions were in position and Hill's force along with the 7th Division were making best speed to join them. The Spanish had four batteries which they deployed along their line on the San Cristóbal feature and with Morillo's Division to the west of Huarte. Douglas's Brigade of 9-pounders was with the 3rd Division to the east of the town, while Sympher's 9-pounders were sited on a rise just off the Huarte to Zabaldica road, the length of which they could sweep from their elevated platform. Moving guns up on to the Narval and Oricain heights in support of the 4th Division was complicated and, with the loss of Da Cunha's guns still preying on minds, both Brandreth's and Cairnes's brigades were deployed with the 6th Division astride the Sorauren to Villava road.

Had Soult been sharper on the 28th (by attacking at day light instead of at one o'cl.) he might *possibly* have succeeded in throwing troops into Pamplona and provisions. But our sixth Division joined us in the forenoon and rendered it impossible.[17]

The battle that followed was largely an infantry affair with the 4th and 6th divisions successfully fighting off six French divisions. On the flanks of the Oricain heights the Gunners had played their part but the brunt of the fighting took place, not on the peripheries of the feature, but onto the frontage of the steep hill itself. By the middle of the afternoon it was clear to Soult that his plan had failed. Fighting petered out along the line and Foy was ordered to fall back. The following day Soult reconsidered his options, desperately waiting for information as to Drouet's whereabouts and anticipated time of arrival. Drouet, realising that the troops to his front were merely a small rearguard from the 2nd Division, moved south but soon received new orders

13. The Battle of Sorauren ~ Situation at 1300 Hours, 28th July 1813

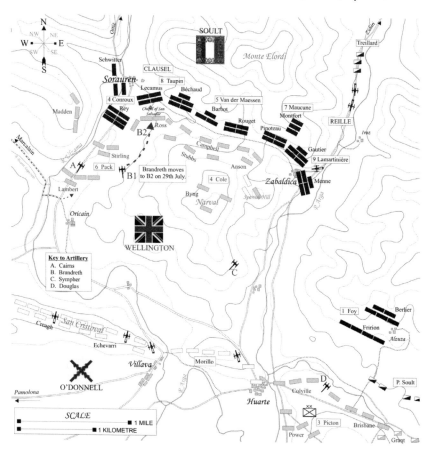

which thrust them from rearguard to vanguard as Soult had given up hope of relieving Pamplona and elected instead to get in between Wellington and Graham's forces and, by so doing, disrupt the siege at San Sebastian. Both Reille and Clausel were to withdraw up the Ostiz road which necessitated the movement of Reille's entire force across the frontage of the 4th and 6th divisions. Wellington issued orders for the 2nd to withdraw on a parallel track and for the 7th Division to close on the position at Sorauren. No additional artillery arrived on the position on the 29th but Brandreth's (heavy) 6-pounder guns were hauled up to a platform in support of Ross's Brigade by the chapel of San Salvador.

As dawn broke on the 30th July Reille's troops were clearly visible moving west. Sergeant Charles Whitman was with Brandreth's guns:

> ... about 5 o'clock began skirmishing with the enemy and by 8 o'clock the action commenced very severe – we drove the enemy from every position but with great loss, being so much among the mountains that our cavalry could do no good, and in several places our artillery could not operate, but they did great execution in parts but lost a number of men and horses by the enemy's riflemen creeping around the mountains.[18]

The 6th Division supported by Cairnes's guns began to pursue the French up the Ostiz road. Wellington had ordered Cairnes's and Brandreth's brigades of guns to move in support and Cairnes recorded that 'we are tumbling them over the mountains in a hasty manner'.[19] But the terrain prevented the guns keeping up with the infantry; Sergeant Whitman recalled that they marched 'on a very bad road being on the sides and up some high mountain hardly passable for infantry much more artillery'.[20] Brandreth was lucky not to lose another gun which had to be unlimbered to negotiate the turn in the track and nearly ran down the precipice. A few days later when Wellington's forces were in full pursuit of Soult's beaten army, William Brereton with 'D' Troop recalled that 'the Troop performed the most extraordinary march to Les Aldudes over a mountain track where no carriage of any sort had at any time been taken, and upon the 9th August from Burguete to Lanz the march, from the nature of the route, could not have been believed within the scope of probability'.[21]

There is little doubting the fact that Sorauren and the battles of the Pyrenees were largely an infantry affair but the contribution of Cairnes's and Brandreth's brigades of guns should not have gone unrecorded. Yet Wellington's lengthy post-battle dispatch makes no mention at all of the artillery. Cairnes was understandably miffed:

> I believe I told you that General Pack had said to me he had had great pleasure in pointing out to Lord W. the essential services we contributed etc. etc. But after all, I find the Artillery are no more mentioned than if there were not a gun within 100 miles of the place ... Mortifying enough to be sure, for after the action Lord Wellington himself asked me what ammunition I had left ... Lord W. knowing the fact of the ammunition and judging as he might have done that other Brigades were also a good deal engaged, should surely make some acknowledgement in general terms, or at one condemn us as useless and inefficient.[22]

One possible explanation for Wellington's oversight was the fact that the CRA was intimately entangled in duties at San Sebastian and it is unclear exactly what role John May played at Army Headquarters during this time. Dickson regretted 'not having been witness of the late brilliant actions' and added, 'but one can't be everywhere'.[23] When he did receive reports from the artillery captains it was clear that some form of mountain guns would be required to keep up with and support the infantry. A few 3-pounders were ordered up from Lisbon and three mountain guns, captured from the French, were provided mules and placed under the command of young Lieutenant William Robe, the son of Colonel William Robe. This young officer was stationed in Gibraltar in 1807 and had volunteered for service in Portugal, joining his father at Vimeiro during the final stages of the battle. He was part of Moore's army, surviving the retreat to return in 1810 as a subaltern in 'D' Troop.

Soult's withdrawal back across the Pyrenees provided the opportunity for Wellington to readjust his forces and to recommence operations at San Sebastian. It also provided Soult a similar breathing space and on 31st August, the same day that the second assault was delivered by the besiegers against San Sebastian, the French Army attacked the allies along the line of the River Bidassoa in the hope of lifting the siege for a second time. The attack had concentrated on the 4th Spanish Army on the heights of San Marcial, who held the allied centre, flanked by the 1st Division on the left, the 7th Division to the right and the Light Division in reserve. It would appear that no British artillery was up with these divisions: Du Bourdieu's Company, the close support artillery for the 1st Division, was at San Sebastian; Cairnes, the close support for the 7th Division, records that he rode over to San Sebastian that morning on one of Lord Dalhousie's nags. However, he notes that 'Ross's, Smith's and Ramsay's Troops were ordered up but did not, I fancy get into action'.[24] Ross's perfunctory entry rather plays down the battle: 'The horse artillery ordered in the night of the 30th to march immediately to the neighbourhood of Yrun. The enemy make an attack along the line of the Bidassoa, but are beat.'[25] But his second captain provides a more illuminating account which highlights the not inconsiderable achievements of the Spanish.

> At the dawn of the day the enemy were discovered crossing the Bidassoa river, which they can always do without encountering any serious opposition, and they soon assembled a sufficient force to make a most vigorous attack upon the Spaniards, which, they repulsed with a steadfastness and bravery, that would have done honour to any troops; but not without the loss of two thousand men, which proves that neither the attack or defence were of a trivial nature.[26]

By the 8th September General Rey hoisted a white flag from the ramparts of the castle at San Sebastian, bringing to an end one of the most difficult sieges of the war. Soult had been surprised that Wellington had not followed up on his successes but, for now, there were other factors to be considered. The blockade at Pamplona was entering its final phase, with the garrison's resources fast dwindling, but it was the allied situation in central Europe which was of greater significance. News had arrived, in late August, of Napoleon's victory at Dresden and the fate of the 6th Coalition hung in the balance. It was another couple of weeks before the news of the allied victories at Kulm and Katzbach was received and, with it, Wellington judged the time was now right to commence the invasion of France. While Wellington and his staff began preparations, orders were given to Dickson to re-equip San Sebastian with suitable garrison artillery, to re-load the balance of the siege train onto the naval transports and to send home all the unserviceable ordnance. In view of the lack of ammunition, Dickson also ordered that 'all English 10 inch, 8 inch, or 24 Pr. shells, either common or spherical, that may be found will be collected near or upon the mole, in order to be embarked and sent to the Battering train ships at Pasajes'.[27]

Preparations for the artillery brigades with the field army were no less frenzied and the shortage of horses was, yet again, proving to be the major concern.

> I see no prospect of getting our horses and mules, 360 in number, from Lisbon, for want of transport. Lord Wellington told me he had written to Lord Bathurst on the subject. It is very provoking.[28]

Provoking indeed, but it was not to prove a show stopper and when Wellington headed north into France on the 7th October the Gunners were ready.

Notes

1. PRO WO 55/1196 pp.40–41, Waller to Wellington from Lisbon, dated 1st July 1813.
2. Ibid., p.42, Fitzroy Somerset to Waller from Lesaca [Lesaka], dated 17th July 1813.
3. Cairnes to Cuppage from Zarranz, dated 22nd September 1813.
4. Frazer (ed. Sabine), letter dated 2nd August 1813.
5. Cairnes to Cuppage from Berrio Plano, dated 25th July 1813.
6. Field officers were to receive 10 shillings per diem and captains 5 shillings.
7. Cairnes to Cuppage from Etulain, dated 19th August 1813.
8. Wellington to Mulgrave from Paris, dated 21st December 1815. Duncan, vol. II, pp.447–48 and papers MD 193.
9. Dickson, vol. V, p.957. Letter from Dickson to MacLeod from Zubieta, dated 10th July 1813.
10. Jenkinson, letter dated 18th July 1813.
11. Whitehead, entry dated 5th July 1813.
12. Gleig, GTS, Roberton, I. (ed.) version p.138.
13. Jenkinson, letter dated 3rd August 1813.
14. Dickson, vol. V, pp.1021–22. Letter from Tulloh to Dickson, dated 16th August 1813.
15. WD, vol. VI, p.757. Wellington to Stewart from Lesaca [Lesaka], dated 13th September 1813. In fact Wellington's claim that these were the only guns lost by troops acting under his command is not strictly correct. Not including the guns lost then recaptured at Albuera and Majadahonda, a howitzer had been lost (and not recovered) at Albuera and Murray had abandoned 18 guns at Tarragona; however, if it is accepted that these troops were not under Wellington's 'direct' command, there is still the matter

of three siege guns and eight captured French pieces left at Burgos and the other 9-pounder that Tulloh lost when withdrawing from the passes.

16. Jenkinson, letter dated 3rd August 1813. This explains Oman's comment that Ross had lost a gun in similar fashion to Tulloh's 9-pounder – Oman, vol. VI. p.682. Ross does not mention it at all and neither does Sgt. Whitehead in the 'A' Troop records. But Dickson records that 'Ross wants a howitzer carriage, his own having been broke to pieces' – Dickson, vol. V, p.980. This would *suggest* that a replacement carriage was procured and that the troop returned to unearth the gun following the conclusion of the battle of the Pyrenees.

17. Cairnes to Cuppage from Villalba, dated 3rd August 1813.

18. Whitman, letter dated 1st August 1813.

19. Cairnes to Cuppage from Villalba, dated 3rd August 1813.

20. Whitman, letter dated 9th August 1813.

21. Brereton Papers, p.v.

22. Cairnes to Cuppage from Zarranz, dated 3rd September 1813.

23. Dickson, vol. V, pp.977–79. Letter from Dickson to MacLeod dated 12th August 1813.

24. Cairnes to Cuppage from Zarranz, dated 3rd September 1813.

25. Ross, p.45. Entry dated 31st August 1813.

26. Jenkinson, letter dated 1st September 1813.

27. Dickson, vol. V, pp.1039–41. Letter from Dickson to Dyer, dated 16th September 1813.

28. Dickson, vol. V, pp.1063–4. Dickson to MacLeod, dated 3rd October 1813.

CHAPTER 21

Frazer's Swank and Lane's Rockets

Wellington had a lot on his mind in the run-up to the invasion. Events on the east coast were less than satisfactory with Lord Bentinck returning to Sicily, amidst rumours of political manoeuvring instigated by the Austrian monarchy, forcing a change of command at a time when a suitable replacement from Wellington's main army was neither readily available nor immediately apparent. The 25,000 strong Spanish force under his command was in a dreadful state of readiness; half starved and poorly equipped, the soldiers were bound to plunder for reasons of personal survival and revenge, behaviour Wellington was determined to avoid at all costs. The garrison at Pamplona were reduced to eating their own horses but still holding out, forcing the need for a large investing force to remain in place. Finally, his concerns over the lack of Royal Naval support in the Bay of Biscay and protection to his new logistic base at Santander had not been resolved as the Admiralty committed yet more ships for the blockade of the east coast of America. Nevertheless, the supply situation had in the main caught up with this adjustment and, leaving aside the perpetual shortage of horses, Wellington's army was ready to tackle the final frontier.

Soult had not been idle in the interim and had ordered the construction of an intricate series of defences along a line extending 22 miles from the Col de Maya westwards to the sea. He divided the line into three sectors. Convinced that the eastern and central sectors were the most likely to be attacked, he deployed the majority of his force to cover these areas. This was a grave error, for Wellington elected to execute a deception upon the eastern sector, occupy the central area and then cross the border by the coast to the west, wrong-footing Soult in the process and leaving the inadequate French reserve badly placed to react. The central sector was dominated by the Grand Rhune, 'a monstrous hump rising to 2,800 feet' which denied any form of artillery support and was thus left to the determined bravery of the Light Division's infantry. The attack across the estuary of the River

Bidassoa was allocated to the 1st and 5th divisions and, to support these assignments, Dickson task organised his artillery as follows:

RHA Troops/RA Companies	Notes	Equipment
Supporting 5th Division: Lt. Col. Hartman KGA		
Lawson's Company	Mosse in command.	5 x heavy 6-pounders 1 x 5½-inch howitzer
Arriaga's Portuguese Company		5 x 9-pounders 1 x 5½-inch howitzer
Supporting 1st Division: Maj. Dyer RA		
'A' Troop (Ross)	In reserve role.	3 x 6-pounders 2 x heavy 6-pounders 1 x 5½-inch howitzer
'F' Troop (Webber Smith)		5 x 9-pounders 1 x 5½-inch howitzer
Carmichael's Company	Dansey in command.	5 x 9-pounders 1 x 5½-inch howitzer
Morrison's Company	Covered the crossing.	6 x 18-pounders
Supporting the Spanish 4th Army: Lt. Col. Frazer RA		
'I' Troop (Bull)	Ramsay in command	3 x 6-pounders 2 x heavy 6-pounders 1 x 5½-inch howitzer
J. Michell's Company	Formerly Stone's Company, not to be confused with C. C. Michell commanding a Portuguese company.	5 x 9-pounders 1 x 5½-inch howitzer

Source: Dickson.

All seemed quiet in the enemy's position. On reaching Irun, Ramsay's troop inclined to the right, leaving the high road. I here learned that Michell's battery was to join me when it came up, which it soon did: and we found 400 infantry waiting to pull the guns over the mountain to the places previously intended. Bull's horses never want assistance; they were soon posted on a height with some Spanish horse artillery. The affair began at 8; a column of our infantry having crossed previously at Fuenterabia, opposite to which place they forded the Bidassoa. Another column crossed by fording just below the burnt bridge at Irun, followed closely by Webber Smith's troop ... Finding the affair was losing all appearance of becoming serious on our right, I quitted Ramsay's and Michell's batteries, sending them orders to cross the burnt bridge at Irun, and crossed myself the river at this point ... I had also previously ordered Ross to leave the mountains and to cross [but] Dickson thought my having moved them hazardous, and I sent Bell off again to stop them where he might find them. Indeed, Ramsay having found out a new ford, had already crossed the Bidassoa, and had gained the road communicating with the main one to Bayonne. At this time the enemy had retired from the river at all points.[1]

Although Dickson had tasked Frazer as his field officer attached to the Spanish 4th Army, he was clearly operating more in the role of Dickson's chief of staff on the ground. Dickson himself was with Wellington's staff and he recorded that the operation was conducted with surprising simplicity.

> The passage of the river was effected and the French position carried with great ease. The Spaniards had the most difficult part but they took it in a very handsome stile [style], and really behaved admirably ... 8 guns of position were taken by us and one or two by the Spaniards. The French behaved ill. I was present with Lord Wellington at this operation which was a very easy one. We expended very little ammunition. The 18 Prs. were got into their position uncommonly well, and had a very good effect.[2]

Included in the eight captured guns were three French 3-pounders which were allocated to young Robe and a demi-brigade of mountain guns was established. At much the same time another six British 3-pounders arrived from Lisbon which were to be manned by Portuguese artillerymen but with British drivers and mules. With neither the Portuguese having gunners to spare nor the British having any mules or drivers the introduction of these nine mountain guns was anything but a straightforward affair. A few weeks after these guns had been employed and seen some service, Dickson wrote (on request) to MacLeod to proffer his opinion on the subject.

> As yet we have not tried them much, but for general purposes I think it may be said, they are more useful from the confidence they give men, than from their own effect, which it is evident must be very uncertain except when employed at very short ranges; soldiers like the noise of Artillery; it gives them confidence when employed in their support, with however little effect, and in like manner it disquiets them when brought against them, and although perhaps the shot only pass over their heads, still they are not able well to judge how high, and feel that if they remain in the same position the practice may become more annoying. Were Armies from a peculiarity of Mountain Country, obliged to wage war for a length of time without being able to employ any other ordnance than the small pieces termed Mountain Guns, I have no doubt that the soldiers would very soon learn the inefficacy and uncertainty of these pieces when employed at a distance, and would grow indifferent about them, but when a country is diversified, and in one action a Corps is fired upon by 9 Prs., in the next by 6 Prs., and in another by 3 Prs., or vice versa, the Soldiers know that it is Artillery that is employed against them, the effect of which they have frequently felt, and will not in the hurry of their occupation make any observation as to its quality, and they will, in the different instances, attribute the success or failure to Ordnance being well or ill directed, more than the real cause. It is also to be observed that the report of small guns in a Mountainous Country appears louder, which serves to add to the illusion. In attack therefore, I think Columns should always in mountain war be supported by Mountain

Guns if no other can be employed. The troops advancing are entertained by their noise, and the force attacked are incommoded by it, but when the attack becomes close the Ordnance of the defenders is then of real efficacy when probably the Guns of the assailants have not been able to keep pace with their Columns. I therefore think that either party would labour under a disadvantage were they without mountain guns.[3]

Henegan confirmed the effect these guns had on the enemy and the illusion they created when operating in the mountains. Robe's guns 'were not, perhaps, capable of doing much mischief, but the moral effect they produced of alarm as their shot came tumbling down from the cloud-topped hills, was fraught with consequences still more important'.[4] The loss of guns during the recent battle for the Pyrenees had highlighted the problems of moving heavier ordnance through the mountains and as Wellington manoeuvred his forces to follow up on their success in crossing the Bidassoa, the artillery commanders posted to support attacks on the right of the line were pressed to the limits in moving their brigades in support of the infantry. Frazer had earlier recorded that 'we are cautious in our movements – this mountain warfare requires us to be so'.[5] Tulloh, who had been allocated with a mixture of 9- and 6-pounders to support General Hill's Corps on the allied right, recorded that 'the road we came over was so difficult and the terrain so terrific a nature, that I am astonished to find guns and cars here, without some serious accident'.[6] Moving guns into position was, of course, only half the problem. Extracting them was always going to be an even greater challenge particularly when undertaken under time pressure, and when the weather conspired against the plan the result was inevitable. Maxwell, whose brigade of 9-pounders was covering the pass at Roncesvalles, suffered just such an ignominy early in November.

In consequence of a recent great fall and drifting of snow in this position having rendered the road between this place and the advanced redoubt on the right of our position entirely impracticable for artillery, and even dangerous and of doubtful communication for infantry, the advanced piquets, by order of Lieut-General Rowland Hill, have been withdrawn and two 9- pounders and one 5½in. heavy howitzer of my brigade, with their limbers and wagons have been, for the present, abandoned, but not destroyed, the guns being spiked with wood and concealed beneath the earth, and the carriages taken to pieces and concealed beneath the snow, so disposed as to be got at and put together, in the most convenient manner, when circumstances will admit our withdrawing them.[7]

These guns were soon recovered with the assistance of the infantry; an (anonymous) soldier of the 71st Highlanders verified that 'General Stewart ordered up a fatigue party to raise them again. We were covered by the picquets, and, with great difficulty, at length got them raised and brought down to the valley. Each man on fatigue got an extra allowance of grog, the only welcome recompense.'[8]

Despite expectations from both attacker and defender, Wellington's follow-up to the remarkable entry into France was, once again, to await encouraging news from central Europe. In the meantime he readjusted his forces for the next phase. During this lull, Pamplona finally succumbed and operations to mop up the isolated French garrisons along the Cantabrian coast were conducted. The small port at Santoña provided safe haven for the increasing number of French privateers running the ever decreasing gauntlet of Royal Navy frigates and gunboats patrolling the area. Lord Aylmer, commanding a brigade which had arrived in August, was sent to capture the structure in mid-October and Dickson selected Captain William Cator and lieutenants George Mainwaring and Henry Palliser with a detachment of four NCOs and 40 gunners to support the operation. In order to attack and penetrate Soult's second line of defence along the River Nivelle, Wellington reorganised his three corps-sized columns under Hope, Beresford and Hill. Accordingly, Dickson issued orders for the artillery task organisation to support those columns.

RHA Troops/RA Companies	Notes	Equipment
Supporting Hope's Corps – Left Flank: Lt. Col. Hartmann KGA and Maj. Dyer RA		
'F' Troop (Webber Smith)		5 x 9-pounders 1 x 5½-inch howitzer
'I' Troop (Bull)	Ramsay in command.	3 x 6-pounders 2 x heavy 6-pounders 1 x 5½-inch howitzer
Carmichael's Company	Dansey in command. Carmichael arrived late October 1813; however, soon after he assumed command of the RA Drivers.	5 x 9-pounders 1 x 5½-inch howitzer
Lawson's Company	Mosse in command.	5 x heavy 6-pounders 1 x 5½-inch howitzer
Brandreth's Company	Greene in command. Brandreth was under arrest for the misconduct of some of his drivers in requisitioning food.	5 x 9-pounders 1 x 5½-inch howitzer
J. Michell's Company		5 x 9-pounders 1 x 5½-inch howitzer
Dickson's Company	Cairnes in command.	5 x 9-pounders 1 x 5½-inch howitzer
Arriaga's Portuguese Company		5 x 9-pounders 1 x 5½-inch howitzer
Morrison's Company		6 x 18-pounders
Supporting Beresford's Corps – Centre: Lt. Col. Frazer RHA and Maj. Buckner RA		
'A' Troop (Ross)	Supporting 4th Division in the attack against Sare.	3 x 6-pounders 2 x heavy 6-pounders 1 x 5½-inch howitzer
Sympher's Company KGA	Supporting 4th and 7th divisions in the attack against Sare.	5 x 9-pounders 1 x 5½-inch howitzer
Douglas's Company	Supporting 4th and 7th divisions in the attack against Sare.	5 x 9-pounders 1 x 5½-inch howitzer

Robe's mountain guns	Supporting 6th Division.	3 x 3-pounders
Half Brigade Portuguese mountain guns	Supporting the Light Division.	3 x 3-pounders
Half brigade Portuguese mountain guns	Supporting Giron's Spanish Army.	3 x 3-pounders
Supporting Hill's Corps – Right Flank: Maj. Carncross RA		
Tulloh's Portuguese Division – Da Cunha Preto's and C. C. Michell's Portuguese companies	Capt. Amado replaced Michell in November 1813 but was soon ill and Michell returned in January 1814 to resume command.	5 x 9-pounders 2 x 6-pounders 1 x 5½-inch howitzer

Sources: Dickson and Teixeira Botelho.

The bulk of the fighting, on this occasion, occurred in the central sector where Ross's Troop was in direct support of the 4th Division.

> … my troop and two 9-Pr. brigades had been moved into the Pass of Vera, preparatory to the attack (which but for the weather was to have taken place sooner than it did), where we remained till the morning of the 10th, when we moved with the 4th Division against the village of Sarre and the strong redoubts the enemy had constructed on all the heights round it. These were soon carried, whilst the Light Division moved down from La Rhune and stormed the lesser mountain of that name, which the enemy had entrenched and occupied in force … before mid-day we had carried their last position, which I can only designate by the heights of Ascani [Ascain], which were very strong, and upon which the enemy had a second line of redoubts, all of which they were compelled to abandon, and in one our advance was so rapid that the garrison, consisting of 500 men, were shut in and obliged to lay down their arms.[9]

Captain John (Boteler) Parker recalled that Ross's 6-pounders were moved to within 700 yards of the redoubt and the 9-pounders of Sympher and Douglas to 1,200 yards and that 'the fire from these 18 pieces of artillery was dreadful and that the garrison were forced to yield and abandon it, but not until they had caused the brigade Ross considerable loss'.[10] Dickson, in his post-battle report to MacLeod, emphasises the importance of this close artillery support. 'However their fire was so active and well directed, and Frazer pushed the guns up so close that the enemy could not stand it, but made off leaving several men dead in the fort, just as the column of the 4th Division approached it.' Ross's guns were the only ones in the sector able to continue in support of the infantry in the subsequent attacks on the redoubts north of La Rhune, a feat which solicited admiration many years after the event, when during a Board of the Ordnance Estimates meeting, Sir Howard Douglas commented that the 'operation was worth all the money the Horse Artillery ever cost the country'.[11] Wellington, having given the Gunners no mention in his Bidassoa dispatch, was full of praise for their achievement following the battle of Nivelle:

> The artillery, which was in the field, was of great use to us; and I cannot sufficiently acknowledge the intelligence and activity with which it was brought to the point

of attack under the directions of Colonel Dickson, over the bad roads through the mountains in this season of the year.[12]

The attack on the allied left was a feint and that on the right too fluid and the terrain too demanding to solicit intricate artillery support from Tulloh's guns but the success in the centre was, by Wellington's design, enough to divide the French force and capture the vital bridge at Amotz forcing Soult into another withdrawal to the line of the River Nive. The captured redoubts furnished 51 guns, including another three French 3-pounders, which Dickson had planned to add to Robe's demi-brigade, but lack of men, mules and other equipment prevented this. The allied divisions moved up in parallel to Soult's withdrawal and established themselves awaiting new orders. As the weather deteriorated, Wellington's intentions of maintaining the advance gave way to the possibility of establishing temporary winter quarters and, in anticipation, he sent his Spanish divisions back south across the border. Wellington, ever mindful of the significance of events playing out in central Europe, was waiting for news on the outcome and strategic implications of the Battle of Nations at Leipzig. As it transpired, it was an attack in early December by Soult on Wellington's rather depleted holding force which sparked the next series of battles across the River Nive.

Once again the bulk of the fighting fell to Beresford's Corps in the centre but involved Hill's Corps on the right flank, with Hope's column pushing up to provide a contiguous line and flank protection to Beresford's left flank. Dickson moved 'A' Troop to assist Tulloh's guns in support of Hill's column, while Ramsay's Troop, less two guns under Captain Cator, which were replaced by two heavier 6-pounders from Lawson's Brigade, provided direct support to the Light Division in the centre. This was to be Hew Ross's last Peninsular battle and it was one where he, and his remarkable troop, conducted themselves with well renowned skill and bravery.

> On the 8th inst. I was ordered to place myself under the orders of Sir Rowland Hill, and to remain with his corps, for which purpose I marched to La Resson, where the following morning I covered General Pringle's and General Buchan's brigades in forcing the fords opposite that place. The rest of Sir Rowland Hill's corps passed the Nive at Combo [Cambo-les-Bains], and Marshal Beresford brought the 5th Division across at Ustaritz, and at every place the fords were carried with very trifling loss, and the enemy driven along the heights over which runs the great road from St. Jean Pied de Port to Bayonne. The armies halted in front of each other in position about a league from Bayonne at dark, to which time firing continued; and at night the enemy withdrew into his entrenched camp on this side, and passing a great deal of his army through Bayonne, attacked our left on the other side of the Nive the following morning …[13]

Soult's attempt to swing west across the Nive and attack the allied left and central columns resulted in a similar conclusion.

> Marshal Soult made an attack on the 10th upon our left near Biarritz, and the Light Division near Arcangues, but he was foiled in all his endeavours, and in this

operation Captain Ramsay's troop assisted by two guns of Capt. Mosse's brigade were very conspicuous. The enemy made a similar attempt on the 11th in which they were equally repulsed. Captain Ramsay's troop and the whole of Captain Mosse's brigade again rendering most valuable assistance in the defence of this position.

Marshal Soult thus disappointed in his hopes of making an impression on our left, drew the greatest part of his force back to Bayonne in the night of the 12th, and early in the morning of the 13th made a desperate attack with great force on Sir Rowland Hill's Corps in position on the right of the Nive; all his attempts were most vigorously repulsed however, by that Corps only, and the enemy were finally driven to their entrenched camp after having sustained severe loss.[14]

Ross, who was on the allied right with Hill, recorded that:

The principal attack was directed against the village of St. Pierre … four times they advanced their columns close up, though under a most destructive fire of artillery, and as often as they were driven back with great slaughter. The brunt of the action fell on General Barnes' Brigade at the village, which lost 47 men, and the General wounded. At this point [Lieutenant] Day's two guns were posted, and lost five men wounded, besides trumpeter Burnett killed. Jenkinson's Division of guns were to the left of the village, and suffered no loss except his own horse wounded in two places. Belson was absent with his division at Assuna, with Col. Vivian's Brigade. My own horse killed. The men wounded were gunners Morgan, Slater, Greaves, Yeates and Francis Clayton.[15]

Wellington once again recognised the contribution made by the artillery, in particular Ross and Tulloh, the latter officer being wounded in the leg. Also receiving a mention in his dispatch was Ramsay who was twice struck by musket balls, the first on the chin and the second on his chest where the projectile flattened a button on his waistcoat. The actions on the 9th–13th December finally convinced Soult of the futility of conducting any further offensive operations and in the wake of these engagements he arrayed his demoralised army along the line of the lower Adour and placed a large force within the structure at Bayonne under General Reille and General Pierre Thouvenot. Both armies once again faced each other and began to settle into a routine and, as the weather worsened, adopt winter quarters.

News of the scale of devastation to the *Grande Armée* following Leipzig was, by now, well known but less clear were the intentions of Napoleon in light of the defeat. He had returned to Paris in November and was knee-deep in trying to patch up relations with Spain by restoring the imprisoned Spanish Ferdinand VII to the throne in Madrid in the hope that this would resolve the crisis on his southern border. News from Leipzig hailed the performance of a British rocket troop from the Royal Horse Artillery which had supported General Levin August Theopil, Count Bennigson's troops in the capture of the villages of Zweiaundorf and Molkau. Captain Richard Bogue, the troop commander, had fallen early in the day but he was to elicit the thanks of allied sovereigns for his performance and contribution at the battle. It was recorded that the King of Sweden rode up to Bogue at a critical juncture and implored him to advance with his rocket brigade as nothing else would save the day. At the conclusion of the battle, Tsar Alexander rode up to Lieutenant Thomas Fox Stangways, the senior surviving officer of the troop, and, removing the Order of Saint Anne from his own breast, pinned it to that young officer in recognition of the troop's services. Lord Londonderry recorded that the effect of the rockets was 'truly astonishing; and produced an impression upon the enemy of something supernatural'[16] while one Russian general stated that 'they look[ed] as if they were made in hell, and surely the devil's own artillery'.[17]

Such sentiments evoked great pride and expectation in this new weapon system and prompted Frazer to note that 'on the 13th [December] when Hill's corps had squeezed his crowded masses into the angle formed by the Nive and the Adour, I would have staked my life in doing great things with a good Rocket corps, which would have scattered dismay into the situation not likely to occur again in many years'.[18] Frazer's wish was to be his command but, as things turned out, the results were not quite as supernatural as he would have hoped. Dickson had noted the intention of the Board of Ordnance to send Captain Henry Lane (back) out to the Peninsula with a small rocket brigade but was unsure if 'Lord Wellington will assent to its coming' for he believed that 'his Lordship thinks very cheaply of rockets, deriving his knowledge of them probably from the use that is made of them from India'.[19]

Wellington did consent and on the day before Christmas Frazer had recorded that:

> Captain Lane, of the Artillery, has arrived at Pasages, with a rocket detachment of fifty men, but no horses. Lord Wellington has permitted a division of rockets to be tried. The division means two carriages of rockets, of which each carriage conveys about fifty rockets, and there will be a couple of carriages in reserve.[20]

Equipping this rocket brigade with horses was an added burden to Dickson and his staff. He calculated that with two carriages, two spare and mounts for the officers and NCO he would need 44 animals. Dickson, ably assisted by his growing staff, set about trying to equip, test and integrate this new troop into the organisation but the best of well-laid plans were thwarted when Wellington ordered artillery headquarters to provide horses to move the two pontoons required to bridge the River Adour. The staff calculated that 576 horses (288 for each bridge) would be required and Dickson was forced, for the second time, to park the guns of Cairnes's Company and use both his men and horses to comply with the commander-in-chief's instructions. Fortunately for Cairnes, his selection for a horse artillery appointment had dovetailed with Ramsay's posting order to command 'H' Troop RHA, and he was able to slip across to assume command of 'I' Troop as Ramsay vacated the post.[21] With that problem resolved Dickson now had to turn his attention to sustaining the Portuguese artillery as their own commissariat system was failing them. Dickson had written to Tulloh expressing his concern: in his opinion he did not 'think Lord Wellington would consent to send the Brigades to the rear, when so much British artillery is in front, and it certainly appears quite ridiculous that the Portuguese cannot feed two or three Brigades in even half a manner'.[22]

With Ross departed for England on a two-month leave pass, Jenkinson had assumed command of 'A' Troop; the large number of changes and presence of artillery field officers within the corps was causing great confusion and complicating the artillery chain of command. Jenkinson, in some frustration, wrote to Brigade Major Robert Ord at the end of February.

> I am now reporting to Lt. Col. May, to Maj Carncross, to Maj Dyer and to you, and I must beg you to ask Colonel Dickson whether it is intended I am to continue a system which has kept me this morning two hours at my desk, instead of attending to the necessary duties of the troop?[23]

It is easy to sympathise with Jenkinson's plight but the reality was that Dickson's command was now very large and spread across Iberia. Furthermore, plans for the renewed allied offensive necessitated splitting the force: 34,000 men under Hope to invest Bayonne and the balance of 45,000 men as the main army with Wellington. Dickson set about dividing the artillery and by late January 1814 until the end of the war in April it remained virtually unchanged. That organisation, excluding the artillery on the east coast under Williamson, was as follows:

CRA: Col. A. Dickson RA
Assistant Adjutant General RA: Lt. Col. J. May RA
Brigade Major RA: Lt. R. H. Ord RA
Adjutants: Lt. J. Pascoe RA and Lt. W. Bell RA
Command of the Horse Artillery: Lt. Col. A. S. Frazer RHA

RA Companies/ RHA Troops	Notes	Equipment
Supporting General Hope's Corps as the Bayonne Investing Force: Lt. Col. Hartmann KGA		
'F' Troop (Webber Smith)		5 x 9-pounders 1 x 5½-inch howitzer
'I' Troop (Bull)	Ramsay in command. Cairnes in command from mid-February 1814.	3 x 6-pounders 2 x heavy 6-pounders 1 x 5½-inch howitzer
Lawson's Company	Mosse in command. Attached to 5th Division.	5 x heavy 6-pounders 1 x 5½-inch howitzer
Carmichael's Company	Dansey in command. Attached to 1st Division.	5 x 9-pounders 1 x 5½-inch howitzer
Arentschildt's Portuguese Division	Composite grouping of three companies – joined main army in mid-March 1814.	9 x 9-pounders 1 x 5½-inch howitzer
Mountain Demi-Brigade	Commanded by Lt. Robe.	3 x 3-pounders
Morrison's Company	Reserve.	6 x 18-pounders
Rocket Brigade	Commanded by Lane. The brigade moved to the main army in mid-March 1814.	231 x 12-pounder rockets 64 x 32-pounder rockets 101 x 32-pounder carcasses
Hutchesson's Company	Reserve ammunition.	

Supporting the Main Army: Maj. Carncross RA and Maj. Dyer RA

'A' Troop (Ross)	Jenkinson in command from 4th January 1814.	3 x 6-pounders 2 x heavy 6-pounders 1 x 5½-inch howitzer
'D' Troop (Bean)		3 x 6-pounders 2 x heavy 6-pounders 1 x 5½-inch howitzer
'E' Troop (Gardiner)	Attached to the Hussar Brigade.	3 x 6-pounders 2 x heavy 6-pounders 1 x 5½-inch howitzer
Maxwell's Company		5 x 9-pounders 1 x 5½-inch howitzer
Brandreth's Company		5 x heavy 6-pounders 1 x 5½-inch howitzer
Douglas's Company	Turner in command from 8th February 1814.	5 x 9-pounders 1 x 5½-inch howitzer
Michell's Company		5 x 9-pounders 1 x 5½-inch howitzer
Sympher's Company KGA	Daniel in command from February 1814, Sympher KIA at Orthez.	5 x 9-pounders 1 x 5½-inch howitzer

Unattached in Iberia – Less for Artillery on East Coast of Spain (see Chapter 18)

Owen's Company	Located at Arcangues, near Bayonne.	Reserve ammunition
May's Company	Elgee in command Located at Calzada near San Sebastian.	Reserve ammunition
Trelawney's Company (formerly Glubb's)	Located at Astigarraga, near San Sebastian.	Reserve ammunition
Bredin's Company	Lisbon.	Garrison duties
Holcombe's Company	Lisbon.	Garrison duties
Gesenius's Company KGA	Lisbon.	Garrison duties
Arentschildt's Company KGA	Lisbon.	Garrison duties

Source: Compilation from Dickson.

Lane had to return home (for legal reasons) from the Peninsula in April 1812. Thompson's Company, in which he had served for the preceding three years, was at this stage part of the artillery group on the east coast; his notification in December 1812 that he was to become a second captain in one of the new rocket brigades of horse artillery was extremely welcome news. However, that contentment would have been tempered with the notification that his rocket detachment was to join Wellington's army in the Peninsula knowing as he did the commander's views on rockets. In addition, the rocket troop being trained for operations in central Europe was to be *primus inter pares* of the pair, receiving the better equipment, men and training. Lane, determined to do well, had his first opportunity to impress Wellington at a test firing at Urrugne on 19th January. Dickson recorded that 'the ground rockets ranged to a very short distance, were very irregular, and altogether answered very badly ... the rockets at higher angles did very tolerably, and went in much more correct direction than I expected'.[24] The weather and unsuitable ground had conspired against the success of the experiment and Lane could not hide his disappointment. While Dickson pondered on how to use the rockets in the high angle and improve the performance in the low angle, they both could take some comfort from the fact that Wellington did not discount their future use completely.

Dickson placed the project under Frazer's watchful eye. Evidently the trial had altered Frazer's view of rockets and he clearly considered their entertainment value outweighed that of their destructive quality.

Like true boys, we could not resist the temptation of burning the pieces, after which, and taking away the shell from the smaller rockets, we set it off without a stick, expecting it would have no range at all; but after running irregularly along the ground, it suddenly mounted into the air, whisked over the end of the village, and fell three or four fields off. We were pleased when we found no mischief had been done. I much doubt these rockets ever being tried in this country, there is prejudice generally against them; but we shall have another trial for our own satisfaction.[25]

The next trial took place at Fuenterrabia on 10th February and Frazer recorded that a good many rockets were fired and that some answered well enough. Certainly, it appears that their performance was satisfactory enough for him to add that 'we shall find them useful on the Adour'.[26] They did not have to wait long to find out, for Wellington's offensive commenced in mid-February with an operation to push back Soult's left wing and force them to abandon the line of the Adour. Once the river line had been vacated he would then bridge the river enabling the Bayonne investing force to cross, contain the city, cut off the three French divisions within and, in so doing, effectively divide Soult's forces. The operation, once completed, would enable Wellington to control the River Adour and with it Soult's vital logistic supply route for his army. However, a bridging operation of this scale at the mouth of a river as wide as the Adour, susceptible to both tide and weather and covered by enemy fire from the north bank, French gunboats and the French naval corvette *Sappho*, was an extreme risk. Storms in the Bay of Biscay delayed the commencement of the bridging operation, but on the afternoon of the 22nd February the wind dropped and the order was given to commence. Morrison's 18-pounders and Lane's rockets were to support the operation. The battery position for the heavy guns had been prepared on the home bank but the movement of the guns and pontoons along the sand paths to the water's edge was fraught with all sorts of difficulties. The 1st Division was at the start point by dawn on the 23rd and the guns were in place but there was no sign of the Royal Navy *chasse-marées* required to anchor groups of the bridging pontoons. Hope decided he could not wait and ordered the pontoons to deploy.

The operation was covered by the 18 pr. brigade under Morrison; and by a detachment of the Guards and rockets which passed over the river in boats – as soon, however, as the passage was discovered, two thousand men came out of Bayonne, and would probably have overpowered our covering force, had not the first discharge of rockets (some of which went into the enemy's column) so paralysed them as to make them absolutely throw away their arms and disperse, when the bridge was established in tranquillity, and the whole of Sir John Hope's corps passed over the river, and the investment of Bayonne was completed.[27]

At the start of the day Frazer had been less than enthusiastic about the Rocket Brigade, considering it to be 'composed of men hastily scrapped together, utterly ignorant of their arm they were to use, the rockets equipped in five varieties of manner and liable to as many mistakes'.[28] By the end of the day, even if not utterly convinced, he was to have a different opinion:

> By 5 p.m. about 500 men had been passed … the enemy pushed down his 27th and 87th Regiments from the citadel; they came on with apparent spirit, but after having a few rockets forced at them (the rocketeers under Captain Lane having been the last troops passed over) hastily retired, not having more than twenty men killed and wounded, of whom several fell by the rockets; one rocket having killed one man and wounded four others seemed the signal for retiring, which they did precipitately.[29]

Lane had every reason to be satisfied and even Wellington concurred that 'the Rocket Brigade was of great use upon this occasion'.[30] They were to get another chance. For now the task of blockading Bayonne was the most pressing issue for Dickson. The huge battering train, which had been loaded on board the transports at Pasajes, consisted of 139 pieces of ordnance and over 160,000 rounds of ammunition. The CRA ordered 70 pieces and over 50,000 rounds to be brought forward in order to commence the siege.[31] To move the guns overland he required horses from across the command. Second Captain Samuel Bolton remained with 'F' Troop's guns while many of the men and the requisite number of horses returned to Pasajes to collect the train.

> We are now on the Paris side of the Bayonne … I expect to remain here for some time as the horses of the Troop are to be employed bringing up the battering train for the purposes of besieging the citadel of Bayonne which, though small, I have no doubt will be well defended as its defences are strong and well provided; already they are keeping a sharp cannonade against our advanced posts not allowing a man to show his head without a cannon shot. Whether I shall be employed I do not know yet but I mean to proffer my services in hopes as the War is nearly at an end that I may have some additional claims to make good my pretentions [sic] to any little grant which may be disposable during a long and ruinous peace – the blight of a soldier's glory.[32]

The companies warned-off to provide men to man the guns came from the reserve ammunition companies of Hutchesson and May (commanded by William Bentham and Peter Faddy respectively) as well as Dansey's, Cairnes's, Owen's and Lawson's (commanded by Charles Mosse) companies of artillery and some Portuguese reserves from Santander. The train and ammunition were complete in the artillery park on the 13th April and ready to commence siege operations but the next day news of the capture of Paris brought an end to the operation but not, as will be seen, to events at Bayonne.

Wellington's offensive against Soult's left was a difficult and demanding operation, aimed at driving the French Army eastwards and isolating Bayonne. It necessitated a rapid and sustained advance across a series of rivers, all of which ran north to south, at right angles to the line of advance. The Joyeuse, the Bidouze, the Saison, the Gave d'Oloron and the Gave de Pau all presented obstacles to the advance and opportunities for the defender but as each successive river was forced, the French fell back and Wellington's plan fell into place. A tactical pause was required between the 18th and 21st February to enable the two advancing columns, under Hill and Beresford, to link up in order to avoid exposing a flank. By the 25th February Beresford's force was on the final obstacle in front of the town of Orthez. Soult indicated that he was not prepared to relinquish his position without a fight and preparations were made for an assault across the Gave de Pau.

> We reached the very commanding heights about Orthez about mid-day, when the enemy made a very ineffectual attempt to destroy the bridge over the Pau, and were in such confusion in the town as can only be properly known to one who witnessed that of Vittoria. Lord Wellington ordered up your troop, which quickly crowned the height, and acquitted itself, as you know so well it always does, to the satisfaction of every person. Their rapid and well-directed fire soon dispersed the enemy's masses of infantry and cavalry, and increased their confusion beyond all conception …
>
> On the morning of the 27th, the 3rd, 4th, 6th, 7th and Light Divisions of Infantry, Lord Ed. Somerset and Colonel Vivian's Brigades of Cavalry, yours and Colonel Gardiner's Troops of Horse Artillery, Maxwell's, Turner's, Michell's and Sympher's Brigades were across the river, and our pontoon bridge established at Berens [Bérenx] … the attack commenced about ten o'clock upon the village of St. Boés [Saint Boès], where the contest was most severe but never doubtful, and as soon as we were possessed of it the other divisions advanced, and the action became general along the whole line, the enemy making such a resistance as I have never before seen … as soon as the ground would admit of it, the artillery began to debouche, and three times was your troop and Gardiner's and Sympher's Brigade in line; keeping up a destructive and most dreadful fire upon the enemy's retiring columns; and you will believe, my dear Ross, what a proud moment it was for me to find myself in a general action, in command of such fine fellows as yours to be.[33]

Corporal Whitehead was with the second division of 'A' Troop during the action when, in the heat of the fight, one of those inexplicable actions occurred:

> … about 2 o'clock to Subdivision No. 2 Troop advancing in column of Subdivisions Right in Front, out of the field to the road under the cross fire of the

enemies guns, at the instance of the Front Rank No. 2 coming on the road, every horse fell down. Lt Belson, Officer of the Division, about half a horse length in front turned around and enquired the cause of it. None could be given excepting that a gun shot having passed close to the horses' muzzles, the effects of which told heavy amongst the infantry on our right.[34]

Dickson, who was embroiled in preparations for the siege of Bayonne, was not up with the main army; responsibility for the artillery lay with Major John Dyer (Beresford's Corps) and major Joseph Carncross (Hill's Corps). Dyer's report to Dickson emphasised the role of the artillery in the battle:

The attack commenced about seven o'clock in the morning, and the Artillery got into action soon after; during the day I received the orders of Marshal Beresford respecting the disposition of the Artillery, and had the satisfaction about one o'clock to get Lieut. Col. Ross's and Major Gardiner's Troops of Horse Artillery, and the German Brigade of Artillery attached to the fourth division, into position opposite the Enemy's strongest Column, the fire from these Guns was tremendous and being admirably served soon caused the Enemy to retire. The Brigades then took up separate positions and annoyed the Enemy … about four o'clock the guns ceased firing, the Enemy retreating in great confusion leaving some pieces of Ordnance. I have to regret the loss of Major Sympher and many valuable Artillery men. Major Sympher was killed by a cannon shot close by me early in the Action; and Lieut. Ward was slightly wounded in the thigh.[35]

Dyer also recorded that Maxwell's Brigade did not make it up in time to get involved in the action but that was of little consequence, Soult was once again on the move, the engagement had been a success and the Gunners had played their part. Wellington wrote, 'The conduct of the artillery throughout the day deserved my highest approbation'.[36] Dickson must have been pleased and not a little relieved at receiving Dyer's report but for now he was more concerned for the welfare of Sympher's widow and children, who were at Lisbon, and he looked to resolve this issue and the family's grief with the same level of immediacy and dedication that he applied to the command of the artillery in general.

Soult's continued withdrawal east of the Pau relinquished the road to Bordeaux and provided Wellington the opportunity of moving to the city in support of the Royalist inspired insurrection. Wellington was understandably cautious; he needed to maintain the momentum on Soult, he was reluctant to risk forces from the Bayonne investment and he was in no position to support a proclamation in the name of Louis XVIII. Nevertheless, it was a clear opportunity and on the 7th March Beresford with the 7th and 4th divisions, General Richard Hussey Vivian's cavalry (he had assumed commanded of one of the Hussar brigades in November 1813) and 'A' Troop RHA received their orders to march for the city. Jenkinson recalled the extraordinary scenes which befell them on their arrival.

On the 12th of March – a memorable day, in truth, should it prove to be that of the restoration of the Bourbons – we moved towards this place … about one mile from it the Mayor, with a mounted retinue in full dress, met the Marshal, and after the usual salutes and ceremonies, he drew a paper from his pocket, which he read in a very audible voice, expressing on the part of the inhabitants the pleasure they felt at the approach of those who might be justly termed as saviours and deliverers of the world. He came also, he said, to solicit the Marshal's permission to hoist the white flag, and allow the inhabitants of Bordeaux to declare for their legitimate sovereign, Louis XVIII … The Marshal then replied, and said that the motives of the English Government were too well known to require any professions on his part. The English troops did not come to force the inhabitants of Bordeaux to declare for one person or another, and he trusted that they had well weighted the consequences of failure before they had made their declarations in favour of Louis XVIII …[37]

'A' Troop's participation in events at Bordeaux was to rob them of an opportunity to share in the final showdown developing near the city of Toulouse. Gardiner, on the other hand, had cogently argued that horse artillery was wasted at the blockade of Bayonne and been permitted to rejoin the main army.[38] It was a shrewd move for the troop was to play a pivotal role in events that were to unfold. *En route* to Toulouse, Wellington had fought actions at Aire on the 2nd March and Tarbes on the 20th March, neither of which had held up the allied main army overly long. Toulouse, however, was a far more formidable objective. On the east bank of the River Garonne, it boasted a well-fortified bridge head at Saint Cyprien and the city itself was ringed by the canal de Languedoc. By early April Dickson had rejoined the main army and in order to support the Spanish divisions, who had recently joined, had called forward Arentschildt's two Portuguese brigades under the command of majors Arriaga and Da Cunha Preto. These supplemented the Portuguese batteries already up in support of the Portuguese Division of Le Cor, commanded by Michell and António da Costa e Silva.

An abortive attempt to attack from the south delayed proceedings but Gardiner recalled that 'on the 9th Lord Wellington made a long reconnaissance along the enemy's front. In the evening he ordered Colonel Vivian's Brigade with ourselves, supported by the Fourth, Sixth and Third divisions, to drive in the enemy's picquets from Lalande and Croixdoudade [Croix Daurade], and made his final arrangements and order of attack for the following day.'[39]

The Portuguese artillery, ten 9 Prs. commanded by Lieut. Colonel Arentschildt, covered the attack made by the Spaniards on the left of the enemy's position; this artillery was warmly engaged during the best part of the day, and distinguished itself much for firmness, and correct firing. In like manner the German Brigade, commanded by Capt. Daniel, and Capt. Brandreth's 9 Pr. Brigade, under Major Dyer, were for some time employed in covering the movement of Marshal Beresford's column in its attack on the right of the position, which, when carried, these brigades moved up to the height, and assisted in taking the remainder of the position, and also opposing the fire of the enemy from the opposite side of the canal which greatly annoyed our troops on the ridge. I had every reason to be satisfied with the conduct of these Brigades.

Major Gardiner's Troop, in the first instance, was employed in supporting the left of the Spanish attack, and afterwards moved to the ridge carried by Marshal Beresford where it was of infinite service.

While these operations were going on, the 3rd and Light Divisions were employed in threatening the enemy's position along the canal towards the point where it joins the Garonne. In this service, Captain Turner's Brigade was a good deal engaged, as were also Captain Bean's Troop and Maxwell's Brigade on the opposite side of the river with Sir Rowland Hill's Corps, in the attack made upon the tête-de-pont.[40]

During the failed Spanish attack on the Grande Redoubt, Charles Michell distinguished himself, for when the Spanish took refuge in a hollow in the road

14. The Battle of Toulouse ~ Early Afternoon, 10th April 1814

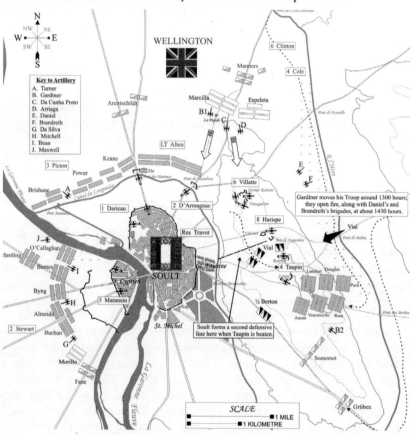

under sustained and accurate artillery fire from the French guns in the two redoubts to their front, Michell ordered his guns forward to cover the Spanish and drive back the French infantry, who were at that juncture venturing forward. During the advance the lead driver of the lead gun was killed almost instantly and Michell leaped into the saddle and drove forward the team and the rest of the battery followed. The Spanish commander wrote to Dickson some time after the battle expressing his admiration and thanks: 'I beg to assure you that Captain Mitchell [sic] was unsurpassed for his great serenity in the action of the 10th, notwithstanding that the guns opposed to him were triple his own force.'[41] Following this action, as events moved to the east and south-east of the city, the Gunners had considerable difficulty keeping up with Beresford's flanking formations due to the sodden and slippery nature of the terrain. In order to expedite the attack, the guns were manoeuvred into position early and did not continue with the forces moving around to the southern flank. The German gunners had to lend their horses to Brandreth's men to enable the heavier 6-pounders to be hauled to their platforms.[42]

Fifty-nine Gunners were killed and wounded in the action against the city. However, the indisputable sadness was that this battle, after six long years of struggle, need not have been fought at all. Allied troops had entered Paris on the 31st March and Napoleon's abdication had been signed on the 4th and ratified on the 6th April but notification had not reached the armies in the south of the country until the 10th. Sergeant Charles Whitman was with Brandreth's guns to the east of the city when, three days later, news of end of the war came through.

> On the morning of the 13th we were surprised to hear two guns fired – blank cartridges on the news of peace. We were all quite overjoyed and went into the French lines, and drank together, as if nothing had been between us.[43]

Lieutenant Richard Hardinge was a few hundred yards to the south of Whitman and was equally jubilant at the news. 'Yesterday morning the news from Paris of Bonaparte's downfall reached us, and today I saw the printed Article decreed by the Senate on which they call Louis XVIII to the throne. I think it is all *glorious* – and three quarters of this Army are certainly devilishly glad it is all over …'.[44] Less glorious were the subsequent actions of two French governors: Thouvenot at Bayonne and Habert at Barcelona who executed sorties from their defences on the 14th and 16th April respectively. Habert had not received news from Paris, but Thouvenot certainly had enough to constitute reasonable doubt. His subsequent actions, which resulted in a large number of allied and French casualties, are a permanent stain.

Notes

1. Frazer (ed. Sabine), letter dated 8th October 1813.
2. Dickson vol. V, p.1073. Letter from Dickson to MacLeod, dated 10th October 1813.
3. Ibid., pp.1119–21, dated 28th November 1813.
4. Henegan, vol. II, p.69.
5. Frazer (ed. Sabine), letter dated 13th October 1813.
6. Dickson, vol. V, pp.1090–91. Letter from Tulloh to Dickson, dated 28th October 1813.
7. Ibid., pp.1093–94. Letter from Maxwell to Carncross, dated 2nd November 1813. These guns were not abandoned, contrary to Duncan's comment (vol. II. p.376), and were recovered a few weeks later.
8. Hibbert (ed.), p.94.
9. Ross, p.51. Letter from Ross to Dalrymple, dated 12th November 1813.
10. Parker letter, filed in Gardiner's Letters (MD 1178/III), dated 14th November 1813.
11. Browne, p.175.
12. WD, vol. VII, pp.131–36. Wellington to Bathurst, dated 13th November 1813.
13. Ross, p.53. Letter from Ross to Dalrymple, dated 14th December 1813.
14. Dickson, vol. V, pp.1143–44. Letter from Dickson to MacLeod, dated 15th December 1813.
15. Ross, p.55.
16. Londonderry, p.221.
17. *Edinburgh Evening Courant*, 20 January 1814.
18. Frazer (ed. Sabine), p.375.
19. Dickson, vol. V, pp.1085–87. Letter from Dickson to MacLeod, dated 24th October 1813.
20. Frazer (ed. Sabine), pp.378–79.
21. In addition, Dickson made some readjustments to the ammunition reserve and reduced Capt. A. Thompson's *ad hoc* company.
22. Dickson, pp.1025. Letter from Dickson to Tulloh, dated 11th January 1814.
23. Dickson. Letter from Jenkinson to Ord, dated 26th February 1814.
24. Ibid. Letter from Dickson to MacLeod, dated 23rd January 1814.
25. Frazer (ed. Sabine), pp.392–93.
26. Ibid., p.403.
27. Jenkinson, letter dated 1st March 1814.
28. Frazer (ed. Sabine), pp.411–17.
29. Ibid.
30. WD, vol. VII, pp.336–41. Wellington to Bathurst, dated 1st March 1814.
31. Jones, vol. II, p.127. It consisted of 26 x 24-pounders, 12 x 10-inch mortars, 12 x 8-inch howitzers and 20 x 4.2-inch coehorn mortars.
32. Bolton, letter dated 19th March 1814.
33. Ross, pp.57–59. Letter from Jenkinson to Ross, dated 11th March 1814.
34. Whitehead, entry 27th February 1814.
35. Dickson. Letter from Dyer to Dickson, dated 3rd March 1814.
36. WD, vol. VII, pp.336–41. Wellington to Bathurst, dated 1st March 1814.

37. Ross, pp.57–59. Letter from Jenkinson to Ross, dated 11th March 1814.

38. Dickson. Letter from Gardiner to Ord, dated 7th April 1814.

39. Gardiner. Letter to MacLeod, dated 15th April 1814.

40. Dickson. Letter from Dickson to MacLeod, dated 13th April 1814.

41. Browne, pp.181–82.

42. Oman, vol. VII, p.484. Interestingly, Oman cites Dickson's report of the 10th April 1814 for this information – that letter appears to be missing from the archives.

43. Whitman, p.108.

44. Hardinge, letter (MD 280) dated 14th April 1814.

CHAPTER 22

Wood's Commitment

Within weeks of Napoleon's abdication he had been dispatched to the island of Elba and the Paris Treaties were signed as an interim measure pending a more formal congress at Vienna. Wellington's Peninsular Army unravelled with alarming speed. The Spanish went home directly but arrangements had to be made to assist the Portuguese; Dickson calculated that 300–400 mules would be required 'to enable the Portuguese artillery to return to Portugal in a respectable manner with its Army'.[1] The KGL marched north to Belgium where they joined thousands of Hanoverian militia and a British detachment under Graham, which had been sent at the end of 1813 to assist the Dutch in their insurrection against French rule.[2] Of the British troops in Iberia and southern France, some sailed for Canada; another divisional-sized formation departed for America under the command of Major General Sir Edward Pakenham; Lord Bentinck's force returned to Sicily; a few were left to enhance the garrison at Gibraltar; and the balance returned to England and Ireland. Politicians wasted little time in cashing-in the peace dividend and, within weeks of repatriation, large scale disbandment was in progress. By the end of 1814, 11 veteran battalions, 24 second battalions and 10,000 foreign troops were discharged. The Board of Ordnance launched into disarmament with unbridled keenness and, in less than a year, 7,000 posts in the Royal Artillery had been cut. The ten battalions of ten companies remained but all their establishments had been reduced.

With the Napoleonic Wars seemingly at an end and the Peninsular Army broken up, Wellington issued his General Order of Thanks to the Army and departed a few weeks later to take up his appointment as British ambassador in Paris.[3] At much the same time Lieutenant Richard Hardinge was in the French capital and he recorded his feelings towards the inhabitants and the Spanish allies:

> I was much gratified in seeing the Parisians well humbled in their capital ... by
> having Russian guards at their gates, theatres and public places. I hate them all for

a set of fickle boasting fellows who will give a great deal of trouble for King and Government. The Spaniards, after their exertions in blood and treasure for Ferdinand, will I dare say tamely submit to a despotic Government under the coward who gave himself up to Napoleon at Bayonne.[4]

His castigation of Ferdinand was rather harsh and there was anything but tame submission in Spain as numerous factions emerged in the wake of national liberation. The war had sparked divisions which were to haunt the country for the next 160 years, until the death of General Francisco Franco in 1975. However, Hardinge's assessment of the fickle nature of the French was to prove a more accurate prediction.

In the meantime, the ongoing war in America was the British main effort. On the 18th June 1812 America had declared war on Great Britain for three reasons: firstly to oppose trade restrictions preventing trade with France; secondly, to end the practice of forced recruitment of American citizens into the Royal Navy; and finally, to confront the overt military support to the indigenous Americans who were resisting American expansion to the north-west. Poor diplomacy and a predetermined political focus on events in Europe had allowed the situation in North American to slide out of Britain's political spotlight and, *ipso facto*, control and by the time the government realised the gravity of the situation, despite rescinding some of the offending Orders in Council in an attempt to mollify the position, it was too little too late.

The War of 1812, as it became known, was initially fought as a combined naval blockade of the American east coast ports and, in Lower Canada, around Lake Erie and Lake Ontario but expanded to the south and Gulf coasts culminating in the landing of an invasion force near New Orleans in 1814. The war was to ebb and flow for two and a half years but, with events in Europe seemingly concluded, it was in neither nation's interest to prolong the struggle. At the outbreak of the war there were nine companies of the Royal Artillery in theatre under the command of Major General George Glasgow.[5] By the end of 1814 this had risen to 19 companies and a rocket detachment under Captain Henry Lane.[6] This detachment and also the companies of captains Robert Pym, Lewis Carmichael, John Michell and Alexander Munro were dispatched to join Pakenham's force for the expedition to New Orleans under the command of his CRA, Dickson. The American forces in the region were the responsibility of a local militia commander, Major General Andrew Jackson, a man with an intense hatred of the British who was, 15 years later, to become the 7th President of the United States. A combination of Jackson's spirited defence and difficult terrain ultimately resulted in defeat for the British. Pakenham made best speed to the area but arrived on the 25th December 1814 only to discover that Admiral Thomas Cochrane had already commenced operations and deployed General John Keane with the army on an isthmus, just over half a mile wide between the Mississippi River and an impenetrable swamp. John Spencer Cooper of the 7th Foot, which had been landed as part of this advanced guard on the 14th December, recalled the rather cavalier way in which the operation was conducted:

The day after we joined the fleet we were conveyed in small craft to the main land. One of our boats, containing sixteen privates and a serjeant, was swamped, and all but one were drowned. After landing we marched towards New Orleans, each man carrying a cannon ball in his haversack, as we had no baggage animals. Now two balls would have been more easily carried than one, because they would have poised each other.[7]

Dickson arrived at the same time as Pakenham and was immediately ordered to silence the American 14-gun schooner *Carolina,* which had bombarded the advance guard with impunity. The Gunners cut embrasures into the levee and on the 27th December, with hot shot fired from the two 9-pounders, succeeded in destroying the vessel.[8] The force was complete ashore (except John Lambert's Brigade) by the 28th December but early probing actions against the American lines revealed the strength of their defences and the accuracy of their gunners. Pakenham decided to breach the line with heavy artillery and instructed Dickson accordingly. The plan relied on the artillery commander's ingenuity to succeed:

> During the attack yesterday the working parties of sailors on the Bayou dragged the two 18 Prs. on their ship carriages as far as Villaré's [canal], and it being now necessary to take them forward, as we are totally unprovided [*sic*] with sling or platform carriages for that purpose, I procured two country bullock carts with high strong spoked wheels, which having been used for moving sugar hogsheads, fortunately had iron axletrees; these with some little alteration made excellent sling-carts, and the guns drawn by sailors and artillerymen were moved by them along the high road part of the way to our new Battery at the picket house, the ammunition amounting to 100 rounds a gun complete, being sent forward the whole way ... After dark the detachment of sailors took the two 18 Prs. and carriages the rest of the way along the high road to the Battery at the Picket house, but the platforms not being ready, they mounted the guns and left them in rear of the Battery, and at three o'clock in the morning Major Michell sent a detachment of his brigade and put them on the platforms.[9]

A total of eight 18-pounders and four 24-pounder carronades were collected but there were problems with the cartridge bags and once again Dickson's inventiveness was required to remedy the situation.

> As the empty paper cartridges were nearly all unserviceable, and the quantity very insufficient, with Sir Edward's permission I caused a search to be made in the different houses for stuff fit to make cartridges, and by this means procured a quantity of hangings, bed-curtains, sheetings [*sic*], etc. that would answer, and a detachment of tailors, part from the Artillery and part from the line, was set to work to make cartridge bags.[10]

The hastily constructed batteries were ready to open on the 1st January but they made little impression upon the American works, which had the advantage of good embrasures, substantially constructed and well riveted. Conversely, the heavier 32- and 24-pounder American guns made short work of the hurriedly built British batteries and, by the end of the day, they were largely destroyed with Dickson's men having taken numerous casualties.[11] Lieutenant Alexander Ramsay, the brother of Norman Ramsay, had been mortally wounded, 12 other gunners killed and 13 wounded.[12] This failure led to a radical reappraisal by Pakenham and his staff. They decided to establish guns on the south bank of the Mississippi from where they could enfilade the American lines in support of another frontal assault. Lambert's Brigade arrived on the 6th January and, with the force at full strength, the attack was made on the 8th. It was an unmitigated failure and Pakenham was killed in the process. Lambert, who had assumed command, sent in a flag of truce prior to organising the re-embarkation of his demoralised force. Major Harry Smith was with the 95th Rifles and, like Dickson, had served throughout the Peninsular War having been at Buenos Aires and now finding himself at New Orleans. 'Never since Buenos Ayres had I witnessed a reverse, and the sight to our eyes, which had looked on victory so often, was appalling indeed.'[13] It was all the more appalling when news arrived on the 14th January that the preliminaries of a peace agreement had been signed between the two nations as early as mid-December 1814: the blood shed on the banks of the mighty Mississippi had been in vain. Both men were now keen to distance themselves from their 'second awful disaster in America' and, as it happened, events in Europe were about to provide just such an opportunity.[14]

The Congress at Vienna was not progressing well; in their quest to redraw the map of Europe, national divisions had turned dialogue to disagreement and accord to argument. The situation in France had steadily deteriorated over the previous months; the restored Bourbon monarchy, which had done little to help their predicament, was becoming increasingly unpopular and the population progressively more bored and disillusioned with their lot. Napoleon sensed the mood, realised his opportunity, and seized it. He stole away from confinement at Elba with his 400-strong personal guard and landed, on the 1st March 1815, in the south of France where initial antipathy soon turned to popular support. He entered Paris 20 days later in triumph; news of his arrival had prompted the departure of Louis XVIII the day prior. It was unadulterated Napoleonic theatre; the delegates at Vienna had greeted Wellington's announcement of Napoleon's escape as some sort of joke. Alarm spread throughout Europe. In Vienna, the reality of the situation, and unfolding events in France in March, refocussed the negotiators and rejuvenated negotiations. Napoleon was declared an outlaw subject to 'public vengeance'. Russia, Prussia, Austria, Sweden, Spain, Portugal, Great Britain and some of the German states created the 7th Coalition determined on restoring Louis XVIII by military force.[15]

Napoleon's appeal to the crowned heads of Europe for peace fell on deaf ears and nations commenced urgent mobilisation. It was patently clear that Napoleon would have to fight if he was to avoid a repetition of the 1814 campaign. He calculated that it would take the allies a significant time to deploy their forces and considered a dynamic offence as the best way to secure his position in Paris. Speed and aggression, gaining local superiority and dealing with the allied armies piecemeal was his policy and from it fell the obvious coalition centre of gravity and point of attack – Belgium. He was able to call upon a number of sources to field his armies and the majority of his old marshals and generals rallied to the cause. His main force was the Army of the

North, consisting of 124,000 men under his own command, but he was also able to mobilise another 20,000 under General Jean Rapp covering the border near Strasbourg. An additional 24,000 men under Suchet were covering the Italian approaches and two further corps, totalling 14,000 men under generals Clausel and Decaen, were covering the Pyrenees. Conversely the allies, particularly the Anglo-Dutch army, were struggling to get up to strength and equip. For Britain, the return of the troops from the American theatre became a national priority and in early April 1815 Wellington had written to Lord Bathurst outlining his requirements.

> If you could let me have 40,000 good British infantry, besides those you insist upon having in garrisons, the proportion settled by treaty that you are to furnish of cavalry, that is to say, the eighth of 150,000 men, including in both the old German legion, and 150 pieces of British field artillery fully horsed, I should be satisfied, and take my chance for the rest, and engage that we would play our part in the game.[16]

If the problems facing Horse Guards were noteworthy, those facing the Board of Ordnance were even more acute. The six brigades of guns with Graham's force, under the command of Colonel Sir George Wood, were to form the nucleus of the artillery for Wellington's army. Wood was not Wellington's choice of CRA, but he had other far greater problems on his hands than to make overtures to the MGO about the suitability of Sir George. 'I might have expected that the Generals and Staff formed by me in the last war would have been allowed to come to me again, but instead of that I am overloaded with people I have never seen before; and it appears to be purposely intended to keep those out of my way whom I wish to have.'[17] Wood was, in fact, no stranger to the Low Countries having served as a subaltern in Flanders under the Duke of York (1793–95) and fought at Walcheren in 1809. He threw himself into the task of resourcing the guns, equipment and horses with enormous zeal and he was assisted in his task by the arrival of Frazer who had been dispatched to command the horse artillery.

At home, MacLeod worked tirelessly to redirect resources to the continent and, on the face of it, resourcing a total of 25 companies of field artillery and troops of horse artillery, from the 114 on paper, should not have presented much of a challenge. However, of the 100 foot artillery companies, they were spread across the globe: 42 were deployed in garrison tasks across Great Britain and Ireland; 12 were in the West Indies; seven remained at Gibraltar; and 21 were still in North America. Other than the six companies already in theatre in the Low Countries, the balance of 12 were spread from Italy to India. Immediate plans were drawn up to redirect three of the four companies from New Orleans direct to Ostend (the British logistic hub), along with five companies withdrawn from North America and 14 companies from across Great Britain and Ireland. In addition, seven troops of horse artillery and one rocket troop were also earmarked for deployment. Wellington must have been impressed with the speed and determination which Wood and his staff displayed in trying to satisfy the commander's requirements; however, his characteristic eye for detail spotted areas for improvement and he had his Adjutant General write to Wood accordingly.

His Grace the Duke of Wellington having noticed the great number of ordnance vessels in this harbour not unloaded, some of which have been here 16 days, requests that more expedition than seems hitherto to have taken place may be used in discharging these vessels, in order that they may return to England. The Commander of the Forces also directs that an active and experienced officer may be stationed at Ostend for the purpose of superintending this duty, which the Duke conceives might be carried on much quicker, particularly as it seems there is no want of craft to receive the stores from the vessels and convey them to their destination. His Grace also noticed that a vessel is being employed as a depot for powder. This cannot be allowed; and the powder or other articles must be moved into the magazines at Antwerp, or some other place.[18]

Wellington had made no secret of the fact that he would not accept local Belgian drivers, urging Wood instead to write to MacLeod to request an additional four companies of artillery to undertake this task. When Wellington received notification that Dickson would arrive in early June from New Orleans, he ordered that three brigades of 18-pounder guns should be established and placed under his former CRA's command. These additional demands placed a huge burden on the Board of Ordnance but Lord Mulgrave, MacLeod, Wood and Frazer worked unstintingly; indeed Frazer took it upon himself to try to equip most of the horse artillery troops with the heavier 9-pounder guns and by mid-June had succeeded in getting three troops equipped accordingly.[19] Whinyates arrived with his rocket troop in early May and was devastated to discover that Wellington was not prepared to entertain rockets with the artillery organisation and he was duly ordered to equip the troop with guns. Wood interceded on Whinyates's behalf and secured agreement that the troop would take to the field with both guns and rockets. The provision of suitable horses was a continual problem but, at the review of the cavalry and horse artillery at Schlendelbeke on the 30th May, it would appear that considerable progress had been made.

We found on our arrival fifteen regiments of British cavalry, with six troops of horse artillery, drawn up in three lines on a beautiful plain on the banks of the Dender. About 1 p.m. the Duke, Marshal Blucher etc. etc., arrived, having come from Brussels by way of Engheim and Grammont. We received the Duke with a salute of nineteen guns. After going down the lines and inspecting the cavalry generally, and the horse artillery very minutely, and repeatedly expressing his approbation of our appearance, the Duke took his station in front of the centre of the first line, and the different corps passed in columns of half squadrons.[20]

According to Second Captain Alexander Cavalie Mercer, the commander of the Prussian Army, Field Marshal Gebhard Leberecht von Blücher, exclaimed, 'Mein Gott, dere is not von orse in dies batterie wich is not goot for Veldt Marshal'.[21] At about this time, Frazer also moved Macdonald from his horse artillery troop to command the horse artillery attached to the Cavalry Corps; his good friend Ramsay assumed command of 'H' Troop to fill this vacancy. He noted in his diary on the 11th June: 'Ramsay arrived at Ghent, he is adored by his men; kind, generous, and manly, he is more than a friend of his soldiers.'[22] Notwithstanding such noble sentiments, Macdonald, who was to struggle with his new appointment, had every reason to question Frazer's motives in removing him from his troop at such a critical juncture.

As it transpired, events unfolded far more rapidly that Wellington and the allies had hoped or anticipated. However, by mid-June, Wood had eight horse artillery troops and seven foot brigades, supplemented by two KGA horse artillery troops and one KGA and two Hanoverian brigades of artillery. They were task organised for the Waterloo Campaign as follows:

CRA: Col. Sir G. A. Wood (Adjutant: Lt. G. Coles RA)
Assistant Adjutant General: Lt. Col. Sir J. May RA
Brigade Major: Capt. H. Baynes RA
Staff: Lt. Col. J. Bloomfield RA
Commanding the RHA: Lt. Col. Sir A. Frazer RHA (Adjutant: Lt. W. Bell RHA)
Commanding the KGA: Lt. Col. Sir G. J. Hartmann KGA

RHA Troops	Notes	Equipment
'A' Troop (Ross)	Reserve.	5 x 9-pounders 1 x 5½-inch howitzer
'D' Troop (Bean)	Reserve.	5 x 6-pounders[23] 1 x 5½-inch howitzer
'E' Troop (Gardiner)	Attached to the Cavalry Corps.	5 x 6-pounders 1 x 5½-inch howitzer
'F' Troop (Webber Smith)	Attached to the Cavalry Corps.	5 x 6-pounders 1 x 5½-inch howitzer
'G' Troop (Dickson)	Mercer in command. Attached to the Cavalry Corps.	5 x 9-pounders 1 x 5½-inch howitzer
'H' Troop (Ramsay)	Attached to the Cavalry Corps.	5 x 9-pounders 1 x 5½-inch howitzer
'I' Troop (Bull)	Attached to the Cavalry Corps.	6 x heavy 5½-inch howitzers
The Rocket Troop RHA	(Whinyates) Attached to the Cavalry Corps.	5 x 6-pounders 13 rocket sections
Horse Artillery KGL	**Notes**	**Equipment**
Sympher's 1st Company KGA	Attached to 2nd Division.	5 x 9-pounders 1 x 5½-inch howitzer
Kühlmann's 2nd Company KGA	Attached to 1st Division.	5 x 9-pounders 1 x 5½-inch howitzer
RA/KGA Companies	**Notes**	**Equipment**
Sandham's Company	Attached to 1st Division.	5 x 9-pounders 1 x 5½-inch howitzer
Alms's Company	Bolton in command. Attached to 2nd Division.	4 x 9-pounders 2 x 5½-inch howitzers
Lloyd's Company	Attached to 3rd Division.	5 x 9-pounders 1 x 5½-inch howitzer

Cleeves's KGA Company	Attached to 3rd Division.	5 x 9-pounders 1 x 5½-inch howitzer
Brome's Company	Attached to 4th Division.	5 x 9-pounders 1 x 5½-inch howitzer
Rettberg's Hanoverian Company[24]	Attached to 4th Division.	5 x 9-pounders 1 x 5½-inch howitzer
Rogers's Company	Attached to 5th Division.	5 x 9 pounders 1 x 5½-inch howitzer
Braun's Hanoverian Company	Attached to 5th Division.	5 x 9-pounders 1 x 5½-inch howitzer
Unett's Company	Attached to 6th Division.	5 x 9-pounders 1 x 5½-inch howitzer
Gordon's Company	Sinclair in command. Reserve.	5 x 9-pounders 1 x 5½-inch howitzer

Sources: Frazer, May (Leslie).

In addition, Hutchesson's, Courtenay Ilbert's and Arthur Hunt's artillery companies formed Dickson's 18-pounder siege train and were supplemented by manpower from (John) Michell's and Carmichael's companies when they landed at Ostend from New Orleans. An additional four companies, Charles Younghusband's, Charles Tyler's, Alexander Munro's and Charles Maitland's (commanding Marsh's Company), provided the Drivers. Thus in a period of just over two months, 24 of the 25 companies or troops of artillery had been resourced; not all were up with the field army and not all were deployed in their primary role and brigaded with guns but, nevertheless, it was a remarkable achievement. Adding the German and Dutch/ Belgian artillery, Wellington had a total of 191 guns, a ratio of two guns per 1,000 troops. The Prussians fielded 296 guns, a ratio of slightly more at two and a half guns per 1,000 troops and the French had 370 guns which provided a ratio of three guns for every 1,000 troops.[25] Thus Wellington's ratio of guns to infantry was better than he had experienced throughout the Peninsula. However, Napoleon's maxim of five guns for every 1,000 infantry had not been met by a considerable margin. Furthermore, as we shall see, the French numerical advantage in artillery was neither capitalised upon nor as effective as it could have been.

Large Russian and Austrian armies were on the move towards France but until they arrived, the Anglo-Dutch and Prussian armies, under the command of Wellington and Blücher respectively, were deployed and operating defensively. Napoleon's plan, to isolate and defeat these two allied armies piecemeal, relied on speed, surprise and the assumption that they would, once pressed, fall back on their respective lines of communication. For the British this was north-west to their logistic hub at Ostend, for the Prussians it was east to Cologne, which suited Napoleon's plan perfectly. Unaware of the French axis of advance, the allies opted to deploy across a wide area in order to defend Belgium and the approaches to Brussels. This was a fundamental error as it failed to take into account Napoleon's manner of waging war by striking at the enemy and not on the seizure of geographical points. By dispersing their forces to protect key locations, Wellington and Blücher needed to get inside the French decision cycle in order to react quickly enough to block any advance with numerical superiority. As it turned out, they failed, despite the defection of one of Napoleon's divisional commanders on the 15th June who provided the Prussians with details of the French plan.

At 0330 hours on the 15th June Napoleon's army converged on the city of Charleroi and the three bridges over the River Sambre. The Prussian screen was driven back and by dusk the French Army was secure on the north bank; Ney, who had arrived in the field the day prior, assumed command of the left wing. Blücher concentrated three of his four corps north, centred on the village of Sombreffe, while Wellington, preoccupied with Napoleonic intentions along the Mons road, hesitated. By the time intelligence reports had confirmed that the entire French effort was concentrated north of Charleroi, Wellington had been caught flat-footed and he had left the Prussians dangerously exposed. He rushed forces to the vital crossroads at Quatre-Bras but, auspiciously, the Chief of Staff of the Prince of Orange had pre-empted the need to move troops to the area. Moreover, a tardy commencement to operations by Ney ensured that for now the crossroads, and with it lateral communications with Blücher, remained in allied hands. At about 0900 hours, when Wellington arrived at Quatre-Bras, the allies had about 6,500 men and eight guns; advancing in their direction were 42,000 Frenchmen consisting largely of General Reille's 2nd Corps, including 7,000 cavalry supported by 92 guns. Ney did not begin his attack on the Dutch–Belgian forces until 1430 hours. There were three reasons for this: firstly, he waited until he had received his confirmatory orders from Napoleon before preparing his own orders and commencing battle preparation; secondly, Ney had only arrived in the field the previous day and had no recognised headquarters staff; and finally, both Ney and Reille had met Wellington before in the Peninsula and both were aware and decidedly wary of his tactic of hiding his troops, prompting a cautious approach to the opening of hostilities.

When the attack finally commenced Wellington's force still only numbered 8,000 men supported by the batteries of Captain Emmanuel Stevenart and Captain Adriaan Bijleveld each with eight guns. The Dutch skirmishers fell back towards the farm of Gemioncourt and it was an anxious moment which, fortuitously for Wellington, coincided with the arrival of Picton's 5th Division and some badly needed cavalry led by the Lieutenant General Prince Friedrich, Duke of Brunswick. Wellington immediately threw Major General Sir James Kempt's Brigade into a counter-attack to secure his left wing while the balance of the division was positioned along the Namur road supported by the batteries of Captain Thomas Rogers and Rettberg. Lieutenant Henry Heise, who was with Rettberg's guns, recalled:

The battery had been attached to the 4th Division; however, during the night of the 15th to the 16th, it received orders to join up with the 5th Division under the command of General Picton. On the morning of the 16th June the battery marched from Brussels with this division and the Brunswick troops and reached the Quatre Bras battlefield at about 3 o'clock in the afternoon. Immediately upon arrival, the battery was positioned on the left flank of the English corps, and participated vigorously in the battle until about 9 o'clock.[26]

The struggle for Quatre-Bras between 1500 and 2100 hours was a most confusing affair. As allied reinforcements arrived they were thrown into action and were able to thwart the piecemeal attacks delivered by Ney. During the first series of attacks Stevenart lost six of his eight guns and was rendered ineffective; Rogers's Gunners had taken heavy losses from the French skirmishers who had taken advantage of the high and dense crops to steal forward.[27] Ney had massed six batteries to soften the allied lines prior to the advance by the French infantry and the subsequent repeated cavalry charges. By the end of the first series of attacks the allies were pushed back to the line of the Namur road and the north end of the Bossu woods. The second attack was preceded by a cavalry charge by General Hippolyte-Marie Piré's chasseurs and lancers and Kellermann's cuirassiers; the allied infantry deployed into squares,

15. The Battle of Quatre Bras ~ Situation at 2030–2100 Hours, 16th June 1815

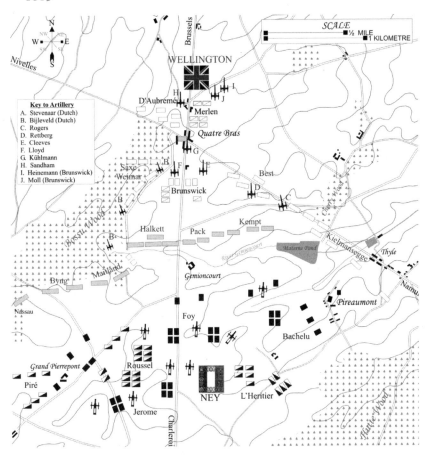

A and B were in location early on the 16th June, but A was withdrawn (badly mauled) at about 1600 hours; C and D arrived at around 1430–1500 hours; E and F at 1730 hours; G arrived at 1800 hours; H at 1830 hours and I and J at 2000 hours. H, I and J were largely held as an artillery reserve.

presenting significant targets for the French gunners. Rogers recalled during this part of the battle:

> ... some French artillery, which opened a heavy fire upon us, in addition to that of musketry, killing and wounding several of our men and horses; the artillery being as we supposed at about the distance of 500 or 600 yards in the direction of the [Hutte] wood ... We were at one time menaced by a body of heavy cavalry, but not charged by them ... Our attention was much engaged in firing spherical case shot at a column which, passing near a piece of water [Materne Pond] ... attempted to turn our left flank.[28]

Although the allies were pressed hard, running short of ammunition and taking heavy casualties, the initiative was slipping from Ney. His orders to Drouet to move his 1st Corps in support of operations against the crossroads had been countermanded by Napoleon who had ordered the corps to assist General Emmanuel de Grouchy at Ligny. The cavalry attacks had largely failed and to make matters worse two additional brigades had just arrived along with Major William Lloyd's and Cleeves's brigades of artillery, which were quickly deployed. The French had moved two batteries to the edge of the Bossu woods and these guns were soon making their presence felt on the Brunswick troops; Wellington immediately ordered Lloyd to deploy his guns to counter the threat.

> The Duke instantly ordered the advance of this battery into the open space between the Charleroi road and the wood, for the purpose of silencing the French guns; but before the British artillerymen could unlimber, several horses of the Battery were killed, wheels were disabled and, from the proximity of the enemy's guns, some of the gunners were literally cut in two by the round shot with which they were so closely assailed. Nevertheless, the Battery succeeded, not only in silencing its opponents, but also in forcing back into the wood a French column of infantry, which, advancing directly towards the Brussels road, had endeavoured to turn its right flank: after which brilliant services, Lloyd, perceiving no adequate support, judged it prudent, in the then crippled state of his Battery, to retire to his former post, abandoning two guns for which he had not sufficient number of horses remaining, and which consequently could not be recovered until the termination of the action.[29]

The arrival of these two additional allied brigades of artillery had already made a significant difference and they were soon supplemented by the arrival of Major Jacob Kühlmann's horse artillery which deployed at the crossroads and went immediately into action, enfilading the road and inflicting a heavy toll on the French heavy cavalry. 'In an instant the whole mass appeared in irretrievable confusion; the road was literally strewed with [the] corpses of these steel clad warriors and their gallant steeds; Kellermann himself was dismounted, and compelled like many of his followers to retire on foot.'[30] As darkness fell the attacks petered out, Ney withdrew to the area around Frasnes while Wellington consolidated his position at Quatre-Bras with a strong piquet line to the south. It had been a difficult six hours for both commanders: Ney had misjudged the situation but Wellington could certainly count his blessings.

To the east, Blücher's Prussians had been defeated by Napoleon and forced to retreat. After some deliberation General August von Gneisenau, Blücher's chief of staff, in the absence of his commander, decided to fall back on Wavre.[31] However, this information was not transmitted to, or at least not received by, Wellington. Consequently, the Anglo-Dutch army continued to concentrate in and around Quatre-Bras and at dawn on the 17th there were 45,000 men preparing to receive the French from the south, unaware that their left flank was wide open. At 0900 hours Wellington finally received notification of Blücher's retrograde movement, realised his predicament and immediately issued orders for a retreat north and simultaneously informed the Prussian liaison officer that he would retire to Mont St. Jean and, if supported by one Prussian corps (he was aware that General Friedrich Bŀlow's Corps had not been engaged at Ligny), he would accept battle.

Napoleon's lassitude on the morning of the 17th June enabled Wellington's forces to break clean from Quatre-Bras and to move north to a defensive position of the commander's own choosing. At Mont St. Jean his Anglo-Dutch army could concentrate but, more critically, it would remain within reach of support from Blücher's Prussians at Wavre. Napoleon had once again decided to divide his army: Grouchy, with over 30,000 men and 96 guns, was to pursue the Prussians while Napoleon with the balance of the *Armée* would move against Wellington. Early on the 17th June all the cards were stacked in favour of the French but within hours that advantage had been squandered. Poor French staff work, confusing orders, contradictory intelligence and the entrenched belief that the Prussians would fall back on their lines of communication, resulted in Grouchy moving north-east and away from the Prussians who had moved north. Not that the staff work in Wellington's army had been much better.

Macdonald, who had been placed in command of the horse artillery attached to the cavalry corps, seemed particularly out of his depth. Horse artillery troops, having been allocated to cavalry brigades, were to move south and link up with those respective brigades at Enghien on the 16th June. However, the urgency of the situation at Quatre-Bras resulted in few, if any, of the horse artillery troops connecting with their respective cavalry formations en route. The cavalry arrived at the crossroads after the last shots had been fired and the horse artillery some time after that; French delays on the morning of the 17th June provided time for the retreat to commence and for orders to be issued to the cavalry to cover the withdrawal. The last of the infantry left Quatre-Bras at about noon with all the infantry moving back on the main road except Major General Karl Alten's 3rd Division which was on the road to the east. Wellington's orders were for the cavalry to cover the retreat in three lines: Major General Sir William Dörnberg's Brigade to the west; Colquhoun Grant's Brigade, Edward Somerset's Household Cavalry Brigade and William Ponsonby's Union Brigade in the centre; and Hussey Vivian's and John Vandeleur's light cavalry brigades to the east. The horse artillery attachments seem somewhat chaotic. Gardiner was supporting Vivian but Ramsay, who should have been supporting Vandeleur, appears to have got lost, prompting Macdonald to offer the task to Mercer, who seems to have taken up the suggestion and, therefore, did not move with Somerset's Brigade, at least initially. Webber Smith's Troop was supporting Grant's Brigade but appears to have moved more with Gardiner to the west, while Grant's hussars were covering the main road in the centre. Whinyates appears to have operated independently while the whereabouts of and orders to Bull are unclear.

When the French advance finally commenced, Napoleon's men pursued Wellington's screen down the Brussels road with vigour in an attempt to bring them to combat. Mercer found himself in the thick of the action and was ordered by the commander of the cavalry, Lord Uxbridge, to 'shoot and scoot'.

'They are just coming up the hill' said Lord Uxbridge. 'Let them get well up before you fire. Do you think you can retire quick enough afterwards?' 'I am sure of it, my lord'. 'Very well, then, keep a good look-out, and point your guns well'. I had often longed to see Napoleon, that mighty man of war – that astonishing genius who had filled the world with his renown. Now I saw him, and there was a degree of sublimity in the interview rarely equalled. The sky had become overcast since the morning, and at this moment presented a most extraordinary appearance … a single horseman, immediately followed by several others, mounted the plateau … For an instant they pulled up and regarded us, when several squadrons, coming rapidly on the plateau, Lord Uxbridge cried out, 'Fire! – fire!' and, giving them a general discharge, we quickly limbered up to retire, as they dashed forward supported by some horse-artillery guns, which opened upon us ere we could complete the manoeuvre …[32]

At the commencement of this action the heavens opened; deafening claps of thunder were interspersed by blinding streaks of lightning and 'the rain came down as if a waterspout had broken'. Mercer withdrew north, narrowly escaping the fire of two French horse artillery batteries and being trapped in a narrow lane with a section of his guns, before arriving at the town of Genappe. Lord Uxbridge was urging the Horse Gunners to make best speed: 'Make haste! – make haste! For God's sake, gallop, or you will be taken!'[33] Crossing the Dyle River, Mercer moved to the north of the village and finally linked up with Somerset's Household Brigade where the 9-pounder guns were brought into action on the right of the 'Blues'. As the French advanced, Mercer's Horse Gunners fired until their ammunition was expended at which point it was decided that Whinyates might as well 'have a go'. Mercer witnessed the scene and rather disparagingly recorded the outcome.

Meanwhile the rocketeers had placed a little iron triangle in the road with a rocket lying on it. The order to fire is given – portfire applied – the fidgety missile begins to splutter out sparks and wriggle its tail for a second or so, and then darts forth straight up the chaussée … I saw the [French] guns standing mute and unmanned, while our rocketeers kept shooting off rockets, none of which ever followed the course of the first; most of them, on arriving about the middle of the ascent, took a vertical direction, whilst some actually turned back upon ourselves – and one of these, following me like a squib until its shell exploded, actually put me in more danger than all of the fire of the enemy throughout the day.[34]

After firing 21 rockets, the French advance brought a rapid halt to rocket practice for the day and forced a further withdrawal. The very heavy rain was hampering progress on both sides. Ingilby, with Gardiner's Troop on the right (east) of the allied withdrawal, noted:

... the rain instantly commenced as it were in torrents, and at the moment the whole of the cavalry received the order and commenced a rapid retreat ... on one occasion a squadron formed to repel some skirmishers who seemed inclined to make a dash at the rear of our troop of guns, by the very heavy rain caused the roads and ground to be so poached and cut up, that they soon ceased to follow us altogether ... At dusk we came upon the infantry who had already reached their bivouac and were in the positions assigned to them. The Troop took up its quarters in the hamlet of Conconbert ... It continued to rain, but in a hovel the officers got into, we found plenty of potatoes and a barrel of beer, we did very well. The only inconvenience I suffered was from having lent my cloak to the Doctor who was ill and had none, by which I got so thoroughly soaked I could get nothing dried, having no change, and my feet began to swell so that I was afraid to take off my boots, fearing I might not be able to put them on again.[35]

Having tempered the enthusiasm of the French advance, the exhausted allied infantry were able to move, unhindered, to their positions astride the Brussels road at Mont St. Jean and the cavalry and horse artillery continued to manoeuvre skillfully, frustrating all attempts to get around the flanks. Lord Uxbridge had every reason to be pleased:

We were received by the Duke of Wellington upon entering the position of Waterloo, having effected the retreat with trifling loss. Thus ended the prettiest Field Day of Cavalry and Horse Artillery that I ever witnessed.[36]

Notes

1. Dickson to MacLeod from Toulouse, dated 23rd April 1814.
2. Later in 1814 these troops were placed under the command of the Prince of Orange pending the final settlement of Europe and the planned congress at Vienna.
3. WD, vol. VII, p.517.
4. Hardinge letters, (MD 280) dated 30th May 1814.
5. Payne's, Story's, Wallace's, Caddy's, Sinclair's, Holcroft's, Phillott's (later Gardner's), Crawford's and St. Clair's.
6. Farrington's, Maxwell's, Trelawney's, Douglas's (later Turner's), Maclachlan's, Addams's, Pym's, Carmichael's, Michell's and Munro's. See Law's *Battery Records*.

7. Spencer Cooper, p.127.

8. Dickson, entries dated 25–27th December 1814. The battery consisted of 2 x 9-pounders, 4 x 6-pounders, 1 heavy and 1 x light 5½-inch howitzer and 1 x 5½-inch mortar.

9. Ibid., entry dated 29th December 1814.

10. Ibid., entry dated 30th December 1814.

11. Kiley, p.249 for a table of British and American artillery.

12. Browne, p.193 records that Alexander Ramsay's nerve failed him and he retreated from the guns and vowed to resign his Commission but returned to his post on the insistence of Maj. Munro, his company commander.

13. Smith, ch. XXII, p.89.

14. Dickson, however, remained in theatre for the attack on (and capture) of Fort Bowyer; which had been achieved by 12th February 1815.

15. Portugal, however, refused to send troops and Spain delayed joining until May 1815.

16. WD, vol. VIII, pp.17–18. Letter from Wellington to Bathurst from Brussels, dated 6th April 1815.

17. Fortescue, vol. X, pp.238–9.

18. Ibid., pp.35–36, letter A.G. to Wood, dated 18th April 1815.

19. Frazer (ed. Sabine), p.551. This decision is often attributed to Wellington but Frazer is clear it was his idea.

20. Ibid., p.521.

21. Mercer, vol. I, p.217.

22. Frazer (ed. Sabine), p.532.

23. The brigade was not equipped with 9-pounder guns as is often listed.

24. The Hanoverian artillery companies were militia units commanded by KGA officers and NCOs. Wellington wanted to use the Hanoverian militia to bring the KGA companies back up to strength but the Hanoverian authorities would not permit this.

25. I have used James (Fortescue) for the figures of French and Prussian guns but I do not agree with his figures for the British/Dutch guns which he calculates at 204 guns, by including the 12 x 18-pounders (which were not in the field) and he credits Whinyates as having six guns when he only had five.

26. Siborne (ed. Glover) – letter from Heise, dated 20th February 1837.

27. Arcq, p.64 quoting from the primary source of Lt. Henckens.

28. Siborne, SWL, pp.231–32 letter from Col. Rogers.

29. Siborne, SWC, pp.174–75.

30. Ibid., p.182.

31. During the closing stages of the battle of Ligny, Blücher was personally leading a cavalry charge when his horse was shot and fell upon him. He was recovered later that day and carried, in a semi-conscious state, from the field.

32. Mercer, vol. I, pp.268–69. The single horseman was reputedly Napoleon himself.

33. Ibid., p.270.

34. Ibid., pp.279–80.

35. Ingilby, Waterloo Diary pp.316–17.

36. Siborne, SWL, Uxbridge – Letters from the General Staff, p.18.

CHAPTER 23

Wellington's Guns and Napoleon's Daughters

The night of the 17th–18th June witnessed unceasing rain, manifesting misery to the many thousands of men in exposed bivouacs across the countryside. In Wellington's army, some of the Peninsular veterans considered the foul weather an omen of impending victory. To the south, Napoleon and his generals did not see it quite the same way. At breakfast Soult's suggestion that part of Grouchy's 30,000 men might well be needed for the impending clash of arms was met with a mixture of scorn and bluster. 'I tell you that he [Wellington] is a bad general and that the English troops are bad troops, and that we will make short work of them.' A subsequent report by Jerome Bonaparte (Napoleon's youngest brother), based on tittle-tattle from a waiter at a Genappe inn, which projected a junction of the Prussian and Anglo-Dutch armies, was dismissed more forcefully by an increasingly irate Emperor. 'After such a battle as Ligny the junction of the English and the Prussians is impossible for another two days; besides the Prussians have Grouchy at their heels. It is very lucky that the English are standing fast. I shall hammer them with my artillery, charge them with my cavalry to make them show themselves, and, when I am quite sure where the actual English are, I shall go straight at them with my Old Guard.'[1] Some seven hours earlier Wellington, at his headquarters in the village of Waterloo, had received the information he eagerly awaited: an assurance from Blücher that at least one Prussian corps would march to his assistance in the course of the day. The components were falling into place for an epic encounter.

Wellington's orders for the defence of the position at Mont St. Jean had been disseminated late on the 17th June. They demonstrated a clear expectation that Napoleon would try and turn the allied right flank and confidence of an early manifestation of Prussian support on the allied left. To that end, 17,000 men, including Lieutenant General Sir Charles Colville's 4th Division, were sent 10 miles west to Hal and Tubize with orders to defend the position for as long as possible. Twenty-eight guns accompanied this force including Joseph Brome's Company but as George Unett's Company had not yet reached the field, Rettberg's Hanoverian Company (the second direct fire unit of the 4th Division) was retained with the main force. Thus Wellington's gun ratio at Mont St. Jean increased slightly to 2.2 guns per 1,000 men; it was the most favourable he had ever enjoyed but was still less than the 3.2 guns per 1,000 which Napoleon was able to field, despite sending 98 guns east with Grouchy.[2]

Early on the 18th, with the rain beginning to abate, Wellington continued to refine the deployment of his forces. Hougoumont was, to all intents and purposes, the centre of his position and his reserve was located to the rear of this point. He was committed to fighting a defensive battle until the Prussians arrived and, in the interim, he needed maximum flexibility to react to each of Napoleon's offensive manoeuvres. As it turned out, Napoleon had no intention of manoeuvring and the battle was actually fought in the confines of a 2-by-2 mile square with the Charleroi–Brussels road forming the central axis. Perpendicular to this axis was the Ohain road, which was sunken in places to various depths and was to play an important but not pivotal role in the proceedings. This road also formed the crest of a slope and was straddled by fields of tall crops as Captain Samuel Rudyard, the second in command of Lloyd's Company, recalled. 'Early on the morning of the 18th our position was taken on the very crest of the slope in front of our division: the Regiments were the 69th and the 33rd in our rear; the grain, I can't say whether wheat or barley, it was above our heads, but soon trodden down.'[3] Exactly how much influence Wellington had regarding the deployment of artillery is unclear. The field companies allocated to their respective divisions had all deployed in direct support with the exception of James Sinclair's and William Braun's companies, which were held in reserve. Also in reserve were the majority of horse artillery troops allocated to the cavalry. Early in the battle, Lord Uxbridge (commanding the cavalry) had given Frazer free rein to use these guns as he saw fit; an order which it is assumed would have been sanctioned by Wellington in the first instance but, as events transpired, may not have been.[4] Wellington's only other orders to Wood and Frazer appear to have been firstly, a restriction on counter-battery fire and secondly, instructions that the Gunners were to take shelter 'within the confines' of the infantry squares when the danger dictated and to return to their guns when it had abated. However, as we shall see, these orders were neither received nor acted upon by all the artillery commanders.

It appears from these arrangements that during the battle Frazer had greater influence than the CRA over the employment of the allied artillery. Certainly in the early stages Frazer deferred to Wood but as the battle developed it is clear that he made arrangements directly with Wellington himself. This can be seen from Frazer's first diary entry of the day:

> Lloyd's battery, forming part of the sixteen pieces placed for the defence of that part of our position, had, by some order of the Prince of Orange, been diverted to guard the point where our line was intersected by the pavé [main road] from

Genappe to Brussels. This weakened Alten: both points required strengthening; and by Wood's leave, Ross's Troop was ordered from the reserve to guard the pavé and I acquainted Alten that Lloyd would not be taken from him … I rejoined the Duke, and was rejoiced to hear that his Grace was determined not to lose the wood [Hougoumont] 300 yards in front of that part of the line, which was in reality our weakest point. I had very hastily, on the preceding day, galloped to this wood, seen its importance, and determined that the heavy-howitzer troop should be brought to this point.[5]

The move of Bull's (howitzer) Troop was instigated soon after hostilities commenced. For now, Ross's and Bean's troops were deployed to the area to cover the Hougoumont – La Haye Sainte gap, at much the same time that loud cheers and wild enthusiasm greeted Napoleon as he rode down the front of his massed formations to the south. The time was a little after 1100 hours; Napoleon's aspiration to commence proceedings at 0900 hours had been thwarted by the heavy rain. The ground was soaked and despite clear skies the loamy soil needed time to dry. The movement of troops was slowed and the progress of artillery carriages severely curtailed. Finally, at about 1130 hours, elements of the massed French ranks moved forward, opening the first of the six subsequent phases of this epic battle.[6]

General Charles-Claude Jacquinot's attempts at Frischermont were merely an attempt to get Wellington to weaken his centre but Jerome's attack on Hougoumont farm was executed with fortitude and purpose. It was clear that this farm, and outlying structures, were going to be pivotal in the day's events. The large walled smallholding was bordered by a 6-foot high stone walled garden which proved capable of withstanding round shot. Earlier in the day, Wellington had strengthened the four light companies in the farm with 300 Hanoverian riflemen and the Nassau Battalion from Saxe-Weimar's Brigade. Jerome's infantry advanced steadily towards the south-west of the enclosure, supported by two of Reille's batteries and two horse artillery batteries, which manoeuvred in support.

Jerome's supporting columns had not advanced far when the Duke of Wellington, with his staff, galloped up to the spot on which the Coldstream Guards were formed; and having directed his glass upon the French columns, the guns of Sandham's Foot Battery, attached to Cooke's Division, were ordered to the front. They instantly unlimbered and opened the cannonade from the Anglo-Allied position. The first discharge was from a howitzer shell of which burst over the head of a column moving towards the Hougoumont inclosures [sic]. The shots from the remaining guns in succession also took effect; and the Battery was soon in full play. It was immediately followed up by an equally well directed fire from Captain Cleeves's Foot Battery of the German legion in front of Alten's Division.[7]

At this juncture Frazer called Bull's Troop forward and they advanced 'handsomely' to the area behind the orchard; their appearance gave encouragement to the many guardsmen who were lying down taking shelter from the incoming artillery fire.

The Duke said, 'Colonel Frazer, you are going to do a deliberate thing; can you depend upon the force of your howitzers? Part of the wood is held by our troops, part by the enemy' and his Grace calmly explained what I already knew. I answered that I could perfectly depend upon the troop; and, after speaking to Major Bull and all his officers, and seeing that they, too, perfectly understood their orders, the troop commenced its fire, and in ten minutes the enemy were driven from the wood.[8]

This was a difficult mission, involving largely unobserved indirect fire, which was skilfully executed. The woods were purged of French infantry, with no friendly casualties, enabling the Guards and Hanoverian Jaegers to reoccupy the vacated ground out to the southern wood line. While this action was ongoing Frazer had ridden back to the area near Mont St. Jean farm and ordered Ramsay's and Mercer's Troops forward to positions east of the Nivelles road. He then readjusted Webber Smith's Troop to fire south down the road against Jerome's left flank and Pire's cavalry. On arrival at his new position, Mercer disparagingly noted that 'the object in bringing us here being to watch a formidable line of lancers drawn up opposite us, and threatening the right flank of our army'.[9] Mercer, one of the most inexperienced RA battery commanders in the battle, had already incurred Macdonald's wrath for having pre-empted his orders to deploy, the first of a number of insubordinate acts Mercer was to perform that day. While the battle for Hougoumont raged, Bull's Troop continued to fire shrapnel shells over the woods and into the French formations as they continued their attacks; Cairnes, directing the howitzers, was killed by a round shot at this stage of the battle. Jerome had called up Jean-Louis Soye's Brigade and it was at this point that the French penetrated the inner farm courtyard, gaining a temporary lodgement through the north gate before being driven back. In the process of this attack, many of the tirailleurs on the periphery engaged Webber Smith's Troop forcing it to retire a short distance up the road. Foy's Division then joined the battle for the farm complex, prompting Wellington to feed more of Major General Peregrine Maitland's Guards to support the defence but as the smoke increased, visibility decreased and the conflict intensified, blurring friend and foe. As it became gradually more difficult for the allied guns to remain involved in the immediate contest for the buildings, they began to lift their fire and concentrate their efforts against Foy's infantry that had started to emerge from the ground to the east of the enclosure.

Watching at a distance and suffering from incoming artillery, Mercer decided, contrary to Wellington's direct order, to try to silence the French battery.

About this time, being impatient of standing idle, and annoyed by the batteries on the Nivelles road, I ventured to commit a folly, for which I should have paid dearly had our Duke chanced to be in our part of the field. I ventured to disobey orders, and open a slow deliberate fire at the battery, thinking with my 9-pounders soon to silence his 4-pounders. My astonishment was great, however, when our first gun was responded to by at least half a dozen gentlemen of very superior calibre, whose presence I had not even suspected, and whose superiority we immediately recognised by their rushing noise and long reach, for they flew far beyond us. I instantly saw my folly, and ceased firing, and they did the same – the 4 pounders alone continuing the cannonade as before.[10]

The attacks on Hougoumont had not been well orchestrated but they had bought time for the French to complete extensive preparations for their main attack. Given the importance of Hougoumont, to both defender and attacker, desperate endeavours to hold and capture the farm were destined to continue. To the south Marshal Ney, who had been designated as the commander for the main attack, sent word a few minutes before 1300 hours to Napoleon that all was ready. The second phase of the battle was about to commence. Military music filled the air and wafted towards the allied lines; many tricolours and military standards coloured the scene, contrasting with the light brown corn carpet on which the massed French formations paraded. Napoleon began his inspection, riding the length of the lines to rapturous acclaim. The massed infantry attacks were, predictably, to be preceded by a heavy artillery

16. The Battle of Waterloo – Situation at 1100–1130 Hours, 18th June 1815

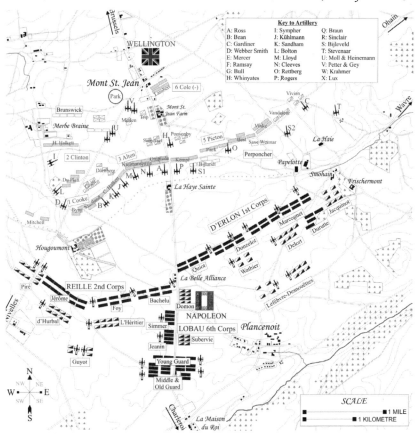

bombardment. On the hill slightly east of La Belle Alliance, 80 guns had been hauled into place, forming a Grand Battery. This incorporated 24 of Napoleon's beloved 12-pounders, affectionately branded by the French gunners as the 'Emperor's Daughters'. At about 1315 hours all the guns began to ply their deadly trade against the allied targets on the Ohain road, between La Haye Sainte and Papelotte, a mere 500 yards distant. It was about this time that news of the Prussians intentions and whereabouts were disclosed to Napoleon by a captured Prussian hussar. Immediate orders were sent to Grouchy, instructing him to close with all speed on the main French Army but, for now, there were more immediate matters to take in hand.

Napoleon's attack formation had shifted the dynamics of the battlefield; the centre was no longer Hougoumont but La Haye Sainte and the central axis now the Brussels road. Facing the Grand Battery on the allied left were Picton's 5th Division and Baron Henri-Georges de Perponcher's 2nd Dutch Division, with Vivian's and Vandeleur's cavalry brigades providing flank protection. Major General William Frederik van Bijlandt's Dutch Brigade, on the exposed southern face, had been ordered to withdraw behind the ridge at about 1230 hours so all the infantry were north of the Ohain road and, if not in the classic Wellington 'rear slope posture', were able to solicit some relief from direct artillery fire by lying down – and this they were instructed to do. However, some of the direct support artillery companies remained exposed and it has been suggested that some of these guns were deployed in the sunken lane for protection but no definitive evidence exists to confirm this.[11] Rettberg recalled that he had 'the most beautiful position that one could wish for artillery ... I stood about 8–10 feet higher than the [Ohain] road. Immediately on the other side of the road the terrain ran gently down towards the enemy. I had arranged to cut down the hedge in the morning to have a view.'[12] Ross, located behind La Haye Sainte, with two guns (under Lieutenant James Day and Lieutenant Phipps Onslow) to the left of the main road behind the sandpit and the balance of the troop on the right of the road, recalled that 'the men serving the four guns in front of the hollow-way retired into it or endeavoured to shelter themselves under the guns'. He goes on to mention that the 'hollow-way was partly blocked up by the wounded horse and limbers of the troop' and this perhaps provides the most accurate indication that the sunken road provided protection for men, horses and artillery equipment but that guns were not actually deployed along the length.[13]

The effect of the massed French guns was quickly felt. Ross had three guns disabled within minutes and the troop sergeant recorded that all of Corporal Armstrong's eight gun horses were killed at the first 'onset of battle'.[14] The barrage lasted about 40 minutes before Drouet's and Reille's tirailleurs began to close with the allied skirmishers and the massed French columns followed in their wake. As the front ranks of Drouet's formations came level with the French gun line, there was a pause while the guns were discharged and batteries reported 'gun's empty'; the infantry completed last minute adjustments before the order was given to advance. They emerged through the remnants of the gun smoke and began to negotiate the last 600–700 yards to the allied lines. Some, but not all, of the massed French guns were able to continue providing fire support once the dense formations reached the lower ground. The French advance took a full 20 minutes and throughout this time the allied artillery mercilessly pounded the exposed and tightly packed formations, first with solid shot, then grape and finally, at a range of 50 yards or less, with canister. The French columns reached the summit and in places infantry closed on infantry, in clashes of bayonet, but for the most part the two sides stood off a short distance and poured deadly fire into their opponents. The Gunners were caught up in this infantry duel and Rogers recalled that his guns fired 'as long as it was possible to continue it' and 'on the enemy coming into close contact with us, by the infantry of the [5th] Division passing between the guns, and receiving them at the point of their bayonets'.[15] One of Rogers's sergeants panicked and spiked his gun and there is some evidence that a quantity of guns were temporarily abandoned at this stage.[16]

The crisis in front of the 5th Division was checked by Picton's orders to Kempt and Pack to move their brigades forward and 'arrest the torrent'. Picton was killed, at this moment of emblematic leadership, by a French musket ball as he drove his Peninsular veterans forward and the situation along the line lay in the balance. With French cuirassiers menacing the centre and right of the allied line the situation demanded a defining moment. It came in the form of a combined charge by the British Union and Household heavy cavalry brigades. Somerset, commanding the latter, swept through the infantry squares of the 3rd Division and smashed into the French cavalry while, to their left, Ponsonby's Union Brigade drove into the massed ranks of French infantry which had just forced the Ohain road and sensed victory. The British cavalry swept all before them but, as had happened all too often with British cavalry charges of the era, 'no sound of voice or trumpet could make the men stop'. The Union Brigade lost all discipline and continued up to the line of the Grand Battery where they sabred many gunners but did not spike a single gun. Whinyates was ordered forward to support the cavalry charge:

> I was in front of my troop when I observed a stir amongst the cavalry ... I suddenly received a communication that the cavalry was going to advance, and that I was to move forward ... The cavalry in all probability had the start, having been prepared before I received my order, and they were certainly across the *chemin creux* before us, as a hollow road with two banks and two hedges would require a little examination and consideration where and how to pass it with guns, and the greatest care to avoid accidents. At this moment, however, Colonel Macdonald of the horse artillery came up, and ordered me to leave my guns and advance with the rocket sections, which I did, down the slope in front of the position until the ground on the French side gave a more favourable chance of effectual rocket practice.[17]

The troop had left two men on each of the guns while the balance, on horseback, moved forward initially to a position just past the road and then, a few minutes later once the French had been pushed back, down the hill to a more suitable launch site. The rockets were fired from the ground, in 'old Indian style', with a total of 52 projectiles being discharged. The results were unclear.

When halted and brought into action, they dismounted from their horses to fire ground rockets, that is rockets not laid at angles of elevation, but rockets that ricocheted along the ground. There were crops of high standing grain in front of the

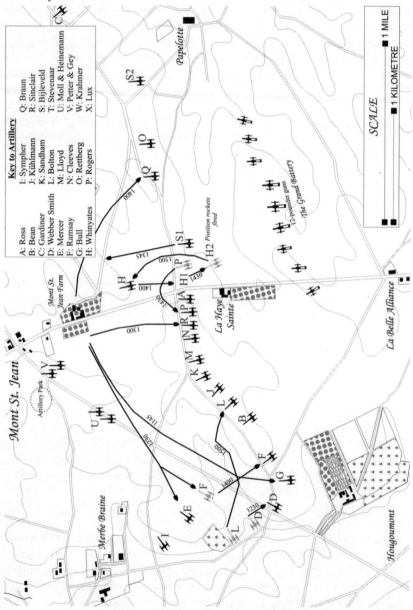

17. The Battle of Waterloo ~ Artillery Moves 1130–1500 Hours, 18th June 1815

Key to Artillery

A: Ross
B: Bean
C: Gardiner
D: Webber Smith
E: Mercer
F: Ramsay
G: Bull
H: Whinyates
I: Sympher
J: Kühlmann
K: Sandham
L: Bolton
M: Lloyd
N: Cleeves
O: Rettberg
P: Rogers
Q: Braun
R: Sinclair
S: Bijleveld
T: Stevenaar
U: Moll & Heinemann
V: Petter & Gey
W: Krahmer
X: Lux

rocket sections when the men dismounted, which screened all objects in front, and the rockets were fired through them in the direction of the enemy's troops in position.[18]

The charge of the British heavy cavalry had been a spectacular success but the subsequent lack of control had extracted a heavy toll on their numbers and ensuing effectiveness. With the French in full flight across the frontage and the French cavalry counter-charge confined to the ground between the Grand Battery and the Ohain road, the opportunity to reorganise the defences along the allied line was seized upon. As early as 1400 hours, Frazer had moved Ramsay to a position overlooking the ground between Hougoumont and La Haye Sainte. As Ramsay's Troop began to unlimber, Bull's Troop, which was by now badly cut up, was sent by Frazer to the artillery park at the rear to refit and repair damaged equipment and carriages. At about 1500 hours Captain Samuel Bolton was also ordered to move his guns from the right and to deploy in front of Colin Halkett's Brigade, with Bean to his right and Captain Charles Freeman Sandham to his left. Finally, Rogers's guns were moved from their position, just left of centre, to just right of centre in between Ross's Troop and Sinclair's 9-pounders. Whinyates's men, having fired off their rockets, returned to their guns north of the road. During this lull a number of ammunition limbers were sent to the rear to replenish. This was contrary to the usual practice of supply being provided from the rear and was most likely instigated because of the congestion on the battlefield; it was, however, to have consequences a little while later and may well have contributed to Wellington's perception of Gunners 'quitting the field'. Wellington had reorganised the infantry by moving Pack's Brigade forward to replace that of Bijlandt, and Lambert's Brigade was moved up from Mont St. Jean to support the 5th Division, now under Kempt's command. The formations on the far right were readjusted to a combination of front line and reserve tasks behind Hougoumont (hence the moves of Ramsay and Bolton) and more riflemen were detached to support the defence of the farm at La Haye Sainte. All of these readjustments were complete by about 1515.

At about this time the French launched another, more determined attack against La Haye Sainte, which was beaten back by the gallant KGL defenders but ammunition was running low. Concurrently, more French batteries were being deployed on both sides of the Brussels road, including three more batteries of the 'Emperor's Daughters' from the Guard Artillery. The batteries opened, not in one mass barrage, but sporadically along the line. They could now reach the entire length of the allied line from behind Hougoumont to the area around Papelotte. Within minutes their effect was beginning to tell, both physically and mentally, on Wellington's men. At about 1550 hours Wellington ordered the more exposed infantry to withdraw behind the ridge; it was the cue for the commencement of the third phase of the battle. Ney, misreading the signs as an indicator of a general retreat by the allies, seized the moment and led 5,000 cavalry to the ground west of the Brussels road to form up for a massed charge. Wellington and his staff watched the French with curiosity, and then incredulity, as it became clear that a massive unsupported cavalry charge was about to be delivered through the Hougoumont–La Haye Sainte gap against infantry in squares, supported by ten batteries of artillery and ample cavalry. Frazer recalled that 'by this time the infantry were entirely formed into squares, the cavalry generally in solid columns, the crest of our position crowned with artillery'.[19] Wellington ordered Frazer to bring up all the reserve horse artillery but, with the reserve long since spent, he readjusted the positions of Bull's and Mercer's troops and they moved into their new locations 'with an alacrity and rapidity most admirable'.[20] This prompted Wellington to remark, 'Ah! That's the way I like to see horse-artillery move'.[21]

> ... Sir Augustus Frazer galloped up, crying out, 'Left limber up, and as fast as you can.' The words were scarcely uttered when my gallant troop stood as desired in column of subdivisions, left in front, pointing towards the main ridge. 'At a gallop, March!' and away we flew, as steadily and compactly as if at a review. I rode with Frazer, whose face was as black as a chimney-sweep's from the smoke, and the jacket sleeve of his right arm torn open by a musket-ball or case-shot, which had merely grazed his flesh. As we went along he told me that the enemy had assembled an enormous mass of heavy cavalry in front of the point to which he was leading us ... and that in all probability we should immediately be charged on gaining our position. 'The Duke's orders, however, are positive', he added, 'that in the event of their persevering and charging home, you do not expose your men, but retire with them into the adjacent squares of the infantry'.[22]

Despite being supported by the French artillery batteries in range, the massed cavalry formations had to squeeze through a gap less than half a mile wide. They were engaged from the outset of their advance by 11 allied batteries, many of which could engage the lines of horsemen in enfilade. Frazer recalled that 'the French cavalry, advancing with intrepidity unparalleled, attacked at once the right and centre of our position, their advance protected by a cannonade more violent than ever'.[23] Swabey remembered that 'the charges in the centre were the most obstinate the French ever made on us ... the guns were repeatedly passed through by the Cuirassiers of the Guard ... we fell back partially several times and never was ground I believe so contested'.[24] Wellington's order for the Gunners to leave their guns and fall back on the security of the infantry squares appeared straightforward enough, yet it is evident that not all artillery commanders had been properly briefed. Some Gunners left their guns and sought sanctuary within the squares, others moved to the lee of the squares and a few even moved some or all their guns within the squares; some left the field completely, with or without their guns, and others executed a combination of these actions.

For example, some of Andrew Cleeves's guns were both withdrawn to the rear, some into squares, while others were left on their platforms when there was no time or the wherewithal to move them. Sergeant Christian Denke, who was commanding the howitzer in Cleeves's Company, had failed to notice the French cavalry encroaching on his left and was unable to 'limber up' in time, so he fired off the loaded round and sought sanctuary under the gun. It was recorded that Driver Eickmann, Denke's limber driver, 'on subsequent attacks ... was equally prompt in bringing the limber up and the gun was able to be withdrawn'.[25] In the same document, Driver Andrew Henke is credited with being 'alert and quick to bring his limber up to the gun so that this alone of the six in the Battery was able to be taken into the squares behind'.[26] Edmund Walcott was the second captain in Webber Smith's Troop:

> That magnificent order which directed artillerymen, when from the closeness of the enemy they could no longer fire canister, to leave their guns in position and fall back in a line with the squares did not reach my ears, and I continued directing a gun of the troop ...[27]

Mercer cannot claim to have not received the order but he elected to remain with his guns and not seek refuge in the squares of the Brunswick infantry, for very different reasons.

> The Brunswickers were falling fast – the shot every moment making great gaps in their squares, which the officers and sergeants were actively employed in filling up by pushing their men together, and sometimes thumping them ere they could make them move. These were the very boys whom I had but yesterday seen throwing away their arms, and fleeing, panic-stricken, from the very sound of our horses' feet. To-day they fled not bodily, to be sure, but spiritually, for their senses seemed to have left them ... To have sought refuge amongst men in such a state were madness – the very moment our men ran from their guns, I was convinced, would be the signal for their disbanding. We had better, then, fall at our posts than in such a situation ... I resolved to say nothing about the Duke's order, and to take our chance – a resolve that was strengthened by the effect of the remaining as they rapidly succeeded in coming into action, making terrible slaughter, and in an instant covering the ground with men and horses ... Many facing about and trying to force their way through the body of the column, that part next to us became a complete mob, into which we kept a steady fire of case-shot from our six pieces. The effect is hardly conceivable, and to paint this scene of slaughter and confusion impossible.
>
> The column now once more mounted the plateau ... on they came in compact squadrons, one behind the other, so numerous that those of the rear were still below the brow when the head of the column was but at some sixty or seventy yards from our guns. Their pace was a slow but steady trot. None of your furious galloping charges was this, but a deliberate advance, at a deliberate pace, as the men resolved to carry their point ... On our part was equal deliberation. Everyman stood steadily at his post, the guns ready, loaded with a round shot first and a [spherical] case over it; the tubes were in the vents; the port-fires glared and sputtered behind the wheels; and my word alone was wanting to hurl destruction on that goodly show of gallant men and noble horses ... 'Fire!' The effect was terrible. Nearly the whole leading rank fell at once; and the round-shot, penetrating the column, carried confusion throughout its extent. The ground, already encumbered with victims of the first struggle, now became almost impassable ... The discharge of every gun was followed by the fall of men and horses like that of grass before the mower's scythe.[28]

Both Wellington and Wood visited Mercer's Troop at various times during the closing stages of this phase of the battle and neither could have failed to notice the physical carnage yards from 'G' Troop's muzzles. In view of Mercer's reasoning for staying with his guns, the fact that it was a decision made in the heat of battle and the undeniably successful upshot, it is hard to comprehend the subsequent censure from the chain of command.

Strangely, there does not appear to have been an officially accepted and practised procedure for the withdrawal of guns or Gunners into infantry squares; instead it depended on the tactical situation, the ground and the commanders' direction and preferences. However, why Wellington's order was not clarified and properly disseminated remains unclear; the failure for this must lie with the artillery chain of command that was convoluted with many layers. Wood retained overall command of the British and German artillery but not that of the Dutch–Belgian, which remained in direct support of their respective divisions. Frazer was acting as the commander of the horse artillery and, as we have seen, had a pivotal role. Major Percy Drummond had been appointed as commander of the artillery reserve but quite what his role was is open to debate. Curiously, Frazer appointed Macdonald to be the artillery commander for the cavalry corps. As this consisted of all but two of the horse artillery troops, the breakdown of responsibility between Frazer and Macdonald was an added confusion, a point borne out by the uncertainty exhibited during the move of the cavalry and horse artillery on the 15th and 16th June and a frequent complaint of Mercer in his journal. Each infantry division (except the 6th) had an artillery field officer appointed, one assumes, to coordinate the two artillery brigades allocated in direct support to that division. These officers were as follows: Lieutenant Colonel Stephen Adye to the 1st Division; Lieutenant Colonel Charles Gold to the 2nd Division; Lieutenant Colonel John Williamson to the 3rd Division; Lieutenant Colonel John Hawker to the 4th Division and Major Henry Heise KGA, to the 5th Division. Cairnes had already questioned the role of these officers following the battle of Vitoria and remained convinced that their appointment served to confuse rather than simplify command and control. Cairnes has a point, but the span of command from CRA direct to battery commander would equally have been too broad for the Waterloo artillery organisation. It would seem that a compromise, consisting of individual commanders for the horse artillery, field artillery and reserve, might have been more practicable. What is evident, however, is that the artillery chain of command in place for the Waterloo campaign did not work well.

The third phase of the Battle commenced at 1600 hours and lasted two hours, with repeated attempts by the massed French cavalry to penetrate the infantry squares. At one stage it is estimated that 10,000 French sabres were in action but, crucially, they were not supported by infantry and artillery effectiveness was severely curtailed by the reverse slope positions. The infantry squares and gun positions were charged repeatedly; Rudyard recalled:

The *cuirassiers* and cavalry might have charged through the battery as often as six or seven times, driving us into the squares, under our guns, wagons, some defending themselves. In general, a squadron or two came up the slope on our immediate front, and on their moving off at the appearance of our cavalry charging, we took advantage to send destruction after them, and when advancing on our fire I have seen four or five men and horses piled upon each other like cards, the men not having been displaced from the saddle, the effect of canister.[29]

Sympher's guns were ordered to move and join the line at about 1700 hours, at about the same time that Sinclair's guns returned from the rear having been re-supplied with ammunition.[30] It is not clear who gave permission for Sinclair to move to the rear or who subsequently redirected the battery to their new position further to the left. It would also appear that they temporarily lost a gun when they withdrew and recovered the piece once they were in their new position. In addition to Sinclair's rearward movement, there is clear evidence in Schwertfeger's account that both of the 1st Division's direct support batteries also quit the field.

> During this time a strong heavy calibre battery deployed about 1,200 paces from our position and fired at us but we did not return fire because of Wellington's earlier order. Later that afternoon we realised that the enemy, some distance from us, was making a heavy attack on the left of our lines but we did not realise how successful this attack was because the progress was masked by the terrain; and afterwards, we realised that our lines were broken and that the enemy cavalry had got in behind unseen by us, and they fell unexpectedly on our left flank and forced us (the two artillery batteries under Lieutenant Colonel Adye) to retreat. After some distance I found some space where other artillery units had arrived along with personnel and carts and here it was possible to reorganise but this took some time. During this time, Lieutenant Colonel Adye arrived with the English battery which had been driven even further back and they now joined us at our position and because that battery had not fired as much as us on the 16th, they had to give us some ammunition. After this, both batteries, under Lieutenant Colonel Adye, as well as all the other artillery which had arrived in the same area, returned to their original positions and re-entered the battle. When they arrived back to the battle line the battle had turned in our favour and the French were retreating.[31]

This is fairly conclusive evidence that three allied artillery batteries quit the field at some stage during the cavalry charges. Wellington undoubtedly would have witnessed this. He would also have witnessed the French cavalry in possession of many of the allied guns that had been left, as directed, on their platforms. Incredibly the French cavalry made little attempt to drag these guns back to their lines. Some of the guns had their near side wheels removed to hinder such exploitation but more perplexing was that fact that none of the guns was spiked *in situ*. This has never been satisfactorily explained and the consequences of this failure seldom fully appreciated. The loss of ten complete batteries, even at this late stage with the Prussians knocking at the door, would have made a critical difference to the next two phases and perhaps even changed the outcome of the battle. There was, after all, plenty of fighting left to be done after the last of the French cavalry charges was repulsed.

Gardiner was stationed with his troop of 6-pounders on the far left of the allied position in support of Vandeleur's and Vivian's light cavalry brigades. It had been a frustrating day for Gardiner who was impatient for involvement. He had ordered

18. The Battle of Waterloo ~ Artillery Moves 1500–2100 Hours,
    18th June 1815

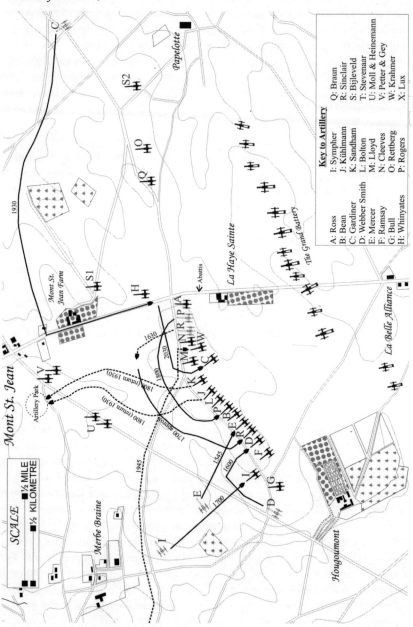

two guns forward to support Ponsonby's Union Brigade in their charge at about 1415 hours but:

> ... the ground, however, was so saturated with the rain and so little capable of bearing the horses without sinking up to their girths nearly, that we had some trouble in bringing the guns into action at all; but scarcely had we opened fire, when a shell from the great French battery, which from its elevated position and large calibre of guns, directed an accurate fire and blew up, by passing through the ammunition boxes of one of the two guns.[32]

The explosion solicited a 'general hurrah' from the delighted French gunners and Gardiner was forced to withdraw in humiliation. The troop's frustrations were to continue, however, as the range of their 6-pounders was insufficient to provide any effective fire support to Saxe-Weimer's infantry in and around the farms of Papelotte and Smohain as these were attacked throughout the afternoon by General Pierre-François Durutte's Division.

Ingilby, with Gardiner's Troop, recalled that 'at about between four and five o'clock in the evening the Prussians did appear, and after some delay they formed and advanced briskly to attack the French right in front of Papelotte'.[33] Some of the French guns on the right of Grand Battery were redirected accordingly. At much the same time, Rettberg had also seen large numbers of French troops being moved towards Plancenoit to counter the arrival of large numbers of Prussian soldiers.[34] However, any hopes that the arrival of the Prussians would bring a rapid change to proceedings in the centre were quickly dispelled as Drouet's infantry divisions again advanced against the farm at La Haye Sainte. It was about 1815 hours and the fourth phase of the battle had commenced.

Major Georg Baring, the commander of the 2nd Light Battalion of the KGL, was entrusted with the defence of La Haye Sainte farm. He had been reinforced by three companies from the 1st Battalion, a company from the 5th Battalion and some Nassauers but they were perilously short of ammunition despite repeated requests for re-supply. French infantry, in great strength and supported by artillery, forced themselves right up to the lower orchard. Allied artillery support was difficult as many of the guns were out of effective range or could not see the target area because of a dip in the ground and the large amounts of smoke obscuration. The order was passed to Captain Whinyates to try to provide assistance and he detached Dansey with two guns.

> When I was detached from the Troop, I had 2 guns as well as rockets; and I went to the front along the high road to look for a place, or rather to form an opinion as to where it would be best to come into action, and I went near the abattis and the fire of Musquetry was very hot, and I resolved not to attempt to bring the guns up. I went back and ordered the men to get their rockets, and follow me on foot with them, Lt. Wright took a rocket under his arm and we all went to the front to the abattis and stuck the rockets among the bushes of it, the moment we began firing I was wounded by a Musquet ball and Lt. Wright had some buttons

knocked off his pocket, we were the only persons of the party mounted and we were both hit, this makes me think the more that the guns could not have been brought up.[35]

In fact, La Haye Sainte had already fallen by the time Dansey and his Gunners had fired off their rockets. With the farm in French hands, and the key to Wellington's centre lost, Ross was forced to move his troop to the right, which he completed by just after 1900 hours. At the same time that Drouet had commenced his attack on La Haye Sainte, Reille had renewed his efforts to capture Hougoumont. Bull's Troop were again firing shrapnel to disrupt the French attacks and it was during this period that Ramsay, who was positioned to Bull's left and had a better view of the target area, reported that 'some of the shells opened a perfect lane' through the French columns.[36] Ramsay also provided some correction to maximise the effect of the shells, in a rare example of observed indirect fire. The battle for Hougoumont continued but with the loss of La Haye Sainte, the French began to press in the centre and moved their guns to within 250 yards of the allied lines. It was now 1900 hours, the battle for Plancenoit was ebbing and flowing and Napoleon was forced to deploy elements of the Old Guard to recapture the village. He could see that Durutte was in control around Papelotte and decided that the supreme moment was at hand. At the head of eight battalions of the Old and Middle Guard, Napoleon ordered an attack across the frontage with the remnants of Reille's and Drouet's corps in support. In direct support to the Guard was a horse artillery battery under the command of Lieutenant Colonel Duchand. He had divided his eight guns into four two-gun sections. The penultimate phase of the battle commenced; it was about 1930 hours.

Wellington moved his reserves in anticipation, recalling General David Hendrik Chassé's Dutch–Belgian Division from the far right and Vandeleur's and Vivian's cavalry brigades from the far left. Gardiner moved with the Hussars and noted that at 'about half past seven o'clock Sir H. Vivian made a circuit to his right and placed his brigade in line, about 20 paces in the rear of the infantry in front of Mont St. Jean, and thus formed in two lines, the whole steadily advanced to attack'.[37] In fact Gardiner's first thoughts were that they had been moved to cover the withdrawal of Wellington's army in the face of the invincible Guard and the initial clash gave credence to his assumption. Duchand's Guard horse artillery deployed within a hundred yards of the allied lines and began to cause considerable destruction; this was so effective that it only remains to speculate on the outcome had better use been made earlier in the battle of the 12 French horse artillery batteries on the field that day. Mercer noted that 'the rapidity and precision' of a battery which had deployed a few hundred yards to his flank was 'quite appalling' and he fully expected the troop to be annihilated.[38] Elements of the Guard reached the muzzles of Lloyd's and Cleeves's guns and for a time overran their positions; Lloyd was killed by a sword thrust delivered by an officer of the Guard and Lieutenant William Harvey lost his arm.

With the arrival of Chassé's Division, his integral guns, under the command of Captain Karl Krahmer, were quickly brought into action on Lloyd's right.[39] There were now a total of 13 allied batteries engaged in the fight; they were exhausted and their ammunition low, but their collective fire was undoubtedly having an effect on the advancing Guard infantry. Lieutenant William Sharpin was deployed with Bolton's Company, which had recently been moved further to the right.

> A few minutes before the French Imperial Guards made their appearance the Duke of Wellington rode up to our battery and hastily asked who commanded it; I replied that Bolton did, but that he was just killed, and that it was then under Napier. His Grace then said, 'Tell him to keep a look to his left, for the French will soon be with him,' and then rode off. I had scarcely communicated the Duke's message when we saw the French bonnets just above the high corn, and within forty or fifty yards of our guns. I believe they were in close columns of grand divisions, and upon reaching the crest of our position they attempted to deploy into line, but the destructive fire of our guns loaded with canister shot, and the well-directed volleys from the infantry, prevented their regular formation. They remained under this fire for about ten minutes, advancing a little, but finding it impossible to force our position they gave way, and went to the right about, upon which the Duke ordered a general charge to be made, and in a moment our infantry and the French were so mixed together that an end was put to our firing for the day.[40]

With their momentum stalled, the Guard hesitated, and then suddenly and unexpectedly they were assailed from the flank by John Colborne's battalion which he wheeled left. Colborne's intention was to make the invincible French troops 'feel our fire'; it was a decisive action, and the Guard wavered and then broke. As Maitland's and Brigadier General Frederick Adam's infantry advanced a number of batteries had to cease firing. Bean had already been killed in action and with William Webber badly wounded, command of the troop's guns fell to Lieutenant John Maunsell, who recorded that 'the troop was prevented firing on the retiring mass as they passed through the gap by a battalion of, I believe, the Guards forming line in front of our guns'.[41] Norman Ramsay had also been killed in action by this stage and Lieutenant Philip Sandilands, now commanding the troop, noted that 'it then ceased, as the Duke of Wellington, who had brought up three infantry regiments from the right, deployed on the flank of the French columns, and shut them out from our view'.[42] Nevertheless, there were plenty of guns to their left that were able to continue firing at the retreating Imperial Guard. Wellington, rising in his saddle, took off his cocked hat and waved it above his head indicating a general advance.

The battle was won, but there was still much to do. The withdrawal of the Imperial Guard was a controlled retreat rather than an ungraceful rout; nevertheless the allied artillery was so decimated that very few batteries were able to assist the infantry and cavalry in their pursuit of the French. Mercer recalled, rather dispiritedly, that:

> On looking round I found we were almost alone. Cavalry and infantry had all moved forward, and only a few guns here and there were to be seen on the position. A little to our right were the remains of Maj M'Donald's ['H'] troop under

Lieutenant Sandilands, which had suffered much, but nothing like us. We were congratulating ourselves on the happy results of the day when an aide-de-camp rode up, crying '*Forward, Sir! – forward! It is of the utmost importance that this movement should be supported by artillery!*' at the same time waving his hat much in the manner of a huntsman laying on his dogs. I smiled at his energy, and, pointing to the remains of my poor troop, quietly asked, '*How, Sir?*' A glance was sufficient to show him the impossibility and away he went.[43]

Ramsay's and Bull's troops were also unable to join the advance and, inexplicably, Webber Smith and Whinyates do not appear to have been ordered to assist. Gardiner's, Bean's and half of Ross's troops thus advanced and they were supported by some of Rogers's guns under the command of Lieutenant George Maule who 'accompanied with two guns the cavalry along a country road diagonally in front of the original, or grand position, coming into action several times on the retreating French'.[44] Gardiner's Troop was still fresh and, having missed much of the day's action, was keen to make its mark. 'Sir Robert Gardiner brought his guns to fire upon the fugitive crowd instantly, and from that period acted independently from [Vivian's] brigade of cavalry, alternately advancing rapidly and halting to fire.'[45] As the light faded it was virtually impossible for the guns to negotiate over the terrain, which was littered with dead and wounded bodies of men and animals, and the detritus of battle.

To the east, before the Imperial Guard commenced their advance, the Prussians had already arrived in force. Their appearance, without doubt, changed the dynamics of the battle. Vivian, commanding his cavalry on the allied far left, certainly thought so, admitting that the Prussian arrival on the right and rear of Napoleon 'gave us the victory at Waterloo'. Rettberg recollected quite joyously that:

In the evening of this for me quite unforgettable day, I was about 7 pm busy at my ammunition wagons ... and I was startled by an unknown bugle call and saw a great number of Prussian cavalry very close to the wood ... leading them was General Lieutenant von Ziethen [Commander 1st Prussian Corps] himself. He asked for the shortest way to the main road that runs along by La Haye Sainte. I rode after him and I showed him my joy that the Prussians came to our aid to which he replied that on his march on the flank of the French army he saw there was already some disquiet and he believed they would be soon retiring.[46]

The arrival of the Prussians from the flank, at a critical moment in the battle, was fraught with dangers. Unfamiliar with each other's equipment and uniforms the likelihood of fratricide was high. Mercer reported that at one stage a Prussian battery fired on his troop who responded in kind. However, there is something in this story which does not ring true as the Prussian artillery had not progressed far enough west by this time to enable their guns to be within range of allied batteries in the allied centre. Nevertheless, it does highlight the difficult nature of an unfamiliar ally conducting a passage of lines from a flank, in fading light and with no real coordinating instructions. At about 2100 hours Wellington met with Blücher at La

Belle Alliance; the two battle-weary but elated commanders shook hands and Wellington agreed that the Prussian Army alone should continue the chase and the band struck up 'God save the King'.

The magnitude of the victory was not immediately apparent but the scale of destruction would have been all too evident; there can be little doubt that the greatest killer on the field of battle that day was artillery.[47] Napoleon, who understood better than any other in his day how best to use this arm, had concentrated his guns to maximise their weight of fire on selected targets. The French enjoyed a superiority in numbers as well as weight and much has been written about 'The Emperor's Daughters' and the havoc they wreaked on the unfortunate infantry on the ridge at Mont St. Jean. Wellington, conversely, did not enjoy superiority in numbers or calibre and as much has been written about this paucity of artillery. Under Wellington's influence and direction, close support artillery was allotted to divisions, thereby reducing the flexibility to relocate those fire units to cover critical points during the battle. Yet, at Waterloo, the allied artillery did more for Wellington than at any other of his battles; furthermore, the tactical employment of the allied artillery was far superior to that used by the French.

Why and how was this so? In short it was because Wellington's defence was more effective than Napoleon's attacks. The French Grand Battery was located on the only suitable terrain and this restricted its fire to the eastern end of the Mont St. Jean ridge. Once Bijlandt's wretched brigade had been moved, Wellington's reverse slope tactics reduced the targets for these massed guns to engage. Individual allied guns were difficult to hit with round shot at ranges of 750 to 1,000 yards, fire control was basic and by word of mouth and the French lacked an effective shrapnel or spherical case round, which denied them the opportunity to engage the massed infantry targets, over the ridge at ranges of between 500 and 700 yards, in much the same way that Bull's howitzers had done so effectively over the farm complex at Hougoumont. Of course, the wet ground also reduced the effectiveness of round shot considerably; many of these rounds, which would otherwise have ricocheted at the top of the ridge and bounced with considerable inertia and destruction into the infantry on the far side, 'plugged' in the earth.[48] Nevertheless, Napoleon's decision not to manoeuvre his 12 French horse artillery batteries to support attacks was unimaginative. The considerable success enjoyed by Duchand's horse artillery battery, in support of the Imperial Guard at the end of the day, underlines this.

Conversely, at no stage during the battle were Wellington's guns neutralised. They were able to respond to every attack and were only found wanting in the final phase, the advance. The plan to keep horse artillery in reserve was, in fact, the concept originally envisaged by Frederick the Great. Wellington's artillery reserve was deployed rapidly at the commencement of the battle and, thus deployed, its mobility was denied (through attrition) during the latter stages of the battle. Nevertheless, throughout the battle, the allied artillery afforded greater fire support to the defence and defenders than that provided by their French counterparts in support of their cavalry and infantry attacks. Guns in defence tend to have greater utility and impact; they can employ an array of munitions descending in range and effectiveness as their attackers close. A higher rate of fire is also important under these circumstances and this is where lighter guns are an advantage; they are also able to be redeployed more rapidly to plug gaps or critical points in the defence. From Wood's ammunition expenditure returns we know that the 107 British and German guns and howitzers under his command fired a total of 5,251 round shot and 3,793 shrapnel, shells and canister (including grape) on the 18th alone.[49] There is no doubt that the French fired more round shot per gun but their expenditure of canister was negligible by comparison. Many of Kellerman's and Milhaud's dead cuirassiers were found with punctured breastplates in rows 50–100 yards from the infantry squares and it has been suggested that these musket holes were the work of the Brown Bess. 'I shall never forget the strange noise our bullets made against the breastplates ... I can only compare it ... to the noise of a violent hailstorm beating upon panes of glass.'[50] This is a dubious assumption, and is far more likely to have been the work of canister packed with musket balls and discharged at a far greater velocity.

Allied artillery losses were 15 per cent, a higher rate than any other battle of the period. Frazer noted that night, amidst the scene of carnage, that:

> I know not the losses of other corps, nor hardly of our own; but Bean, Cairnes and Ramsay, are among the horse artillery dead. Whinyates, Bull, Macdonald (junior), Webber [Smith], Strangways, Parker, Day, and, I am sorry to say, many others, including Robe, are among our wounded. Many of the troops are almost without officers, and almost all the guns were repeatedly in the enemy's hands ...[51]
>
> Are you not tired of battles? Are you not sick of the sanguinary description? Judge then what must have been the reality. The Duke himself said in the evening he had never seen such a battle, and hoped he never should again. To this hope we will all say: Amen.[52]

Notes

1. Girod de l'Ain, pp.278–79.
2. Based upon an allied army at Waterloo of 73,200 and 163 guns and a French army of 77,500 and 246 guns.
3. Siborne, SWL, p.229.
4. Frazer (ed. Sabine), p.556.
5. Ibid., pp.554–55.
6. These phases were used by Sir John Shaw-Kennedy in his published work in 1865, and provide a good basis for examination.
7. Siborne, SWC, pp.375–76.
8. Frazer (ed. Sabine), p.556.
9. Mercer, vol I, p.297.
10. Ibid., pp.301–02.
11. Hughes, HOF, p.77 provides the suggestion. Much has been written about the sunken road and some French (secondary) accounts have suggested that this was so deep as to became a 'ravine of death' to Ney's cavalry. However, while the evidence was largely

removed when the battlefield was 'landscaped' for the erection of the Lion Mound, it is fairly clear that the average depth was about 3 feet. This would not have been an obstacle to cavalry but it would have afforded some protection to the gunners. See Roberts, RNLG, p.86.

12. Glover, p.150.

13. Siborne, SWL, pp.221–22.

14. Whitehead, p.99.

15. Siborne, SWL, p.232.

16. Fortescue, vol. X, p.364 and Weller, p.101 make this assertion based on letters of Capt. Clark Kennedy of the 1st Royal Dragoons (who captured the Eagle of the 105e Ligne) – Siborne, SWL. pp.75 and 76. Both Fortescue and Weller allude to a general 'desertion' of guns and 'streaming to the rear' of the gunners, but I can find no evidence to support this in letters from any of the infantry officers in either Kempt's or Pack's brigades or from the artillery units themselves. It is true that Bijleveld's Battery, supporting Bijlandt's Brigade, fled with that formation but the gunners seem to have at least made an attempt to stand. Therefore, Weller's conclusion that this was the catalyst for Wellington's subsequent letter – see Chapter 24 – is flawed.

17. Siborne, SWL, pp.201–02.

18. Ibid., p.205.

19. Frazer (ed. Sabine) p.558.

20. Ibid.

21. Mercer vol. I, p.313.

22. Ibid., pp.309–10.

23. Frazer (ed. Sabine), p.558.

24. Swabey, in RAI. Proccedings, vol. XLII, pp.150–55. Leslie, Maj. J. H., *Centenary of the Battle of Waterloo*. Letter Swabey to his brother, dated 24th June 1815.

25. Vigors, *Voices from the Napoleonic Wars*, p.139.

26. Ibid., pp.138–39.

27. Siborne, SWL, p.192.

28. Mercer, vol. I, pp.312–21.

29. Siborne, SWL, p.230.

30. Ibid., p.235.

31. Schwertfeger, vol. II, pp.312–14.

32. Siborne, SWL. p.198.

33. Ingilby, Waterloo Diary, p.321.

34. Glover, p.150.

35. Siborne, SWL. Letter from Dansey to Siborne, dated 2nd February 1843.

36. Siborne, SWL, p.190. There is some disagreement as to exactly when this assistance took place but it seems logical that it was at this time rather than during the cavalry charges.

37. Ibid., p.199.

38. Mercer, vol. I, p.325.

39. The other battery appears to have got tied up with the ditches when traversing the ground and come into action somewhere near Mercer.

40. Siborne, SWL, pp.224–26.

41. Ibid., p.222.
42. Ibid., pp.220–21.
43. Mercer, vol. I, pp.330–31.
44. Siborne, SWL, pp.234–35.
45. Ibid., p.200.
46. Glover, p.150.
47. It is impossible to confirm or dispute this statement with any degree of certainty, but three excellent studies conducted by Hughes, Weller and Adkin all reach the same conclusion.
48. Adkin, in his excellent work, considers that 3,600 shots were fired during the Grand Battery's 30-minute bombardment and about half of these rounds 'plugged' on the south side of the ridge.
49. MD 2809. Mercer, vol. I, p.339 estimated that he fired 700 rounds per gun – which given the overall figures is far too high.
50. Fletcher, citing Gronow, *Reminiscences*, p.46.
51. Frazer (ed. Sabine), p.547.
52. Ibid., p.553.

CHAPTER 24

Wellington's Gunners

George Bean, Robert Cairnes, Norman Ramsay, Samuel Bolton and Lieutenant Charles Detlef von Schulzen (KGA) were also killed in action; while William Lloyd, Robert Manners and young William Robe all died within days of their wounds. Another 27 officers were wounded, some severely. A total of 62 British and German artillery NCOs and gunners were also killed in action and 228 wounded, some of whom succumbed to their wounds. Of the artillery horses, 356 were killed and 173 wounded or missing. Wellington's celebrated post-battle dispatch, penned on the 19th June, ran to many pages; the Gunners merited half a sentence and that they shared with the Royal Engineers.[1] Wellington was satisfied with their performance. Such faint praise far from satisfied many in the artillery and Frazer noted, rather irately, a few days later that 'The Duke *might* have mentioned the horse artillery, which really was of essential service'.[2] However, if the dispatch was a disappointment, the lack of recommendations for brevet rank was nothing short of shameful. Tom Scott, who had been the second in command of Rogers's Company, captured the feeling when the list was published.

> Rode towards Passy, met Williamson and went together to Sir G Wood's to make enquiries about the review. Sat there an hour and a half listening to the Knight's anecdotes. Went to the library, found the gazette containing the brevets for Waterloo – very few indeed – many grievously disappointed and with some reason as there are names among the few that were in England during the action and deserving characters left out such as Lloyd. It's cruel hard but justice is rarely an inhabitant of great men's breasts.[3]

Long before this list had been prepared Wood had fallen foul of Wellington for failing to organise the capture of the French guns. He wrote to Dickson four days after the battle. 'My sun is set and I shall ask leave to return to England having received the most severe reprimand before the whole Staff and servants for not bringing off the artillery taken by us … but more when we meet.'[4] It was a cruel and ill-handled snub by Wellington to a man who, following his performance prior to and during the battle, merited more respect than to receive a dressing down in front of junior officers and servants. In fact, Frazer had secured the guns during the night of the 20th June:

> On the evening of that day, the Duke being anxious that the captured guns should be parked, I offered, together with Colonel May, to our friend Sir George Wood to go and collect and park the captured guns and carriages during the night. It was feared that whilst our chief attention had been paid to re-equipping our troops and batteries, and sending them forward, and to getting up the battering-train and small arm and gun ammunition, the Prussians had run away with the trophies of our victory … but at last near Genappe we found 161 guns, with some hundreds of ammunition and other carriages. They were regularly parked with Prussian sentries. After much difficulty we found the Prussian officer, who was asleep under some straw, and evidently did not wish us to see him; however, after distinctly stating our errand, and showing our return of the guns taken by the British, (which return was made by Lieut.-Colonel Williamson of the artillery,) the officer assented readily to our receiving them, and we drew them and parked them near Waterloo.[5]

From Le Cateau on the 24th June, Wood wrote his full post-campaign and battle report to the secretary of the Board of Ordnance. To this dispatch he attached a private letter to MacLeod in which he concluded: 'I do assure you, I have not words to express the extreme good conduct of the Corps. All exerted themselves, both officers and men, and such a conflict of guns never was in the memory of man.'[6] In particular he singled out lieutenant colonels Frazer, Dickson, Hartmann and May, Captain Henry Baynes and lieutenants George Coles, William Bell and Henry Miëlmann. However, the praise heaped upon many officers of the artillery by the formation commanders is perhaps more telling. Hill furnished the highest approbation on Gold, Sympher and Captain Charles Napier. While Kempt spoke equally favourably of Rodgers and Heise, Grant could not speak highly enough of the conduct of Webber Smith and Walcott.

Following the battle, the French Army fled in disorder towards France closely pursued, in the first instance, by the Prussians. Wellington's army was not far behind. They met little resistance for the *Grande Armée* was broken. In Paris, on the 22nd June, Napoleon abdicated in favour of his son and vacated the Elysée Palace three days later, while 60,000 French troops concentrated to defend the nation's capital. The allied advance was rapid: Cambrai was captured on the 24th June by the British 4th Division, assisted in the process by Unett's Brigade of 9-pounders; Peronne and St. Quentin fell two days later. The Prussians, keen to take Paris ahead of Wellington's force, overextended their lines and were counter-attacked at Villers-Cotterêts but this was a temporary setback. Blücher crossed the River Seine at Saint-Germain on the 30th June and although he met stiff resistance, the defenders' determination was short lived; on the 3rd July, the defence collapsed when an early morning attack on the Prussians at Issy (les Moulineaux) was beaten back with ease. The Anglo-Prussian forces entered the city on the 7th July and Louis XVIII returned the following day amidst little rejoicing.

At the commencement of the pursuit, Wellington had given orders to Dickson to organise a siege train. Lieutenant Robert Ord was Dickson's Brigade Major and recalled that 'the Army was in march for Paris while Sir Alexander remained behind, by order of the Duke, to disembark a large Battering Train which lay in the canal on board *Schuyts* as well as to equip and land two 18 pdr. brigades of 4 guns each to accompany the Army'.[7] Ilbert's and Hutchesson's companies manned the 18-pounders while the companies of Michell and Carmichael, recently arrived from New Orleans, provided the manpower for the train. The train consisted of 70 pieces of ordnance including 40 24-pounders, six 8-inch howitzers, six 68-pounder carronades, nine 10-inch mortars and nine 8-inch mortars. So large in fact that two additional companies of artillery, Younghusband's and Munro's, were also seconded to provide manpower for the train. Five French fortresses were besieged and captured between the 14th July and the 16th August after which Dickson was tasked to bring forward a second siege train to tackle Givet but before the train was in place the governor capitulated on the 11th September.[8]

The British naval blockade thwarted Napoleon's attempt to escape by sea and ultimately he decided to throw himself at the mercy of British justice and boarded HMS *Bellerophon* on the 14th July. The war which had raged in Europe for over 20 years was finally at an end. A lengthy letter from Gardiner to MacLeod summed up the mood and the situation:

> In detailing its events we should not withhold our tribute of testimony and praise to the bravery and devoted conduct of the Emperor's Army. His own conduct was that of a man who sees his last hope of fortune falling from him. From every account I have heard, as well as from prisoners, as from people who profess to have been near him in the battle, he certainly headed two charges made by the Imperial Guard. It will always be in the recollection of his Army also that the Duke personally received and resisted these charges. He appeared to be ever in the midst of those who were supporting the most unequal and hazardous conflict.
>
> I believe no person was at first aware either of the extent of our victory or of the important consequences to which it would lead. These have since appeared in the events that followed the capitulation of the French Army and the capital. We may hope that the result may be secured and rendered lasting to the world. Much however remains yet to be done. Not a man of the allied armies should be withdrawn from France till Napoleon Bonaparte is secured beyond the possibility of returning to its Government.[9]

Consigned to the island of St. Helena, Napoleon was considered beyond the possibility of return and this story closes very much as it opened at the end of the 18th century, with extensive reductions across the armed forces. At the final curtain, Britain was burdened with the greatest national debt (£861,000,000) ever incurred by any nation. Hardly surprising therefore that the army was reduced from 190,767 men to 72,140 by 1823, a reduction of over 62 per cent; the artillery, including the driver corps, was reduced from 23,085 to 6,365 in 1823, a reduction of 72.4 per cent.[10] For the artillery two guiding principles were adopted when deciding how to achieve these savings: firstly, the less capable units were selected for reduction and secondly, where possible, units (either a battalion or company) were to be retained but their establishment size was to be reduced. By and large this second principle was followed resulting in the disbandment of five of the 13 horse artillery troops, one of the ten artillery battalions and 18 of the 100 field companies. However, each of the remaining troops and companies retained only sufficient manpower to man two to three guns. Sadly, the first principle was not adhered to as strictly as the second. Many good units were disbanded quickly with soldiers being discharged and pensioned only to be replaced over the coming months by the overseas companies who returned to Woolwich having adopted 'the habits and manners of an idle garrison where wine and spirits were cheap and abundant'.[11] Many were found unsuitable for service, while others were suffering from the deleterious and debilitating effects of their previous climate. Large numbers were necessarily discharged and the artillery was forced to recruit to find sufficient men to man the companies and assume their garrison duties. This unnecessary additional cost to the public purse was high and there can be little doubt that cashing-in on the peace dividend had, not for the first or last time, been bungled politically and bureaucratically.

From the perspective of the Duke of Wellington and his immediate post-war relationship with his Gunners, there is little to report. It was particularly ironic that, four years after Waterloo, Wellington assumed the post of MGO. Although a political appointment, it brought him face to face with Gunner business and politics, neither of which he understood or tolerated. When MacLeod (who was still DAG RA) visited Wellington in 1821 to discuss artillery drivers, Fitzroy Somerset was instructed by the MGO that 'It is very little use my seeing him, for he neither understands me nor I him.'[12] Indeed, there the matter of Wellington's relationship with his Gunners would have faded had a letter, written by the Duke a few months after Waterloo, not surfaced many years later. It caused a sensation in Gunner (and wider) circles, re-opening old wounds and re-igniting the debate. The letter, written in Paris on the 21st December 1815 to the then MGO, the Earl of Mulgrave, surfaced in 1872 when the second Duke published the *Supplementary Letters and Dispatches of the Duke of Wellington*.

Paris, 21st December, 1815.

My Dear Lord,

I received yesterday your Lordship's letter of the 10th, regarding the claim of the field officers of the Artillery present in the battle of Waterloo, to the same measure of favour granted to those in the battle of Vittoria.

In my opinion you have done quite right to refuse to grant this favour, and that you have founded your refusal on the best grounds. I cannot recommend that you should depart from the ground you have taken. To tell you the truth, I was not very well pleased with the Artillery in the battle of Waterloo.

The army was formed in squares immediately on the slope of the rising ground, on the summit of which the Artillery was placed, with orders not to engage with artillery, but to fire only when bodies of troops came under their fire. It was very difficult to get them to obey this order. The French cavalry charged, and were formed on the same ground with our Artillery in general, within a few yards of our guns. In some instances they were in actual possession of our guns. We could not expect the artillerymen to remain at their guns in such a case; but I had a right to expect that the officers and men of the Artillery would do as I did, and as all the staff did, that is, to take shelter in the squares of the Infantry till the French cavalry should be driven off the ground, either by our Cavalry or Infantry. But they did no such thing; they ran off the field entirely, taking with them limbers, ammunition, and everything: and when, in a few minutes, we had driven off the French cavalry, and had regained our ground and our guns, and could have made good use of our artillery, we had no artillerymen to fire them; and, in point of fact, I should have had no Artillery during the whole of the latter part of the action if I had not kept a reserve in the commencement.

Mind, my dear Lord, I do not mean to complain; but what I have above mentioned is a fact known to many; and it would not do to reward a corps under such circumstances. The Artillery, like others, behaved most gallantly; but when a misfortune of this kind has occurred, a corps must not be rewarded. It is on account of these little stories, which must come out, that I object to all the propositions to write what is called a history of the battle of Waterloo.

If it is to be a history, it must be the truth, and the whole truth, or it will do more harm than good, and will give as many false notions of what a battle is, as other romances of the same description have. But if a true history is written, what will become of the reputation of half of those who have acquired reputation, and who deserve it for their gallantry, but who, if their mistakes and casual misconduct were made public, would not be so well thought of? I am certain that if I were to enter into a critical discussion of everything that occurred from the 14th to the 19th June, I could show ample reasons for not entering deeply into these subjects.

The fact is, that the army that gained the battle of Waterloo was an entirely new one, with the exception of some of the old Spanish troops. Their inexperience occasioned the mistakes they committed, the rumours they circulated that all was destroyed, because they themselves ran away, and the mischief which ensued; but they behaved gallantly, and I am convinced, if the thing was to be done again, they would show what it was to have the experience of even one battle.
Believe me, &c.

WELLINGTON.
P.S. – I am very well pleased with the field officers for not liking to have their application referred to me. They know the reason I have not to recommend them for a favour.

There are few who would challenge Jac Weller's assertion that 'Wellington's artillery did more for him at Waterloo than any other of his battles'.[13] An article in the

United Services Journal in 1884 which examined the Waterloo campaign and battle concluded that:

> If we admit that during this arduous and terrible day the British infantry acted up to the right standard of soldiership [*sic*] which their long career of victory had established, it must be added that the artillery actually surpassed all expectation, high as, from their previous conduct, that expectation naturally was. In point of zeal and courage the officers and men of the three arms were of course fully upon a par; but the circumstances of the battle were favourable to the artillery; and certainly the skill, spirit, gallantry, and indefatigable exertion which they displayed almost surpasses belief.[14]

A detailed examination of the battle would certainly seem to support this assertion and it is therefore quite extraordinary that Wellington, who was at the heart of things throughout the day, could have viewed the situation so differently. Many historians, authors and military men have, over the last 140 years, dissected this letter and discredited much of the detail. In the most part, they have been correct in their analysis and individual conclusions, but on the whole most have considered the Royal Artillery companies and Royal Horse Artillery troops only and have not included an examination of the Hanoverian, King's German Legion and Dutch–Belgian batteries. This, as it turns out, is a crucial omission. As hurtful and unjust as this letter was of the artillery at Waterloo, it was not a mere criticism. It was the culmination of Wellington's many years of frustration at having to endure a separate chain of command; a questionable procurement policy (executed by the Board of Ordnance) that resulted in a paucity of equipment on the one hand or unsuitable equipment on the other; the appointment of incompatible CRAs; artillery officers playing both ends against the middle; and a justifiable claim that Gunner officers had a tendency to disregard or even countermand his direct orders. The letter, and the charges therein, require examination but the fact that the letter was not wholly uncharacteristic of Wellington's pen provides a suitable basis with which to bring this chronicle to a close.

Leaving aside, for the moment, the main thrust of the letter, Wellington makes four accusations against his Gunners. The first is that had *he* not kept a reserve at the commencement of the battle there would have been no artillery during the latter part of the battle. This is a very odd statement. We know that even before battle commenced, at 1130 hours, some of the troops/companies in reserve had already been deployed leaving four horse artillery troops (including Whinyates's Rocket Troop in a reverse slope position) and two artillery batteries, those of Sinclair and Braun, as the reserve. By 1400 hours all of these units had been deployed and *ipso facto* no reserve existed from that point on. Curiously, at the commencement of the cavalry attacks at about 1600 hours, Wellington ordered Frazer to bring up all the reserve horse artillery. It is an order which clearly demonstrated that Wellington was unaware that he had no artillery reserve. However, perhaps this tells us more about the problems within the Gunners' own battlefield chain of command rather than Wellington's recollection and state of mind on the issue. It is clear that the CRA was not used properly by Wellington as his primary artillery advisor and conduit; instead Frazer seems to have acted more in this capacity with Wellington, frequently giving direct orders during the battle to the individual artillery sub unit commanders.

The second point of issue concerns the order not to engage in counter-battery fire. We have Mercer's rather boastful account of events to confirm that indeed Wellington's direct order not to engage the French batteries was ignored. Moreover, there is also evidence that Sandham ignored the order and was witnessed in the act by Wellington who ordered that Sandham be placed under arrest.[15] This latter order was not acted upon but it indicates Wellington's determination to have his orders adhered to at all costs even at the questionable expense of removing a commander from his post in the heat of battle.

Furthermore, it sets the tone for the third accusation: that the Gunners failed to take shelter in the infantry squares during the French cavalry attacks and the connected fourth accusation that, in failing to so do, they 'ran off the field completely'. These are particularly damning indictments which merit thorough examination. Wellington's order was, in fact, confusing. Frazer is clear that the order was to take refuge 'within the squares', while Bloomfield (one of Wood's staff officers) states that it was 'out of reach of the French cavalry' and other sources state it was 'behind the squares'.[16] Hime concludes that only Mercer (again quite boastfully but undeniably to great effect) disobeyed this order but we know from Walcott that the order, in whatever form, had not reached Webber Smith's Troop and that they too remained at their guns during the cavalry attacks. However, there is overwhelming evidence from countless (all arms) sources that the balance sought shelter either in or alongside the infantry squares. Lieutenant Basil Jackson of the Royal Staff Corps informs us that 'Major Lloyd with his officers and men sought refuge in the Guards' square. Lloyd did not enter the square, but found shelter under its lee'.[17] General Sir James Shaw-Kennedy wrote that when the French cavalry charged 'the officers and men of two Brigades (Bolton's RA and Cleeve's [sic] KGL) took shelter within the oblong'.[18] Similar opinions are recorded in numerous other letters collected by Siborne in his detailed study. Where the confusion may lie is in the interpretation of 'refuge' and the expectations of Wellington in this regard. He is quite specific in the letter that he expected the officers and men of the artillery to take shelter *as I did in* the squares of the infantry.

We know that the order to take refuge was not received by all artillery commanders; we also know that there were three interpretations of that order. Assuming that all non-essential wagons and equipment was being held well to the rear, a six-gun battery would have been positioned immediately behind the guns and the six limber wagons (six or eight horses each) with the first line ammunition. A little way behind that would be up to nine ammunition wagons (six or eight horses each), one for each gun and a spare for each division. Generally, each battery would have about 100 men manning the guns with another 100 horses and 15 wagons. As there were about twice as many infantry squares as artillery batteries on the allied centre right, this would have meant that each infantry square could expect to 'shelter' 50 men, 50 horses and up to eight wagons. This is clearly nonsense. Although there is conflicting evidence, the assumption is that the limbers and ammunition wagons moved to the rear of the squares while the officers and gunners manning the guns took refuge within. However, there is a problem with an expectation that the gunners man their guns until the last safe moment and then move to the squares. In order to do this, the gun limbers would have been retained at the gun position with the men using them to expedite their extraction. Many would, understandably, have chosen to ride on these vehicles rather than running to the squares for refuge. It is precisely this that Wellington would have witnessed through the intense smoke and dust of the cavalry charges. It is this that gave rise to his accusation that the Gunners 'ran off the field entirely, taking with them limbers, ammunition, and everything'.

Wellington's perception of this rearward movement may have been the result of the unusual manner adopted during the battle by the allied artillery to re-supply their ammunition. The standard procedure on a Napoleonic battlefield was for the second line ammunition wagons to move from the park, or ammunition store, forward to re-supply the first line ammunition wagons (or caissons) and the front line limbers. Under certain circumstances, the re-supply of the front line limbers would have been undertaken by the first line ammunition wagons once they had been re-supplied. At Waterloo the allied ammunition re-supply did not work rear to front but vice-versa and it is not clear why this was the case. Some eyewitness accounts record that, during the French cavalry charges, ammunition wagons and limbers moved back behind the squares and then, quite sensibly, took the opportunity to move further back and complete their ammunition re-supply at this time.

The lack of guns being manned, once the French cavalry had been driven off or retired, is due to the fact that many Gunners and the only available ammunition were still on the limbers and ammunition wagons. In the wake of the French cavalry withdrawals, it took time for the Gunners and these means of transport to assume their positions. Furthermore, we know from Schwertfeger's account (Chapter 23) that Sandham's and Kühlmann's companies withdrew completely, with their guns, during this phase of the battle under the pretext that they were surrounded and cut off. We also know from Lieutenant Wilson's account (in a letter to Siborne) that Sinclair's Brigade had done the same thing (less one gun which was surrounded) at about 1500 hours.[19] Leaving aside the withdrawal of Bijleveld's Dutch battery early in the battle, did Wellington witness these rearward movements? If so, he clearly has grounds for his accusation.

By the time the letter was published, Wellington and most of the Gunner protagonists were dead. Since publication many artillery officers, infuriated at Wellington's snub, have argued and dismissed each point in turn. Wellington was clearly wrong about the artillery reserve but it is clear that he was correct, to a degree, regarding the other three accusations. What is less clear is why the Gunner orders seem confused, why they were not received by all the artillery commanders on the field and why his principal artillery advisor was not keeping the commander-in-chief informed, explaining circumstances as they developed if necessary. Nevertheless, there were 18 RA, KGA and Hanoverian artillery sub units on the field that day: only one, aware of Wellington's order, positively engaged in counter-battery fire; only two of the sub units chose deliberately not to seek some form of refuge during the cavalry attacks, and one of these wreaked carnage on the French cavalry as a result; and up to three sub units may have quit the field completely, for the sensible reason of ammunition re-supply, before rejoining the battle. This hardly merits the castigation of the entire artillery. Colonel Lynedoch Gardiner, son of Sir Robert Gardiner, wrote to the 2nd Duke in 1872 and made the pertinent point that 'if a regiment of infantry had ran away, and all the others had behaved splendidly, would the whole arm have been similarly condemned?'[20] Quite so! So why did Wellington write the letter and why, when he had the chance, did he not remove and destroy it, as he did with so many other contentious letters in his correspondence?

The answer as to why he wrote the letter is straightforward enough. The officers of the RA present at Waterloo had written directly to the MGO requesting the same award as had been forthcoming following the battle of Vitoria. On that occasion Lord Mulgrave had acted on his own initiative and had petitioned the Prince Regent who had readily agreed to the pension. Wellington had been furious, considering it duplicitous and 'having an irritating effect on the rest of the army'. Wood alluded to the subject in a letter to the MGO from Paris in August 1815, in which he informed the general of Lloyd's death and broached the subject in roundabout terms: 'should Lord Mulgrave, in his goodness, be inclined to grant pensions to field officers and captains commanding brigades, similar to the battle of Vittoria …'[21] Mulgrave, however, was unsure how to proceed, for at Vitoria every artillery brigade had been in action while at Waterloo some were detached; he therefore wrote to Wellington for guidance. Wellington's response was designed to kill the idea stone dead and prevent any form of retrospective resurrection. His letter certainly achieved that.

The reason why he chose not to remove it from his official papers is less clear, for by the middle of the 19th century it had achieved its purpose and by preserving it he must have known that when it came to light, it would cause unnecessary ill-feeling. The 2nd Duke, in his correspondence about the issue with Captain Duncan, closed with the following summary of Wellington's relationship with his Gunners: 'his approbation of the R. Artillery was not unmeasured, and I daresay the R. Artillery did not love him …'[22] It was, without doubt, a difficult relationship but there existed a huge respect, bordering on adoration, for Wellington amongst his artillery officers. Frazer's comment following Waterloo that the 'Duke's forte is in pursuit of a beaten enemy' could not have been further from the truth yet he clearly felt it.[23] Swabey dismissed Wellington's lack of praise in his dispatches with the words: 'People in general affect to be dissatisfied with the measure of his praise; his dispatches however have no right to be compared to those of our officers commanding what we term "an expedition" who make their own fame, deal out encomiums to those under them.'[24] There are countless other examples, many quoted in this work, which demonstrate a huge respect for their commander-in-chief and a recognition that he was prepared to fight on their behalf for better equipment, more horses, larger and more capable guns, brevet rank and better promotion rules and regulations. He created the concept of integrated army artillery, in effect bringing the artillery in closer contact with the other arms and allocating it to divisions. He was instrumental in raising the first heavy battery with his 18-pounder brigades as part of the field army and, later in the Peninsular campaign, by supporting the establishment of mountain guns for the battles in the Pyrenees. Conversely, his conduct of siege warfare and handling of artillery during sieges was poor as was his ability to grasp the force-multiplication effect of Shrapnel's spherical case rounds.

Wellington was not an easy man. He treated his subordinates harshly and Napier noted that he had a policy never to admit he was wrong. Consider his unforgiving relationship with his wife Kitty which overshadowed much of this period of his life.[25] The 7th Duke wrote of his ancestor: 'His reticence and aversion from displays of sentiment, his bursts of irritability at incompetence, his intolerance of human weakness like late rising or gambling, make his character as repulsive to some people as a love of publicity and a lack of reticence to others.'[26] John Fuller wrote of Wellington in 1938 that 'he was a believer in the divine right of blue blood. Although he was an aristocrat to his fingertips, he loathed ostentation and outward show. Possessed of a profound sense of duty, he was autocratic and dictatorial and was never able to suffer fools gladly.'[27] His inability to suffer fools and irritability at incompetence were at the heart of his failed relationships with his CsRA. Larpent, Wellington's Judge Advocate General, noted that the post of CRA 'should be a general's command to be done properly with proper officers under him; others say the old artillery officers have rather changed their sex and are somewhat of old women. Lord Wellington seems to favour the latter opinion a little.'[28] This failure to appoint a 'suitable' commander of artillery must be shared by the Board of Ordnance and the DAG RA. However, it is unlikely that any man selected would have been acceptable to Wellington – he wanted his own man. That was the nature of the Duke and the crux of the problem of Wellington's relationship with his Gunners and the colours they served.

Epilogue

My hand trembles whilst I take up my pen to announce the sad event of the death of a dear friend. I need not say that your brother has fallen. You will know that to this sad blow I allude. Poor Norman fell in the glorious struggle of yesterday, and fell like himself, gallantly resisting one of the many attacks made on the part of our position confided to his defence. I cannot, if I would, describe the anguish of my feelings nor the deep silent sorrow with which he was buried in the field by the soldiers, who looked up to him with pride and admiration. In the midst of all that deadens feeling on most occasions it was trembling alive yesterday, and the tears of honest and unaffected sorrow yet flow at the recollection of a dear friend who can never be forgotten.[29]

On the morning of the battle of Waterloo, the Duke, who had not seen Ramsay since his arrival in Belgium, accosted him cheerfully, something to the effect of 'Very Good' or 'Well done Ramsay'. The latter saluted profoundly bowing until his head almost touched his horse's mane, and then passed to the position where he nobly fell.[30] Ramsay had been unable to reply to Wellington's salutations that morning. He had still not come to terms with his treatment at the hands of the man he worshipped – such *was* the relationship between Wellington and his Gunners.

Six weeks after Captain David Ramsay was informed of the death of his son Norman, he received another notification that his son David had died on the Jamaica station in July 1815. Another son, John, had died while serving in the Royal Navy off the Leeward Islands in May 1807 and his youngest boy, Alexander, a lieutenant in the RA, had died in the batteries before New Orleans in January 1815. All four of his sons had died in service of their country; he was a broken man – such *is* the price of war.

Notes

1. WD, vol. VIII, p.150.
2. Frazer (ed. Sabine), p.593.
3. Scott, entry Sunday 23rd July 1815, Clichy.
4. Dickson, ch.11, p.1711.
5. Frazer (ed. Sabine), pp.562–64.
6. Vigors, vol. II, ch.26.
7. Ord p.3.
8. The other towns were: Maubeuge captured on 14th July; Landrecies on 23rd July; Mariembourg on 30th July; Philippeville on 10th August; and Rocroi on 16th August.
9. Gardiner, letter No. 21, from Paris, dated 15th July 1815.
10. Hime, pp.17–18.
11. Ibid., p.21.
12. Ibid., p.59.
13. Weller, p.164.
14. Browne, p.195.
15. Duncan Boxes and Papers, MD 193, p.9. Duncan in his examination incorrectly concludes that Mercer was located close to Sandham at the time and that it was Mercer's guns *only* that had fired against the French guns. In fact, when the incident occurred Mercer was positioned well to the west of Sandham and his guns were pointed south-west and not south-east (the direction of Sandham's barrels). Lt. Bloomfield, who was acting on Wood's staff and was with Wellington and Wood when the incident took place, recorded that 'one or more of these shots [from Sandham's guns] *appeared* to be directed against the French artillery …' Once Wellington was satisfied that this action had not been intentional he rescinded his original order to place Sandham under arrest.
16. Ibid., letter 2nd Duke of Wellington to Duncan p.26.
17. Hime, p.131, quoting B. Jackson & R. C. Seaton, *Notes and Reminiscences of a Staff Officer* (London, 1903) p.50.
18. Ibid., quoting General Sir James Shaw-Kennedy, *Notes on the Battle of Waterloo (London, 1865)* p.116.
19. Siborne, SWL, p.235.
20. Duncan Boxes and Papers, p.31.
21. Duncan, vol. II, p.446.

22. Duncan Boxes and Papers, p.36.
23. Frazer, pp.549–51.
24. Swabey (ed. Whinyates), p.171.
25. See Wellesley, J., pp.176–97 for an excellent insight into this aspect of his life.
26. Roberts, RN&W, p.292.
27. Fuller, p.1.
28. Larpent, vol. II, pp.141–42.
29. Ramsay Papers, unpublished letters, Frazer to Miss Ramsay, dated 19th June 1815.
30. Swabey (ed. Whinyates), p.243.

Appendices

Appendix 1

List of the Royal Horse Artillery and Royal Artillery Officers, by Troop and Battalion/Company, who served in the Peninsula 1808–14

† *kia* = Killed in action (including year)

† = Died (including year)

Kane's officer number is provided where there might be confusion.

Officers in **italics** have produced eyewitness accounts, diaries or memoirs used in this history.

Dates in theatre given for each sub unit. Dates officers served in sub unit are given where known.

Sources: Compilation from PRO WO 10/782 – 1050 (Artillery Muster Books/Pay Lists) and all primary sources used in this book.

First Captain	Second Captain	Lieutenants/Second Lieutenants
'A' Troop RHA 1809–14		
H. D. Ross 1806–15	***G. Jenkinson 1807–13***	G. Belson 1806–14
	J. B. Parker 1813–15	A. Macdonald (1174) 1808–13
		G. B. Smyth (1299) 1808–13¹
		W. Saunders 1811–14
		W. Bell 1813–14
		J. Day 1813–15

First Captain	Second Captain	Lieutenants/Second Lieutenants
'B' Troop RHA 1808–09		
T. Downman 1802–09	*R. Bogue 1806–? †kia 1813*[II]	W. Loring †1812
		W. C. Lempriere 1805–13
		H. Forster 1807–14[III]
'C' Troop RHA 1808–09		
H. Evelegh 1802–10	J. Chester 1806–13	E. Y. Walcott 1809–11[IV]
		W. Webber 1804–12[V]
		E. Barlow (1178) 1804–13
'D' Troop RHA 1810–14		
G. Lefebure 1807–†12	E. C. Whinyates 1808–13	W. Dunn 1804–13
G. Bean 1812–14	A. Macdonald (1174) 1813–14	H. Mallett (1224) 1805–12[VI]
		W. Brereton 1813–14
		W. L. Robe 1810–14[VII]
		M. T. Cromie 1808–09
		J. A. MacLeod 1811–14[VIII]
		M. Louis 1813–14
		T. Carter (1220) 1810–11
		W. H. Bent 1812–13[IX]
'E' Troop RHA 1811–14		
R. Macdonald 1806–13	*T. Dyneley 1808–13*	R. Harding (1322) ?–1814
R. W. Gardiner 1813–14		*W. Swabey 1811–13*
		R. Newland (1229) 1805–14
		R. Hardinge (1318) 1813–14
'F' Troop RHA 1813–14		
J. Webber Smith 1806–14	S. Bolton 1806–14	W. Saunders 1805–14
		D. Craufurd 1804–15
		D . J. Edwardes 1806–15
'I' Troop RHA 1809–14		
R. Bull 1805–14[X]	W. N. Ramsay 1806–14	P. Stanhope 1804–12
	R. M. Cairnes 1814	G. Browne (1395) ?–1813
		C. Blachley (1171) 1809–12
		H. Blachley (1221) 1812–14
		H. R. Moor 1810–12
		M. Louis 1814
		J. Townsend 1813–?
		J. M. Weatherall 1813–14
		M. T. Cromie 1813–14
Lane's Rocket Brigade RHA 1814		
	H. Bowyer Lane 1814	J. Crawley
		E. Morgan (1558)
1st Battalion/2nd Company: May's Company March 1809 – June 1814		
J. May 1807–14[XI]	H. Baynes 1808–11	W. Elgee 1806–14
	P. Faddy 1811–14	H. Wyatt †*kia* 1809
		J. Pascoe 1809–14
		W. F. Lindsay (1183)
		W. Dennis 1809–13

First Captain	Second Captain	Lieutenants/Second Lieutenants
		H. Hough 1812–13

2nd Battalion/2nd Company: P. Campbell's Company August 1802 – January 1810 in Gibraltar and March 1810 – August 1814

P. Campbell 1806–14[XII]	A. Hunt (1023) 1806–14	S. P. Brett 1804–†*kia* 12
	T. Atchison 1814	H. Pester ?–1812
		T. Grantham 1804–?
		A. Carter 1808–?[XIII]
		D. N. Martin †1815
		W. Greenwood
		W. Furneaux 1811–13[XIV]

3rd Battalion/1st Company: A. Campbell's Company March 1813 – June 1814

A. Campbell (819) 1804–14	D. J. Skelton 1808–15	N. R. Drewry †1814
		J. C. Burton
		W. H. Lawrence

3rd Battalion/4th Company: Drummond's Company September 1808 – January 1809

P. Drummond 1806–14	C. F. Sandham 1806–14	F. Macbean (1228) 1805–14
		W. A. Raynes

3rd Battalion/5th Company: Bean's/Hutchesson's Company November 1808 – January 1809 and March 1813 – June 1814

G. Bean 1808–12	T. A. Brandreth 1805–12	J. Darby
T. Hutchesson 1812–14	W. Bentham 1812–?	W. E. Maling
		T. R. Cookson
		G. A. Moore (1410) 1813–†*kia* 14
		R. Manners 1813–14
		J. Christie 1813–†14[XV]

3rd Battalion/6th Company: Truscott's Company November 1808 – January 1809

R. Truscott 1805–†14	S. Du Bourdieu 1805–†*kia* 13	G. Lear †1809
	T. Greatly 1813–16	J. Wilson (1361) †1809
		J. Davies (1414)

3rd Battalion/8th Company: Wilmot's Company September 1808 – January 1809

E. Wilmot 1808–11	J. Gomm 1808–?	J. Sinclair
		A. M. Campbell (1273)

4th Battalion/1st Company: Hawker's/Maxwell's Company November 1810 – May 1814

J. Hawker 1803–12	W. Latham 1808–†*kia* 12	P. Faddy 1805–11
S. Maxwell 1812–14	*W. Webber 1812–14*	T. Trotter †1812
		W. H. Bent 1810–12
		H. F. Cubitt (1310) 1812–?
		R. Litchfield
		C. R. Baldock

4th Battalion/6th Company: Skyring's/Morrison's Company August 1802 – July 1808 in Gibraltar, September 1808 – January 1809 and November 1812 – June 1814

G. Skyring 1804–11	C. H. Godby 1804–08	E. T. Michell (1152)
W. Morrison 1811–14	C. P. Deacon 1809–11	M. C. W. Aytoun
	J. Lloyd 1811– ?	L. Woodyear †1813
		H. M. Leathes 1811–?
		H. Stanway 1812–13

First Captain	Second Captain	Lieutenants/Second Lieutenants
		R. W. Story 1812–13
		F. Monro (1498) 1813–14

5th Battalion/4th Company: Geary's/Carthew's/Lacy's Company August 1808 – January 1809 and December 1812 – June 1814

First Captain	Second Captain	Lieutenants/Second Lieutenants
H. Geary 1802–†*kia*08	W. G. Eliot 1804–09[XVI]	W. B. Patten 1812–17
R. Carthew 1808–†09	W. M. G. Colebrook 1810–?[XVII]	W. E. Locke 1806–09
R. J. J. Lacy 1809–14		W. H. Hill (1371) 1812–?
		G. S. Maule 1812–?

5th Battalion/8th Company: Glubb's/Trelawney's Company March 1809 – June 1814

First Captain	Second Captain	Lieutenants/Second Lieutenants
F. Glubb 1808–†13	W. G. Power 1807–15	D. M. Bourchier
H. Trelawney 1813–14		J. G. Martin (1339) †1811
		J. Love
		C. A. Oldham 1813–?
		C. Shaw (1468)
		E. Morgan

5th Battalion/10th Company: Owen's Company March 1810 – June 1814

First Captain	Second Captain	Lieutenants/Second Lieutenants
H. Owen 1803–14	W. Cator 1809–13	W. Brereton 1810–13
	H. Festing 1813–?	G. H. Mainwaring 1810–?
		H. Morgan (1459)
		H. R. Wright
		H. Hutchins 1813–?

6th Battalion/2nd Company: Crawford's Company September 1808 – January 1809

First Captain	Second Captain	Lieutenants/Second Lieutenants
G. Crawford 1805–14	J. Taylor (1029) 1806–09[XVIII]	A. F. Crawford 1804–10
		J. Eyre

6th Battalion/3rd Company: Holcombe's Company November 1808 – January 1809 and May 1811 – January 1815

First Captain	Second Captain	Lieutenants/Second Lieutenants
H. F. Holcombe 1807–14	F. Knox 1806–11	T. N. King (1346) 1806–09
	W. B. Dundas (1150) 1811[XIX]	T. Cox (1349) 1809–14[XX]
	E. Y. Walcott (1127) 1811–12	P. W. Foster 1808–10[XXI]
	W. B. Dundas 1812–14	J. M. Weatherall 1809–10 and 1812–14
		J. Townsend (1456)
		G. James 1812–14
		R. Grimes (1462) 1810–12

7th Battalion/2nd Company: Thornhill's Company September 1808 – January 1809

First Captain	Second Captain	Lieutenants/Second Lieutenants
R. Thornhill 1801–10	J. D. Blundell 1805–09	F. Wright (1280)

7th Battalion/4th Company: Wall's Company November 1808 – January 1809

First Captain	Second Captain	Lieutenants/Second Lieutenants
A. Wall 1808–14	W. Romer 1806–†09	W. E. Byne
		J. N. Charles[XXII]

7th Battalion/6th Company: Sillery's/Thomson's Company March 1809 – June 1814

First Captain	Second Captain	Lieutenants/Second Lieutenants
C. D. Sillery 1804–†09	H. Bowyer Lane 1806–12	*R. Woollcombe 1808–14*
G. Thomson (964) 1809–†14	F. Arabin 1812–14	W. C. Johnston (1303) †1811[XXIII]
		J. Mercier †1814
		F. Bayly (1473) 1809–12
		K. C. Wulfe
		H. Palliser 1812–14

APPENDICES

First Captain	Second Captain	Lieutenants/Second Lieutenants
8th Battalion/1st Company: Bredin's Company September 1808 – December 1814		
A. Bredin 1804–14	T. C. Terrell 1808 -?	B. Wills 1803–11
		W. Arbuthnot
		F. Dawson 1809–?
		J. Mercier (1440) 1811–14
		J. Bloomfield 1810–14
8th Battalion/6th Company: Williamson's Company September 1812 – May 1814		
J. S. Williamson 1808–14	C. Gilmour 1806–14	T. Wynn 1808–14
		J. Hill (1483) 1813–14
		T. Scott 1804–14
		J. Trotter (1454) 1812–?
8th Battalion/7th Company: Lawson's Company August 1808 – June 1814		
R. Lawson (943) 1808–14[XXIV]	J. Taylor (1029) ? –1809[XXV]	H. Festing 1804–12
	A. Thompson (1141) 1809–13	J. W. Johnson (1193) 1808–14
	C. Mosse 1813–14	H. G. Macleod (1392) 1809–12
		W. B. Ingilby 1810–12
		B. R. Heron 1812–14
		P. Thompson (1501) 1813–14
		A. Macbean (1529) 1812–14
8th Battalion/9th Company: Raynsford's/Gardiners's/Du Bourdieu's/Carmichael's Company August 1808 – January 1809 and May 1811 – May 1814		
R. T. Raynsford 1804–11[XXVI]	*R. W. Gardiner 1808–10*	E. Hawker †*kia* 1811
R. W. Gardiner 1811–13	*C. C. Dansey 1812–14*	C. Graham 1806–09[XXVII]
S. Du Bourdieu †*kia* 1813		F. Weston 1809–14
L. Carmichael 1813–14		J. Christie 1810–14[XXVIII]
		G. B. Willis (1420) ?–1812
		R. Hardinge (1318) 1812–13
		J. J. Connell (1452)
		F. Monro (1498) 1812–13
		P. V. England 1813–14
8th Battalion/10th Company: Meadows's/Eligé's/Brandreth's Company November 1810 – July 1814		
P. Meadows 1807–†11	J. S. Byers 1809–14	F. Dawson 1809–14
J. P. Eligé 1811–†*kia*12		G. M. Baynes (1375) 1807–14
T. A. Brandreth 1812–14		J. H. Castleman 1810–14
		E. Seward
		R. B. Hunt (1155) 1810–12
		W. Furneaux 1810–11
9th Battalion/5th Company: Stone's/Michell's Company April 1812 – May 1814		
H. Stone (not in Peninsula)	J. B. Parker 1808–13	R. H. Ord 1806–13[XXIX]
J. Michell (1004) 1813–14	W. C. Lempriere 1813–14	T. G. T. Williams (1527) 1810–?
		G. Browne (1395) 1812–?
		H. Stanway 1811–12
		F. Bayly (1473) 1812–14
9th Battalion/8th Company: Douglas's Company April 1812 – May 1814		
R. Douglas 1810–14	W. Greene 1808–14	J. H. Wood (1281) 1805–14
G. Turner 1814		J. Grant (1441) 1813–14
		C. J. Downman 1812–14
		R. F. Phillips 1812–13

First Captain	Second Captain	Lieutenants/Second Lieutenants
		H. Slade 1812–14
		A. Ward (1428) 1814

9th Battalion/9th Company: Hughes's Company February 1810 – July 1814

First Captain	Second Captain	Lieutenants/Second Lieutenants
P. J. Hughes 1808–19	F. Bedingfeld 1810–14	J. Maxwell (1286) †1812
		C. Manners 1806–14
		A. R. Harrison (1429) 1808–14[XXX]
		F. Warde 1809–11 and 1812–14
		J. Apreece 1810–14

10th Battalion/4th Company: Dickson's Company April 1810 – June 1814

First Captain	Second Captain	Lieutenants/Second Lieutenants
A. Dickson 1808–14[XXXI]	*R. M. Cairnes 1808–13*	P. J. Woolcombe †1811
R. H. Birch 1812–13[XXXII]	C. Close 1814	W. A. Raynes 1806–14
R. M. Cairnes 1813–14		L. Talbot 1809–13
		E. J. Bridges 1808–14

10th Battalion/5th Company: Shenley's/Chester's Company April 1810 – August 1814

First Captain	Second Captain	Lieutenants/Second Lieutenants
W. Shenley 1808–†13	J. Mallet (1107) 1808–12	B. J. Maitland (1274) 1805–?
J. Chester 1813–17[XXXIII]	C. E. Gordon (1162) 1812–14	R. Godby 1806–†10
		W. Cator (1134) 1804–14
		T. O. Cater (1465) 1810–11
		J. Trotter (1454) 1808–12[XXXIV]
		E. H. Bland 1812–14
		A. R. Harrison

10th Battalion/6th Company: Roberts's Company April 1810 – August 1814

First Captain	Second Captain	Lieutenants/Second Lieutenants
W. Roberts 1808–17	H. Gardner 1806–10	W. B. Dundas (1150) 1810–12
	R. W. Gardiner 1810–11	R. J. Home 1805–†11
	C. Clarke 1811–?	W. Cozens 1809–13[XXXV]
		J. N. Colquhoun 1808–14
		H. M. Parrat (1445) 1808–?

Notes

I. Lt. Smyth resigned 1st December 1813.

II. Capt. Bogue was killed at the battle of Leipzig, 18th October 1813.

III. Lt. Forster joined 'F' Troop for Waterloo.

IV. Lt. Walcott became adjutant to the CRA in May 1811.

V. Webber's diary covers the period when he was second captain with Maxwell's Company of the 4th Battalion.

VI. Lt. Mallett resigned March 1813.

VII. Lt. William Robe was the son of Lt. Col. William Robe, the first CRA in the Peninsula (see Chapter 20).

VIII. Lt. John MacLeod was the son of General John MacLeod, the DAG RA.

IX. Lt. Bent was also seconded to 'I' Troop in 1812.

X. Capt. Bull came back to England for medical reasons from 12th to 13th November.

XI. Lt. Col. John May actually never commanded his company in the Peninsula. He was always on the staff. His company was never brigaded and acted as a reserve normally dedicated to ammunition duties.

APPENDICES

XII. Lt. Col. Campbell did not command his company in the Peninsula but was attached throughout with the Spanish Army.

XIII Lt. Carter remained in England throughout.

XIV. Lt. Furneaux served on the east coast 1812–13 as Brigade Major RA.

XV. Lt. Christie had been in Raynsford's/Gardiner's Company and was subsequently in Carmichael's Company in 1814 and died at New Orleans 1st March 1815 from wounds.

XVI. 2nd Capt. Eliot joined the Portuguese artillery in April 1809.

XVII. 2nd Capt. Colebrook was serving in the East Indies/Ceylon.

XVIII. 2nd Capt. Taylor stayed in Peninsula following Moore's withdrawal and joined Lawson's Company – see note XXV.

XIX. 2nd Capt. Dundas lost an arm at Badajoz.

XX. Cox served in the Portuguese artillery as a 2nd Capt. and commanded an artillery company on the east coast.

XXI. Foster resigned his Commission on 22nd March 1810.

XXII. Lt. Charles served with the Portuguese artillery in 1809 and resigned in 1811.

XXIII. Lt. Johnson drowned in Portugal (River Tagus) 15th June 1811.

XXIV. Capt. Morrison commanded Lawson's Company in 1808 until Lawson arrived in early 1809.

XXV. Taylor was injured at Talavera in 1809 and captured and taken as a POW until the end of the war.

XXVI. Capt. Raynsford resigned his Commission in November 1811.

XXVII. Lt. Graham resigned his Commission in November 1809.

XXVIII. See note XV.

XXIX. Lt. Ord became the CRA's ADC in October 1813.

XXX. Lt. Harrison was part-time adjutant to Maj. Duncan.

XXXI. Dickson never really commanded this company having exchanged companies with Richard Dyas in 1808.

XXXII. Capt. Birch had his own company (10th Battalion/8th Company) which he commanded from 1808 until it was disbanded in June 1817. From April 1810 until April 1817 the company was based in Gibraltar. Birch assumed temporary command of Dickson's Company in 1812 until he handed over to 2nd Capt. Cairnes in 1813.

XXXIII. Capt. Chester did not join the company until it returned to England in August 1814.

XXXIV. Lt. Trotter then joined Williamson's Company on the east coast.

XXXV. Lt. Cozens lost a leg at Cadiz in 1812 and passed to the Invalid Battalion in 1813.

Appendix 2

List of the Royal Horse Artillery and Royal Artillery Officers, by Troop and Battalion/Company, who served during the Waterloo Campaign 1815

†*kia* = Killed in action

† = Died of wounds

+ = Wounded.

Officers in **italics** have produced eyewitness accounts, diaries or memoirs used in this history.

Dates in theatre given for each sub unit. Dates officers served in sub unit are given where known.

Sources: Waterloo Roll Call (not accurate), Leslie and all primary sources used in this book.

Troops of Royal Horse Artillery First Captain	Second Captain	Lieutenants/Second Lieutenants
'A' Troop *H. D. Ross*	J. B. Parker + (leg amputated)	P. V. Onslow J. Day (1380) + R. Hardinge (1318)[I] F. Warde G. Foot[II]
'D' Troop G. Bean †*kia*	*W. Webber* +	J. E. Maunsell J. R. Bruce M. T. Cromie † (both legs amputated)
'E' Troop *R. W. Gardiner*	*T. Dyneley*	W. B. Ingilby R. Harding (1322) *W. Swabey*
'F' Troop *J. Webber Smith* +	E. Y. Walcott	D. Craufurd + D. J. Edwardes H. Forster (1329) +
'G' Troop *A. C. Mercer*	R. Newland	J. Hincks H. M. Leathes J. F. Breton W. Bell[III]
'H' Troop *W. N. Ramsay* †*kia*	A. Macdonald (1174) +	*W. Brereton* +

First Captain	Second Captain	Lieutenants/Second Lieutenants
		P. Sandilands
		W. L. Robe †

First Captain	Second Captain	Lieutenants/Second Lieutenants
'I' Troop		
R. Bull +	*R. M. Cairnes* †*kia*	M. Louis
		W. Smith (1340) +
		J. Townsend
The Rocket Troop		
E. C. Whinyates +	*C. C. Dansey* +	A. Wright (1359)
		T. Strangways +
		A. Ward (1428)

Companies of Royal Artillery First Captain	Second Captain	Lieutenants/Second Lieutenants
3rd Battalion/2nd Company: Rogers' Company		
T. Rogers	*T. Scott*	G. Coles[IV]
		R. G. Wilson (1559)
		R. Manners †
		H. Dunnicliffe
		G. S. Maule[V]
3rd Battalion/3rd Company: Brome's Company		
J. Brome	J. E. G. Parker	R. J. Saunders
		T. O. Cater
		A. O. Molesworth
3rd Battalion/4th Company: Gordon's Company		
J. Sinclair[VI]	F. MacBean	R. B. Burnaby
		W. H. Poole+
		J. A. Wilson (1543)
3rd Battalion/7th Company: Unett's Company		
G. W. Unett	T. G. Browne	D. Lawson
		W. Montagu
		C. G. Kett
3rd Battalion/9th Company: Sandham's Company		
C. F. Sandham	W. H. Stopford	G. Foot (1355)
		G. M. Baynes
		D. Jago
9th Battalion/4th Company: Alms's Company		
S. Bolton[VII] †*kia*	C. G. Napier (1160) +	G. Pringle (1296)
		W. C. Anderson
		W. Sharpin
		C. Spearman (1477) †[VIII]
		B. Cuppage
10th Battalion/2nd Company: Lloyd's Company		
W. J. Lloyd †	S. Rudyerd	F. Wells
		S. Phelps
		W. H. Harvey + (r. arm amputated)

Notes

I. Richard Hardinge was appointed as ADC to his brother who was Wellington's Staff Officer at the Prussian HQ.

II. Confirmed by 'A' Troop records but not on Waterloo roll call.

III. Lt. Bell was acting as adjutant to Lt. Col. Sir Augustus Frazer.

IV. Lt. Coles was acting as adjutant to Col. Sir G. Wood.

V. From Ilbert's Company.

VI. Capt. Gordon in Canada, Capt. J. Sinclair in command.

VII. Capt. Alms in Ceylon, Capt. S. Bolton commanding. Capt. Bolton never actually joined his own company – 9th Battalion/2nd Company – as he was kia at Waterloo.

VIII. Not the author of *British Gunner* as written in Asquith – that was J. M. Spearman (1612).

Appendix 3

Royal Artillery Recipients of the Army Gold Cross for Peninsula Service

The Army Gold Cross is arguably the most coveted campaign award. It was approved by the Prince Regent in 1813 and was granted to generals and officers of field rank for service in four or more battles during the Peninsular War. The four battles were annotated, one on each arm, with service at additional battles annotated by a clasp on the ribbon, which was crimson edged with a dark blue central band. Only three crosses had six clasps; one of these was earned by Major General Alexander Dickson. Wellington himself had the highest number with nine clasps.

(Key to Battle clasps: Alb – Albuera; Bad – Badajoz; Bar – Barrosa; Bus – Buçaco; Cor – Coruña; CR – Ciudad Rodrigo; FdO – Fuentes de Oñoro; Nil – Nivelle; Niv – Nive; Ort – Orthez; Pyr – Pyrenees; SanS – San Sebastian; Sal-Salamanca; Tal – Talavera; Tou – Toulouse; Vim – Vimeiro; Vit – Vitoria.)

Name	Rank[I]	Kane's No.	Clasps
Joseph Hugh Carncross	Major	727	Sal, Vit, Pyr, Nil, Niv, Ort.
Alexander Dickson	Lieutenant Colonel	844	Alb, Bus, CR, Bad, Sal, Vit, SanS, Nil, Niv, Tou.
Robert Douglas	Captain	958	Sal, Vit, Pyr, Nil.[II]
Thomas Downman	Lieutenant Colonel	742	Cor, Pyr, Nil, Niv, Ort, Tou.[III]
John Dyer	Lieutenant	751	Pyr, SanS, Niv, Ort, Tou.
Hoylett Framingham	Colonel	624	Tal, Bus, FdO, Bad, Sal.
Augustus Frazer	Lieutenant Colonel	765	Vit, SanS, Nil, Niv, Tou.
Robert Gardiner	Major	979	Bar, Bad, Sal, Vit, Ort, Tou.
Robert Lawson	Major	943	Tal, Bus, FdO, Sal, Vit.
John May	Lieutenant Colonel	883	Bad, Sal, Vit, SanS, Nil, Niv, Tou.
William Robe	Lieutenant Colonel	654	Vim, Tal, Bus, Bad, Sal.
Hew Dalrymple Ross	Lieutenant Colonel	890	Bus, Bad, Sal, Vit, Nil, Niv.
Alexander Tulloh	Captain	801	Bad, Vit, Nil, Niv.[IV]

Notes

I. Rank given is the highest rank attained during the campaign.
II. Douglas also received the MGSM with a clasp for SanS.
III. Downman also received the MGSM with clasps for S/B, Cor and CR.
IV. Tulloh served throughout in the Portuguese artillery.

Royal Artillery Recipients of the Army Gold Medal for Service in the Peninsula

The Maida Gold Medal, issued for the battle of Maida in Calabria in 1806, established a precedent for the series of medals instituted in 1810. The name of the battle was inscribed on the reverse of the medal (although that for Badajoz was die-struck) and second or third battles were denoted by an appropriately inscribed clasp. There were two sizes of the Army Gold Medal, the larger being conferred on officers of general rank and the smaller on officers of field rank. There were only two clasps as officers were able to exchange their Gold Medal for a Gold Cross when they qualified for a fourth award (although many chose to keep both!). Interestingly, although not instituted solely for the war in the Peninsula, they did cease to be issued in 1814 when the Companion of the Bath was instituted.

(Key to Battle clasps: Alb – Albuera; Bad – Badajoz; Bar – Barrosa; Bus – Buçaco; Cor – Coruña; CR – Ciudad Rodrigo; FdO – Fuentes de Oñoro; Nil – Nivelle; Niv – Nive; Ort – Orthez; Pyr – Pyrenees; SanS – San Sebastian; Sal-Salamanca; Tal – Talavera; Tou – Toulouse; Vim – Vimeiro; Vit – Vitoria.)

Name	Rank[I]	Kane's No.	Clasps
Recipients of the Large Medal			
William Borthwick	Major General	552	CR.
Edward Howorth	Major General	484	Tal, Bus, FdO.
Recipients of the Small Medal			
Henry Baynes	Second Captain	1092	Tal.
George Bean	Captain	914	Vit, Ort.
Thomas Alston Brandreth	Captain	990	Pyr, Tou.
Richard Buckner	Major	746	Vit, SanS, Nil.
Robert Bull	Captain	845	Bus, FdO, Sal.
Robert Cairnes	Second Captain	1106	Vit, Pyr.
Lewis Carmichael	Captain	1007	Niv.
Saumarez du Bourdieu	Captain	1001	Vit.
Alexander Duncan	Major	740	Bar.
William Granville Eliot	Second Captain	971	Vim.[II]
William Greene	Second Captain	1105	Sal.[III]
John Harding	Colonel	542	Cor.
James Hawker	Captain	771	Alb.
Harcourt Fort Holcombe	Captain	895	Bad.
Philip J. Hughes	Captain	915	Bar.
George Jenkinson	Second Captain	1032	Ort.
Henry Bowyer Lane[IV]	Second Captain	1062	Tou.

Name	Rank[I]	Kane's No.	Clasps
Robert Macdonald	Captain	858	Sal.
Stewart Maxwell	Captain	966	Vit, Niv, Ort.
Charles Cornwallis Michell	First Lieutenant	1486	Vit, Tou.[V]
John Michell	Captain	1004	Ort, Tou.[VI]
William Morrison	Captain	934	Vim.
Charles Mosse	Second Captain	1101	Niv.
John Boteler Parker	Second Captain	1117	Vit.[VII]
William Norman Ramsey	Second Captain	1019	Vit, Niv.
Richard T. Raynsford	Captain	809	Vim.
William Livingstone Robe	First Lieutenant	1390	Nil, Niv.
William Roberts	Captain	928	Bar.
Charles Doyne Sillery	Captain	827	Tal.
James Webber Smith	Captain	877	Vit, SanS.[VIII]
George Turner	Captain	974	Ort, Tou.
James Viney	Major	685	Rol, Vim, Cor.
Edward Wilmot	Captain	912	Cor.

Notes

I. Rank given is the rank at the time of the first award.

II. Eliot also received the MGSM for Rol, Vim and Tal.

III. Greene also received the MGSM for FdO, CR and Pyr.

IV. Bowyer Lane had also been at Talavera and was wounded early on the 28th July 1809. He died on the 28th January 1837 and was therefore never awarded his MGSM.

V. Michell C. also received the MGSM for Bad. (He served with the Portuguese artillery throughout.)

VI. Michell J. also received the MGSM for Bad.

VII. Parker also received the MGSM for Vit, SanS, Ort and Tou.

VIII. Webber Smith also received the MGSM for Nil and Niv.

Royal Artillery Officer Recipients of the Military General Service Medal for Service in the Peninsula

The Military General Service Medal was not sanctioned until 1847 and awarded the following year; it was granted for all ranks but only for the survivors. The Duke of Wellington was against the issue and it was public opinion which won the day, enabling the medal to be struck with the head of Victoria, a sovereign who had not even been born when some of the earlier engagements had been fought. There were a total of 29 battle or campaign clasps, 21 were issued for the Peninsula and these were all added to the ribbon which was crimson edged with a dark blue central stripe. The list of all the Royal Artillery recipients would be extensive, so only the officer recipients are depicted below. Gunner Thomas Rolland earned the greatest number of clasps in the Royal

Artillery. He served throughout the entire war with Captain Robert Lawson's Company and earned a total of 13 for his extraordinary contribution to events in Iberia.

(Key to Battle clasps: Alb – Albuera; Bad – Badajoz; Bar – Barrosa; Ben-Benavente; Bus – Buçaco; Cor – Coruña; CR – Ciudad Rodrigo; FdO – Fuentes de Oñoro; Nil – Nivelle; Niv – Nive; Ort – Orthez; Pyr – Pyrenees; SanS – San Sebastian; Sal-Salamanca; S/B-Sahagún/Benavente; Tal – Talavera; Tou – Toulouse; Vim – Vimeiro; Vit – Vitoria.)

Name	Rank[1]	Kane's No.	Clasps
William Arbuthnott	First Lieutenant	1217	Tal, Bus.
George Smyth Barttelot	First Lieutenant	1299	Bus, FdO, CR, Bad, Sal.
Frederick Bayly	Second Lieutenant	1473	Bus.
George Macleod Baynes	First Lieutenant	1375	Pyr, Nil, Tou.
Francis Bedingfield	Second Captain	1087	Bar.
William Bell	First Lieutenant	1242	Nil, Niv, Tou.
George John Belson	First Lieutenant	1235	Bus, FdO, CR, Bad, Vit, Pyr, Nil, Niv, Ort.
William Henry Bent	Second Lieutenant	1449	Alb, Bad.
Charles Blachley	First Lieutenant	1171	Bus, FdO, Sal.
Henry Blachley	First Lieutenant	1221	Sal, Vit, SanS, Nil, Niv.
John Bloomfield	Second Lieutenant	1516	Vit, SanS, Nil, Niv, Ort, Tou.
Daniel Macnamara Bourchier	First Lieutenant	1166	Bus, CR, Bad.
William Brereton	First Lieutenant	1258	Bar, Vit, Pyr, SanS, Ort, Tou.
Edward Jacob Bridges	First Lieutenant	1438	Vit, Pyr, Nil, Niv.
Patrick Campbell[II]	Captain	879	Tal.
Thomas Carter	First Lieutenant	1220	Bus.
Thomas Orlando Cater	Second Lieutenant	1465	Bar.
William Cator	Second Captain	1134	Bar.
John Chester	Second Captain	1010	Ben.
Thomas Cox	First Lieutenant	1349	Cor, Bad.[III]
Charles Cornwallis Dansey	Second Captain	1138	Bad, Sal, Vit, SanS, Nil, Niv.
Joseph Darby	First Lieutenant	1126	Cor.
Charles Parke Deacon	Second Captain	1124	SanS.
William Boden Dundas	Second Captain	1150	CR, Bad.
William Dunn	First Lieutenant	1188	Bus, Alb.
Thomas Dyneley	Second Captain	1114	CR, Sal, Vit, Pyr.
David John Edwardes	First Lieutenant	1297	Vit, SanS, Nil, Niv.
William Elgee	First Lieutenant	1384	Tal, FdO.
Poole Vallancey England	First Lieutenant	1261	Vit, Nil.
Henry Evelegh	Captain	747	S/B.

Name	Rank[1]	Kane's No.	Clasps
John Eyre	First Lieutenant	1381	Cor.
Peter Faddy	Second Captain	1157	SanS.[IV]
George Ford	Second Lieutenant	1550	Tou.
Henry Forster	First Lieutenant	1329	S/B, Cor.
William Furneaux	First Lieutenant	1455	CR.
Charles Edward Gordon	Second Captain	1162	SanS, Nil, Niv, Ort.
Robert Graham	First Lieutenant	1312	Rol, Vim, Cor.
Thomas Greatley	Second Captain	1080	S/B, Cor.
Robert Grimes[V]	Second Lieutenant	1462	CR, Bad.
Robert Harding	First Lieutenant	1322	Sal, Vit, SanS, Ort, Tou.
Richard Hardinge	First Lieutenant	1318	Vit, SanS, Ort, Tou.
Richard Burges Hunt	Second Captain	1155	Bad.
William Bates Ingilby	Second Lieutenant	1464	Bus, FdO, CR, Sal.
George James	Second Lieutenant	1503	Vit, Pyr, Nil, Ort.
Henry Mussenden Leathes	First Lieutenant	1268	Cor.
William C Lempriere	First Lieutenant	1205	S/B, Cor.
William F. Lindsay[VI]	First Lieutenant	1185	FdO.
Richard Litchfield	First Lieutenant	1453	Vit, Ort, Tou.
Walter Elphinstone Locke	First Lieutenant	1338	Rol, Vim.
James Love	Second Lieutenant	1489	CR, Bad, Sal.
Matthew Louis	First Lieutenant	1244	Vit, SanS, Nil, Niv.
Archibald Macbean	Second Lieutenant	1529	Vit, SanS, Nil, Niv.
Forbes Macbean	First Lieutenant	1228	Cor.
Alexander MacDonald	First Lieutenant	1174	Bus, FdO, Sal, Vit, SanS, Ort, Tou.
Henry George MacLeod	First Lieutenant	1392	Tal, Bus.
Charles Manners	First Lieutenant	1397	Bar.
Frederick Monro	Second Lieutenant	1498	Sal, Vit, Nil, Niv.
Hassell Richard Moor	First Lieutenant	1176	Bus, FdO, CR, Bad, Sal.
Evan Morgan	Second Lieutenant	1558	Tou.
Hugh Morgan	First Lieutenant	1459	Pyr, SanS, Tou.
Robert Newland	First Lieutenant	1229	Sal, Vit, Ort, Tou.
Henry Palliser	Second Lieutenant	1523	Vit, SanS, Ort, Tou.
Hillebrant M. Parratt	First Lieutenant	1445	SanS, Nil, Niv, Ort, Tou.
John Pascoe	Second Lieutenant	1415	Bus, Bad, Sal, Vit, SanS, Nil, Niv.
Henry Pester	Second Lieutenant	1470	Bar.
Robert Fryer Phillips	Second Lieutenant	1353	Sal, Vit, Pyr, SanS, Nil.
William Greenshields Power	Second Captain	1074	Tal, CR, Bad, Sal, Pyr, SanS, Nil, Niv.

Name	Rank[I]	Kane's No.	Clasps
John Powers	Quarter-Master[VII]	36	Cor.
William Augustus Raynes	First Lieutenant	1313	Cor, Bar, Vit, Pyr, Nil, Niv.
Claudius Shaw	First Lieutenant	1468	SanS, Nil, Niv.
James Sinclair	First Lieutenant	1207	Cor, Bad, Vit, Pyr, SanS, Nil, Niv.
William Swabey	First Lieutenant	1327	CR, Sal, Vit.
Robert William Story	First Lieutenant	1488	SanS.
John Townsend	First Lieutenant	1456	Nil, Niv.
Michael Tweedie	First Lieutenant	1471	Tou.
Edward Charles Whinyates	Second Captain	1002	Bus, Alb.
George Brander Willis	First Lieutenant	1420	Bad.
James Humphreys Wood	First Lieutenant	1281	Vit, Pyr, SanS, Nil, Ort, Tou.
Robert Woollcombe	First Lieutenant	1325	FdO.
Frederick Wright	First Lieutenant	1280	Cor.

In addition, 1st Lt. Thomas Newton King (1346) was entitled to the clasp for Coruña; he died on 8th May 1854. 1st Lt. Henry Finlay Cubitt (1310) was also entitled to the medal with four clasps: Vitoria, Pyrenees, Orthez and Toulouse; he died on 12th August 1848. It is assumed that neither officer applied for the medal.

Notes

I. Rank given is the rank at the time of the first award.
II. Patrick Campbell was serving with the Spanish Army and commanding a regiment of artillery: he was known as Don Patricio Campbell.
III. Cox served throughout with the Portuguese Artillery.
IV. Faddy's medal was in fact the Naval GSM as he was attached to the RN at the time.
V. Grimes changed his surname to Cholmley in 1852.
VI. Lindsey assumed the additional surname 'Carnegie' in 1816.
VII. The Board of Ordnance abolished purchase of a Quarter-Master's commission in February 1783 and ruled that future appointees should be recommended from the ranks of NCO on merit. The first vacancy occurred in 1793.

Appendix 4

Ordnance Allocation to Batteries – Badajoz 3rd–10th June 1811

(Source: Compilation from Jones)
Maj. Dickson had the following guns available for the siege: 30 x 24-pdr guns (24G), 4 x 16-pdr guns (16G), 4 x 10in. howitzers (10H) and 8 x 8in. howitzers (8H).[1]

Battery No.	Battery Task	June 1811						
		3rd	4th	5th	6th	7th	8th	9th
Battery 1	San Cristóbal.	5 x 24G	5 x 24G[IV]	4 x 24G	4 x 24G / 2 x 8H	2 x 8H[VII] / 2 x 8H[IX]	4 x 24G	3 x 24G / 2 x 8H
Battery 2	San Cristóbal.	4 x 24G / 4 x 8H[II]	4 x 24G / 3 x 8H[V]	4 x 24G / 3 x 8H	6 x 24G / 1 x 8H[VII]	5 x 24G[X]	4 x 24G	4 x 24G
Battery 3	San Cristóbal.	4 x 24G	4 x 24G	4 x 24G	-	-	-	-
Battery 4	San Cristóbal – to enfilade the bridge.	4 x 16G / 2 x 10H[III]	4 x 16G / 1 x 10H[III]	4 x 16G	4 x 16G	4 x 16G	4 x 16G	4 x 16G[I]
Battery 5	Castle.	14 x 24G / 2 x 10H / 4 x 8H	14 x 24G / 1 x 10H / 4 x 8H	14 x 24G / 1 x 10H / 4 x 8H[VI]	2 x 24G / 2 x 10H / 3 x 8H[VIII]	2 x 10H / 3 x 8H[VIII]	2 x 10H / 1 x 8H	2 x 10H / 1 x 8H
Battery 6	Castle.	-	-	-	7 x 24G	6 x 24G	7 x 24G[XI]	5 x 24G
Battery 7	Castle.	-	-	-	-	3 x 24G	9 x 24G / 1 x 8H[IX XII]	8 x 24G / 1 x 8H

Notes

I. The 16-pdr guns were old Portuguese pieces.

II. 8in. howitzer disabled by French counter-battery fire.

III. These two 10in. howitzers' carriages were disabled by the (Portuguese) artillery officer firing at greater than 30 degrees elevation.

IV. One of these guns became unserviceable through drooping muzzle.

V. One 24-pdr carriage disabled.

VI. Two 24-pdr guns unserviceable through metal fatigue – many of the 24-pdr guns moved this night to Battery 6.

VII. One 24-pdr gun in each battery unserviceable through drooping muzzle and one 8in. howitzer destroyed by enemy fire.

VIII. One 8in. howitzer unserviceable.

IX. One 24-pdr gun in each battery unserviceable due to drooping muzzle.

X. These six additional guns arrived on 7th June and were iron 24-pdr Portuguese naval guns.

XI. Two 24-pdr guns unserviceable due to drooping muzzle.

XII. One iron 24-pdr disabled by enemy fire.

Ordnance Allocation to Batteries - Ciudad Rodrigo 8th–19th January 1812

(Source: Jones)

Maj. Dickson had the following guns: 34 x 24-pdr guns (24G) and 4 x 18-pdr guns (18G).

Battery No.	Battery Task	January 1812						
		13th	14th	15th	16th	17th	18th	19th
Battery 1	Initially San Francisco then main breach.	2 x 18G	2 x 18G	2 x 18G 3 x 24G	3 x 24G	3 x 24G	3 x 24G	3 x 24G
Battery 2	Main breach.	2 x 18 G 7 x 24G	2 x 18 G 7 x 24G	2 x 18 G 9 x 24G	2 x 18 G 9 x 24G	2 x 18 G 4 x 24G[I]	2 x 18 G 4 x 24G	1 x 18 G 4 x 24G
Battery 3	Main breach.	16 x 24G	16 x 24G	16 x 24G	16 x 24G	16 x 24G	15 x 24G[II]	15 x 24G[II]
Battery 4	Second breach.						7 x 24G	7 x 24G
Battery 5	To prevent repairs to both breaches during the night of 18–19th Jan 1812.							[III]

Notes

I. Struck in the muzzle and destroyed; four additional 24-pdrs were temporarily immobilised.
II. Gun burst through having a shot jammed half way down the bore.
III. This battery was originally intended for 6 x 24-pdrs but was manned with 1 x 6-pdr and 1 x 5½in. howitzer from a field brigade.

Ordnance Allocation to Batteries ~ Badajoz 23rd March – 6th April 1812
(Sources: Jones and Dickson)

Maj. Dickson had the following guns available for the siege¹: 16 x 24-pdr guns (24G), 20 x 18-pdr guns (18G) and 16 x 24-pdr howitzers (24H).

Battery No.	Battery Task	March 1812 23rd	24th	25th	26th	27th	28th	29th	30th	31st	April 1812 1st	2nd	3rd	4th	5th	6th
Battery 1	To enfilade left face of Picurina, howitzers to fire on interior.	3x18G 3x24H	3x18G 3x24H	3x18G 3x24H	3x18G 3x24Hᴵᴵᴵ	3x18G 3x24Hᴵᴵᴵ	3x18G to 9 By 3x24Hᴵᴵᴵ	3x18G 3x24H	3x24H	3x24H	-	3x24H	3x24H	3x24H	3x24H	3x24H
Battery 2	Direct fire on Picurina.	4x24G	4x24G	4x24G	4x24Gᴵᴵᴵ	4x24Gᴵᴵᴵ	4x24Gᴵᴵᴵ	4x24Gᴵᴵᴵ 1x24G	4x24Gᴵᴵᴵ 1x24G to Bty 7 3x24G to Bty 8	-	-	-	-	-	-	-
Battery 3	Direct fire on San Roque Lunette.	-	4x18G	4x18G	3x18Gᴵⱽ	3x18G	3x18G	3x18G	3x18G	3x18G	3x18G to Bty 11	-	-	-	-	-
Battery 4	To enfilade the right face of Trinidad Bastion.	-	6X24G 1X24H	5x24Gᴵᴵ	5x24G	5x24G	5x24G	5x24G	5x24G to Bty 8	-	-	-	-	-	-	-
Battery 5	To enfilade the right face of San Pedro Bastion.	-	4X18G	4X18G	3x18Gᴵⱽ	3x18G	3x18G	3x18G	3x18G	3x18G	1x18G 3x24Hᵛ 2x18G to Bty 11	1x18G 3x24H	1x18G 3x24H	1x18G 3x24H	1x18G 3x24H	1x18G 3x24H
Battery 6	To enfilade the right face of San Roque Lunette.	-	-	3X24H	3X24H	3X24H	3X24H	3X24H	3X24H to Bty 10	-	-	-	-	-	-	-
Battery 7	To breach right face of Trinidad.	-	-	-	-	-	-	-	12x24G	-	12x24G	12x24G	12x24G	12x24G	12x24G	12x24G

Battery No.	Battery Task	March 1812									April 1812					
		23rd	24th	25th	26th	27th	28th	29th	30th	31st	1st	2nd	3rd	4th	5th	6th
Battery 8	To enfilade Santa Maria Bastion.								3x18G 3x24G	3x18G 3x24G	3x18G 3x24G	3x18G 3x24G	3x18G 3x24G	3x18G 3x24G	3x18G 3x24G	3x18G 3x24G
Battery 9	To breach left flank of the Santa Maria Bastion.							8x18G	8x18G	8x18G	8x18G	8x18G	8x18G	8x18G	8x18G	8x18G
Battery 10	To enfilade ditch in front of main breach.							3x24H	3x24H	3x24H	3x24H	3x24H	3x24H	3x24H	3x24H	3x24H
Battery 11	To neutralise the San Roque Lunette.										6x18G	5x18G^{IV}	5x18G	5x18G	5x18G	5x18G
Battery 12	To fire in direct support of the assault.	14x24H	14x24H												14x24H	14x24H

Notes

I. The ten British 18-pdr guns were also brought up and in the park but were not used.
II. One 24-pdr gun and one 24-pdr howitzer disabled overnight.
III. The guns/howitzers in batteries 1 & 2 were not used from 26th March onwards.
IV. One piece of ordnance disabled.
V. Received from the Artillery Park.

Ordnance Allocation to Batteries ~ Tarragona 3rd–12th June 1813

(Source: Scott – not authoritative)

Maj. Williamson had the following ordnance: 14 x 24-pdr guns (24G), 9 x 8in. howitzers (8H) and 5 x 10in. mortars (10M).

Battery No.	Battery Task	June 1813						
		5th	6th	7th	8th	9th	10th	11th
Battery 1	To prevent repairs to Fort Royal and San Carlos Bastion.	4 x 8H	4 x 8H	4 x 8H	4 x 8H	4 x 8H	4 x 8H	4 x 8H
Battery 2	To engage Fort Royal and San Carlos Bastion.	2 x 24G	2 x 24G	2 x 24G	2 x 24G	2 x 24G	2 x 24G	2 x 24G
Battery 3	To commence breaching against the west wall.			2 x 24G	6 x 24G	6 x 24G	6 x 24G	6 x 24G	6 x 24G
Batteries 4 & 5	To breach the north wall.					6 x 24G 5 x 10M 5 x 8H	6 x 24G 5 x 10M 5 x 8H	6 x 24G 5 x 10M 5 x 8H

Ordnance Allocation to Batteries ~ First Siege of San Sebastian 13th–25th July 1813

(Sources: Jones and Dickson)

Lt. Col. Dickson had the following guns for the siege; 14 x 24-pdr guns (24G), 5 x 24-pdr short guns (24GS), 6 x 18-pdr guns (18G), 6 x 8in. howitzers (8H), 4 x 68-pdr carronades (68C) and 4 x 10in. mortars (10M).[1]

Battery No.	Battery Task	13th	14th	15th	16th	17th	18th (July 1813)	19th	20th	21st	22nd	23rd	24th	25th
Battery 1	Engage San Bartolomé.	4 x 18G	4 x 18G	4 x 18G	4 x 18G	4 x 18G	4 x 18G							
Battery 2	Engage San Bartolomé.	2 x 8H	2 x 8H	2 x 8H	2 x 8H	2 x 8H	2 x 8H							
Battery 3	Enfilade fire on eastern wall.								6 x 18G	6 x 18G	6 x 18G	6 x 18G	6 x 18G	6 x 18G
Battery 4	Enfilade fire on eastern wall.								2 x 8H	2 x 8H	2 x 8H	2 x 8H	2 x 8H	2 x 8H
Battery 11	Counter Miradór Bty and fire against the castle.					2 x 24GS	2 x 24GS	2 x 24G	2 x 24G	2 x 24G	2 x 24G	2 x 24G	2 x 24G	2 x 24G
						2 x 8H	2 x 8H	4 x 8H	4 x 8H	4 x 8H	4 x 8H	4 x 8H	4 x 8H	4 x 8H
Battery 12	Against the town defences.							2 x 24G	2 x 24G	2 x 24G				
Battery 13	To create a breach.							4 x 24G	4 x 24G	4 x 24G	4 x 24G	4 x 24G	4 x 24G	4 x 24G
Battery 14	To create a breach.							8 x 24G	8 x 24G	7 x 24G	9 x 24G	9 x 24G	9 x 24G	9 x 24G
								3 x 24GS	3 x 24GS	3 x 24GS[ll]	3 x 24GS	3 x 24GS	3 x 24GS	3 x 24GS

Battery No.	Battery Task	13th	14th	15th	16th	17th	July 1813 18th	19th	20th	21st	22nd	23rd	24th	25th
Battery 15	Direct fire against breach and harassing fire.										4 x 68C	4 x 68C	4 x 68C	4 x 68
Battery 16	To engage the town and castle.											4 x10M	4 x10M	4 x10M

Notes

I. It appears that only five of the short 24-pdrs were landed from HMS *Surveillante*.

II. One 24G was knocked out and one had a blocked vent, which was not repaired until later on 21st July. In addition, the 3 x 24GS were mounted on land carriages.

Ordnance Allocation to Batteries ~ Second Siege of San Sebastian 22nd August – 8th September 1813

(Source: Jones)
Lt. Col. Dickson had the following guns for the siege; 56 x 24-pdr guns (24G), 14 x 18-pdr guns (18G), 18 x 8in. howitzers (8H), 12 x 68-pdr carronades (68C), 16 x 10in. mortars (10M), and 1 x 12in. mortar (12M).[1]

Battery No.	Battery Task	22nd	23rd	24th	August 1813 25th	26th	27th	28th	29th	30th	31st
Battery 5	To breach the face of the left demi-bastion and the curtain above it.		6 x 18G	6 x 18G	6 x 18G	6 x 18G	6 x 18G	6 x 18G	6 x 18G	6 x 18G	6 x 18G
Battery 6	Guns – to breach the face of the left demi-bastion and the curtain above it. Howitzers – general purposes of annoyance.	7 x 24G	7 x 24G	7 x 24G 2 x 8H	7 x 24G 2 x 8H	7 x 24G 2 x 8H	3 x 24G 2 x 8H	3 x 24G 2 x 8H	3 x 24G 2 x 8H	3 x 24G 2 x 8H	3 x 24G 2 x 8H
Battery 7	To breach the face of the main bastion and the high curtain of the hornwork.							3 x 24G[IV]	3 x 24G[IV]	3 x 24G	3 x 24G
Battery 10	To enfilade the rear of the castle.[II]									1 x 24G 1 x 8H	1 x 24G 1 x 8H
Battery 11	To counter Mirador Bty and fire against the castle.	2 x 8 H[III]	2 x 8H	2 x 8H	2 x 8H	2 x 8H	2 x 8H	2 x 8H	2 x 8H	2 x 8H	2 x 8H
Battery 13	To fire behind the breach and against the town defences and castle.				1 x 12M 5 x 10M	1 x 12M 5 x 10M	1 x 12M 5 x 10M	1 x 12M 5 x 10M	1 x 12M 5 x 10M	1 x 12M 5 x 10M	1 x 12M 5 x 10M

Battery No.	Battery Task	August 1813									
		22nd	23rd	24th	25th	26th	27th	28th	29th	30th	31st
Battery 14	Guns – to fire at the breaches A to C. Carronades and howitzers – to enfilade the curtain and land front between A and C.	2 x 24 G 4 x 8H[III] 2 x 24 G	2 x 24 G 4 x 8H 4 x 68C	6 x 24 G 5 x 8H 4 x 68C	6 x 24 G 5 x 8H 4 x 68C	6 x 24 G 5 x 8H 4 x 68C	6 x 24 G 5 x 8H 4 x 68C	6 x 24 G 5 x 8H 4 x 68C	6 x 24 G 5 x 8H 4 x 68C	6 x 24 G 5 x 8H 4 x 68C	6 x 24 G 5 x 8H 4 x 68C
Battery 15	To fire at the breaches A to C.	4 x 24G	8 x 24G	15 x 24G	15 x 24G	15 x 24G	15 x 24G	15 x 24G	15 x 24G	15 x 24G	15 x 24G
Battery 16	To engage the land front and castle.				4 x 10M	4 x 10M	4 x 10M	4 x 10M	4 x 10M	4 x 10M	4 x 10M
Battery 17	To engage the town, land front and castle.								6 x 10M	6 x 10M	6 x 10M

Battery No.	Battery Task	September 1813							
		1st	2nd	3rd	4th	5th	6th	7th	8th
Battery 5	To engage the castle.	6 x 18G	6 x 18G	6 x 18G	6 x 18G	6 x 18G	3 x 18G	3 x 18G	3 x 18G
Battery 6	This battery was not used beyond 6th September.	3 x 24G 2 x 8H	3 x 24G 2 x 8H	3 x 24G 2 x 8H	3 x 24G 2 x 8H	3 x 24G 2 x 8H[VI]	2 x 8H	2 x 8H	2 x 8H
Battery 7	To breach the Mirador Bty.	3 x 24G	3 x 24G	3 x 24G	3 x 24G	3 x 24G	3 x 24G	3 x 24G	3 x 24G
Battery 8	To neutralise/destroy the Reyna Bty.						3 x 18G	3 x 18G	3 x 18G
Battery 9	To neutralise/destroy the Reyna and Mirador batteries.						17 x 24G	17 x 24G	17 x 24G
Battery 10	To enfilade the rear of the castle and its lower defences.	1 x 24G 1 x 8H	1 x 24G 1 x 8H	1 x 24G 1 x 8H	1 x 24G 1 x 8H	1 x 24G 1 x 8H	1 x 24G 1 x 8H[VII]	1 x 24G 1 x 8H	1 x 24G 1 x 8H
Battery 11	Counter Mirador Bty.	2 x 8 H	2 x 8 H	2 x 8 H	2 x 8 H	2 x 8 H	2 x 8 H	2 x 8 H	2 x 8 H

Battery No.	Battery Task	1st	2nd	3rd	September 1813 4th	5th	6th	7th	8th
Battery 13	Fire behind the castle.	1 x 12M 5 x 10M	1 x 12M 5 x 10M	1 x 12M 5 x 10M	1 x 12M 5 x 10M	1 x 12M 5 x 10M	1 x 12M 5 x 10M	1 x 12M 5 x 10M	1 x 12M 5 x 10M
Battery 14	Guns – to counter the Mirador Bty. Carronades and howitzers – to engage the castle.	6 x 24 G 5 x 8H 4 x 68C	6 x 24 G 5 x 8H 4 x 68C	6 x 24 G 5 x 8H 4 x 68C	6 x 24 G 5 x 8H 4 x 68C	6 x 24 G 5 x 8H 4 x 68C	6 x 24 G 5 x 8H 4 x 68C	6 x 24 G 5 x 8H 4 x 68C	6 x 24 G 5 x 8H 4 x 68C
Battery 15	This battery was not used beyond 3rd September.	15 x 24G	15 x 24G	15 x 24G [v]					
Battery 16	At the castle and behind.	4 x 10M	4 x 10M	4 x 10M	4 x 10M	4 x 10M	4 x 10M	4 x 10M	4 x 10M
Battery 17	At the castle and behind.	6 x 10M	6 x 10M	6 x 10M	6 x 10M	6 x 10M	6 x 10M	6 x 10M	6 x 10M

Notes

I. It is assumed that the five short-barrelled 24-pdrs were returned to HMS *Surveillante* in August. The one 12in. mortar was a Spanish piece. Despite such a large train, Wellington gave orders that the siege artillery destined for Cuxhaven was not to be used: this included 15 x 24-pdr guns, 8 x 18-pdr guns and 4 x 10in. mortars. Note one additional 10in. mortar was lost in the harbour during unloading.

II. It was the original intention to have 5 x 24-pdr guns and an 8in. howitzer in this battery.

III. These guns and howitzers were left in place from the previous siege.

IV. Four guns were moved from Battery 6; only three were in place on the night of 27th August and one gun was destroyed on 28th August, replaced the same night by the remaining 24-pdr.

V. The 15 x 24-pdr guns were brought across the riverbed of the Urumea over the next couple of days and placed in the hornwork.

VI. The third 24-pdr gun was sent to Battery 10.

VII. A further 24-pdr gun was mounted in Battery 10 on the island; yet another gun was lost during unloading.

Glossary and Abbreviations

Glossary

Abattis	Trees cut and arranged to leave the branches facing outwards to form a barrier.
Bastion	A construction with two front faces protruding into the ditch from the curtain to facilitate flanking fire from both sides along the ditch.
Bátardeau	A wall built across the ditch of a fortification, with a sluice gate to regulate the height of water in the ditch on both sides of the wall.
Caisson	A chest or wagon for holding or conveying ammunition.
Casemate	A vaulted chamber for artillery guns.
Caudle	A warm drink consisting of thin gruel, mixed with wine or ale, sweetened and spiced.
Chasse-marée	A decked commercial sailing vessel or fast lugger – for the Adour River crossing they were to be used to anchor groups of pontoons upstream.
Chevaux de frise	The *chevaux de frise* (singular: *cheval de frise*) were medieval defensive obstacles consisting of a portable frame (sometimes just a simple log) covered with many long iron or wooden spikes or even actual spears. They were principally intended as an anti-cavalry obstacle but could also be moved quickly to help block a breach.
Creeping barrage	A (slowly) moving artillery barrage acting as a defensive curtain for infantry following closely behind.

Demi-lune	A triangular outwork built to protect the curtain wall and to provide cover to the flanks of a bastion. (See also *ravelin*)
En potence	The movement of any part of the left or right wing formed at a projecting angle with the line.
Generalissimo	The supreme commander of the Spanish forces.
Glanders	A rare contagious disease that mainly affects horses, characterised by swellings below the jaw and mucous discharge from the nostrils.
Hornwork	A defensive work detached from the main defensive structure, normally to the front.
Ordenança	Portuguese Home Guard.
Palisade	Strong wooden stake, about 10 feet long, driven into the ground short of the parapet of the glacis.
Park	An old term which essentially referred to the artillery attached to the army. In the Napoleonic era it was a depot which moved with the army from where ammunition was re-supplied and where repairs were made to guns, carriages, limbers and ammunition wagons. It would also contain the heavier guns, such as the 12-pounder, which were less mobile and kept centrally.
Portfire	A short stick wrapped at the top end with a slow match and used to ignite the gun.
Postilion	The rider who drove the post chaise mounted (normally on the left) of one of the drawing horses.
Prime movers	Prime movers were the animals required to haul the wagons. These were generally bullocks or cart horses but due to the paucity of both in Iberia at this time, ordinary horses and mules were also utilised.
Ravelin	A triangular outwork built to protect the curtain wall and to provide cover to the flanks of a bastion. (See also *demi-lune*)
Saucisson	Literally French sausage – an early form of slow burning fuse which had the appearance of a thin black sausage.
Slowmatch	A composition of gunpowder, sulphur and saltpetre driven into a paper casing which, depending on the size of the casing, would burn slowly for a 'precise' period of time.
Subaltern	An officer below the rank of captain i.e. a first or second lieutenant.
Terreplein/Terre-pleine	Surface of the rampart behind the parapet, where guns are mounted.
Tête-du-pont	Bridgehead

Toise	A measurement of distance just over 6 feet.
Train	The artillery train was the pool of drivers formed and trained to drive the horse teams to pull the foot artillery limbers and carriages.
Windage	The gap between the bore of the barrel and the projectile.

Abbreviations

AG	Adjutant General
CRA	Commander Royal Artillery
DAG	Deputy Adjutant General
KGA	King's German (Legion) Artillery
KGL	King's German Legion
MGO	Master General of the Ordnance
NCO	Non Commissioned Officer
OR	Other Ranks
QMG	Quarter Master General
RA	Royal Artillery
RE	Royal Engineers
RHA	Royal Horse Artillery

Bibliography

Short titles are used in the endnotes as follows (see below for publication details):

BS   Hughes, Maj. Gen. B. P., *British Smooth-Bore Artillery*

GTH   Gleig, G. R., (ed.). *Sergeant Norbert Landsheit – The Hussar, A German Cavalryman in British Service throughout the Napoleonic Wars*

GTS   Gleig, G. R., *The Subaltern, A Chronicle of the Peninsular War*

HFI   Hughes, Maj. Gen. B. P., *Firepower*

HHT   Hughes, Maj. Gen. B. P, *Honour Titles of the Royal Artillery*

HOF   Hughes, Maj. Gen. B. P., *Open Fire, Artillery Tactics from Marlborough to Wellington*

KAR   Kincaid, Capt. J., *Adventures in the Rifle Brigade in the Peninsula, France and the Netherlands from 1809 to 1815*

KRS   Kincaid, Cap J., *Random Shots from a Rifleman*

LBR   Laws, Lt. Col. M. E. S., *Battery Records of the Royal Artillery, 1716–1859*

LKH   Leslie, K. H., *Military Journal of Colonel Leslie, K H, of Balquhain*

LRA   Laws, Lt. Col. M. E. S., *The Royal Artillery at Barrosa*

OHP   Oman, Sir Charles, *A History of the Peninsular War*

OWA   Oman, Sir Charles, *Wellington's Army 1809–1814*

RN&W   Roberts, A., *Napoleon and Wellington*

RNLG   Roberts, A., *Waterloo, Napoleon's Last Gamble*

SD   Wellington, The Duke of, *Supplementary Dispatches and Memoranda of Field Marshal Arthur Duke of Wellington KG*

SWC   Siborne, W., *The Waterloo Campaign*

SWL   Siborne, H. J., *The Waterloo Letters*

WCS   Whinyates, F. A., *From Coruna to Sevastopol*

WD   Wellington, Arthur Wellesley, *The Dispatches of Field Marshal The Duke of Wellington, During his Various Campaigns in India, Denmark, Portugal, Spain, the Low Countries, and France*

James Clavell Library, Woolwich

Primary Sources

Adye, Capt. R. W., *The Bombardier and the Pocket Gunner*, eight editions (London, 1800–27).

Bent, Lt. W., *Various Letters from Lt William Henry Bent*. MD 632.

Bogue, Capt. R., *The Diary of 2nd Captain Richard Bogue, Serving in 'B' Troop, Royal Horse Artillery, September 22, 1808 to February 1, 1809*. MD 343.

Bolton S., *The Papers and Letters of Captain Samuel Bolton RA*. MD 2602.

Bowyer Lane, Maj. H., *Letters of Major Henry Bowyer Lane RA*. The location of the letters is unknown; Edward Whinyates summarised the key points from the letters in an undated manuscript and, according to Duncan, these are held in Cleaveland's MSS. However, there is no record of this at the James Clavell Library. I received a copy of the summary from the current Battery (46 Talavera Battery RA) historical sources.

Brereton, Lieutenant General Sir W., *Operations of D Troop RHA: Notes on Brereton's Diary* (unknown editor). MD 2405.

Bull, Col. R, *Letters of Colonel Robert Bull in the Peninsula and Waterloo, 1810–15*. MD 2005.

Coates, Cpl. J., *Manuscript Notes of Service of Corporal Joseph Coates, Corps of RA Drivers, 1803–16*. MD 1836.

Colquhoun, N., *Colonel J. N. Colquhoun Papers 1791–1853*. MD 915.

Congreve, W., *The Details of the Rocket System* (London, 1814).

Cookson, Gen. G., *The Journals of Lieutenant General George Cookson: The Retreat to Corunna*. MD 2566.

Dickson, Maj. Gen. Sir Alexander. *The Dickson Manuscripts* are a series of diaries, letters, accounts books, officers' squad books, orders and returns, maps and drawings. They commence in 1794 and end in 1840. Series A covers 'Notes on Artillery' from 1294 to 1794 (the year of Dickson's commission) and consists of notes compiled for Dickson by Capt. R. H. Ord, his personal staff officer for many years. Maj. Murdoch edited these and they were published in the Proceedings of the Royal Artillery Institute (RAI) between 1899 and 1903. Series B, covering the years 1794 to 1808, was edited by Lt. Col. Desmond Vigors and sent to the RAI in 1989. Series C, covering the years 1809 to 1813, was edited and published part by part by Lt. Col. Leslie between 1906 and 1914. Lt. Col. Desmond Vigors continued the series from 1814 to 1818 in four volumes between 1986 and 1991 (Chapter 9, Jan–Apr 1814; Chapter 10, May–Dec 1814; Chapter 11, Jan–Dec 1815; and Chapter 12, 1816–1818). Lt. Col. Vigors was subsequently allowed an additional Chapter 13, 1819–1840, published in 1992. The references used in this book refer to Series C as published by Leslie (five volumes) and the additional work (chapters 9–12) as yet unpublished by Vigors.

Dyneley, T., *The Letters written by Lieutenant-General Thomas Dyneley, While on Active Service Between the Years 1806 and 1815*, MD 1050/1 and 1050/1(2).

Evelegh, Capt. H., *The Diary of Captain H. Evelegh RHA, C Troop RHA during the Corunna Campaign 1808–1809*. MD 1254.

Gardiner, Gen. Sir Robert, *Letters of Sir Robert Gardiner 1806–1814*. MD 1178 Parts I, II and III.

Hardinge, Lt. R., *Extract from the Diary of Lieut. Richard Hardinge, RA*. MD 280.

Hough, Lt. H., *The Diary of Lieutenant H. Hough, RA, 1812–13 (Peninsular War)*. MD 83.

Jenkinson, Maj. G., *Letters from the Peninsular War 1809–1814, Major George Jenkinson RA*. MD 212 Parts I, II and III.

Lawson, Capt. R., *Diary of Captain Robert Lawson, Royal Artillery: 14 May 1812 – 26 August 1813*. MD 81. Part of Dickson's boxes: the diary was reproduced in the 1990 (Ken Trotman) reprint of part of Series C in vol. IV, pp.696–727.

Mercer, Maj. A. C., *Mercer Notes and Papers*. MD 88/1–4.

Ord, Capt. R., *Diary of Captain Robert Ord RA: June to August 1815*. MD 1438. Part of the Leslie Papers. Copied from the original diary lent to Major Leslie by the Reverend F. Penny in 1923.

Ramsay, Maj. N., *Ramsay Papers 1792–1815*. MD 340.

Robe, Lt. Col. Sir William, *Papers of Colonel Sir William Robe, 1793–1818*. MD 914.

Sandilands, Lt. P., *Notes Recorded from Waterloo*. MD 638.

Unger Lt. W., *Papers and Maps of Lieutenant William Unger, KGL*. MD 228.

Whitehead, Sergeant T., *Record of the Services of The Chestnut Troop R.H.A. under Sir H. D. Ross K.C.B. from 1st June 1806 to 1st September 1825*. MD 1270 (filed in MD 917).

Wood, Col. G., *Ammunition Expenditure at Waterloo*. MD 2809.

Secondary Sources
Duncan, Capt. F., Boxes and Papers. MD 193.

Letter Latham to Bidwell dated 10 Sep 1971. MD 224/1.

Leslie, Maj. J., Papers. MD 1438.

RA Personnel Present at Battle (Waterloo). MD 1107.

Royal Artillery Institution (RAI), Royal Artillery Historical Society (RAHS) Proceedings and Royal Artillery Journal (RAJ)

Primary Sources
Ingilby, Lt. I., *Diary of Lieutenant Ingilby, R.A., in the Peninsular War*, ed. Major E.A. Lambert RA, RAI Proceedings, vol. XX, pp.241–62.

Ingilby, Lt. I., *Extracts from the Diary of Lieut. Ingilby, RHA During the Waterloo Campaign*, RAI Proceedings, pp.315–23 – see MD 797.

Wall, Capt. A., *Diary of the Operations in Spain under Sir John Moore by Captain Adam* Unger, Lt., *Battle of Albuera*, RAI Proceedings, vol. XIII, p.126. MD 228).

Wall RA, RAI Proceedings, vol. XIV, p.329.

BIBLIOGRAPHY

Secondary Sources

Becke, Capt. A. F., *The British Artillery at Waterloo*, RAJ vol. XXXIV, pp.313–28.

Dering Majendie, Capt. V., *On the Validity of General Shrapnel's Claim to the Invention of Shells in which the True Principle of Shrapnel Fire was first Enunciated and Applied*, RAI Proceedings, vol. III, pp.398–408.

Gardiner, Maj. Gen. W. B., *Hints for the Application of Shrapnel Shell*, Minutes of RAI Proceedings, vol. IV, pp.33–46.

Gilman, Lt. Col. H. C. R., *Waterloo 1815*, RAJ vol. LXXX, pp.225–31.

Headlam, Maj. Gen. Sir John, *The Duke and the Regiment*, RAJ vol. LXXI, pp.1–11.

Hime, Lt. H. W. L., *The Mobility of Field Artillery, Past and Present*, RAI Proceedings, vol. VI.

Holmes, Capt. C., *The Campaign of Corunna*, RAI Proceedings, vol. XXXI, pp.391–98.

Latham, Brig. H. B., *Major-General Sir John May, K.C.B., K.C.H. 1779–1847*, RAI Proceedings, vol. LXXXII, pp.25–30.

Laws, Lt. Col. M. E. S., *The Royal Artillery at Barrosa*, RAI Proceedings, vol. LXXVIII, pp.196–206. (LRA in endnotes)

Laws, Lt. Col. M. E. S., *A Waterloo Letter*, RAJ vol. LXXXI, No. 4, pp.305–07.

Leslie, Maj, J. H., *Some Remarks concerning The Royal Artillery at the Battle of Talavera, July 27–28, 1809*, RAI Proceedings, vol. XXXIV, pp.503–08.

Leslie, Maj. J. H., *Notes on the Artillery Units engaged at Waterloo*, RAJ vol. XXXVI, pp.180–87.

Lipscombe, Col. N. J., *Wellington's Gunner in the Peninsula – Lieutenant Colonel Alexander Dickson*, Proceedings of the Royal Artillery Historical Society, vol. 10, No. 3, Dec 2009.

Marshall-Cornwell, Gen. Sir James, *The Royal Regiment in the Waterloo Campaign*, RAJ vol. XCII, pp.1–21.

Maurice Jones, Col. K. W., *Wellington in 1815*, RAJ vol. LXXXI, pp.257–67.

Minto, Capt. G. A., *The Waterloo Dispatch*, RAJ vol. LXIII, pp.47–52.

Oman, Sir Charles, *Albuera*, RAI Proceedings, vol. XXXVI, pp.49–69.

Parsons, Maj. Gen. Sir C. S. B., *Extract from Letter of Captain John Charlton, Royal Artillery*, RAI Proceedings, vol. XXXII, pp.334–36.

Vigors, Lt. Col. D., *Voices from the Napoleonic Wars*, RAJ vol. CXI, pp.137–40. Quoting L. Von Wissel, *Ruhmwurdig Thateu welche in der letzten Kreigen von Unterofficieren und Soldaten der englisch-deutchen Legion und der hannoverschenm Armee Werichtet Sind* (Hannover, 1846).

Vigors, Lt. Col. D., *The Battle of Albuera, Dickson's Missing Letter of 22 May 1811*, RAJ vol. CXXVIII, pp.43–45.

Whinyates, Col. F. A., *The British Artillery in the Waterloo Campaign*, RAI Proceedings, vol. XVI, pp.579–81.

Whinyates, Col. F. A., *Horse Artillery Guns at Waterloo*, RAI Proceedings, vol. XX, pp.627–31.

Unpublished Sources

Corkerry, S., *Personnel and Training in the Royal Artillery 1741–1815*, MA dissertation, De Montford University, Bedford.

Ebke, G. E. and H., *Andrew Cleeves: Life as an Officer of the King's German Legion*, dated 15th March 2011.

Freer, W., *Letters from the Peninsular Wars*, Leicestershire Records Office, Ref: 16D52 N.

Vigors, Lieutenant Colonel D., *History of the Royal Regiment of Artillery*, two volumes.

British Library

Moore, Sir John, Papers, MSS 57320–57330.

Wyld J., *Wyld's Atlas – Map Showing the Principal Movements, Battles and Sieges in which the British Army was Engaged During the War from 1808–1814 in the Spanish Peninsula and the South of France* (London 1840).

National Army Museum

Belson, Capt. G., – NAM 1992-03-51-32/33/34. *Diaries kept by Captain George John Belson 1787–1868 relating to the Peninsular War.* (From a collection of documents and photographs of the Belson family, 1733–1989.)

Eliot – NAM 1959-03-127-1. *Correspondence of William Granville Eliot RA.*

Whitman, Sgt C., – NAM 1984-08-37-1. *Journal of Campaigns in the Peninsula by Charles Whitman.*

National Archives (Public Record Office)

Artillery Letters and Letter Book, from Officers, Foreign: PRO WO 55/1193 to 1197.

Artillery Letters and Letter Book, to Officers, Foreign: PRO WO 55/1200 to 1202.

Artillery Muster Books and Pay Lists RA: PRO WO 10/782 to 1050.

Artillery Muster Books and Pay Lists Horse (RHA): PRO WO 10/788 to 789.

Monthly Returns: PRO WO 17/2464 to 2476.

Other Sources

Primary Sources

Burgoyne, Sir John, *Life and Correspondence of Sir John Fox Burgoyne*, two volumes (London, 1873).

BIBLIOGRAPHY

Costello, E., *Adventures of a Soldier, or Memoirs of Edward Costello. K.S.F. formerly a Non-Commissioned Officer in the Rifle Brigade and Late Captain in the British Legion Comprising Narratives of the Campaign in the Peninsular Wars under the Duke of Wellington and the Recent Civil Wars in Spain* (London, 1841).

Cowell Stepney, Sir John, *Leaves from the Diary of an Officer of the Guards* (London, 1854).

Downman, Maj. T., *The Diary of Major Thomas Downman RHA in the Peninsula, 30 April 1811 to 17 August 1812*, published in the Journal of the Society for Army Historical Research, vol. V, pp.178–86.

Foy, Gen. M., *History of the War in the Peninsula under Napoleon*, two volumes (Paris, 1829).

Frazer, Sir Augustus, *Remarks on the Organisation of a Corps of Artillery in British Service* (London, 1818).

Gleig, G. R., *The Subaltern, A Chronicle of the Peninsular War* (London, 1826). (GTS in endnotes)

Gleig, G. R. (ed.), *Sergeant Norbert Landsheit – The Hussar, A German Cavalryman in British Service throughout the Napoleonic Wars* (London, 1837). (GTH in endnotes)

Glover, G. (ed.), *Letters from the Battle of Waterloo – unpublished correspondence from the Siborne Papers* (London, 2004).

Glover, G. (ed.), *The Letters of Second Captain Charles Dansey Royal Artillery 1806– 1813* (2006).

Grattan, Lt. W., *Adventures with the Connaught Rangers, 1809–1814* (London, 1847).

Henegan, Sir Richard, *Seven Years Campaigning in the Peninsula and the Netherlands 1808–1815*, two volumes (London, 1846).

Heron, Capt. F., *A Concise Review of the Present State of the British Artillery* (London, 1823).

Hibbert, C. (ed.), Anon, *A Soldier of the 71st, The Journal of a Soldier in the Peninsular War* (London, 1996).

Jones, Sir John, *Journal of Sieges carried on by the Army under the Duke of Wellington in Spain, Between the Years 1811 and 1814*, three volumes (London, 1846).

Kincaid, Capt. J., *Adventures in the Rifle Brigade in the Peninsula, France and the Netherlands from 1809 to 1815* (London, 1830). (KAR in endnotes)

Kincaid, Cap J., *Random Shots from a Rifleman* (London, 1835). (KRS in endnotes)

Larpent, F. S., *The Private Journal of F. Seymour Larpent, Judge-Advocate General Attached to the Head-quarters of Lord Wellington During the Peninsular War from 1812 to its Close*, three volumes (London, 1853).

Leach, J., *Rough Sketches of the Life of an Old Soldier During a Service in the East Indies, at the Siege of Copenhagen in 1807, in the Peninsula and the South of France in the Campaign from 1808 to 1814 with the Light Division, in the Netherlands in 1815, including the Battles of Quatre Bras and Waterloo, with a Slight sketch of Three Years passed by the Army of Occupation in France* (London, 1831).

Leslie, K. H., *Military Journal of Colonel Leslie, K H, of Balquhain, while Serving with the Twenty-Ninth Regiment in the Peninsula and the Sixth Rifles in Canada, 1807–1832* (Aberdeen, 1887). (LKH in endnotes)

Liddell Hart, Capt. B. H. (ed.), *The Letters of Private Wheeler, 1809–1828* (London, 1951).

Londonderry, Lord, *The War in Germany and France in 1813 and 1814* (London 1830).

May, Lt. Col. J., *A Few Observations on the Mode of Attack and Employment of the Heavy Artillery at Ciudad Rodrigo, Badajoz in 1812 and San Sebastian in 1813* (London, 1819).

Mercer, Gen. A. C., *Journal of the Waterloo Campaign*, two volumes (London, 1870).

Miller, Sergeant B., *The Adventures of Serjeant Benjamin Miller* (London, 1813) – Naval & Military reprint (ed.) by Dacombe & Rowe.

Napier, W. F. P., *History of the War in the Peninsula and in the South of France, 1807–1814,* six volumes (London, 1828–45).

Parlby, Capt. S., *British Indian Military Repository*, vol. III (Calcutta, 1824).

Ross, Sir Hew Dalrymple, *Memoir of Field Marshal Sir Hew Dalrymple Ross, Royal Horse Artillery* (Woolwich, 1871). Later version by Ken Trotman Publishing, introduction by Howie Muir (Godmanchester, 2008).

Sabine, E. (ed.), *Letters of Colonel Sir Augustus Simon Frazer, KCB, Commanding the Horse Artillery in the Army under the Duke of Wellington* (London, 1859).

Schaumann, A. L. F., *On the Road with Wellington, the Diary of a War Commissary in the Peninsular Campaigns* (London, 1924 translated version).

Scott, Maj. T., *The Diary of Major Thomas Scott RA.* This diary was discovered in 1940 at Draycott House, Kempsey, Worcester by Lt. Col. Frederick Scott Garwood RE who set about transcribing the work. It consists of 23 volumes but unfortunately volumes III and IV are missing, covering 6th July 1813 – 1st June 1814.

Siborne, H. J., *The Waterloo Letters* (2009 reprint). (SWL in endnotes)

Siborne, W., *The Waterloo Campaign* – third edition (London, 1848). (SWC in endnotes)

Simmons, G., *A British Rifle Man, The Journals and Correspondence of Major George Simmons, Rifle Brigade, During the Peninsular War and the Campaign of Waterloo* (London, 1899).

Smith, Sir Harry, The *Autobiography of Lieutenant-General Sir Harry Smith, Baronet of Aliwal on the Sutlej, G.C.B.* (London, 1903).

Spencer Cooper, J., *Rough Notes of Seven Campaigns in Portugal, Spain, France and America, During the Years 1809–1815* (London, 1869).

Tomkinson, Lt. Col. W., *Diary of a Cavalry Officer in the Peninsular War and Waterloo Campaign 1809–1815* (London, 1895).

Ward, S. G. P. (ed.), *The Diary of Lieutenant Robert Woollcombe, R.A. 1812–1813,* published by the Journal of the Society for Army Historical Research, vol. LII (1974).

Wellington, Arthur Wellesley, *The Dispatches of Field Marshal The Duke of Wellington, During his Various Campaigns in India, Denmark, Portugal, Spain, the Low Countries, and France,* eight volumes (Gurwood, London 1844–47). (WD in endnotes)

BIBLIOGRAPHY

Wellington, The Duke of, *Supplementary Dispatches and Memoranda of Field Marshal Arthur Duke of Wellington KG,* ed. A. R. Wellesley, Second Duke of Wellington, 15 volumes (London, 1858–72). (SD in endnotes)

Whinyates, F. A., (ed.), *Diary of Campaigns in the Peninsula for the Years 1811, 12 and 13, by Lieutenant William Swabey, An Officer of 'E' Troop Royal Horse Artillery* (London, 1895).

Whittingham, F., (ed.), *A Memoir of the Services of Lieutenant-General Sir Samuel Ford Whittingham* (London, 1868).

Wollocombe, R.H., (ed.), *The Peninsular War Journal of Captain William Webber, Royal Artillery* (London, 1991).

Secondary Sources

Arcq, A., *Les Quatre-Bras 16 Juin 1815 Le second prelude à Waterloo* (Saint-Thonan, 2009).

Asquith Gen. W. H., *List of Officers of the Royal Regiment of Artillery from the Year 1716 to the Year 1899,* fourth edition (London, 1900).

Bailey, Maj. Gen. J. B. A., *Field Artillery and Firepower* (Annapolis, 2004).

Barbero, A., *The Battle, A History of the Battle of Waterloo* – English version translated by Cullen, J. (London, 2006).

Bassford, C., Moran, D. and Pedlow, G. W., *On Waterloo, Clausewitz, Wellington and the Campaign of 1815* (USA, 2010).

Batty, R., *A Historical Sketch of the Campaign of 1815* (London, 1820).

Beatson, Maj Gen F. C., *With Wellington in the Pyrenees* (London 1914).

Beatson, Maj Gen F. C., *The Bidassoa and Nivelle* (London 1931).

Beatson, Maj Gen F. C., *The Crossing of the Gaves and the Battle of Orthez* (London 1925).

Bidwell, Brig. S., *The Royal Horse Artillery* (London, 1973).

Black, J., *Waterloo, The Battle that Brought Down Napoleon* (London, 2010).

Bowyer Lane, Maj. F. W., *Memoir of Major Henry Bowyer Lane of the Royal Artillery* (London, 1883).

Browne, J. A., *England's Artillerymen, Historical Narrative of the RA, from the Formation of the Regiment to the Amalgamation of the Royal and Indian Artilleries in 1862* (London, 1865).

Bryant, A., *The Years of Endurance 1793–1802* (London, 1942).

Chambers, G., *Bussaco* (London, 1910).

Chartrand, R., *Fuentes de Oñoro, Wellington's Liberation of Portugal* (Oxford, 2002).

Coss, E., *All For the King's Shilling, The British Soldier under Wellington, 1808–1814* (University of Oklahoma Press, 2010).

Davies, H., *Wellington's Wars, The Making of a Military Genius* (London, 2012).

Dawson, A. L., Dawson, P. L. and Summerfield, S., *Napoleonic Artillery* (Marlborough, 2007).

Dawson, Maj. H. M., *The History of 'G' Troop Royal Horse Artillery* (London, 1919).

Dempsey, G., *Albuera 181,1 the Bloodiest Battle of the Peninsular War* (London, 2008).

Duncan, Capt. F., *History of the Royal Regiment of Artillery*, two volumes (London, 1873).

Fletcher, I., *A Desperate Business, Wellington, the British Army and the Waterloo Campaign* (Stroud, 2001).

Fortescue, J., *A History of the British Army 1645–1870*, 20 volumes (London, 1899–1930).

Franklin, C. E., *British Napoleonic Field Artillery* (Stroud, 2008).

Franklin, C. E., *British Rockets of the Napoleonic and Colonial Wars 1085–1901* (Staplehurst, 2005).

Fuller, J. F. C., *The Duke of Wellington* (The Coast Artillery Journal, Nov–Dec 1938).

Girod de l'Ain, M., *Vie Militaire de Général Foy* (Paris, 1900).

Glover, M. *Wellington as a Military Commander* (London, 1968).

Graham, Brig. C. A. L., *The Story of the Royal Regiment of Artillery*, sixth edition (Woolwich, 1944).

Haythornthwaite, P., *The Armies of Wellington* (London, 1994).

Henry, C., *British Napoleonic Artillery 1793–1815*, two books – *Field Artillery* and *Siege and Coastal Artillery* (Oxford, 2002–03).

Hime, Lt. Col. H. W. L., *History of the Royal Regiment of Artillery 1815–1853* (London, 1908).

Hogg, Brig. O. F. G., *English Artillery 1326–1716* (London, 1963).

Hughes, Maj. Gen. B. P., *British Smooth-Bore Artillery* (London, 1969). (BS in endnotes)

Hughes, Maj. Gen. B. P., *Firepower* (London, 1974). (HFI in endnotes)

Hughes, Maj. Gen. B. P., *Open Fire, Artillery Tactics from Marlborough to Wellington* (Chichester, 1983). (HOF in endnotes)

Hughes, Maj. Gen. B. P, *Honour Titles of the Royal Artillery* (Dorchester, 1988). (HHT in endnotes)

Kennedy, Sir J. Shaw, *Notes on the Battle of Waterloo* (London, 1865).

Kiley, K. F., *Artillery of the Napoleonic Wars 1792–1815* (London, 2004).

Laws, Lt. Col. M. E. S., *Battery Records of the Royal Artillery, 1716–1859* (Woolwich, 1952). LBR in endnotes)

Leslie, Maj. J., *The Services of the Royal Regiment of Artillery in the Peninsular War 1808–1814* (Woolwich, 1908).

Lipscombe, Col. N. J., *The Peninsular War Atlas* (Oxford, 2010).

Longford, E., *Wellington* (London, 1969).

Ludlow Beamish, N., *History of the Kings German Legion*, two volumes (London, 1832–37).

Marriott Smith, Maj. H., *The History of the 13th Battery Royal Field Artillery From 1759 – 1913* (Naval & Military Press reprint).

Martin Lanuza, J. A., *Diccionario Biográfico del Generalto Español, Reinados de Carlos IV y Fernando VII (1788–1833)* (Madrid, undated).

BIBLIOGRAPHY

Norris, J., *Artillery, a History* (Stroud, 2000).

Norris and Bremner, *The Lines of Torres Vedras*, The British Historical Society of Portugal (Lisbon, 1986).

Nosworthy, B., *With Musket, Cannon and Sword, Battle Tactics of Napoleon and His Enemies* (New York, 1996).

Oman, Sir Charles, *A History of the Peninsular War*, seven volumes (Oxford, 1902–30). (OHP in endnotes)

Oman, Sir Charles, *Wellington's Army 1809–1814*, (London, 1913). (OWA in endnotes)

Roberts, A., *Napoleon and Wellington* (London, 2001). (RN&W in endnotes)

Roberts, A., *Waterloo, Napoleon's Last Gamble* (London, 2005). (RNLG in endnotes)

Robinson, H. B., *Memoires of Lieutenant General Sir Thomas Picton, Including his Correspondence*, two volumes (London, 1836).

Rogers, Col. H. C. B., *Artillery through the Ages* (London, 1971).

Schwertfeger, B., *Geschichte Der Königlich Deutschen Legion, 1803–1816*, two volumes (Hannover and Leipzig, 1907).

Smirinov, A., *Russian Field Artillery Systems in 1805* (Moscow, 1998).

Southey, R., *History of the Peninsular War 1807–1811*, four volumes (London, 1823–32).

Strachan, H., *The Politics of the British Army* (Oxford, 1997).

Teixeira Botelho, J. J., *História da Artilaria Portugesa*, two volumes (Lisbon, 1944).

Uffindell, A., *The Eagle's Last Triumph, Napoleon's Victory at Ligny, June 1815* (London, 2006).

Urban, M., *The Man Who Broke Napoleon's Codes, The Story of George Scovell* (London, 2001).

Vieira Borges, J., *A Arilharia na Guerra Peninsular* (Lisbon, 2009).

Weller, J., *Wellington at Waterloo*, (London, 1967).

Wellesley, J., *Wellington, A Journey through My Family* (London, 2008)

Whinyates, F. A., *From Coruna to Sevastopol, The History of 'C' Battery, 'A' Brigade (Late 'C' Troop), Royal Horse Artillery* (London, 1883). (WCS in endnotes)

Wilkinson-Latham, R., *British Artillery on Land and Sea 1790–1820* (Newton Abbot, 1973).

Wilson, Lt. A. W., *The Story of the Gun* (Woolwich, 1944).

Winter, F. H., *The First Golden Age of Rocketry* (Washington, 1990).

Index